POCKET

PCRef

D1236255

by

Thomas J. Glover
Millie M. Young

Third Edition

Sequoia Publishing, Inc.
Littleton, Colorado   U.S.A.

This PCRef belongs to:

NAME:

HOME ADDRESS:

HOME PHONE:

WORK PHONE:

BUSINESS ADDRESS:

In case of accident or serious illness, please notify:
Name:
Phone Number:

ISBN 0–9622359–7–0

Books by
Sequoia Publishing, Inc.

POCKET REF
by Thomas J. Glover
April 1989, 496p
ISBN 0-9622359-0-3

POCKET PCRef
by Thomas J. Glover and Millie M. Young
3rd Edition, November 1993, 496 pages
ISBN 0-9622359-7-0

DESKRef
by Thomas J. Glover
1st Edition, January 1993
ISBN 0-9622359-1-1

Send your Name and Address to:

Mailing List Group
Sequoia Publishing, Inc
P.O. Box 620820
Littleton, CO   80162-0820

Receive news when Sequoia's new titles and up-dates are available at your favorite store.

Preface

Sequoia Publishing, Inc. has made a serious effort to provide accurate information in this book. However, the probability exists that there are errors and misprints. Sequoia Publishing, Inc. and the authors do not represent the information as being exact and make no warranty of any kind with regard to the content of Pocket PCRef. Sequoia Publishing, Inc. and the authors shall not be held liable for any errors contained in Pocket PCRef or for incidental or consequential damages in connection with any use of the material herein.

The publishers would appreciate being notified of any errors, omissions, or misprints which may occur in this book. ***Your suggestions for future editions would also be greatly appreciated.***

The information in this manual was collected from numerous sources and if not properly acknowledged, Sequoia Publishing, Inc. and the authors would like to express their appreciation for those contributions. See page 6 for specific trade name, trade mark, and credit information.

Sequoia Publishing, Inc.
Department 101
P.O. Box 620820
Littleton, Colorado 80162–0820
(303) 972-4167

Acknowledgements

POCKET PCRef would not have been possible without the efforts and endless patience of our families and many co-workers. Our deepest love and thanks to all of you.

Our deepest gratitude to Dave Derby, co-owner of Sequoia Publishing and Chief Financial Officer, for his technical editing, suggestions, and effort in tracking down the true meaning of Keyboard Scan Codes (a task no less difficult than tracking down the true meaning of life!).

Thanks to Liz Young, Trish Glover and Laurie Vendryes for their help in compiling and verifying the Phone Book. Thanks to Donna Baumgarten and Ken Sweet for their help in updating the Hard Drive section.

POCKET PCRef was produced using Ventura Publisher, Version 3, by Xerox Desktop Software, Inc.

◆━━━◆━━━◆

Thank you never seems to be enough when you're saying it to the ones you care about the most! My wonderful wife, Georgia, and my kids, Trish and Carrie, have supported and loved me through the whole monumental process of writing and publishing a book ... *Thank you and I love you*. A very special thank you to my dear friend and co-author Millie, who has taught me the true meanings of courage, dedication and perseverance. *Thomas*

◆━━━◆━━━◆

It is amazing to me, what one person can accomplish when that accomplishment is based on the faith another person has in you. I share only in a small part of this book, the DOS Commands section, and though that may seem insignificant to some, it is a major accomplishment to this novice in the computer world. To the man I love, my gentle and patient husband Richard and our understanding offspring, Elizabeth, Christopher, and Stephanie, none of this would have been possible without you. And, especially to my mentor and friend Thomas, who doesn't know the meaning of limitations. To all of you who have had great faith in me and have allowed *this humble sparrow to soar as an eagle*, I give my sincerest thanks. *Millie*

REFERENCES, TRADE NAMES and TRADE MARKS

The following books were used as references during the writing of Pocket PCRef. (They are all excellent references and should be added to any good reference library):

DOS Power Users Guide by Kris Jamsa
    McGraw Hill, 1988, ISBN 0-07-881310-7
Hard Disk Handbook by Alfred Glossbrenner and Nick Anis
    Osborne McGraw Hill, 1989, ISBN 0-07-881604-1
The Hard Disk Technical Guide by Douglas T. Anderson
    PCS Publications, 1991
The Micro House Hard Drive Encyclopedia, Edited by Douglas
    T. Anderson, Micro House, 1992, 1993
Inside the IBM PC by Peter Norton
    Brady Books, 1986, ISBN0-89303-583-1
PC Magazine DOS Power Tools by Paul Somerson
    Bantam Computer Books, 1988, ISBN 0-553-34526-5
Que's Computer User's Dictionary by Bryan Pfaffenberger
    Que Corporation, 1990, ISBN 0-88022-540-8
MSDOS User's Guide and Reference, Ver 2.11, 3.0, 3.1, 3.2, 3.3, 4.01, 5.0 by Microsoft Corporation. (Ver 5.0 is excellent !)
Pocket Ref by Thomas J. Glover
    Sequoia Publishing, Inc, 1989, ISBN 0-9622359-0-3
Supercharging MSDOS by Van Wolverton
    Microsoft Press, 1986, ISBN 0-914845-95-0
The Winn Rosch Hardware Bible by Winn L. Rosch
    Brady Books, 1989, ISBN 0-13-160979-3

See page 223 for additional hard drive references.

NOTE: There are many more references, most of which are referenced on specific pages in Pocket PCRef. If we have omitted a reference, we apologize, please let us know and we will include it in the next printing of Pocket PCRef.

TABLE OF CONTENTS

NOTES

POCKET PCRef

ASCII and Numerics

COMPUTER ASCII CODES

The following ASCII (American Standard Code for Information Interchange) tables are used by most of the microcomputer industry. The codes occur in two sets: the "low–bit" set, from Dec 0 to Dec 127, and the "high–bit" set, from Dec 128 to Dec 255. The "low–bit" set is standard for almost all microcomputers but the "high–bit" set varies between the different computer brands. For instance, in the case of Apple computers and Epson printers, the "high–bit" set repeats the "low–bit" set except that the alphabetic characters are italic. In the case of IBM and many other MSDOS systems, the "high–bit" set is composed of foreign language and box drawing characters and mathematic symbols.

Hex	Dec	Description	Abbr		Character
00	0	Null	Null	☻	Control @
01	1	Start Heading	SOH	☺	Control A
02	2	Start of Text	STX	☻	Control B
03	3	End of Text	ETX	♥	Control C
04	4	End Transmit	EOT	♦	Control D
05	5	Enquiry	ENQ	♣	Control E
06	6	Acknowledge	ACK	♠	Control F
07	7	Beep	BEL	•	Control G
08	8	Back space	BS	■	Control H
09	9	Horizontal Tab	HT	○	Control I
0A	10	Line Feed	LF	◙	Control J
0B	11	Vertical Tab	VT	♂	Control K
0C	12	Form Feed	FF	♀	Control L
0D	13	Carriage Ret.	CR	♪	Control M
0E	14	Shift Out	SO	♫	Control N
0F	15	Shift In	SI	☼	Control O
10	16	Device Link Esc	DLE	►	Control P
11	17	Dev Cont 1 X-ON	DC1	◄	Control Q
12	18	Dev Control 2	DC2	↕	Control R
13	19	Dev Cont 3 X-OFF	DC3	‼	Control S
14	20	Dev Control 4	DC4	¶	Control T
15	21	Negative Ack	NAK	§	Control U
16	22	Synchronous Idle	SYN	▬	Control V
17	23	End Trans Block	ETB	↨	Control W
18	24	Cancel	CAN	↑	Control X
19	25	End Medium	EM	↓	Control Y
1A	26	Substitute	SUB	→	Control Z
1B	27	Escape	ESC	←	Control [

COMPUTER ASCII CODES

Hex	Dec	Description		Abbr	Character
1C	28	Cursor Right	FS	←	Control /
1D	29	Cursor Left	GS	↔	Control]
1E	30	Cursor Up	RS	▲	Control ^
1F	31	Cursor Down	US	▼	Control –

Hex	Dec	Character	Description
20	32		Space (SP)
21	33	!	Exclamation Point
22	34	"	Double Quote
23	35	#	Number sign
24	36	$	Dollar sign
25	37	%	Percent
26	38	&	Ampersand
27	39	'	Apostrophe
28	40	(	Left parenthesis
29	41	)	Right parenthesis
2A	42	*	Asterisk
2B	43	+	Plus sign
2C	44	,	Comma
2D	45	–	Minus sign
2E	46	.	Period
2F	47	/	Right or Front slash
30	48	0	Zero
31	49	1	One
32	50	2	Two
33	51	3	Three
34	52	4	Four
35	53	5	Five
36	54	6	Six
37	55	7	Seven
38	56	8	Eight
39	57	9	Nine
3A	58	:	Colon
3B	59	;	Semicolon
3C	60	<	Less than
3D	61	>	Greater than
3E	62	=	Equal sign
3F	63	?	Question mark
40	64	@	"at" symbol

COMPUTER ASCII CODES

Hex	Dec	Character	Description
41	65	A	Uppercase A
42	66	B	Uppercase B
43	67	C	Uppercase C
44	68	D	Uppercase D
45	69	E	Uppercase E
46	70	F	Uppercase F
47	71	G	Uppercase G
48	72	H	Uppercase H
49	73	I	Uppercase I
4A	74	J	Uppercase J
4B	75	K	Uppercase K
4C	76	L	Uppercase L
4D	77	M	Uppercase M
4E	78	N	Uppercase N
4F	79	O	Uppercase O
50	80	P	Uppercase P
51	81	Q	Uppercase Q
52	82	R	Uppercase R
53	83	S	Uppercase S
54	84	T	Uppercase T
55	85	U	Uppercase U
56	86	V	Uppercase V
57	87	W	Uppercase W
58	88	X	Uppercase X
59	89	Y	Uppercase Y
5A	90	Z	Uppercase Z
5B	91	[	Left bracket
5C	92	\	Left or Back Slash
5D	93	]	Right bracket
5E	94	^	Caret
5F	95	_	Underline
60	96	`	Accent
61	97	a	Lowercase a
62	98	b	Lowercase b
63	99	c	Lowercase c
64	100	d	Lowercase d
65	101	e	Lowercase e
66	102	f	Lowercase f
67	103	g	Lowercase g

COMPUTER ASCII CODES

Hex	Dec	Standard Character	Description
68	104	h	Lowercase h
69	105	i	Lowercase i
6A	106	j	Lowercase j
6B	107	k	Lowercase k
6C	108	l	Lowercase l
6D	109	m	Lowercase m
6E	110	n	Lowercase n
6F	111	o	Lowercase o
70	112	p	Lowercase p
71	113	q	Lowercase q
72	114	r	Lowercase r
73	115	s	Lowercase s
74	116	t	Lowercase t
75	117	u	Lowercase u
76	118	v	Lowercase v
77	119	w	Lowercase w
78	120	x	Lowercase x
79	121	y	Lowercase y
7A	122	z	Lowercase z
7B	123	{	Left bracket
7C	124			Vertical line
7D	125	}	Right bracket
7E	126	~	Tilde
7F	127	DEL	Delete

Hex	Dec	Standard Character	IBM Set	Standard Description
80	128	Null	Ç	Null
81	129	SOH	ü	Start Heading
82	130	STX	é	Start of Text
83	131	ETX	â	End of Text
84	132	EOT	ä	End Transmit
85	133	ENQ	à	Enquiry
86	134	ACK	å	Acknowledge
87	135	BEL	ç	Beep
88	136	BS	ê	Back Space
89	137	HT	ë	Horiz Tab
8A	138	LF	è	Line Feed

COMPUTER ASCII CODES

Hex	Dec	Standard Character	IBM Set	Standard Description
8B	139	VT	ï	Vertical Tab
8C	140	FF	î	Form Feed
8D	141	CR	ì	Carriage Return
8E	142	SO	Ä	Shift Out
8F	143	SI	Å	Shift In
90	144	DLE	É	Device Link Esc
91	145	DC1	æ	Device Cont 1 X–ON
92	146	DC2	Æ	Device Control 2
93	147	DC3	ô	Device Cont 3 X–OFF
94	148	DC4	ö	Device Control 4
95	149	NAK	ò	Negative Ack
96	150	SYN	û	Synchronous Idle
97	151	ETB	ù	End Transmit Block
98	152	CAN	ÿ	Cancel
99	153	EM	Ö	End Medium
9A	154	SUB	Ü	Substitute
9B	155	ESC	¢	Escape
9C	156	FS	£	Cursor Right
9D	157	GS	¥	Cursor Left
9E	158	RS	Pt	Cursor Up
9F	159	US	ƒ	Cursor Down
A0	160	Space	á	Space
A1	161	!	í	Italic Exclamation point
A2	162	"	ó	Italic Double quote
A3	163	#	ú	Italic Number sign
A4	164	$	ñ	Italic Dollar sign
A5	165	%	Ñ	Italic Percent
A6	166	&	ª	Italic Ampersand
A7	167	'	º	Italic Apostrophe
A8	168	(	¿	Italic Left parenthesis
A9	169	)	⌐	Italic Right parenthesis
AA	170	*	¬	Italic asterisk
AB	171	+	½	Italic plus sign
AC	172	,	¼	Italic comma
AD	173	–	¡	Italic minus sign
AE	174	.	«	Italic period
AF	175	/	»	Italic right slash
B0	176	0	░	Italic Zero
B1	177	1	▒	Italic One

COMPUTER ASCII CODES

Hex	Dec	Standard Character	IBM Set	Standard Description
B2	178	2	▓	Italic Two
B3	179	3	│	Italic Three
B4	180	4	┤	Italic Four
B5	181	5	╡	Italic Five
B6	182	6	╢	Italic Six
B7	183	7	╖	Italic Seven
B8	184	8	╕	Italic Eight
B9	185	9	╣	Italic Nine
BA	186	:	║	Italic colon
BB	187	;	╗	Italic semicolon
BC	188	<	╝	Italic less than
BD	189	=	╜	Italic equal
BE	190	>	╛	Italic greater than
BF	191	?	┐	Italic question mark
C0	192	@	└	Italic "at" symbol
C1	193	A	┴	Italic A
C2	194	B		Italic B
C3	195	C	┬	Italic C
C4	196	D	─	Italic D
C5	197	E	┼	Italic E
C6	198	F	╞	Italic F
C7	199	G	╟	Italic G
C8	200	H	╚	Italic H
C9	201	I	╔	Italic I
CA	202	J	╩	Italic J
CB	203	K	╦	Italic K
CC	204	L	╠	Italic L
CD	205	M	═	Italic M
CE	206	N	╬	Italic N
CF	207	O	╧	Italic O
D0	208	P	╨	Italic P
D1	209	Q		Italic Q
D2	210	R	╤	Italic R
D3	211	S	╥	Italic S
D4	212	T	╙	Italic T
D5	213	U	╘	Italic U
D6	214	V	╒	Italic V
D7	215	W	╓	Italic W
D8	216	X	╫	Italic X

COMPUTER ASCII CODES

Hex	Dec	Standard Character	IBM Set	Description
D9	217	Y	┘	Italic Y
DA	218	Z	┌	Italic Z
DB	219	[	■	Italic left bracket
DC	220	\	■	Italic left or back slash
DD	221	]	▌	Italic right bracket
DE	222	^	■	Italic caret
DF	223	_	▀	Italic underline
E0	224	'	α	Italic accent / alpha
E1	225	a	β	Italic a / beta
E2	226	b	Γ	Italic b / gamma
E3	227	c	π	Italic c / pi
E4	228	d	Σ	Italic d / sigma
E5	229	e	σ	Italic e / sigma
E6	230	f	μ	Italic f / mu
E7	231	g	γ	Italic g / gamma
E8	232	h	Φ	Italic h / phi
E9	233	i	θ	Italic i / theta
EA	234	j	Ω	Italic j / omega
EB	235	k	δ	Italic k / delta
EC	236	l	∞	Italic l / infinity
ED	237	m	$\emptyset$	Italic m / slashed zero
EE	238	n	$\in$	Italic n
EF	239	o	$\cap$	Italic o
F0	240	p	$\equiv$	Italic p
F1	241	q	$\pm$	Italic q
F2	242	r	$\geq$	Italic r
F3	243	s	$\leq$	Italic s
F4	244	t	$\int$	Italic t
F5	245	u	$\int$	Italic u
F6	246	v	$\div$	Italic v
F7	247	w	$\approx$	Italic w
F8	248	x	°	Italic x
F9	249	y	•	Italic y
FA	250	z	•	Italic z
FB	251	{	$\sqrt{}$	Italic left bracket
FC	252	|	^{n}	Italic vertical line
FD	253	}	2	Italic right bracket
FE	254	~		Italic tilde
FF	255	Blank	Blank	Blank

NUMERIC PREFIXES

Prefix	Abbreviation	Pronounce	Multiplier
atto	a	at–to	10^{-18}
femto	f	fem–to	10^{-15}
pico	p	pe–ko	10^{-12}
nano	n	nan–o	10^{-9}
micro	μ	mi–kro	10^{-6}
milli	m	mil–l.	10^{-3}
centi	c	sent–ti	10^{-2}
deci	d	des–l	10^{-1}
deka	da	dek–a	10^{1}
hecto	h	hek–to	10^{2}
kilo	k	kil–o.	10^{3}
mega	M	meg–a	10^{6}
giga	G	ji–ga	10^{9}
tera	T	ter–a	10^{12}
peta	P	pe–ta	10^{15}
exa	E	ex–a	10^{18}
		sextillion	10^{21}
		septillion	10^{24}
		octillion	10^{27}
		nonillion	10^{30}

MEGABYTES AND KILOBYTES

1 kilobyte = 2^{10} bytes = exactly 1,024 bytes
1 megabyte = 2^{20} bytes = exactly 1,048,576 bytes
1 gigabyte = 2^{30} bytes = 1 billion bytes
1 terabyte = 2^{40} bytes = 1 trillion bytes
1 byte = 8 bits (bit is short for binary digit)

8 bit computers (such as the 8088)
    move data in 1 byte chunks
16 bit computers (such as the 80286 and 80386SX)
    move data in 2 byte chunks
32 bit computers (such as the 80386DX)
    move data in 4 byte chunks

POWERS OF 2

n	2^n	Hexadecimal
0	1	1
1	2	2
2	4	4
3	8	8
4	16	10
5	32	20
6	64	40
7	128	80
8	256	100
9	512	200
10	1024	400
11	2048	800
12	4096	1000
13	8192	2000
14	16384	4000
15	32768	8000
16	65536	10000
17	131072	20000
18	262144	40000
19	524288	80000
20	1048576	100000
21	2097152	200000
22	4194304	400000
23	8388608	800000
24	16777216	1000000
25	33554432	2000000
26	67108864	4000000
27	134217728	8000000
28	268435456	10000000
29	536870912	20000000
30	1073741824	40000000
31	2147483648	80000000
32	4294967296	100000000

POWERS OF 2

n	2^n	Hexadecimal
33	8589934592	200000000
34	17179869184	400000000
35	34359738368	800000000
36	68719476736	1000000000
37	137438953472	2000000000
38	274877906944	4000000000
39	549755813888	8000000000
40	1099511627776	10000000000
41	2199023255552	20000000000
42	4398046511104	40000000000
43	8796093022208	80000000000
44	17592186044416	100000000000
45	35184372088832	200000000000
46	70368744177664	400000000000
47	140737488355328	800000000000
48	281474976710656	1000000000000
49	562949953421312	2000000000000
50	1125899906842624	4000000000000
51	2251799813685248	8000000000000
52	4503599627370496	10000000000000
53	9007199254740992	20000000000000
54	18014398509481984	40000000000000
55	36028797018963968	80000000000000
56	72057594037927936	100000000000000
57	144115188075855872	200000000000000
58	288230376151711744	400000000000000
59	576460752303423488	800000000000000
60	1152921504606846976	1000000000000000
61	2305843009213693952	2000000000000000
62	4611686018427387904	4000000000000000
63	9223372036854775808	8000000000000000
64	18446744073709551616	10000000000000000

HEX to DECIMAL CONVERSION

Example: To convert the Hex number 1F7 to its decimal equivalent (Decimal 503), find 1F in the shaded left column of Hex numbers and follow the 1F row to the right, until it intersects the column with the shaded 7 at the top. The number at the intersection (503) is the decimal equivalent of Hex 1F7.

Standard Hex notation, using A through F to denote decimal values 10 through 15, is used in this table.

↓ Hex→ 0	1	2	3	4	5	6	7
00	0	1	2	3	4	5	6	7
01	16	17	18	19	20	21	22	23
02	32	33	34	35	36	37	38	39
03	48	49	50	51	52	53	54	55
04	64	65	66	67	68	69	70	71
05	80	81	82	83	84	85	86	87
06	96	97	98	99	100	101	102	103
07	112	113	114	115	116	117	118	119
08	128	129	130	131	132	133	134	135
09	144	145	146	147	148	149	150	151
0A	160	161	162	163	164	165	166	167
0B	176	177	178	179	180	181	182	183
0C	192	193	194	195	196	197	198	199
0D	208	209	210	211	212	213	214	215
0E	224	225	226	227	228	229	230	231
0F	240	241	242	243	244	245	246	247
10	256	257	258	259	260	261	262	263
11	272	273	274	275	276	277	278	279
12	288	289	290	291	292	293	294	295
13	304	305	306	307	308	309	310	311
14	320	321	322	323	324	325	326	327
15	336	337	338	339	340	341	342	343
16	352	353	354	355	356	357	358	359
17	368	369	370	371	372	373	374	375
18	384	385	386	387	388	389	390	391
19	400	401	402	403	404	405	406	407
1A	416	417	418	419	420	421	422	423
1B	432	433	434	435	436	437	438	439
1C	448	449	450	451	452	453	454	455
1D	464	465	466	467	468	469	470	471
1E	480	481	482	483	484	485	486	487
1F	496	497	498	499	500	501	502	503
20	512	513	514	515	516	517	518	519
21	528	529	530	531	532	533	534	535
22	544	545	546	547	548	549	550	551
23	560	561	562	563	564	565	566	567
24	576	577	578	579	580	581	582	583
25	592	593	594	595	596	597	598	599

HEX to DECIMAL CONVERSION

Large number conversion: (Up to five Hexidecimal digits)
Find the fourth and fifth Hexidecimal significant digits in the
following table and add their decimal equivalent to the value in
the primary table. For example:

CB13F (Hex) = 786432 + 45056 + 319 = 831807 (Dec)

Hex	Dec	Hex	Dec	Hex	Dec	Hex	Dec
1000	4096	9000	36864	20000	131072	A0000	655360
2000	8192	A000	40960	30000	196608	B0000	720896
3000	12288	B000	45056	40000	262144	C0000	786432
4000	16384	C000	49152	50000	327680	D0000	851968
5000	20480	D000	53248	60000	393216	E0000	917504
6000	24576	E000	57344	70000	458752	F0000	983040
7000	28672	F000	61440	80000	524288		
8000	32768	10000	65536	90000	589824		

↓ Hex→	8	9	A	B	C	D	E	F
00	8	9	10	11	12	13	14	15
01	24	25	26	27	28	29	30	31
02	40	41	42	43	44	45	46	47
03	56	57	58	59	60	61	62	63
04	72	73	74	75	76	77	78	79
05	88	89	90	91	92	93	94	95
06	104	105	106	107	108	109	110	111
07	120	121	122	123	124	125	126	127
08	136	137	138	139	140	141	142	143
09	152	153	154	155	156	157	158	159
0A	168	169	170	171	172	173	174	175
0B	184	185	186	187	188	189	190	191
0C	200	201	202	203	204	205	206	207
0D	216	217	218	219	220	221	222	223
0E	232	233	234	235	236	237	238	239
0F	248	249	250	251	252	253	254	255
10	264	265	266	267	268	269	270	271
11	280	281	282	283	284	285	286	287
12	296	297	298	299	300	301	302	303
13	312	313	314	315	316	317	318	319
14	328	329	330	331	332	333	334	335
15	344	345	346	347	348	349	350	351
16	360	361	362	363	364	365	366	367
17	376	377	378	379	380	381	382	383
18	392	393	394	395	396	397	398	399
19	408	409	410	411	412	413	414	415
1A	424	425	426	427	428	429	430	431
1B	440	441	442	443	444	445	446	447
1C	456	457	458	459	460	461	462	463
1D	472	473	474	475	476	477	478	479
1E	488	489	490	491	492	493	494	495
1F	504	505	506	507	508	509	510	511
20	520	521	522	523	524	525	526	527
21	536	537	538	539	540	541	542	543
22	552	553	554	555	556	557	558	559
23	568	569	570	571	572	573	574	575
24	584	585	586	587	588	589	590	591
25	600	601	602	603	604	605	606	607

HEX to DECIMAL CONVERSION

↓ Hex→	0	1	2	3	4	5	6	7
26	608	609	610	611	612	613	614	615
27	624	625	626	627	628	629	630	631
28	640	641	642	643	644	645	646	647
29	656	657	658	659	660	661	662	663
2A	672	673	674	675	676	677	678	679
2B	688	689	690	691	692	693	694	695
2C	704	705	706	707	708	709	710	711
2D	720	721	722	723	724	725	726	727
2E	736	737	738	739	740	741	742	743
2F	752	753	754	755	756	757	758	759
30	768	769	770	771	772	773	774	775
31	784	785	786	787	788	789	790	791
32	800	801	802	803	804	805	806	807
33	816	817	818	819	820	821	822	823
34	832	833	834	835	836	837	838	839
35	848	849	850	851	852	853	854	855
36	864	865	866	867	868	869	870	871
37	880	881	882	883	884	885	886	887
38	896	897	898	899	900	901	902	903
39	912	913	914	915	916	917	918	919
3A	928	929	930	931	932	933	934	935
3B	944	945	946	947	948	949	950	951
3C	960	961	962	963	964	965	966	967
3D	976	977	978	979	980	981	982	983
3E	992	993	994	995	996	997	998	999
3F	1008	1009	1010	1011	1012	1013	1014	1015
40	1024	1025	1026	1027	1028	1029	1030	1031
41	1040	1041	1042	1043	1044	1045	1046	1047
42	1056	1057	1058	1059	1060	1061	1062	1063
43	1072	1073	1074	1075	1076	1077	1078	1079
44	1088	1089	1090	1091	1092	1093	1094	1095
45	1104	1105	1106	1107	1108	1109	1110	1111
46	1120	1121	1122	1123	1124	1125	1126	1127
47	1136	1137	1138	1139	1140	1141	1142	1143
48	1152	1153	1154	1155	1156	1157	1158	1159
49	1168	1169	1170	1171	1172	1173	1174	1175
4A	1184	1185	1186	1187	1188	1189	1190	1191
4B	1200	1201	1202	1203	1204	1205	1206	1207
4C	1216	1217	1218	1219	1220	1221	1222	1223
4D	1232	1233	1234	1235	1236	1237	1238	1239
4E	1248	1249	1250	1251	1252	1253	1254	1255
4F	1264	1265	1266	1267	1268	1269	1270	1271
50	1280	1281	1282	1283	1284	1285	1286	1287
51	1296	1297	1298	1299	1300	1301	1302	1303
52	1312	1313	1314	1315	1316	1317	1318	1319
53	1328	1329	1330	1331	1332	1333	1334	1335
54	1344	1345	1346	1347	1348	1349	1350	1351
55	1360	1361	1362	1363	1364	1365	1366	1367
56	1376	1377	1378	1379	1380	1381	1382	1383
57	1392	1393	1394	1395	1396	1397	1398	1399
58	1408	1409	1410	1411	1412	1413	1414	1415
59	1424	1425	1426	1427	1428	1429	1430	1431
5A	1440	1441	1442	1443	1444	1445	1446	1447
5B	1456	1457	1458	1459	1460	1461	1462	1463
5C	1472	1473	1474	1475	1476	1477	1478	1479

HEX to DECIMAL CONVERSION

↓Hex→	8	9	A	B	C	D	E	F
26	616	617	618	619	620	621	622	623
27	632	633	634	635	636	637	638	639
28	648	649	650	651	652	653	654	655
29	664	665	666	667	668	669	670	671
2A	680	681	682	683	684	685	686	687
2B	696	697	698	699	700	701	702	703
2C	712	713	714	715	716	717	718	719
2D	728	729	730	731	732	733	734	735
2E	744	745	746	747	748	749	750	751
2F	760	761	762	763	764	765	766	767
30	776	777	778	779	780	781	782	783
31	792	793	794	795	796	797	798	799
32	808	809	810	811	812	813	814	815
33	824	825	826	827	828	829	830	831
34	840	841	842	843	844	845	846	847
35	856	857	858	859	860	861	862	863
36	872	873	874	875	876	877	878	879
37	888	889	890	891	892	893	894	895
38	904	905	906	907	908	909	910	911
39	920	921	922	923	924	925	926	927
3A	936	937	938	939	940	941	942	943
3B	952	953	954	955	956	957	958	959
3C	968	969	970	971	972	973	974	975
3D	984	985	986	987	988	989	990	991
3E	1000	1001	1002	1003	1004	1005	1006	1007
3F	1016	1017	1018	1019	1020	1021	1022	1023
40	1032	1033	1034	1035	1036	1037	1038	1039
41	1048	1049	1050	1051	1052	1053	1054	1055
42	1064	1065	1066	1067	1068	1069	1070	1071
43	1080	1081	1082	1083	1084	1085	1086	1087
44	1096	1097	1098	1099	1100	1101	1102	1103
45	1112	1113	1114	1115	1116	1117	1118	1119
46	1128	1129	1130	1131	1132	1133	1134	1135
47	1144	1145	1146	1147	1148	1149	1150	1151
48	1160	1161	1162	1163	1164	1165	1166	1167
49	1176	1177	1178	1179	1180	1181	1182	1183
4A	1192	1193	1194	1195	1196	1197	1198	1199
4B	1208	1209	1210	1211	1212	1213	1214	1215
4C	1224	1225	1226	1227	1228	1229	1230	1231
4D	1240	1241	1242	1243	1244	1245	1246	1247
4E	1256	1257	1258	1259	1260	1261	1262	1263
4F	1272	1273	1274	1275	1276	1277	1278	1279
50	1288	1289	1290	1291	1292	1293	1294	1295
51	1304	1305	1306	1307	1308	1309	1310	1311
52	1320	1321	1322	1323	1324	1325	1326	1327
53	1336	1337	1338	1339	1340	1341	1342	1343
54	1352	1353	1354	1355	1356	1357	1358	1359
55	1368	1369	1370	1371	1372	1373	1374	1375
56	1384	1385	1386	1387	1388	1389	1390	1391
57	1400	1401	1402	1403	1404	1405	1406	1407
58	1416	1417	1418	1419	1420	1421	1422	1423
59	1432	1433	1434	1435	1436	1437	1438	1439
5A	1448	1449	1450	1451	1452	1453	1454	1455
5B	1464	1465	1466	1467	1468	1469	1470	1471
5C	1480	1481	1482	1483	1484	1485	1486	1487

HEX to DECIMAL CONVERSION

↓ Hex→0	1	2	3	4	5	6	7
5D	1488	1489	1490	1491	1492	1493	1494	1495
5E	1504	1505	1506	1507	1508	1509	1510	1511
5F	1520	1521	1522	1523	1524	1525	1526	1527
60	1536	1537	1538	1539	1540	1541	1542	1543
61	1552	1553	1554	1555	1556	1557	1558	1559
62	1568	1569	1570	1571	1572	1573	1574	1575
63	1584	1585	1586	1587	1588	1589	1590	1591
64	1600	1601	1602	1603	1604	1605	1606	1607
65	1616	1617	1618	1619	1620	1621	1622	1623
66	1632	1633	1634	1635	1636	1637	1638	1639
67	1648	1649	1650	1651	1652	1653	1654	1655
68	1664	1665	1666	1667	1668	1669	1670	1671
69	1680	1681	1682	1683	1684	1685	1686	1687
6A	1696	1697	1698	1699	1700	1701	1702	1703
6B	1712	1713	1714	1715	1716	1717	1718	1719
6C	1728	1729	1730	1731	1732	1733	1734	1735
6D	1744	1745	1746	1747	1748	1749	1750	1751
6E	1760	1761	1762	1763	1764	1765	1766	1767
6F	1776	1777	1778	1779	1780	1781	1782	1783
70	1792	1793	1794	1795	1796	1797	1798	1799
71	1808	1809	1810	1811	1812	1813	1814	1815
72	1824	1825	1826	1827	1828	1829	1830	1831
73	1840	1841	1842	1843	1844	1845	1846	1847
74	1856	1857	1858	1859	1860	1861	1862	1863
75	1872	1873	1874	1875	1876	1877	1878	1879
76	1888	1889	1890	1891	1892	1893	1894	1895
77	1904	1905	1906	1907	1908	1909	1910	1911
78	1920	1921	1922	1923	1924	1925	1926	1927
79	1936	1937	1938	1939	1940	1941	1942	1943
7A	1952	1953	1954	1955	1956	1957	1958	1959
7B	1968	1969	1970	1971	1972	1973	1974	1975
7C	1985	1986	1986	1987	1988	1989	1990	1991
7D	2000	2001	2002	2003	2004	2005	2006	2007
7E	2016	2017	2018	2019	2020	2021	2022	2023
7F	2032	2033	2034	2035	2036	2037	2038	2039
80	2048	2049	2050	2051	2052	2053	2054	2055
81	2064	2065	2066	2067	2068	2069	2070	2071
82	2080	2081	2082	2083	2084	2085	2086	2087
83	2096	2097	2098	2099	2100	2101	2102	2103
84	2112	2113	2114	2115	2116	2117	2118	2119
85	2128	2129	2130	2131	2132	2133	2134	2135
86	2144	2145	2146	2147	2148	2149	2150	2151
87	2160	2161	2162	2163	2164	2165	2166	2167
88	2176	2177	2178	2179	2180	2181	2182	2183
89	2192	2193	2194	2195	2196	2197	2198	2199
8A	2208	2209	2210	2211	2212	2213	2214	2215
8B	2224	2225	2226	2227	2228	2229	2230	2231
8C	2240	2241	2242	2243	2244	2245	2246	2247
8D	2256	2257	2258	2259	2260	2261	2262	2263
8E	2272	2273	2274	2275	2276	2277	2278	2279
8F	2288	2289	2290	2291	2292	2293	2294	2295
90	2304	2305	2306	2307	2308	2309	2310	2311
91	2320	2321	2322	2323	2324	2325	2326	2327
92	2336	2337	2338	2339	2340	2341	2342	2343
93	2352	2353	2354	2355	2356	2357	2358	2359

HEX to DECIMAL CONVERSION

↓Hex→	8	9	A	B	C	D	E	F
5D	1496	1497	1498	1499	1500	1501	1502	1503
5E	1512	1513	1514	1515	1516	1517	1518	1519
5F	1528	1529	1530	1531	1532	1533	1534	1535
60	1544	1545	1546	1547	1548	1549	1550	1551
61	1560	1561	1562	1563	1564	1565	1566	1567
62	1576	1577	1578	1579	1580	1581	1582	1583
63	1592	1593	1594	1595	1596	1597	1598	1599
64	1608	1609	1610	1611	1612	1613	1614	1615
65	1624	1625	1626	1627	1628	1629	1630	1631
66	1640	1641	1642	1643	1644	1645	1646	1647
67	1656	1657	1658	1659	1660	1661	1662	1663
68	1672	1673	1674	1675	1676	1677	1678	1679
69	1688	1689	1690	1691	1692	1693	1694	1695
6A	1704	1705	1706	1707	1708	1709	1710	1711
6B	1720	1721	1722	1723	1724	1725	1726	1727
6C	1736	1737	1738	1739	1740	1741	1742	1743
6D	1752	1753	1754	1755	1756	1757	1758	1759
6E	1768	1769	1770	1771	1772	1773	1774	1775
6F	1784	1785	1786	1787	1788	1789	1790	1791
70	1800	1801	1802	1803	1804	1805	1806	1807
71	1816	1817	1818	1819	1820	1821	1822	1823
72	1832	1833	1834	1835	1836	1837	1838	1839
73	1848	1849	1850	1851	1852	1853	1854	1855
74	1864	1865	1866	1867	1868	1869	1870	1871
75	1880	1881	1882	1883	1884	1885	1886	1887
76	1896	1897	1898	1899	1900	1901	1902	1903
77	1912	1913	1914	1915	1916	1917	1918	1919
78	1928	1929	1930	1931	1932	1933	1934	1935
79	1944	1945	1946	1947	1948	1949	1950	1951
7A	1960	1961	1962	1963	1964	1965	1966	1967
7B	1976	1977	1978	1979	1980	1981	1982	1983
7C	1992	1993	1994	1995	1996	1997	1998	1999
7D	2008	2009	2010	2011	2012	2013	2014	2015
7E	2024	2025	2026	2027	2028	2029	2030	2031
7F	2040	2041	2042	2043	2044	2045	2046	2047
80	2056	2057	2058	2059	2060	2061	2062	2063
81	2072	2073	2074	2075	2076	2077	2078	2079
82	2088	2089	2090	2091	2092	2093	2094	2095
83	2104	2105	2106	2107	2108	2109	2110	2111
84	2120	2121	2122	2123	2124	2125	2126	2127
85	2136	2137	2138	2139	2140	2141	2142	2143
86	2152	2153	2154	2155	2156	2157	2158	2159
87	2168	2169	2170	2171	2172	2173	2174	2175
88	2184	2185	2186	2187	2188	2189	2190	2191
89	2200	2201	2202	2203	2204	2205	2206	2207
8A	2216	2217	2218	2219	2220	2221	2222	2223
8B	2232	2233	2234	2235	2236	2237	2238	2239
8C	2248	2249	2250	2251	2252	2253	2254	2255
8D	2264	2265	2266	2267	2268	2269	2270	2271
8E	2280	2281	2282	2283	2284	2285	2286	2287
8F	2296	2297	2298	2299	2300	2301	2302	2303
90	2312	2313	2314	2315	2316	2317	2318	2319
91	2328	2329	2330	2331	2332	2333	2334	2335
92	2344	2345	2346	2347	2348	2349	2350	2351
93	2360	2361	2362	2363	2364	2365	2366	2367

↓ Hex→ 0	1	2	3	4	5	6	7
94	2368	2369	2370	2371	2372	2373	2374	2375
95	2384	2385	2386	2387	2388	2389	2390	2391
96	2400	2401	2402	2403	2404	2405	2406	2407
97	2416	2417	2418	2419	2420	2421	2422	2423
98	2432	2433	2434	2435	2436	2437	2438	2439
99	2448	2449	2450	2451	2452	2453	2454	2455
9A	2464	2465	2466	2467	2468	2469	2470	2471
9B	2480	2481	2482	2483	2484	2485	2486	2487
9C	2496	2497	2498	2499	2500	2501	2502	2503
9D	2512	2513	2514	2515	2516	2517	2518	2519
9E	2528	2529	2530	2531	2532	2533	2534	2535
9F	2544	2545	2546	2547	2548	2549	2550	2551
A0	2560	2561	2562	2563	2564	2565	2566	2567
A1	2576	2577	2578	2579	2580	2581	2582	2583
A2	2592	2593	2594	2595	2596	2597	2598	2599
A3	2608	2609	2610	2611	2612	2613	2614	2615
A4	2624	2625	2626	2627	2628	2629	2630	2631
A5	2640	2641	2642	2643	2644	2645	2646	2647
A6	2656	2657	2658	2659	2660	2661	2662	2663
A7	2672	2673	2674	2675	2676	2677	2678	2679
A8	2688	2689	2690	2691	2692	2693	2694	2695
A9	2704	2705	2706	2707	2708	2709	2710	2711
AA	2720	2721	2722	2723	2724	2725	2726	2727
AB	2736	2737	2738	2739	2740	2741	2742	2743
AC	2752	2753	2754	2755	2756	2757	2758	2759
AD	2768	2769	2770	2771	2772	2773	2774	2775
AE	2784	2785	2786	2787	2788	2789	2790	2791
AF	2800	2801	2802	2803	2804	2805	2806	2807
B0	2816	2817	2818	2819	2820	2821	2822	2823
B1	2832	2833	2834	2835	2836	2837	2838	2839
B2	2848	2849	2850	2851	2852	2853	2854	2855
B3	2864	2865	2866	2867	2868	2869	2870	2871
B4	2880	2881	2882	2883	2884	2885	2886	2887
B5	2896	2897	2898	2899	2900	2901	2902	2903
B6	2912	2913	2914	2915	2916	2917	2918	2919
B7	2928	2929	2930	2931	2932	2933	2934	2935
B8	2944	2945	2946	2947	2948	2949	2950	2951
B9	2960	2961	2962	2963	2964	2965	2966	2967
BA	2976	2977	2978	2979	2980	2981	2982	2983
BB	2992	2993	2994	2995	2996	2997	2998	2999
BC	3008	3009	3010	3011	3012	3013	3014	3015
BD	3024	3025	3026	3027	3028	3029	3030	3031
BE	3040	3041	3042	3043	3044	3045	3046	3047
BF	3056	3057	3058	3059	3060	3061	3062	3063
C0	3072	3073	3074	3075	3076	3077	3078	3079
C1	3088	3089	3090	3091	3092	3093	3094	3095
C2	3104	3105	3106	3107	3108	3109	3110	3111
C3	3120	3121	3122	3123	3124	3125	3126	3127
C4	3136	3137	3138	3139	3140	3141	3142	3143
C5	3152	3153	3154	3155	3156	3157	3158	3159
C6	3168	3169	3170	3171	3172	3173	3174	3175
C7	3184	3185	3186	3187	3188	3189	3190	3191
C8	3200	3201	3202	3203	3204	3205	3206	3207
C9	3216	3217	3218	3219	3220	3221	3222	3223
CA	3232	3233	3234	3235	3236	3237	3238	3239

↓Hex→8	9	A	B	C	D	E	F
94	2376	2377	2378	2379	2380	2381	2382	2383
95	2392	2393	2394	2395	2396	2397	2398	2399
96	2408	2409	2410	2411	2412	2413	2414	2415
97	2424	2425	2426	2427	2428	2429	2430	2431
98	2440	2441	2442	2443	2444	2445	2446	2447
99	2456	2457	2458	2459	2460	2461	2462	2463
9A	2472	2473	2474	2475	2476	2477	2478	2479
9B	2488	2489	2490	2491	2492	2493	2494	2495
9C	2504	2505	2506	2507	2508	2509	2510	2511
9D	2520	2521	2522	2523	2524	2525	2526	2527
9E	2536	2537	2538	2539	2540	2541	2542	2543
9F	2552	2553	2554	2555	2556	2557	2558	2559
A0	2568	2569	2570	2571	2572	2573	2574	2575
A1	2584	2585	2586	2587	2588	2589	2590	2591
A2	2600	2601	2602	2603	2604	2605	2606	2607
A3	2616	2617	2618	2619	2620	2621	2622	2623
A4	2632	2633	2634	2635	2636	2637	2638	2639
A5	2648	2649	2650	2651	2652	2653	2654	2655
A6	2664	2665	2666	2667	2668	2669	2670	2671
A7	2680	2681	2682	2683	2684	2685	2686	2687
A8	2696	2697	2698	2699	2700	2701	2702	2703
A9	2712	2713	2714	2715	2716	2717	2718	2719
AA	2728	2729	2730	2731	2732	2733	2734	2735
AB	2744	2745	2746	2747	2748	2749	2750	2751
AC	2760	2761	2762	2763	2764	2765	2766	2767
AD	2776	2777	2778	2779	2780	2781	2782	2783
AE	2792	2793	2794	2795	2796	2797	2798	2799
AF	2808	2809	2810	2811	2812	2813	2814	2815
B0	2824	2825	2826	2827	2828	2829	2830	2831
B1	2840	2841	2842	2843	2844	2845	2846	2847
B2	2856	2857	2858	2859	2860	2861	2862	2863
B3	2872	2873	2874	2875	2876	2877	2878	2879
B4	2888	2889	2890	2891	2892	2893	2894	2895
B5	2904	2905	2906	2907	2908	2909	2910	2911
B6	2920	2921	2922	2923	2924	2925	2926	2927
B7	2936	2937	2938	2939	2940	2941	2942	2943
B8	2952	2953	2954	2955	2956	2957	2958	2959
B9	2968	2969	2970	2971	2972	2973	2974	2975
BA	2984	2985	2986	2987	2988	2989	2990	2991
BB	3000	3001	3002	3003	3004	3005	3006	3007
BC	3016	3017	3018	3019	3020	3021	3022	3023
BD	3032	3033	3034	3035	3036	3037	3038	3039
BE	3048	3049	3050	3051	3052	3053	3054	3055
BF	3064	3065	3066	3067	3068	3069	3070	3071
C0	3080	3081	3082	3083	3084	3085	3086	3087
C1	3096	3097	3098	3099	3100	3101	3102	3103
C2	3112	3113	3114	3115	3116	3117	3118	3119
C3	3128	3129	3130	3131	3132	3133	3134	3135
C4	3144	3145	3146	3147	3148	3149	3150	3151
C5	3160	3161	3162	3163	3164	3165	3166	3167
C6	3176	3177	3178	3179	3180	3181	3182	3183
C7	3192	3193	3194	3195	3196	3197	3198	3199
C8	3208	3209	3210	3211	3212	3213	3214	3215
C9	3224	3225	3226	3227	3228	3229	3230	3231
CA	3240	3241	3242	3243	3244	3245	3246	3247

HEX to DECIMAL CONVERSION

↓ Hex→ 0	1	2	3	4	5	6	7
CB	3248	3249	3250	3251	3252	3253	3254	3255
CC	3264	3265	3266	3267	3268	3269	3270	3271
CD	3280	3281	3282	3283	3284	3285	3286	3287
CE	3296	3297	3298	3299	3300	3301	3302	3303
CF	3312	3313	3314	3315	3316	3317	3318	3319
D0	3328	3329	3330	3331	3332	3333	3334	3335
D1	3344	3345	3346	3347	3348	3349	3350	3351
D2	3360	3361	3362	3363	3364	3365	3366	3367
D3	3376	3377	3378	3379	3380	3381	3382	3383
D4	3392	3393	3394	3395	3396	3397	3398	3399
D5	3408	3409	3410	3411	3412	3413	3414	3415
D6	3424	3425	3426	3427	3428	3429	3430	3431
D7	3440	3441	3442	3443	3444	3445	3446	3447
D8	3456	3457	3458	3459	3460	3461	3462	3463
D9	3472	3473	3474	3475	3476	3477	3478	3479
DA	3488	3489	3490	3491	3492	3493	3494	3495
DB	3504	3505	3506	3507	3508	3509	3510	3511
DC	3520	3521	3522	3523	3524	3525	3526	3527
DD	3536	3537	3538	3539	3540	3541	3542	3543
DE	3552	3553	3554	3555	3556	3557	3558	3559
DF	3568	3569	3570	3571	3572	3573	3574	3575
E0	3584	3585	3586	3587	3588	3589	3590	3591
E1	3600	3601	3602	3603	3604	3605	3606	3607
E2	3616	3617	3618	3619	3620	3621	3622	3623
E3	3632	3633	3634	3635	3636	3637	3638	3639
E4	3648	3649	3650	3651	3652	3653	3654	3655
E5	3664	3665	3666	3667	3668	3669	3670	3671
E6	3680	3681	3682	3683	3684	3685	3686	3687
E7	3696	3697	3698	3699	3700	3701	3702	3703
E8	3712	3713	3714	3715	3716	3717	3718	3719
E9	3728	3729	3730	3731	3732	3733	3734	3735
EA	3744	3745	3746	3747	3748	3749	3750	3751
EB	3760	3761	3762	3763	3764	3765	3766	3767
EC	3776	3777	3778	3779	3780	3781	3782	3783
ED	3792	3793	3794	3795	3796	3797	3798	3799
EE	3808	3809	3810	3811	3812	3813	3814	3815
EF	3824	3825	3826	3827	3828	3829	3830	3831
F0	3840	3841	3842	3843	3844	3845	3846	3847
F1	3856	3857	3858	3859	3860	3861	3862	3863
F2	3872	3873	3874	3875	3876	3877	3878	3879
F3	3888	3889	3890	3891	3892	3893	3894	3895
F4	3904	3905	3906	3907	3908	3909	3910	3911
F5	3920	3921	3922	3923	3924	3925	3926	3927
F6	3936	3937	3938	3939	3940	3941	3942	3943
F7	3952	3953	3954	3955	3956	3957	3958	3959
F8	3968	3969	3970	3971	3972	3973	3974	3975
F9	3984	3985	3986	3987	3988	3989	3990	3991
FA	4000	4001	4002	4003	4004	4005	4006	4007
FB	4016	4017	4018	4019	4020	4021	4022	4023
FC	4032	4033	4034	4035	4036	4037	4038	4039
FD	4048	4049	4050	4051	4052	4053	4054	4055
FE	4064	4065	4066	4067	4068	4069	4070	4071
FF	4080	4081	4082	4083	4084	4085	4086	4087

Hex→	8	9	A	B	C	D	E	F
CB	3256	3257	3258	3259	3260	3261	3262	3263
CC	3272	3273	3274	3275	3276	3277	3278	3279
CD	3288	3289	3290	3291	3292	3293	3294	3295
CE	3304	3305	3306	3307	3308	3309	3310	3311
CF	3320	3321	3322	3323	3324	3325	3326	3327
D0	3336	3337	3338	3339	3340	3341	3342	3343
D1	3352	3353	3354	3355	3356	3357	3358	3359
D2	3368	3369	3370	3371	3372	3373	3374	3375
D3	3384	3385	3386	3387	3388	3389	3390	3391
D4	3400	3401	3402	3403	3404	3405	3406	3407
D5	3416	3417	3418	3419	3420	3421	3422	3423
D6	3432	3433	3434	3435	3436	3437	3438	3439
D7	3448	3449	3450	3451	3452	3453	3454	3455
D8	3464	3465	3466	3467	3468	3469	3470	3471
D9	3480	3481	3482	3483	3484	3485	3486	3487
DA	3496	3497	3498	3499	3500	3501	3502	3503
DB	3512	3513	3514	3515	3516	3517	3518	3519
DC	3528	3529	3530	3531	3532	3533	3534	3535
DD	3544	3545	3546	3547	3548	3549	3550	3551
DE	3560	3561	3562	3563	3564	3565	3566	3567
DF	3576	3577	3578	3579	3580	3581	3582	3583
E0	3592	3593	3594	3595	3596	3597	3598	3599
E1	3608	3609	3610	3611	3612	3613	3614	3615
E2	3624	3625	3626	3627	3628	3629	3630	3631
E3	3640	3641	3642	3643	3644	3645	3646	3647
E4	3656	3657	3658	3659	3660	3661	3662	3663
E5	3672	3673	3674	3675	3676	3677	3678	3679
E6	3688	3689	3690	3691	3692	3693	3694	3695
E7	3704	3705	3706	3707	3708	3709	3710	3711
E8	3720	3721	3722	3723	3724	3725	3726	3727
E9	3736	3737	3738	3739	3740	3741	3742	3743
EA	3752	3753	3754	3755	3756	3757	3758	3759
EB	3768	3769	3770	3771	3772	3773	3774	3775
EC	3784	3785	3786	3787	3788	3789	3790	3791
ED	3800	3801	3802	3803	3804	3805	3806	3807
EE	3816	3817	3818	3819	3820	3821	3822	3823
EF	3832	3833	3834	3835	3836	3837	3838	3839
F0	3848	3849	3850	3851	3852	3853	3854	3855
F1	3864	3865	3866	3867	3868	3869	3870	3871
F2	3880	3881	3882	3883	3884	3885	3886	3887
F3	3896	3897	3898	3899	3900	3901	3902	3903
F4	3912	3913	3914	3915	3916	3917	3918	3919
F5	3928	3929	3930	3931	3932	3933	3934	3935
F6	3944	3945	3946	3947	3948	3949	3950	3951
F7	3960	3961	3962	3963	3964	3965	3966	3967
F8	3976	3977	3978	3979	3980	3981	3982	3983
F9	3992	3993	3994	3995	3996	3997	3998	3999
FA	4008	4009	4010	4011	4012	4013	4014	4015
FB	4024	4025	4026	4027	4028	4029	4030	4031
FC	4040	4041	4042	4043	4044	4045	4046	4047
FD	4056	4057	4058	4059	4060	4061	4062	4063
FE	4072	4073	4074	4075	4076	4077	4078	4079
FF	4088	4089	4090	4091	4092	4093	4094	4095

ALPHABET-DEC-HEX-EBCDIC

Hex	Dec	Alph	EBCDIC
00	0	Null	00
01	1	SOH	01
02	2	STX	02
03	3	ETX	03
04	4	EOT	37
05	5	ENQ	2D
06	6	ACK	2E
07	7	BEL	2F
08	8	BS	16
09	9	HT	05
0A	10	LF	25
0B	11	VT	0B
0C	12	FF	0C
0D	13	CR	0D
0E	14	SO	0E
0F	15	SI	0F
10	16	DLE	10
11	17	DC1	11
12	18	DC2	12
13	19	DC3	13
14	20	DC4	3C
15	21	NAK	3D
16	22	SYN	32
17	23	ETB	11
18	24	CAN	18
19	25	EM	19
1A	26	SUB	3F
1B	27	ESC	27
1C	28	FS	22
1D	29	GS	—
1E	30	RS	35
1F	31	US	—
20	32	space	40
21	33	!	5A
22	34	"	7F
23	35	#	7B
24	36	$	5B
25	37	%	6C
26	38	&	50
27	39	'	7D
28	40	(	4D
29	41	)	5D
2A	42	*	5C
2B	43	+	4E
2C	44	,	6B
2D	45	-	60
2E	46	.	4B
2F	47	/	61
30	48	0	F0
31	49	1	F1
32	50	2	F2
33	51	3	F3
34	52	4	F4
35	53	5	F5
36	54	6	F6
37	55	7	F7
38	56	8	F8
39	57	9	F9
3A	58	:	7A
3B	59	;	5E
3C	60	<	4C
3D	61	=	7E
3E	62	>	6E
3F	63	?	6F
40	64	@	7C
41	65	A	C1
42	66	B	C2
43	67	C	C3
44	68	D	C4
45	69	E	C5
46	70	F	C6
47	71	G	C7
48	72	H	C8
49	73	I	C9
4A	74	J	D1
4B	75	K	D2
4C	76	L	D3
4D	77	M	D4
4E	78	N	D5
4F	79	O	D6
50	80	P	D7
51	81	Q	D8
52	82	R	D9
53	83	S	E2
54	84	T	E3
55	85	U	E4
56	86	V	E5
57	87	W	E6
58	88	X	E7
59	89	Y	E8
5A	90	Z	E9
5B	91	[	—
5C	92	\	E0
5D	93	]	—
5E	94	^	—
5F	95	_	6D
60	96	`	—
61	97	a	81
62	98	b	82
63	99	c	83
64	100	d	84
65	101	e	85
66	102	f	86
67	103	g	87
68	104	h	88
69	105	i	89
6A	106	j	91
6B	107	k	92
6C	108	l	93
6D	109	m	94
6E	110	n	95
6F	111	o	96
70	112	p	97
71	113	q	98
72	114	r	99
73	115	s	A2
74	116	t	A3
75	117	u	A4
76	118	v	A5
77	119	w	A6
78	120	x	A7
79	121	y	A8
7A	122	z	A9
7B	123	{	C0
7C	124			6A
7D	125	}	D0
7E	126	~	A1
7F	127	DEL	07

POCKET PCRef

PC Hardware

VIDEO STANDARDS

Video Standard (year)	Mode	Horz x Vert Resolution (pixels)	Simultaneous Colors	Vert Freq Hz	Horz Freq kHz	Band Width mHz
MDA (1981)	Text	720x350	1	50Hz	18.43	16.257
HGC	Text	640x400	1	50	18.43	16.257
	Graph	720x348	1	50	"	"
CGA (1981)	Text	320x200	4	60	15.75	14.318
	Graph	320x200	4	60	"	"
	Graph	640x200	1	60	"	"
EGA Color (1985)	Text	640x350	16	60	15.75	14.318
	Graph	640x350	16	60	to	to
	Graph	320x200	16	60	21.85	16.257
	Graph	640x350	64	60	"	"
EGA Mono	Graph	640x350	1	50	"	"
MCGA (1987)	Text	320x400	4	70	31.50	25.175
	Text	640x400	2	70	"	"
	Graph	640x480	2	60	"	"
	Graph	320x200	256	70	"	"
VGA (1987)	Text	720x400	16	70	31.50	25.175
	Text	720x400	16	70	"	to
	Text	360x400	16	70	"	28.322
	Graph	640x480	16	60	"	"
	Graph	640x480	2	60	"	"
	Graph	320x200	256	70	"	"
Super VGA (1989)	Graph	800x600	16	50,60	35,37	
	Graph	800x600	256	and	and	
	Graph	1024x768	16	72	60,80	
8514-A (1987)	Graph	1024x768	16	43.48	35.52	44.897
	Graph	640x480	256	43.48	"	"
	Graph	1024x768	256	43.48	"	"
XGA (1990)	Graph	640x480	256	43.48	35.52	
	Graph	1024x768	256	43.48	"	
	Graph	640x480	65536	43.48	"	
	Graph	1024x768	16	43.48	"	

Note: Most video cards built around the standards listed above are downward compatible and will function in the modes of the earlier standards. For example, most VGA cards will operate in all of the MDA, CGA, and EGA modes.

VIDEO STANDARDS

Abbreviations for the graphics standards defined on the previous page are as follows:

MDA......	Monochrome Display Adapter
HGC......	Hercules Graphics Card
CGA......	Color Graphics Adapter
EGA......	Enhanced Graphics Adapter
PGA......	Professional Graphics Adapter
MCGA....	Multi Color Graphics Array
VGA......	Video Graphics Array
Super VGA.	Super Video Graphics Array, VESA
XGA......	Extended Graphics Array

Pixels are coded by assigning bits to the colors. 1 bit/pixel boards can only display 1 color, monochrome (the bit is either on or off). 2 bits/pixel boards can display 4 colors (CGA for example). 8 bits/pixel can display 256 colors (VGA for example). 24 bits/pixel can display 16,777,216 simultaneous colors. Video board memory limits the number of colors that a graphics adapter can store; for example, a 1024x768 adapter requires 786,432 bytes of memory in order to display 256 colors. Needless to say, future video memory requirements will continue to grow. Consider that a 4096x4096 image with 24 bit/pixel color will require nearly 50 meg of video RAM.

KEYBOARD SCAN CODES

Generally, expanded PC/XT, AT and PS/2 keyboard scan codes are converted to PC/XT standard scan codes prior to ROM BIOS ASCII Code conversion. Notable exceptions are the F11 and F12 keys, which generate new scan codes (see table below). Extended ASCII characters and some special "characters" are achieved by combining 2 or more key presses.

Shaded areas in the table represent keys and scan codes of the standard 84 key PC/XT keyboard, however, the "Key #" listed in column 1 of the table is not the correct Key # for the XT class keyboard. See your computer's keyboard documentation for verification of the correct Key # to Key Name assignments. AT Scan Codes are only relevant to AT class and PS/2 (Models 50 and above) computers.

Key # for 101 Keybd	Key Name	XT scan codes Down • Up	AT hardware scan codes Down • Up
1	Esc	01 • 81	76 • F0 76
2	F1	3B • BB	05 • F0 05
3	F2	3C • BC	06 • F0 06
4	F3	3D • BD	04 • F0 04
5	F4	3E • BE	0C • F0 0C
6	F5	3F • BF	03 • F0 03
7	F6	40 • C0	0B • F0 0B
8	F7	41 • C1	83 • F0 83
9	F8	42 • C2	0A • F0 0A
10	F9	43 • C3	01 • F0 01
11	F10	44 • C4	09 • F0 09
12	F11	57 • D7	78 • F0 78
13	F12	58 • D8	07 • F0 07

Special Keys (expanded keyboards only)

14	*PrtScn / SysReq*		
14	–PRINT SCRN	E0 2A E0 37•	E0 12 E0 7C•
14		E0 B7 E0 AA	E0 F0 7C E0 F0 12
14	–Sys Req (+ CTRL)	E0 37 • E0 B7	E0 7C • E0 F0 7C
14	–Sys Req (+ ALT)	54 • D4	84 • F0 84
15	*ScrollLock*	46 • C6	7E • F0 7E
16	*Pause / Break*		
16	–PAUSE (key alone)	4E11 1D45 E19DC5•	3E11 1477 E1 F0 14 F0 77•
16	(No Auto Repeat)	No Up Code	No Up Code
16	–BREAK (+ CTRL)	E0 46 E0 C6•	E0 7E E0 F0 7E•
16	(No Auto Repeat)	No Up Code	No Up Code
31	*Insert Key*	E0 52• E0 D2	E0 70 • E0 F0 70
31	–LEFT SHIFT case	E0 AA E0 52•	E0 F0 12 E0 70•
31		E0 D2 E0 2A	E0 F0 70 E0 12
31	–RIGHT SHIFT case	E0 B6 E0 52•	E0 F0 59 E0 70•
31		E0 D2 E0 36	E0 F0 70 E0 59
31	–NUM LOCK ON case	E0 2A E0 52•	E0 12 E0 70•
31		E0 D2 E0 AA	E0 F0 70 E0 F0 12

Key # for 101 Keybd	Key Name	XT scan codes Down • Up	AT hardware scan codes Down • Up
32	**Home**	E0 47 • E0 C7	E0 6C • E0 F0 6C
32	–LEFT SHIFT case	E0 AA E0 47•	E0 F0 12 E0 6C•
32		E0 C7 E0 2A	E0 6C E0 12
32	–RIGHT SHIFT case	E0 B6 E0 47•	E0 F0 59 E0 6C•
32		E0 C7 E0 36	E0 6C E0 59
32	–NUM LOCK ON case	E0 2A E0 47•	E0 12 E0 6C•
32		E0 C7 E0 AA	E0 F0 6C E0 F0 12
33	**PageUp**	E0 49 • E0 C9	E0 7D • E0 F0 7D
33	–LEFT SHIFT case	E0 AA E0 49•	E0 F0 12 E0 7D•
33		E0 C9 E0 2A	E0 7D E0 12
33	–RIGHT SHIFT case	E0 B6 E0 49•	E0 F0 59 E0 7D•
33		E0 C9 E0 36	E0 7D E0 59
33	–NUM LOCK ON case	E0 2A E0 49•	E0 12 E0 7D•
33		E0 C9 E0 AA	E0 F0 7D E0 F0 12
52	**Delete**	E0 53 • E0 D3	E0 71 • E0 F0 71
52	–LEFT SHIFT case	E0 AA E0 53•	E0 F0 12 E0 71•
52		E0 D3 E0 2A	E0 71 E0 12
52	–RIGHT SHIFT case	E0 B6 E0 53•	E0 F0 59 E0 71•
52		E0 D3 E0 36	E0 71 E0 59
52	–NUM LOCK ON case	E0 2A E0 53•	E0 12 E0 71•
52		E0 D3 E0 AA	E0 F0 71 E0 F0 12
53	**End**	E0 4F • E0 CF	E0 69 • E0 F0 69
53	–LEFT SHIFT case	E0 AA E0 4F•	E0 F0 12 E0 69•
53		E0 CF E0 2A	E0 69 E0 12
53	–RIGHT SHIFT case	E0 B6 E0 4F•	E0 F0 59 E0 69•
53		E0 CF E0 36	E0 69 E0 59
53	–NUM LOCK ON case	E0 2A E0 4F•	E0 12 E0 69•
53		E0 CF E0 AA	E0 F0 69 E0 F0 12
54	**PageDown**	E0 51 • E0 D1	E0 7A • E0 F0 7A
54	–LEFT SHIFT case	E0 AA E0 51•	E0 F0 12 E0 7A•
54		E0 D1 E0 2A	E0 7A E0 12
54	–RIGHT SHIFT case	E0 B6 E0 51•	E0 F0 59 E0 7A•
54		E0 D1 E0 36	E0 7A E0 59
54	–NUM LOCK ON case	E0 2A E0 51•	E0 12 E0 7A•
54		E0 D1 E0 AA	E0 F0 7A E0 F0 12
87	**UpArrow**	E0 48 • E0 C8	E0 75 • E0 F0 75
87	–LEFT SHIFT case	E0 AA E0 48•	E0 F0 12 E0 75•
87		E0 C8 E0 2A	E0 75 E0 12
87	–RIGHT SHIFT case	E0 B6 E0 48•	E0 F0 59 E0 75•
87		E0 C8 E0 36	E0 75 E0 59
87	–NUM LOCK ON case	E0 2A E0 48•	E0 12 E0 75•
87		E0 C8 E0 AA	E0 F0 75 E0 F0 12
97	**LeftArrow**	E0 4B • E0 CB	E0 6B • E0 F0 6B
97	–LEFT SHIFT case	E0 AA E0 4B•	E0 F0 12 E0 6B•
97		E0 CB E0 2A	E0 6B E0 12
97	–RIGHT SHIFT case	E0 B6 E0 4B•	E0 F0 59 E0 6B•
97		E0 CB E0 36	E0 6B E0 59
97	–NUM LOCK ON case	E0 2A E0 4B•	E0 12 E0 6B•
97		E0 CB E0 AA	E0 F0 6B E0 F0 12

Key # for 101 Keybd	Key Name	XT scan codes Down • Up	AT hardware scan codes Down • Up
98	*DownArrow*	E0 50• E0 D0	E0 72• E0 F0 72
98	–LEFT SHIFT case	E0 AA E0 50•	E0 F0 12 E0 72•
98		E0 D0 E0 2A	E0 F0 72 E0 12
98	–RIGHT SHIFT case	E0 B6 E0 50•	E0 F0 59 E0 72•
98		E0 D0 E0 36	E0 F0 72 E0 59
98	–NUM LOCK ON case	E0 2A E0 50•	E0 12 E0 72•
98		E0 D0 E0 AA	E0 F0 72 E0 F0 12
99	*RightArrow*	E0 4D• E0 CD	E0 74• E0 F0 74
99	–LEFT SHIFT case	E0 AA E0 4D•	E0 F0 12 E0 74•
99		E0 CD E0 2A	E0 F0 74 E0 12
99	–RIGHT SHIFT case	E0 B6 E0 4D•	E0 F0 59 E0 74•
99		E0 CD E0 36	E0 F0 74 E0 59
99	–NUM LOCK ON case	E0 2A E0 4D•	E0 12 E0 74•
99		E0 CD E0 AA	E0 F0 74 E0 F0 12

Alpha–Numeric Primary Keyboard Keys
(includes expanded keys)

17	` ~ (accent, tilde)	29 • A9	0E • F0 0E
18	1 !	02 • 82	16 • F0 16
19	2 @	03 • 83	1E • F0 1E
20	3 #	04 • 84	26 • F0 26
21	4 $	05 • 85	25 • F0 25
22	5 %	06 • 86	2E • F0 2E
23	6 ^ (6, caret)	07 • 87	36 • F0 36
24	7 &	08 • 88	3D • F0 3D
25	8 * (8, asterisk)	09 • 89	3E • F0 3E
26	9 (	0A • 8A	46 • F0 46
27	0)	0B • 8B	45 • F0 45
28	– _ (dash,underline)	0C • 8C	4E • F0 4E
29	= + (equal, plus)	0D • 8D	55 • F0 55
30	Bkspace	0E • 8E	66 • F0 66
38	Tab	0F • 8F	0D • F0 0D
39	q Q	10 • 90	15 • F0 15
40	w W	11 • 91	1D • F0 1D
41	e E	12 • 92	24 • F0 24
42	r R	13 • 93	2D • F0 2D
43	t T	14 • 94	2C • F0 2C
44	y Y	15 • 95	35 • F0 35
45	u U	16 • 96	3C • F0 3C
46	i I	17 • 97	43 • F0 43
47	o O	18 • 98	44 • F0 44
48	p P	19 • 99	4D • F0 4D
49	[{	1A • 9A	54 • F0 54
50	] }	1B • 9B	5B • F0 5B
51	\	(backslash,bar)	2B • AB	5D • F0 5D
59	CapsLock	3A • BA	58 • F0 58
60	a A	1E • 9E	1C • F0 1C
61	s S	1F • 9F	1B • F0 1B
62	d D	20 • A0	23 • F0 23
63	f F	21 • A1	2B • F0 2B
64	g G	22 • A2	34 • F0 34

KEYBOARD SCAN CODES (cont.)

Key # for 101 Keybd	Key Name	XT scan codes Down • Up	AT hardware scan codes Down • Up
65	h H	23 • A3	33 • F0 33
66	j J	24 • A4	3B • F0 3B
67	k K	25 • A5	42 • F0 42
68	l L	26 • A6	4B • F0 4B
69	; : (semicolon,colon)	27 • A7	4C • F0 4C
70	' " (single quote,double)	28 • A8	52 • F0 52
71	Enter	1C • 9C	5A • F0 5A
75	Shift(left)	2A • AA	12 • F0 12
76	z Z	2C • AC	1A • F0 1A
77	x X	2D • AD	22 • F0 22
78	c C	2E • AE	21 • F0 21
79	v V	2F • AF	2A • F0 2A
80	b B	30 • B0	32 • F0 32
81	n N	31 • B1	31 • F0 31
82	m M	32 • B2	3A • F0 3A
83	, < (comma,less than)	33 • B3	41 • F0 41
84	. > (period,greater than)	34 • B4	49 • F0 49
85	/ ? (forward slash, ?)	35 • B5	4A • F0 4A
86	Shift(right)	36 • B6	59 • F0 59
92	Ctrl(left)	1D • 9D	14 • F0 14
93	Alt(left)	38 • B8	11 • F0 11
94	Space	39 • B9	29 • F0 29
95	Alt(right)	E0 38 • E0 B8	E0 11 • E0 F0 11
96	Ctrl(right)	E0 1D • E0 9D	E0 14 • E0 F0 14

Keypad keys
(Includes expanded keyboard layout)

34	NumLock	45 • C5	77 • F0 77
35	/	E0 35 • E0 B5	E0 4A • E0 F0 4A
35	–LEFT SHIFT case	E0 AA E0 35 •	E0 F0 12 E0 4A •
35		E0 B5 E0 2A	E0 F0 4A E0 12
35	–RIGHT SHIFT case	E0 B6 E0 35 •	E0 F0 59 E0 4A •
35		E0 B5 E0 36	E0 F0 4A E0 59
36	* (PrtSc 84 key)	37 • B7	7C • F0 7C
37	–	4A • C4	7B • F0 7B
55	Home 7	47 • C7	6C • F0 6C
56	UpArrow 8	48 • C8	75 • F0 75
57	PageUp 9	49 • C9	7D • F0 7D
58	+	4E • CE	79 • F0 79
72	LeftArrow 4	4B • CB	6B • F0 6B
73	5	4C • CC	73 • F0 73
74	RightArrow 6	4D • CD	74 • F0 74
88	End 1	4F • CF	69 • F0 69
89	DownArrow 2	50 • D0	72 • F0 72
90	PageDown 3	51 • D1	7A • F0 7A
91	Enter	E0 1C • E0 9C	E0 5A • E0 F0 5A
100	Ins 0	52 • D2	70 • F0 70
101	Del .	53 • D3	71 • F0 71

PARALLEL PRINTER INTERFACE

Printer Pin Number	Signal Description	Function	Signal Direction At Printer
1	STROBE	Reads in the data	Input
2	DATA Bit 0	Data line	Input
3	DATA Bit 1	Data line	Input
4	DATA Bit 2	Data line	Input
5	DATA Bit 3	Data line	Input
6	DATA Bit 4	Data line	Input
7	DATA Bit 5	Data line	Input
8	DATA Bit 6	Data line	Input
9	DATA Bit 7	Data line	Input
10	ACKNLG	Acknowledge receipt of data	Output
11	Busy	Printer is busy	Output
12	Paper Empty	Printer out of paper	Output
13	SLCT	Online mode indicator	Output
14	Auto Feed XT		Input
15	Not Used	Not Used	
16	Signal ground	Signal ground	
17	Frame ground	Frame ground	
18	+5 volts	+5 volts	
19-30	Ground	Return signals of pins 1–12, twisted pairs.	
31	Input Prime or INIT	Resets printer, clears buffer & initializes	Input
32	Fault or Error	Indicates offline mode	Output
33	Signal ground	External ground	
34	Not Used	Not Used	
35	+5 Volts	+5 Volts (3.3 K-ohm)	
36	SLCT IN	TTL high level	Input

The above pinout is at the printer plug, computer side pinouts are on the next page. The "Parallel" or "Centronics" configuration for printer data transmission has become the de facto standard in the personal computer industry. This configuration was developed by a printer manufacturer (Centronics) as an alternative to serial data transmission. High data transfer rates are the main advantage of parallel and are attained by simultaneous transmission of all bits of a binary "word" (normally an ASCII code). Disadvantages of the parallel transfer are the requirement for 8 separate data lines and computer to printer cable lengths of less than 12 feet.

PARALLEL PINOUTS @ COMPUTER

DB25 Systems

Computer Pin Number	Signal Description	Function	Signal Direction At Computer
1	STROBE	Reads in the data	Output
2	DATA Bit 0	Data line	Output
3	DATA Bit 1	Data line	Output
4	DATA Bit 2	Data line	Output
5	DATA Bit 3	Data line	Output
6	DATA Bit 4	Data line	Output
7	DATA Bit 5	Data line	Output
8	DATA Bit 6	Data line	Output
9	DATA Bit 7	Data line	Output
10	ACKNLG	Acknowledge receipt of data	Input
11	Busy	Printer is busy	Input
12	Paper Empty	Printer out of paper	Input
13	SLCT	Online mode indicator	Input
14	Auto Feed XT		Input
15	Fault or Error	Indicates offline mode	Input
16	Input Prime or INIT	Resets printer, clears buffer & initializes	Output
17	SLCT IN	TTL high level	Output
18-25	Ground	Return signals of pins 1–12, twisted pairs.	

PS-8 and 9 POWER CONNECTOR

Pin #	PS-8 (XT)	PS-8 (AT)	PS-9 (XT & AT)
1	Power ground	Power good	Ground
2	Align Key	+5 volt	Ground
3	+12 volt	+12 volt	−5 volt
4	−12 volt	−12 volt	+5 volt
5	Ground	Ground	+5 volt
6	Ground	Ground	+5 volt

DISK DRIVE POWER CONNECTOR

Pin #	Description (4 pin molex)
1	+12 volt
2	Ground
3	Ground
4	+5 volt

SERIAL I/O INTERFACES (RS232C)

Standard DB25 Pin Connector

Serial Pin Number	Signal Description	Function	Signal Direction At Device
1	FG	Frame ground	
2	TD	Transmit Data	Output
3	RD	Receive Data	Input
4	RTS	Request to Send	Output
5	CTS	Clear to Send	Input
6	DSR	Data Set Ready	Input
7	SG	Signal Ground	
8	DCD	Data Carrier Detect	Input
9	+V	+DC test voltage	Input
10	– V	– DC test voltage	Input
11	QM	Equalizer Mode	Input
12	(S)DCD	2nd Data Carrier Detect	Input
13	(S)CTS	2nd Clear to Send	Input
14	(S)TD	2nd Transmitted Data	Output
15	TC	Transmitter Clock	Input
16	(S)RD	2nd Received Data	Input
17	RC	Receiver Clock	Input
18	Not used	Not used	
19	(S)RTS	2nd Request to Send	Output
20	DTR	Data Terminal Ready	Output
21	SQ	Signal Quality Detect	Input
22	RI	Ring Indicator	Input
23		Data Rate Selector	Output
24	(TC)	External Transmitter Clk.	Output
25	Not used	Not used	

IBM® Standard DB9 Pin Connector

Serial Pin Number	Signal Description	Function	Signal Direction At Device
1	DCD	Data Carrier Detect	Input
2	RD	Receive Data	Input
3	SD	Transmit Data	Output
4	DTR	Data Terminal Ready	Output
5	SG	Signal Ground	
6	DSR	Data Set Ready	Input
7	RTS	Request to Send	Output
8	CTS	Clear to Send	Input
9	RI	Ring Indicator	Input

NOTES ON SERIAL INTERFACING

Printers and asynchronous modems are relatively unsophisticated pieces of electronic equipment. Although all 25 pins of the **Standard DB25** serial connector are listed 1 page back, only a few of the pins are needed for normal applications. The following pins list gives the necessary pins for each of the indicated applications.

1. "Dumb Terminals" – 1,2,3, & 7
2. Printers and asynchronous modems – 1,2,3,4,5,6,7,8, & 20
3. "Smart" and synchronous modems – 1,2,3,4,5,6,7,8,13,14,
   15,17,20,22, & 24

Cable requirements also differ, depending on the particular hardware being used. The asynchronous modems normally use the 9 pin or 25 pin cables and are wired 1 to 1 (ie, pin 1 on one end of the cable goes to pin 1 on the other end of the cable.) Serial printers, however, have several wires switched in order to accommodate "handshaking" between computer and printer. The rewired junction is called a "Modem Eliminator". In the case of Standard DB25 the following are typical rewires:

DB25 @ Computer Standard	DB25 @ Printer IBM PC		DB25 @ Computer Second Standard	DB25 @ Printer PC
1	1		1	1
3	2		3	2
2	3		2	3
8	4		20	5, 6 & 8
4	8		7	7
5 & 6	20		5, 6 & 8	20
20	5 & 6			
7	7			

PC to Terminal			Std Hewlett-Packard	
1	1		1	1
2	3		2	3
3	2		3	2
4	5		4 & 5	8
5	4		8	4 & 5
6 & 8	20		6	20
20	6 & 8		7 & 22	7 & 22
7	7		17	15
.			11	12
.			12	11
.			15 & 24	17
.			20	6

VIDEO CARD PINOUTS

Pin Number	Description

Monochrome Display Adapter (MDA and HGC)

1 & 2	Ground
3, 4, & 5	Not Used
6	+ Intensity
7	+ Video
8	+ Horizontal Drive
9	– Vertical Drive

Color Graphics Display Adapter (CGA)

1 & 2	Ground
3	Red
4	Green
5	Blue
6	+ Intensity
7	Reserved
8	+ Horizontal Drive
9	– Vertical Drive

CGA Composite Video (RCA phono jack)

1 (pin)	1.5 volt DC video signal
2 (shell)	Ground

Enhanced Graphics Adapter (EGA)

1	Ground
2	Secondary Red
3	Red
4	Green
5	Blue
6	Secondary Green / Intensity
7	Secondary Blue / Monochrome
8	Horizontal Drive
9	Vertical Drive

Video Graphics Array (VGA)

Color VGA		Monochrome VGA	
1	Red (Output)	1	Not Used
2	Green (Output)	2	Monochrome Video
3	Blue (Output)	3	Not Used
4	Reserved	4	Not Used
5	Digital Ground	5	Ground
6	Red Return (Input)	6	Key
7	Green Return (Input)	7	Monochrome Ground
8	Blue Return (Input)	8	Not Used
9	Plug	9	No Connection
10	Digital Ground	10	Horizontal Sync Ground
11	Reserved	11	Not Used
12	Reserved	12	Vertical Sync Ground
13	Horizontal Sync (Output)	13	Horizontal Sync
14	Vertical Sync (Output)	14	Vertical Sync
15	Reserved	15	No Connection

GAME CONTROL CABLE

Joystick Pin Number	Signal Description	Function	Signal Direction At Joystk
1.	+5 Volts	Supply voltage	Input
2.	Button 1	Push Button 1	Output
3.	Position 0	X Coordinate	Output
4.	Ground	Ground	
5.	Ground	Ground	
6.	Position 1	Y Coordinate	Output
7.	Button 2	Push Button 2	Output
8.	+5 Volts	Supply voltage	Input
9.	+5 Volts	Supply voltage	Input
10.	Button 3	Push Button 3	Output
11.	Position 2	X Coordinate	Output
12.	Ground	Ground	
13.	Position 3	Y Coordinate	Output
14.	Button 4	Push Button 4	Output
15.	+5 Volts	Supply voltage	Input

LIGHT PEN INTERFACE

Pin #	Description
1.	– Light Pen Input
2.	No connection
3.	– Light Pen Switch
4.	Chassis Ground
5.	+5 Volts
6.	+12 Volts

KEYBOARD CONNECTOR

Pin #	Description
1.	Clock (TTL signal)
2.	Data (TTL signal)
3.	Not used
4.	Ground
5.	Power (+5 volt)

286/386/486 BATTERY CONNECTOR

Pin #	Description
1.	Ground
2.	Not used
3.	Not used, or alignment key
4.	+6 volt

SPEAKER CONNECTOR

1.	Audio
2.	Alignment key
3.	Ground
4.	+5 volt

HAYES COMPATIBLE MODEM COMMAND SETTINGS

Command	Function
>>>>>Note: all commands are **not** available on all modems!<<<<<	
+++.....	Default escape code, wait for modem to return state
A.......	Force answer mode; Immediate answer on ring
A /......	Repeat last command line (Replaces AT)
AT	Attention code
Cn	n=Ø is Transmitter off, n=1 is on, (1=default)
Bn.....	n=Ø is CCITT answer tone, n=1 is US/Canada Tone
Dn	Dial telephone number
	n=Ø to 9 for phone numbers
	n=T is Touch Tone Dial, P is Pulse Dial
	n=R is Originate Only, n= , is Pause
	n=! is xfer call to following extension
	n=" is dial letters that follow
	n=@ is Dial, Wait for answer, & continue
	n= ; is Return to command mode after dialing
En......	n=Ø is no character echo in command state
	n=1 is echo all characters in command state
Fn.....	n=Ø is Half Duplex; n=1 if Full Duplex
Hn	n=Ø is On Hook (Hang Up), n=1 is Off Hook
	n=2 is Special Off Hook
In	n=Ø is Display product code, n=1 show Check Sum
	n=2 is show RAM test, n=3 is show call time length
	n=4 is show current modem settings
Kn.....	n=Ø at AT13 show last call length, n=1 show time
Ln.....	Speaker volume control: n=Ø or 1 is low volume
	n=2 is medium volume; n=3 is high volume.
Mn	n=Ø is Speaker always off, n=2 is always on
	n=1 is Speaker on until carrier detected (default)
	n=3 is Speaker on during CONNECT sequence only.
Nn	Auto data standard/speed adjust; n=Ø is connect at S37,
	n=1 auto data standard and speed adjust to match
On	n=Ø is return to on-line; n=1 is return to on-line & retain
Qn	n=Ø is send Result Codes; n=1 is do not send code
	n=2 is send result code only when originating call.
SØ=n ..	n=Ø to 255 rings before answer (see switch 5)
S1=n ..	Counts rings from Ø to 255
S2=n ..	Set escape code character, n=Ø to 127, 43 default
S3=n ..	Set carriage return character, n=Ø to 127, 13 default
S4=n ..	Set line feed character, n=Ø to 127, 10 default
S5=n ..	Set backspace character, n=Ø to 127, 8 default
S6=n ..	Wait time for dial tone, n=2 to 255 seconds
S7=n ..	Wait time for carrier, n=2 to 255 seconds
S8=n ..	Set duration of "," pause character, n=Ø to 255 sec.
S9=n ..	Carrier detect response time, n=1 to 255 1/10 secs.
S10=n ..	Delay time carrier loss to hang-up, n=1 to 255 1/10 s.
S11=n ..	Duration & space of Touch Tones, n=50 to 255 ms.
S12=n ..	Escape code guard time, n=50 to 255 1/50 seconds
S13=n ..	UART Status Register Bit Mapped (reserved)
S14=n ..	Option Register, Product code returned by AT1Ø

HAYES COMPATIBLE MODEM COMMAND SETTINGS

Command	Function
S15=n . .	*Flag Register (reserved)*
S16=n . .	Self test mode. n=Ø is data mode (default), n=1 is Analog Loopback, n=2 is dial test, n=4 is Test Pattern, n=5 is Analog Loopback and Test Pattern.
S18=n . .	Test timer for modem diagnostic tests
S37=n . .	Set line speed. Used in conjunction with Nn. n=Ø Attempt at speed of last AT command; n=1 to 3 attempt at 300bps; n=4 reserved; n=5 attempt 1200bps; n=6 attempt 2400bps; n=7 reserved; n=8 use 4800bps; n=9 use 9600; =10-12200bps; =11-14400bps; =12-7200
Sn ?. . . .	Send contents of Register n (Ø to 16) to Computer
Vn	n=Ø is send result codes as digits, n=1 is words
Wn	Protocol negotiation progress report; n=Ø is progress is not reported; n=1 is reported; n=2 is not reported but CONNECT XXXX message reports DCE speed
Xn	Send normal or extended result codes: n=Ø send basic set/blind dial; n=1 extended/blind dial; n=2 extended/dial tone; n=3 extended/blind & busy; n=4 extended/dial tone, busy.
Yn	Long space disconnect; n=Ø is disabled; n=1 is enabled.
Zn	Modem reset: n=Ø is power on; =1 to 3 user; =4 is factory
&Cn . . .	n=Ø is DCD always active; n=1 active during connect
&Dn . . .	n=Ø DTR always ignored, =1 DTR causes return to command, =2 DTR disconnects, =3 disconnect/reset
&F	Get Factory Configuration
&Gn . . .	n=Ø Disable Guard Tone, =1 is 550hz, =2 is 1800hz
&Kn . . .	DTE: n=Ø is disable flow control, n=3 Enable RTS/CTS flow control; n=4 enable XON/XOFF flow control; n=5 enable transparent XON/XOFF flow control.
&Ln . . .	n=Ø or 1 Speaker Volume Low, =2 medium, =3 high
&Mn . . .	Communications mode (same as &Qn).
&Pn . . .	n=Ø Pulse Make/Break Ratio USA 39% / 61% n=1 Pulse Make/Break Ratio UK 33% / 67%
&Qn . . .	Communication mode: n=Ø is Async, Direct mode; n=4 modem issues OK result code; n=5 Error correction mode; n=6 Async, Normal mode; n=8 MNP; n=9 V.42 and V.42bis modes.
&Rn . . .	n=Ø is CTS always active, n=1 CTS always active
&Sn . . .	n=Ø is DSR always active, n=1 DSR active at connect
&Tn . . .	Test Commands: n=Ø end test, =1 local analog loopback, =3 local digital loopback, =4 enable Rmt digital loopback, =5 disable digital loopback, =6 request Rmt digital loop, =7 request Rmt dig loop & enter self test, =8 local analog loop & self test
&Vn . . .	View current configuration
&W . . .	Write Configuration to Memory
&Yn . . .	n=Ø is Default is user configuration at NVRAM Ø ; n=1 default is user configuration at NVRAM location 1.
&Zn=x . .	Store Phone Number "x" at location "n". n=0,1,2, or 3

GPIB I/O INTERFACE (IEEE-488)

The HPIB/GPIB/IEEE-488 standard is a very powerful interface developed originally by Hewlett-Packard (HP-IB). The interface has been adopted by a variety of groups, such as IEEE, and is known by names such as HP-IB, GPIB, IEEE-488 and IEC Standard 625-1 (outside the US). Worldwide use of this standard has come about due to its ease of use, handshaking protocol, and precisely defined function.

Information management is handled by three device types: Talkers, Listeners, and Controllers. Talkers send information, Listeners receive data, and Controllers manage the interactions. Up to 15 devices can be interconnected, but are usually located within 20 feet of the computer. Additional extenders can be used to access more than 15 devices.

GPIB 24 Line Bus

Pin Number	Signal Description	Function
1	DATA I/O 1	Data line I/O bus
2	DATA I/O 2	Data line I/O bus
3	DATA I/O 3	Data line I/O bus
4	DATA I/O 4	Data line I/O bus
5	EIO	End or Identify
6	DAV	Data valid
7	NRFD	Not Ready For Data
8	NDAC	Data Not Accepted
9	SRQ	Service Request
10	IFC	Interface Clear
11	ATN	Attention
12	Shield	or wire ground
13	DATA I/O 5	Data line I/O bus
14	DATA I/O 6	Data line I/O bus
15	DATA I/O 7	Data line I/O bus
16	DATA I/O 8	Data line I/O bus
17	REN	Remote Enable
18	Ground	Ground
19	Ground	Ground
20	Ground	Ground
21	Ground	Ground
22	Ground	Ground
23	Ground	Ground
24	Logic Ground	Logic Ground

Devices can be set up in star, linear or other combinations and are easily set up using male/female stackable connectors.

PC MEMORY MAP

Address Range	Size	Description
00000-003FF	1K	Interrupt Vectors
00400-7FFFF	512K	Bios, DOS, 512K RAM Expansion
80000-9FFFF	128K	128K RAM Expansion (Top of 640K)
A0000-AFFFF	64K	EGA Video Buffer
B0000-B7FFF	32K	Monochrome & other screen buffers
B8000-B8FFF	32K	CGA and EGA Buffers
AT LIM Expanded Memory 64K page is between 768K and 896K		
C0000-C3FFF	16K	EGA Video Bios
C4000-C7FFF	16K	ROM Expansion Area
XT LIM Expanded Memory 64K page is between 800K and 960K		
C8000-CCFFF	20K	XT Hard Disk Controller Bios
CD000-CFFFF	12K	User PROM, Memory mapped I/O
D0000-DFFFF	64K	User PROM, normal LIM Location for Expanded Memory
E0000-EFFFF	64K	ROM expansion, I/O for XT
F0000-FDFFF	56K	ROM BASIC
FE000-FFFD9	8K	BIOS
FFFF0-FFFF4	4	1st Code run after system power on
FFFF5-FFFFC	8	BIOS Release Date
FFFFE-FFFFF	2	Machine ID (Top of 1 Meg RAM)
100000-FFFFFF	15Meg	AT Extended Memory

PC HARDWARE INTERRUPTS

NMI		Non-Maskable Interrupt (Parity)

Interrupt Controller 1:

IRQ0	Timer Output
IRQ1	Keyboard
IRQ2	XT – Reserved
	AT – Route to Interrupt Controller 2, IRQ8 to 15
IRQ3	Serial Port COM2: or SDLC
IRQ4	Serial Port COM1: or SDLC
IRQ5	XT – Hard Disk Controller
	AT – Parallel Printer Port 2
IRQ6	Floppy Disk Controller
IRQ7	Parallel Printer Port LPT1:

Interrupt Controller 2 (AT Only):

IRQ8	Real Time Clock
IRQ9	Software redirect to IRQ2 (Int 0A Hex)
IRQ10	Reserved
IRQ11	Reserved
IRQ12	Reserved
IRQ13	80287 Math Coprocessor
IRQ14	Hard Disk Controller
IRQ15	Some hard drive and SCSI controllers

PC HARDWARE I/O MAP

8088 Class Systems

Address	Function
000–00F	DMA Controller (8237A)
020–021	Interrupt controller (8259A)
040–043	Timer (8253)
060–063	PPI (8255A)
080–083	DMA page register (74LS612)
0A0–0AF	NMI – Non Maskable Interrupt
200–20F	Game Port Joystick controller
210–217	Expansion Unit
2E8–2EF	COM4: Serial Port
2F8–2FF	COM2: Serial Port
300–31F	Prototype Card
320–32F	Hard Disk
378–37F	Parallel Printer Port 1
380–38F	SDLC
3B0–3BF	MDA – Monochrome Adapter and printer
3D0–3D7	CGA – Color Graphics Adapter
3E8–3EF	COM3: Serial Port
3F0–3F7	Floppy Diskette Controller
3F8–3FF	COM1: Serial Port

80286 /386/486 Class Systems

Address	Function
000–01F	DMA Controller #1 (8237A–5)
020–03F	Interrupt controller #1 (8259A)
040–05F	Timer (8254)
060–06F	Keyboard (8042)
070–07F	NMI – Non Maskable Interrupt & CMOS RAM
080–09F	DMA page register (74LS612)
0A0–0BF	Interrupt controller #2 (8259A)
0C0–0DF	DMA Controller #2 (8237A)
0F0–0FF	80287 Math Coprocessor
1F0–1F8	Hard Disk
200–20F	Game Port Joystick controller
258–25F	Intel Above Board
278–27F	Parallel Printer Port 2
2E8–2EF	COM4: Serial Port
2F8–2FF	COM2: Serial Port
300–31F	Prototype Card
378–37F	Parallel Printer Port 1
380–38F	SDLC or Bisynchronous Comm Port 2
3A0–3AF	Bisynchronous Comm Port 1
3B0–3BF	MDA – Monochrome Adapter
3BC–3BE	Parallel Printer on Monochrome Adapter
3C0–3CF	EGA – Reserved
3D0–3D7	CGA – Color Graphics Adapter
3E8–3EF	COM3: Serial Port
3F0–3F7	Floppy Diskette Controller
3F8–3FF	COM1: Serial Port

PC SOFTWARE INTERRUPTS

Address	Int #	Interrupt Name
000-003	0	Divide by zero
004-007	1	Single Step IRET
008-00B	2	NMI Non Maskable Interrupt
00C-00F	3	Breakpoint
010-013	4	Overflow IRET
014-017	5	Print Screen
018-01F	6	Reserved 018-01B and 01C-01F
020-023	8	Time of Day Ticker IRQ0
024-027	9	Keyboard IRQ1
028-02B	A	XT Reserved, AT IRQ2 direct to IRQ9
02C-02F	B	COM2 communications, IRQ3
030-033	C	COM1 communications, IRQ4
034-037	D	XT Hard disk, AT Parallel Printer, IRQ5
038-03B	E	Floppy Diskette, IRQ6
03C-03F	F	Parallel Printer 1, IRQ7, slave 8259, IRET
040-043	10	ROM Handler – Video
044-047	11	ROM Handler – Equipment Check
048-04B	12	ROM Handler – Memory Check
04C-04F	13	ROM Handler – Diskette I/O
050-053	14	ROM Handler – COMM I/O
054-057	15	XT Cassette, AT ROM Catchall Handlers
058-05B	16	ROM Handler – Keyboard I/O
05C-05F	17	ROM Handler – Printer I/O
060-063	18	ROM Handler – Basic Startup
064-067	19	ROM Handler – Bootstrap
068-06B	1A	ROM Handler – Time of Day
06C-06F	1B	ROM Handler – Keyboard Break
070-073	1C	ROM Handler – User Ticker
074-077	1D	ROM Pointer, Video Initialization
078-07B	1E	ROM Pointer, Diskette Parameters
07C-07F	1F	ROM Pointer, Graphics Characters Set 2
080-083	20	DOS – Terminate Program
084-087	21	DOS – Function Call
088-08B	22	DOS – Program's Terminate Address
08C-08F	23	DOS – Program's Control–Break Address
090-093	24	DOS – Critical Error Handler
094-097	25	DOS – Absolute Disk Read
098-09B	26	DOS – Absolute Disk Write
09C-09F	27	DOS – TSR Terminate & Stay Ready
0A0-0FF	28-3F	DOS – Idle Loop, IRET
100-103	40	Hard Disk Pointer – Original Floppy Handler
104-107	41	ROM Pointer, XT Hard Disk Parameters
108-10B	42-45	Reserved
10C-10F	46	ROM Pointer, AT Hard Disk Parameters
110-17F	47-5F	Reserved
180-19F	60-67	Reserved for User (67 is Expanded Mem)
1A0-1BF	68-6F	Not Used
1C0-1C3	70	AT Real Time Clock, IRQ8
1C4-1C7	71	AT Redirect to IRQ2, IRQ9, LAN Adapter 1
1C8-1CB	72	AT Reserved, IRQ10
1CC-1CF	73	AT Reserved, IRQ11
1D0-1D3	74	AT Reserved, IRQ12
1D4-1D7	75	AT 80287 Error to NMI, IRQ13
1D8-1DB	76	AT Hard Disk, IRQ14
1DC-1DF	77	AT Reserved, IRQ15
1E0-1FF	78-7F	Not Used
200-217	80-85	Reserved for BASIC
218-21B	86	NetBIOS, Relocated Interrupt 18H
218-3C3	87-F0	Reserved for BASIC Interpreter
3C4-3FF	F1-FF	Not Used

AUDIO ERROR CODES

A variety of tests are executed automatically when XT/AT class computers are first turned on. Initially, the "Power-On Self Test" (POST) is run. It provides error or warning messages whenever a faulty component is encountered. Typically, two types of messages are issued: **audio codes** and **display screen** messages or codes.

    Audio codes consist of a series of beeps that identify a faulty component. If your computer is functioning normally, you will hear one short beep when the system is turned on. However, if a problem is detected, a series of beeps will occur. These audio codes define the problem and are typically the following:

Beep Code	Problem
No beep, continuous beep, or repeating short beeps	Power Supply
1 long beep and 1 short beep	System Board
1 long beep and 2 short beeps, or 1 short beep and blank	Monitor adapter card and/or monitor cable and/or wrong display.
1 short beep and either the red drive LED staying on or Personal Computer BASIC statement	Drive and/or drive adapter card

    If the system completes the POST process, then additional errors are reported in the form of display error messages.

IBM® PC/XT MOTHERBOARD SWITCH 1 SETTINGS

See the next page for typical codes and their descriptions.

Switch #	On/Off	Function
1	Off	Always off
2	On	Coprocessor NOT present in system
2	Off	Coprocessor present in system
		Switch 3,4 System motherboard memory
3,4	3 On, 4 On	PC=16K XT=64K
3,4	3 Off, 4 On	PC=32K XT=128K
3,4	3 On, 4 Off	PC=48K XT=192K
3,4	3 Off, 4 Off	PC=64K XT=256K
5,6	5 On, 6 On	EGA/VGA video adapter present
5,6	5 Off, 6 Off	Monochrome video adapter present
5,6	5 On, 6 Off	CGA video adapter present, 80x25 mode
5,6	5 Off, 6 On	CGA video adapter present, 40x25 mode
7,8	7 On, 8 On	One floppy disk drive present
7,8	7 Off, 8 On	Two floppy disk drives present
7,8	7 On, 8 Off	Three floppy disk drives present

IBM® PC MOTHERBOARD SWITCH 2 SETTINGS (MEMORY)

7,8	7 Off, 8 Off	Four floppy disk drives present				
System Memory Size	sw2-1	sw2-2	sw2-3	sw2-4	256K board sw2-5	64K board sw2-5
64K	On	On	On	On	On	Off
96K	Off	On	On	On	On	Off
128K	On	Off	On	On	On	Off
160K	Off	Off	On	On	On	Off
192K	On	On	Off	On	On	Off
224K	Off	On	Off	On	On	Off
256K	On	Off	Off	On	On	Off
288K	Off	Off	Off	On	On	Off
320K	On	On	On	Off	On	Off
352K	Off	On	On	Off	On	Off
384K	On	Off	On	Off	On	Off
416K	Off	Off	On	Off	On	Off
448K	On	On	Off	Off	On	Off
480K	Off	On	Off	Off	On	Off
512K	On	Off	Off	Off	On	Off
544K	Off	Off	Off	Off	On	Off
576K	On	On	On	On	Off	N/A
608K	Off	On	On	On	Off	N/A
640K	On	Off	On	On	Off	N/A
704K	On	On	Off	On	Off	N/A

Notes:

1. Switch 2 listed on this page is not used on an IBM® XT.

2. The 256K board listed at the head of column 6 is the PC2 motherboard. The 64K board at the head of column 7 is the PC1 motherboard.

3. Switch 1-3 and 1-4 on the previous page must both be OFF if the motherboard is fully populated with memory chips on either the 64K or 256K motherboard.

4. Switch 1 on the IBM® AT, is a single switch that selects whether the installed video adapter is color or monochrome.

IBM XT/AT CLASS ERROR CODES

Code	Description
01x	Undetermined problem errors
02x	Power supply errors
1xx	**System board error**
101	Interrupt failure
102	Timer failure
103	Timer interrupt failure
104	Protected mode failure
105	Last 8042 command not accepted
106	Converting logic test
107	Hot NMI test
108	Timer bus test
109	Direct memory access test error
121	Unexpected hardware interrupts occurred
131	Cassette wrap test failed
152	
161	System Options Error-(Run SETUP) [Battery failure]
162	System options not set correctly-(Run SETUP)
163	Time and date not set-(Run SETUP)
164	Memory size error-(Run SETUP)
199	User indicated configuration not correct
2xx	**Memory (RAM) errors**
201	Memory test failed
202	Memory address error
203	Memory address error
3xx	**Keyboard errors**
301	Keyboard did not respond to software reset correctly or a stuck key failure was detected. If a stuck key was detected, the scan code for the key is displayed in hexadecimal. For example, the error code 49 301 indicates that key 73, the PgUp key has failed (49 Hex = 73 decimal)
302	User indicated error from the keyboard test or AT system unit keylock is locked
303	Keyboard or system unit error
304	Keyboard or system unit error; CMOS does not match system
4xx	**Monochrome monitor errors**
401	Monochrome memory test, horizontal sync frequency test, or video test failed
408	User indicated display attributes failure
416	User indicated character set failure
424	User indicated 80X25 mode failure
432	Parallel port test failed (monochrome adapter)
5xx	**Color monitor errors**
501	Color memory test failed, horizontal sync frequency test, or video test failed
508	User indicated display attribute failure
516	User indicated character set failure
524	User indicated 80X25 mode failure
532	User indicated 40X25 mode failure
540	User indicated 320X200 graphics mode failure
548	User indicated 640X200 graphics mode failure
6xx	**Diskette drive errors**

IBM XT/AT CLASS ERROR CODES

Code	Description
601	Diskette power on diagnostics test failed
602	Diskette test failed; boot record is not valid
606	Diskette verify function failed
607	Write protected diskette
608	Bad command diskette status returned
610	Diskette initialization failed
611	Time-out - diskette status returned
612	Bad NEC - diskette status returned
613	Bad DMA - diskette status returned
621	Bad seek - diskette status returned
622	Bad CRC - diskette status returned
623	Record not found - diskette status returned
624	Bad address mark - diskette status returned
625	Bad NEC seek - diskette status returned
626	Diskette data compare error
7xx	**8087 or 80287 math coprocessor errors**
9xx	**Parallel printer adapter errors**
901	Parallel printer adapter test failed
10xx	**Reserved for parallel printer adapter**
11xx	**Asynchronous communications adapter errors**
1101	Async communications adapter test failed
12xx	**Alternate asynchronous communications adapter errors**
1201	Alternate asynchronous communications adapter test failed
13xx	**Game control adapter errors**
1301	Game control adapter test failed
1302	Joystick test failed
14xx	**Printer errors**
1401	Printer test failed
1404	Matrix printer failed
15xx	**Synchronous data link control (SDLC) comm adapter errors**
1510	8255 port B failure
1511	8255 port A failure
1512	8255 port C failure
1513	8253 timer 1 did not reach terminal count
1514	8253 timer 1 stuck on
1515	8253 timer 0 did not reach terminal count
1516	8253 timer 0 stuck on
1517	8253 timer 2 did not reach terminal count
1518	8253 timer 2 stuck on
1519	8273 port B error
1520	8273 port A error
1521	8273 command/read time-out
1522	Interrupt level 4 failure
1523	Ring Indicate stuck on
1524	Receive clock stuck on
1525	Transmit clock stuck on
1526	Test indicate stuck on
1527	Ring indicate not on
1528	Receive clock not on
1529	Transmit clock not on
1530	Test indicate not on
1531	Data set ready not on

IBM XT/AT CLASS ERROR CODES

Code	Description
1532	Carrier detect not on
1533	Clear to send not on
1534	Data set ready stuck on
1536	Clear to send stuck on
1537	Level 3 interrupt failure
1538	Receive interrupt results error
1539	Wrap data mis-compare
1540	DMA channel 1 error
1541	DMA channel 1 error
1542	Error in 8273 error checking or status reporting
1547	Stray interrupt level 4
1548	Stray interrupt level 3
1549	Interrupt presentation sequence time-out
16xx	**Display emulation errors (327x, 5520, 525x)**
17xx	**Fixed disk errors**
1701	Fixed disk POST error
1702	Fixed disk adapter error
1703	Fixed disk drive error
1704	Fixed disk adapter or drive error
1780	Fixed disk 0 failure
1781	Fixed disk 1 failure
1782	Fixed disk controller failure
1790	Fixed disk 0 error
1791	Fixed disk 1 error
18xx	**I/O expansion unit errors**
1801	I/O expansion unit POST error
1810	Enable/Disable failure
1811	Extender card wrap test failed (disabled)
1812	High order address lines failure (disabled)
1813	Wait state failure (disabled)
1814	Enable/Disable could not be set on
1815	Wait state failure (disabled)
1816	Extender card wrap test failed (enabled)
1817	High order address lines failure (enabled)
1818	Disable not functioning
1819	Wait request switch not set correctly
1820	Receiver card wrap test failure
1821	Receiver high order address lines failure
19xx	**3270 PC attachment card errors**
20xx	**Binary synchronous communications (BSC) adapter errors**
2010	8255 port A failure
2011	8255 port B failure
2012	8255 port C failure
2013	8253 timer 1 did not reach terminal count
2014	8253 timer 1 stuck on
2016	8253 timer 2 did not reach terminal count or timer 2 stuck on
2017	8251 Data set ready failed to come on
2018	8251 Clear to send not sensed
2019	8251 Data set ready stuck on
2020	8251 Clear to send stuck on
2021	8251 hardware reset failed
2022	8251 software reset failed
2023	8251 software "error reset" failed

IBM XT/AT CLASS ERROR CODES

Code	Description
2024	8251 transmit ready did not come on
2025	8251 receive ready did not come on
2026	8251 could not force "overrun" error status
2027	Interrupt failure - no timer interrupt
2028	Interrupt failure - transmit, replace card or planar
2029	Interrupt failure - transmit, replace card
2030	Interrupt failure - receive, replace card or planar
2031	Interrupt failure - receive, replace card
2033	Ring indicate stuck on
2034	Receive clock stuck on
2035	Transmit clock stuck on
2036	Test indicate stuck on
2037	Ring indicate stuck on
2038	Receive clock not on
2039	Transmit clock not on
2040	Test indicate not on
2041	Data set ready not on
2042	Carrier detect not on
2043	Clear to send not on
2044	Data set ready stuck on
2045	Carrier detect stuck on
2046	Clear to send stuck on
2047	Unexpected transmit interrupt
2048	Unexpected receive interrupt
2049	Transmit data did not equal receive data
2050	8251 detected overrun error
2051	Lost data set ready during data wrap
2052	Receive time-out during data wrap
21xx	**Alternate binary synchronous communications adapter errors**
2110	8255 port A failure
2111	8255 port B failure
2112	8255 port C failure
2113	8253 timer 1 did not reach terminal count
2114	8253 timer 1 stuck on
2115	8253 timer 2 did not reach terminal count or timer 2 stuck on
2116	8251 Data set ready failed to come on
2117	8251 Clear to send not sensed
2118	8251 Data set ready stuck on
2119	8251 Clear to send stuck on
2120	8251 hardware reset failed
2121	8251 software reset failed
2122	8251 software "error reset" failed
2123	8251 transmit ready did not come on
2124	8251 receive ready did not come on
2125	8251 could not force "overrun" error status
2126	Interrupt failure - no timer interrupt
2128	Interrupt failure - transmit, replace card or planar
2129	Interrupt failure - transmit, replace card
2130	Interrupt failure - receive, replace card or planar
2131	Interrupt failure - receive, replace card
2133	Ring indicate stuck on
2134	Receive clock stuck on
2135	Transmit clock stuck on

IBM XT/AT CLASS ERROR CODES

Code	Description
2136	Test indicate stuck on
2137	Ring indicate stuck on
2138	Receive clock not on
2139	Transmit clock not on
2140	Test indicate not on
2141	Data set ready not on
2142	Carrier detect not on
2143	Clear to send not on
2144	Data set ready stuck on
2145	Carrier detect stuck on
2146	Clear to send stuck on
2147	Unexpected transmit interrupt
2148	Unexpected receive interrupt
2149	Transmit data did not equal receive data
2150	8251 detected overrun error
2151	Lost data set ready during data wrap
2152	Receive time-out during data wrap
22xx	**Cluster adapter errors**
24xx	**Enhanced graphics adapter errors**
29xx	**Color matrix printer errors**
2901	
2902	
2904	
33xx	**Compact printer errors**

IBM is a registered trademark of the International Business Machine Corporation.

IBM HARDWARE RELEASES

Date	Code	Hardware Release
04-24-81	FF	PC (the original!)
10-19-81	FF	PC (fixed bugs)
08-16-81	FE	XT
10-27-82	FF	PC with hard drive support and 640k
11-08-82	FE	PC-XT portable
06-01-83	FD	PC jr
01-10-84	FC	AT
06-10-85	FC	AT revision 1
09-13-85	F9	PC Convertible
11-15-85	FC	AT w/speed control, 30 meg hard disk
01-10-86	FB	XT revision 1
04-21-86	FC	XT-286 model 2
05-09-86	FB	XT revision 2
09-02-86	FA	PS/2 Model 30
02-13-87	FC	PS/2 Model 50 model 4
02-13-87	FC	PS/2 Model 60 model 5
03-30-87	F8	PS/2 Model 80 16 mhz
10-07-87	F8	PS/2 Model 80 20 mhz

STD 286/386/486 HARD DISK TYPES

Drive Type	# of Cylinders	# of Heads	Write Precomp	Land Zone	Size in Megabytes
1	306	4	128	305	10
2	615	4	300	615	21
3	615	6	300	615	31
4	940	8	512	940	63
5	940	6	512	940	47
6	615	4	65535	615	21
7	462	8	256	511	31
8	733	5	65535	733	31
9	900	15	65535	901	112
10	820	3	65535	820	21
11	855	5	65535	855	36
12	855	7	65535	855	50
13	306	8	128	319	21
14	733	7	65535	733	43
15	0	0	0	0	0
16	612	4	0	663	21
17	977	5	300	977	41
18	977	7	65535	977	57
19	1024	7	512	1023	60
20	733	5	300	732	31
21	733	7	300	732	43
22	733	5	300	733	31
23	306	4	0	336	10
24	698	7	300	732	42
25	615	4	0	615	21
26	1024	4	65535	1023	34
27	1024	5	65535	1023	43
28	1024	8	65535	1023	68
29	512	8	256	512	34
30	615	2	615	615	10
31	732	7	300	732	44
32	1023	5	65535	1023	44
33	306	4	0	340	10
34	976	5	488	977	42
35	1024	9	1024	1024	77
36	1024	5	512	1024	43
37	830	10	65535	830	69
38	823	10	256	824	68
39	615	4	128	664	21
40	615	8	128	664	41
41	917	15	65535	918	114
42	1023	15	65535	1024	127
43	823	10	512	823	68
44	820	6	65535	820	41
45	1024	8	65535	1024	68
46	925	9	65535	925	69
47	699	7	256	700	41

Note: Drive types over #24 vary between computer manufacturers

DMA CHANNELS

Channel	Function
0	Memory refresh
1	SDLC
2	Floppy disk drive
3	Unassigned
4	Unassigned
5	Unassigned
6	Unassigned
7	Unassigned

XT and 286/386/486 (channels 0-3)

286/386/486 only (channels 4-7)

CPU PROCESSOR TYPES

CPU Type	Maker & Date	Maximum Memory	Bus Int/Ext	Number of Transistors	Speeds Mhz
8086	Intel, 8-76	1Mb	16/16	29K	4.77,8,10
V30	NEC, 3-84	1Mb	16/16	63K	8,10
8088	Intel, 6-79	1Mb	16/8	29K	4.77,8
V20	NEC, 3-84	1Mb	16/8	63K	8,10
80286	Intel, 2-82	16Mb	16/16	130K	8,10,12
80386SX	Intel, 6-88	16Mb	32/16	275K	16,20,25,33
AM386SX	AMD, 7-91	4Gb	32/16	161K	25,33,40
80386SL	Intel, 10-90	4Gb	32/16	855K	20,25
80386SLC	IBM, 12-91	16Mb	32/16	800K	20
80386DX	Intel, 10-85	4Gb	32/32	275K	16,20,25,33
AM386DX	AMD, 3-91	4Gb	32/32	161K	25,33,40
80486SX	Intel, 4-91	4Gb*	32/32	900K	16,20,25,33
AM486SX	AMD, 7-93	4Gb*	32/32	?	33,40
AM486SXLV	AMD, 7-93	4Gb*	32/32	?	20,33 (3.3V)
CY486SLC	Cyrix, 4-92	16Mb	32/16	600K	20,25,33
80486SLC2	IBM, 9-92	16Mb	32/16	1,425K	20/40,25/50-doubler
80486DX	Intel, 4-89	4Gb*	32/32	1,200K	25,33,50
CY486DLC	Cyrix, 6-92	4Gb*	32/32	600K	25,33,40
80486DX2	Intel, 3-92	4Gb*	32/32	900K	25/50,33/66-doubler
CY486DRU	Cyrix, 10-92	4Gb*	32/32	600K	16/32,20/40, 25/50-doubler
Blue Lightning	IBM, ?-93?	?	32/32	?	25/75,33/99-tripler

* = 4Gb addressable, 64Tb virtual memory

MATH CoPROCESSOR TYPES

CPU Type	CoProcessor Type
8086, 8088, V20 & V30	8087
80286	80287XL
80386SX & SL	80387SX
80386DX	80387DX
80486SX	80487SX
80486DX	Built In

POCKET PCRef

Printer Control Codes

Printer Control Codes

Since the PC boom started, there have been more than a thousand different printer makes and models released. With each new generation of printer, more and more bells and whistles have been introduced. All of a printers' functions can normally be accessed through a set of decimal or hex control codes and this chapter has been designed to provide the reader with some of the more standardized control code sets. "Standardized" simply means that the particular printer listed in this chapter has codes that are also used by other manufacturers, for example, the Panasonic 2124, 24 pin, dot matrix printer, can be configured to use either Epson LQ860 codes or IBM Proprinter X24E codes.

Please note that your particular printer may have additional, specialized codes which are unique to your printer and are not included in the standardized set. If in doubt, always refer to the printer manual that came with your printer.

Some control codes included in this chapter have been drastically simplified, particularly in the "Graphics" sections. Simplified sections are noted and you are told to refer to the manual that came with your printer for more details.

Sequoia welcomes your suggestions concerning the inclusion of other "Standardized" code sets in future editions of Pocket PCRef.

DIABLO 630 PRINTER CODES

Code	Hex	Decimal	Command
Page Format Control:			
ESC 9	1B 39	27 57	Set left margin at current position
ESC Ø	1B 3Ø	27 48	Set right margin at current position
ESC T	1B 54	27 84	Set top margin at current position
ESC L	1B 4C	27 76	Set bottom margin at current position.
ESC C	1B 43	27 67	Clear top and bottom margins
ESC FF #	1B ØC #	27 12 #	Set lines/page, # is 1 to 126 lines
Horizontal Movement and Spacing Control:			
CR	ØD	13	Carriage return
ESC M	1B 4D	27 77	Enable auto justify
ESC =	1B 3D	27 61	Enable auto center
ESC ?	1B 3F	27 63	Enable auto carriage return
ESC !	1B 21	27 33	Disable auto carriage return
ESC /	1B 2F	27 47	Enable auto backward printing
ESC \	1B 5C	27 92	Disable auto backward printing
ESC <	1B 3C	27 6Ø	Enable reverse printing
ESC >	1B 3E	27 62	Disable reverse printing
ESC 5	1B 35	27 53	Enable forward printing
ESC 6	1B 36	27 54	Enable backward printing
SP	2Ø	32	Space
BS	Ø8	Ø8	Backspace
ESC BS	1B Ø8	27 Ø8	Backspace 1/12Ø inch
HT	Ø9	Ø9	Horizontal tab
ESC HT #	1B Ø9 #	27 Ø9 #	Absolute horizontal tab, # is column 1 to 126
ESC DC1 #	1B 11 #	27 17 #	Spacing offset, # is 1 to 126 (1/12Ø" units), where #1 = offset 1 to # 63 = offset 63, # 64 = offset Ø, # 65 = offset –1 to # 126 = offset –62
ESC 1	1B 31	27 49	Set horizontal tab stop at current position
ESC 8	1B 38	27 56	Clear horizontal tab at current position

DIABLO 630 PRINTER CODES

Code	Hex	Decimal	Command
Horizontal Movement and Spacing Control: (Continued)			
ESC 2	1B 32	27 5Ø	Clear all vertical and horizontal tab stops
ESC US #	1B 1F #	27 31 #	Set horizontal motion index, # is 1 to 126, where (#−1)/12Ø inch is the column spacing.
ESC S	1B 53	27 83	Return HMI control to spacing switch
Vertical Movement and Spacing Control:			
LF	ØA	1Ø	Line feed
ESC LF	1B ØA	27 1Ø	Reverse line feed
ESC U	1B 55	27 85	Half line feed
ESC D	1B 44	27 68	Reverse half line feed
FF	ØC	12	Form feed
VT	ØB	11	Vertical tab
ESC VT #	1B ØB #	27 11 #	Absolute vertical tab, # is line 1 to 126
ESC _	1B 2D	27 45	Set vertical tab stop at current position
ESC 2	1B 32	27 5Ø	Clear all vertical and horizontal tab stops
ESC RS #	1B 1E #	27 3Ø #	Set vertical motion index, # is 1 to 126, where #/48 inch is the line spacing.
Character Selection:			
ESC P	1B 5Ø	27 8Ø	Enable proportional print spacing
ESC Q	1B 51	27 81	Disable proportional print spacing
ESC SO DC2	1B ØE 12	27 14 18	Enable printwheel down-load mode
DC4	14	28	Exit printwheel down-load
SO	ØE	14	Enable ESC mode, supplementary characters
SI	ØF	15	Disable ESC mode, primary characters
ESC A	1B 41	27 65	Select red ribbon (secondary font)
ESC B	1B 42	27 66	Select black ribbon (primary font)
ESC X	1B 58	27 88	Cancel all WP modes except Proportional

DIABLO 630 PRINTER CODES

Code	Hex	Decimal	Command
Character Selection: (Continued)			
ESC Y	1B 59	27 89	Printwheel Spoke Ø char.
ESC Z	1B 5A	27 9Ø	Printwheel Spoke 95 char.
Character Highlight Selection:			
ESC E	1B 45	27 69	Enable underscore print
ESC R	1B 52	27 82	Disable underscore print
ESC O	1B 4F	27 79	Enable bold printing
ESC W	1B 57	27 87	Enable shadow printing
ESC &	1B 26	27 38	Disable bold and shadow printing
Graphics:			
ESC 3	1B 33	27 51	Enable graphics mode
ESC 4	1B 34	27 52	Disable graphics mode
ESC G	1B 47	27 71	Enable HyPLOT mode
Miscellaneous:			
ESC CR P	1B ØD 5Ø	27 13 8Ø	Reset all modes to default
ESC SUB I	1B 1A 49	27 27 73	Reset all modes to default
ESC EM	1B 19	27 25	Enable auto sheet feeder
ESC SUB	1B 1A	27 26	Enable remote diagnostics
ESC N	1B 4E	27 78	Restore normal carriage settling time
ESC %	1B 25	27 37	Increase carriage settling time
ESC 7	1B 37	27 55	Enable print suppression
ESC SO M	1B ØE 4D	27 14 77	Enable program mode

EPSON FX-80 PRINTER CODES (9 PIN)

Code	Hex	Decimal	Command
Page Format Control:			
ESC l #	1B 6C #	27 1Ø8 #	Set Left Margin at Col #
ESC Q #	1B 51 #	27 81 #	Set Right Margin at Col #
ESC C #	1B 43 #	27 67 #	Set Form Length to # Lines (or n inches)
ESC C Ø #	1B 43 ØØ #	27 67 Ø #	Set Form Length to # inches
ESC N #	1B 4E #	27 78 #	Set Skip-over Perforation to # lines
ESC O	1B 4F	27 79	Turn Skip-over Perforation Off

EPSON FX–80 PRINTER CODES (9 PIN)

Code	Hex	Decimal	Command
Horizontal Movement and Spacing Control:			
CR	ØD	13	Carriage return
BS	Ø8	Ø8	Backspace
HT	Ø9	Ø9	Horizontal tab
ESC a Ø	1B 61 ØØ	1B 61 Ø	Alignment Left Justified
ESC a 1	1B 61 Ø1	1B 61 1	Alignment Auto Centering
ESC a 2	1B 61 Ø2	1B 61 2	Alignment Right Justified
ESC a 3	1B 61 Ø3	1B 61 3	Alignment Auto Justified
ESC D # Ø	1B 44 # Ø	27 68 # ØØ	Set Horizontal Tab(s), # can be 1 or a series of tabs
ESC D Ø	1B 44 Ø	27 68 ØØ	Release Horizontal Tab
ESC e Ø #	1B 44 Ø #	27 68 ØØ #	Set Horizontal Unit Tab(s), # is repeating Tab distance in columns.
ESC e ØØ	1B 44 ØØ	27 68 ØØ ØØ	Release Horiz Tab Unit
ESC f Ø #	1B 66 ØØ #	27 1Ø2 Ø #	Move print position # cols
ESC \ #1#2	1B 5C #1#2	27 92 #1#2	Move print position in increments of 1/12Ø inch
ESC $ #1#2	1B 24 #1#2	27 36 #1#2	Move print position in1/6Ø inch increments from left margin
ESC SP #	1B 2Ø #	27 32 #	Add space after each character in units of 1/24Ø inch where # is from 1 to 63
ESC <	1B 3C	27 6Ø	One Line Unidirectional Printing Mode On
ESC U	1B 55	27 85	Select Continuous Print Unidirectional Mode
Vertical Movement and Spacing Control:			
LF	ØA	1Ø	Line feed
ESC j #	1B 6A #	27 1Ø6 #	Reverse Line Feed of #/216 Inch
ESC J #	1B 4A #	27 74 #	Forward Line Feed of #/216 inches
ESC f 1 #	1B 66 Ø1 #	27 1Ø2 1 #	Forward Line Feed # lines
FF	ØC	12	Form feed
ESC Ø	1B 3Ø	27 48	Set Line Spacing to 1/8" (9 points or 8 lpi)
ESC 1	1B 31	27 49	Set Line Spacing to 7/72" (7 points)
ESC 2	1B 32	27 5Ø	Set Line Spacing to 1/6" (12 points, 6 lpi)
ESC 3 #	1B 33 #	27 51 #	Set Line Spacing to #/216"

EPSON FX-80 PRINTER CODES (9 PIN)

Code	Hex	Decimal	Command
Vertical Movement and Spacing Control: (Continued)			
ESC A #	1B 41 #	27 65 #	Set Line Spacing to # Points (#/72 inch)
VT	ØB	11	Vertical tab
ESC b#1#2#3 Ø	1B 62 #1#2#3 ØØ	27 98 #1#2#3 Ø	Set Vertical Tabs Format Units in Specific Channel, see the manual for details
ESC b #1 Ø	1B 62 #1 ØØ	27 98 #1 Ø	Release Vertical Tab Format Unit
ESC / #	1B 2F #	27 47 #	Select Vertical Tab Channel #
ESC B#1#2Ø	1B 42 #1#2 Ø	27 66 #1 #2 Ø	Set Vertical Tabs for Channel #1, #2 etc
ESC B Ø	1B 42 Ø	27 66 Ø	Release Vertical Tabs for Channels
ESC e 1 #	1B 65 Ø1 #	27 1Ø1 1 #	Set Vertical Tab Unit at # of equal space intervals
ESC e 1 1	1B 65 Ø1 Ø1	27 1Ø1 1 1	Release Vertical Tab Unit of equal space intervals
Character Selection:			
ESC I 1	1B 49 Ø1	27 73 1	Select Characters (Ø–31, 128–159) to Print
ESC I Ø	1B 49 ØØ	27 73 Ø	Disable Characters (Ø–31, 128–159) from Printing
ESC M	1B 4D	27 77	Enable Elite Pitch Mode
ESC P	1B 5Ø	27 8Ø	Enable Pica Pitch Mode
ESC o	1B 6F	27 111	Enable Elite Pitch Mode
ESC n	1B 6E	27 11Ø	Enable Pica Pitch Mode
ESC w #	1B 77 #	27 119 #	Direct Pitch Selection, #=Ø is 1Øcpi, #=1 is 12cpi, #=2 is 15cpi, #=3 is 17cpi, #=4 is proport.
ESC p 1	1B 7Ø Ø1	27 112 1	Select Proportional Spac
ESC p Ø	1B 7Ø ØØ	27 112 Ø	Release Proportional Spa
ESC W 1	1B 57 Ø1	27 87 1	Select Expanded Pitch
ESC W Ø	1B 57 ØØ	27 87 Ø	Release Expanded Pitch
SO or ESC SO	ØE	14	Enable 1-line Expanded Print Mode
DC4	14	28	Disable one-line Expanded Print Mode
SI or ESC SI	ØF	15	Enable Compressed Print
DC2	12	18	Disable Compressed Print
ESC :	1B 3A	27 58	Duplicate Internal Font

EPSON FX-80 PRINTER CODES (9 PIN)

Code	Hex	Decimal	Command
Character Selection: (Continued)			
ESC ! #	1B 21 #	27 33 #	Print Mode Selection, # determines mode, #=128 is underline, #=64 is italic, #=32 is double wide, #=16 is double strike, #=8 is bold, #=4 is compressed, #=2 is proportional, #=1 is Elite, #=Ø is Pica. Add numbers for multiples, eg, 129 is Underlined Elite
ESC %	1B 25	27 37	Select Character Set Bank
ESC &	1B 26	27 38	Define User Font
ESC 6	1B 36	27 54	Enable printing High Bit Symbols (Dec128–Dec159)
ESC 7	1B 37	27 55	Disable printing High Bit Symbols (Dec128–Dec159)
ESC 4	1B 34	27 52	Enable Italics printing
ESC 5	1B 35	27 53	Disable Italics printing
ESC R #	1B 52 #	27 82 #	Select International Character Set, #=Ø is USA, 1 is France, 2 is Germany, 3 is England, 4 is Denmark A, 5 is Sweden, 6 is Italy, 7 is Spain, 8 is Japan, 9 is Norway, 1Ø is Denmark B
ESC S 1	1B 53 Ø1	27 83 1	Select Subscripting
ESC S Ø	1B 53 ØØ	27 83 Ø	Select Superscripting
ESC T	1B 54	27 84	Release Super or Subscripting
Character Highlight Selection:			
ESC – 1	1B 2D Ø1	27 45 1	Turn underline mode on
ESC – Ø	1B 2D ØØ	27 45 Ø	Turn underline mode off
ESC E	1B 45	27 69	Enable Bold Print Mode
ESC F	1B 46	27 7Ø	Disable Bold Print Mode
ESC G	1B 47	27 71	Enable Double-strike
ESC H	1B 48	27 72	Disable Double-strike
Graphics:			
For values for #1 and #2 below, see printer manuals			
ESC K#1#2	1B 4B #1#2	27 75 #1#2	Enable Single-density Graphics Mode, 6Ø dpi
ESC L#1#2	1B 4C #1#2	27 76 #1#2	Enable Double-density Graphics Mode, 12Ø dpi
ESC Y#1#2	1B 59 #1#2	27 89 #1#2	Enable Double-density, 12Ø dpi, High-speed Graphics Mode

EPSON FX80 PRINTER CODES (9 PIN)

Code	Hex	Decimal	Command
Graphics: (Continued)			
ESC Z #1#2	1B 5A #1#2	27 90 #1#2	Enable Quadruple – density Graphics Mode, 240 dpi
ESC ★ #1#2#3	1B 2A #1#2#3	27 42 #1#2#3	Set Graphics Mode
ESC ∧ #1#2#3	1B 5E #1 #2 #3	27 94 #1#2#3	9 pin Graphics Mode
ESC ? #1#2	1B 3F #1#2	27 63 #1#2	Bit Image Mode Reassignment
Miscellaneous:			
CAN	18	24	Cancel
DC1	11	17	Remote Printer Select
DC3	13	19	Remote Printer Deselect
DEL	7F	127	Delete
ESC @	1B 40	27 64	Master Reset
ESC #	1B 23	27 35	Read Bit 7 of Received Word Normally
ESC =	1B 3D	27 61	Set Received Bit 7 to 0
ESC >	1B 3E	27 62	Set Received Bit 7 to 1
ESC 8	1B 38	27 56	Out of Paper Sensor Off
ESC 9	1B 39	27 57	Out of Paper Sensor On
ESC i	1B 69	27 105	Enable Immediate Printing
ESC s	1B 73	27 115	Half Speed Printing
ESC s 1	1B 73 01	27 115 1	Sets Half Speed Printing
ESC s 0	1B 73 00	27 115 0	Releases Half Speed Printing
ESC EM #	1B 19 #	27 25 #	Paper Cassette Selection, #=E is envelope, #=1 is Lower Cassette, #=2 is Upper Cassette, #=R is eject page

EPSON LQ860 PRINTER CODES (24 PIN)

Code	Hex	Decimal	Command
Page Format Control:			
ESC l #	1B 6C #	27 108 #	Set Left Margin at Col #
ESC Q #	1B 51 #	27 81 #	Set Right Margin at Col #
ESC C #	1B 43 #	27 67 #	Set Form Length to # Lines (or n inches)
ESC C 0 #	1B 43 00 #	27 67 0 #	Set Form Length to # inches

EPSON LQ860 PRINTER CODES (24 PIN)

Code	Hex	Decimal	Command
Page Format Control: (Continued)			
ESC N #	1B 4E #	27 78 #	Set Skip-over Perforation to # lines
ESC O	1B 4F	27 79	Turn Skip-over Perforation Off
Horizontal Movement and Spacing Control:			
CR	ØD	13	Carriage return
BS	Ø8	Ø8	Backspace
HT	Ø9	Ø9	Horizontal tab
ESC a Ø	1B 61 ØØ	1B 61 Ø	Alignment Left Justified
ESC a 1	1B 61 Ø1	1B 61 1	Alignment Auto Centering
ESC a 2	1B 61 Ø2	1B 61 2	Alignment Right Justified
ESC a 3	1B 61 Ø3	1B 61 3	Alignment Auto Justified
ESC D # Ø	1B 44 # Ø	27 68 # ØØ	Set Horizontal Tab(s), # can be 1 or a series of tabs
ESC D Ø	1B 44 Ø	27 68 ØØ	Release Horizontal Tab
ESC e Ø #	1B 44 Ø #	27 68 ØØ #	Set Horizontal Unit Tab(s), # is repeating Tab distance in columns
ESC e ØØ	1B 44 ØØ	27 68 ØØ ØØ	Release Horiz Tab Unit
ESC f Ø #	1B 66 ØØ #	27 1Ø2 Ø #	Move print position in # cols
ESC \ #1#2	1B 5C #1#2	27 92 #1#2	Move print position in increments of 1/12Ø inch
ESC $ #1#2	1B 24 #1#2	27 36 #1#2	Move print position in 1/6Ø inch increments from left margin
ESC SP #	1B 2Ø #	27 32 #	Add space after each character in units of 1/24Ø inch where # is from 1 to 63
ESC <	1B 3C	27 6Ø	One Line Unidirectional Printing Mode On
ESC U	1B 55	27 85	Select Continuous Print Unidirectional Mode
ESC U Ø	1B 55 ØØ	27 85 Ø	Releases unidirectional printing
ESC U 1	1B 55 Ø1	27 85 1	Sets unidirectional printing
Vertical Movement and Spacing Control:			
LF	ØA	1Ø	Line feed
ESC j #	1B 6A #	27 1Ø6 #	Reverse Line Feed of #/216 Inch
ESC J #	1B 4A #	27 74 #	Forward Line Feed of #/216 inches
ESC f 1 #	1B 66 Ø1 #	27 1Ø2 1 #	Forward Line Feed # lines

Code	Hex	Decimal	Command
Vertical Movement and Spacing Control: (Continued)			
FF	ØC	12	Form feed
ESC Ø	1B 3Ø	27 48	Set Line Spacing to 1/8" (9 points or 8 lpi)
ESC 1	1B 31	27 49	Set Line Spacing to 7/72" (7 points)
ESC 2	1B 32	27 5Ø	Set Line Spacing to 1/6" (12 points, 6 lpi)
ESC 3 #	1B 33 #	27 51 #	Set Line Spacing to #/216"
ESC A #	1B 41 #	27 65 #	Set Line Spacing to # Points (#/72 inch)
ESC + #	1B 2B	27 43	Sets paper feed to #/360 inch
VT	ØB	11	Vertical tab
ESC b #1#2#3 Ø	1B 62 #1#2#3 ØØ	27 98 #1#2#3 Ø	Set Vertical Tabs Format Units in Specific Channel, see the manual for details
ESC b #1 Ø	1B 62 #1 ØØ	27 98 #1 Ø	Release Vertical Tab Format Unit
ESC / #	1B 2F #	27 47 #	Select Vertical Tab Channel #
ESC B #1#2Ø	1B 42 #1#2 Ø	27 66 #1 #2 Ø	Set Vertical Tabs for Channel #1, #2 etc
ESC B Ø	1B 42 Ø	27 66 Ø	Release Vertical Tabs for Channels
ESC e 1 #	1B 65 Ø1 #	27 1Ø1 1 #	Set Vertical Tab Unit at # of equal space intervals
ESC e 1 1	1B 65 Ø1 Ø1	27 1Ø1 1 1	Release Vertical Tab Unit of equal space intervals
Character Selection:			
ESC I 1	1B 49 Ø1	27 73 1	Select Characters (Ø–31, 128–159) to Print
ESC I Ø	1B 49 ØØ	27 73 Ø	Disable Characters (Ø–31, 128–159) from Printing
ESC M	1B 4D	27 77	Enable Elite Pitch Mode
ESC P	1B 5Ø	27 8Ø	Enable Pica Pitch Mode
ESC o	1B 6F	27 111	Enable Elite Pitch Mode
ESC n	1B 6E	27 11Ø	Enable Pica Pitch Mode
ESC w #	1B 77 #	27 119 #	Direct Pitch Selection, #=Ø is 1Øcpi, #=1 is 12cpi, #=2 is 15cpi, #=3 is 17cpi, #=4 is proport.
ESC p 1	1B 7Ø Ø1	27 112 1	Select Proportional Spacing
ESC p Ø	1B 7Ø ØØ	27 112 Ø	Release Proportional Spacing

EPSON LQ860 PRINTER CODES (24 PIN)

Code	Hex	Decimal	Command
Character Selection: (Continued)			
ESC W 1	1B 57 Ø1	27 87 1	Select Expanded Pitch
ESC W Ø	1B 57 ØØ	27 87 Ø	Release Expanded Pitch
SO or	ØE	14	Enable 1-line Expanded
ESC SO			Print Mode
DC4	14	28	Disable one-line Expanded Print Mode
SI or ESC SI	ØF	15	Enable Compressed Print
DC2	12	18	Disable Compressed Print
ESC :	1B 3A	27 58	Duplicate Internal Font
ESC : Ø # Ø	1B 3A ØØ	27 58	Copies internal ROM CG font into download CG
ESC ! #	1B 21 #	27 33 #	Print Mode Selection, # determines mode, #=128 is underline, #=64 is italic, #=32 is double wide, #=16 is double strike, #=8 is bold, #=4 is compressed, #=2 is proportional, #=1 is Elite, #=Ø is Pica. Add numbers for multiples, eg, 129 is Underlined Elite
ESC %	1B 25	27 37	Select Character Set Bank
ESC % Ø	1B 25	27 37	Selects ROM CG
ESC % 1	1B 25	27 37	Selects download CG
ESC &	1B 26	27 38	Define User Font
ESC 6	1B 36	27 54	Enable printing High Bit Symbols (Dec128–Dec159)
ESC 7	1B 37	27 55	Disable printing High Bit Symbols (Dec128–Dec159)
ESC 4	1B 34	27 52	Enable Italics printing
ESC 5	1B 35	27 53	Disable Italics printing
ESC R #	1B 52 #	27 82 #	Select International Character Set, #=Ø is USA, 1 is France, 2 is Germany,3 is England, 4 is Denmark A, 5 is Sweden, 6 is Italy, 7 is Spain, 8 is Japan, 9 is Norway, 1Ø is Denmark B
ESC S 1	1B 53 Ø1	27 83 1	Select Subscripting
ESC S Ø	1B 53 ØØ	27 83 Ø	Select Superscripting
ESC T	1B 54	27 84	Release Super or Subscripting

EPSON LQ860 PRINTER CODES (24 PIN)

Code	Hex	Decimal	Command
Character Selection: (Continued)			
ESC t #	1B 74	27 116	Selects character set, #=Ø is Italic set, #=1 is Graphic set #=2 remaps downloaded characters from 0-127 to 128-255
ESC g	1B 67	27 1Ø3	Sets micron (15 cpi) printing
ESC x #	1B 78	27 12Ø	Selects print quality, #=Ø is Draft mode, #=1 is LQ mode, #2 is SLQ mode.
ESC k #	1B 6B	27 1Ø7	Selects print typeface (NOTE: these may vary between printers.)
			#=Ø is Roman
			#=1 is Sans Serif
			#=2 is Courier
			#=3 is Prestige
			#=4 is Script
			#=5 is OCR-B
			#=6 is Bold PS
			#=7 is Orator
Character Highlight Selection:			
ESC – 1	1B 2D Ø1	27 45 1	Turn underline mode on
ESC – Ø	1B 2D ØØ	27 45 Ø	Turn underline mode off
ESC E	1B 45	27 69	Enable Bold Print Mode
ESC F	1B 46	27 7Ø	Disable Bold Print Mode
ESC G	1B 47	27 71	Enable Double–strike
ESC H	1B 48	27 72	Disable Double–strike
ESC w 1	1B 77 Ø1	27 119 1	Sets Double-High Printing
ESC w Ø	1B 77 ØØ	27 119 Ø	Releases Double-High Printing
ESC q #	1B 71	27 113	Sets Outline & Shadow Printing
Graphics:			
For values for #1 and #2 below, see printer manuals			
ESC K#1#2	1B 4B #1#2	27 75 #1#2	Enable Single–density Graphics Mode, 6Ø dpi
ESC L#1#2	1B 4C #1#2	27 76 #1#2	Enable Double–density Graphics Mode, 12Ø dpi
ESC Y#1#2	1B 59 #1#2	27 89 #1#2	Enable Double–density, 12Ø dpi, High–speed Graphics Mode

EPSON LQ860 PRINTER CODES (24 PIN)

Code	Hex	Decimal	Command
ESC Z #1#2	1B 5A #1#2	27 90 #1#2	Enable Quadruple – density Graphics Mode, 24Ø dpi
ESC * #1#2#3	1B 2A #1#2#3	27 42 #1#2#3	Set Graphics Mode
ESC ^ #1#2#3	1B 5E #1 #2 #3	27 94 #1#2#3	9 pin Graphics Mode
ESC ? #1#2	1B 3F #1#2	27 63 #1#2	Bit Image Mode Reassignment

Miscellaneous:

Code	Hex	Decimal	Command
CAN	18	24	Cancel
DC1	11	17	Remote Printer Select
DC3	13	19	Remote Printer Deselect
DEL	7F	127	Delete
ESC @	1B 4Ø	27 64	Master Reset
ESC "#"	1B 23	27 35	Set to receive Bit 8 as is.
ESC =	1B 3D	27 61	Set Received Bit 7 to Ø
ESC >	1B 3E	27 62	Set Received Bit 7 to 1
ESC 8	1B 38	27 56	Out of Paper Sensor Off
ESC 9	1B 39	27 57	Out of Paper Sensor On
ESC i	1B 69	27 1Ø5	Enable Immediate Printing
ESC s	1B 73	27 115	Half Speed Printing
ESC EM #	1B 19 #	27 25 #	Paper Cassette Selection, #=E is envelope, #=1 is Lower Cassette, #=2 is Upper Cassette, #=R is eject page
BEL	Ø7	7	Sounds the buzzer for approx. Ø.5 seconds
ESC r #	1B 72	27 114	Selects print color (Note: may vary between printers) #=Ø is Black #=1 is Red #=2 is Blue #=3 is Violet #=4 is Yellow #=5 is Orange #=6 is Green

NEC PINWRITER PRINTER CODES

Code	Hex	Decimal	Command

NEC Pinwriters use most of the same codes as the Epson LQ1500, except for the following FS Codes:

Code	Hex	Decimal	Command
FS 3 #	1C 33 #	28 51 #	Line space Ø-255 #/360
FS C #	1C 43 #	28 67 #	Set Font Cartridge, #=Ø is resident font, #=1 is slot 1, #=2 is slot 2
FS E #	1C 45 #	28 69 #	Ø=Cancel horiz enlarge., 1=2X horiz enlargement, 2=3X horiz enlargement
FS F	1C 46	28 7Ø	Release Enhanced Print
FS I #	1C 49 #	28 73 #	Ø=Italic Set, 1=IBM Set
FS R	1C 52	28 82	Set Reverse Line Feed
FS S #	1C 53 #	28 83 #	Ø=Draft 12,1=high speed
FS V 1	1C 56 31	28 86 49	Set double vertical enlarge
FS V Ø	1C 56 3Ø	28 86 48	Release double vertical enlargement
FS Z #1 #2	1C 6Ø #1 #2	28 9Ø #1 #2	Set 360 dpi graphics
FS @	1C 4Ø	28 64	Initialize except user buffer

Code	Hex	Decimal	Command
Page Format Control:			
ESC & l 0 O	1B 26 6C 30 4F	27 38 108 48 79	Portrait Orient.
ESC & l 1 O	1B 26 6C 31 4F	27 38 108 49 79	Landscape Orient.
ESC & l #P	1B 26 6C # 50	27 38 108 # 80	Page length, # of lines
ESC & l #E	1B 26 6C # 45	27 38 108 # 69	Top Margin, # of lines
ESC & l #F	1B 26 6C # 46	27 38 108 # 70	Text Length, # of lines
ESC & l 1L	1B 26 6C 31 4C	27 38 108 49 76	Skip Perforation, On
ESC & l 0L	1B 26 6C 30 4C	27 38 108 48 76	Skip Perforation, Off
ESC & l #D	1B 26 6C # 44	27 38 108 # 68	Lines Per Inch, # of lines/inch
ESC & l #C	1B 26 6C # 43	27 38 108 # 67	Vertical Motion Index # of 1/48 inch
ESC &k#H	1B 26 6B # 48	27 38 107 # 72	Horizontal Motion Index, # of 1/120 inch
ESC &a#L	1B 26 61 # 4C	27 38 97 # 76	Left Margin, Left column #
ESC &a#M	1B 26 61 # 4D	27 38 97 # 77	Right Margin, Right column #
ESC 9	1B 39	27 57	Clear Margins
Horizontal Movement and Spacing Control:			
BS	08	8	Backspace
CR	0D	13	Carriage Return
ESC & k # G	1B 26 6B # 47	27 38 107 # 71	CR/LF/FF Line Termination Action

	Line Termination Action		
#	CR	LF	FF
0	CR	LF	FF
1	CR+LF	LF	FF
2	CR	CR+LF	CR+FF
3	CR+LF	CR+LF	CR+FF

Code	Hex	Decimal	Command
ESC & s 0 C	1B 26 73 30 43	27 38 115 48 67	Set Wrap Around
ESC & s 1 C	1B 26 73 31 43	27 38 115 49 67	Release Wrap Around
ESC & a # C	1B 26 61 # 43	27 38 97 # 67	Move Print Position to Column #
ESC & a # H	1B 26 61 # 48	27 38 97 # 72	Move Print Position Horizontal # of Decipoints
ESC *p # X	1B 2A 70 # 58	27 42 112 # 88	Move Print Position Horizontal # of Dots

HP LASERJET PCL3 CODES

Code	Hex	Decimal	Command
Vertical Movement and Spacing Control:			
LF	ØA	1Ø	Line Feed
FF	ØC	12	Formfeed
ESC =	1B 3D	27 61	Half Line Feed
ESC & a # R	1B 26 61 # 52	27 38 97 # 82	Move Print Position to Row #
ESC & a # V	1B 26 61 # 56	27 38 97 # 86	Move Print Position Vertical # of Decipoints
ESC * p # Y	1B 2A 7Ø # 59	27 42 112 # 89	Move Print Position Vertical # of Dots
Font Selection:			
ESC (# X	1B 28 # 58	27 4Ø # 88	Symbol Set, Primary, # is Character ID
ESC) # X	1B 29 # 58	27 41 # 88	Symbol Set, Secondary, # is Character ID

Character ID's:

Roman-8bit = 8U		Kana-8bit = 8K,	
Math-8bit = 8M		ANSI-8bit = 9U	
USASCII = ØU		Line Draw = ØB	
Math Symbols =ØA		US Legal = 1U	
Roman Ext =ØE		ISO Denmark = ØD	
ISO Italy = ØI		ISO United Kingdom = 1E	
ISO France = ØF		ISO Germany = ØG	
ISO Sweden = ØS		ISO Spain = 1S	

Code	Hex	Decimal	Command
ESC (s Ø P	1B 28 73 3Ø 5Ø	27 4Ø 115 48 8Ø	Spacing, Primary Fixed
ESC (s 1 P	1B 28 73 31 5Ø	27 4Ø 115 49 8Ø	Spacing, Primary Proportional
ESC) s Ø P	1B 29 73 3Ø 5Ø	27 41 115 48 8Ø	Spacing, Secondary Fixed
ESC) s 1 P	1B 29 73 31 5Ø	27 41 115 49 8Ø	Spacing, Secondary Proportional
ESC (s # H	1B 28 73 # 48	27 4Ø 115 # 72	Print Pitch, Primary, # is characters/inch
ESC) s # H	1B 29 73 # 48	27 41 115 # 72	Print Pitch, Secondary, # is characters/inch
ESC & k # S	1B 26 6B # 53	27 38 1Ø7 # 83	Print Pitch, Prim. & Secondary, #=Ø is 1Ø cpi, #=1 is 16.66 cpi

Code	Hex	Decimal	Command
ESC (s # V	1B 28 73 # 56	27 40 115 # 86	Print Point Size, Primary, # is points
ESC) s # V	1B 29 73 # 56	27 41 115 # 86	Print Point Size, Secondary, # is points
ESC (s Ø S	1B 28 73 3Ø 53	27 40 115 48 83	Print Style, Primary, Upright
ESC (s1S	1B 28 73 31 53	27 40 115 49 83	Print Style, Primary, Italic
ESC) sØS	1B 29 73 3Ø 53	27 41 115 48 83	Print Style, Secondary, Upright
ESC) s1S	1B 29 73 31 53	27 41 115 49 83	Print Style, Secondary, Italic
ESC (s # B	1B 28 73 # 42	27 40 115 # 66	Stroke Weight, Primary, # is –7 to +7
ESC) s # B	1B 29 73 # 42	27 41 115 # 66	Stroke Weight, Secondary, # is –7 to +7 –1 to –7=light, Ø =Medium, 1 to 7 =Bold
ESC (s # T	1B 28 73 # 54	27 40 115 # 84	Typeface, Primary # is typeface
ESC) s # T	1B 29 73 # 54	27 41 115 # 84	Typeface, Secondary # is typeface:

Typeface ID's:

Ø=Line printer	6=Gothic
1=Pica	7=Script
2=Elite	8=Prestige
3=Courier	9=Caslon
4=Swiss 721	1Ø=Orator
5=Dutch	23=Century 7Ø

Font Control:

Code	Hex	Decimal	Command
SI	ØF	15	Shift In Primary
SO	ØE	14	Shift In Secondary
ESC (# X	1B 28 # 58	27 4Ø # 88	Define Font, Primary # is Font ID number
ESC) # X	1B 29 # 58	27 41 # 88	Define Font, Secondar # is Font ID numbr
ESC ★c # F	1B 2A 63 # 46	27 42 99 # 7Ø	Font/Character Control, see printer manual
ESC (# @	1B 28 # 4Ø	27 4Ø # 64	Primary Font, Default see printer manual

HP LASERJET PCL3 CODES

Code	Hex	Decimal	Command

Font Control: (Continued)

ESC) # @	1B 29 # 4Ø	27 41 # 64	Secondary Font
		Default, see printer manual
ESC *c # D	1B 2A 63 # 44	27 42 99 # 68	Define Font ID, # is the ID
ESC) s # W	1B 29 73 # 57	27 41 115 # 87	Font Header, # is byte number of font attribute
ESC *c # E	1B 2A 63 # 45	27 42 99 # 69	Define Character Code to download # is Ø to 255
ESC (s # W	1B 28 73 # 57	27 4Ø 115 # 87	Produce Download Character see printer manual

Character Highlight Selection:

ESC & d D	1B 26 64 44	27 38 1ØØ 68	Turn underline on
ESC & d @	1B 26 64 4Ø	27 38 1ØØ 64	Turn underline off

Graphics:

ESC * t # R	1B 2A 74 # 52	27 42 116 # 82	Resolution, # is 75, 1ØØ, 15Ø, or 3ØØ Dots/inch
ESC * r # A	1B 2A 72 # 41	27 42 114 # 65	Graphics Start, #=Ø is start vertical from left end of print area, #=1 is start from present position.
ESC * b # W	1B 2A 62 # 57	27 42 98 # 87	Sending Graphics data, # is number of bytes of bit image data.
ESC * r B	1B 2A 72 42	27 42 114 66	End Raster Graphics Mode
ESC * c # A	1B 2A 63 # 41	27 42 99 # 65	Set Horizontal Rule Width to # dots (1 dot=1/3ØØ inch)
ESC * c # H	1B 2A 63 # 48	27 42 99 # 72	Set Horizontal Rule Width to # decipoints (1 decipoint=1/72Ø inch)
ESC *c # B	1B 2A 63 # 42	27 42 99 # 66	Set Vertical Rule Width to # dots (1 dot=1/3ØØ inch)

Code	Hex	Decimal	Command
Graphics: (Continued)			
ESC *c # V	1B 2A 63 # 56	27 42 99 # 86	Set Vertical Rule Width to # decipoints (1 decipoint= 1/72Ø inch)
ESC *c # G	1B 2A 63 # 47	27 42 99 # 71	Set Gray Scale or Hatch Pattern ID #, see printer manual for a sample of each pattern/hatch and its associated ID #
ESC *c # P	1B 2A 63 # 5Ø	27 42 99 # 8Ø	Set Print Pattern #
Macro's:			
ESC &f # Y	1B 26 66 # 59	27 38 1Ø2 # 89	Set Macro ID #
ESC &f Ø X	1B 26 66 3Ø 58	27 38 1Ø2 48 88	Start Macro
ESC &f 1 X	1B 26 66 31 58	27 38 1Ø2 49 88	End Macro
ESC &f 2 X	1B 26 66 32 58	27 38 1Ø2 5Ø 88	Jump to Macro
ESC &f 3 X	1B 26 66 33 58	27 38 1Ø2 51 88	Call Macro
ESC &f 4 X	1B 26 66 34 58	27 38 1Ø2 52 88	Set Overlay Macro
ESC &f 5 X	1B 26 66 35 58	27 38 1Ø2 53 88	Release Overlay Macro
ESC &f 6 X	1B 26 66 36 58	27 38 1Ø2 54 88	Release all Macro
ESC &f 7 X	1B 26 66 37 58	27 38 1Ø2 55 88	Release all temporary Macro
ESC &f 8 X	1B 26 66 38 58	27 38 1Ø2 56 88	Release current Macro
ESC &f 9 X	1B 26 66 39 58	27 38 1Ø2 57 88	Assign temporary attribute to Macro
ESC &f 1ØX	1B 26 66 31 3Ø 58	27 38 1Ø2 49 48 88	Assign permanent attribute to Macro
Miscellaneous:			
ESC Y	1B 59	27 89	Set Display Function of control codes
ESC Z	1B 5A	27 9Ø	Release Display Function of control codes
ESC & p # X	1B 26 7Ø # 58	27 38 112 # 88	Transparent Print Data (no ESC commands exist)
ESC & f Ø S	1B 26 66 3Ø 53	27 38 1Ø2 48 83	Push Printing Position. Puts present printing

HP LASERJET PCL3 CODES

Code	Hex	Decimal	Command
Miscellaneous: (Continued)			
			position on the top of the stack
ESC & f 1 S	1B 26 66 31 53	27 38 102 49 83	Pop Printing Position. Recall stored printing position and put on the top of the stack
ESC & l # X	1B 26 6C # 58	27 38 108 # 88	Set Number of Copies to #
ESC & l # H	1B 26 6C # 48	27 38 108 # 72	Paper Input Control.

#=Ø is Feed out current page
#=1 is Lower Cassette supplies paper
#=3 is Envelope feeder supplies envelope
#=4 is Upper Cassette supplies paper

Code	Hex	Decimal	Command
ESC E	1B 45	27 69	Reset Printer
ESC z	1B 7A	27 122	Start Printer Self Test

HP LASERJET PCL5 CODES

Code	Hex	Decimal	Command
Page Format Control:			
ESC & l ØO	1B 26 6C 3Ø 4F	27 38 108 48 79	Portrait Orient.
ESC & l 2O	1B 26 6C 32 4F	27 38 108 5Ø 79	Reverse Portrait
ESC & l 1O	1B 26 6C 31 4F	27 38 108 49 79	Landscape Orient.
ESC & l 3O	1B 26 6C 33 4F	27 38 108 51 79	Reverse Landscape
ESC & l #P	1B 26 6C # 5Ø	27 38 108 # 8Ø	Page length, # of lines
ESC & l #E	1B 26 6C # 45	27 38 108 # 69	Top Margin, # of lines
ESC & l #F	1B 26 6C # 46	27 38 108 # 7Ø	Text Length, # of lines
ESC & l 1L	1B 26 6C 31 4C	27 38 108 49 76	Skip Perforation, Set on
ESC & l ØL	1B 26 6C 3Ø 4C	27 38 108 48 76	Skip Perforation, Set off
ESC & l #D	1B 26 6C # 44	27 38 108 # 68	Lines Per Inch, # of lines/inch

HP LASERJET PCL5 CODES

Code	Hex	Decimal	Command
Page Format Control: (Continued)			
ESC & l #C	1B 26 6C # 43	27 38 108 # 67	Vertical Motion Index, # of 1/48 inch
ESC &k #H	1B 26 6B # 48	27 38 107 # 72	Horizontal Motion Index, # of 1/120 inch
ESC &a #L	1B 26 61 # 4C	27 38 97 # 76	Left Margin, Left column #
ESC &a #M	1B 26 61 # 4D	27 38 97 # 77	Right Margin, Right column #
ESC &a #P	1B 26 61 #...#50	27 38 97 #...# 080	# Degrees of Rotation(counter-clockwise/90 degree increments only)
ESC 9	1B 39	27 57	Clear Margins

Horizontal Movement and Spacing Control:			
BS	08	8	Backspace
CR	0D	13	Carriage Return
ESC &k # G	1B 26 6B # 47	27 38 107 # 71	CR/LF/FF Line Termination Action

	CR	LF	FF
		Line Termination Action	
#	CR	LF	FF
0	CR	LF	FF
1	CR+LF	LF	FF
2	CR	CR+LF	CR+FF
3	CR+LF	CR+LF	CR+FF

Code	Hex	Decimal	Command
ESC &s0C	1B 26 73 30 43	27 38 115 48 67	Set Wrap Around
ESC &s1C	1B 26 73 31 43	27 38 115 49 67	Release Wrap Around
ESC &a #C	1B 26 61 # 43	27 38 97 # 67	Move Print Position to Column #
ESC &a #H	1B 26 61 # 48	27 38 97 # 72	Move Print Position Horizontal # of Decipoints
ESC *p #X	1B 2A 70 # 58	27 42 112 # 88	Move Print Position Horizontal # of Dots
ESC & l # U	1B 26 6C #...# 55	27 038 108 #...# 085	Long-edge (left) Offset Registration

HP   LASERJET PCL5 CODES

Code	Hex	Decimal	Command
Vertical Movement and Spacing Control:			
LF	ØA	1Ø	Line Feed
FF	ØC	12	Formfeed
ESC =	1B 3D	27 61	Half Line Feed
ESC &a #R	1B 26 61 # 52	27 38 97 # 82	Move Print Position to Row #
ESC &a #V	1B 26 61 # 56	27 38 97 # 86	Move Print Position Vertical # of Decipoints
ESC *p #Y	1B 2A 7Ø # 59	27 42 112 # 89	Move Print Position Vertical # of Dots
ESC & l # Z	1B 26 6C #...# 5A	27 Ø38 1Ø8 #...# Ø9Ø	Short-edge (top) Offset Registration
Font Selection:			
ESC (#	1B 28 #	27 4Ø #	Symbol Set, Primary, # is Character ID
ESC) #	1B 29 #	27 41 #	Symbol Set, Secondary, # is Character ID

Character ID's:

Ø D = ISO 6Ø:Norwegian 1	5M=PS Math
1E=ISO 4:United Kingdom	6M=Ventura Math
1F=ISO 69:French	8M=Math-8
G=ISO 21:German	ØN=ECMA-94 Latin 1
Ø1=ISO 15:Italian	ØS=ISO 11:Swedish
6J=Microsoft Publishing	2S=ISO 17:Spanish
7J=DeskTop	ØU=ISO 6:ASCII
1ØJ=PS Text	1U=Legal
13J=Ventura International	8U=Roman8
14J=Ventura US	9U=Windows
9L=Ventura ITC Zapf Dingbats	1ØU=PC-8
1ØL=PS ITC Zapf Dingbats	11U=PC-8 D/N
11L=ITC Zapf Dingbats(S100)	12U=PC 850
12L=ITC Zapf Dingbats(S200)	15U=Pi Font
13L=ITC Zapf Dingbats(S300)	

ESC (s ØP	1B 28 73 3Ø 5Ø	27 4Ø 115 48 8Ø	Spacing, Primary Fixed
ESC (s 1P	1B 28 73 31 5Ø	27 4Ø 115 49 8Ø	Spacing, Primary Proportional

HP LASERJET PCL5 CODES

Code	Hex	Decimal	Command
Font Selection: (Continued)			
ESC) s ØP	1B 29 73 3Ø 5Ø	27 41 115 48 8Ø	Spacing, Secondary Fixed
ESC) s 1P	1B 29 73 31 5Ø	27 41 115 49 8Ø	Spacing, Secondary Proportional
ESC (s # H	1B 28 73 # 48	27 4Ø 115 # 72	Print Pitch, Primary, # is characters/inch
ESC) s # H	1B 29 73 # 48	27 41 115 # 72	Print Pitch, Secondary, # is characters/inch
ESC & k # S	1B 26 6B # 53	27 38 1Ø7 # 83	Print Pitch, Prim.
ESC & k ØS	1B 26 6B 31 53	27 38 1Ø7 49 83	1Ø.Ø CPI
ESC & k 1S	1B 26 6B 31 53	27 38 1Ø7 49 83	16.66 CPI
ESC & k 2S	1B 26 6B 32 53	27 38 1Ø7 5Ø 83	Compressed (16.5 - 16.7 CPI)
ESC & k 4S	1B 26 6B 34 53	27 38 1Ø7 52 83	Elite (12.Ø CPI)
ESC (s # V	1B 28 73 # 56	27 4Ø 115 # 86	Print Point Size, Primary, # is points
ESC) s # V	1B 29 73 # 56	27 41 115 # 86	Print Point Size, Secondary, # is points
ESC (sØS	1B 28 73 3Ø 53	27 4Ø 115 48 83	Upright (Solid)
ESC (s1S	1B 28 73 31 53	27 4Ø 115 49 83	Italic
ESC (s4S	1B 28 73 34 53	27 4Ø 115 52 83	Condensed
ESC (s5S	1B 28 73 35 53	27 4Ø 115 53 83	Condensed Italic
ESC (s8S	1B 28 73 38 53	27 4Ø 115 56 83	Compressed (Extra Condensed)
ESC (s24S	1B 28 73 32 34 53	27 4Ø 115 5Ø 52 83	Expanded
ESC (s32S	1B 28 73 33 32 53	27 40 115 51 5Ø 83	Outline
ESC (s64S	1B 28 73 36 34 53	27 4Ø 115 54 52 83	Inline
ESC (s128S	1B 28 73 31 32 38 53	27 4Ø 115 49 5Ø 56 83	Shadowed
ESC (s16ØS	1B 28 73 31 36 30 53	27 4Ø 115 49 54 48 83	Outline Shadowed
ESC (s # B	1B 28 73 # 42	27 4Ø 115 # 66	Stroke Weight, Primary, # is –7 to +7

See Stroke Weights on next page:

Code	Hex	Decimal	Command

Font Selection: (Continued)

Stroke Weights

-7=Ultra Thin	1=Semi Bold
-6=Extra Thin	2=Demi Bold
-5=Thin	3=Bold
-4=Extra Light	4=Extra Bold
-3=Light	5=Black
-2=Demi Light	6=Extra Black
-1=Semi Light	7=Ultra Black
Ø=Medium (book or text)	

Code	Hex	Decimal	Command
ESC) s # B	1B 29 73 # 42	27 41 115 # 66	Stroke Weight, Secondary, # is −7 to +7, −1 to −7=light Ø =Medium 1 to 7 =Bold
ESC (s # T	1B 28 73 # 54	27 4Ø 115 # 84	Typeface,Primary # is typeface (see below)
ESC) s # T	1B 29 73 # 54	27 41 115 # 84	Typeface,Secondary # is typeface:

Typeface ID's:

Ø=Line printer	7=Script
1=Pica	8=Prestige
2=Elite	9=Caslon
3=Courier	1Ø=Orator
4=Swiss 721	23=Century 7Ø
5=Dutch	4 14 8 = Universe
6=Gothic	4 1Ø 1 = CG Times

Font Control:

Code	Hex	Decimal	Command
SI	ØF	15	Shift In Primary
SO	ØE	14	Shift In Secondary
ESC (# X	1B 28 # 58	27 4Ø # 88	Define Font, Primary # is the Font ID number
ESC) # X	1B 29 # 58	27 41 # 88	Define Font, Secondary, # is the Font ID numbr

Code	Hex	Decimal	Command
ESC ∗c # F	1B 2A 63 # 46	27 42 99 # 7Ø	Font/Character Control, see printer manual
Font Control: (Continued)			
ESC (# @	1B 28 # 4Ø	27 4Ø # 64	Primary Font Default, see printer manual
ESC) # @	1B 29 # 4Ø	27 41 # 64	Secondary Font Default, see printer manual
ESC ∗c # D	1B 2A 63 # 44	27 42 99 # 68	Define Font ID, # is the ID
ESC) s # W	1B 29 73 # 57	27 41 115 # 87	Font Header, # is byte number of font attribute
ESC ∗c # E	1B 2A 63 # 45	27 42 99 # 69	Define Character Code to download, # is Ø to 255
ESC (s # W	1B 28 73 # 57	27 4Ø 115 # 87	Produce Download Character, see printer manual
ESC∗c # R	1B 2A 63 #...#52	27 4Ø 99 #...# 82	ID #
ESC (f # W	1B 2A 66 #...#46	27 4Ø 1Ø2 #...87	# of Bytes
ESC ∗ c ØS	1B 24 63 30 53	27 4Ø 99 48 83	Delete all symbol sets
ESC ∗c1S	1B 2A 63 31 53	27 4Ø 99 49 83	Delete all temporary symbol sets
ESC ∗c 2S	1B 2A 63 32 53	27 4Ø 99 5Ø 83	Delete current soft symbol sets (last ID#)
ESC ∗c 4S	1B 2A 63 34 53	27 4Ø 9Ø 52 83	Make current soft symbol set temporary
ESC ∗c 5S	1B 2A 63 35 53	27 4Ø 9Ø 53 83	Make current soft symbol set permanent
Character Highlight Selection:			
ESC & d D	1B 26 64 44	27 38 1ØØ 68	Turn underline on
ESC & d @	1B 26 64 4Ø	27 38 1ØØ 64	Turn underline off
Graphics:			
ESC ∗r #A	1B 2A 72 # 41	27 42 114 # 65	Graphics Start,

#=Ø is start vertical from left end of print area
#=1 is start from present position.

HP LASERJET PCL5 CODES

Code	Hex	Decimal	Command
Graphics: (Continued)			
ESC *c #A	1B 2A 63 # 41	27 42 99 # 65	Set Horizontal Rule Width to # dots (1 dot=1/3ØØ inch)
ESC *c #B	1B 2A 63 # 42	27 42 99 # 66	Set Vertical Rule Width to # dots (1 dot=1/3ØØ inch)
ESC *c # H	1B 2A 63 # 48	27 42 99 # 72	Set Horizontal Rule Width to # decipoints (1 decipoint=1/72Ø inch)
ESC *c # V	1B 2A 63 # 56	27 42 99 # 86	Set Vertical Rule Width to # decipoints (1 decipoint= 1/72Ø inch)
ESC%Ø A	1B 25 3Ø 41	27 37 48 65	Use previous PCL cursor position
ESC%1A	1B 25 31 41	27 37 49 65	Use current HP-GL/2 pen position for cursor position
ESC%ØB	1B 25 30 42	27 37 48 66	Use previous HP-GL/2 pen position. Use current PCL cursor position
ESC *c #K	1B 2A 63 #...# 48	27 42 99 #...#75	Horizontal size in inches
ESC *c #L	1B 2A 63 #...# 4C	27 42 99 #...#76	Vertical size in inches
ESC *cØT	1B 2A 63 3Ø 54	27 42 99 84	Set anchor point to cursor position
ESC *c #X	1B 2A 63 #...# 58	27 42 99 #...# 88	Decipoints Horiz.
ESC *c #Y	1B 2A 63 #...#59	27 42 99 #...#89	Decipoints Vert.
ESC * t 75R	1B 2A 74 37 35 52	27 42 116 55 53 82	75 dots/inch
ESC * t 1Ø ØR	1B 2A 74 31 3Ø 3Ø 52	27 42 116 49 48 48 82	100 dots/inch
ESC * t 15 ØR	1B 2A 74 31 35 3Ø 52	27 42 116 49 53 48 82	150 dots/inch
ESC * t 3 Ø ØR	1B 2A 74 33 30 3Ø 52	27 42 116 51 48 48 82	300 dots/inch
ESC * rØF	1B 2A 72 3Ø 46	27 42 114 48 7Ø	Follows orientation
ESC * r3F	1B 2A 72 33 46	27 42 114 51 7Ø	Follows physical page
ESC * b#Y	1B 2A 62 #...# 59	27 42 98 #...# 89	# of Raster Lines of vertical movement

HP LASERJET PCL5 CODES

Code	Hex	Decimal	Command
Graphics: (Continued)			
ESC*b0M	1B 2A 62 30 4D	27 42 98 48 77	Unencoded
ESC*b1M	1B 2A 62 31 4D	27 42 98 49 77	Run-Length Encoded
ESC*b2M	1B 2A 62 32 4D	27 42 98 50 77	Tagged Image Format
ESC*b3M	1B 2A 62 33 4D	27 42 98 51 77	Delta Row
ESC*b5M	1B 2A 62 35 4D	27 42 98 53 77	Adaptive compression
ESC*b#W	1B 2A 62 #...# 57	27 42 98 #...# 87	# of Bytes
ESC*r B	1B 2A 72 42	27 42 114 66	End Raster Graphics
ESC*r # T	1B 2A 72 #...# 54	27 42 114 #...# 84	# Raster Rows
ESC*r # S	1B 2A 72 #...#53	27 42 114 #...# 83	# Pixels of the specified resolution
ESC*v0 T	1B 2A 76 30 54	27 42 118 48 84	Solid Black (default)
ESC*v1T	1B 2A 76 31 54	27 42 118 49 84	Solid White
ESC*v2T	1B 2A 76 32 54	27 42 118 50 84	HP-defined shading pattern
ESC*v3T	1B 2A 76 33 54	27 42 118 51 84	HP-defined Cross-Hatched Pattern
ESC*y4T	1B 2A 76 34 54	27 42 118 52 84	User defined pattern
ESC*v0 N	1B 2A 76 30 4E	27 42 118 48 78	Transparent Source
ESC*v1N	1B 2A 76 31 4E	27 42 118 49 78	Opaque Source
ESC*v0 O	1B 2A 76 30 4F	27 42 118 48 79	Transparent Pattern
ESC*v1O	1B 2A 76 31 4F	27 42 118 49 79	Opaque Pattern
ESC*c0P	1B 2A 63 30 50	27 42 99 48 80	Solid Black
ESC*c1P	1B 2A 63 31 50	27 42 99 49 80	Erase (solid white fill)
ESC*c2P	1B 2A 63 32 50	27 42 99 50 80	Shaded Fill
ESC*c3P	1B 2A 63 33 50	27 42 99 51 80	Cross-hatched Fill
ESC*c5P	1B 2A 63 35 50	27 42 99 53 80	Current Pattern
ESC*c#G	1B 2A 63 #...# 47	27 42 99 #...# 71	% Shading or Type of Pattern
ESC*c2G	1B 2A 63 32 47	27 42 99 50 71	2% Gray
ESC*c10G	1B 2A 63 31 30 47	27 42 99 49 48 71	10% Gray
ESC*c15G	1B 2A 63 31 35 47	27 42 99 49 53 71	15% Gray
ESC*c30G	1B 2A 63 33 30 47	27 42 99 51 48 71	30% Gray
ESC*c45G	1B 2A 63 34 35 47	27 42 99 52 53 71	45% Gray
ESC*c70G	1B 2A 63 37 30 47	27 42 99 55 48 71	70% Gray
ESC*c90G	1B 2A 63 39 30 47	27 42 99 57 48 71	90% Gray
ESC*c100G	1B 2A 6 331 30 30 47	27 42 99 49 48 48 71	100% Gray
ESC*c1G	1B 2A 63 31 47	27 42 99 49 71	1 Horiz. Line
ESC*c2G	1B 2A 63 32 47	27 42 99 50 71	2 Vert Lines
ESC*c3G	1B 2A 63 33 47	27 42 99 51 71	3 Diagonal Lines
ESC*c4G	1B 2A 63 34 47	27 42 99 52 71	4 Diagonal Lines
ESC*c5G	1B 2A 63 35 47	27 42 99 53 71	5 Square Grid
ESC*c6G	1B 2A 63 36 47	27 42 99 54 71	6 Diagonal Grid

HP LASERJET PCL5 CODES

Code	Hex	Decimal	Command
Graphics: (Continued)			
ESC *c# W	1B 2A 63 31 51	27 42 99 #...# 87	# of Bytes
ESC *c# Ø Q	1B 2A 63 32 51	27 42 99 48 81	Delete all patterns
ESC *c#1Q	1B 2A 63 31 51	27 42 99 49 81	Delete all temp-orary patterns
ESC *c#2Q	1B 2A 63 32 51	27 42 99 50 81	Delete current pat.
ESC *c#4Q	1B 2A 63 34 51	27 42 99 52 81	Make pattern temporary
ESC *c#5Q	1B 2A 63 34 51	27 42 99 53 81	Make pattern permanent
ESC *pØR	1B 2A 7Ø 3Ø 52	27 42 112 48 82	Rotate with orientation
ESC *p1 R	1B 2A 7Ø 31 52	27 42 112 49 82	Follow physical page
Macros:			
ESC &f#Y	1B 26 66 # 59	27 38 1Ø2 # 89	Set Macro ID #
ESC &fØX	1B 26 66 3Ø 58	27 38 1Ø2 48 88	Start Macro
ESC &f1X	1B 26 66 31 58	27 38 1Ø2 49 88	End Macro
ESC &f2X	1B 26 66 32 58	27 38 1Ø2 5Ø 88	Jump to Macro
ESC &f3X	1B 26 66 33 58	27 38 1Ø2 51 88	Call Macro
ESC &f4X	1B 26 66 34 58	27 38 1Ø2 52 88	Set Overlay Macro
ESC &f5X	1B 26 66 35 58	27 38 1Ø2 53 88	Release Overlay Macro
ESC &f6X	1B 26 66 36 58	27 38 1Ø2 54 88	Release all Macro
ESC &f7X	1B 26 66 37 58	27 38 1Ø2 55 88	Release all temporary Macro
ESC &f8X	1B 26 66 38 58	27 38 1Ø2 56 88	Release current Macro
ESC &f9X	1B 26 66 39 58	27 38 1Ø2 57 88	Assign temporary attribute to Macro
ESC &f1ØX	1B 26 66 31 3Ø 58	27 38 1Ø2 49 48 88	Assign permanent attribute to Macro
Miscellaneous:			
ESC Y	1B 59	27 89	Set Display Function of control codes
ESC Z	1B 5A	27 9Ø	Release Display Function of control codes
ESC & p # X	1B 26 7Ø # 58	27 38 112 # 88	Transparent Print Data (no ESC commands exist)
ESC &fØS	1B 26 66 3Ø 53	27 38 1Ø2 48 83	Push Printing Position. Puts present printing

HP LASERJET PCL5 CODES

Code	Hex	Decimal	Command
Miscellaneous: (Continued)			
			position on the top of the stack
ESC &f1S	1B 26 66 31 53	27 38 102 49 83	Pop Printing Position. Recall stored printing position and put on the top of the stack
ESC & l #X	1B 26 6C # 58	27 38 108 # 88	Set Number of Copies to #
ESC & l #H	1B 26 6C # 48	27 38 108 # 72	Paper Input Control.
	#=Ø is feed out current page		
	#=1 is Lower Cassette supplies paper		
	#=3 is Envelope		
ESC & l ØH	1B 26 6C 30 48	27 Ø38 1Ø8 Ø48 Ø72	Eject Page
ESC & l 1H	1B 26 6C 31 48	27 Ø38 1Ø8 Ø49 Ø72	MP Tray
ESC & l 2H	1B 26 6C 32 48	27 Ø38 1Ø8 Ø5Ø Ø72	Manual Feed
ESC & l 3H	1B 26 6C 33 48	27 Ø38 1Ø3 Ø51 Ø72	Manual Envelope Feed
ESC & l 4H	1B 26 6C 34 48	27 Ø38 1Ø8 Ø52 Ø72	Lower Tray
ESC & l 6H	1B 26 6C 36 48	27 Ø38 1Ø8 Ø54 Ø72	Lower Cassette feeder supplies envelope, #=4 is Upper Cassette supplies paper
ESC & l 1G	1B 26 6C 31 47	27 Ø38 1Ø8 Ø49 Ø71	Upper Output Bin
ESC & l 1A	1B 26 6C 31 41	27 Ø38 1Ø8 Ø49 Ø65	Executive
ESC & l 2A	1B 26 6C 32 41	27 Ø38 1Ø8 Ø5Ø Ø65	Letter size
ESC & l 3A	1B 26 6C 33 41	27 Ø38 1Ø8 Ø51 Ø65	Legal size
ESC & l 26A	1B 26 6C 32 36 41	27 Ø38 1Ø8 Ø5Ø Ø54 Ø65	A4 size
ESC & l 8ØA	1B 26 6C 38 30 41	27 Ø38 1Ø8 Ø56 Ø48 Ø65	Monarch size
ESC & l 81A	1B 26 6C 38 31 41	27 Ø38 1Ø8 Ø56 Ø49 Ø65	COM 10 size
ESC & l 9ØA	1B 26 6C 39 3Ø 41	27 Ø38 1Ø8 Ø57 Ø48 Ø65	DL size
ESC & l 91A	1B 26 6C 39 31 41	27 Ø38 1Ø8 Ø57 Ø49 Ø65	C5 size
ESC E	1B 45	27 69	Reset Printer
ESC z	1B 7A	27 122	Start Printer Self Test

HP-GL GRAPHICS LANGUAGE CODES

HP-GL Command	Description [Parameters]	Syntax
ESC %#A	Enter PCL Mode	Ø-Retain previous PCL cursor position
		1-Use current HP-GL/2 pen position
ESC E	Reset	None
AA	Arc Absolute	**AA** X,Y,arc angle (,chord tolerance)
		[X,Y = coordinates, range -32768 to +32767]
		[arc angle = coordinates, range -360 to 360 degrees]
		[Chord Tolerance - Angle, range 0.1 to 180 degrees Deviation, range -32768 to +32767]
AP	Automatic Pen Operations	**AP** n, or **AP**;
		[n = coordinates, range 0 to 31]
AR	Arc Relative	**AR** X,Y arc angle (,chord tolerance)
		[X,Y = coordinates, range -32768 to 32767]
		[arc angle = coordinates, range -360 to +360 degrees]
		[Chord Tolerance - Angle, range 0.1 to 180 degrees Deviation, range -32768 to +32767]
CA	Designate Alternate Character Set	**CA** set, or **CA**;
		[set = coordinates, range 0-9, 30-39, 61, 99, 100 & 101]
CI	Circle	**CI** radius(,chord tolerance)
		[Radius = coordinates, range -32768 to 32767]
		[Chord Tolerance-angle, range 0.1 to 180 degrees Deviation, range -32768 to 32767]
CM	Character Selction Mode	**CM** switch mode (,fallback mode); or **CM**;
		[Switch Mode = coordinates, range 0 to 3]
		[Fallback Mode = coordinates, range 0 or 1]
CP	Character Plot	**CP** spaces,lines; or **CP**
		[spaces = coordinates, range -32768.9999 to +32767.9999]
		[lines = coordinates, range -32768.9999 to +32767.9999]
CS	Designate Standard Character Set	**CS** set; or **CS**;
		[set = coordinates, range 0-9, 30-39, 61, 99, 100 & 101]
CT	Chord Tolerance	**CT** n; or **CT**;
		[n = coordinates, range 0 to 1]
DC	Digitize Clear	**DC**;
DF	Default	**DF**;
DI	Direction Absolute	**DI** run,rise; or **DI**;
		[run = coordinates, range -32768.9999 to +32767.9999]
		[rise = coordinates, range -32768.9999 to +32767.9999]
DP	Digitize Point	**DP**;

HP-GL GRAPHICS LANGUAGE CODES

HP-GL Command	Description *[Parameters]*	Syntax
DR	Direction Relative	**DR** *run,rise;* or **DR;**
	[run = coordinates, range -32768.9999 to +32767.9999]	
	[rise = coordinates, range -32768.9999 to +32767.9999]	
DS	Designate Character Set Into Slot	**DS** *slot,set;* or **DS;**
	[slot = coordinates, range 0 to 1 (HP modes)	
	0 to 3 (ISO modes)	
	set = coordinates, range 0-9, 30-39, 61, 99, 100 & 101]	
DT	Define Label Terminator	**DT** *label terminator*
	[label terminator = coordinates, range any character	
	except NUL, ENQ, LF, ESC, and ; (decimal codes	
	0, 5, 10, 27, and 59, respectively]	
DV	Direction Vertical	**DV** *n;* or **DV;**
	[n = coordinates, range 0 or 1]	
EA	Edge Rectangle Absolute	**EA** *X,Y;*
	[X,Y coordinates, range -32768 to +32767]	
EP	Edge Polygon	**EP;**
ER	Edge Rectangle Relative	**ER** *X,Y;*
	[X,Y coordinates, range -32768 to +32767]	
ES	Extra Space	**ES** *spaces(,lines);* or **ES;**
	[spaces = coordinates, range -.05 to +1 char. plot cells]	
	[lines = coordinates, range -.05 to +2 char. plot cells]	
EW	Edge Wedge	**EW** *radius,start angle,sweep*
		angle, (,chord tolerance)
	[radius = coordinates, range -32768 to +32767]	
	[start angle = coordinates, range -360 to +360 degrees]	
	[sweep angle = coordinates, -360 to +360 degrees]	
	[chord tolerance-angle = coordinates range 0.1 to 180 deg.]	
	[deviation = coordinates, range -32768 to +32767]	
FI	Primary Font	Font ID
FP	Fill Polygon	**FP;**
FT	Fill Type	**FT** *type(,spacing (,angle));* or **FT;**
	[type = coordinates, range 1-4]	
	[spacing = coordinates, range 0 to 32767]	
	[angle = coordinates, range 0 to 90 degrees]	
GM	Graphics Memory	**GM** *(polygon buffer)*
		(,reserved buffer)
		(,reserved buffer)
		(,reserved buffer)
		(,pen sort buffer); or **GM;**
	[polygon buffer = coordinates, range 0 to 31887 bytes]	
	[reserved = coordinates, range 0]	
	[reserved = coordinates, range 0]	
	[reserved = coordinates, range 0]	
	[pen sort buffer = coordinates, range 12 to 31889 bytes]	

HP-GL GRAPHICS LANGUAGE CODES

HP-GL Command	Description [Parameters]	Syntax
IM	Input Mask	**IM** *E-mask value (,S-mask value (,P-mask value)); or* **IM;**
	[E-mask value = coordinates, range 0 to 255]	
	[S-mask value = coordinates, range 0 to 255]	
	[P-mask value = coordinates, range 0 to 255]	
IN	Initialize	**IN;**
IP	Input P1 and P2	**IP** *P1x,P1y(,P2x,P2t); or* **IP**
	[X, Y = coordinates, range -32678 to 32767 plotter units]	
IV	Invoke Character Slot	**IV** *(slot, (left)); or* **IV;**
	[slot = coordinates, range 0 to 1 (HP modes)	
	0 to 3 (ISO modes)]	
	[left = coordinates, range 0 to 1]	
IW	Input Window	**IW** *X1,Y1,X2, Y2; or* **IW;**
	[X1, Y1,X2, Y2 = coordinates, range -32768 to 32767]	
LB	Label	**LB** *c...x CHR$(3)*
	[c...c = coordinates, range any ASCII character]	
LO	Label Origin	**LO** *position number;*
	[position number = coordinates, range 1 to 9 or 11 to 19]	
LT	Line Type	**LT** *pattern number (, pattern length); or* **LT;**
	[pattern number = coordinates, range -6 to +6]	
	[pattern length = coordinates, range 0 to 100 percentage]	
NR	Not Ready	**NR;**
OA	Output Actual Pen Status	**OA;** *X, Y, pen status*
	[X, Y = coordinates, range -32678 to +32767]	
	[pen status = coordinates, range 0 (up) or 1 (down)]	
OC	Output Commanded Pen Status	**OC;** *X, Y, pen status*
	[X, Y = coordinates, range -32678 to +32767]	
	[pen status = coordinates, range 0 (up) or 1 (down)]	
OD	Output Digitized Point and Pen Status	**OD;** *X, Y, pen status*
	[X, Y = coordinates, range -32678 to 32767]	
	[pen status = coordinates, range 0 (up) or 1 (down)]	
OE	Output Error	**OE;** *error number*
	[error number = coordinates, range 0 to 7]	
OF	Output Factors	**OF;** *40,40*
	[40,40 = coordinates, range none]	
OH	Output Hard-Clip Limits	**OH;** *XLL,YLL,YUR,YUR*
	[YLL, YLL,YUR,YUR = coordinates, range -32678 to +32767]	
OI	Output Identification	**OI;** *model number*
	[model number = coordinates, range 7575A or 7576A]	
OO	Output Options	**OO;** *n,n,n,n,n,n,n,n*
	[none = coordinates, range 0 or 1]	

HP-GL GRAPHICS LANGUAGE CODES

HP-GL Command	Description [Parameters]	Syntax
OP	Output P1 and P2	**OP:** *P1X, P1Y, P2X, P2Y*
	[P1X, P1Y, P2X, P2Y = coordinates, range -32678 to +32767]	
OS	Output Status	**OS;** *status number*
	[status number = coordinates, range 0 to 255]	
OT	Output Carousel Type	**OT:** *-1, 255*
	[-1, 255 = coordinates, range none]	
OW	Output Window	**OW;** *XLL, YLL, XUR, YUR*
	[YLL, YLL,XUR, YUR = coordinates, range -32678 to +32767]	
PA	Plot Absolute	**PA** *X, Y (. . . ,X, Y)* or **PA;**
	[X, Y = coordinates, range -32768 to +32767]	
PD	Pen Down	**PD** *X,Y(,...);* or **PD;**
	[X, Y = coordinates, range -32768 to +32767]	
PE	Encoded Polyline	**PE** *(flag)(value)X, Y... (flag)value)X, Y,*
	[flag = coordinates, range ':', '<', '>', '=', or '7']	
	[value = coordinates, range flag dependent]	
	[X, Y = coordinates, range -32768 to +32767]	
PM	Polygon Mode	**PM** *n;* or **PM;**
	[n = coordinates, range 0,1, and 2]	
PR	Plot Relative	**PR** *X,Y(,...);* or **PR;**
	[X, Y increments = coordinates, range -8388608.9999 to +8388607.9999]	
PT	Pen Thickness	**PT** *pen thickness;* or **PT;**
	[pen thickness = coordinates, range 0.1 to 5.0 millimetres]	
PU	Pen Up	**PU** *X,Y(,...);* or **PU;**
	[X, Y = coordinates, range -32768 to +32767]	
RA	Fill Rectangle Absolute	**RA** *X, Y;*
	[X, Y = coordinates, range -32768 to +32767]	
RO	Rotate Coord System	**RO** *n;* or **RO;**
	[n = coordinates, range 0 or 90 degrees]	
RR	Fill Relative Rectangle	**RR** *X, Y*
	[X, Y increments = coords, range -32768 to +32767]	
SA	Select Alt. Character Set	**SA;**
SC	Scale	**SC** *Xmin,Xmax, Ymin, Ymax;* or **SC**
	[Xmin, Xmax, Ymin, Ymax = coordinates, range -8388608 to +8388607]	
SG	Select Pen Group	**SG** *pen number;*
	[pen number = coordinates, range 0 to 8]	
SI	Absolute Character Size	**SI** *width, height;* or **SI;**
	[width = coordinates, range -110 to +110]	
	[height = coordinates, range -100 to +110]	

HP-GL GRAPHICS LANGUAGE CODES

HP-GL Command	Description [Parameters]	Syntax
SL	Slant Character	**SL** *tangent;* or **SL;**
	[tangent = coordinates, range -3.5 to +3.5]	
SM	Symbol Mode	**SM** *character(character);* or **SM;**
	[character = coordinates, range most printing characters (decimal codes 33-58 and 60-126)]	
SP	Select Pen	**SP** *pen number;* or **SP;**
	[pen number = coordinates, range 0 to 8]	
SR	Relative Character Size	**SR** *width, height;* or **SR;**
	[width = coordinates, range -100 to 100 percent of P2X - P1X]	
	[height = coordinates, range -100 to 100 percent of P2X - P1X]	
SS	Select Std Character Set	**SS;**
TL	Tick Length	**TL** *positive tick(,negative tick);* or **TL;**
UC	User-defined Character	**UC** *(pen control,)X-increment, Y-increment(,...)(,pen control) (,...);* or **UC;**
VS	Velocity Select	**VS** *pen velocity(,pen number);* or **VS;**
	[pen velocity = coordinates, range 1 to 80]	
	[pen number = coordinates, range 1 to 8]	
WG	Wedge Fill	**WG** *radius, start angle, sweep angle(,chord tolerance);*
	[radius = coordinates, range -32768 to +32767]	
	[start angle = coordinates, range -360 to +360 degrees]	
	[sweep angle = coordinates, range -360 to +360 degrees]	
	[chord tolerance-angle = coordinates, range 0.1 to 180 degrees]	
	[chord deviation = coordinates, range -32768 to +32767]	
XT	X-Tick	**XT;**
YT	Y-Tick	**YT;**

IBM PROPRINTER PRINTER CODES

Code	Hex	Decimal	Command
Page Format Control:			
ESC C Ø #	1B 43 ØØ #	27 67 Ø #	Page Length, # is in Inch
ESC C #	1B 43 #	27 67 #	Page Length, # is in Lines
ESC X #1#2	1B 58 #1#2	27 88 #1#2	Left/Right Margins Set, #1 is left inches, #2 is right inches
ESC N #	1B 4E #	27 78 #	Skip Perforation Set, # is Top + Bottom
ESC O	1B 4F	27 79	Skip Perforation Release
ESC 4	1B 34	27 52	Top of Page Set
Horizontal Movement and Spacing Control:			
BS	Ø8	8	Backspace
CR	ØD	13	Carriage Return
ESC D # Ø	1B 44 # ØØ	27 68 # Ø	Horizontal Tab Set, # is the column, can use more than one #
ESC D Ø	1B 44 ØØ	27 68 Ø	Horizontal Tab Release
HT	Ø9	9	Horizontal Tab, moves to next preset tab
ESC R	1B 52	27 82	Reset all Tabs
Vertical Movement and Spacing Control:			
ESC Ø	1B 3Ø	27 48	Set Line Spacing to 1/8 inch (9 points or 8 lpi)
ESC 1	1B 31	27 49	Set Line Spacing to 7/72 inch (7 points)
ESC 2	1B 32	27 5Ø	Execute a Line Feed, must follow ESC A # command
ESC 3 #	1B 33 #	27 51 #	Set Line Spacing to #/216 inch
ESC A #	1B 41 #	27 65 #	Set Line Spacing to # Points (#/72 inch)
LF	ØA	1Ø	Line feed
ESC 5 1	1B 35 Ø1	27 53 1	Set Auto Line Feed
ESC 5 Ø	1B 35 ØØ	27 53 Ø	Release Auto Line Feed
ESC j #	1B 6A #	27 1Ø6 #	Reverse Line Feed of #/216 Inches
ESC J #	1B 4A #	27 74 #	Forward Line Feed of #/216 Inches
FF	ØC	12	Form feed
ESC B # Ø	1B 42 # ØØ	27 66 # Ø	Vertical Tab Set, # is the line, can use more than one #
ESC B Ø	1B 42 ØØ	27 66 Ø	Vertical Tab Release

IBM PROPRINTER PRINTER CODES

Code	Hex	Decimal	Command
Vertical Movement and Spacing Control (Continued):			
VT	ØB	11	Vertical Tab, moves to next preset tab
ESC R	1B 52	27 82	Reset all Tabs
Character Selection:			
DC2	12	18	Pica Pitch (12 pt,1Ø cpi)
ESC :	1B 3A	27 58	Elite Pitch (1Ø pt, 12 cpi)
SI	ØF	15	Compressed Print
ESC SI	1B ØF	27 15	Compressed Print
SO	ØE	14	Set Double Width for a single line
ESC SO	1B ØE	27 14	Set Double Width for a single line
DC4	14	2Ø	Release Double Width for a single line
ESC WØ	1B 57 ØØ	27 87 Ø	Release Double Wide Line
ESC W1	1B 57 Ø1	27 87 1	Set Double Width Line
ESC SØ	1B 53 ØØ	27 83 Ø	Set Superscript Mode On
ESC S1	1B 53 Ø1	27 83 1	Set Subscript Mode On
ESC T	1B 54	27 84	Release Superscript and Subscript
ESC 7	1B 37	27 55	Set IBM Character Set 1
ESC 6	1B 36	27 54	Set IBM Character Set 2
ESC ^	1B 5E	27 94	Select 1 Character from the All Character Chart
ESC \ #1 #2	1B 5C	27 92	Select Print Continuously from All Character Chart for a total of (#2 X 256) + #1
Character Highlight Selection:			
ESC – 1	1B 2D Ø1	27 45 1	Turn Underline Mode On
ESC – Ø	1B 2D ØØ	27 45 Ø	Turn Underline Mode Off
ESC _ 1	1B 5F Ø1	27 95 1	Enable Overline Mode
ESC _ Ø	1B 5F ØØ	27 95 Ø	Disable Overline Mode
ESC E	1B 45	27 69	Enable Bold Print Mode
ESC F	1B 46	27 7Ø	Disable Bold Print Mode
ESC G	1B 47	27 71	Enable Double–strike
ESC H	1B 48	27 72	Disable Double–strike

IBM PROPRINTER PRINTER CODES

Code	Hex	Decimal	Command
Graphics:			

For values of #1 and #2 below, see printer manuals

Code	Hex	Decimal	Command
ESC K#1#2	1B 4B #1#2	27 75 #1#2	Enable Single–density Graphics Mode, 6Ø dpi
ESC L#1#2	1B 4C #1#2	27 76 #1#2	Enable Double–density Graphics Mode, 12Ø dpi
ESC Y#1#2	1B 59 #1#2	27 89 #1#2	Enable Double–density, 12Ø dpi, High–speed Graphics Mode
ESC Z#1#2	1B 5A #1#2	27 9Ø #1#2	Enable Quad–density Graphics Mode, 24Ø dpi

Miscellaneous:

Code	Hex	Decimal	Command
CAN	18	24	Cancel
DC1	11	17	Remote Printer Select
ESC Q3	1B 51 Ø3	27 8 3	Remote Printer Deselect
ESC EM #	1B 19 #	27 25 #	Paper Cassette Selection, #=E is envelope #=1 is Lower Cassette #=2 is Upper Cassette #=R is eject page
NUL	ØØ	Ø	Null
BEL	Ø7	7	Sound Beeper

POCKET PCRef

Miscellaneous

RESISTOR COLOR CODES

Color	1st Digit(A)	2nd Digit(B)	Multiplier(C)	Tolerance(D)
Black	0	0	1	
Brown	1	1	10	1%
Red	2	2	100	2%
Orange	3	3	1,000	3%
Yellow	4	4	10,000	4%
Green	5	5	100,000	
Blue	6	6	1,000,000	
Violet	7	7	10,000,000	
Gray	8	8	100,000,000	
White	9	9	10^9	
Gold			0.1 (EIA)	5%
Silver			0.01 (EIA)	10%
No Color				20%

Example: Red–Red–Orange = 22,000 ohms, 20%

Additional information concerning the Axial Lead resistor can be obtained if Band A is a wide band. Case 1: If only Band A is wide, it indicates that the resistor is wirewound. Case 2: If Band A is wide and there is also a blue fifth band to the right of Band D on the Axial Lead Resistor, it indicates the resistor is wirewound and flame proof.

Axial Lead Resistor

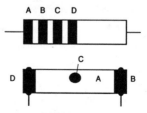

Radial Lead Resistor

PAPER SIZES

Paper Size	Standard	Millimeters	Inches
Eight Crown	IMP	1461 x 1060	57-1/2 x 41-3/4
Antiquarian	IMP	1346 x 533	53 x 21
Quad Demy	IMP	1118 x 826	44 x 32-1/2
Double Princess	IMP	1118 x 711	44 x 28
Quad Crown	IMP	1016 x 762	40 x 30
Double Elephant	IMP	1016 x 686	40 x 27
B0	ISO	1000 x 1414	39.37 x 55.67
Arch-E	USA	914 x 1219	36 x 48
Double Demy	IMP	889 x 572	35 x 22-1/2
➤ E.	ANSI	864 x 1118	34 x 44
A0	ISO	841 x 1189	33.11 x 46.81
Imperial	IMP	762 x 559	30 x 22
Princess	IMP	711 x 546	28 x 21-1/2
B1	ISO	707 x 1000	27.83 x 39.37
Arch-D	USA	610 x 914	24 x 36
A1	ISO	594 x 841	23.39 x 33.11
Demy	IMP	584 x 470	23 x 18-1/2
➤ D.	ANSI	559 x 864	22 x 34
B2	ISO	500 x 707	19.68 x 27.83
Arch-C	USA	457 x 610	18 x 24
➤ C.	ANSI	432 x 559	17 x 22
A2	ISO	420 x 594	16.54 x 23.39
B3	ISO	353 x 500	13.90 x 19.68
Brief	IMP	333 x 470	13-1/8 x 18-1/2
Foolscap folio	IMP	333 x 210	13-1/8 x 8-1/4
Arch-B	USA	305 x 457	12 x 18
A3	ISO	297 x 420	11.69 x 16.54
➤ B.	ANSI	279 x 432	11 x 17
Demy quarto	IMP	273 x 216	10-3/4 x 8-1/2
B4	ISO	250 x 353	9.84 x 13.90
Crown quarto	IMP	241 x 184	9-1/2 x 7-1/4
Royal octavo	IMP	241 x 152	9-1/2 x 6
Arch-A	USA	229 x 305	9 x 12
Demy octavo	IMP	222 x 137	8-3/4 X 5-3/8
➤ A.	ANSI	216 x 279	8.5 x 11
A4	ISO	210 x 297	8.27 x 11.69
Foolscap quarto	IMP	206 x 165	8-1/8 x 6-1/2
Crown Octavo	IMP	181 x 121	7-1/8 x 4-3/4
B5	ISO	176 x 250	6.93 x 9.84
A5	ISO	148 x 210	5.83 x 8.27
	USA	140 x 216	5.5 x 8.5
	USA	127 x 178	5 x 7
A6	ISO	105 x 148	4.13 x 5.83
	USA	102 x 127	4 x 5
	USA	76 x 102	3 x 5
A7	ISO	74 x 105	2.91 x 4.13
A8	ISO	52 x 74	2.05 x 2.91
A9	ISO	37 x 52	1.46 x 2.05
A10	ISO	26 x 37	1.02 x 1.46

Abbreviations for the above table are:

ISO	International Standards Organization
ANSI	American National Standards Institute
USA	United States
IMP	Imperial paper and plan sizes
Arch	United States architectural standards

DOS HISTORY

DOS Type	Release Date	Command. COM	io ibmbio	msdos ibmdos	Loaded System (if High)
		System File Sizes			
PC 1.0 MS 1.0	8-4-81	3,231	1,920	6400	13,312
PC 1.1 MS 1.25	5-7-82	4,959	1,920	6400	14,336
Zenith		4,986	1,713	6,138	
PC 2.0 MS 2.0	3-8-83	17,792	4,608	17,152	40,960
PC 2.1 MS 2.11	10-20-83	17,792	4,736	17,024	40,960
?mfg	11-17-83	15,957	6836	17,176	25,680
PC 2.11 MS 2.25	11-17-83				
PC 3.0 MS 3.0	8-14-84	22,042	8,964	27,920	60,416
PC 3.1 MS 3.1	3-7-85	23,210	9,564	27,760	62,464
PC 3.2	12-30-85	23,791	16,369	28,477	69,632
MS 3.2	7-7-86	23,612	16,138	28,480	55,568
MS 3.21	5-1-87				
PC 3.3	3-17-87	25,307	22,100	30,159	78,848
MS 3.3	7-24-87	25,276	22,357	30,128	55,440
MS 3.3a	2-2-88				
MS 4.0	10-6-88				
PC 4.01	3-89				
MS 4.01	11-30-88				
MS 4.01a	4-7-89	37,557	33,337	37,376	73,232
PC 5.0	6-91				
MS 5.0	4-9-91	33,430	37,394	47,845	62,576 (21,776)
MS 6.0	3-10-93	52,925	40,470	38,138	63,065 (17,197)
PC 6.1					
MS 6.2	Fall 93?				

NOTE: According to Microsoft, there were no official versions of MS-DOS prior to version 3.2. Prior to version 3.2, only OEM versions were sold with computers by the computer manufacturers. Slight variations in size do occur, so use these as a general reference only. If you have one of the OEM versions listed above, for which there is no data, we would appreciate hearing from you so we can fill in the gaps. See page iv (4) for a contact address and phone number.

POCKET PCRef

DOS COMMANDS

Including MS-DOS® Version 6.0

The section is a concise general reference of DOS commands, listed in alphabetic order. Page 102 contains a guide to conventions used in this section, in order to assist you in using the reference more effectively. A list of all DOS commands, grouped by command type, is located on page 103. Since most users will never need all of the DOS commands, a shaded sidebar has been provided that lists the most important commands every user should know.

Editors Note: We highly recommend that you upgrade your operating system with an official copy of MS-DOS 5.0 or 6.0. They have numerous functions and features not included in previous versions, particularly the high memory management functions. The Users Guide and Reference is well written and is an excellent resource. See page 6 for additional references. *If you are using Version 6.0, it is strongly recommended that you do not use DBLSPACE or SMARTDRV. Both of these programs cause a variety of problems with hard drives and are not safe to use.* Several aftermarket programs are available which can safely provide the same features.

Command descriptions in this chapter are based on the following notation:

5 New switch or parameter for DOS Version 5.0 or
6 Version 6.0

New V5.0 New Command for DOS Version 5.0
New V6.0 or Version 6.0

COMMAND NAME

Short Description: Long description

Syntax (shaded is optional):

COMMAND   Drive: \Path, **/switches parameters**

(Shaded areas indicate optional paramaters and switches)

     Examples: Samples of the syntax and command

Syntax Options:

Drive:\Path . . .	Drive & Directory containing command.
/switches	*Switches* modify the way a command performs its particular function.
parameters . . .	Data (usually numeric) passed to the command when it's started.

Command Type and Version:

External command	DOS commands stored as files on a disk. All externals end in either .EXE or .COM
Internal command	DOS commands contained in COMMAND.COM. These are loaded into the system on startup.
Batch command	A script (text) file containing a sequence of commands to be run. The file always ends in .BAT
Config.sys command . . .	Script (text) file containing start-up system configuration information and device drivers.
Network command	Will function on a network.
Introduced with Ver X.XX	The DOS version in which a command became available.

DOS COMMANDS, DRIVERS AND UTILITIES

External

Append
Assign
Attrib
Backup
Basic
Basica
Chkdsk
Command
Comp
Dblspace
Debug
Defrag
Deltree
Diskcomp
Diskcopy
Doskey
Dosshell
Edit
Edlin
Emm386
Exe2bin
Expand
Fasthelp
Fastopen
FC
Fdisk
Find
Format
Graftabl
Graphics
GW-Basic
Help
Interlnk
Intersvr
Join
Keyb
Keybxx
Label
Link
Loadfix
Mem
Memmaker
Mirror
Mode
More
Move
Msav/Mwav

Msbackup
MWbackup
Mscdex
Msd
Msherc
NLsfunc
Power
Print
Qbasic
Recover
Replace
Restore
Select
Setver
Share
Sort
Vsafe

External Continued

Subst
Sys
Tree
Undelete
Unformat
Xcopy

Internal

CD (Chdir)
Chcp
Chdir (CD)
Cls
Copy
Ctty
Date
Del (Erase)
Dir
Echo
Erase (Del)
Exit
Loadhigh
MD (Mkdir)
Mkdir (MD)
Path
Prompt
RD (Rmdir)
Rem

Ren (Rename)
Rename (Ren)
Rmdir (RD)
Set
Time
Type
Ver
Verify
Vol

Config.sys

Ansi.sys
Break
Buffers
Country (sys)
Dblspace.sys
Device
Devicehigh
DOS
Display.sys
Driver.sys
Drivparm
EGA.sys
Emm386.exe
FCBS
Files
Himem.sys
Include
Install
Interlnk
Keyboard.sys
Lastdrive
Menucolor
Menudefault
Menuitem
Numlock
Power
Printer.sys
Ramdrive.sys
Rem
Setver.exe
Shell
Smartdrv.sys
Stacks
Submenu
Switches
Vdisk.sys
Xma2ems.sys

Can Not Use on a Network

Chkdsk
Diskcomp
Diskcopy
Fastopen
Fdisk
Format
Join
Label
Recover
Subst
Sys
Unformat

Batch

@
Break
Call
Choice
Echo
For-In-Do
Goto
IF
   IF..errorlevel
   IF..exist
Pause
Rem
Shift

Operating System

See page 286
Command.com
Io.sys
Msdos.sys
Ibmbio.com
Ibmdos.com

ANSI.SYS

A device driver loaded through CONFIG.SYS that allows the user to control the computers display and keyboard. Once the ANSI.SYS driver has been loaded, ANSI escape code sequences can be used to customize both the display and keyboard. This was developed by the American National Standards Institute (ANSI).

Syntax (shaded is optional):

DEVICE = Drive:\Path\ANSI.SYS /x /k

    Examples: device=c:\dos\ansi.sys /x

    If ANSI.SYS is loaded, try the following example for some enhancement of a color display:
        PROMPT $e[35;44;1m$pge[33;44;1m

Syntax Options:

Drive: . . . . Letter of drive containing *\Path*.

\Path . . . . Directory containing ANSI.SYS.

/x . . . . Remaps 101-key keyboards so that the extended keys operate independently.

/k .🖑 . . . . Extended keys on the 101-key keyboards will be ignored. This is particularly important on systems that do not accurately handle extended keyboard functions.

Command Type and Version:

CONFIG.SYS command; Introduced with Ver 2.0

Notes:

1. The user has a lot of control over screen colors at the DOS level when the ANSI.SYS driver is loaded. See also PROMPT, p. 244.

2. The .SYS extension must be used in the syntax.

3. Using the Escape Code sequences is sometimes not an easy task. See PC Magazines book *DOS Power Tools, page 420,* for an example of how to write simple programs to send these codes.

ANSI.SYS (cont.)

ANSI escape sequences are a series of characters beginning with the ESCAPE (character 27) key, followed by open left bracket (**[**), followed by parameters sometimes, and ending with a letter or number. Note that the ending letter must be used in the correct upper or lower case format.

Parameters used in the escape sequences are as follows:

pl	Line number (decimal value)
pc	Column number (decimal value)
pn	Specifies parameter is numeric.
ps	Specific decimal number for a function. Multiple *ps* functions are separated with a **;**

ANSI escape sequences:

ESC [*pl* ; *pc* H .. Moves cursor to a specific line (*pl* parameter) and column (*pc* parameter). If no *pl* or *pc* is specified, the cursor goes to the Home position.

ESC [*pl* ; *pc* f ... Functions same as **ESC [*pl* ; *pc* H.**

ESC [*pn* A ..... Moves Cursor Up *pn* number of lines. If cursor is on top line, ANSI.SYS ignores this sequence.

ESC [*pn* B ..... Moves Cursor Down *pn* number of lines. If the cursor is on the bottom line, ANSI.SYS ignores this sequence.

ESC [*pn* C ..... Moves Cursor Forward *pn* number of columns. If the cursor is at the farthermost right column, ANSI.SYS ignores this sequence.

ESC [*pn* D ..... Moves Cursor Backward *pn* number of lines. If the cursor is at the farthermost left column, ANSI.SYS ignores this sequence.

ESC [s . . . . Save Cursor Position. The cursor may be moved to the saved position by using the Restore Cursor sequence.

ESC [u . . . . Restore Cursor Position. Moves the cursor to the Save Cursor Position.

ESC [2 J . . . . Erase Display. Erases the screen and returns the cursor to the home position.

ESC [K . . . . Erase Line. Erases all characters from the cursor to the end of the line.

ESC [*ps* ; .. ; *ps* m Sets graphics functions (text attributes and foreground and background colors). Note: These functions stay active until a new set of parameters is issued with this command.

Text Attributes:
All attributes off	0
Bold On	1
Underscore	4 (Mono adapter only)
Blink on	5
Reverse Video On	7
Concealed On	8

Colors	Foreground	Background
Black	30	40
Red	31	41
Green	32	42
Yellow	33	43
Blue	34	44
Magenta	35	45
Cyan	36	46
White	37	47

Example: Try using the following PROMPT command if you have a color monitor and ANSI.SYS has been loaded in CONFIG.SYS.

PROMPT $e[35;44;1m$pge[33;44;1m

ESC [= *ps* h .... Set Mode function. The active screen width and graphics mode type is changed with this sequence using the following values: ("mono" means monochrome).

Mode		Mode	
ps	(Graphics unless noted)	*ps*	(Graphics unless noted)
0	40 x 25 mono (text)	13	320 x 200 color
1	40 x 25 mono (text)	14	640 x 200 color (16 color)
2	80 x 25 mono (text)	15	640 x 350 mono (2 color)
3	80 x 25 color (text)	16	640 x 350 color (16 color)
4	320 x 200 (4-color)	17	640 x 480 mono (2 color)
5	320 x 200 mono	18	640 x 480 (16 color)
6	640 x 200 mono	19	320 x 200 color (256 color)
7	Enables line wrapping		

ESC [= *ps* l (l in the sequence to the left is a lower case **L**) This sequence resets the Mode sequence described above. The *ps* parameter uses the same values as those shown in the Set Mode sequence above.

ANSI.SYS (cont.)

ESC [*code* **;** *string* **;...P**   Redefine a specific keyboard key with a
specific string of characters. *code* is one of the values in the ASCII
Key Code table, on the next three pages, that represent keyboard
keys or combinations of keys. Gray keys, keypad keys or codes
shown in ( ) in the table may not function on some keyboards (try
using the /x switch on the ANSI.SYS command line). *string* is
either the decimal ASCII code for a single character (76 is the
letter "C") or a string of characters in quotes ("<"). For example:

   ESC ["<" ; "+" p ESC ["+" ; "<" p
   ESC [60 ; 43 p ESC [43 ; 60 p

Both of the above sequences do the same task, they exchange
the < and + keys.
Note that it is not possible to alter the ALT and Caps Lock keys.

*NOTE: Some values listed in the ASCII Key
Codes table below may not be valid for all
computers! If in doubt, be sure to check the
computers documentation for verification.*

ASCII Key Codes for ANSI.SYS

Key	*K means Key ➡* K Code	SHIFT+K Code	CTRL+K Code	ALT+K Code
F1	0;59	0;84	0;94	0;104
F2	0;60	0;85	0;95	0;105
F3	0;61	0;86	0;96	0;106
F4	0;62	0;87	0;97	0;107
F5	0;63	0;88	0;98	0;108
F6	0;64	0;89	0;99	0;109
F7	0;65	0;90	0;100	0;110
F8	0;66	0;91	0;101	0;111
F9	0;67	0;92	0;102	0;112
F10	0;68	0;93	0;103	0;113
F11	0;133	0;135	0;137	0;139
F12	0;134	0;136	0;138	0;140
Home	0;71	55	0;119	—
Up Arrow	0;72	56	(0;141)	—
Page Up.	0;73	57	0;132	—
Left Arrow	0;75	52	0;115	—
Right Arrow	0;77	54	0;116	—
End	0;79	49	0;117	—
Down Arrow.	0;80	50	(0;145)	—
Page Down	0;81	51	0;118	—

Key	*K means Key* ➡ K Code	SHIFT+K Code	CTRL+K Code	ALT+K Code
Insert	0;82	48	(0;146)	—
Delete	0;83	46	(0;147)	—
Home (gray key) . . .	224;71	224;71	224;119	224;151
Up Arrow (gray key)	224;72	224;72	224;141	224;152
Page Up (gray key) .	224;73	224;73	224;132	224;153
Left Arrow (gray key)	224;75	224;75	224;115	224;155
Right Arrow (gray K)	224;77	224;77	224;116	224;157
End (gray key)	224;79	224;79	224;117	224;159
Down Arrow (gray key)	224;80	224;80	224;145	224;154
Page Down (gray key)	224;81	224;81	224;118	224;161
Insert (gray key) . . .	224;82	224;82	224;146	224;162
Delete (gray key). . .	224;83	224;83	224;147	224;163
Print Screen	—	—	0;114	—
Pause/Break	—	—	0;0	—
Backspace	8	8	127	(0)
Enter	13	—	10	(0;28)
Tab	9	0;15	(0;148)	(0;165)
Null	0;3	—	—	—
A	97	65	1	0;30
B	98	66	2	0;48
C	99	66	3	0;46
D	100	68	4	0;32
E	101	69	5	0;18
F	102	70	6	0;33
G	103	71	7	0;34
H	104	72	8	0;35
I	105	73	9	0;23
J	106	74	10	0;36
K	107	75	11	0;37
L	108	76	12	0;38
M	109	77	13	0;50
N	110	78	14	0;49
O	111	79	15	0;24
P	112	80	16	0;25
Q	113	81	17	0;16
R	114	82	18	0;19
S	115	83	19	0;31
T	116	84	20	0;20
U	117	85	21	0;22
V	118	86	22	0;47
W	119	87	23	0;17

ASCII Key Codes for ANSI.SYS (cont.)

Key	K Code	SHIFT+K Code	CTRL+K Code	ALT+K Code
X	120	88	24	0;45
Y	121	89	25	0;21
Z	122	90	26	0;44
1.	49	33	—	0;120
2.	50	64	0	0;121
3.	51	35	—	0;122
4.	52	36	—	0;123
5.	53	37	—	0;124
6.	54	94	30	0;125
7.	55	38	—	0;126
8.	56	42	—	0;127
9.	57	40	—	0;128
0.	48	41	—	0;129
– (minus sign)	45	95	31	0;130
= (equal sign)....	61	43	—	0;131
[(left bracket)	91	123	27	0;26
] (right bracket) ...	93	125	29	0;27
\ (back slash)	92	124	28	0;43
; (semi-colon)....	59	58	—	0;39
' (apostrophe)	39	34	—	0;40
, (comma)	44	60	—	0;51
. (period)	46	62	—	0;52
/ (forward slash)...	47	63	—	0;53
` (accent)	96	126	—	(0;41)
ENTER (on keypad)	13	—	10	(0;166)
/ (on keypad)	47	47	(0;142)	(0;74)
* (on keypad)	42	(0;144)	(0;78)	—
– (on keypad).....	45	45	(0;149)	(0;164)
+ (on keypad)....	43	43	(0;150)	(0;55)
5 (on keypad).....	(0;76)	53	(0;143)	—

APPEND

Sets directory search order: Searchs specified directories on specified drives to locate files outside of the current directory that have extensions <u>other than</u> .COM, .EXE, or .BAT. *Use Caution!*

Syntax (shaded is optional):

APPEND **Drive: \Path /X /E ;**

Examples: APPEND /X /E
APPEND C:\WORDDATA; D:\PFS
APPEND ;

Syntax Options:

Drive:	Letter of drive to be searched.
\Path	Directory searched for data files.
/X :on or :off . .	Extends the DOS search path for specified files when executing programs. Processes SEARCH FIRST, FIND FIRST, and EXEC functions. :ON and :OFF, new to Version 5.0, toggles this switch on and off.
/Path :on or :off	If path is already included for a program file, :on tells program to also search in-appended directories. Default= :on
/E	Causes the appended path to be stored in the DOS environment and searched for there.
;	Use ";" to separate multiple Drive:\Path statements on one line. APPEND ; by itself will cancel the APPEND list.

⑤

Command Type and Version:

External command; Network; Introduced with Ver 3.2

Notes:

1. /X and /E switches can only be used the first time you use Append. The line following the APPEND /X /E line contains the Drive:\Path.
2. You can not use any paths on the same command line as /X & /E.
3. :ON and :OFF swithches are valid for Ver 5.0 and later.

Assign disk drive: Instructs DOS to redirect disk operations on one drive to a different drive.

Syntax (shaded is optional):

ASSIGN   Source = Target /status

> Examples: ASSIGN A = B   or   ASSIGN A: = B:
> ASSIGN A = B B = C
> ASSIGN
> ASSIGN /status

Syntax Options:

ASSIGN . . . . . . ASSIGN with no switch cancels redirected drive assignments and sets them back to their origional drives.

Source . . . . Letter(s) of source drive(s).

Target . . . . Letter(s) of target drive(s). Starting with Version 5.0, a colon can be used with each assigned drive letter. For example; ASSIGN A: = B:

/Status . . . . Lists current drive assignments.

Command Type and Version:

External command; Network; Introduced with Ver 2.0 Removed from Version 6.0, considered to dangerous.

Notes:

1. DO NOT use a colon after a drive letter in versions prior to 5.0.
2. FORMAT, DISKCOPY, DISKCOMP, BACKUP, JOIN, LABEL, RESTORE, PRINT and SUBST cannot be used on ASSIGNed drives.
3. Be careful to reassign drives back to their original designations before running other programs.
4. If ASSIGN and APPEND are both used, the APPEND command must be used first.
5. See also the SUBST command.

ATTRIB

Changes or displays file attributes: Sets, displays or clears a files read-only, archive, system, and hidden attributes.

Syntax (shaded is optional):

ATTRIB `+r-r +a-a +s-s +h-h` Drive:\Path\Filename `/s`

> Examples: ATTRIB wordfile.doc
> ATTRIB +r wordfile.doc
> ATTRIB +r d:\worddata*.* /s

Syntax Options:

Drive:	Letter of drive containing \path\filename.
\Path	Directory containing *filename*.
Filename	Filename(s) of which attributes are to be displayed or changed. Wildcards (? and *) can be used for groups of files.
+ r	Sets file to read-only.
− r	Removes read-only attribute.
+ a	Sets the archive file attribute.
− a	Removes the archive file attribute.
+ s	Sets file as a system file.
− s . . **⑤**	Removes system file attribute.
+ h	Sets file as a hidden file.
− h	Removes the hidden file attribute.
/s	ATTRIB command processes files in the current directory and its subdirectories.

Command Type and Version:

External command; Network; Introduced with Ver 3.0

Notes:

1. When the system or hidden attribute is set , the read-only and *archive* attributes cannot be changed.

2. The *archive* attribute is used by the DOS BACKUP, RESTORE, and XCOPY commands when their /m switch is used and also the XCOPY command when the /a switch is used.

@ (at)

Turns off the command echo function: In a batch file, placing the @ symbol at the start of a command line surpresses the echoed display of the command on the screen.

Syntax (shaded is optional):

> @ command

> Examples: @xcopy a:*.* b:

> @ECHO off

Syntax Options:

command . . . . Any DOS command.

Command Type and Version:

Batch command; Introduced with Ver 3.3

Notes:

1. Useful in preventing the words ECHO OFF from displaying on the screen when ECHO OFF is used in a Batch file. This command is useful if all screen echos need to be turned off in a Batch file.

2. See also ECHO.

Removed V6.0

Back up files: Backs up files from one drive to another drive. Source and target drives may be either hard disks or floppy disks. DOSV6 use MSBACKUP.

Syntax (shaded is optional):

BACKUP Source:\Path\Filename Target: **/s /m /a /d:date /t:time /f:size /L:LogDrive\Path\Log**

> Examples: BACKUP C:*.* B: /s
> BACKUP C:\DATA*.* B: /s /L:C:\LOG

Syntax Options:

Source:\Path . .	Source drive & directory to be backed up.
Filename	Filename (s) to be backed up. Use of Wild cards (? and *) is allowed.
Target:	Target drive for backed up files.
/s	Backs up all files in *Source:\Path* and subdirectories under *Source:\Path*
/m	Backs up all files that have changed since the last backup (backup looks at the files archive attribute) and then turns off the files archive attribute.
/a	Adds new backup files to the existing backup disk (existing files are not deleted.) If a backup was made with DOS 3.2 or earlier, the /a switch is ignored.
/d:date	Only files created or modified after *date* are backed up. The way *date* is written depends on COUNTRY.SYS settings.
/t:time	Only files created or modified after *time* are backed up. The way *time* is written depends on COUNTRY.SYS settings. Always use the */d:date* switch when */t:time* is used.

/f:size	Format backup disk to the following *size*. (*size* can also be with k or kb, e.g. 160 can be 160k or 160kb; or 1200 can be 1200k, 1200kb, 1.2, 1.2m or 1.2mb, etc)

size	Disk size and type
160	160k single sided DD 5.25" disk
180	180k single sided DD 5.25" disk
320	320k double sided DD 5.25" disk
360	360k double sided DD 5.25" disk
720	720k double sided DD, 3.5" disk
1200 . . .	1.2meg double sided HD, 5.25"
1440 . . .	1.44meg double sided QD, 3.5"
2880 . . .	2.88meg double sided, 3.5" disk

(DD=Double Density, QD=Quad Density)

/L:	Creates a log file during a specific backup operation.
Logdrive:\Path .	Drive & Directory where backup *Log* is to be sent.
Log	Text file log of a backup operation.

Command Type and Version:

External command; Network; Introduced with Ver 2.0
Removed from Version 6.0, replaced with MSBACKUP.

Notes:
1. See also RESTORE, COPY, XCOPY, DISKCOPY, IF
2. The sequence number of a backup disk can be checked by doing a DIR of the backup disk (Valid for version after DOS 3.3)
3. BACKUP does not backup the 3 system files, COMMAND.COM, MSDOS.SYS (or IBMDOS.SYS) , and IO.SYS (or IBMBIO.SYS).
4. BACKUP/RESTORE commands are not very compatible between pre DOS 5.0 version. DOS 5.0 will restore previous versions.
5. Do not use BACKUP when the ASSIGN, JOIN, or SUBST commands have been used.
6. When the IF ERRORLEVEL functions are used, BACKUP Exit Codes can be used to show why a backup failed (see IF):

Exit Code	Code Meaning
0	Successful backup
1	No files found to be backed up
2	File-sharing conflict, some files not backed up
3	BACKUP terminated by user with CTRL-C
4	Error terminated BACKUP procedure

7. Backup floppies are not readable by DOS, a special file format is used.

BASIC® and BASICA®

BASIC Computer Language: Depending on the system in use and version of DOS, it will run one of the BASIC interpreters (BASIC, BASICA, GW-BASIC, or QBASIC) and provide an environment for programming in the BASIC language. BASIC and BASICA are versions that were shipped with IBM® systems and were simply entry programs that started BASIC from the systems ROM. GW-BASIC is Microsoft's own version of BASIC that is shipped with MS-DOS versions through 4.01. For specifics on DOS 5.0/6.0 QBASIC, refer to page 245.

Syntax (shaded is optional):

BASIC `Filename`

> Examples: BASIC Test.bas
>   BASICA

Syntax Options:

BASIC . . . .   BASIC without a filename just starts the BASIC Interpreter.

Filename . . . . .   A program written in BASIC that is loaded and run when the BASIC interpreter starts. The files normally end with .BAS

Command Type and Version:

External command; Network; Introduced with Ver 1.0

Notes:

1. See also QBASIC and GW-BASIC.

BREAK

Turns on/off the DOS check for Control-C or Control-Break. Determines when DOS looks for a Ctrl-C or Ctrl-Break more frequently in order to stop a program.

Syntax (shaded is optional):

BREAK on off

    Examples: BREAK
                  BREAK = ON (syntax for CONFIG.SYS)
                  BREAK ON (syntax at DOS prompt)

Syntax Options:

BREAK . . . . . . BREAK, with no switches or options, displays the current setting of BREAK.

ON . . . . Tells DOS to check for Ctrl-C or Ctrl-Break from the keyboard, during disk reads and writes, and during screen and printer writes.

OFF . . . . Tells DOS to check for Ctrl-C or Ctrl-Break only from the keyboard or screen and printer writes.

Command Type and Version:

Internal command; CONFIG.SYS and Batch command; Introduced with Ver 2.0

Notes:

1. If BREAK is ON, your system will run slightly slower.
2. The default setting is BREAK=OFF.

BUFFERS

Sets number of disk buffers in memory: A disk buffer is a block of RAM memory that DOS uses to hold data while reading and writing data to a disk.

Syntax (shaded is optional):

BUFFERS = X **Y**

Examples: BUFFERS = 35
BUFFERS = 35,8

Syntax Options:

X . . . . The number of disk buffers allocated. The total may range from 1 to 99 for versions Ver 4.0 to 5.0. Versions prior to 4.0 can be in the range from 2 to 255. Default values are as follows:

Buffers	Drive Configuration
2	<128K RAM & 360k drive only
3	<128K RAM & Disks over 360K
5	128K to 255K RAM
10	256K to 511K RAM
15	512K or more RAM

Y . . . . The number of secondary cache buffers. The total may range from 1 to 8, the default is 1.

Command Type and Version:

CONFIG.SYS command; Introduced with Ver 2.0

Notes:

1. Each buffer takes up approximately 532 bytes of RAM.
2. Standard buffer sizes should range from 20 to 30, unless more are required by a specific application (such as Dbase III Plus®).
3. If a disk cache program, such as SMARTDRV.SYS is used, the number of buffers can be set at 8 to 15 (sometimes lower).
4. In Ver 5.0, if DOS is in high memory, buffers are also in high mem.
5. The number of buffers (up to 35) significantly affects system speed; over 35, speed still increases but at much slower rate.
6. /X switch from earlier DOS versions is no longer available.

CALL

Calls a batch program. Starts one batch program from inside another batch program, without causing the initial batch program to stop.

Syntax (shaded is optional):

CALL Drive:\Path\ Filename Parameters

    Examples: CALL C:\TEST %1

Syntax Options:

Drive: . . . . Letter of drive containing path.

\Path . . . . Path containing filename.

Filename . . . . . Filename specifies name of the batch program to be called. *Filename* must have a .BAT extension.

Parameters . . . Specifies command-line information required by the batch program, including switches, filenames, pass through parameters such as %1, and variables.

Command Type and Version:

Internal command; Batch; Introduced with Ver 3.3

Notes:

1. Any information that can be passed to a batch program can be contained in the *Batch-parameters*, including switches, filenames, replaceable parameters %1 through %9, and variables such as % Parity %

2. Pipes and redirection symbols cannot be used with CALL.

3. If a recursive call (a program that calls itself) is created, an exit condition must be provided or the two batch programs will loop endlessly.

CD or CHDIR

Change directory: Changes (moves) to another directory or shows the name of the current directory path.

Syntax (shaded is optional):

CD **Drive:\Path**

Examples: CD (displays current drive and directory)
CD D:\PFS (change to PFS directory on
D: drive)
CD\ (changes to root directory)

Syntax Options:

Drive: . . . . Drive containing the subdirectory to be changed. CD does not move to *Drive:*, it remains on the current drive.

\Path . . . . Directory path name to be made current, if *Drive:* is the current drive. If *Drive:* is not the current drive, *\Path* is simply the active path on *Drive:* and the current drive and directory remain unchanged. Pathname can be no longer than 63 characters and (\) is to be used as the path's first character to move to the root directory.

Command Type and Version:

Internal command; Network; Introduced with Ver 2.0

Notes:

1. When a drive letter is not specified, the current drive is assumed.
2. **CD ..** specifies move up one directory level.

CHCP

Change code page: Displays or changes the number of the active code page for the command processor COMMAND.COM.

Syntax (shaded is optional):

CHCP `ccc`

> Examples: CHCP   (reports current *ccc* setting)
> CHCP 863

Syntax Options:

ccc . . . . These are the numbers that represent the prepared system code pages defined by the COUNTRY.SYS command in the CONFIG.SYS file. Valid code page numbers are as follows:

> 437 . . . . United States
> 850 . . . . Multilingual (Latin I)
> 852 . . . . Slavic (Latin II)
> 860 . . . . Portuguese
> 863 . . . . Canadian-French
> 865 . . . . Nordic

Command Type and Version:

Internal command; Network; Introduced with Ver 3.3

Notes:

1. Once a specified code page has been selected, all programs that are started will use that new code page.

2. NLSFUNC (national language support functions) must be installed before a code page can be switched with CHCP.

3. MODE SELECT can also be used to change code pages.

4. See also DOS commands COUNTRY.SYS, NLSFUNC, DEVICE, and MODE.

CHKDSK

Checks disk: Scans the disk and reports size, disk memory available, RAM available and checks for and corrects logical errors. A status report is displayed on screen.

Syntax (shaded is optional):

CHKDSK Drive:\Pathname\Filename / f / v

Examples: CHKDSK C: / f
(If no Drive: is specified, the current drive is used.)

Syntax Options:

Drive: . . . . Drive letter of the disk to be checked.

Path . . . . Directory path containing file to be checked.

Filename . . . . . Name of file to be checked by CHKDSK for fragmentation. Wildcards * & ? are allowed.

/ f . . . . Fixes logical errors on the disk.

/ v . . . . Verbose switch. Displays CHKDSK progress by listing each file in every directory as it is being checked.

Command Type and Version:

External command; Can NOT check a Network drive; Introduced with Ver 1.0

Notes:

1. CHKDSK analyzes a disks File Allocation Table (FAT) and file system. / f must be specified in order to fix errors. If / f is not used, CHKDSK reports the error, but does not fix the error, even if you answer yes to fixing the error at the CHKDSK prompt.
2. When CHKDSK / f finds an error, it asks if you want to covert the "lost clusters" to files. If you answer Yes, files in the form FILE0001.CHK are created and the lost areas dumped into those files. You must then determine if any valuable info is in that file. If they don't contain useful information, delete them.
3. Do not use CHKDSK from inside any other program, especially Windows.
4. Only logical errors are repaired by CHKDSK, not physical errors.
5. CHKDSK will not work when SUBST, JOIN or ASSIGN has been used.

Pauses the system and prompts the user to make a choice in a batch file: This command can only be used in batch programs.

Syntax: (shaded is optional)

CHOICE /C:keys /N /S /T:c,nn text

Examples: CHOICE /C:T,F / S

Syntax Options:

/C:keys .... Defines which keys are allowed in the prompt. The : is optional. Displayed keys are separated by commas and will be enclosed in [ ] brackets. Multiple keystroke characters are allowed. Default is [YN] (yes/no).

/N .... Prevents display of prompt, but the specified keys are still valid.

/S .... Specifies that CHOICE is case sensative.

/T:c,nn ...... Forces CHOICE to pause for *nn* seconds before defaulting to a specified key *(c)*. nn can range from 0 to 99. The *c* key specified must be included in the */C:keys* definition.

text .... Defines what text is displayed before the prompt. Quotation marks ("") must be used if a "/" character is included in the prompt. Default for CHOICE is not text displayed.

Command Type and Version:

Internal Batch command; Network; Introduced with Ver 6.0

Notes:

1. ERRORLEVEL 0 is returned if Control-C or Control-Break are pressed.

CLS

Clears or Erases Screen: All information is cleared from the DOS screen and the prompt and cursor is returned to the upper left corner of the screen.

Syntax:

CLS

Examples: CLS

Syntax Options:

None

Command Type and Version:

Internal command; Network; Introduced with Ver 2.0

Notes:

1. Screen colors set by ANSI.SYS will remain set.
2. If more than one video display is attached to the system, only the active display is cleared.
3. If ANSI.SYS is not loaded on the system, CLS will clear the screen to gray (or amber on an amber monitor, etc) on black.

COMMAND

Start a new DOS command processor: The command processor is responsible for displaying the prompt on the computers display and contains all of the Internal DOS commands. It is also used to set variables such as environment size. Use the EXIT command to stop the new processor.

Syntax (shaded is optional):

COMMAND `Drive:\Path\Device / e:xxxx / p / c text / msg / k`

In CONFIG.SYS use the following:

SHELL = `Drive:\Path\` COMMAND.COM `/ e:xxxx / p`

> Examples: COMMAND /e:1024 /p
> (use the following in CONFIG.SYS with SHELL)
> SHELL = Drive:\Path\COMMAND.COM /e:512 /p

Syntax Options:

Drive:\Path	Drive and \Path of the command device. Must be included if COMMAND.COM is not located in the root directory.
\Device	Device for command input or outpur (see the CTTY command on page 131.
/ e:xxxx	Set environment size in bytes (xxxx). Default for Ver 5.0 = 256 bytes; default for versions before 5.0 is 160 bytes. Range is 160 to 32768 bytes.
/ p	Makes the new command processor the permanent processor.
/ c text	Forces the command processor to perform the commands specified by *text*. On completion, it returns to the primary command processor.
/ msg	Causes error messages to be stored in memory. The */ p* switch must also be used when */ msg* is used.

/k .... ⑥ Execute a command, but after the command is executed, do not terminate the second COMMAND.COM that is running.

Command Type and Version:

External command;

CONFIG.SYS command when used with SHELL;

Introduced with Ver 1.0

Notes:

1. See also CTTY, EXIT and SHELL
2. Default environment sizes are commonly not large enough. Try setting the environment to 512 or 1024.
3. In Version 6.0, if DOS is unable to find COMMAND.COM, a warning message is issued that allows the user to "Enter correct name of Command Interpreter (e.g., C:\COMMAND.COM). This is a much improved error handling function and allows the system to complete the booting process.
4. Exercise caution when you are "messing around" with COMMAND.COM. It can get the user into some dangerous situations!
5. The SHELL command in CONFIG.SYS is the preferred method of increasing the environment size with the /e:xxxx switch.

COMP   Removed V6.0

Compare files: Compares the contents of two sets of disk files to see if they are the same or different. The comparison is made on a byte by byte basis. COMP displays filenames, locations and the differences found during the compare process .

Syntax (shaded is optional):

COMP   **Drive1:\Path1\File1 Drive2:\Path2\File2**
/d /a /L /n=xx /c

Examples: COMP (prompts for file locations)
COMP C:\File1 D:\File2 /a

Syntax Options:

Drive1: Drive2:. Letters of drives containing the file (s) to be compared.

\Path1 \Path2.. Paths of files to be compared.

File1 File2 .... Filenames to be compared. The names may be the same if they are in different locations. Wild cards (*?) are allowed.

/d ... Displays file differences in decimal format, the default format is hexadecimal.

/a ... File differences displayed as characters.

/L ... ⑤ ... Display Line numbers with different data instead of byte offsets.

/n=xx ...... Compares the first number of lines (*xx*) in each file, even if files are different sizes.

/c ... Upper and lower case is ignored.

Command Type and Version:

External command; Network; Introduced with Ver 1.0
Removed from Ver 6.0, replaced by FC.

Notes:

1. If the drive, path and filename information is not specific enough, COMP will prompt for the correct information
2. If more than 10 mismatches are found, COMP ends the compare.
3. See also DISKCOMP (for floppy disk comparisons) and FC.

COPY

Copies file(s) from one location to another:
Files can also be combined (concatenated) using COPY.

Syntax (shaded is optional):

COPY /a Source /a /b + Source /a /b +...
Target /a /b /v

> Examples: COPY C:\Test*.* D:\Test2
> COPY Test1.txt + Text2.txt Test3.txt /a

Syntax Options:

Source.......	Source Drive, Directory, and File(s) or Devices to be copied **from**.
Target	Destination Drive, Directory, and File(s) or Devices being copied **to**.
/a	Denotes an ASCII text file. If /a preceeds a filename, that file and all following files are treated as ASCII files until a /b switch is encountered, then files that follow are considered to be binary files. If /a follows a filename, it applies to all files before and after the /a until a /b switch is encountered, then files that follow are considered to be binary files.
/b	Denotes a Binary file. If /b preceeds a filename, that file and all following files are treated as binary files until a /a switch is encountered, then files that follow are considered to be ASCII files. If /b follows a filename, it applies to all files before and after the /b until a /a switch is encountered, then files that follow are considered to be ASCII files. /b forces copy to read exactly the number of bytes allocated to the files size in the directory.
/v	Verifies files were copied correctly.

Command Type and Version:

Internal command; Network; Introduced with Ver 1.0

Notes:

1. COPY will only copy the contents of 1 directory. If a directory and its subdirectories need to be copied, use the XCOPY command.

2. COPY will not copy files 0 bytes in length, use XCOPY instead.

3. Both *Source* and *Destination* can be a device such as COM1: or LPT1:, however, when sending to *Destination*, if the /b switch is used, all characters, including control codes, are sent to the device as data. If no switch is used, the data transfers as ASCII data and the transmitted control codes may perform their special function on the device. For example, if a Ctrl + L code is sent to a printer on LPT1:, the printer will form feed.

4. If Destination Filename is not specified, COPY will create a file with the same name and date and time of creation in the current directory (*Target*). If a file with the same name as *Filename* exists in the current directory, DOS will not copy the file and display an error message that says "File cannot be copied onto itself. 0 Files Copied".

5. If the + function is used to combine files, it is assumed that the files are ASCII files. Normally you should NOT combine binary files since the internal format of binary files may be different.

6. /v slows down the copy process. If a verify error occurs, the message is displayed on the screen.

7. In order to change the date and time of a file during the copy process, use the following syntax:
   COPY /b Source + , ,

8. See also DISKCOPY and XCOPY.

COUNTRY (.SYS also)

Country dependent information: Enables DOS to use international time, date, currency, and case conversions.

Syntax (shaded is optional):

COUNTRY= ccc ppp Drive:\Path \Filename

    Examples: COUNTRY = 002

Syntax Options:

ccc..........	Country code number. Default 001, USA
ppp	Code page number.
Drive:\Path ...	Drive & subdirectory containg *Filename*..
Filename......	File containing country information.

Command Type and Version:

CONFIG.SYS; Introduced with Ver 3.2

Notes:

1. COUNTRY is put in CONFIG.SYS . If the *Drive:\Path\Filename* option is not used to specify which file contains country information, COUNTRY.SYS must be in the root directory of the systems boot drive so that COUNTRY can retrieve the country data.

Country Code	Country or Language	Code Page	Time Format	Date Format
001	United States	437, 850	2:35:00.00p	06/20/1991
002	Canadian-French	863, 850	14:35:00,00	1991-20-06
003	Latin America	850, 437	2:35:00.00p	06/20/1991
031	Netherlands	850, 437	14:35:00,00	06-20-1991
032	Belgium	850, 437	14:35:00,00	06.20.1991
033	France	850, 437	14:35:00,00	06.20.1991
034	Spain	850, 437	14:35:00,00	06/20/1991
036	Hungary	852, 850	14:35:00,00	1991-20-06
038	Yugoslavia	852, 850	14:35:00,00	1991-20-06
039	Italy	850, 437	14.35.00,00	06/20/1991
041	Switzerland	850, 437	14,35.00,00	06.20.1991
042	Czechoslovakia	852, 850	14:35:00,00	1991-20-06
044	United Kingdom	437, 850	14:35:00,00	06/20/1991
045	Denmark	850, 865	14:35:00,00	06-20-1991
046	Sweden	850, 437	14.35.00,00	1991-20-06
047	Norway	850, 865	14:35:00,00	06.20.1991
048	Poland	852, 850	14:35:00,00	1991-20-06
049	Germany	850, 437	14:35:00,00	06.20.1991
055	Brazil	850, 437	14:35:00,00	06/20/1991
061	International English	437, 850	14:35:00,00	06/20/1991
351	Portugal	850, 860	14:35:00,00	06-20-1991
358	Finland	850, 437	14.35.00,00	06.20.1991

CTTY

Change to a remote console. Allows you to choose the device from which you issue commands. USE WITH CAUTION, you could loose control of your system!

Syntax: (shaded is optional)

CTTY   Device

        Examples: CTTY aux
                     CTTY com1
                     CTTY con

Syntax Options:

Device . . . . Any valid DOS device for issuing commands. Examples include prn, com1, com2, com3, com4, con, aux.

Command Type and Version:

Internal command; Network; Introduced with Ver 2.0

Notes:

1. *Device* refers to a character-oriented remote unit, or secondary terminal, that will be used for command input and *output*. This device name must be a valid MS/PC-DOS name, specifically, AUX, COM1, COM2, COM3, COM4, CON. The use of a colon after the device name is optional.

2. *ctty con* moves the input and output back to the main terminal (the local console screen and keyboard).

3. *When redirected, some programs that are designed to work with the video display's control codes may not function correctly.*

4. Other redirected IO or piping is not affected by CTTY.

5. CAUTION: the command CTTY NUL will disconnect the screen and keyboard !!!! Do not use unless the CTTY CON command is executed under some type of program control, such as a batch file.

DATE

Date: Change and /or display the system date.
(Note: This does not reset the computer's battery
powered clock if DOS 3.21 or earlier is used.)

Syntax (shaded is optional):

DATE **month-day-year**

> Examples: **date mm-dd-yy** (for North America)
> Note: If COUNTRY in config.sys is set for a coun-
> try other than a North American country, then the
> following syntax is used:
> > **DATE dd-mm-yy** for Europe
> > **DATE yy-mm-dd** for Far East

Syntax Description and Options:

month . . . . . . One or two digit number (1 to 12)

day . . . . One or two digit number (1 to 31*)*. DOS
knows the correct number of days in
each month (28, 29, 30 or 31).

year . . . . Two or four digit number (80 to 99 – The
19 is assumed for 1980 to 1999).

Command Type and Version:

Internal command; Network; Introduced with Ver 1.0

Notes:

1. You may separate the day, month and the year by the use of
   hyphens, periods or slashes.
2. If a system does not have an AUTOEXEC.BAT file in the root
   directory of the boot drive, the date and time functions are
   activated automatically when the system starts and the user is
   prompted for change or confirmation.
3. DOS has been programmed to change the year, month and day
   and adjusts the number of days in a month accordingly. DOS
   also knows which months have 28, 29, 30, or 31 days. DOS will
   issue errors if valid dates are not used.
4. Beginning with DOS 3.3, DATE and TIME both set the systems
   CMOS (battery powered) calendar.
5. See also TIME

Utility to compress both hard and floppy disk drives so that there is more available storage space on the drive: Once the .EXE program has been run, DBLSPACE.SYS must be included in CONFIG.SYS. *Many problems have been reported with the DOS 6.0 version of this program. USE WITH CAUTION or not at all, you could loose data on your drive!*

Syntax: (shaded is optional)

DBLSPACE `/Automount /Chkdsk /Compress /Convstac /Create /Defragment /Delete /Format /Info /List /Mount /Ratio /Size /Unmount`

Syntax Options:

/Automount . . .	Automatically mount a compressed disk.
/Chkdsk.	Check the validity of a compressed disks directory and FAT and report the status of the drive.
/Compress . . .	Start the compression process on a drive.
/Convstac	Converts a Stacker compressed drive to a DBLSPACE compressed drive.
/Create	Creates a new compressed drive in the free space of an existing drive.
/Defragment . .	Defragment the files on an existing drive.
/Delete	Remove a compressed drive.
/Format	Format a compressed drive.
/Info.	Display detailed information on a compressed drive.
/List.	Display a list of both compressed and uncompressed drives on a system. It does not report network drives.

/ Mount	......	Mount a compressed drive.
/ Ratio	....	Display and change the estimated compression ratio of a compressed drive.
/ Size	....	Change the size of a compressed drive.
/ Unmount	....	Unmount a compressed drive.

Command Type and Version:

External command; Introduced with Ver 6.0

Notes:

1. DBLSPACE can be run as a menu driven utility or with the command line switches listed under Syntax Options.

2. The maximum size of a DBLSPACE volume is 512 MB.

3. Default cluster size of a compressed volume is 8k.

4. When DBLSPACE.EXE is run, DBLSPACE.SYS is automatically placed in CONFIG.SYS as part of the installation process.

5. See Also DBLSPACE.SYS

Device driver that activates a compressed drive. DBLSPACE.SYS determines the final memory location of DBLSPACE.BIN, which provides access to the compressed drives *Many problems have been reported with the DOS 6.0 version of this program. USE WITH CAUTION or not at all, you could loose data on your drive!*

Syntax: (shaded is optional)

DEVICE = `Drive:\Path\` DBLSPACE.SYS `/ Move`

Examples: DEVICE = C:\DBLSPACE.SYS

It may also be loaded high using:
DEVICEHIGH = C:\DBLSPACE.SYS / Move

Syntax Options:

Drive:\ Path... Drive and Path of the DBLSPACE.SYS

/ Move .... Moves the DBLSPACE.BIN file to a different location in memory. By default it is loaded at the top of conventional memory. /Move moves it to the bottom of conventional memory. Note that if DEVICEHIGH is used, it can be moved to upper memory, thereby freeing up conventional memory.

Command Type and Version:

CONFIG.SYS command; Introduced with Ver 6.0

Notes:

1. DBLSPACE can be run as a menu driven utility or with the command line switches listed under Syntax Options.
2. DBLSPACE.SYS is automatically inserted into CONFIG.SYS the DBLSPACE.EXE installation program is run.
3. See also DBLSPACE.EXE and DEVICEHIGH.

DEBUG

Starts a debugging program: Debug is a program that provides a testing environment for binary and executable programs, i.e. all programs that have .EXE or .COM extensions . It is also commonly used to run executable programs that are in memory, such as a hard drives setup program stored in ROM on a hard drive controller. The full use of DEBUG is beyond the scope of this book. Refer to books such as Microsoft's *DOS Manuals* or PC Magazine's *DOS Power Tools*.

Syntax (shaded is optional):

There are two methods of starting DEBUG.

Method 1:

DEBUG **Drive:\Path** Filename **Parameter**

Method 2:

DEBUG

Examples:

Method 1: DEBUG C:\test.exe

Method 2: DEBUG (run in command line mode)

Syntax Options:

Method 1:

Drive:\Path ... Drive and Path of the executable *Filename* to be tested.

Filename ..... Name of executable file to be tested.

Parameter .... Command line information needed by *Filename*.

Method 2:

Debug .... Starts DEBUG in the command line mode where debug commands are given at the DEBUG hyphen prompt (–).

Command Type and Version:

External command; Introduced with Ver 1.0

Debug Commands for Method 2:

Case makes no difference: *address* and *range* is in hex

?.	Display list of all DEBUG commands.
A *address*	Assemble 8086/8087/8088 mnemonics directly into memory at *address* (hex).
C *range address*	Compares contents of two memory blocks. *range* is the starting and ending address or starting address and length of Block 1 and *address* is the starting address of Block 2.
D *range*.	Dump (display) contents of memory with starting and ending addresses of *range*.
E *address data*	Enter data into memory starting at *address*. *data* is entered into successive bytes of memory.
F *range data* . .	Fill memory with *data* (hex or ASCII) in starting and ending addresses or starting address & length defined by *range*.
G=*address bkp*.	Run program in memory starting at *address*. *bkp* defines 1 to 10 temporary breakpoints.
H *hex1 hex2* . .	Does hexadecimal math on *hex1* & *hex2*. Two results are returned, first the sum of *hex1* and *hex2*; second, *hex1* minus *hex2*.
I *port*.	Read (input) & display 1 byte from *port*.
L *address drive:start number*	Load a file or specific drive sectors into memory. *address* is the memory location you want to load to. *drive* contains the sectors to be read. *start* is the hex value of the first sector to be read. *number* is the number of consecutive sectors to load.
M *range address*	Copies memory contents from the starting and ending address or starting address and length of *range*. *address* is the starting address of the destination.

N d:\path\file parameters	Name the *drive:\path\file-name* of an executable file for Debug *L* or *W*. Also used to specify *parameters* for the executable file. *N* by itself clears the current specification.
O *port data* ...	Output *data* to a *port* (by address).
P=address value	Run a loop, string instruction, subroutine, or software interrupt starting at *address* and for *value* number of instructions.
Q	Stop DEBUG without saving the file being tested. Returns to DOS.
R *register*	Display or alter CPU (central processing units) *register*. *R* by itself displays contents of all registers.
S *range data* ..	Search for *data* at the beginning and ending address of *range*.
T=address value	Trace instructions starting at *address* and for *value* number of instructions.
U *range*	Unassemble code at the start & end address or start address & length of *range*.
W *address drive:start number*	Write a file or specific drive sectors into memory. *address* is the memory location you want to write to. *drive* contains the sectors to be written. *start* is the hex value of the first sector to be written. *number* is the number of consecutive sectors to write.
XA count	Allocate count number of 16k expanded memory pages.
XD handle	Deallocate a handle to expanded memory
XM Lpage Ppage handle	Map a Lpage logical page of expanded memory belonging to handle, to a Ppage physical page of expanded memory.
XS	Display status information of expanded memory.

DEBUG ERROR MESSAGES: BF=Bad Flag; BP=Too many breakpoints; BR=Bad Register; DF=Double Flag

Reorganizes or defragments a disk in order to optimize disk drive performance.

Syntax (shaded is optional):

DEFRAG **Drive: /F /U /S:order /B /Skiphigh /LCD /BW /GØ /A /H**

Examples: DEFRAG C: /U /B

Syntax Options:

Drive:	Drive letter to be defragmented.
/F	Insures that no emptdy disk space remains between files.
/U	Leaves empty space, if any, between files.
/S:order ..	Sort files in a specific sort *"order"*.
	N .. In alphabetic order by name
	-N .. In reverse alphabetic name order
	E .. In alphabetic order by extension order
	-E .. In reverse alphabetic order by extension
	D .. By date & time, earliest first
	-D .. By date & time, latest first
	S .. By size, smallest first
	-S .. By size, largest first
/ B	Reboot system after DEFRAG is done.
/ Skiphigh .	Load DEFRAG into conventional memory, instead of the default upper memory
/ LCD	Start DEFRAG in LCD color scheme mode.
/ BW.....	Start DEFRAG in black & white color mode.
/ GØ	Disable graphics mouse and character set.
/ A	Start in DEFRAG in Automatic mode.
/ H	Moves hidden files.

Command Type and Version:

External command; Network; Introduced with Ver 6.0

Notes:

1. Do not use DEFRAG while Windows is running.

DEL or ERASE

Delete (erase): Deletes specified files from a directory.

Syntax (shaded is optional):

DEL `Drive:\Path` Filename `/p`

Examples: DEL *.*
DEL *.exe
DEL C:\budget\1990 /p
ERASE C:\Bin*.dbf

Syntax Options:

Drive:. . . . .   Drive letter containing \Path
\Path . . . .   Subdirectory containing \Filename
\Filename . . . .   Filename(s) to be deleted.
/P. . . . .   Screen prompts user for confirmation of the file(s) to be deleted.

Command Type and Version:

Internal command; Network; Introduced with Ver 1.1

Notes:

1. Use of wildcards * and ? is allowed. Use DEL *.* with caution, it will delete all files in the current directory. If you happen to be in the root directory of your boot drive when DEL *.* is used, COMMAND.COM, AUTOEXEC.BAT, CONFIG.SYS, etc will be deleted and the system will probably not start.
2. Files may be UNDELETED in DOS Versions 5.0 and 6.0.
3. See also RMDIR, MIRROR, and UNDELETE.

DELTREE

Deletes a directory and all the files and subdirectories that are in it: Exercise caution when using this command.

Syntax (shaded is optional):

DELTREE   `/ Y  Drive:\Path\Filename`

     Examples: DELTREE / Y A:*.*
                    DELTREE / Y C:\DATA

Syntax Options:

Drive: . . . . Drive letter containing *Path*

Path . . . . Subdirectory containing *Filename*

Filename . . . . Filename(s) to be deleted.

/ Y . . . . Completes DELTREE without first prompting for confirmation of the deletion. Don't use this switch if you can avoid it.

Command Type and Version:

External command; Network; Introduced with Ver 6.0

Notes:

1. If a filename is not specified, all files and subdirectories in the Drive:\Path are deleted.

2. Wild card are supported in the filenames.

3. Attributes such as read only, system and hidden are ignored when a filename is specified.

4. See also DEL and RMDIR.

DEVICE

Loads a device driver into memory. Device drivers are loaded by way of CONFIG.SYS.

Syntax (shaded is optional):

DEVICE = Drive:\Path\ Filename Parameters

Examples: DEVICE = C:\Dos\Himem.sys
DEVICE = Smartdrv.sys 1024 512

Syntax Options:

Drive:\Path ... Drive and directory(s) containing *Filename.*

\Filename .... Driver to be loaded.

Parameters ... Switches and/or parameters needed by the device driver.

Command Type and Version:

CONFIG.SYS command; Introduced with Ver 2.0

Notes:

1. Standard installable device drivers are: ANSI.SYS, DISPLAY.SYS, DRIVER.SYS, EGA.SYS, PRINTER.SYS, RAM.SYS, EMM386, HIMEM.SYS, AND SMARTDRV.SYS

2. COUNTRY.SYS and KEYBOARD.SYS are files, not device drivers. Do not try to load either of these files using the DEVICE command or your system will lock up and DOS will not be able to restart.

3. When new devices are purchased, such as a mouse or scanner, you will usually receive device driver software. Use DEVICE to install these drivers, making certain that the device driver is in the specified directory.

4. Install third party console drivers before DISPLAY.SYS.

5. See also DEVICEHIGH.

Load a device driver into upper memory: After DOS=umb and HIMEM.SYS have been loaded in CONFIG.SYS, DEVICEHIGH makes it possible to load device drivers into the upper memory area. Loading devices high will free up conventional memory for other programs.

Syntax (shaded is optional):

DEVICEHIGH = Drive:\Path\ Filename dswitch

or

DEVICEHIGH ⑤ SIZE=hexsize Drive:\Path \Filename dswitch

DEVICEHIGH ⑥ /L:(see below) / S Drive:\Path\ \Filename dswitch

Examples: DEVICEHIGH = C:\Filename.sys
DEVICEHIGH SIZE=FF C:\Filename.sys

Syntax Options:

Drive:\Path. . . . Drive and Path of driver to be loaded high.

Filename . . . . . Device driver to be loaded high.

dswitch. . . . . . . Command line switches required by the device driver being loaded.

SIZE= *hexsize* . ⑤ Minimum number of bytes (in hex) that must be available for DEVICEHIGH to try to load a driver in high memory.

/ L:*region1[,minsize1][;region2[,minsize2]* . . . ⑥ This switch specifies one or more memory regions into which to load a device driver. Normally, DOS loads the driver into the largest free UMB. / L allows a specific region to be selected. See your DOS manual for detailed information on using this switch.

/S ... **❻** ..... Use / S only in conjunction with / L.
/ S shrinks the UMB to its minimum
size while a driver is loading and therefore makes the most efficient use of
memory.

Command Type and Version:

CONFIG.SYS command; Introduced with Ver 5.0

Updated with different switches in Ver 6.0

Notes:

1. DOS=umb and HIMEM.SYS must be loaded before DEVICE-
   HIGH in order to function. The following is typical in CONFIG.SYS:
   DEVICE = C:\HIMEM.SYS
   DOS = umb
   DEVICE = C:\DOS\EMM386.EXE
   DEVICEHIGH = C:\Filename.sys

2. If the driver being loaded high requires more high memory than is
   available, the system may lock-up. Use SIZE= to specify the
   memory required by the driver, after determining how much
   memory the driver normally takes by using MEM /DEBUG.

3. See also DOS, LOADHIGH, HIMEM.SYS and EMM386.

4. In DOS Ver 6.0, see also MEMMAKER.

Directory: Displays the list of files and subdirectories within the current or a designated directory.

Syntax (shaded is optional):

DIR **Drive:\Path\Filename /p /w /a:attrib / o:sort /s /b /L /c**

> Examples: DIR or DIR *.* (wild cards are allowed)
> DIR *.exe /p

Syntax Options:

Drive:\Path . . . . Drive and subdirectory to be listed

\Filename . . . . . File name(s) and/or extension to display.

/ p . . . . Displays one screen of information, then pause until any key is pressed.

/ w . . . . Displays a wide screen list of files and subdirectories, but the file creation date & time, file size, and <DIR> subdirectory indicator are not shown.

/ a : attrib . . . . **⑤** Displays only files with *attrib* attributes: h=hidden, –h=not hidden, s=system, –s=not system, d=directories, –d=files, a=files ready for archive, –a=files not changed, r=read only, –r=not read only.

/ o : sort . . . . . **⑤** Displays by *sort* order: n=alphabetic by name, –n=reverse alphabetic, e=alphabetic by extension, –e=reverse extension alphabetic, d=earliest date/time 1st, –d=latest date/time 1st, s=smallest first, –s=largest 1st, g=group directories before files, –g=group directories after.

⠀⠀⠀⠀⠀⠀⠀⠀⠀⠀c=compression ratio (least compressed **⑥** first), –c=compression ratio (most compressed first)

/s . . . **⑤** . . . . . Show all occurrences in both the current directory and all subdirectories below it.

/b . . . . **⑤** . . . . Displays directory 1 line at a time.

/L . . . **⑤** . . . . Displays unsorted names in lowercase.

/ c **⑥** . . . . Sort directory by compression ratio.

Command Type and Version:

Internal command; Network; Introduced with Ver 1.0

Notes:

1. The date and time formats displayed by the *DIR* command will vary, depending on which COUNTRY code is in CONFIG.SYS.

DISKCOMP

Compares Disks. Compares the contents of the
floppy disk in the Source drive to the contents of
the floppy disk in the Target drive.

Syntax (shaded is optional):

DISKCOMP **Source: Target: /1 /8**

> Examples:
> DISKCOMP (first floppy disk drive is used)
> DISKCOMP A: B: /1

Syntax Options:

Source: . . . . . . Source drive containing one of the floppy
disks to be compared.

Target: . . . . Target drive containing the other disk to
be compared.

/ 1 . . . . Compares only the first side of disks.

/ 8 . . . . Compares first 8 sectors per track.

Command Type and Version:

External command; Introduced with Ver 1.0

Notes:

1. DISKCOMP must be used with identical size floppy disks. It
cannot be used with a hard drive.

2. If a target drive is not specified, DISCOMP uses the current drive.

3. DISCOMP prompts you when to swap disks as necessary.

4. DISCOMP cannot compare double-sided disk with single-sided
disk, or double-density disk with high-density disk.

5. Do not use DISKCOMP on a drive that is affected by the ASSIGN,
JOIN, or SUBST commands or DISCOMP will display an error
message. Do not use DISCOMP on a network drive.

6. When using DISCOMP to compare a disk made with the COPY
comand, although it is duplicate information, COPY may not put the
information in the same location on the target disk and DISCOMP
will display an error message.

7. The DOS 6.0 FC command is basically the same as DISKCOMP
DISKCOMP is still included for backward compatibility only.

DISKCOPY

Copies disks. Copies entire contents of the disk (including the DOS system files) in the source drive onto the disk in the target drive.

Syntax (shaded is optional):

DISKCOPY **Source: Target: /1 / v**

    Examples:
        DISKCOPY   (current drive must be A: or B:)
        DISKCOPY A: B: /1
        DISKCOPY A: A: (prompts to change disks)

Syntax Options:

Source: . . . . . . The floppy disk to be copied.

Target:. . . . . . . The floppy disk to be copied to.

/1 . . . . Copies one side of disk.

/ v . **❺** . . . . . . Verifies that information is correctly copied.

Command Type and Version:

External command; Introduced with Ver 1.0

Notes:

1. DISKCOPY must be used with identical size floppy disks only. It will not work with a hard disk.

2. If you do not enter a target drive, DOS uses the default drive as the target drive and DISKCOPY will overwrite all information that is on the target disk.

3. DISKCOPY will cause further disk fragmentation when using an already fragmented disk causing delays in finding, reading or writing a file. Using the COPY command or the XCOPY command will give you a new disk that will be in sequential order and will not be fragmented.

DISPLAY.SYS

Driver that supports code page switching for the display: Supported types include Mono, CGA, EGA (includes VGA), and LCD.

Syntax (shaded is optional):

DEVICE = **Drive:\Path** DISPLAY.SYS CON **:= (type, hwcp, (n,m))**

> Examples:
> DEVICE = DISPLAY.SYS con:=(ega,437,2)

Syntax Options:

Drive:\Path . . . . Drive & directory containing DISPLAY.SYS

type . . . . Type of display adapter,

hwcp . . . . The number assigned to a particular code page. Choices are as follows:
- 437 . . . . United States
- 850 . . . . Multilingual (Latin I)
- 852 . . . . Slavic (Latin II)
- 860 . . . . Portuguese
- 863 . . . . Canadian-French
- 865 . . . . Nordic

n . . . . Number of code pages supported by the hardware: Range is 0 through 6, max for EGA is 6, LCD is 1.

m . . . . Number of subfonts supported by the hardware. Default=2 for EGA, 1 if LCD. If the *m* option is omitted, the parentheses around *n,m* can be omitted.

Command Type and Version:

CONFIG.SYS command; Introduced with Ver 3.3

Notes:

1. Code-page switching has no effect with monochrome and CGA display adapters.
2. If 3rd party console drivers are installed, make sure they are installed <u>before</u> DISPLAY.SYS.

Forces DOS to keep a link with the upper memory area or to load itself into high memory.:
HIMEM.SYS must be loaded before DOS= can be used. DOS is useful in that it is part of the program set that frees up conventional memory.

Syntax (shaded is optional):

DOS = high or low **, umb or noumb**
or
DOS = **high or low,** umb or noumb

    Examples: DOS = high
                  DOS = umb
                  DOS = high, umb or DOS = umb, high

Syntax Options:

high	Loads a portion of DOS into high memory.
low	Forces DOS to stay in conventional mem.
umb	Forces DOS to maintain a link between high (upper) memory and conventional memory.
noumb	Breaks the link between upper memory and conventional memory.

Command Type and Version:

CONFIG.SYS command: Introduced with Ver 5.0

Notes:

1. See also DEVICEHIGH and LOADHIGH.
2. UMB must be used in order to load either DOS or drivers into upper memory.
3. DOS can be placed anywhere in the CONFIG.SYS file.
4. UMB or NOUMB can be combined with HIGH or LOW in the same DOS = command line, see the example above.

Starts the DOSKEY program, which allows the user to edit command lines, create macros, and recall DOS commands.

Syntax (shaded is optional):

DOSKEY /reinstall /bufsize=nnn /macros
/history /insert /overstrike /macroname=text

    Examples: DOSKEY   (start DOSKEY with defaults)
                DOSKEY / history > special.bat

Syntax Options:

/reinstall	Installs DOSKEY again. If DOSKEY is currently running, this command clears the buffer.
/bufsize=nnn . .	Sets the size of the buffer where DOS-KEY store commands. Default=512 bytes, minimum=256 bytes.
/macros or */m* .	Displays the current list of DOSKEY macros.
/history or */h* . .	Displays a list of all commands that were stored in memory.
/insert	Sets typing to insert mode (text is not overwritten as typing occurs)
/overstrike	Sets typing to overstrike mode (text <u>is</u> overwritten as typing occurs)
/macroname= .	Name of file created to hold *text* macro.
text.	The commands and text to be recorded in the file named *macroname*.

Command Type and Version:

  External command; Network; Introduced with Ver 5.0

Notes:

1. */macros* and */history* can be used with DOS redirection to a file. e.g. DOSKEY */macros* > Macro.txt creates a text file list of macros.

2. DOSKEY is a very powerful program, see the Microsoft *Users Guide and Reference* for detailed comments and examples.

When DOSKEY is on, the following can be used to recall/edit commands from its command buffer:

Up Arrow	Recall command issued before currently displayed command.
Down Arrow . .	Recall command issued after the currently displayed command.
Page Up	Recall oldest command in current session.
Page Down . . .	Recall most recent command in current session.
Left Arrow	Moves cursor left one character.
Right Arrow . . .	Moves cursor right one character.
Ctrl+Left Arrow	Moves cursor left one word.
Ctrl+Rght Arrow	Moves cursor right one word.
Home	Moves cursor to start of line.
End	Moves cursor to end of line.
Esc	Clears the display command line.
F1	Copy one character from last command buffer to the command line.
F2	Look forward for the next key typed after pressing F2.
F3	Copies the remainder of the current template line at the current cursor position to the command line.
F4	Delete all characters of the current template line, up to but not including the character pressed after F4 is pressed
F5	Copy current line to template and clear command line
F6	Put Ctrl+Z (end of line marker) at the end of the current line.
F7	Displays all commands and numbers, beginning with the oldest, currently stored in the command buffer.
Alt+F7	Delete all commands in command buffer.
F8	Locate the most recently used command in the buffer that begins with a specific

character(s). At the DOS prompt, simply type those beginning characters and then press *F8*.

F9	Display the command associated with a specific command line number in buffer.
Alt+F10	Delete all macros.

The following are special codes that can be used in creating macros. Code letters shown can be used in either upper or lower case.

$G	Redirect output (same as >) to a device other than the screen. e.g. a printer.
GG	Append output data (same as >>) to the end of a file instead of overwriting file.
$L	Redirect input (same as <) to read from a device other than the keyboard.
$B	Send output from macro to another command (same as I).
$T	Used to separate commands in either a macro or at the DOSKEY command line.
$$	Used to specify the $ character
$1 to *$9*	Batch parameters (similar to %1) for passing command line info to the macro when it's run.
$ *	A replaceable parameter similar to *$1* to *$9*, except that everything that is typed on the command line after *macroname* is substituted for the *$ ** in the macro.

Macros are run by simply typing the *macroname* at the DOS prompt, followed by any parameter info such as *$1* or *$**. If a macro is created that has the same name as a normal DOS command, the DOS command is started by typing a space and then the command name, whereas with the macro, simply type the *macroname* without a space preceding it.

Starts the MS-DOS 5.0 graphical user interface shell.

Syntax (shaded is optional):

DOSSHELL /t or /g :Res n /b

    Examples: DOSSHELL / t
              DOSSHELL / g:m
              DOSSHELL / g /b

Syntax Options:

/t .... Directs DOSSHELL to start in text mode.

/g .... Directs DOSSHELL to start in graphics mode.

:Res .... Screen resolution class. /(lowercase L) for Low, *m* for medium and *h* for high resolution.

n .... If there is more than one resolution available in the *Res* category, *n* provides additional information concerning which category to use. *n* is hardware dependent.

/b .... Starts Shell in black and white mode.

Command Type and Version:

External command; Network; Introduced with Ver 5.0

Notes:

1. If SHELL has already been started, the screen resolution can be changed from the options menu.

2. SHELL is very useful for such tasks as renaming subdirectories.

DRIVER.SYS

Defines a logical drive from an existing physical drive: A logical drive is simply a drive letter used to point to the actual physical drive. The new drive letter established by DRIVER.SYS is the next highest drive letter above the systems highest current drive.

Syntax (shaded is optional):

DEVICE = `Drive:\Path` DRIVER.SYS /d:number `/c / f:factor /h:heads /s:sectors / t:tracts`

> Examples:
> DEVICE=C:\dos\driver.sys /d:1 /f:2 /h:2 /s:9 /t:80
> (above configures a 3.5" 720k floppy drive, if the last hard drive was drive E:, then the 3.5 inch would be designated as drive F:)

Syntax Options:

Drive:	Drive letter containig *\Path*
\Path	Subdirectory containing *DRIVER.SYS*
/d: number	Specifies physical drive number. Values must be in the range of 0 to 127. Normally, Drive A=0, Drive B=1, etc.
/c	Specifies that the driver will be able to tell that the floppy disk drive door is open.
/ f: factor	Specifies type of drive. Default value= 2

Factor	Description
0	160K/180K or 320K/360
1	1.2 megabyte (MB)
2	720K (3.5in. disk)
7	1.44MB (3.5in. disk)
9	2.88MB (3.5in.disk)

/h: heads	Specifies max. number of heads. Value for **heads** must be in the 1 to 99 range.

/s: sectors	Number of sectors per track, ranging in value from 1 to 99. The default varies according to the /f factor selected above. Normal values are 360k and 720k = 9 sectors, 1.44 meg = 18 sector, 1.2 meg = 15 sectors and 2.8 meg = 36 sector.
/t: tracks	Number of tracks per side on the block device, ranging from 1 to 999. Default values vary according to the /f factor selected above. Normal values are 360k = 40 track, 720k, 1.44 meg, and 1.2 meg = 80 track.

Command Type and Version:

CONFIG.SYS command; Introduced with Ver 3.2

Notes:

1. DRIVER.SYS is commonly used to set up a 3.5 inch floppy drives on a system that does not support 3.5 inch drives directly. Setting up external 3.5 inch drives is also common.

2. See also the DRIVEPARM command, it is used to modify existing parameters of a physical device.

3. DRIVER.SYS can not be used to define hard drives. If hard drive logical drive assignments need to be changed, see the SUBST command.

4. If two DRIVER.SYS command lines are used for the same physical drive, then two logical drive letters will be assigned to the single physical drive.

5. XT class systems, with standard floppy controllers, will still need either a special driver or special controller in order to recognize a 1.44 or 2.8 meg 3.5 inch floppy or 1.2 meg 5-1/4 inch floppy.

DRIVPARM

Defines block device parameters: Driveparm allows the default or original device driver settings to be overridden when DOS is started.

Syntax (shaded is optional):

DRIVEPARM=/d:number /c /f:factor /h:heads /i /n /s:sectors /t:tracks

Examples: DRIVEPARM=/d:1 /c /f:2 /h:2 /s:9 /t:80
(above configures a 3.5" 720k floppy drive)

Syntax Options:

/d: number	Specifies physical drive number. Numbers must be in the range of 0 to 255. Normally, Drive A=0, Drive B=1, etc.
/c	Specifies that the driver will be able to tell that the floppy disk drive door is open.
/f: factor	Specifies type of drive. Default value= 2

Factor .	Description
0	160K/180K or 320K/360
1	1.2 megabyte (MB)
2	720K (3.5in. disk)
5	Hard disk
6	Tape
7	1.44MB (3.5in. disk)
8	Read/write optical disk
9	2.88MB (3.5in.disk)

/h: heads	Specifies max. number of heads. Value for **heads** must be in the 1 to 99 range.
/i	Specifies an electronically-compatible 3.5 in. floppy disk drive. Use the / i switch
/n	Non-removable block device.

DRIVPARM (cont.)

/s: sectors . . . . Number of sectors per track, ranging in value from 1 to 99. The default varies according to the /f factor selected above. Normal values are 360k and 720k = 9 sectors, 1.44 meg = 18 sector, 1.2 meg = 15 sectors and 2.8 meg = 36 sector.

/t: tracks . . . . . Number of tracks per side on the block device, ranging from 1 to 999. Default values vary according to the /f factor selected above. Normal values are 360k = 40 track, 720k, 1.44 meg, and 1.2 meg = 80 track.

Command Type and Version:
CONFIG.SYS command; Introduced with Ver 3.2

Notes:
1. DRIVEPARM is particularly useful in configuring 3.5 inch floppy drives.
2. Settings in DRIVEPARM will override any settings specified for a device prior to the DRIVEPARM command line.
3. Although DRIVEPARM is listed as an option in DOS Ver 3.3, the command will not function in that version.
4. DRIVEPARM does not create new logical drives, it can only modify existing physical drive parameters.
5. See also DRIVER.SYS

ECHO

Display a message or turn command echo feature on or off: When batch files are run, DOS usually displays (echos) the name of the program being run to the display. This feature can be turned on or off with the ECHO command.

Syntax (shaded is optional):

ECHO   Message on | off

> Examples: ECHO off
> ECHO Enter program name to be run!
> ECHO on

Syntax Options:

Message:..... Text to be displayed on screen.

on........... Turn display echo on.

off........... Turn display echo off.

Command Type and Version:

Internal and Batch command; Introduced with Ver 2.0

Notes:

1. Use the @ symbol in front of a batch file command in order to turn the screen echo function off.

2. **NOTE: in DOS 6.0, ECHO by iteself on a command line will output a blank line. 6**

Starts MS-DOS Editor: EDIT is a full-screen text editor which can create, save, edit and print ASCII text files.

Syntax (shaded is optional):

EDIT `Drive:\Path \Filename /b /g /h /nohi`

>　　Examples:　EDIT C:\Autoexec.bat
>　　　　　　　　EDIT D:\Bin\Test.bat /h

Syntax Options:

Drive:\Path . . .	Location of *Filename.*
\Filename	Name of ASCII text file to be edited.
/b	Editor displayed in black and white.
/g	Provides CGA monitors with the fastest screen update.
/h	Allows monitor to display maximum number of lines on the screen.
/nohi	Normally, DOS uses a 16 color mode for monitors. This switch enables the use of 8 color monitors.

Command Type and Version:

External command; Network; Introduced with Ver 5.0

Notes:

1. QBASIC.EXE must be in the same directory as EDIT or included in the DOS path. If it is not, EDIT will not function.
2. Shortcut keys that are shown on the bottom line of the screen may not display properly. If this occurs, use the */b* and */nohi* switches.

Line oriented text editor. Edlin is an editor used to insert, change, copy, move and delete lines of text in an ASCII file. If a full screen editor is required, use EDIT (page 160). 24 lines of text can be displayed on the screen at one time.

Syntax (shaded is optional):

EDLIN **Drive:\Path** Filename **/b**

     Examples: EDLIN Test
                  EDLIN C:\Autoexec.bat

Syntax Options:

Drive:\Path. . . . Drive and directory containing the file to be edited.

Filename . . . . . File to be edited. If Edlin cannot fine the file named *Filename*, it will automatically create the file in the specified *Drive:\Path* location.

/b. . . . . Causes EDLIN to ignore Ctrl–Z (end of file character).

Command Type and Version:

External command; Network; Introduced with Ver 1.0
Removed from DOS Ver 6.0, use the EDIT command.

Notes:

1. Edlin can handle a maximum of 253 characters per line.
2. A full description of EDLIN is beyound the scope of this book, see a full DOS manual for additional details and instructions.
3. EDLIN uses an asterisk • prompt on a line by itself to ask for a command. If the • occurs after a line number, it indicated that that line number is the current line.

EDLIN Commands:(case doesn't matter)

?. . . . . Displays the list of EDLIN commands.

Line . . . . Just typing a number, at the prompt, displays the text contained in that line #.

Ctrl–C . . . . Exits user out of the insert (I) mode.

n A	Append n number of lines into memory from disk. Edlin will load till 75% of available memory is full.
L1,L2,L3,count C . . .	Copy a block of lines. L1=first line to copy, L2=last line to copy, L3=line before which EDLIN is to insert the block, count=number of times to copy.
L1, L2 D	Delete from line L1 to line L2.
E	Write current file to disk and stop EDLIN.
L1 I	Insert lines before line L1. Ctrl-C stops.
L1, L2 L	List (display) lines between L1 and L2.
L1, L2, L3 M . . or L1,+n,L3 M .	Move a block of lines. L1=first line to move, L2=last line to move, L3=line before which EDLIN is to move the block, +n=include the next n lines.
L1, L2 P	Display all or part of the file one full screen of text at a time. L1=first line and L2=last line.
Q	Quit EDLIN without saving the current file to disk. Return to DOS.
L1,L2 ? R S1 S2 S3 . . .	Replace a block of lines with a string. L1=first line to replace, L2=last line to replace, ?=prompt user to confirm replacement, S1=string to be replaced, S2=Ctrl–Z separator, S3=string to replace S1.
L1,L2 ? S S1 .	Search between L1 first line and L2 last line for string S1. ?=prompt user when string S1 is located.
L1 T D:\Path\Filename . . .	Transfer (merge) contents of a second file from disk into the current edited file. L1=line in current file before which user wants inserted file to be placed. D:\Path\Filename=name and directory location of file to be inserted into current file.
n W	Write n number of lines, starting at the first line, to disk.

When usingTask Swapper with an EGA monitor, the EGA.SYS command saves and restores the display.

Syntax (shaded is optional):

DEVICE = **Drive\path** EGA.SYS

   Examples: DEVICE=C:\Dos\EGA.SYS

Syntax Options:

Drive:\ Path . . . Specifies the location of the EGA.SYS file.

Command Type and Version:

CONFIG.SYS command; Introduced with Ver 5.0

Notes:

1. To save memory when using a mouse on a system, install
   EGA.SYS before installing the mouse driver.

Activates or deactivates expanded memory emulator for 80386 and higher systems:
EMM386 is both a device driver loaded through CONFIG.SYS and an External command. It also enables or disables support of the Weitek coprocessor.

Syntax (shaded is optional):

To load EMM386 initially in CONFIG.SYS:
Device= **Drive:\Path** EMM386.EXE **on** *or* **off** *or* **auto memory w=on** *or* **w=off mx** *or* **frame = address** *or* **/pmmm pn=address x=mm-nn i=mm-nn b=address L=minXMS a=altregs h=handles d=nnn ram noems altboot**

To use EMM386 as an External command:
EMM386 **on** *or* **off** *or* **auto w=on** *or* **w=off /?**

    Examples: Device=C:\EMM386.EXE noems
    EMM386 on   (at DOS prompt)
    EMM386   (at DOS prompt to show status)

Syntax Options:

Drive:\Path . . .	Drive and directory containing EMM386
EMM386	At the DOS prompt this displays the current status of EMM386.
on	Activates EMM386 driver. (default)
off	Deactivates EMM386 driver.
auto	Places EMM386 driver in auto mode, where expanded memory support is turned on when a program needs expanded memory.
memory	kbytes of memory allocated to EMM386. Default=256, Range=16 to 32768, use multiples of 16. This memory is in addition to low-memory backfilling.

w=on	Enable Weitek coprocessor support.
w=off	Disable Weitek coprocessor support.
m*x*	Address of page frame. Values for *x* can be 1 to 14 below. On systems with only 512k of memory, only 10 to 14 can be used.

1=C000 hex	8=DC00 hex
2=C400 hex	9=E000 hex
3=C800 hex	10=8000 hex
4=CC00 hex	11=8400 hex
5=D000 hex	12=8800 hex
6=D400 hex	13=8C00 hex
7=D800 hex	14=9000 hex

frame=*address*	Specific page-frame segment address for base page. *address* can be C000h to E000h and 8000h to 9000h, in increments of 400h.
/p*mmm*.	Address of page frame. *mmm* can range from C000h to E000h and 8000h to 9000h, in increments of 400h.
p*n*=*mmm*	Specific segment address (*mmm*) of a specific page *n*. *n* can range from 0 to 255. *mmm* can range from 8000h to 9C00h and C000h to EC00h, in increments of 400h.
x=*mm–nn*.	Excludes a range of segment addresses from EMS page use. *mm* and *nn* can both range from A000h to FFFFh, and are rounded off to the nearest 4k. x overrides i when two ranges overlap.
i=*mm–nn*	Includes a range of segment addresses for EMS page or RAM use. *mm* and *nn* can both range from A000h to FFFFh, and are rounded off to the nearest 4k. x overrides i when two ranges overlap.
b=*address*	Lowest segment address that can be used for bank swapping of 16k EMS pages. Default=4000h, range=1000h to 4000h.

EMM386.EXE (cont.)

L=*minXMS* . . .	Specifies that *minXMS* kbytes of extended memory will remain after EMM386 has been loaded. Default=0
a=*altregs*	*altregs* number of fast alternate register sets are allocated to EMM386. Default= 7, range=0 to 254. Each register uses an additional 400 bytes of memory.
h=*handles*	Number of handles EMM386 can have. Default=64, range=2 to 255.
d=*nnn*	Kbytes of memory reserved for buffered DMA (direct memory access). Default= 16, range=16 to 256.
ram	Upper memory and expanded memory access is provided.
noems	Upper memory access provided but not to expanded memory.
altboot . . . . ⑥	Provides an alternate boot sequence for some computers with compatibility problems. Used if computer doesn't recognize Ctrl-Alt-Del.
/ ?	Help with command line switches.

Command Type and Version:

External and CONFIG.SYS command;
Introduced with Ver 4.0

Notes:

1. HIMEM.SYS must be loaded before EMM386.EXE is loaded.
2. The .EXE extension of EMM386 must be used to load the driver.
3. The order of switches and parameters is not important.
4. Device=EMM386.EXE must preceed DEVICEHIGH commands.
5. If enough memory is not available to set up a 64k page frame, the "Unable to set base address" error message will display.
6. DOS=umb must be used in CONFIG.SYS to provide access to the upper memory block.
7. See also DOS, HIMEM.SYS, DEVICEHIGH, and LOADHIGH.
8. Using EMM386.EXE and the Note 7 commands is a very complicated task. It is strongly recommended that the user spend a great deal of time with Microsofts *MS-DOS 5.0 User's Guide and Reference* learning about memory management and system optimization.

EXE2BIN

Converts an executable file to a binary file:
Converting executable files (.EXE extension) to
files with a binary format, is only useful to software
developers and is of no value to general users.

Syntax (shaded is optional):

EXE2BIN **Drive1:\Path1** INfile
Drive2:\Path2 OUTfile

Examples: EXE2BIN C:\Test.exe C:\test.bin

Syntax Options:

Drive1:\Path1 . . Drive and directory of input .EXE file.

Drive2:\Path2 . . Drive and directory of output binary file.

INfile . . . . Input .EXE file to be converted.

OUTfile . . . . . . Output binary file.

Command Type and Version:

External command; Introduced with Ver 1.1
Removed from DOS Ver 6.0, call Microsoft if needed.

Notes:

1. EXE2BIN is not for the general computer user, only programmers.
2. Default extensions for INfile is .EXE and for OUTfile is .BIN.
3. INfile must have been produced by LINK and must not be a packed
4. See also LINK

EXIT

Exits a secondary command processor and returns to the primary processor if one exists.

Syntax (shaded is optional):

EXIT

Examples: EXIT

Syntax Options:
No options

Command Type and Version:
Internal; Network; Command processor function;
Introduced with Ver 2.0

Notes:
1. If a secondary command processor is not loaded (or /P is used with COMMAND.COM), the EXIT command will have no effect.
2. See Also COMMAND

Expands a compressed DOS version 5.0 file:
Compressed files are not usable unless exanded.
Use EXPAND to retrieve files from DOS 5.0 instal-
lation or update disks.

Syntax (shaded is optional):

EXPAND Drive:\Path\ Filename Destination

> Examples:
> EXPAND B:\Dos\FIND.EX_ C:\Dos\FIND.EXE

Syntax Options:

Drive:\Path . . . Specifies location and name of a
                     compressed file to be expanded.

Filename . . . . . File to be expanded.

Destination. . . . . Target location where expanded files are
                        to be placed. Destination can be a
                        drive letter and colon, a filename, a di-
                        rectory name <u>or</u> a combinaton. A desti-
                        nation filename can only be used if a
                        single compressed *Filename* is used.

Command Type and Version:

External command; Network; Introduced with Ver 5.0

Notes:

1. Wildcards (* and ?) **cannot** be used.

2. Compressed files, such as installation or update files, have a
   file extention which ends with an underscore character (_)

3. Although EXPAND is normally used by the DOS 5.0 Upgrade
   program to install all DOS 5.0 files, you can copy a single
   compressed file, such as FIND.EX_ , from an upgrade disk to the
   hard drive and EXPAND it for full use. A complete list of all files
   and what disk they are on is included in the file named
   PACKING.LST on upgrade disk 1 or 2.

Displays a list and gives a brief description of all DOS 6.0 commands: This command is a direct replacement for the DOS Ver 5.0 DOSHELP.

Syntax (shaded is optional):

FASTHELP   command   /?

> Examples: FASTHELP Chkdsk
> FASTHELP /?
> FASTHELP

Syntax Options:

command . . . . The particular DOS command that you want help about.

/? . . . . Displays a quick help for a specific command.

Command Type and Version:

External command; Network; Introduced with Ver 6.0

Notes:

1. FASTHELP without a command displays a list and brief description of all DOS 6.0 commands.
2. Detailed information on DOS commands is available with the HELP command.
3. FASTHELP is a direct replacement for the DOS Ver 5.0 DOSHELP command.

FASTOPEN

Fast opening of files: Decreases the amount of time to open frequently used files by keeping directory information in memory. FASTOPEN can be started in either a Batch file or CONFIG.SYS

Syntax (shaded is optional):

To start in a Batch file or at the DOS Prompt:
   FASTOPEN Drive1: = nnn Drive2:= nnn ... /x
To start in CONFIG.SYS use the following:
   Install=Drive:\Path\FASTOPEN.EXE
                  Drive1: = nnn Drive2:=nnn ... /x

   Examples: FASTOPEN C:=97 /x
              Install=C:\DOS\FASTOPEN C:=97

Syntax Options:

Drive1: Drive2:. One or more drives FASTOPEN tracks.

nnn. . . . . Number of files FASTOPEN can work with at the same time. The valid values are 10 through 999. 48 is the default.

/x . . . . Creates the *name cache* in expanded memory rather than conventional memory. *name cache* is a buffer where names and locations of open files are stored.

Drive:\Path. . . . . Drive and directory containing FASTOPEN.

Command Type and Version:

External and CONFIG.SYS command; NOT for Network Introduced with Ver 3.3

Notes:

1. When placed in CONFIG.SYS, FASTOPEN.EXE must be used, not FASTOPEN without the extension.
2. FASTOPEN uses approximately 48 bytes of memory for each file that it tracks.
3. Deactivate FASTOPEN **BEFORE** disk compaction is used!!!!!
4. FASTOPEN works with hard drives only, not floppy drives.

Compare two files and report the differences:
FC reports the differences it finds between two
files and displays them on screen. The comparison can be of ASCII or binary files.

Syntax (shaded is optional):

FC /a /c /L /Lbx /n /t /w /nnn
   Drive1:\Path\ File1 Drive2:\Path\ File2

or

FC /b Drive1:\Path\ File1 Drive2:\Path\ File2

Examples: FC /a C:\DATA\Test.txt D:\Master.txt

Syntax Options:

Drive1:\Path ..	Drive and directory of first file *(File1)*.
Drive2:\Path ..	Drive and directory of second file *(File2)*.
File1 & File2 ..	The two files to be compared.
/a	Abbreviate ASCII comparison output, will only display first and last line of different block.
/c	Ignore upper/ lower case.
/L	Files comparred in ASCII mode.
/Lbx	Set *x* lines of internal line buffer.
/n	During ASCII compare, displays line #s.
/t	Do not expand tabs to spaces. Default is to treat tabs as spaces with stops at every 8th position.
/w	During compression, tabs and spaces are compressed. Also causes FC to ignore space that occurs at the beginning and end of lines.
/nnn	Set the number of consecutively matching lines before files are resynchronized.
/b	Files comparred in binary mode. This is the default for all files ending in .EXE, .COM, .SYS, .OBJ, .LIB and .BIN.

FC (cont.)

Command Type and Version:

External command; Network;
Introduced with MS-DOS® Ver 2.1

Notes:

1. See also COMP and DISKCOMP.

2. Use of wild cards (* or ?) is allowed.

3. For ASCII comparisons, the *File1* name is displayed, then the lines from *File1* that are different are displayed, then the first line to match in both files, then the *File2* name is displayed, then the lines from *File2* that are different, and finally, the first line to match in *File2*. FC uses a 100 line buffer to hold the lines being comparred, if there are more than 100 lines of differences, FC cannot complete the comparison and issues a Resynch Failed error message.

4. For binary comparisons, the differences are reported on a single line as **xxxxxxxx: yy zz**, where xxxxxxxx is the hex address from the beginning of the file where the difference occurs. **yy** is the byte that is different in *File1* and **zz** is the byte that is different in *File2*. FC uses the same line buffer as Note 4 for binary comparisons, however if it runs out of memory, it will overlay portions of the memory until the comparison is completed.

5. FC is only available with MS-DOS®, not PC-DOS.

Sets number of file control blocks that DOS can have open at the same time:

Syntax (shaded is optional):

FCBS = x

    Examples: FCBS = 10

Syntax Options:

x . . . . File control blocks that DOS can have open at one time. Default = 4. Values can range from 1 through 255.

Command Type and Version:

CONFIG.SYS command; Introduced with Ver 3.1

Notes:

1. Normally, this command should only be used if a program specifically requires that FCBS be set to a specific value.

2. DOS may close a file opened earlier if there are not enough FCBs set aside.

3. The "Y" Syntax Option available in DOS Versions 4.01 and earlier, is no longer a valid option.

FDISK

Configures hard disk: After the low level format of a hard drive, FDISK is used to partition the drive for DOS. A series of menus are displayed to assist in partitioning process. *Caution:* When a partition is deleted, all of the data stored on that partition is also deleted.

Syntax (shaded is optional):

FDISK **/ status**

      Examples: FDISK

Syntax Options:

/ status . . **⑥** . . Display partition table info for hard drives installed in the system.

Command Type and Version:

External command; Network, introduced with Ver 2.0

Notes:

1. Using the FDISK command, you can accomplish the following:
   Create a primary DOS partition on a hard drive.
   Create an extended DOS partition on a hard drive.
   Delete a partition on a hard drive.
   Change the active partition on a hard drive.
   Displays partition data for a hard drive.
   Selects a different hard disk for partitioning.

2. Maximum partition size is 2 gigabytes.

3. In order to change the size of a partition, the partition must be deleted first, and a new partition created.

4. Drives formed by ASSIGN, SUBST, or JOIN cannot be partictioned with FDISK.

5. USE WITH CAUTION, backup hard drive data files before changing or deleting a partition.

6. The formatting of a hard drive for use by DOS is a three step process: Low level format, FDISK, then FORMAT. Note that IDE hard drives have been low level formatted at the factory, do not re-low level format these drives, only use FDISK then FORMAT.

7. See also FORMAT.

FILES

Sets the number of open files DOS can access.

Syntax (shaded is optional):

FILES = nnn

    Examples: FILES=20

Syntax Options:

nnn . . . . Number of files DOS can access, at one
                    time, with valid values ranging from
                    8-255. The Default is 8.

Command Type and Version:

CONFIG.SYS command; Introduced with Ver 2.0

Notes:

1. The standard value for files is FILES=20, however, many software
   packages, such as database managers, will require values in the
   range of 35 to 40. See the documentation for each program you
   wish to run and verify that your FILES= statement is not smaller
   than that required by the program. It is all right if FILES= is
   larger than a program requires.

FIND

Looks for a text string in a file(s): Once the text string is located that FIND is searching for, it displays those lines of text containing the text string.

Syntax (shaded is optional):

FIND /v /c /n /i text Drive:\Path\ Filename

Examples: FIND /v /i "Dear Sir" C:\Test.doc
   FIND "Dear Sir" Test.doc
   FIND "Dear Sir" "Sincerely" "Help" C:\Test.doc

Syntax Options:

Drive:\Path. . . . Drive and directory containing *Filename*.

Filename . . . . . File being searched for *Text*.

text. . . . . Text string being searched for.

/ v. . . . . Display lines that do not contain *Text*.

/ c. . . . . Display line count of lines containing *Text*.

/ n. . . . . Files line number containing *Text*.

/ i . . . . ❺ . . . . Ignor upper/lower case during search.

Command Type and Version:

External command; Network; Introduced with Ver 2.0

Notes:

1. Wild cards (* and ?) cannot be used in filenames being searched for by FIND. See the FOR command for help in this area.

2. FIND ignores carriage returns, so *Text* must be a string that does not contain any carriage returns.

3. If /c and /n are used together, the /n is disregarded.

4. If Filename is not specified, FIND will act as a filter for any standard device (keyboard, file, pipe, etc) and display those lines containing *Text*.

5. DOS provides three filter commands, FIND, MORE, and SORT.

6. /c /v used together will return a count of lines that do not contain *Text*.

FOR..IN..DO

A logical batch command that runs a specific command for each file in a group: FOR can be run from inside a batch file or at the DOS prompt.

Syntax (shaded is optional):

If used in a batch file, use the following:
FOR %%variable IN (set) DO command `cpar`
If used at the DOS prompt, use the following:
FOR %variable IN (set) DO command `cpar`

> Examples:
> FOR %T IN (*.doc, *.asc) DO DEL %T
> (deletes all .doc and .asc files in current directory)

Syntax Options:

%variable . . . . Replaceable variable for use at the DOS prompt. The *variable* name can be any character(s) except the numbers 0 to 9. FOR replaces *variable* with each text string contained in *(set)* and runs *command* over and over until all are processed.

%%variable . . . Same as %variable, except for use in batch files only.

(set) . . . . One or more files or text strings on which *command* is to operate. ( ) is required

command . . . . Any DOS command to be run on each item listed in *(set)*.

cpar . . . . Parameters for *command*.

Command Type and Version:

Batch and Internal command; Introduced with Ver 2.0

Notes:

1. FOR..IN..DO commands cannot be nested on a single command line.
2. Wild cards (* and ?) are allowed in *(set)*.
3. Multiple %variable names are allowed.

Format a floppy or hard disk: A disk must be formatted before DOS can recognize it.

Syntax (shaded is optional):

There are 4 different syntax choices:

FORMAT Drive: /v:name /q /u /f:size /b /s
FORMAT Drive: /v:name /q /u /t:trak /n:sect /b /s
FORMAT Drive: /v:name /q /u /1 /4 /b /s
FORMAT Drive: /q /u /1 /4 /8 /b /s /autotest

    Examples: FORMAT A: / s /autotest
               FORMAT / B: / f:720k / s

Syntax Options:

Drive:	Drive to be formatted. If no switches are used, the drive is formatted according to its system drive type.
/v:name	Assign the disk the volume label *name*. *name* can be up to 11 characters long. If /v is not used, DOS will automatically prompt the user for a volume name when the format process is finished. /v is not compatible with /8. See also the VOL, DIR, and LABEL commands.
/q . . . **❺**	Quick format a disk by deleting the FAT (File Allocation Table) and root directory. Only use this on disks that have already been formatted.
/u . . . **❺**	Unconditional format. Destroys all data and UNFORMAT will not work. Use if read or write errors occur with this disk or when a new disk is to be formatted.
/1	Format 1 side of floppy only.
/4	Formats a DSDD (double-sided double-density) 5-1/4 inch, 360k floppy in a 1.2 m floppy drive. Warning: some 1.2m drives can not reliably do this format!
/8	Formats a 5-1/4 disk with 8 sectors per track. 8 sectors per track are necessary

	for use with pre DOS 2.0 operating systems.
/f:size	Floppy disk size. Use instead of /t and /n switches if possible:

160, 160k or 160kb	160k SSDD, 5-1/4
180, 180k or 180kb	180k SSDD, 5-1/4
320, 320k or 320kb	320k DSDD, 5-1/4
360, 360k or 360kb	360k DSDD, 5-1/4
720, 720k, or 720kb	720k DSDD, 3.5"
1200, k, kb, 1.2, 1.2m, 1.2mb ...	1.2m DSQD, 5-1/4
1440, k, kb, 1.44, 1.44m, 1.44mb	1.44m DSQD, 3.5"
❺ 2880, k, kb, 1.88, 2.88m, 2.88mb	2.88m DS, 3.5"

/b	Obsolete switch used to reserve space for the system files. No longer generally used, retained for compatibility only.
/s	Copies all 3 system files, [IO.SYS and MSDOS.SYS] or [IBMBIO.COM and IBMDOS.COM] and COMMAND.COM) to the disk after formatting has finished. The DBLSPACE.BIN file is also copied to the target drive (if you are not using the DBLSPACE program, you can remove the hidden, system, read-only attributes from DBLSPACE.BIN on the target disk and then delete it.)
/t:trak	Number of tracks on disk, must be used with the /n switch. Use /f:size switch if possible.
/n:sect.	Number of sectors on disk, must be used with the /t switch. Use /f:size switch if possible.
/ autotest . ❻ .	Bypasses prompts during formatting. Note that this is an undocumented command.

Command Type and Version:

External command; Introduced with Ver 1.0

Notes:

1. New floppy disks need only be formatted in order to make the disk useable by DOS. Hard drives, however, require a 2 or 3 step format process which includes a low level format (Not on IDE drives), then partitioning with FDISK, and finally FORMAT.

2. If the / U switch is **not** used, UNFORMAT can unformat the disk. See also UNFORMAT

3. Format issues a warning when a hard drive is to be formatted.

4. Do not format Network drives or drives that have had ASSIGN, JOIN or SUBST used on the drive.

5. FORMAT / S and the DOS "SYS" command both copy the DBLSPACE.BIN file to the Target Disk.

6. FORMAT Exit codes are:

0	Successful FORMAT
3	Aborted with Ctrl+C by user
4	Fatal error other than 0,3, or 5
5	No response to Proceed?

GOTO

Directs DOS to process commands starting with the line after a specified label: Within a Batch program, when DOS finds the specified label, it processes the commands beginning with the next line after that label.

Syntax (shaded is optional):

GOTO Label
:Label

Examples: GOTO Start
Test.bat   (bypassed by GOTO)
:Start   (must begin with :)

Syntax Options:

Label . . . . Directs DOS to a specific line in a batch
file. Valid values for *Label* can include
spaces but cannot include other separators, such as equal signs and
semicolons. GOTO will recognize only
the first 8 characters of the Label
name. *Label,* on the GOTO command
line, does not begin with a colon and it
must have a matching *Label* line in the
batch program. The *Label* line in the
batch program must begin with a colon.
You can also substitute an environment
variable enclosed in percent signs, e.g.
%RETURN%, for *Label.*

Command Type and Version:

Internal command; only used in a Batch program;
Introduced with Ver 2.0

Notes:

1. A batch-program line beginning with a colon (:) is a label line,
and will not be processed as a command. When the line begins
with a (:) colon, DOS ignores any commands on that line.

GRAFTABL

Allows a display to show extended characters in graphics mode from a specific code page:
This command is required when a monitor is not able to display extended characters in graphics mode. (Most monitors do not need GRAFTABL.)

Syntax (shaded is optional):

GRAFTABL nnn
    or
GRAFTABL /status

    Examples:
        GRAFTABL 860   (Portuguese code page)

Syntax Options:

nnn. . . . . Code page used to define extended characters.

                437 . . . . United States
                850 . . . . Multilingual
                852 . . . . Slavic
                860 . . . . Portuguese
                863 . . . . Canadian-French
                865 . . . . Nordic

/status . . . . Identifies current country code page.

Command Type and Version:

External command; Network; Introduced with Ver 3.0
Removed from DOS Ver 6.0, not used anymore.

Notes:

1. The active code page is not changed when GRAFTABL is run.
2. GRAFTABL uses approximately 1K of RAM.
3. GRAFTABL exit codes are as follows:
            0 . . . . . . Successful load of character set.
            1 . . . . . . Current character set replaced by new table.
            2 . . . . . . File error has occurred.
            3 . . . . . . Incorrect parameter, new table not loaded.
            4 . . . . . . Incorrect DOS version, 5.0 required.

GRAPHICS

Configures DOS so that Print Screen (Shift+Print Scrn) can print a graphics screen to a printer. GRAPHICS supports CGA, EGA, and VGA display modes:

Syntax (shaded is optional):

GRAPHICS **Type Drive:\Path** Filename **/r /b /Lcd /pb:std or /pb:Lcd**

Examples: GRAPHICS color4 /b

Syntax Options:

Type	Printer type (HP=Hewlett-Packard)
color1	IBM Color Printer with black ribbon
color4	IBM Color Printer with RGB ribbon
color8	IBM Color Printer with CMY ribbon
hpdefault	Any HP PCL printer
deskjet	HP DeskJet printer
graphics	IBM Graphics, Proprinter or Quietwriter
graphicswide . .	IBM Graphics Printer with 11inch carriage
laserjet	HP LaserJet printer
laserjetii	HP LaserJet II printer
paintjet	HP PaintJet printer
quietjet	HP QuietJet printer
quietjetplus . . .	HP QuietJet Plus printer
ruggedwriter . . .	HP Rugged Writer printer
ruggedwriterwide	HP Rugged Writerwide printer
thermal	IBM PC-convertible Thermal Printer
thinkjet	HP ThinkJet printer

Drive:\Path . . .	Drive and directory containing Filename.
Filename	Printer profile where graphics screen is to be printed to. Default is GRAPHICS.PRO.

/r	Prints the image as white characters on a black background (black characters on a white background is the Default).
/b	Prints the background in color. (only color4 and color8 types are valid)
/Lcd	Prints image using an LCD screen aspect ratio instead of a CGA screen aspect ratio.
/pb:std	Sets printbox size. If this switch is used,
or /pb:Lcd . . .	you must check the GRAPHICS.PRO file and change each printbox line to *std* or *Lcd* so that it matches what you selected for *pb*:

Command Type and Version:

External command; Network; Introduced with Ver 2.0

Notes:

1. The GRAPHICS command does use a limited amout of conventional RAM when it is loaded.

2. Four shades of gray are printed if *color1* or *graphics* is in effect and the screen is in the 320x200 mode.

3. If a printer profile such as GRAPHICS.PRO is already loaded, and you wish to load a different .PRO file, the new .PRO must be smaller than the currently loaded .PRO. If it is larger, your system must be re-booted first in order for the larger profile to be loaded.

4. Use the Graphics or Graphicswide printer types if the printer you are using is an Epson.

5. Supported displays include EGA and VGA.

6. See also PRINT

GW-BASIC®

BASIC language intrepreter: GW-BASIC® is Microsoft's own version of BASIC that shipped with MS–DOS versions prior to Ver 5.0. Starting with Ver 5.0, QBASIC is shipped with DOS.

Syntax (shaded is optional):

GWBASIC **Drive:\Path\Filename < Input >> Output /f:n /i /s:n /c:n /m:n,n /d**

Examples: GWBASIC   (starts BASIC)
           GWBASIC C:\BAS\test.bas /f:4 /d

Syntax Options:

Drive:\Path . . .	Drive and directory containing *Filename*.
Filename	The BASIC program file to be run. The default file extension is .BAS
< Input	Standard input is read from *Input* file.
> Output	Output is redirected to *Output* file or a device (screen, printer, etc)
>>	Causes *Output* to be appended.
/ f:n	Max number *n* of simultaneously open files while a BASIC program is running. Default is 3. */ i* must be used at the same time. Size requirement includes 194 bytes (File Control Block) plus 128 bytes (data buffer).
/ i	Forces static allocation of memory for file operations.
/ s:nn	Max record length *nn* for a file. Default is 128 bytes, maximum is 32,767 bytes.
/ c:nn	Allocates *nn* bytes of Receive buffer and 128 bytes of Transmit buffer for RS-232 (serial) communications. */c:0* disables support. Defaults are 256 byte receive buffer and 128 byte transmit buffer for each RS-232 card.

/m:x,y .... Sets the highest memory location *x* and
              the maximum block size *y* in bytes.
              Block size is in multiples of 16.

/d. .... Activates double-precision for the
              following functions: ATN, COS, EXP,
              LOG, SIN, SQR and TAN.

Command Type and Version:

External command; Network; Introduced with Ver 1.0

Notes:

1. See also BASIC, BASICA, and QBASIC.
2. Variables n, nn, x, and y listed above are all given in decimal
   values. If you wish to use hexadecimal values, preceed the
   value with &H. If you wish to use octal values, preceed the
   value with &O (O is the letter O, not zero).
3. A complete discussion of GW-BASIC is beyond the scope of this
   book. If you need information on GW-BASIC commands and how
   to program in BASIC, refer to Microsoft's manual on GW-BASIC
   or other texts on BASIC.
4. Different versions of GWBASIC were released and each needs
   to be run with its correct version of DOS.
5. Programs written in BASIC (IBM's version) may require small
   adjustments in order to run correctly under GW-BASIC

Online Information about MS-DOS version 5.0 commands:

Syntax (shaded is optional):

HELP **command**

> Examples: HELP   (brief description of commands)
> HELP chkdsk
> DISKCOPY / ?   (see Note: 1 below)

Syntax Options:

Command. . . .   Any specific DOS version 5.0 command on which more information is desired.

Command Type and Version:

External command; Network; Introduced with Ver 5.0
FASTHELP in Ver 6.0 is the same as HELP in Ver 5.0

Notes:

1. You can get online HELP in two ways. Either specify the name of the command on the HELP command line or type the command name and the /? switch at the command prompt.

Online information about MS-DOS Version 6.0 commands and a list of all DOS commands:
The Ver 6.0 information for HELP is much more detailed than FASTHELP or DOS Ver 5.0 HELP.

Syntax (shaded is optional):

HELP command /B /G /H /nohi

    Examples: HELP   (List of commands)
                 HELP chkdsk
                 DISKCOPY   / ?   (see Note: 1 below)

Syntax Options:

Command .... Any specific DOS version 6.0 command on which more information is desired.
/B . . . . Display in black-and-white mode.
/G . . . . Display in CGA color mode.
/H . . . . Display HELP with the maximum number of lines that the display supports.
/nohi . . . . Turn high-intensity display off.

Command Type and Version:

External command; Network; Introduced with Ver 6.0
FASTHELP in Ver 6.0 is the same as HELP in Ver 5.0

Notes:

1. You can get online HELP in two ways. Either specify the name of the command on the HELP command line or type the command name and the /? switch at the command prompt.

HIMEM.SYS

Extended memory and HMA (high memory area) manager: HIMEM.SYS prevents programs from using the same memory locations at the same time.

Syntax (shaded is optional):

Device= Drive:\Path\ HIMEM.SYS /hmamin=m /numhandles=n /int15=xxx /machine:xxx /a20control:on or off /shadowram:on or off /cpuclock:on or off /EISA /verbose

Examples: Device=C:\Dos\HIMEM.SYS

Syntax Options:

Drive:\Path ... Drive and directory containing HIMEM.

/hmamin=m ... Minimum *m* kilobytes of memory a program must use before it can use the HMA. Default=0, Range=0 to 63. The most efficient use of HMA is accomplished by setting m to the amount of memory required by the program that uses the most HMA.

/numhandles=n Maximum number (*n*) of EMB (extended memory block) handles that can be used at the same time. Each handle uses 6 bytes of RAM. Default=32, Range=1 to 128.

/int15=xxx .... *xxx* kilobytes of memory are assigned to the Interrupt 15h interface. Programs must recognize VDisk headers in order to use this switch.

/machine:xxx.. Defines a specific A20 handler *xxx* to be used. Normally, HIMEM automatically detects which A20 is to be used. Default=1. If the required handler is not listed in the following table, see the README.TXT file in your DOS directory for additional information.

Number	Code	A20 handler
1	at	IBM PC/AT
2	ps2	IBM PS/2
3	pt1cascade	Phoenix Cascade Bios
4	hpvectra	HP Vectra, A and A+
5	att6300plus	AT&T 6300 Plus
6	acer1100	Acer 1100
7	toshiba	Toshiba 1600 and 1200XE
8	wyse	Wyse 12.5 MHz 286
9	tulip	Tulip SX
10	zenith	Zenith ZBIOS
11	at1	IBM PC/AT
12	at2	IBM PC/AT (alt. delay)
12	css	CSS Labs
13	at3	IBM PC/AT (alt. delay)
13	philips	Philips
14	fasthp	HP Vectra
15	ibm7552	IBM 7552 Industrial Comp.
16	bullmicral	Bull Micral 60
17	dell	Dell XBIOS

❻ (brace grouping rows 15–17)

/a20control:on : *off* allows HIMEM.SYS to take control of
or */a20control:off* the A20 line only if A20 was off when
HIMEM.SYS was loaded. Default=:*on*

/shadowram:on If your system has Shadow RAM, :*off*
or */shadowram:off* switches the Shadow RAM off and
returns control of that RAM to HIMEM.
Default=:*off* if your system has a less
than 2 megabytes of RAM.

/cpuclock:on If your system slows down when
HIMEM.SYS is loaded, specifying :*on*
might correct the problem. :*on* will slow
down HIMEM.SYS.

/EISA ❻ Used only on EISA systems to specify
that HIMEM allocates all available extended memory.

/verbose or */v* HIMEM displays status and error messages
❻ while loading. Hold ALT key down dur-
ing system startup to disable /verbose.

Command Type and Version:

Config.sys command; Introduced with Ver 4.0

Notes:

1. Only one program at a time can use the high memory area.

2. HIMEM.SYS, or another XMS driver such as 386MAX or QEMM must be loaded before DOS can be loaded into HMA with the DOS=high command.

3. In most cases, command line switches do not need to be used. since the defaults are designed to work with most computer hardware.

IF

Performs a command based on the result of a condition in batch programs: If a conditional statement is true, DOS executes the command, if the condition is false, DOS ignores the command.

Syntax (shaded is optional):

Three syntax formats are valid:

    IF not errorlevel nnn *command*
    IF not string1==string2 *command*
    IF not exist filename *command*

Examples: IF errorlevel 3 goto end

Syntax Options:

not . . . . The command is to be carried out only if the statement is false.

errorlevel *nnn*. . True, only if, the previous program executed by COMMAND.COM had an exit code equal to or greater than *nnn*.

command. . . . . The specified command that DOS is to perform if the preceding condition is met.

string1==string2 True, only if *string1* and *string2* are the same. The values of *string1* and *string2* can be literal strings or batch variables. Strings may not contain separators, such as commas, semicolons, spaces, etc.

exist *filename*. . True condition if *filename* exists.

Command Type and Version:

Internal command; Introduced with Ver 2.0

Notes:

1. The *errorlevel* parameter allows you to use exit codes as conditions. An exit code is returned to DOS whenever a program stops.

2. Use " " quotes around strings when comparing, it's safer.

Includes the contents of one configuration block within another configuration block: This is one of five special CONFIG.SYS commands used to define multiple configurations.

Syntax (shaded is optional):

INCLUDE=blockname

Syntax Options:

blockname . . . . The name of the configuration block to be included.

Command Type and Version:

CONFIG.SYS command; Introduced with Ver 6.0

Notes:

1. See also MENUITEM, MENUDEFAULT, MENUCOLOR, and SUBMENU. These are the other four special CONFIG.SYS commands used to define multiple configurations

2. Refer to your DOS 6.0 manual for more information on setting up the special multiple configuration menus.

INSTALL

Loads a memory-resident program when DOS is started: Use the INSTALL command to load FASTOPEN, KEYB, NLSFUNC, or SHARE in CONFIG.SYS.

Syntax (shaded is optional):

INSTALL = Drive: \Path\ Filename parameters

   Examples: INSTALL = C:\Dos\NLSFUNC

Syntax Options:

Drive.\Path. . . .   Drive and directory containing *Filename*.

\Filename. . . . .   Name of memory-resident program that you want to run.

Parameters . . .   Command parameters, if any, required by *Filename*.

Command Type and Version:

External command; Network; Introduced with Ver 4.0

Notes:

1. Less memory is used when you load a program with INSTALL instead of loading from AUTOEXEC.BAT file since an environment for a program is not created by INSTALL .

2. Do not use INSTALL to load programs that use shortcut keys, environment variables, or require COMMAND.COM for error handling.

3. Not all programs will function properly if loaded with INSTALL.

4. See also FASTOPEN, KEYB, NLSFUNC, SHARE, CONFIG.SYS.

New V6.0

Link computers to share resources:
INTERLNK.EXE must be installed as a device
driver in the CONFIG.SYS file before the
INTERLNK and INTERSVR commands can be run.

Syntax (shaded is optional):

Device= **Drive: \Path** INTERLNK.EXE **/drives:n
/noprinter /com:n\address /lpt:n\address
/auto /noscan /low /baud:rate /v**

Examples: Device=C:\ INTERLNK.EXE /drives:4

Syntax Options:

Drive:\Path. . . . . Drive and directory containing the
INTERLNK.EXE program.

/drives:n. . . . . . . The number of redirected drives.
Default is n=3. If n=0, only the printers
are redirected.

/noprinter . . . . No printers are to be redirected. Default
is INTERLNK redirects all ports.

/com:n\address Specifies that serial port *n* be used to
transfer data. If *n* or the address is
omitted, INTERLNK scans for the first
available port. Default is INTERLNK redirects all ports.

/lpt:n\address . Specifies that serial port n be used to
transfer data. If *n* or the address is
omitted, INTERLNK scans for the first
available port. Default is INTERLNK redirects all ports.

/auto . . . . INTERLNK.EXE is installed in memory
only if *client* can make a connection
when the *server* starts up. Default is IN-
TERLNK is installed whether or not
server is there.

/noscan	INTERLNK.EXE driver is installed, but a connection between *client* and *server* is prevented.
/low	INTERLNK.EXE forces driver to be loaded into conventional memory. Default is driver loaded into upper memory if it is available.
/baud:rate	Sets baud rate for com serial ports. Default=115200. Valid values are 9600, 19200, 38400, 57600, & 115200.
/v	Used to resolve problems conflicts between *com* and *lpt* ports and the computers timer.

Command Type and Version:

External CONFIG.SYS command; Network;
Introduced with Ver 6.0

Notes:

1. See also INTERSVR and INTERLNK the command.

Link computers to share resources:
INTERLNK.EXE must be installed as a device driver in the CONFIG.SYS file before the INTERLNK and INTERSVR commands can be run.

Syntax (shaded is optional):

INTERLNK **client :** = **server :**

Examples: INTERLNK C: = F:

Syntax Options:

client : . . . . The drive letter of the client drive that is
redirected to a drive on the server.

server : . . . . . . The drive letter on the server that will be
redirected. If a letter is not specified,
the client drive will no longer be redirected.

Command Type and Version:

External command; Network; Introduced with Ver 6.0

Notes:

1. See also INTERLNK.EXE and INTERSVR.
2. Note, the LASTDRIVE command may need to be used if drive letters greater than E are used.

Starts the INTERLNK server so that resources can be shared between linked computers: INTERLNK.EXE must be installed as a device driver in the CONFIG.SYS file before the INTERLNK and INTERSVR commands can be run.

Syntax (shaded is optional):

INTERSVR drive: /X=drive /lpt:n/address /com:n/address /baud:rate /b /v /rcopy

    Examples: INTERSVR / rcopy

Syntax Options:

/X=drive	Specifies those drives that will not be redirected. Default is all drives are redirected.
/lpt:n/address .	Specifies that serial port n be used to transfer data. If *n* or the address is omitted, INTERLNK scans for the first available port. Default is INTERSVR scans all ports.
/com:n/address	Specifies that serial port n be used to transfer data. If *n* or the address is omitted, INTERLNK scans for the first available port. Default is INTERSVR scans all ports.
/baud:rate	Sets baud rate for com serial ports. Default=115200. Valid values are 9600, 19200, 38400, 57600, & 115200.
/b.	Display stat screen in black-and-white.
/v.	Used to resolve problems conflicts between *com* and *lpt* ports and the computers timer.

/rcopy . . . . Copies all INTERLNK files from one
                      computer to another. Note that a full 7
                      wire null-modem serial cable must be
                      installed on the *com* port and the DOS
                      MODE command must be available.

Command Type and Version:

External command; Network; Introduced with Ver 6.0

Notes:

1. See also INTERLNK.EXE and INTERLNK.

2. If port numbers for com and lpt are not specified, INTERLNK will scan and select the first port it finds.

Joins a disk drive to a specific directory on another disk drive: Once joined, DOS treats the directories and files of the first drive as the contents of the second drive and path.

Syntax (shaded is optional):

Two syntax formats are valid:
JOIN `Drive1: Drive2:\Path`
JOIN Drive: /d

    Examples: JOIN C: D:\Notes
               JOIN C: D:\Notes\Bin (valid for DOS 5.0 only)

Syntax Options:

Drive1: . . . . Drive to be joined to *Drive2:\Path.*
Drive2:\Path. . . Drive and Path to which you want to
. . . . JOIN *Drive1:*. Drive2:\Path must be empty and other than the root directory. With DOS Ver 5.0, you can JOIN to a subdirectory also, e.g. C:\Notes\Bin
Drive: . . . . Drive on which JOIN is to be canceled.
/ d . . . . Cancels the JOIN command.

Command Type and Version:

External command; Introduced with Ver 3.1
Removed from DOS Version 6.0, deemed to dangerous.

Notes:

1. Once you use the JOIN command, Drive1: becomes invalid.
2. If a specified path already exists before using JOIN, that directory cannot be used while JOIN is in effect. The specified directory must be empty or the JOIN operation will be incomplete and an error message will be displayed.
3. Commands that do not work with drives formed by JOIN are: ASSIGN, BACKUP, CHKDSK, DISKCOMP, DISKCOPY, FDISK, FORMAT, LABEL, MIRROR, RECOVER, RESTORE, SYS.
4. Use JOIN without parameters to show a list of the currently joined drives.

Configures a keyboard for use with a specific language (Installs alternate keyboard layout):

Syntax (shaded is optional):

If started in a batch file or at the DOS prompt:
  KEYB xx,yyy,Drive:\Path\Filename /e / id:nn

If started in CONFIG.SYS:
  install = Drive1:\Path1\KEYB.COM xx, yyy, Drive:\Path\Filename /e / id:nn

> Examples: KEYB fr,850,437,C:\Dos\Keyboard.sys
> install = C:\KEYB.COM fr , , C:\Dos\Keyboard.sys

Syntax Options:

xx.	Keyboard code. See table on next page.
yyy.	Code page. See table on next page.
Drive:\Path . . .	Drive and directory containing *Filename*.
Filename	Keyboard definition file. Default=KEYBOARD.SYS
/e . . **5**	Enhanced keyboard is being used.
/id:nn	Defines which keyboard is in use. See table on next page.
Drive1:\Path1 .	Drive and directory containing KEYB.COM

Command Type and Version:

External command; Network; Introduced with Ver 3.3

Notes:

1. When KEYB is installed through CONFIG.SYS, KEYB.COM with the .COM must be used. See also the CHCP command.
2. The Code Page specified with yyy must already be loaded on your system before KEYB is used.
3. You can switch from the default keyboard configuration to the KEYB configuration by pressing Ctrl+Alt+F2. To switch to the default keyboard configuration, press Ctrl+Alt+F1
4. The following are KEYB exit codes:

0.	KEYB definition file loaded successfully.
1.	Invalid Keyboard Code, Code Page, or syntax.
2.	Bad or missing keyboard definition file.
4.	Communication error with CON device.
5.	Requested Code Page has not been prepared.

The following table lists xx, yyy, and nnn values for different countries and languages.

Country or language	Keyboard Code *xx*	Code Page *yyy*	Keyboard ID *nnn*
Belgium	be	850,437	
Brazil	br	850,437	
Canadian-French	cf	850,863	
Czechoslovakia (Czech)	cz	852,850	
Czechoslovakia (Slovak)	sl	852,850	
Denmark	dk	850,865	
Finland	su	850,437	
France	fr	850,437	120,189
Germany	gr	850,437	
Hungary	hu	852,850	
Italy	it	850,437	141,142
Latin America	la	850,437	
Netherlands	nl	850,437	
Norway	no	850,865	
Poland	pl	852,850	
Portugal	po	850,860	
Spain	sp	850,437	
Sweden	sv	850,437	
Switzerland (French)	sf	850,437	
Switzerland (German)	sg	850,437	
United Kingdom	uk	850,437	166,168
United States	us	850,437	
Yugoslavia	yu	852,850	

Loads a keyboard program for a specific country or keyboard type:

Syntax (shaded is optional):

KEYBxx

> Examples: KEYBGR
> KEYBUK

Syntax Options:

xx. . . . . Code for a specific keyboard type:

KEYBdv . . . . Dvorak keyboard
KEYBfr . . . . . France
KEYBgr . . . . Germany
KEYBit . . . . . Italy
KEYBsp . . . . Spain
KEYBuk . . . . United Kingdom

Command Type and Version:

External command; Network; Introduced with Ver 3.0

Notes:

1. KEYBxx was discontinued after DOS version 3.2 and was replaced by KEYB.

2. Only one keyboard program can be loaded at a time.

3. You can switch from the default keyboard configuration to the KEYBxx configuration by pressing Ctrl+Alt+F2. To switch to the default keyboard configuration, press Ctrl+Alt+F1.

4. If you need to change from one keyboard type to another, restart the system after the changes have been made.

LABEL

Creates, changes or deletes the name or volume label of a disk: DOS displays the volume label and serial number, if it exists, as part of the directory listing.

Syntax (shaded is optional):

LABEL `Drive: Label`

Examples: LABEL
            LABEL A: datadisc

Syntax Options:

Drive: . . . . Drive or diskette to be named.

Label . . . . New volume label, up to 11 characters.
                        A colon (:) must be included between the drive letter and label.

Command Type and Version:

External command; Introduced with Ver 3.0

Notes:

1. Using the LABEL command without a label displays the following:

          Volume in Drive A is nnnnnnnnnnn
          Volume Serial Number is nnnn-nnnn
          Volume Label (11 characters, ENTER for none)?

2. The Volume label cannot include tabs. Spaces are allowed, but consecutive spaces may be treated as a single space.

3. **Do not** use the following characters in a volume label:

        * ? / \ | . , ; : + = [ ] ( ) & ^ < > "

4. LABEL is not case sensitive. (lower case is automatically converted to upper case.)

5. LABEL does not work on a drive created by ASSIGN, JOIN or SUBST.

LASTDRIVE

Number of drives installed: By default, the last drive is the one *after* the last drive used by your computer.

Syntax (shaded is optional):

LASTDRIVE = parameter

   Examples: LASTDRIVE = F

Syntax Options:

parameter . . . .   A drive letter in the range of A through Z to correspond to the number of logical drives installed. The default is the last drive being used by the computer.

Command Type and Version:

CONFIG.SYS command; Introduced with Ver 3.0

Notes:

1. Memory is allocated by DOS for each drive specified by LASTDRIVE, therefore, don't specify more drives than are necessary.

8086 Object Linker that creates executable pro-grams from Microsoft Macro Assembler (MASM) object files: LINK is for the experienced programmer and is not used by the general user.

Syntax (shaded is optional):

```
LINK          (LINK prompts for file names, etc)
LINK object , execute , map , library options ;
```

Examples: LINK file /se:192 , , ;

Syntax Options:

object	Object files to be linked together.
execute	Name for created executable file.
map	Map listing file.
library	Name(s) of library files to LINK.
options	Options for the LINK program
;	Terminates command line.

Command Type and Version:

External command; Introduced with Ver 1.0
Removed from Ver 6.0

Notes:

1. Further discussion of LINK is beyound the scope of POCKET PCRef.

Forces a program to load above the first 64k of conventional memory and then runs the program.

Syntax (shaded is optional):

LOADFIX **Drive: \Path** Filename **parameters**

Examples: LOADFIX C:\TEST.EXE

Syntax Options:

Drive\Path . . . Drive and directory containing *Filename*.

Filename . . . . . Name of program that you want to run.

Parameters . . . Command parameters, if any, required by *Filename*.

Command Type and Version:

External command; Introduced with Ver 5.0

Notes:

1. Use LOADFIX when the error message "Packed file corrupt" is reported during the execution of a program.

Loads programs into upper memory: Loading programs into upper memory frees up conventional memory for other programs. An upper memory manager such as EMM386 must be loaded first in order for LOADHIGH to function. LH and LOADHIGH are equivalent commands.

Syntax (shaded is optional):

LOADHIGH **Drive:\Path** Filename **/L:region**
parameters

Examples: LOADHIGH C:\Dos\doskey.com
LH C:\Dos\doskey.com

Syntax Options:

Drive:\Path . . .	Drive and directory containing *Filename*.
\Filename.	Program to be loaded into high memory.
/L:region.	Load the device driver into a specific upper memory region.
parameters . . .	Command line parameters required by *Filename*.

Command Type and Version:

Internal command; Network; Introduced with Ver 5.0

Notes:

1. DOS=umb must be included in your CONFIG.SYS in order for LOADHIGH to function.
2. HIMEM.SYS and EMM386.EXE must be loaded in CONFIG.SYS on a 386/486 system in order to provide upper memory management for 386/486 systems. (Programs such as 386MAX and QEMM will provide the same capabilities.)
3. If there is not enough upper memory to load a program, DOS will load the program into conventional memory (no notice is given).
4. See also DEVICEHIGH, DOS, HIMEM.SYS, and EMM386.
5. When LOADHIGH is used, it is typically placed in the AUTOEXEC.BAT file.
6. Use MEM /c to see where programs are loaded.

MD or MKDIR

Makes a Directory: Creates a new subdirectory under the current directory (if no Drive:\Path is specified). A new subdirectory on a different drive or under a different path can also be created. MD and MKDIR are equivalent commands.

Syntax (shaded is optional):

MD Drive:\Path\ subdirectory

> Examples: MD contract
> MKDIR contract
> MD C:\contract\bin

Syntax Options:

Drive: . . . . Letter of drive for *subdirectory*.

\Path . . . . Path where subdirectory is to be made. If no path is specified, e.g. C:\ only, the new directory is made a subdirectory under the root directory.

subdirectory. . . Name of the *subdirectory* being created.

Command Type and Version:

Internal command; Network; Introduced with Ver 2.0

Notes:

1. DOS will always assume that the MD command is on the current directory if no path is specified.
2. The maximum length of any path to the final subdirectory is 63 characters, including backslashes.

***Display information about used and free
system memory:*** Options are available that will
display items such as which programs are loaded,
the order of loaded programs, free memory, etc.

Syntax (shaded is optional):

MEM **/program /page /d /c /f /m progname**

Examples: MEM
MEM /classify

Syntax Options:

MEM . . . . Without any switches, the status of used
and free memory is displayed.

/ program or */ p* **DOS Version 4/5 only:** Displays the status
of programs currently loaded into mem-
ory. This switch can not be used at the
same time as */debug* and */classify*.

/ page or */ p* **(6)** **DOS Version 6 only.** Pauses display
output after each screen.

/ d or */ debug* . Displays the status of programs and
drivers currently loaded into memory.
This switch can not be used at the
same time as */program* and */classify*.

/ c or */ classify* . Displays the status of all programs and
(5) drivers currently loaded into conven-
tional and upper memory. Other info,
such as memory use and largest memory blocks available are also displayed.
This switch can not be used at the
same time as */program* and */debug*.

/ f or */ free* . . . . Lists free regions in upper memory.
/ free can not be used with other
switches, except */module*.

/m progname or */module progname* . . . Display info on a
particular program loaded in memory.
This switch can not be used with any
other switches except */page*.

Command Type and Version:

External command; Network; Introduced with Ver 4.0

Notes:

1. Extended memory usage is displayed only if the installed system memory is 1 meg or greater. Only LIM 4.0 expanded memory use is displayed.

2. Total conventional memory=first 640k of RAM. Extended = mem- above 1 meg. Expanded = bank switched LIM 4.0 memory.

3. If information is needed on hard drive available space, see the CHKDSK command.

MEMMAKER

Optimizes computer memory by moving device drivers and memory-resident programs (TSR's) into upper memory: The system must be either a 386 or 486 and have extended memory available.

Syntax (shaded is optional):

MEMMAKER /b /batch /session /swap:drive
/T /undo /w:size1,size2

Examples: MEMMAKER
MEMMAKER /undo

Syntax Options:

/b . . . . Display in black-and-white mode. Use if there are problems with your monochrome monitor.

/batch . . . . Run MEMMAKER in unattended mode. This forces acceptance of defaults at all prompts. If an error occurs during the process, MEMMAKER restores the original AUTOEXEC.BAT, CONFIG.SYS, and Windows SYSTEM.INI. Status messages and errors are reported in the MEMMAKER.STS file.

/session . . . . . . This switch is only used by MEMMAKER during the optimizing process.

/swap:drive . . . Specifies the drive letter of the system startup drive, if it has changed since the system started up. (encountered with some disk swapping programs)

/T . . . . If problems are encountered between MEMMAKER and an IBM Token Ring network, use this switch. It disables the Token-Ring detection function.

/undo	Forces MEMMAKER to undo the most recent changes it has made to the system. This switch is normally used if problems are encountered after MEMMAKER has been run and you with the system to be returned to its original confituration.
/w:size1,size2.	Sets the upper memory size reserved for Windows translation buffers. Windows needs two separate areas of upper memory for the buffers. size1 is the size of the first area, size2 is the size of the second area. The default is no buffers are created (/w:0,0).

Command Type and Version:

External command; Introduced with Ver 6.0

Notes:

1. See also DEVICEHIGH and LOADHIGH.
2. **WARNING: Do not run this program if Windows is running!**
3. CHKSTATE.SYS is a CONFIG.SYS command line that is automatically created by MEMMAKER during the optimization process. At the end of the process, it is automatically removed from CONFIG.SYS.

Command line to set text and background colors for the DOS startup menu in the CONFIG.SYS file: The startup menu is a list of system configuration choices that appear when your system is started. Each menu item is a set of CONFIG.SYS commands and is called a "configuration block". See your DOS manual for details of setting up and using the startup menu.

Syntax (shaded is optional):

MENUCOLOR = X ,Y

  Examples: MENUCOLOR 7, 9

Syntax Options:

X	Sets menu text color. Valid values are 0 to 15.
, Y	Sets screen background color. Valid values are 0 to 15. Default=0 (black).

Color Values . .

0=Black	8=Gray
1=Blue .	9=Bright blue
2=Green	10=Bright green
3=Cyan.	11=Bright cyan
4=Red. .	12=Bright Red
5=Magenta	13=Bright magenta
6=Brown	14=Yellow
7=White	15=Bright white

  Note: colors 8 to 15 blink on some displays.

Command Type and Version:

CONFIG.SYS command; Network; Introduced with Ver 6.0

Notes:

1. See also MENUDEFAULT, MENUITEM, NUMLOCK, INCLUDE and SUBMENU. All are used by the startup menu.
2. Don't make X and Y the same number, text won't show!

MENUDEFAULT   New V6.0

Command line to set the default menu item for the DOS startup menu in CONFIG.SYS: The startup menu is a list of system configuration choices that appear when your system is started. Each menu item is a set of CONFIG.SYS commands and is called a "configuration block". See your DOS manual for details of setting up and using the startup menu.

Syntax (shaded is optional):

   MENUDEFAULT = blockname **, timeout**

   Examples: MENUDEFAULT = NET, 20

Syntax Options:

blockname. . . . Sets the default menu item. If no default is specified, item 1 is selected.

, timeout . . . . . The number of seconds DOS waits before starting your computer with a default configuration.

Command Type and Version:

   CONFIG.SYS command; Network; Introduced with Ver 6.0

Notes:

1. See also MENUCOLOR, MENUITEM, NUMLOCK, INCLUDE and SUBMENU. All are used by the startup menu.

MENUITEM

Command line to define a menu item for the DOS startup menu in CONFIG.SYS: The startup menu is a list of system configuration choices that appear when your system is started. Each menu item is a set of CONFIG.SYS commands and is called a "configuration block". See your DOS manual for details of setting up and using the startup menu.

Syntax (shaded is optional):

MENUITEM   blockname **, menutext**

    Examples: MENUITEM NET, Start your Network

Syntax Options:

blockname . . . . Defines a menu item on the startup menu. It is usable only within a menu block and there can be a maximum of nine menu items per menu. If DOS cannot find a specified name, the item will not appear on the startup menu. blockname can be up to 70 characters long but you cannot use spaces, \ (backslashes), / (forward slashes), commas, semicolos, equal signs or square brackets.

, menutext . . . . Up to 70 characters of text to display for the menu item. If no text is given, DOS displays *blockname* as the menu item.

Command Type and Version:

CONFIG.SYS command; Network; Introduced with Ver 6.0

Notes:

1. See also MENUCOLOR, MENUDEFAULT, NUMLOCK, INCLUDE and SUBMENU. All are used by the startup menu.

Records information about 1 or more disks for use by UNFORMAT and UNDELETE commands:

Syntax (shaded is optional):

Three syntax formats are valid:

MIRROR **Drives: /1 /Tdrive – entries . . .**
MIRROR **/u**
MIRROR **/partn**

      Examples: MIRROR /u
               MIRROR C: /Ta /Tc

Syntax Options:

Drives: . . . . The drive or drives to be MIRRORed.

/1 . . . . Instructs MIRROR to retain only the
latest information about a disk. The de-
fault causes MIRROR to make a
backup of existing information before
new information is recorded.

/Tdrive – entries Loads a deletion-tracking program that
maintains information so that the UN-
DELETE command can recover files.
drive is required and is the drive to be
MIRRORed. *entries* is optional and is
the maximum number of entries in
PCTRACKR.DEL (the deletion tracking
file). *entries* can range from 1 to 999
and the *entries* defaults are as follows:

Disk Size	Default Entry	File Size
360k	25	5k
720k	50	9k
1.2 meg	75	14k
1.44k	75	14k
20 meg	101	18k
32 meg	202	36k
>32 meg	303	55k

MIRROR (con't)

/u. . . . . Unload and disable the deletion tracking program. If other memory resident programs have been loaded after MIRROR, the /u switch will not function.

/partn . . . . Save partitioning information for the UNFORMAT command. The information is saved on a floppy disk for use at a later time if partitions need to be rebuilt by UNFORMAT. The default drive to save the information to is A:, although a different drive can be specified at the prompt.

Command Type and Version:

External command; Network; Introduced with Ver 5.0 Removed from DOS Ver 6.0, functionally replace by the UNDELETE / T command.

Notes:

1. If MIRROR is used without any switches, it saves information about the disk in the current drive.

2. Do not use MIRROR on any drive that has been redirected using the JOIN or SUBST commands. If ASSIGN is used, it must be used before MIRROR.

3. MIRROR saves a copy of a drive's FAT (file allocation table) and a copy of the drive's root directory. Since this information may change regularly, it is recommended that you use MIRROR regularly in order to maintain current information for UNFORMAT can use. It is recommended that MIRROR be placed in your AUTOEXEC.BAT file so that current information is saved every time your system is turned on or re-booted.

4. See also UNFORMAT and UNDELETE.

5. **DOS 6.0 Note:** MIRROR is still available from Microsoft as a supplemental disk, call them for details.

MODE

Controls system devices such as display, serial ports, printer ports, and system settings:

NOTE: Since there are many functions that MODE addresses, they will each be treated separately in the following pages.

Command Type and Version:

External command; Network; Introduced with Ver 1.0

MODE to Display Device Status

Syntax (shaded is optional):

MODE **device /status**

Examples:
MODE (Display status of all system devices)
MODE con (Display console status)
MODE lpt1 /status

Syntax Options:

device . . . . Device for which status is requested.

/status or */sta.* . . Displays status of redirected parallel printers.

Notes:

None

MODE to Configure Printer

Configures parallel port printers: Ports that can be addressed include PRN, LPT1, LPT2, and LPT3. Printer types that can be configured are IBM compatibles and Epson compatibles.

Syntax (shaded is optional):

MODE Lptn **: c , L , r**
MODE Lptn **: cols=c lines=L retry=r**

     Examples: MODE Lpt2:132,6
                    MODE Lpt1 cols=132 lines=8

Syntax Options:

Lptn . . . . Parallel port to be configured. Valid numbers for *n* are 1, 2, and 3.

c or *cols=* . . . . . Number of character columns per line. Default=80, Values=80 or 132.

L or *lines=* . . . . Number of vertical lines per inch. Default=6, Values=6 or 8.

r or *retry=* . . . . . Type of retry if time-out error occurs. This option leaves a memory resident piece of MODE in RAM. Valid /s are:

  e . . . . Return busy port error from status check.
  b . . . . Return busy port "Busy" from status check.
  p . . . . Continue retry until printer accepts data.
  r . . . . Return "Ready" from busy port status check.
  n . . . . Disable retry (Default). "none" is also valid.

Notes:

1. *retry=b* is equivalent to the "p" parameter in earlier DOS versions.
2. Ctrl+C will break out of a time-out loop.
3. PRN and LPT1 can be used interchangeably.
4. Do not use any *retry* options over a network.
5. The colon (:) with Lptn is optional.

MODE to Configure Serial Port

Configures a serial communications port:
Ports that can be addressed include COM1,
COM2, COM3, and COM4.

Syntax (shaded is optional):

```
MODE COMn : b , p , d , s , r
MODE COMn : baud=b parity=p data=d
            stop=s retry=r
```

Examples: MODE COM1:24,N,8,1

Syntax Options:

COMn	Asynchronous serial port to be configured. Valid values are 1, 2, 3, and 4.
b or baud=. . . .	Transmission rate in bits per second. Only the first 2 digits are required. Valid values are 11=110 baud, 15=150, 30=300, 60=600, 12=1200, 24=2400, 48=4800, 96=9600, & 19=19,200 baud.
p or parity= . .	Parity check. N=none, E=even, O=odd, M=mark, S=space. Default=E
d or data=	Number of data bits in a character. Valid values are 5, 6, 7, 8. Default=7
s or stop=	Number of stop bits for end of character. Valid values are 1, 1.5 or 2. Default=1 (Default at 110 baud=2)
r or retry=	Type of retry if time-out error occurs. This option leaves a memory resident piece of MODE in RAM. Valid r's are:
e	Return busy port error from status check.
b	Return busy port "Busy" from status check.
p	Continue retry until printer accepts data.
r	Return "Ready" from busy port status check.
n	Disable retry (Default). "none" is also valid.

Notes:

1. If any parameters are omitted in the MODE statement, the most recent setting is used.
2. Do not use *retry* values over a network.
3. *retry=b* is equivalent to the "p" parameter in earlier DOS versions.

MODE to Redirect Printing

Redirects output from a parallel port to a serial port:

Syntax (shaded is optional):

MODE Lptn: = COMn:

> Examples: MODE Lpt1: = COM1:
> MODE Lpt1 = COM2

Syntax Options:

Lptn . . . .   The parallel port to be redirected.
Valid *n* values are 1, 2, and 3.

COMn . . . .   The serial port to be redirected to.
Valid *n* values are 1, 2, 3, and 4

Notes:

1. In order to break redirection, type MODE Lptn, where *n* is the port number to stop redirection from.

MODE to Set Device Code Pages

Selects, refreshes, prepares, or displays code page numbers for parallel printers and the console:

Syntax (shaded is optional):

MODE device codepage prepare= yyy
                              Drive:\Path\Filename
MODE device codepage select=yyy
MODE device codepage refresh
MODE device codepage /status

> Examples:
> MODE CON codepage prepare = 860
> MODE LPT1 codepage /status

Syntax Options:

device . . . . Device to be affected. Valid values are
CON, LPT1, LPT2, and LPT3.

codepage prepare or *cp prep* Prepares the code page for
the specific *device*. Use *codepage
select* after this command.

Drive:\Path\Filename Drive, directory and file containing
code page information (.CPI files)
needed to prepare a code page.

EGA.CPI	Enhanced graphics adapter or PS2
4201.CPI	IBM Proprinters II and III, Model 4201
	IBM Proprinters II & III, Model 4202
4208.CPI	IBM Proprinter X24E Model 4207
	IBM Proprinter XL24E Model 4208
5202.CPI	IBM Quietwriter III Printer
LCD.CPI	IBM PC Convertible Liquid Crystal Disp.

codepage select or *cp sel* Selects a code page for a
specific device. *cp prep* above must be
run first.

codepage refresh or *cp ref* If a code page is lost, this
command reinstates it.

codepage . . . . When used alone, codepage displays
the numbers of the code pages that
have been prepared for a specific device.

/status or */sta.* . Displays the current code page numbers

Notes:
1. See also NLSFUNC and CHCP.

MODE to Set Display Mode

Reconfigure or select active display adapter:

Syntax (shaded is optional):

```
MODE adapter , shift , t
MODE adapter , n
MODE CON : cols=c lines=n
```

Examples: MODE co80,r
MODE CON:cols=40 lines=43

Syntax Options:

adapter . . . . . . Display adapter category as follows:

40 or 80 . . . . Number of characters/line.

bw40 or bw80 . . . . CGA (color graphics with color disabled. Characters per line = 40 or 80

co40 or co80 . . . . . Color display with color enabled. Characters per line = 40 or 80.

mono . . . . Monochrome display with 80 characters per line.

shift . . . . Shift CGA screen left or right. Valid values are L for left, R for right.

t . . . . Starts a test pattern for screen alignment.

n. . . . . Vertical lines per screen. Valid values are 25, 43, and 50. ANSI.SYS must be loaded in CONFIG.SYS for this to work.

cols= . . . . Characters or columns per line. Valid values are 40 and 80.

lines=. . . . . Vertical lines per screen. Valid values are 25, 43, and 50. ANSI.SYS must be loaded in CONFIG.SYS for this to work.

Notes:

1. Some monitors do not support 43 and 50 vertical lines per screen.

MODE to Set Typematic Rate

Set the rate at which DOS repeats a character when a keyboard key is held down: Some keyboards do not recognize this command.

Syntax (shaded is optional):

MODE con **: rate= r delay= d**

Examples: MODE con : rate=20 delay=2

Syntax Options:

con or con: ...	Keyboard
rate=*r*.	The rate that a character is repeated on the display when a key is held down. *r* Default=20 for AT keyboards, Default=21 for PS2 keyboards. *r* Range = 1 to 32, which is equivalent to 2 to 30 characters per second.
delay=*d*.	The amount of time, after a key is held down, before the repeat function activates. *d* Default=2, *d* valid values are 1, 2, 3 and 4 (equivalent to 0.25, 0.50, 0.75, and 1 second respectively). If a delay is specified, rate must also be specified.

Notes:
1. The keyboard must be an AT or PS/2 class or higher keyboard in order for this command to work.

MORE

Displays output one screen at a time: MORE reads standard input from a pipe or redirected file and is typically used to view lengthy files. Each screen of information ends with the prompt -More- and you can press any key to view the next screen.

Syntax (shaded is optional):

MORE < ` Drive: \Path\ ` Filename

or

command I MORE

>   Examples: MORE < C:\Data.txt
>   DIR I MORE

Syntax Options:

Drive:\Path. . . . Drive and directory containing *Filename*.

Filename . . . . . Name of file that supplies data to be displayed.

command. . . . . Name of command that supplies data to be displayed, for example, DIR

Command Type and Version:

External command; Network; Introduced with Ver 2.0

Notes:

1. When using the pipe (I) for redirection, you are able to use DOS commands, such as DIR, SORT, and TYPE with MORE, but the TEMP environment variable in AUTOEXEC.BAT file should be set first.

2. MORE saves input information in a temporary file on disk until the data is ready to be displayed. If there is no room on the disk, MORE will not work. Also, if the current drive is a write-protected drive, MORE will return an error.

Move files from one drive or directory to an-other: You can also move and rename complete directories, along with their files and subdirectories, to other drives or directories. **Warning:** DOS does not warn you if it is about to overwrite files with the same name.

> MOVE **/Y Drive: \Path** Filename
> **, Drive: \Path\ . . .** Filename Destination

Examples: M

Syntax (shaded is optional):

Syntax Options:

Drive.\Path . . .   Drive and directory containing *Filename*.

Filename . . . . .   Name of file(s) that you want to move.

Destination . . .   The new location of the file(s) being moved. This can be a drive, subdirectory, or combination of the two.

Command Type and Version:

External command; Network; Introduced with Ver 6.0

Notes:

1. If more than one file is being moved, the Destination must be a drive and subdirectory.

*Microsoft Anti-Virus scanners for DOS (MSAV)
and Windows (MWAV).*

Syntax (shaded is optional):

MSAV **Drive: /S /C /R /A /L /N /P /F /ss
/video /IN /BW /mono /LCD /FF /BF /NF
/BT /NGM /LE /PS2**

    Examples: MSAV C: /A /N /F

Syntax Options:

Drive:	Drive to be scanned. The Default is the current drive.
/S	Scan but do not remove viruses.
/C	Scan and remove viruses.
/R	Create a MSAV.RPT report that lists the number of files scaned, the number of viruses found, and the number of viruses removed. Default=no report.
/A	Scan all drives except A and B.
/L	Scan all logical drives except network drives.
/N	Run in command mode, not graphical. Also, display contents of a MSAV.TXT file if its present.
/P	Run in command line mode w/ switches.
/F	Do not display file names during scan.
/ss	Set screen display size: /25=25 lines, this is the default /28=28 lines, use with VGA /43=43 lines, use with EGA or VGA /50=50 lines, use with VGA /60=60 lines, use with VGA and Video7
/ video	Display list of valid video screen switches.

/IN.	Run MSAV using a color cheme.
/BW	Run MSAV in black-and-white mode.
/mono	Run MSAV in monochrome mode.
/LCD.	Run MSAV in LCD mode.
/FF	Run MSAV in fast screen mode for CGA monitors. Screen quality is worse.
/BF.	Use computer BIOS to display video.
/NF.	Disable use of alternate screen fonts.
/BT.	Enable graphics mouse in Windows.
/NGM	Use default mouse character instead of the graphics character.
/LE	Switch left and right mouse buttons.
/PS2	Reset mouse if the mouse cursor locks up or disappears.

Command Type and Version:

External command; Network; Introduced with Ver 6.0

Notes:

1. MSAV is actually Central Point Software's Anti-Virus program which has been licensed to Microsoft.

Microsofts menu driven program to backup and restore one or more files from one disk to another disk : This program is a replacement for BACKUP and RESTORE used in previous DOS versions.

Syntax (shaded is optional):

MSBACKUP setup_file /BW /LCD /MDA

    Examples: MSBACKUP /BW

Syntax Options:

setup_file	Predefined setup that specifies which files to backup and tye type of backup to be performed. MSBACKUP automatically creates this file if "save program settings". During the "save program" function, if no file name is specified, the file name DEFAULT.SET is used.
/BW	Run screen in black-and-white mode.
/LCD	Run screen in LCD mode.
/MDA	Run screen in monochrome mode.

Command Type and Version:

External command; Network; Introduced with Ver 6.0

Notes:

1. MSBACKUP does not support the use of tape backups.
2. Backups and catalog files are compatible between MSBACKUP and MWBACKUP.

MSCDEX

Microsofts CD-ROM Extensions : MSCDEX is used in conjunction with the CD-ROM device driver that was shipped with the drive. It is normally executed in the AUTOEXEC.BAT file.

Syntax (shaded is optional):

MSCDEX /D:driver /D:driver2 ... /E /K /S /V /L:letter /M:number

Examples: MSCDEX /D:1

Syntax Options:

/D:driver	Drive signature for the first CD-ROM drive. Typically this is MSCD000Ø. The drive signature must match that of the CD-ROM driver in CONFIG.SYS.
/D:driver2	Drive signature of the second CD-ROM drive. Typically this is MSCD0001.
/E	CD-ROM drive can use expanded memory, if available, to store sector buffers.
/K	Provide Kanji support for CD-ROM.
/S	Share CD-ROM on MS-NET network or Windows for workgroup servers.
/V	Display MSCDEX memory stats with the program starts.
/L:letter	Specifies drive letter for first CD-ROM. more than one CD-ROM, DOS assigns the subsequent drive letters.
/M:number . . .	Specifies the number of sector buffers.

Command Type and Version:

External command; Network; Introduced with Ver 6.0

Notes:

1. Do not start MSCDEX after Windows has been started.

MSD

Microsofts menu driven system diagnostics:
This program provides detailed technical information about your system.

Syntax (shaded is optional):

MSD **/I /B [/F drive:\path\filename]**
   [/P drive:\path\filename]
   [/S drive:\path\filename]

   Examples: MSD
   MSD / B / I

Syntax Options:

/I . . . . Forces MSD to not initially detect hardware when it starts. This may be necessary if MSD is not running properly or locks up.

/B . . . . Run MSD in black-and-white mode.

drive:\path . . . . Drive and path where a MSD report file is to be written.

/F *drive:\path\filename*. . Prompts for a company, address, & phone to be written on the MSD report named *filename*.

/P *drive:\path\filename*. . Writes a complete MSD report to a file named *filename*.

/S *drive:\path\filename*. . Writes a summary MSD report to a file named *filename*.

Command Type and Version:

External command; Network; Introduced with Ver 6.0

Notes:

1. MSD has shipped with Windows for quite some time and is an excellent diagnostics tool.

MSHERC

Installs support for Qbasic graphics programs using the Herculese graphics card :

Syntax (shaded is optional):

MSHERC / half

    Examples: MSHERC / half

Syntax Options:

/ half. . . . . Use this switch if a color adapter card is also installed in the system.

Command Type and Version:

External command; Network; Introduced with Ver ?

Notes:

NLSFUNC

**National language support function, which
loads country-specific information and codepage switching:** Use NLSFUNC from either the
command line or through **CONFIG.SYS.**

Syntax (shaded is optional):

At the DOS prompt:
  NLSFUNC `Drive:\Path\ Filename`
If loaded through CONFIG.SYS:
INSTALL= `Drive1:\Path1\` NLSFUNC.EXE
  `country`

      Examples: NLSFUNC C:\Bin\Newcode.sys

Syntax Options:

Drive:\Path....	Drive and directory containing *Filename.*
Filename	File containing country-specific information.
Drive1:\Path1..	Drive and directory containing NSLFUNC.
country.......	Same as *Filename.*

Command Type and Version:

External command; Network; Introduced with Ver 3.3

Notes:

1. The COUNTRY command in CONFIG.SYS defines the default
   value for Drive:\Path \Filename. If there is no COUNTRY
   command in CONFIG.SYS, NLSFUNC looks for COUNTRY.SYS
   in the root directory of the start up drive.

2. See also CHCP and MODE.

Command line to set the NUM LOCK key to ON or OFF for the DOS startup menu in the CONFIG.SYS file: The startup menu is a list of system configuration choices that appear when your system is started. Each menu item is a set of CONFIG.SYS commands and is called a "configuration block". See your DOS manual for details of setting up and using the startup menu.g: Use NLSFUNC from either the command line or through **CONFIG.SYS**.

Syntax (shaded is optional):

NUMLOCK = **ON or OFF**

Examples: NUMLOCK = ON

Syntax Options:

ON. . . . . Turns NUM LOCK key on.
OFF. . . . . Turns NUM LOCK key off.

Command Type and Version:

CONFIG.SYS command; Network; Introduced with Ver 6.0

Notes:

1. See also MENUDEFAULT, MENUITEM, MENUCOLOR, INCLUDE and SUBMENU. All are used by the startup menu.

PATH

Sets a directory search path: DOS uses the path command to search for executable files in specified directories. The default is the current working directory.

Syntax (shaded is optional):

PATH `Drive1: \Path1; Drive2: \Path2;...`

Examples: PATH C:\ ;D:\ ;D:\Dos;D:\Utility\test
PATH   (displays the current search path)
PATH ;   (clears search-path settings other than default setting (current directory).

Syntax Options:

Drive1: Drive2: Specifies drive letters to be included in the search path

\Path1 \Path 2. Specifies directory (s) in the search path where DOS should look for files.

; .... Must be used to separate multiple *Drive:\Path* locations or if used as *Path ;* it clears search-path settings other than the default setting.

Command Type and Version:

Internal command; Network; Introduced with Ver 2.0

Notes:

1. The maximum number of characters allowed in the PATH statement is 127. See SUBST for ways to get around this limit. Also see the SET Path statement.

2. If files have the same name but different extensions, DOS searches for files in the following order: .COM, .EXE, .BAT.

3. If identical file names occur in different directories, DOS looks in the current directory first, then in locations specified in PATH in the order they are listed in the PATH statement.

4. A PATH command is usually included in the AUTOEXEC.BAT file so that it is issued at the time the system starts.

Reduces power consumption in a computer when applications and devices are idle :
This driver conforms to the Advanced Power Management (APM) specifications and is loaded through the CONFIG.SYS file.

Syntax (shaded is optional):

Device = **Drive:\Path** POWER.EXE
ADV[:MAX or REG or MIN] or STD or OFF /low

Examples: Device = POWER.EXE

Syntax Options:

Drive1\Path . . Specifies the location of POWER.EXE

ADV[:MAX or REG or MIN] . . . Conserves power when devices are idle. MAX=maximum power conservation, REG=default, balance conservation with device performance, MIN=higher device performance is needed.

STD . . . . If the computer supports APM, STD conserves power. If not supported, it turns off the power.

OFF . . . . Turns off power management.

/low . . . . Loads driver into conventional memory, even if upper memory is available. The default is load into upper memory.

Command Type and Version:

CONFIG.SYS command; Network; Introduced with Ver 6.0

Notes:

1. See also POWER.
2. If the computer does not support APM, using STD will disable the power completely.

Reduces power consumption in a computer when applications and devices are idle :
Once the POWER.EXE driver is loaded through the CONFIG.SYS file, POWER at the command line turns power on/off, reports status and sets conservation levels.

Syntax (shaded is optional):

POWER
   ADV[:MAX or REG or MIN] or STD or OFF

   Examples: POWER (displays current settings)
              POWER OFF

Syntax Options:

ADV[:MAX or REG or MIN] . . . Conserves power when devices are idle. MAX=maximum power conservation, REG=default, balance conservation with device performance, MIN=higher device performance is needed.

STD . . . . If the computer supports APM, STD conserves power. If not supported, it turns off the power.

OFF . . . . Turns off power management.

Command Type and Version:

CONFIG.SYS and External command;
Network; Introduced with Ver 6.0

Notes:

1. See also POWER.EXE.
2. If the computer does not support APM, using STD will disable the power completely.

PAUSE

Pauses the processing of a batch file. Sus-
pends processing of a batch file and prompts the
user to press any key to continue.

Syntax (shaded is optional):

PAUSE

Examples: PAUSE

Syntax Options:

None

Command Type and Version:

Internal command; Batch; Introduced with Ver 1.0

Notes:

1. Earlier versions of PAUSE indicated that a text comment could be
   inserted after PAUSE and the message would display when
   PAUSE ran, for example "PAUSE This is a test". This message
   function is not functional.

2. Ctrl+C or Ctrl Break will stop a Batch program while running or at
   PAUSE.

PRINT

Prints a text file to a line printer, in the background. Other DOS commands can be executed at the same time PRINT is running.

Syntax (shaded is optional):

PRINT /d:device /b:size /u:ticks1 /m:ticks2
s:ticks3 /q:qsize /t
Drive:\Path\ Filename ... /c /p

Examples: PRINT C:\Test.txt /c C:\test2.txt /p
PRINT /d:Lpt1 /u:25

Syntax Options:

/d:device	Name of printer device. **Parallel Ports:** Lpt1, Lpt2, Lpt3. **Serial Ports:** com1,com2, com3, com4. PRN and Lpt1 refer to the same parallel port. Default=PRN **/d must precede Filename.**
/b:size	Sets size (in bytes) of internal buffer. Default=512, Range=512 to 16384.
/u:ticks1	Maximum number of clock ticks PRINT is to wait for a printer to become available. Default=1, Value Range=1 to 255.
/m:ticks2	Maximum number of clock ticks PRINT can take to print a character on printer. Default=2, Value Range=1 to 255.
/s:ticks3	Maximum number of clock ticks allocated for background printing. Default=8, Value Range=1 to 255.
/q:qsize	Maximum number of files allowed in the print queue. Default=10 Value Range=4 to 32.

/t	Removes files from the print queue.
/c	Removes files from the print queue. Both the /c and /p switches can be used on the same command line. When the /c **precedes** the *Filenames* on the command line, it applies to all the files that follow until PRINT comes to a /p, in which case the /p switch applies to the file preceding the /p. When the /c switch **follows** the *Filenames*, it applies to the file that precedes the /c and all files that follow until PRINT comes to a /p switch.
/p	Adds files to the print queue. Both the /c and /p switches can be used on the same command line. When the /p **precedes** the *Filenames* on the command line, it applies to all the files that follow until PRINT comes to a /c, in which case the /c switch applies to the file preceding the /c. When the /p switch **follows** the *Filenames*, it applies to the file that precedes the /p and all files that follow until PRINT comes to a /c switch.

Command Type and Version:

External command; Introduced with Ver 2.0

Notes:

1. You can use the /d,/b,/u,/m,/s and /q switches only the first time you use PRINT. DOS must be restarted to use them again.

2. Use a program's own PRINT command to print files created with that program. PRINT only functions correctly with ASCII text.

3. Each queue entry includes a drive, directory and subdirectory and must not exceed 64 characters per entry.

Installable device driver that supports code-page switching for parallel ports PRN, LPT1, LPT2, AND LPT3.

Syntax (shaded is optional):

DEVICE = `Drive:\Path\` PRINTER.SYS
LPTn = (type `, hwcp , n`)

Examples:
DEVICE=C:\Dos\PRINTER.SYS LPT1:=(4201,437,2)

Syntax Options:

Drive:\Path	Drive and directory containing PRINTER.SYS
LPT*n*	LPT1, LPT2, or LPT3
type	Type of printer in use. Valid values for *type* and the printer represented by each value are as follows:

    4201 . . . IBM Proprinters II and III M.4201
    . IBM Proprinters II and III XL M.4202
    4208 . . . IBM Proprinters X24E M.4207
    IBM Proprinters XL24E M.4208
    5202 . . . IBM Quietwriter III M.5202

hwcp	Code-page supported by your hardware. DOS supports the following code pages:

    437 . . . . United States
    850 . . . . Multilingual (Latin I)
    852 . . . . Slavic (Latin II)
    860 . . . . Portuguese
    863 . . . . Canadian-French
    865 . . . . Nordic

n	Number of additional code-pages.

Command Type and Version:

CONFIG.SYS command; Introduced with Ver 3.3

Notes:

None

PROMPT

Change Prompt: Customizing prompt to display text or information and change color. Example: time or date, current directory or default drive.

Syntax (shaded is optional):

PROMPT **Text $Characters**

> Examples: PROMPT pg (Most commonly used)
> If ANSI.SYS is loaded and you have a color monitor, try the following for colors at the DOS level:
> PROMPT $e[35;44;1m$pge[33;44;1m

Syntax Options:

PROMPT.....	PROMPT by itself resets to default prompt.
Text	*Text* can be any typed message.
$Characters...	Type in special characters from the table below to create special prompts.

Typed character	displayed prompt
$q	The = character
$$	The $ sign
$t	Current time
$d	Current date
$p	Current drive and path
$v	DOS version number
$n	Current drive
$g	>Greater-than symbol
$l	<Less-than symbol
$b	(l) vertical bar
$_	Enter, first position of next line
$e	ASCII escape code (code 27)
$h	Backspace (deletes a **prompts** command line character)

Command Type and Version:

Internal command; Network; Introduced with Ver 2.0

Notes:

1. See also ANSI.SYS
2. The PROMPT command is typically inserted in AUTOEXEC.BAT

Basic computer language. A program that reads instructions and interprets those instructions into executable computer code. A complete environment for programming in the Basic language is provided by the QBASIC program.

Syntax (shaded is optional):

QBASIC `/b /editor /g /h /mbf /nohi /run` `Drive:\Path \Filename`

Examples: QBASIC
QBASIC C:\Qb\Bin\Test

Syntax Options:

Drive\Path. . . .	Drive and directory containing *Filename.*
\Filename.	Name of file to load when QBASIC starts.
/b	QBASIC is displayed in black and white.
/editor.	Invokes EDIT, DOS full-screen text Editor.
/g	Fastest screen update of a CGA monitor.
/h	Displays max. number of display lines.
/mbf	Converts the resident functions MKS$, MKD$, CVS, and CVD to MKSMBF$, MKDMBF$, CVSMBF, and CVDMBF.
/nohi.	Allows use of monitor without high-intensity video support. COMPAQ laptop computers cannot use this switch.
/run	The specified BASIC program is run before being displayed.

Command Type and Version:

External command; Network; Introduced with Ver 5.0

Notes:

1. QBASIC.EXE must be in the current directory, search path, or in same directory as EDIT.COM in order to use the DOS Editor.
2. Consecutive Basic programs can be run from a Batch file if the Basic system command and the /run switch is used.
3. If GW-BASIC programs need to be converted to QBASIC, read REMLINE.BAS in QBASIC's subdirectory.
4. If a monitor does not support shortcut keys, use */b* and */nohi*.

RAMDRIVE.SYS or VDISK.SYS

Creates a simulated hard disk from the systems RAM memory: RAM disks are much faster than hard disks but they are temporary (if the system shuts down, the data is lost).

Syntax (shaded is optional):

Device=Drive:\Path\ RAMDRIVE.SYS `disksize` `sectorsize numentry /e /a`

Examples:
    Device=C:\Dos\RAMDRIVE.SYS 4096 / a

Syntax Options:

Drive:\Path . . .	Drive and directory containing RAMDRIVE.SYS
disksize	Sets size of RAM disk in kilobytes. Valid sizes range from 16 to 4096. Default=64
sectorsize	Sets sector size in bytes. Valid sizes are 128, 256, and 512. Default=512. Do not change default if possible.
numentry	Sets the number of files and directories that the RAM disk's root directory can hold. Default=64, range=2 to 1024. If this parameter is used, *disksize* and *sectorsize* must also be set.
/e	RAM disk uses extended memory. Default= uses conventional memory
/a	RAM disk uses expanded memory. Default= uses conventional memory

Command Type and Version:

CONFIG.SYS command; Introduced with Ver 3.1(Vdisk=3.0)

Notes:

1. Multiple RAM disks are allowed.
2. Always try to use /e or /a so that conventional RAM is not used.
3. A memory manager like HIMEM.SYS must be used if /e is used.
4. An expanded memory manager must be installed if /a is used.

RD or RMDIR

Removes a directory. You cannot delete a directory without first deleting its files and subdirectories. The directory must be empty except for the "." and ".." symbols which represent the directory itself and the parent directory. RD and RMDIR are equivalent commands.

Syntax (shaded is optional):

RD Drive: \Path

      Examples: RD \Data
                  RD \Data\Smith

Syntax Options:

Drive . . . . Drive containing *Path*.
\Path . . . . Directory to be deleted.

Command Type and Version:

Internal command; Network; Introduced with Ver 2.0

Notes:

1. Use DIR to list hidden and system files and ATTRIB to remove hidden and system file attributes in order to empty directory.

2. When a backslash (\) is used before the first directory name in *Path*, DOS treats the directory as a subdirectory of the root directory. Omit the backslash (\) before the first directory name and DOS treats the directory as a subdirectory of the current directory.

3. The directory being deleted cannot be the current directory and must be used on an empty directory.

Recovers readable information from a disk containing bad sectors: When CHKDSK reports bad sectors on a disk, use the RECOVER command to read a file, sector by sector, and recover data from the good sectors.

Syntax (shaded is optional):

RECOVER **Drive:\Path** Filename

Examples: RECOVER A:

Syntax Options:

Drive:\Path ... Drive and directory containing *Filename*.

\Filename .... *Filename* to be recovered. If no *Filename* or *Path* is specified, the entire drive is recovered.

Command Type and Version:

External command; Introduced with Ver 2.0
Removed from Ver 6.0, deemed to dangerous.

Notes:

1. Wildcards (* and ?) cannot be used with the RECOVER command.

2. When an entire disk is recovered, each file is placed in the root directory in a FILEnnnn.REC file. The 4 digit numbering sequence on each recovered file is as follows: FILE0001.REC, FILE0002, etc.

3. Since all data in bad sectors is lost when you recover a file, it is best to recover files one at a time, allowing you to edit each file and re-enter missing information.

4. If a drive was formed by the ASSIGN, JOIN or SUBST command, the RECOVER command will not work. It will not work with the BACKUP or RESTORE command since you must use RESTORE with backup files that you created with the BACKUP command.

5. RECOVER cannot recover files on a network drive.

6. If an entire drive is recovered, it is possible that some files will be lost, since the recovered files are written to the root directory and a limited number of files will fit in the root directory.

7. See also CHKDSK

REM

Allows use of remarks (comments) in a Batch file or in CONFIG.SYS. : Any BATCH command or CONFIG.SYS line beginning with REM is ignored by DOS.

Syntax (shaded is optional):

REM **Comment**

> Examples: REM begin files here

Syntax Options:

Comment. . . . . Line of text that you want to include as a comment.

Command Type and Version:

Internal command;

Batch command; Introduced with Ver 1.0

CONFIG.SYS command; Introduced with Ver 4.0

Notes:

1. ECHO ON must be used in the Batch or CONFIG.SYS file for a comment to be displayed.
2. REM can be used without a comment to add vertical spacing to a Batch file, but you can also use blank lines. Blank lines are ignored by DOS.
3. Do not use redirection characters (>or <) or pipe (l) in a Batch file comment.
4. a ";" can be used in place of REM in the WIN.INI file.

REN or RENAME

Renames a file(s): Changes the name(s) on all files matching a specified Filename. REN and RE-NAME are equivalent commands.

Syntax (shaded is optional):

REN `Drive:\Path\` Filename1 Filename2

Examples: REN C:\ data*.dbf *.db2

Syntax Options:

Drive:\Path . . . Drive and directory containing *Filename*.

Filename1 . . . . File(s) to be renamed.

Filename2 . . . . New name for file(s). You cannot rename Drive or Path.

Command Type and Version:

Internal command; Network; Introduced with Ver 1.0

Notes:

1. The use of Wildcards (* and ?) are allowed.
2. You cannot duplicate a *Filename*.
3. See also LABEL, COPY and XCOPY.

REPLACE

Replaces files in the target drive with files from the source drive when the filenames are the same: If same name files are not on the target drive, the new files will be added to the target drive.

Syntax (shaded is optional):

REPLACE **Source:\ Path** Filename
Target\Path2 /a /p /r /w

REPLACE **Source:** Filename
Target:\Path2 /p /r /s /w /u

Examples: REPLACE A:*.* C:\Test /a /s

Syntax Options:

Source:\Path1 .	Source drive and directory containing *Filename*.
Filename	Name of source file.
Target:\Path2 . .	Location of the destination file(s).
/a	Adds, instead of replacing, new files to the destination file. This switch **cannot** be used with */s* or */u*.
/p	Prompts for confirmation before adding a source file or replacing the destination file.
/r	Replaces read-only and unprotected files.
/s	Searches subdirectories of the destination directory and replaces matching files with the source file. The */s* switch **cannot** be used with */a*.
/w	Waits for a disk to be inserted before REPLACE starts copying. If */w* is not specified, REPLACE begins immediately.
/u	Updates or replaces files in the destination directory that are older than files in the source directory.

Command Type and Version:

External command; Network; Introduced with Ver 3.2

Notes:

1. REPLACE issues a message concerning the number of files that have been added or replaced when the operation is complete.

2. Use /w if you need to change disks during REPLACE.

3. REPLACE does not function on system or hidden files.

4. REPLACE returns the following exit codes: (see IF errorlevel)

```
0 . . . . . . . Files successfully added or replaced
2 . . . . . . . Source files could not be found
3 . . . . . . . Source or destination path could not be found
5 . . . . . . . User does not have access to files being replaced
8 . . . . . . . Insufficient system memory to complete command
11 . . . . . . Wrong command line syntax
```

RESTORE

Restores files that were backed up using the BACKUP command: The "backed up" and "restored to" disk types do not have to be identical. In Ver 6.0, RESTORE will only restore backups made with previous versions of DOS. It will **NOT** restore backups made with the Ver 6.0 MSBACKUP program!

Syntax (shaded is optional):

RESTORE Drive1: Drive2: \Path\ Filename /s /p /b:date /a:date /e:time /L:time /m /n /d

> Examples: RESTORE A: C:*.* /s
> RESTORE B: D:\Data*.dbf /s / m

Syntax Options:

Drive1:	Drive on which backed-up files are stored.
Drive2\Path. . .	Drive and directory to which backed-up files will be restored.
Filename	Name(s) of backed-up file(s) to be restored.
/s	Restores all subdirectories.
/p	Prompts for permission to restore files that are read-only or files that have changed since last backup.
/b:*date*	Restores files changed or modified on or before a specified *date*.
/a :*date*	Restores files changed or modified on or after a specified *date*.
/e:*time*	Restores files changed or modified at or earlier than a specified *time*.
/L :*time*	Restores files changed or modified at or later than a specified *time*.
/m	Restores only files changed or modified since the last backup.
/n	Restores files that no longer exist on the destination disk. (Drive2)

/d ... **5** .... Without restoring, */d* displays a list of files on the backup disk that match names specified in *Filename*.

Command Type and Version:

External command; Network; Introduced with Ver 2.0

Notes:

1. RESTORE does not restore the system files (IO.SYS and MSDOS.SYS or IBMBIO.COM and IBMDOS.COM).

2. RESTORE will not function on drives that have been redirected with ASSIGN, JOIN, or SUBST.

3. MS-DOS RESTORE Version 5.0 will restore backups made with all previous versions of BACKUP.

4. RESTORE returns the following exit codes: (see IF errorlevel)

    0 . . . . . . Files successfully restored
    1 . . . . . . Files to be restored could not be found
    3 . . . . . . RESTORE stopped by user Ctrl+C
    4 . . . . . . RESTORE ended in error.

5. BACKUP is not included in DOS Ver 6.0, see the MSBACKUP utility program.

SELECT

Installs DOS on a new disk along with country specific information such as time and date formats and collating sequences. Select also formats the target disk, creates CONFIG.SYS and AUTOEXEC.BAT on a new disk and copies the source disk to the target disk.

Syntax (shaded is optional):

SELECT Source Target\Path yyy xx

Examples: SELECT B: A: 045 dk

Syntax Options:

Source	Drive containing Information to be copied.
Target	Drive containing disk onto which DOS is to be copied.
\Path	Name of directory containing information to be copied.
yyy	Country code. See COUNTRY Command.
nn.	Keyboard code. See KEYB Command.

Command Type and Version:

External command; Introduced with Ver 3.0

Notes:

1. WARNING: SELECT is used to install DOS for the first time. Everything on the *target* disk is erased. SELECT is not available for use on Version 5.0 and should be used with caution in earlier versions.

2. The *Source Drive* can be either Drive A: or Drive B:.

3. If a hard disk is used in the Target Drive, DOS will prompt for the correct internal label for that disk. If the wrong label is typed in, SELECT ends.

Sets, removes or displays environment variables: SET is normally used in the AUTOEXEC.BAT file to set environment variables when the system starts.   With DOS Ver 6.0, SET can be used in CONFIG.SYS. ❻

Syntax (shaded is optional):

SET `variable = string`

    Examples:
    SET   (displays current environment settings)
    SET TEMP=E:\Windows\Temp
    SET variable =
        (above clears *string* associated with *variable*)

Syntax Options:

variable . . . . . .   The *variable* to be set or modified.
string . . . .   Text *string* to be associated with
                variable.

Command Type and Version:

    Internal command; Network; Introduced with Ver 2.0

Notes:

1. If SET is used to define values for both *variable* and *string*, DOS adds *variable* to the environment and associates *string* with it. If *variable* already existed, the new *variable* replaces the old one.
2. In a Batch file, SET can be used to create variable that can be used in the same way as %1 through %9. In order to use the new variable, it must be enclosed with %, e.g. %variable%
3. The SET command uses memory from the environment space. If the environment space is too small, DOS will issue the error message "Out of Environment Space". See the SHELL command and COMMAND.COM for ways to increase environment space.
4. See also PATH, PROMPT, SHELL and DIR for additional information on environment variables.

*Sets the DOS version number that is reported
to a program by MS-DOS® 5.0:* If a program will
not run under Ver 5.0 and issues the error "Incorrect DOS Version", adding the program to the
SETVER file may allow the program to run.

Syntax (shaded is optional):

To initially load the SETVER table in CONFIG.SYS
　Device = `Drive:\Path\` SETVER.EXE
At DOS prompt or in Batch file:
SETVER `Drive:\Path` (Displays current table)
SETVER `Drive:\Path Filename v.vv`
SETVER `Drive:\Path Filename /delete /quiet`

　Examples:　Device=C:\DOS SETVER.EXE

　　SETVER C:\DOS　　(Displays current ver. table)
　　SETVER C:\DOS TEST.EXE 3.30
　　　(above adds TEST.EXE to the version table)
　　SETVER C:\DOS TEST.EXE /delete
　　　(above deletes TEST.EXE from the version table)

Syntax Options:

Drive:\Path. . . . .　Drive and directory containing SETVER.

Filename . . . . .　Program file to be added to version table.
　　　　　　　　　　Must be a .EXE or .COM file. Wild
　　　　　　　　　　cards are not allowed.

v.vv . . . .　The DOS version number that should be
　　　　　　　　　　reported to the program when it is run.

/delete . . . .　Delete the version table entry for the
　　　　　　　　　　Filename program.

/quiet . . . .　Hides the message normally displayed
　　　　　　　　　　during the deletion process.

Command Type and Version:

External and CONFIG.SYS command;
Network; Introduced with Ver 5.0

Notes:

1. When loaded in CONFIG.SYS, the .EXE extension with SETVER.EXE must be used.

2. In order for SETVER to function at the DOS prompt or in a Batch file, it must first be loaded through CONFIG.SYS. SETVER is automatically added to CONFIG.SYS by the MS-DOS 5.0 setup program.

3. If you set a version number for your MS-DOS 5.0 COMMAND.COM, your system may not start.

4. If changes or additions or deletions are made to the SETVER table, your system must be restarted in order for the chages to take affect.

5. If a program starts correctly after it has been added to the SETVER table, the program may still not run correctly under Ver 5.0 if a compatibility problem exists.

6. If a program is added to the SETVER table and the program name is already in the table, the new entry and version number will replace the existing entry.

7. The following SETVER exit codes can be used in conjunction with the IF errorlevel command to report completion and error codes:

   0 . . . . SETVER function completed successfully

   1 . . . . Invalid command switch.

   2 . . . . Invalid *Filename*.

   3 . . . . Insufficient system memory to complete command.

   4 . . . . Invalid version number (*v.vv*) format specified.

   5 . . . . Specified entry not currently in version table.

   6 . . . . SETVER could not find the SETVER.EXE file.

   7 . . . . Invalid drive specified.

   8 . . . . Too many command line parameters specified by user.

   9 . . . . Missing command line parameter.

   10 . . . . . . Error whie reading SETVER.EXE file.

   11 . . . . . . Corrupt SETVER.EXE file.

   12 . . . . . . Specified SETVER.EXE file does not support a version table.

   13 . . . . . . Insufficient space in version table to add a new entry.

   14 . . . . . . Error detected while writing to the SETVER.EXE file.

SHARE

Program that installs file-sharing and locking capabilities on hard disk: The share command is installed through AUTOEXEC.BAT and CONFIG.SYS and can only be seen when networking is active.

Syntax (shaded is optional):

In a Batch file or at the DOS prompt:
SHARE `/f:space /L:locks`
In CONFIG.SYS:
INSTALL= `Drive:\Path\` SHARE.EXE
`/f:space /L:locks`

Examples: SHARE / f:4096 /L:40
INSTALL=C:\Dos\SHARE.EXE

Syntax Options:

Drive:\Path. . . .	Drive and directory containing the SHARE.EXE file.
/f:space	File space allocated in bytes for the DOS storage area used to record file-sharing information. Default=2048
/L:locks	Number of files that are to be locked. Default=20

Command Type and Version:

External command; Network; Introduced with Ver 3.0

Notes:

1. In CONFIG.SYS, the .EXE extension must be included with SHARE.EXE
2. SHARE allows DOS to check and verify all read and write requests from programs.
3. The average length of a file name and its Path is 20 bytes. Use that value when calculating the */f:space* switch.
4. Beginning with Ver 5.0, SHARE is no longer required to support drive partitions >32mb.

Specifies the name and location of a command Interpreter, other than COMMAND.COM:
Include the SHELL command to CONFIG.SYS to add different Command Interpreter.

Syntax (shaded is optional):

SHELL = `Drive:\Path\` Filename `parameters`

Examples:
SHELL=C:\COMMAND.COM /e:1024 /p

Syntax Options:

Drive:Path . . . . Drive and directory containing *Filename*.

\Filename . . . . Command Interpreter to be used.

Parameters . . . Command-line parameters or switches to be used with Command Interpreter.

Command Type and Version:

CONFIG.SYS command; Introduced with Ver 2.0

Notes:

1. The SHELL command does not use or accept any switches, only the Command Interpreter uses switches .

2. The default Command Interpreter is COMMAND.COM.

3. SHELL must be used if the Command Interpreter is in a location other than the Root directory or if you need to change the environment size of COMMAND.COM.

4. **DOSSWAP** is the DOS Task Swapper and is used internally by the SHELL command. There are no switches for DOSSWAP and it should not be run from the DOS command line.

SHIFT

Allows a change in the position of replaceable command line parameters in a Batch file: Specifically, SHIFT copies the value of each replaceable parameter to the next lowest parameter (for example, %1 is copied to %0, %2 is copied to %1, etc).

Syntax (shaded is optional):

SHIFT

    Examples: SHIFT

Syntax Options:

None

Command Type and Version:

Internal command; Batch command;
Introduced with Ver 2.0

Notes:

1. Batch files, usually limited to ten parameters (%0 through %9) on the command line, can now use more than 10. This is made possible because if more than 10 parameters are used, those appearing after the 10th will be shifted one at a time into %9.

2. Once the parameters are shifted, they cannot be shifted back.

SIZER.EXE

SIZER is used only by MEMMAKER during the memory optimizing process. It is used to determine the size, in memory, of device drivers and memory resident programs. It is added automatically to AUTOEXEC.BAT or CONFIG.SYS in order to determine the memory size, and when MEMMAKER is finished, SIZER is automatically removed.

SMARTDRV.SYS

Creates a disk cache in extended or expanded memory: A disk cache can significantly increase the speed of any disk operations.

Syntax (shaded is optional):

DEVICE = **Drive:\Path** SMARTDRV.SYS
initsize   minsize   /a

Examples:
DEVICE=C:\Dos\SMARTDRV.SYS 1024 512

Syntax Options:

Drive:\Path. . . .	Drive and directory containing SMARTDRV.SYS.
initsize	Initial size of disk cache in kilobytes. Default=256; Range=128 to 8192. Size is rounded off to 16k blocks.
minsize	Minimum size of disk cache in kilobytes. Default=no minimum size. This option is important to programs such as Windows, which can reduce the cache size as required for its own use.
/a.	Specifies that the disk cache is to be set up in expanded memory. The Default places the cache in extended memory.

Command Type and Version:

CONFIG.SYS command; Introduced with Ver 4.0

Notes:

1. If no sizes are specified with SMARTDRV, then all available extended and expanded memory is allocated to the cache.
2. In order to use extended memory, HIMEM.SYS or another extended memory manager must be installed. HIMEM.SYS must precede SMARTDRV in CONFIG.SYS.
3. On 80286 / 386 / 486 systems, extended memory is probably the best choice for SMARTDRV.
4. Do not use disk compaction programs while SMARTDRV is loaded.

SORT

A filtering program that reads the input, sorts the data and then writes the results to a screen, file or another device: The SORT command alphabetizes a file, rearranges in ascending or descending order by using a collating table based on Country Code and Code Page settings.

Syntax (shaded is optional):

SORT /r /+n < Drive1:\ Path1\ Filename1 >
                 Drive2:\ Path2\ Filename2

command | SORT /r +n > Drive2:\ Path2\
                 Filename2

Examples: SORT < C:\Data\Text.txt
          DIR | SORT > C:\Sortdata.txt

Syntax Options:

Drive1:\Path1 .	Drive and directory containing *Filename*.
Filename1	File containing data to be sorted.
\Drive2:\Path2	Drive and directory containing *Filename2*.
Filename2	File in which to store sorted data.
Command	Specific command whose output is data to be sorted.
/r	Reverses sorting order: Z to A and 9 to 0.
/+n	Sorts according to character in column *n*.

Command Type and Version:

External command; Network; Introduced with Ver 2.0

Notes:

1. Use the pipe (I) or the less-than (<) to direct data through SORT from a command or filename. Before using a pipe for redirection, set the TEMP environment variable in AUTOEXEC.BAT.

2. Specify the MORE command to display information one screen at a time. You are prompted to continue after one screen is shown.

3. SORT is not case sensitive.

4. Files as large as 64K can be accommodated by SORT.

5. ASCII characters with codes higher than 127 are sorted based on the systems configuration with CONTRY.SYS.

STACKS

Supports the dynamic use of data stacks. The STACK command is used in CONFIG.SYS.

Syntax (shaded is optional):

STACKS = n,s

    Examples: STACKS = 8, 512

Syntax Options:

n. . . . . Defines the number of STACKS. Valid values for *n* are 0 and numbers in the range 8 to 64.

s. . . . . Defines STACK size in bytes. Valid values for *s* are 0 and numbers in the range 32 to 512.

Command Type and Version:

CONFIG.SYS; Introduced with Ver 3.2

Notes:

1. Default setting for the STACK command are as follows:

COMPUTER	STACKS
IBM PC, IBM PC/XT	0,0
IBM PC-PORTABLE.	0,0
OTHER	9, 128

2. When the values for *n* and *s* are specified at 0, DOS allocates no stacks. If your computer does not seem to function properly when STACKS are set to 0, return to the default values.

SUBMENU New V6.0

Command line to setup an item to display an-other set of choices for the DOS startup menu in CONFIG.SYS: The startup menu is a list of system configuration choices that appear when your system is started. Each menu item is a set of CONFIG.SYS commands and is called a "configuration block". See your DOS manual for details of setting up and using the startup menu.

Syntax (shaded is optional):

SUBMENU = blockname , menutext

Examples: SUBMENU = NET, Network Choices

Syntax Options:

blockname . . . . Sets the name of the associated menu block. The menu block must be defined somewhere else in the CONFIG.SYS file and can contain other menu definition commands. *Blockname* can be up to 70 characters but without spaces, backslashes, forward slashes, commas, semicolons, equal signs and square brackets.

, menutext . . . . Text to be displayed for the menu item. If no text is defined, DOS displays the *blockname* as the menu item. menutext can be up to 70 characters long.

Command Type and Version:

CONFIG.SYS command; Network; Introduced with Ver 6.0

Notes:

1. See also MENUCOLOR, MENUITEM, NUMLOCK, INCLUDE and MENUDEFAULT. All are used by the startup menu.

Substitutes a path with a drive letter: The SUBST command lets you use a drive letter (also known as a virtual drive) in commands as though it represents a physical drive.

Syntax (shaded is optional):

SUBST (Lists the virtual drives in effect)

SUBST **Drive1: Drive2:\ Path**

SUBST Drive1: /d (deletes virtual drive)

    Examples: SUBST
                  SUBST R: B: \Data\Text.txt

Syntax Options:

Drive1:	Virtual drive to which a path is assigned.
Drive2:	Physical drive that contains the specified path.
\Path	Path to be assigned to the virtual drive named *Drive1:*
/d	Deletes the *Drive1:* virtual drive.

Command Type and Version:

External command; Introduced with Ver 3.1

Notes:

1. Commands that do not work on drives where SUBST has been used are as follows:

ASSIGN	DISKCOPY	MIRROR
BACKUP	FDISK	RECOVER
CHKDSK	FORMAT	RESTORE
DISKCOMP	LABEL	SYS

2. A virtual drive letter must be included in the LASTDRIVE command in CONFIG.SYS.

3. Use SUBST rather than ASSIGN to ensure compatibility with future DOS versions.

2. If using drive letters higher than E, the LASTDRIVE command must also be used.

Forces enhanced keyboard to function like a conventional keyboard: This command is used in the CONFIG.SYS file.

Syntax (shaded is optional):

SWITCHES = /W /K /N /F

Examples: SWITCHES = / k

Syntax Options:

/W	If Windows 3.0 is used in enhance mode and you have moved the WINA20.386 file, use this switch to tell DOS that the file has been moved.
/K	Ignores extended keys on 101-key keyboards.
/N	Disables the F5 and F8 keys so that you cannot bypass startup commands.
/F	Skips the 2 second system delay after "Starting MS-DOS . . ." is displayed during startup.

Command Type and Version:

CONFIG.SYS command; Introduced with Ver 5.0

Notes:

1. Use the switches command when there is a program that does not properly interpret input from an enhanced keyboard. This command enables the enhanced keyboard to use conventional keyboard functions.

2. If SWITCHES=/k is used in a system that uses ANSI.SYS, be sure to also use the /k switch on the ANSI.SYS command.

SYS

*Copies the DOS system files (IO.SYS and
MSDOS.SYS on MS-DOS systems or
IBMBIO.COM and IBMDOS.COM on PC-DOS
systems) and the Command Interpreter from
one disk drive to another disk drive.*

Syntax (shaded is optional):

SYS `Drive1:\Path` Drive2

> Examples: SYS A: (current drive to drive A:)
> SYS D:\ A: (copy from disk in D: to A:)

Syntax Options:

Drive1:\Path. . . Drive and directory where system files
are located. If a path is not specified,
DOS searches the root directory. If a
drive is not specified, DOS uses the current drive as the system files source
drive.

Drive2:. . . . . . . Drive to which system files are to be
copied. These files can be copied
to a root directory only.

Command Type and Version:

External command; Introduced with Ver 1.0

Notes:

1. The order in which the SYS command files are copied are as
   follows: IO:SYS, MSDOS.SYS and COMMAND.COM.

2. The two system files no longer need to be "contiguous" in Ver 5.0.
   In simple terms, this means that pre DOS 3.3 disks do not need
   to be reformatted in order to install the Ver 5.0 operating system.

3. The SYS command will not work on drives redirected by
   ASSIGN, JOIN or SUBST.

4. The SYS command does not work on Network drives.

5. See also DISKCOPY, which duplicated disks of the same size
   (including transfer of the operating system). See also COPY
   and XCOPY for information on copying all files except system and
   hidden files.

❻ 6. With **DOS 6.0**, DBLSPACE.BIN is also copied to the target drive.

TIME

Enter or change current system time: DOS uses the internal clock to update the directory with date and time when a file is created or changed.

Syntax (shaded is optional):

TIME **Hours: Minutes: Seconds: Hundredths**

> Examples: TIME
> TIME 13:45 or TIME 1:45 p
> TIME 11:28p

Syntax Options:

Hours: . . . . Specifies the hour. One or two digit number with valid values from 0-23.

Minutes: . . . . . . Specifies the minute. One or two digit number with valid values from 0-59.

Seconds: . . . . . Specifies the seconds. One or two digit number with valid values from 0-59.

Hundredths: . . . Specifies hundredths of a second. One or two digit number with valid values from 0-99.

a or *p* . . . . When a 12 hour time format is used instead of the 24 hour format, use **a** or **p** to specify A.M. or P.M. When a valid 12 hour time is entered and a parameter is not entered, *time* uses **a** (A.M.).

Command Type and Version:

Internal command; Network; Introduced with Ver 1.0

Notes:

1. Using *time* without parameters will display the current time and prompt you for a time change.

2. Use a colon (:) to separate hours, minutes, (seconds and hundredths of a second are optional), if as defined in COUNTRY, dependent information file for the United States.

3. With all versions of DOS 3.3 and later, the TIME command will update the systems battery powered clock.

TREE

Displays the directory structure of a path on a specific drive.

Syntax (shaded is optional):

TREE `Drive:\ Path  /f /a`

> Examples: TREE (all directories and subdirectories)
> TREE \   (names of all subdirectories)
> TREE D:\ /f | MORE
> TREE D:\ / f PRN

Syntax Options:

Drive:\Path....	Drive and directory containing disk for display of directory structure.
/f	Displays file names in each directory.
/a..........	Text characters used for linking lines, instead of graphic characters. */a* is used with code pages that do not support graphic characters and to send output to printers that do not properly interpret graphic characters.

Command Type and Version:

External command; Network; Introduced with Ver 2.0

Notes:

1. The path structure displayed by the TREE command will depend upon the specified parameters on the command line.
2. See also DIR
3. The TREE command in MS-DOS 5.0 has been greatly enhanced.

TYPE

Screen display of a text file's contents: The
TYPE command is used to view a text file without
modifying it.

Syntax (shaded is optional):

TYPE **Drive:\ Path**

Examples: TYPE C:\Act\Receivbl.dat
TYPE C:\Act\Receivbl.dat | MORE

Syntax Options:

Drive:\Path . . . Drive and directory containing Filename.
\Filename . . . . Name of text file to be viewed.

Command Type and Version:

Internal command; Network; Introduced with Ver 1.0

Notes:

1. Avoid using the TYPE command to display binary files or files
   created using a program as you may see strange characters on
   the screen which represent control codes used in binary files.
2. Use DIR to find the name of a file and EDLIN or EDIT to change
   its contents.
3. When using the pipe (|) for redirection, set the TEMP environ-
   ment variable in AUTOEXEC.BAT.
4. See also DIR and MORE.

Recovers files that have been deleted with the DEL command: UNDELETE is the DOS version and MWUNDEL is the Windows version.

Syntax (shaded is optional):

UNDELETE **Drive:\Path** Filename **/List or /all /purge:drive /status /load [/dos or /dt or /ds] /sentry:drive /tracker:driveentries /U**

    Examples: UNDELETE /all
                  UNDELETE C:\Data*.*

Syntax Options:

Drive:\Path. . . . Drive and directory containing *Filename*.

Filename . . . . . File to be undeleted. By default, all files in the current directory will be undeleted. Wild cards * and ? are allowed.

/List. . . . . Lists all deleted files the *Drive:\Path* that can be undeleted, but does not undelete them.

/all. . . . . Recovers all deleted files without a confirmation prompt. If the deletion tracking file is present, it is used, otherwise deleted file information is taken from the DOS directory. See Note: 3.

/purge:drive. **❻** Deletes all files in the sentry directory on the specified *drive*.

/status. . **❻**. . . Displays the current UNDELETE protection level that is enabled.

/load . . . **❻**. . . Load UNDELETE as memory resident, in order to track deleted files.

/U . . . . . **❻**. . . Unload the resident portion of the UNDELETE delete tracker.

/dos. . . . . Causes UNDELETE to ignore the deletion tracking file and recover only those files listed as deleted by DOS. A confirmation prompt occurs with each undelete.

/ dt	Causes UNDELETE to ignore the files listed as deleted by DOS and only recover those files listed in the deletion tracking file. A confirmation prompt occurs with each undelete.
/ ds . . . **⑥**	UNDELETE only the files in the /Sentry directory.
/ Sentry:drive . . **⑥**	Specify the drive to be used for delete sentry files.
/ Tracker:drive-entries . . . **⑥**	Specify the drive to track deleted files on. The maximum number of deleted files to track can range from 1 to 999.

Command Type and Version:

External command; Introduced with Ver 5.0

Notes:

1. For best results, use MIRROR and the deletion tracking system.

2. When a file is recovered, it is assigned a # for the first character of its name, if a duplicate exists, another letter is selected, in order from the following list, until a unique filename is possible:
   #%&–1234567890ABCDEFGHIJKLMNOPQRSTUVWXYZ

3. If a switch is not specified with UNDELETE, the deletion tracking file is automatically used. If the deletion tracking file is not present, the DOS directory information is used. The deletion tracking system is much more accurate.

4. UNDELETE cannot undelete a directory.

5. UNDELETE cannot undelete a file if its directory has been deleted. A possible exception to this rule exists if the deleted directory was a main directory under the root directory and not a subdirectory of some other directory. If this is the case, see the UNFORMAT command. It is possible the directory and file can be saved. Use extreme caution with UNFORMAT and understand exactly what you are doing!!! If not used correctly, UNFORMAT can loose data and you might be worse off than when you started!

6. UNDELETE may not be able to recover a deleted file if data of any kind has been written to the disk since the file was deleted. If you accidentally delete a file, stop what you are doing immediately and run the UNDELETE program.

7. Some MIRROR command from DOS 5.0 are included in the DOS 6.0 UNDELETE command.

7. See also the UNFORMAT command.

Restores a disk that has been reformatted or restructured by the RECOVER command:
UNFORMAT can also rebuild disk partition tables that have been corrupted. Do not use UNFORMAT on a network drive.

Syntax (shaded is optional):

UNFORMAT Drive: **/ J**
UNFORMAT Drive: **/ U / L / test / P**
UNFORMAT **/partn / L**

Examples: UNFORMAT C: / J
UNFORMAT A: / test

Syntax Options:

Drive:	Drive containing disk to be unformatted.
/ J. Removed V6.0	Check the file created by MIRROR for use with UNFORMAT to make sure it agrees with the system information. Use this switch only by itself.
/ U Removed V6.0	UNFORMAT a disk without using the MIRROR file.
/L	If */partn* is not used, */L* lists every file and directory found by UNFORMAT. Use if the MIRROR file is to be ignored. If */partn* is used also, */L* displays the complete partition table of the drive. Standard 512 byte sectors are assumed when the partition table size is displayed.
/ test.	Displays how UNFORMAT would rebuild information on the disk, but it does NOT unformat the disk. Use this switch only if you want UNFORMAT to ignore the MIRROR file.
/ P	Outputs messages to the LPT1 printer.

/ *partn* . . . . Rebuilds and restores a corrupted partition table of a hard drive. This switch will only work if MIRROR was run previously and the PARTNSAV.FIL file is available to UNFORMAT.

Command Type and Version:

External command; Introduced with Ver 5.0

Notes:

1. Although UNFORMAT is a very powerful tool, it can also do a lot of damage if not used correctly. BE CAREFUL!

2. UNFORMAT normally restores a disk based on MIRROR information. If disk information has changed since MIRROR was run, UNFORMAT may not be able to recover it. Use MIRROR frequently in order to assure an accurate restoration of the disk.

3. If FORMAT with its /u switch was used, UNFORMAT cannot restore the disk.

4. Per Microsofts Ver 5.0 User's Guide: "The only case in which you would want to use a prior mirror file is the following: you use the MIRROR command, then the disk is corrupted, then you use the FORMAT command. If you use the MIRROR command and the FORMAT command after the disk is corrupted, the UNFORMAT command will not work. UNFORMAT searches the disk for the MIRROR file. Because UNFORMAT searches the disk directly, the disk does not have to be "readable" by MS-DOS for UNFORMAT to work. Do not use the FDISK command before using UNFORMAT; doing so can destroy information not saved by the MIRROR program."

5. If UNFORMAT does not use the MIRROR file, the restore will take much longer and be less reliable.

6. Without a MIRROR file, UNFORMAT cannot recover a file that is fragmented. It will recover what it can, then prompt for truncation of the file or delete the file.

7. If DOS displays the message "Invalid drive specification", the problem might be a corrupted disk partition table, which UNFORMAT can probably repair. In order to recover the disk partition table, the MIRROR file must be available.

8. When the /partn switch is used, you are prompted to insert a system disk in drive A: and press ENTER to restart. The restart will allow DOS to read the new partition table data. Once the system has been restarted, use UNFORMAT without the /partn switch to recover directories and the FAT (file allocation table).

9. See also UNDELETE, MIRROR, FORMAT, and FDISK.

VER

Displays DOS version number. Type **ver** and the version number will display on the screen.

Syntax (shaded is optional):

VER ⬛**/R**

> Examples: VER

Syntax Options:

/R ... **❻** ..... Provides a more detailed report.

Command Type and Version:

Internal command; Network; Introduced with Ver 2.0

Notes:
None

VERIFY

Disk verification: Verifies that the files are written correctly to a disk.

Syntax (shaded is optional):

VERIFY **on / off**

    Examples: VERIFY on

Syntax Options:

Verify . . . .   **Verify** without an option will state whether verification is turned on or off.

on . . . .   Forces DOS to confirm that information is being written correctly. The verify command will function until the system is rebooted or **verify off** is used.

off . . . .   Turns verification off once it is on.

Command Type and Version:

Internal command; Network; Introduced with Ver 2.0

Notes:

1. When the VERIFY command is used, DOS verifies data as it is written to a disk. This will slow writing speed slightly.

2. COPY / V or XCOPY / V can also be used to verify that files are being copied correctly but on a case by case basis.

3. Verify does not perform a physical disk to disk comparison.

VOL

Displays disk Volume label: The VOL command displays the name of volume label given to a disk when it was formatted. DOS Version 4.0 and greater will also display a volume serial number.

Syntax (shaded is optional):

VOL **Drive:**

> Examples: VOL A:
> VOL

Syntax Options:

VOL . . . . VOL, without options, displays the volume label and volume serial number of the disk in current drive.

Drive: . . . . Specifies the drive that contains the disk whose label is to be displayed.

Command Type and Version:

Internal command; Network; Introduced with Ver 2.0
Volume serial numbers introduced with DOS Ver 4.0

Notes:

1. See also FORMAT and LABEL.

*Continuously monitors a system for viruses
and displays a warning if it finds one.*

VSAFE is a memory resident program that uses
approximately 22k of memory. See Windows
Note below.

Syntax (shaded is optional):

VSAFE **/option + or - /NE /NX /A# /C# /N
/D /U**

Example: VSAFE / 2+ /NE /AV

Syntax Options:

/ option + or - .. Specifies how VSAFE looks for viruses.
The + or - is used to either turn on or
turn off the option. Options are as follows:

1 - Warn of a formatting request. Default=On

2 - Warn if a program tries to stay resident. Default=Off

3 - Disable all disk writes. Default=Off

4 - Check executable files that DOS opens. Default=On

5 - Check for boot sector viruses. Default=On

6 - Warns if a program tries to write to the boot sector or
partition table of a hard disk. Default=On

7 - Warns if a program tries to write to the boot sector of
a floppy disk. Default=Off

8 - Warns if an attempt is made to modify an executable
file. Default=Off

/ NE . . . . Prevents VSAFE from loading into
expanded memory.

/ NX . . . . Prevents VSAFE from loading into
extended memory.

/ A# . . . . Sets the VSAFE hot key as Alt plus the
key specified by #.

/ C# . . . . Sets the VSAFE hot key as Ctrl plus the
key specified by #.

/N .... Enable network drive monitoring.

/D .... Disable CRC checksumming.

/U .... Unloads VSAFE from memory.

Command Type and Version:

External command; Network; Introduced with Ver 6.0

Notes:

1. If VSAFE is to be used when Windows 3.1 is running, you must include " load=MWAVTSR.EXE" in the WIN.INI file.

The WINA20.386 file must be located in the root directory in order for Microsoft Windows Ver. 3.0 to run in enhanced mode. It is automatically placed in the root directory by Windows during the installation process.

If the file is not in the root directory, you will receive the message "You must have the file WINA20.386 in the root of your boot drive to run Windows in Enhanced Mode."

WINA20.386 must remain in the root directory unless the SWITCHES /W command is used to tell DOS that it has been moved. You must also add a DEVICE command under the [386Enh] section of your Windows SYSTEM.INI file, which specifies where WINA20.386 is now located.

Command Type and Version:

External Windows command; Introduced with Ver ?

XCOPY

Copies file, directories, and subdirectories from one location to another location. XCOPY will not copy system or hidden files.

Syntax (shaded is optional):

XCOPY Source **Destination /a /m /d:date /p /s /e /v /w**

   Examples: XCOPY C:\Dos*.* D:\Dos2\ /s

Syntax Options:

Source	Location and names of files to be copied.
Destination	Destination of the files to be copied.
/a	Copies *Source* files that have their archive file attributes set **without** modifying it.
/m	Copies *Source* files that have their archive file attributes set and turns them off.
/d:date	Copies *Source* files that have been modified on or after a specific date.
/p	Prompts whether you want to create each destination file.
/s	Copies directories and subdirectories, unless they are empty.
/e	Copies subdirectories even if empty.
/v	Verifies each file, as it is written, to confirm that the destination and source files are identical.
/w	Displays "Press any key to begin copying file (s)", and waits for response before starting to copy files.

Command Type and Version:

External command; Network; Introduced with Ver 3.2

XCOPY (cont.)

Notes:

1. The default *Destination* is the current directory.

2. If the *Destination* subdirectory does not end with a " \ ", DOS will prompt you to find out if the subdirectory is a subdirectory or a file.

3. XCOPY will not copy system or hidden files.

4. When a file is copied to *Destination*, the archive attribute is turned on, regardless of the file attribute in *Source*.

5. In order to copy between disks that are different formats, use XCOPY, not DISKCOPY, but remember that XCOPY does not copy the hidden or system files.

6. XCOPY exit codes are as follows: (see IF errorlevel)

0	Files copied successfully
1	Source files not found
2	XCOPY stopped by user Ctrl+C
4	a. Initialization error
	b. not enough disk space
	c. insufficient memory available
	d. invalid drive name
	e. invalid syntax was used.
5	Disk write error occurred.

7. When a files size is larger than 64k, use XCOPY instead of the COPY command.

XMA2EMS.SYS

Device driver that supports LIM 4.0 expanded memory under MS-DOS® 4.0. This driver will only work on those systems that have an IBM 2MB Expanded Memory Adapter, PS2 80286 Expanded Memory Adapter/A, or PS2 80286 Memory Expansion Option.

Syntax (shaded is optional):

Device = Drive:\Path\ XMA2EMS.SYS Pn=mm
　　　　Frame=xx P254=yy P255=zz /x:n

　　Examples:
　　Device=C:\XMA2EMS.SYS Frame=D000
　　　　　　P254=C000 P255=C400 /x:4

Syntax Options:

Drive:\Path. . . .	Drive and directory containing XMA2EMS.
P*n=mm*	Addresses for Pages P0, P1, P2, and P3. All 4 must be used.
Frame=*xx*	xx is the address of the Page Frame, for example D000, that is a single 64k contiguous block of memory.
P254=*yy*	Address, *yy* and *zz*, for a Fixed length 16k block of memory that represent pages.
P255=*zz*	P254 and P255 are reserved for DOS. Example: if P254 is specified, FAS-TOPEN can run in expanded memory if /x is specified.
/x:*n*.	Sets the minimum number of 16k pages. /x:4 = four 16k pages.

Command Type and Version:

CONFIG.SYS command; Introduced with Ver 4.01

Notes:

1. XMA2EMS is documented in the DOS 4.01 text file README.TXT on one of the installation disks.

OPERATING SYSTEM FILES

The following files, in addition to COMMAND.COM on page 125 , are the required DOS files that contain the operating system. The four files below have attributes of "read only", "system" and "hidden" and are located in the root directory on the systems boot drive (hard drive or floppy drive).

If any of these files are deleted, the system will not start.

On MS-DOS systems, the files are named:

MSDOS.SYS and IO.SYS

On PC-DOS systems (such as IBM and Compaq) the files are named:

IBMBIO.COM and IBMDOS.COM

POCKET PCRef

Hard Drive Specifications

See page 370 for comments on the hard drive data included in this chapter and a hard drive resource list. The following are descriptions of the information contained in the hard drive tables.

1. Format Size MB . . . . Formatted drive size in megabytes.
2. Heads. . . . . Number of data heads
3. Cyl . . . . Number of cylinders
4. Sect/Trac . . . . . . Number of sectors per track, V=Variable
5. Translate . . . . . . Head-Cyl-Sector/Track Translation. *UNIV is a Universal Translation where any drive setup can be used as long as the total translated sectors is less than total drive sectors (Total drive sectors=physical heads x physical cylinders x physical sectors per track)
6. RWC . . . . Start Reduced Write Current cylinder
7. WPC. . . . . Start Write Precompensation cylinder
8. Land zone . . . . . . Safe cylinder for parking drive heads
9. Seek Time . . . . Avg. drive head access time, milliseconds
10. Interface . . . . . . Type of drive interface used
     ST412/506, ESDI, SCSI, IDE AT, IDE XT
11. Encode . . . . . . Data encoding method used on drive
     MFM, 2,7RLL, 1,7 RLL, RLL ZBR, ERLL
12. Form Factor . Physical diameter and height of drive
     5.25HH, 3.5HH, 3.5/3H, 2.5
13. Cache . . . . Read ahead cache/buffer, in k bytes
14. mtbf. . . . . Mean time between failures in hours
15. RPM . . . . Drive motor Revolutions Per Minute
16. Obs Y/N . . . . . Is the drive obsolete? Yes or No

Drive Model	Format Size MB	Head	Cyl	Sect/ Trac	Translate H/C/S	RWC/ WPC	Land Zone
ALPS AMERICA							
DR311C	106	2	2108	V		NA/NA	AUTO
DR311D	106	2	2108	V		NA/NA	AUTO
DR312C	212	4	2108	V		NA/NA	AUTO
DR312D	212	4	2108	V		NA/NA	AUTO
DRND-10A	11	2	615	17		616/616	
DRND-20A	21	4	615	17		616/616	
DRPO-20A	16	4	615	26		616/616	
DRPO-20D	16	2	615	26		616/616	
AMPEX							
PYXIS-7	6	2	320	17		132/132	
PYXIS-13	11	4	320	17		132/132	
PYXIS-20	17	6	320	17		132/132	
PYXIS-27	22	8	320	17		132/132	
AREAL TECHNOLOGY, INC							
A90	92	2	1430	62	10/715/25	NA/NA	NONE
A120	132	4	1070	63	10/535/50	NA/NA	NONE
A130	130	2	1453			---/---	
A180	183	4	1430	62	10/715/50	NA/NA	NONE
A260	260	4	1453			---/---	
BP50 (Never made)						---/---	
BP100 (Never made)						---/---	
BP200 (Never made)						---/---	
MD2050 (Never made)						---/---	
MD2060	62	2	1024	59	7/1024/17	NA/NA	NONE
MD2065	62	2	1024			---/---	
MD2080	81	2	1330	59	14/665/17	NA/NA	NONE
MD2085	86	2	1410	59	14/705/17	NA/NA	NONE
MD2100 (Never made)						---/---	
ATASI TECHNOLOGY, INC							
519	159	15	1224	17		NA/NA	
519R	244	15	1224	26		NA/NA	
638	338	15	1225	36		NA/NA	AUTO
676	676	15	1632	54		NA/NA	AUTO
738	336	15	1225	36		NA/NA	AUTO
776	668	15	1632	54		NA/NA	AUTO
3020	17	3	645	17		320/320	
3033	28	5	645	17		320/320	
3046	39	7	645	17		320/320	644
3051	43	7	704	17		---/352	703
3051+	44	7	733	17		---/368	732
3053	44	7	733	17		350/368	
3075	67	8	1024	17		1025/1025	
3085	72	8	1024	17		---/512	1023
3128	128	8	1024	26		---/---	1023
6120	1051	15	1925	71		NA/NA	AUTO
7120	1034	15	1919	71		NA/NA	AUTO
AURA ASSOCIATES							
AU43	42	2				---/---	
AU63	62	2				---/---	
AU85	85	4				---/---	
AU126	125	4				---/---	

Drive Model	Seek Time	Interface	Encode	Form Factor	cache kb	mtbf	RPM	Obsolete?
ALPS AMERICA								
DR311C	13	IDE AT	1,7 RLL	3.5 3H		150k		
DR311D	13	SCSI-2	1,7 RLL	3.5 3H		150k		
DR312C	13	IDE AT	1,7 RLL	3.5 3H		150k		
DR312D	13	SCSI-2	1,7 RLL	3.5 3H		150k		
DRND-10A	60	ST412/506	MFM	3.5 HH				
DRND-20A	60	ST412/506	MFM	3.5 HH				
DRPO-20A	60	ST412/506	2,7 RLL	3.5 HH				
DRPO-20D	60	ST412/506	2,7 RLL	3.5 HH				
AMPEX								
PYXIS-7	90	ST412/506	MFM	5.25 FH				Y
PYXIS-13	90	ST412/506	MFM	5.25 FH				Y
PYXIS-20	90	ST412/506	MFM	5.25 FH				Y
PYXIS-27	90	ST412/506	MFM	5.25 FH				Y
AREAL TECHNOLOGY, INC								
A90	15	IDE XT-AT	2,7 RLL	2.5 4H	32k	100k	2981	N
A120	15	IDE AT	2,7-1,7 RL	2.5 4H	32k	100k	2981	N
A130		IDE AT	1,7 RLL	2.5 4H		100k	2981	
A180	17	IDE XT-AT	2,7 RLL	2.5 4H	32k	100k	2981	N
A260		IDE AT	1,7 RLL	2.5 4H		100k	2981	
BP50 (Never made)								Y
BP100 (Never made)								Y
BP200 (Never made)								Y
MD2050 (Never made)								Y
MD2060	19	IDE AT	2,7 RLL	2.5 4H	32k	45k	1565	N
MD2065		IDE AT	RLL	2.5 4H		100k	2504	
MD2080	19	IDE AT	2,7 RLL	2.5 4H	32k	100k	1565	N
MD2085	19	IDE AT	2,7 RLL	2.5 4H	32k	100k	2504	N
MD2100 (Never made)								
ATASI TECHNOLOGY, INC								
519	22	ST412/506	MFM	5.25 FH		40k		
519R	22	ST412/506	2,7 RLL	5.25 FH		40k		
638	18	ESDI		5.25 FH		40k	3600	N
676	16	ESDI		5.25 FH		150k	3600	N
738	18	SCSI		5.25 FH		40k	3600	N
776	16	SCSI		5.25 FH		150k	3600	N
3020		ST412/506	MFM	5.25 FH				Y
3033	30	ST412/506	MFM	5.25 FH				
3046	30	ST412/506	MFM	5.25 FH				
3051	33	ST412/506	MFM	5.25 FH				
3051+		ST412/506	MFM	5.25 FH				
3053		ST412/506	MFM	5.25 FH				Y
3075		ST412/506	MFM	5.25 FH				Y
3085		ST412/506	MFM	5.25 FH				
3128		ST412/506	2,7 RLL	5.25 FH				
6120	14	ESDI	2,7 RLL	5.25 FH		150k	3600	N
7120	14	SCSI	2,7 RLL	5.25 FH		150k	3600	N
AURA ASSOCIATES								
AU43	17	IDE AT	1,7 RLL	1.8 4H	32k	100k	5400	
AU63	17	PCMCIA-ATA	1,7 RLL	1.8 4H	32k	100k	5400	
AU85	17	IDE AT	1,7 RLL	1.8 4H	32k	100k	5400	
AU126	17	PCMCIA-ATA	1,7 RLL	1.8 4H	32k	100k	5400	

Drive Model	Format Size MB	Head	Cyl	Sect/ Trac	Translate H/C/S	RWC/ WPC	Land Zone
BASF							
6185	23	6	440	17		220/220	
6186	15	4	440	17		220/220	
6187	8	2	440	17		220/220	
6188-R1	10	2	612	17		---/---	
6188-R3	21	4	612	17		---/---	
BRAND TECHNOLOGIES							
9121A (Never made)	107	5	1166	36		NA/NA	AUTO
9121S (Never made)	107	5	1166	36		NA/NA	AUTO
9121E (Never made)	107	5	1166	36		NA/NA	AUTO
9170E	150	7	1166	36		NA/NA	AUTO
9170A	150	7	1165	36		NA/NA	AUTO
9170S	150	7	1166	36		NA/NA	AUTO
9220E	200	9	1210	38		NA/NA	AUTO
9220A	200	9	1209	36		NA/NA	AUTO
9220S	200	9	1210	36		NA/NA	AUTO
BT8085	71	8	1024	17		NA/NA	AUTO
BT8128	109	8	1024	26		NA/NA	AUTO
BT8170E	142	8	1024	34		NA/NA	AUTO
BT8170S	142	8	1024	34		NA/NA	AUTO
BT9400A (Never made)	400	6	1800	36		NA/NA	AUTO
BT9400S (Never made)	400	6	1800	36		NA/NA	AUTO
BT9650A (Never made)	650	10	1800	36		NA/NA	AUTO
BT9650S (Never made)	650	10	1800	36		NA/NA	AUTO
BULL							
D530	25	3	987	17		988/988	
D550	43	5	987	17		988/988	
D570	60	7	987	17		988/988	
D585	71	7	1166	17		1166/1166	
C.ITOH ELECTRONICS, INC							
SEE YE-DATA							
CARDIFF							
F3053	44	5	1024	17		---/---	
F3080E	68	5	1024	26		NA/NA	
F3080S	68	5	1024	26		NA/NA	
F3127E	109	5	1024	35		NA/NA	
F3127S	109	5	1024	35		NA/NA	
CDC							
94161-151 WREN III	151	9	969	34		NA/NA	AUTO
94151-25 WREN II	25	3	921			---/---	
94151-27 WREN II	26	3	921	19		---/---	
94151-42 WREN II	42	5	921			---/---	
94151-44 WREN 11	44	5	921	19		---/---	
94151-59 WREN II	59	7	921			---/---	
94151-62 WREN II	62	7	921	19		---/---	
94151-76 WREN II	76	9	921			---/---	
94151-80 WREN II	80	9	921	19		---/---	
94151-80SA	72	9	921			---/---	
94151-80SC	70	9	921			---/---	
94151-86	72	9	925	17		925/925	
94155-021 WREN I	18	5	697	17		697/697	
94155-025 WREN I	24	4	697	17		697/128	
94155-028 WREN I	24	3	697	17		698/128	
94155-029 WREN I	25	3	925			---/---	

Drive Model	Seek Time	Interface	Encode	Form Factor	cache kb	Obsolete? mtbf	RPM

BASF

Drive Model	Seek Time	Interface	Encode	Form Factor	cache kb	mtbf	RPM
6185	150/70?	ST412/506	MFM	5.25 FH			
6186	70	ST412/506	MFM	5.25 FH			
6187	70	ST412/506	MFM	5.25 FH			
6188-R1	70	ST412/506	MFM	5.25 FH			
6188-R3	70	ST412/506	MFM	5.25 FH			

BRAND TECHNOLOGIES

Drive Model	Seek Time	Interface	Encode	Form Factor	cache kb	mtbf	RPM	Obsolete?
9121A (Never made)	16.5	IDE AT	2,7 RLL	3.5 HH		50k		Y
9121S (Never made)	16.5	SCSI	2,7 RLL	3.5 HH		50k		Y
9121E (Never made)	16.5	ESDI	2,7 RLL	3.5 HH		50k		Y
9170E	16.5	ESDI	2,7 RLL	3.5 HH		50k	3565	N
9170A	16.5	IDE AT	2,7 RLL	3.5 HH	64k	50k		N
9170S	16.5	SCSI	2,7 RLL	3.5 HH	64k	50k		N
9220E	16.5	ESDI	2,7 RLL	3.5 HH		50k	3565	N
9220A	16.5	IDE AT	2,7 RLL	3.5 HH	64k	50k	3565	N
9220S	16.5	SCSI	2,7 RLL	3.5 HH	64k	50k		N
BT8085	25	ST412/506	MFM	5.25 FH		50k		Y
BT8128	25	ST412/506	2,7 RLL	5.25 FH		50k		Y
BT8170E	25	ESDI	2,7 RLL	5.25 FH		50k		Y
BT8170S	25	SCSI	2,7 RLL	5.25 FH		50k		Y
BT9400A (Never made)	12	IDE AT	1,7 RLL	5.25 FH				Y
BT9400S (Never made)	12	SCSI-2	1,7 RLL	5.25 FH				Y
BT9650A (Never made)	12	IDE AT	1,7 RLL	5.25 FH				Y
BT9650S (Never made)	12	SCSI-2	1,7 RLL	5.25 FH				Y

BULL

Drive Model	Seek Time	Interface	Encode	Form Factor	cache kb	mtbf	RPM	Obsolete?
D530		ST412/506	MFM	5.25 FH				Y
D550		ST412/506	MFM	5.25 FH				Y
D570		ST412/506	MFM	5.25 FH				Y
D585		ST412/506	2,7 RLL	5.25 FH				Y

C.ITOH ELECTRONICS, INC

SEE YE-DATA

CARDIFF

Drive Model	Seek Time	Interface	Encode	Form Factor
F3053	20	ST412/506	MFM	3.5 HH
F3080E	20	ESDI	2,7 RLL	3.5 HH
F3080S	20	SCSI	2,7 RLL	3.5 HH
F3127E	20	ESDI	2,7 RLL	3.5 HH
F3127S	20	SCSI	2,7 RLL	3.5 HH

CDC

Drive Model	Seek Time	Interface	Encode	Form Factor	mtbf
94161-151 WREN III	16.5	SCSI	2,7 RLL	5.25 FH	100k
94151-25 WREN II				5.25 FH	
94151-27 WREN II				5.25 FH	
94151-42 WREN II				5.25 FH	
94151-44 WREN 11				5.25 FH	
94151-59 WREN II				5.25 FH	
94151-62 WREN II				5.25 FH	
94151-76 WREN II				5.25 FH	
94151-80 WREN II				5.25 FH	
94151-80SA	38	SASI		5.25 FH	
94151-80SC	38	SCSI		5.25 FH	
94151-86	38	ST412/506	MFM	5.25 FH	
94155-021 WREN I		ST412/506	MFM	5.25 FH	
94155-025 WREN I		ST412/506	MFM	5.25 FH	
94155-028 WREN I	28	ST412/506	MFM	5.25 FH	
94155-029 WREN I	28	ST412/506	MFM	5.25 FH	

Drive Model	Format Size MB	Head	Cyl	Sect/ Trac	Translate H/C/S	RWC/ WPC	Land Zone
94155-036 WREN I	31	5	733	17		697/128	
94155-037 WREN I	32	4	925	17		---/---	
94155-038 WREN I	31	5	733	17		734/0	
94155-048 WREN II	40	5	925	17		926/128	
94155-051 WREN II	43	5	989	17		990/128	
94155-057 WREN II	48	6	925	17		926/128	
94155-057P WREN II	48	6	925	17		926/128	AUTO
94155-067 WREN II	56	7	925	17		926/128	
94155-067P WREN II	56	7	925	17		926/128	AUTO
94155-077 WREN II	64	8	925	17		926/128	AUTO
94155-085 WREN II	71	8	1024	17		1025/128	AUTO
94155-085P WREN II	71	8	1024	17		1025/128	AUTO
94155-086 WREN II	72	9	925	17		926/128	AUTO
94155-087 WREN II	72	9	925			---/---	
94155-092 WREN II	77	9	989	17		---/-1.0	
94155-092P WREN II	77	9	989	17		---/128	
94155-096 WREN II	80	9	1024	17		---/---	AUTO
94155-120 WREN II	120	8	960	26		961/128	AUTO
94155-130 WREN II	122	9	1024	26		---/128	AUTO
94155-135 WREN II	115	9	960	26		961/128	AUTO
94156-048 WREN II	40	5	925	17		926/128	AUTO
94156-067 WREN II	56	7	925	17		926/128	AUTO
94156-086 WREN II	72	9	925	17		926/128	AUTO
94161-086 WREN III	86	5	969	35		NA/NA	AUTO
94161-101 WREN III	84	5	969	34		NA/NA	
94161-103 WREN III	104	6	969	35		NA/NA	
94161-121 WREN III	121	7	969	35		NA/NA	
94161-138 WREN III	138	8	969	35		NA/NA	
94161-141 WREN III	118	7	969	35		NA/NA	AUTO
94161-155 WREN III	132	9	969	35		---/-1.0	
94161-156 WREN III	132	9	969	36		---/-1.0	
94161-182 WREN III	156	9	969	35		NA/NA	AUTO
94161-182M WREN III	160	9	969			---/---	
94166-086 WREN III	86	5	969	35		---/-1.0	
94166-101 WREN III	86	5	969	35		NA/NA	AUTO
94166-103 WREN III	104	6	969	35		---/-1.0	
94166-121 WREN III	107	6	969	36		NA/NA	
94166-138 WREN III	138	8	969	35		---/-1.0	
94166-141 WREN III	125	7	969	36		NA/NA	
94166-161 COMPAQ	160	9	969	36		NA/NA	
94166-161 WREN III	142	8	969	36		NA/NA	
94166-182 WREN III	161	9	969	36		NA/NA	
94171-300 WREN IV	300	9	1412			NA/NA	
94171-307 WREN IV	300	9	1412			NA/NA	
94171-327 WREN IV	300	9	1412			NA/NA	
94171-344 WREN IV	323	9	1549	V		NA/NA	
94171-350 WREN IV	307	9	1412	V		NA/NA	
94171-375 WREN IV	330	9	1549	V		NA/NA	
94171-376 WREN IV	330	9	1546	V		NA/NA	
94171-376D WREN IV	323	9	1549	V		NA/NA	
94181-383 WREN IV	330	15	1224			---/---	
94181-385H WREN V	337	15	791	V		NA/NA	
94181-385D WREN V	337	15	791	V		NA/NA	
94181-574 WREN V	574	15	1549	V		NA/NA	
94181-702 WREN V	613	15	1546	V		NA/NA	
94181-702D WREN V	601	15	1546	V		NA/NA	
94181-702M WREN V	613	15	1549			---/---	
94186-265 WREN V	234	9	1412	36		NA/NA	AUTO
94186-324 WREN V	278	11	1412	35		NA/NA	AUTO
94186-383 WREN V	338	7	1747	35		NA/NA	AUTO
94186-383H WREN V	338	7	1747	35		NA/NA	AUTO
94186-383S WREN V	338	13	1412	36		NA/NA	AUTO
94186-442 WREN V	380	15	1412	35		NA/NA	AUTO

Drive Model	Seek Time	Interface	Encode	Form Factor	cache kb	mtbf	RPM	Obsolete?
94155-036 WREN I		ST412/506	MFM	5.25 FH				
94155-037 WREN I	28	ST412/506	MFM	5.25 FH				
94155-038 WREN I	28	ST412/506	MFM	5.25 FH				
94155-048 WREN II	28	ST412/506	MFM	5.25 FH				
94155-051 WREN II	28	ST412/506	MFM	5.25 FH				
94155-057 WREN II	28	ST412/506	MFM	5.25 FH		40k		
94155-057P WREN II	28	ST412/506	MFM	5.25 FH		40k		
94155-067 WREN II	28	ST412/506	MFM	5.25 FH		40k		
94155-067P WREN II	38	ST412/506	MFM	5.25 FH		40k		
94155-077 WREN II	28	ST412/506	MFM	5.25 FH		40k		
94155-085 WREN II	28	ST412/506	MFM	5.25 FH		40k		
94155-085P WREN II	28	ST412/506	MFM	5.25 FH		40k		
94155-086 WREN II	28	ST412/506	MFM	5.25 FH		40k		
94155-087 WREN II	38	ESDI		5.25 FH				
94155-092 WREN II	38	ST412/506	MFM	5.25 FH				
94155-092P WREN II	38	ST412/506	MFM	5.25 FH				
94155-096 WREN II	28	ST412/506	MFM	5.25 FH		40k		
94155-120 WREN II	28	ST412/506	2,7 RLL	5.25 FH		40k		
94155-130 WREN II	28	ST412/506	RLL	5.25 FH				
94155-135 WREN II	28	ST412/506	2,7 RLL	5.25 FH		40k		
94156-048 WREN II	28	ESDI	MFM	5.25 FH		40k		
94156-067 WREN II	28	ESDI	MFM	5.25 FH		40k		
94156-086 WREN II	28	ESDI	MFM	5.25 FH		40k		
94161-086 WREN III	16.5	SCSI	2,7 RLL	5.25 FH		100k		
94161-101 WREN III	16.5	SCSI	2,7 RLL	5.25 FH		100k		
94161-103 WREN III	16.5	SCSI	2,7 RLL	5.25 FH		100k		
94161-121 WREN III	16.5	SCSI	2,7 RLL	5.25 FH		100k		
94161-138 WREN III	16.5	SCSI	2,7 RLL	5.25 FH		100k		
94161-141 WREN III	16.5	SCSI	2,7 RLL	5.25 FH		100k		
94161-155 WREN III	17	SCSI	RLL	5.25 FH				
94161-156 WREN III	17	SCSI	RLL	5.25 FH				
94161-182 WREN III	16.5	SCSI	2,7 RLL	5.25 FH		100k		
94161-182M WREN III	17	SCSI	ZBR	5.25 FH				
94166-086 WREN III	25	ESDI	RLL	5.25 FH				
94166-101 WREN III	16.5	ESDI	2,7 RLL	5.25 FH		100k		
94166-103 WREN III	25	ESDI	RLL	5.25 FH				
94166-121 WREN III	16.5	ESDI	2,7 RLL	5.25 FH		100k		
94166-138 WREN III	25	ESDI	RLL	5.25 FH				
94166-141 WREN III	16.5	ESDI	2,7 RLL	5.25 FH		100k		
94166-161 COMPAQ		ESDI	2,7 RLL	5.25 FH		100k		
94166-161 WREN III		ESDI	2,7 RLL	5.25 FH		100k		
94166-182 WREN III	16.5	ESDI (10)	2,7 RLL	5.25 FH		100k		
94171-300 WREN IV	17	SCSI		5.25 FH				
94171-307 WREN IV	17	SCSI		5.25 FH				
94171-327 WREN IV	17	SCSI		5.25 FH				
94171-344 WREN IV	18	SCSI	RLL ZBR	5.25 FH				
94171-350 WREN IV	16.5	SCSI	RLL ZBR	5.25 FH		100k		
94171-375 WREN IV	16	SCSI	RLL ZBR	5.25 FH		100k		
94171-376 WREN IV	17.5	SCSI	RLL ZBR	5.25 FH		100k		
94171-376D WREN IV		SCSI	RLL ZBR	5.25 HH		100k		
94181-383 WREN IV	18	SCSI	ZBR	5.25 FH				
94181-385H WREN V	10.7	SCSI	RLL ZBR	5.25 FH		100k		
94181-385D WREN V		SCSI	RLL ZBR	5.25 FH		100k		
94181-574 WREN V	16	SCSI	RLL ZBR	5.25 FH		100k		
94181-702 WREN V	16.5	SCSI	RLL ZBR	5.25 FH		100k		
94181-702D WREN V		SCSI	RLL ZBR	5.25 FH		100k		
94181-702M WREN V	17	SCSI	ZBR	5.25 FH				
94186-265 WREN V	16.5	ESDI (10)	2,7 RLL	5.25 FH		100k		
94186-324 WREN V		ESDI (10)	2,7 RLL	5.25 FH		100k		
94186-383 WREN V		ESDI (10)	2,7 RLL	5.25 FH		100k		
94186-383H WREN V		ESDI (10)	2,7 RLL	5.25 FH		100k		
94186-383S WREN V	19	ESDI (10)	2,7 RLL	5.25 FH		100k		
94186-442 WREN V		ESDI (10)	2,7 RLL	5.25 FH		100k		

Drive Model	Format Size MB	Head	Cyl	Sect/ Trac	Translate H/C/S	RWC/ WPC	Land Zone
94186-442S WREN V	390	15	1412	36		NA/NA	AUTO
94191-766 WREN VI	677	15	1632	54		NA/NA	AUTO
94191-766D WREN VI	677	15	1632	54		NA/NA	AUTO
94196-383 WREN VI	338	7	1747	54		NA/NA	AUTO
94196-766 WREN V	677	15	1632	54		NA/NA	AUTO
94204-051 WREN II	43	5	989	26		NA/NA	AUTO
94204-065 WREN II	63	5	948	26		NA/NA	AUTO
94204-071 WREN II	63	5	1032	27		NA/NA	AUTO
94204-074 WREN II	63	5	948	26		NA/NA	AUTO
94204-081 WREN II	71	5	1032	27		NA/NA	AUTO
94205-030 WREN II	26	3	989	17		989/---	AUTO
94205-041 WREN II	43	4	989	17		990/128	AUTO
94205-051 WREN II	43	5	989	17		990/128	AUTO
94205-053 WREN II	43	5	1024	17		990/128	AUTO
94205-071 WREN II	43	5	989	26		990/128	AUTO
94205-075 WREN II	62	5	966	25		966/128	AUTO
94205-077 WREN II	66	5	989	26		---/---	AUTO

Conversion Chart: Part I
Old CDC/Imprimis model # to new Seagate model

CDC/Imprimis ➡	Seagate	Seagate ➡	CDC/Imprimis
94155-135	ST4135R	ST1090A	94354-090
94155-85	ST4085	ST1090N	94351-090
94155-86	ST4086	ST1100	94355-100
94155-96	ST4097	ST1111A	94354-111
94161-182	ST4182N	ST1111E	94356-111
94166-182	ST4182E	ST1111N	94351-111
94171-350	ST4350N	ST1126A	94354-126
94171-376	ST4376N	ST1126N	94351-126
94181-385H	ST4385N	ST1133A	94354-133
94181-702	ST4702N	ST1133NS	94351-133S
94186-383	ST4383E	ST1150R	94355-150
94186-383H	ST4384E	ST1156A	94354-155
94186-442	ST4442N	ST1156E	94356-155
94191-766	ST4766N	ST1156N	94351-155
94196-766	ST4766E	ST1156NS	94351-155S
94204-65	ST274A	ST1162A	94354-160
94204-71	ST280A	ST1162N	94351-160
94204-74	ST274A	ST1186A	94354-186
94204-81	ST280A	ST1186NS	94351-186S
94205-51	ST253	ST1201A	94354-200
94205-77	ST279R	ST1201E	94356-200
94211-106	ST2106N	ST1201N	94351-200
94216-106	ST2106E	ST1201NS	94351-200S
94221-125	ST2125N	ST1239A	94354-239
94241-502	ST2502N	ST1239NS	94351-230S
94244-274	ST2274A	ST2106E	94216-106
94244-383	ST2383A	ST2106N	94211-106
94246-182	ST2182E	ST2125N	94221-125
94246-383	ST2383E	ST2182E	94246-182
94351-090	ST1090N	ST2274A	94244-274
94351-111	ST1111N	ST2383A	94244-383
94351-126	ST1126N	ST2383E	94246-383
94351-133S	ST1133NS	ST2502N	94241-502
94351-155	ST1156N	ST253	94205-51
94351-155S	ST1156NS	ST274A	94204-74
94351-160	ST1162N	ST274A	94204-65
94351-186S	ST1186N	ST279R	94205-77
94351-200	ST1201N	ST280A	94204-81
94351-200S	ST1201NS	ST280A	94204-71
94351-230S	ST1239NS	ST4085	94155-85
94354-090	ST1090A	ST4086	94155-86

Drive Model	Seek Time	Interface	Encode	Form Factor	cache kb	mtbf	Obsolete? RPM
94186-442S WREN	15	SCSI	2,7 RLL	5.25 FH			
94191-766 WREN VI	15.5	SCSI	2,7 RLL	5.25 FH		100k	
94191-766D WREN VI		SCSI	2,7 RLL	5.25 FH		100k	
94196-383 WREN VI		ESDI (15)	2,7 RLL	5.25 FH		100k	
94196-766 WREN V		ESDI (15)	2,7 RLL	5.25 FH		100k	
94204-051 WREN II		IDE AT	2,7 RLL	5.25 HH		40k	
94204-065 WREN II		IDE AT	2,7 RLL	5.25 HH		40k	
94204-071 WREN II		IDE AT	2,7 RLL	5.25 HH		40k	
94204-074 WREN II	28	IDE AT	2,7 RLL	5.25 HH		40k	
94204-081 WREN II	28	IDE AT	2,7 RLL	5.25 HH		40k	
94205-030 WREN II		ST412/506	MFM	5.25 FH		40k	
94205-041 WREN II		ST412/506	MFM	5.25 HH		40k	
94205-051 WREN II	28	ST412/506	MFM	5.25 HH		40k	
94205-053 WREN II		ST412/506	MFM	5.25 HH		40k	
94205-071 WREN II		ST412/506	RLL	5.25 HH		40k	
94205-075 WREN II	28	ST412/506	RLL	5.25 HH		40k	
94205-077 WREN II	28	ST412/506	2,7 RLL	5.25 HH		40k	

Conversion Chart: Part II
Old CDC/Imprimis model # to new Seagate model

CDC/Imprimis ➡	Seagate	Seagate ➡	CDC/Imprimis
94354-111	ST1111A	ST4097	94155-96
94354-126	ST1126A	ST41200N	94601-12G/M
94354-133	ST1133A	ST41201J	97500-12G
94354-155	ST1156A	ST41201K	97509-12G
94354-160	ST1162A	ST4135F	94155-135
94354-186	ST1186A	ST41520N	97501-12G
94354-200	ST1201A	ST4182E	94166-182
94354-239	ST1239A	ST4182N	94161-182
94355-100	ST1100	ST4350N	94171-350
94355-150	ST1150R	ST4376N	94171-376
94356-111	ST1111E	ST4383E	94186-383
94356-155	ST1156E	ST4384E	94186-383H
94356-200	ST1201E	ST4385N	94181-385H
94601-12G/M	ST41200N	ST4442E	94186-442
94601-767H	ST4767N	ST4702N	94181-702
97100-80	ST683J	ST4766E	94196-766
97150-160	ST6165J	ST4766N	94191-766
97150-300	ST6315J	ST4767N	94601-767H
97150-340	ST6344J	ST6165J	97150-160
97150-500	ST6516J	ST6315J	97150-300
97200-1130	ST81123J	ST6344J	97150-340
97200-12G	ST81236J	ST6516J	97150-500
97200-23G	ST82272K	ST683J	97100-80
97200-25G	ST82500J	ST81123J	97200-1130
97200-368	ST8368J	ST81154K	97229-1150
97200-500	ST8500J	ST81236J	97200-12G
97200-736	ST8741J	ST81236K	97209-12G
97200-850	ST8851J	ST81236N	97201-12G
97201-12G	ST81236N	ST82105K	97289-21G
97201-25G	ST82500N	ST82272K	97200-23G
97201-368	ST8368N	ST82368N	97299-23G
97201-500	ST8500N	ST82500J	97200-25G
97201-736	ST8741N	ST82500K	97209-25G
97201-850	ST8851N	ST82500N	97201-25G
97209-12G	ST81236K	ST8368J	97200-368
97209-25G	ST82500K	ST8368N	97201-368
97229-1150	ST81154K	ST8500J	97200-500
97289-21G	ST82105K	ST8500N	97201-500
97299-23G	ST82368K	ST8741J	97200-736
97500-12G	ST41201J	ST8741N	97201-736
97501-12G	ST41520N	ST8851J	97200-850
97509-12G	ST41201K	ST8851N	97201-850

Drive Model	Format Size MB	Head	Cyl	Sect/Trac	Translate H/C/S	RWC/WPC	Land Zone
94208-062 WREN II	60	5	989	17		—/—	
94208-075 WREN II	66	5	989	26		NA/NA	
94208-951 WREN II	42	5	989	17		990/128	
94211-086 WREN III	72	5	1024			—/—	
94211-091 WREN III	77	5	1024	17		970/970	
94211-106 WREN III	92	5	1024	35		NA/NA	AUTO
94211-106M WREN III	94	5	1024			1025/1025	
94211-209 WREN III	183	5	1547			1548/1548	
94216-106 WREN III	90	5	1024	34		NA/NA	AUTO
94221-125 WREN V	110	5	1544	V		NA/NA	AUTO
94221-169 WREN V	159	5	1310	V		NA/NA	AUTO
94221-190 WREN V	190	5	1547	V		NA/NA	AUTO
94221-209 WREN V	183	5	1544	V		NA/NA	AUTO
94241-383 WREN VI	338	7	1400	V		NA/NA	AUTO
94241-502 WREN VI		7	1765	V		NA/NA	AUTO
94241-502M WREN VI		7	1765	V		NA/NA	AUTO
94244-219 WREN VI	186	4	1747	54		1748/-1.0	
94244-274 WREN VI	233	5	1747	52		NA/NA	AUTO
94244-383 WREN VI	338	7	1747	54		NA/NA	AUTO
94246-182 WREN VI	161	4	1453	54		NA/NA	AUTO
94246-383 WREN VI	338	7	1747			NA/NA	AUTO
94311-136 SWIFT SL	120	5				NA/NA	
94311-136S SWIFT SL	120	5	1247	36		NA/NA	
94314-136 SWIFT SL	120	5				NA/NA	
94316-111 SWIFT	98	5		36		NA/NA	
94316-136 SWIFT SL	120	5		36		NA/NA	
94316-155 SWIFT	138	7	1072	36		NA/NA	AUTO
94316-200 SWIFT	177	5		36		NA/NA	AUTO
94335-055 SWIFT SL	46	5				—/—	
94335-100 SWIFT	85	9	1072	17		—/—	
94335-150 SWIFT	128	9		26		—/—	
94351-090 SWIFT	80	5	1068			—/—	
94351-111 SWIFT	98	5	1068	36		NA/NA	AUTO
94351-126 SWIFT	111	7	1068	29		NA/NA	AUTO
94351-128 SWIFT	111	7	1068	36		NA/NA	AUTO
94351-133S SWIFT	117	5	1268	36		NA/NA	AUTO
94351-134 SWIFT	120	7	1268			—/—	
94351-135 SWIFT	121	6	1068			—/—	
94351-155 SWIFT	138	7	1068	36		NA/NA	AUTO
94351-155S SWIFT	138	5	1268	36		NA/NA	AUTO
94351-160 SWIFT	143	9	1068	29		NA/NA	AUTO
94351-172 SWIFT	177	7	1068	36		NA/NA	AUTO
94351-186S SWIFT	164	7	1268	36		NA/NA	AUTO
94351-200 SWIFT	178	7	1068	36		NA/NA	AUTO
94351-200S SWIFT	177	9	1068	36		NA/NA	AUTO
94351-230 SWIFT	210	9	1268	36		NA/NA	AUTO
94351-230S SWIFT	210	9	1268	36		NA/NA	AUTO
94354-090 SWIFT	80	5	102	29		—/-1.0	
94354-111 SWIFT	99	5	1072	36		NA/NA	AUTO
94354-126 SWIFT	111	7	1072	29		NA/NA	AUTO
94354-133 SWIFT	117	5	1272	36		NA/NA	AUTO
94354-155 SWIFT	138	7	1072	36		NA/NA	AUTO
94354-160 SWIFT	143	9	1072	29		NA/NA	AUTO
94354-186 SWIFT	164	7	1272	36		NA/NA	AUTO
94354-200 SWIFT	178	9	1072	36		NA/NA	AUTO
94354-239 SWIFT	211	9	1272	36		NA/NA	AUTO
94355-055 SWIFT II	46	5		17		—/—	AUTO
94355-100 SWIFT	84	9	1072	17		1073/300	AUTO
94355-150 SWIFT	128	9	1072	26		1073/300	AUTO
94356-111 SWIFT	99	5	1072	36		NA/NA	AUTO
94356-155 SWIFT	138	7	1072	36		NA/NA	AUTO
94356-200 SWIFT	178	9	1072	36		NA/NA	AUTO
94601-12D WREN VII	1035	15	1931	V		NA/NA	AUTO

Drive Model	Seek Time	Interface	Encode	Form Factor	cache kb	Obsolete? mtbf	RPM ⇓
94208-062 WREN II	28	COMPAQ	MFM	5.25 HH			
94208-075 WREN II	30	IDE AT	2,7 RLL	5.25 HH			
94208-951 WREN II	28	COMPAQ	MFM	5.25 FH			
94211-086 WREN III	18	SCSI	RLL	5.25 HH			
94211-091 WREN III	18	SCSI	MFM	5.25 HH			
94211-106 WREN III	18	SCSI	2,7 RLL	5.25 HH		100k	
94211-106M WREN III	18	SCSI	ZBR	5.25 FH			
94211-209 WREN III	18	SCSI	ZBR	3.5 HH			
94216-106 WREN III	18	ESDI (10)	2,7 RLL	5.25 HH		100k	
94221-125 WREN V	18	SCSI	RLL ZBR	5.25 HH		100k	
94221-169 WREN V	18	SCSI	RLL ZBR	5.25 HH		100k	
94221-190 WREN V	18	SCSI	RLL ZBR	5.25 HH		100k	
94221-209 WREN V	18	SCSI	RLL ZBR	5.25 HH		100k	
94241-383 WREN VI	14	SCSI	RLL ZBR	5.25 HH		100k	
94241-502 WREN VI	16	SCSI	RLL ZBR	5.25 HH		100k	
94241-502M WREN VI	16	SCSI(MAC)	RLL ZBR	5.25 HH		100k	
94244-219 WREN VI	16	AT	RLL	5.25 HH			
94244-274 WREN VI	16	IDE AT	2,7 RLL	5.25 HH		100k	
94244-383 WREN VI	16	IDE AT	2,7 RLL	5.25 HH		100k	
94246-182 WREN VI	16	ESDI (20)	2,7 RLL	5.25 HH		100k	
94246-383 WREN VI	16	SCSI (20)	2,7 RLL	5.25 HH		100k	
94311-136 SWIFT SL	15	SCSI	2,7 RLL	3.5 3H		70k	
94311-136S SWIFT SL	15	SCSI-2	2,7 RLL	3.5 3H		70k	
94314-136 SWIFT SL	15	IDE AT	2,7 RLL	3.5 3H		70k	
94316-111 SWIFT	23	ESDI	2,7 RLL	3.5 HH		70k	
94316-136 SWIFT SL	15	ESDI	2,7 RLL	3.5 3H		70k	
94316-155 SWIFT	15	ESDI	2,7 RLL	3.5 HH		70k	
94316-200 SWIFT	15	ESDI	2,7 RLL	3.5 HH		70k	
94335-055 SWIFT SL	25	ST412/506	RLL	3.5 HH			
94335-100 SWIFT	25	ST412/506	MFM	3.5 HH			
94335-150 SWIFT	25	ST412/506	RLL	3.5 HH			
94351-090 SWIFT	15	SCSI	RLL	3.5 HH			
94351-111 SWIFT	15	SCSI	2,7 RLL	3.5 HH		70k	
94351-126 SWIFT	15	SCSI	2,7 RLL	3.5 HH		70k	
94351-128 SWIFT	15	SCSI	2,7 RLL	3.5 HH		70k	
94351-133S SWIFT	15	SCSI-2	2,7 RLL	3.5 HH		70k	
94351-134 SWIFT	15	SCSI	RLL	3.5 HH			
94351-135 SWIFT	15	SCSI	RLL	3.5 HH			
94351-155 SWIFT	15	SCSI	2,7 RLL	3.5 HH		70k	
94351-155S SWIFT	15	SCSI-2	2,7 RLL	3.5 HH		70k	
94351-160 SWIFT	15	SCSI	2,7 RLL	3.5 HH		150k	
94351-172 SWIFT	15	SCSI	2,7 RLL	3.5 HH		70k	
94351-186S SWIFT	15	SCSI-2	2,7 RLL	3.5 HH		150k	
94351-200 SWIFT	15	SCSI	2,7 RLL	3.5 HH		150k	
94351-200S SWIFT	15	SCSI-2	2,7 RLL	3.5 HH		150k	
94351-230 SWIFT	15	SCSI		3.5 HH		70k	
94351-230S SWIFT	15	SCSI-2	2,7 RLL	3.5 HH		70k	
94354-090 SWIFT	15	AT	RLL	3.5 HH			
94354-111 SWIFT	15	IDE AT	2,7 RLL	3.5 HH		70k	
94354-126 SWIFT	15	IDE AT	2,7 RLL	3.5 HH		150k	
94354-133 SWIFT	15	IDE AT	2,7 RLL	3.5 HH		70k	
94354-155 SWIFT	15	IDE AT	2,7 RLL	3.5 HH		150k	
94354-160 SWIFT	15	IDE AT	2,7 RLL	3.5 HH		150k	
94354-186 SWIFT	15	IDE AT	2,7 RLL	3.5 HH		150k	
94354-200 SWIFT	15	IDE AT	2,7 RLL	3.5 HH		150k	
94354-239 SWIFT	15	IDE AT	2,7 RLL	3.5 HH		70k	
94355-055 SWIFT II	25	ST412/506	MFM	3.5 HH		70k	
94355-100 SWIFT	15	ST412/506	MFM	3.5 HH		70k	
94355-150 SWIFT	15	ST412/506	2,7 RLL	3.5 HH		150k	
94356-111 SWIFT	15	ESDI (10)	2,7 RLL	3.5 HH		150k	
94356-155 SWIFT	15	ESDI (10)	2,7 RLL	3.5 HH		70k	
94356-200 SWIFT	15	ESDI (10)	2,7 RLL	3.5 HH		70k	
94601-12D WREN VII	15	SCSI	2,7 RLL	5.25 FH		150k	

Drive Model	Format Size MB	Head	Cyl	Sect/ Trac	Translate H/C/S	RWC/ WPC	Land Zone
94601-12G WREN VII	1037	15	1937	V		NA/NA	AUTO
94601-12GM WREN VII	1037	15	1937	V		NA/NA	AUTO
94601-767H WREN VII	676	15	1356	V		NA/NA	AUTO
9720-368 SABRE	368		1635			1218/1218	AUTO
9720-500 SABRE	500	10	1217			1218/1218	AUTO
9720-736 SABRE	736	15	1635			1636/1636	AUTO
9720-850 SABRE	727	15	1381			1382/1382	AUTO
97155-036	30			17		—/—	AUTO
9720-1123 SABRE	964	19				—/—	AUTO
9720-1130 SABRE	1050	15	1635			—/—	AUTO
9720-2270 SABRE	1948	19				—/—	AUTO
9720-2500 SABRE	2145	19				—/—	AUTO
97229-1150 WREN V	990	19				—/—	AUTO
97501-15G ELITE	1500	17				NA/NA	AUTO
97509-12G ELITE	1050	17				—/—	AUTO
SABRE 368	368	10	1635			—/—	AUTO
SABRE 500	500	10	1217			—/—	AUTO
SABRE 736	741	15	1217			—/—	AUTO
SABRE 850	851	15	1635			—/—	AUTO
SABRE 1123	964	19				—/—	AUTO
SABRE 1150	990	19				—/—	AUTO
SABRE 1230	1050	15	1635			—/—	AUTO
SABRE 2270	1948	19				—/—	AUTO
SABRE 2500	2145	19				—/—	AUTO
BJ7D5A/77731600	18	3	697	17		—/128	
BJ7D5A/77731601	18	3	697	17		—/128	
BJ7D5A/77731602	30	5	697	17		—/128	
BJ7D5A/77731603	30	5	697	17		—/128	
BJ7D5A/77731604	36	5	697			—/128	
BJ7D5A/77731605	30	5	697	17		—/128	
BJ7D5A/77731606	27			17		—/128	
BJ7D5A/77731607	18	3	697	17		—/128	
BJ7D5A/77731608	29	5	670	17		—/128	
BJ7D5A/77731609	30	5	697	17		—/128	
BJ7D5A/77731610	18	3	697	17		—/128	
BJ7D5A/77731611	30	5	697	17		—/128	
BJ7D5A/77731612	24	4	697	17		—/128	
BJ7D5A/77731613	31	5	733	17		—/128	
BJ7D5A/77731614	23	4	670	17		—/128	
BJ7D5A/77731615	24	4	697	17		—/128	
BJ7D5A/77731616	31	5	733	17		—/128	
BJ7D5A/77731617	30	5	697	17		—/128	
BJ7D5A/77731618	30	5	697	17		—/128	
BJ7D5A/77731619	30	5	697	17		—/128	
BJ7D5A/77731620	30	5	697	17		—/128	

CENTURY DATA

Drive Model	Format Size MB	Head	Cyl	Sect/ Trac	Translate H/C/S	RWC/ WPC	Land Zone
CAST-10203E	55	3	1050	35		NA/NA	AUTO
CAST-10203S	55	3	1050	35		NA/NA	AUTO
CAST-10304E	75	4	1050	35		NA/NA	AUTO
CAST-10304S	75	4	1050	35		NA/NA	AUTO
CAST-10305E	94	5	1050	35		NA/NA	AUTO
CAST-10305S	94	5	1050	35		NA/NA	AUTO
CAST-14404E	114	4	1590	35		NA/NA	AUTO
CAST-14404S	114	4	1590	35		NA/NA	AUTO
CAST-14405E	140	5	1590	35		NA/NA	AUTO
CAST-14405S	140	5	1590	35		NA/NA	AUTO
CAST-14406E	170	6	1590	35		NA/NA	AUTO
CAST-14406S	170	6	1590	35		NA/NA	AUTO
CAST-24509E	258	9	1599	35		NA/NA	AUTO
CAST-24509S	258	9	1599	35		NA/NA	AUTO
CAST-24611E	315	11	1599	35		NA/NA	AUTO
CAST-24611S	315	11	1599	35		NA/NA	AUTO

Drive Model	Seek Time	Interface	Encode	Form Factor	cache kb	Obsolete? mtbf RPM
94601-12G WREN VII	15	SCSI	RLL ZBR	5.25 FH		150k
94601-12GM WREN VII	15	SCSI(MAC)	RLL ZBR	5.25 FH		150k
94601-767H WREN VII	15	SCSI(MAC)	RLL ZBR	5.25 FH		100k
9720-368 SABRE	18	SMD/SCSI	2,7 RLL	8.0 FH		30k
9720-500 SABRE	18	SMD/SCSI	2,7 RLL	8.0 FH		30k
9720-736 SABRE	15	SMD/SCSI	2,7 RLL	8.0 FH		50k
9720-850 SABRE	15	SMD/SCSI	2,7 RLL	8.0 FH		50k
97155-036		ST412/506	MFM	8.0 FH		70k
9720-1123 SABRE	15	SMD	2,7 RLL	8.0 FH		70k
9720-1130 SABRE	15	SMD/SCSI	2,7 RLL	8.0 FH		100k
9720-2270 SABRE	12	SMD	2,7 RLL	8.0 FH		100k
9720-2500 SABRE	12	SMD/SCSI	2,7 RLL	8.0 FH		100k
97229-1150 WREN V	15	IPI-2		8.00		100k
97501-15G ELITE	12	SCSI-2	RLL	5.25 FH		100k
97509-12G ELITE	12	IPI-2		5.25 FH		100k
SABRE 368	18					30k
SABRE 500	18					30k
SABRE 736	15					50k
SABRE 850	15					50k
SABRE 1123	15					100k
SABRE 1150	15					100k
SABRE 1230	15					100k
SABRE 2270	12					100k
SABRE 2500	12					100k
BJ7D5A/77731600		ST412/506	MFM	5.25 FH		
BJ7D5A/77731601			MFM	5.25 FH		
BJ7D5A/77731602			MFM	5.25 FH		
BJ7D5A/77731603		ST412/506	MFM	5.25 FH		
BJ7D5A/77731604		ST412/506	MFM	5.25 FH		
BJ7D5A/77731605		ST412/506	MFM	5.25 FH		
BJ7D5A/77731606		ST412/506	MFM	5.25 FH		
BJ7D5A/77731607		ST412/506	MFM	5.25 FH		
BJ7D5A/77731608		ST412/506	MFM	5.25 FH		
BJ7D5A/77731609		ST412/506	MFM	5.25 FH		
BJ7D5A/77731610			MFM	5.25 FH		
BJ7D5A/77731611		ST412/506	MFM	5.25 FH		
BJ7D5A/77731612		ST412/506	MFM	5.25 FH		
BJ7D5A/77731613		ST412/506	MFM	5.25 FH		
BJ7D5A/77731614		ST412/506	MFM	5.25 FH		
BJ7D5A/77731615		ST412/506	MFM	5.25 FH		
BJ7D5A/77731616		ST412/506	MFM	5.25 FH		
BJ7D5A/77731617		ST412/506	MFM	5.25 FH		
BJ7D5A/77731618		ST412/506	MFM	5.25 FH		
BJ7D5A/77731619		ST412/506	MFM	5.25 FH		
BJ7D5A/77731620		ST412/506	MFM	5.25 FH		

CENTURY DATA

Drive Model	Seek Time	Interface	Encode	Form Factor	cache kb	Obsolete? mtbf RPM
CAST-10203E	28	ESDI	2,7 RLL	5.25 FH		
CAST-10203S	28	SCSI	2,7 RLL	5.25 FH		
CAST-10304E	28	ESDI	2,7 RLL	5.25 FH		
CAST-10304S	28	SCSI	2,7 RLL	5.25 FH		
CAST-10305E	28	ESDI	2,7 RLL	5.25 FH		
CAST-10305S	28	SCSI	2,7 RLL	5.25 FH		
CAST-14404E	25	ESDI	2,7 RLL	5.25 HH		
CAST-14404S	25	SCSI	2,7 RLL	5.25 HH		
CAST-14405E	25	ESDI	2,7 RLL	5.25 HH		
CAST-14405S	25	SCSI	2,7 RLL	5.25 HH		
CAST-14406E	25	ESDI	2,7 RLL	5.25 HH		
CAST-14406S	25	SCSI	2,7 RLL	5.25 HH		
CAST-24509E	18	ESDI	2,7 RLL	5.25 FH		
CAST-24509S	18	SCSI	2,7 RLL	5.25 FH		
CAST-24611E	18	ESDI	2,7 RLL	5.25 FH		
CAST-24611S	18	SCSI	2,7 RLL	5.25 FH		

Drive Model	Format Size MB	Head	Cyl	Sect/ Trac	Translate H/C/S	RWC/ WPC	Land Zone
CAST-24713E	372	13	1599	35		NA/NA	AUTO
CAST-24713S	372	13	1599	35		NA/NA	AUTO

CMI

Drive Model	Format Size MB	Head	Cyl	Sect/ Trac	Translate H/C/S	RWC/ WPC	Land Zone
CM3412	10	4	306	17		306/256	
CM3426	20	4	615	17		616/256	
CM5018H	15	2		17		---/---	
CM5205	4	2	256	17		128/128	
CM5206	5	2	306	17		307/256	
CM5410	8	4	256	17		128/128	
CM5412	10	4	306	17		307/128	
CM5616	14	6	256	17		257/257	
CM5619	16	6	306	17		307/128	
CM5826	20	8	306	17		---/---	
CM6213	11	2	640	17		641/256	
CM6426	22	4	615	17		---/300	615
CM6426S	22	4	615	17		256/300	615
CM6640	33	6	615	17		616/300	615
CM7000	44	7	733	17		733/512	
CM7030	25	4	733	17		733/512	
CM7038	31	5	733	17		733/512	
CM7053	44	7	733	17		733/512	
CM7085	71	8	1024	17		1024/512	
CM7660	50	6	960	17		961/450	
CM7880	67	8	960	17		961/450	

CMS ENHANCEMENTS, INC

Drive Model	Format Size MB	Head	Cyl	Sect/ Trac	Translate H/C/S	RWC/ WPC	Land Zone
D20XT-OK	21	4	615	17		---/---	
D30XT-OK	32	4	615	26		---/---	
D40XT-OK	42	5	977	17		---/---	
F70ESDI-T	73	7	583	35		---/---	AUTO
F115ESD1-T	115	7	915	35		---/---	AUTO
F150AT-CA	150	9	969	34		---/---	
F150AT-WCA	151	9	969	34		---/---	AUTO
F150EQ-WCA	151	9	969	34		---/---	AUTO
F320AT-CA	320	15	1224	34		---/---	AUTO
H40M50-P	42	4	977	17		---/---	
H60286D-P	64	5	948	27		---/---	
H60SCSI-S	65	6	628	34		---/---	
H65M50-P	65	9	1072	17		---/---	
H80AT	84	6	1072	17		---/---	
H80SCSI-S	85	6	820	34		---/---	
H100286D-P	105	8	776	34		---/---	
H100386S-P	105	8	776	34		---/---	
H330E1 (PS Express)	330	7	1780	54		---/---	AUTO
H340E1 (PS Express)	340	7	1780	54		---/---	AUTO
HD20AT-S	21	4	615	17		---/---	
HD30AT-S	32	6	615	17		---/---	
HD40AT-S1	43	6	820	17		---/---	
K20M25-WS	21	2	636	34		---/---	
K20M25/30-OK	21	4	615	17		---/---	
K20M25/30-WS	21	4	615	17		---/---	
K30M25/30-OK	32	6	615	17		---/---	
K30M25/30-WS	32	6	615	17		---/---	
K30M30E-P	31	4	615	25		---/---	
K40M25/30-WS	42	5	977	17		---/---	
K40M25/30-WS	42	5	977	17		---/---	
K45M30286-ZS	48	6	615	26		---/---	
K50M50Z/70P	63	6	767	27		---/---	
K60M30286-ZS	61	5	921	26		---/---	
K80M30286-WS	84	7	906	26		---/---	
K80M25Z/30	84	9	1072	17		---/---	

Drive Model	Seek Time	Interface	Encode	Form Factor	cache kb	mtbf	Obsolete? RPM
CAST-24713E	18	ESDI	2,7 RLL	5.25 FH			
CAST-24713S	18	SCSI	2,7 RLL	5.25 FH			

CMI

Drive Model	Seek Time	Interface	Encode	Form Factor	cache kb	mtbf	Obsolete? RPM
CM3412		ST412/506	MFM	5.25 FH			Y
CM3426	85	ST412/506	MFM	5.25 FH			Y
CM5018H	85	ST412/506	MFM	5.25 FH			Y
CM5205		ST412/506	MFM	5.25 FH			Y
CM5206	102	ST412/506	MFM	5.25 FH			Y
CM5410	102	ST412/506	MFM	5.25 FH			Y
CM5412	85	ST412/506	MFM	5.25 FH			Y
CM5616	102	ST412/506	MFM	5.25 FH			Y
CM5619	85	ST412/506	MFM	5.25 FH			Y
CM5826	102	ST412/506	MFM	5.25 FH			Y
CM6213	48	ST412/506	MFM	5.25 FH			Y
CM6426	39	ST412/506	MFM	5.25 FH			Y
CM6426S	39	ST412/506	MFM	5.25 FH			Y
CM6640	39	ST412/506	MFM	5.25 FH			Y
CM7000	42	ST412/506	MFM	5.25 FH			Y
CM7030	42	ST412/506	MFM	5.25 FH			Y
CM7038	42	ST412/506	MFM	5.25 FH			Y
CM7053	42	ST412/506	MFM	5.25 FH			Y
CM7085	42	ST412/506	MFM	5.25 FH			Y
CM7660	28	ST412/506	MFM	5.25 FH			Y
CM7880	28	ST412/506	MFM	5.25 FH			Y

CMS ENHANCEMENTS, INC

Drive Model	Seek Time	Interface	Encode	Form Factor	cache kb	mtbf	Obsolete? RPM
D20XT-OK	62	ST412/506	MFM	3.5 HH			
D30XT-OK	62	ST412/506	2,7 RLL	3.5 HH			
D40XT-OK	24	ST412/506	MFM	3.5 HH			
F70ESDI-T	30	ESDI	2,7 RLL	5.25 FH		25k	
F115ESD1-T	30	ESDI	2,7 RLL	5.25 FH		25k	
F150AT-CA	17	ESDI	2,7 RLL	5.25 FH		40k	
F150AT-WCA	17	ESDI	2,7 RLL	5.25 FH		40k	
F150EQ-WCA	17	ESDI	2,7 RLL	5.25 FH		40k	
F320AT-CA	18	ESDI	2,7 RLL	5.25 FH		40k	
H40M50-P	24	ST412/506	MFM	3.5 HH		45k	
H60286D-P	29	IDE AT		5.25 HH		40k	
H60SCSI-S	28	SCSI		5.25 HH		45k	
H65M50-P	15	ST412/506	MFM	3.5 HH		30k	
H80AT	15	SCSI		5.25 HH		30k	
H80SCSI-S	28	SCSI		5.25 HH		45k	
H100286D-P	25	IDE AT		5.25 HH		20k	
H100386S-P	25	IDE AT		5.25 HH		20k	
H330E1 (PS Express)	14	ESDI	2,7 RLL	5.25 FH		150k	
H340E1 (PS Express)	14	ESDI	2,7 RLL	5.25 FH		150k	
HD20AT-S	65	ST412/506	MFM	5.25 HH		50k	
HD30AT-S	40	ST412/506	MFM	5.25 HH		50k	
HD40AT-S1	28	ST412/506	MFM	5.25 HH		50k	
K20M25-WS	27	IDE AT		3.5 HH		20k	
K20M25/30-OK	62	ST412/506	MFM	3.5 HH		20k	
K20M25/30-WS	40	ST412/506	MFM	3.5 HH		20k	
K30M25/30-OK	62	ST412/506	MFM	3.5 HH		50k	
K30M25/30-WS	40	ST412/506	MFM	3.5 HH		50k	
K30M30E-P	39	IDE AT		3.5 HH		25k	
K40M25/30-WS	24	ST412/506	MFM	3.5 HH		45k	
K40M25/30-WS	24	ST412/506	MFM	3.5 HH		45k	
K45M30286-ZS	28	SCSI		3.5 HH		45k	
K50M50Z/70P	27	MCA	2,7 RLL	3.5 HH			
K60M30286-ZS	24	SCSI		3.5 HH		40k	
K80M30286-WS	24	SCSI		3.5 HH		40k	
K80M25Z/30	15	ST412/506	MFM	3.5 HH			

Drive Model	Format Size MB	Head	Cyl	Sect/ Trac	Translate H/C/S	RWC/ WPC	Land Zone
K120M50Z-70P	125	8	925	33		---/---	
LDSNECMS-20	20	4	575	32		---/---	
LDZE386-100	100	8	776	33		---/---	
PSEXPRESS 150	150					---/---	AUTO
PSEXPRESS 320	320					---/---	AUTO
SENTRY 90	90	5	1024			---/---	
SENTRY 180	180	5	1546			---/---	
SENTRY 300	290	9	1546			---/---	
SENTRY 600	600	15	1546			---/---	

COGITO

Drive Model	Format Size MB	Head	Cyl	Sect/ Trac	Translate H/C/S	RWC/ WPC	Land Zone
CG906	5	2	306	17		128/128	
CG912	10	4	306	17		128/128	
CG925	21	4	612	17		307/307	
PT912	11	4	612	17		307/307	
PT925	21	4	612	17		307/307	

COMPORT

Drive Model	Format Size MB	Head	Cyl	Sect/ Trac	Translate H/C/S	RWC/ WPC	Land Zone
2040	44	4	820	26		---/---	
2041	44	4	820	26		---/---	
2082	86	8	820	34		---/---	

CONNER PERIPHERALS, INC.

Drive Model	Format Size MB	Head	Cyl	Sect/ Trac	Translate H/C/S	RWC/ WPC	Land Zone
CP320	20	2	752	26		NA/NA	AUTO
CP321	20	2	752	26	4/615/17	NA/NA	AUTO
CP323	20	2	752	26	4/615/17	NA/NA	AUTO
CP324	20	2	752	26	4/615/17	NA/NA	AUTO
CP340	42	4	788	26		NA/NA	AUTO
CP341	42	4	805	26	5/977/17	NA/NA	AUTO
CP341I	42	4	805	26	5/977/17	NA/NA	AUTO
CP342	43	4	805	26	5/977/17	NA/NA	AUTO
CP343 (ZENITH)	43	4	805		5/977/17	NA/NA	AUTO
CP344	43	4	805	26	5/977/17	NA/NA	AUTO
CP2020 (KATO)	21	2	653	32		NA/NA	AUTO
CP2022	20	2	653	32	4/615/17	NA/NA	AUTO
CP2024 (KATO)	21	2	653	32	4/615/17	NA/NA	AUTO
CP2034 (PANCHO)	32	2	823	38	4/615/17	NA/NA	AUTO
CP2040	43	4	548	38		NA/NA	AUTO
CP2044 (PANCHO)	42	4	548	38	5/977/17	NA/NA	AUTO
CP2060	64	4	823	38		NA/NA	AUTO
CP2064 (PANCHO)	64	4	823	38	4/615/17	NA/NA	AUTO
CP2084 (PANCHO)	85	4	1096	38	8/548/38	NA/NA	AUTO
CP2124 (PANCHO)	120	4	1123	53	*UNIV T	NA/NA	AUTO
CP2304	209	8	1348	39	*UNIV T	NA/NA	AUTO
CP3000	42	2	1045	40	5/980/17	NA/NA	AUTO
CP3020	21	2	623	33		NA/NA	AUTO
CP3022	21	2	636	33	4/615/17	NA/NA	AUTO
CP3024	22	2	636	33	4/615/17	NA/NA	AUTO
CP3040	42	2	1026	40		NA/NA	AUTO
CP3041	42	2	1047	40	5/977/17	NA/NA	AUTO
CP3044	42	2	1047	40	5/977/17	NA/NA	AUTO
CP3181	84	6	832	33		NA/NA	AUTO
CP3100	104	8	776	33		NA/NA	AUTO
CP3102	104	8	776	33	*UNIV T	NA/NA	AUTO
CP3104	104	8	776	33	13/925/17	NA/NA	AUTO
CP3111	107	8	832	33	*UNIV T	NA/NA	AUTO
CP3114	107	8	832	33	*UNIV T	NA/NA	AUTO
CP3150	52	4	776	33		NA/NA	AUTO
CP3180	84	6	832	33		NA/NA	AUTO
CP3184	84	6	832	33	9/1024/17	NA/NA	AUTO
CP3200	209	8	1348	38		NA/NA	AUTO
CP3200F	212	8	1366	38		NA/NA	AUTO

Drive Model	Seek Time	Interface	Encode	Form Factor	cache kb	mtbf	RPM	Obsolete?
K120M50Z-70P	23	MCA	2,7 RLL	3.5 HH				
LDSNECMS-20	28	IDE AT	2,7 RLL	3.5 HH		20k		
LDZE386-100	25	IDE AT		3.5 HH		20k		
PSExpress 150	17	ESDI	2,7 RLL	5.25 FH		40k		
PSExpress 320	15	ESDI	2,7 RLL	5.25 FH		40k		
SENTRY 90	18	SCSI		5.25 FH		40k		
SENTRY 180	18	SCSI		5.25 FH		40k		
SENTRY 300	16.5	SCSI		5.25 FH		30k		
SENTRY 600	16	SCSI		5.25 FH		30k		
COGITO								
CG906	93	ST412/506	MFM	5.25 HH				
CG912	93	ST412/506	MFM	5.25 HH				
CG925	93	ST412/506	MFM	5.25 HH				
PT912	93	ST412/506	MFM	5.25 HH				
PT925	93	ST412/506	MFM	5.25 HH				
COMPORT								
2040	35	ST412/506	2,7 RLL	5.25 HH		30k		
2041	29	IDE AT		5.25 HH		30k		
2082	29	SCSI		5.25 HH		30k		
CONNER PERIPHERALS, INC.								
CP320		SCSI	2,7 RLL	3.5 3H				Y
CP321		IDE AT	2,7 RLL	3.5 3H				Y
CP323		ZENITH		3.5 3H				Y
CP324		IDE AT	2,7 RLL	3.5 3H				Y
CP340	29	SCSI	2,7 RLL	3.5 HH	1k	20k	3600	Y
CP341	29	IDE AT	2,7 RLL	3.5 HH				Y
CP341I	29	IDE AT	2,7 RLL	3.5 HH				Y
CP342	29	IDE AT	2,7 RLL	3.5 HH				Y
CP343 (ZENITH)	29	ZENITH		3.5 HH				Y
CP344	29	IDE AT	2,7 RLL	3.5 HH	8k	20k	3600	Y
CP2020 (KATO)	23	SCSI	2,7 RLL	2.5 4H	8k	100k		Y
CP2022	23	IDE AT	2,7 RLL	3.5 HH				
CP2024 (KATO)	23	IDE AT	2,7 RLL	2.5 4H	8k	100k	3433	Y
CP2034 (PANCHO)	19	IDE AT	2,7 RLL	2.5 4H	32k	100k	3433	Y
CP2040	17	SCSI	2,7 RLL	2.5 4H	32k	50k	3486	
CP2044 (PANCHO)	19	IDE AT	2,7 RLL	2.5 4H	32k	50k	3486	Y
CP2060	19	SCSI	2,7 RLL	2.5 4H	32k	50k	3486	
CP2064 (PANCHO)	19	IDE AT	2,7 RLL	2.5 4H	32k	50k	3486	
CP2084 (PANCHO)	19	IDE AT	1,7 RLL	2.5 4H	32k	150k	3486	
CP2124 (PANCHO)	26	IDE AT	1,7 RLL	2.5	32k	150k		N
CP2304	19	IDE AT	RLL	3.5 HH				
CP3000	28	IDE AT	2,7 RLL	2.5 4H	8k	100k	3557	Y
CP3020	27	SCSI	2,7 RLL	3.5 3H	8k	50k	3575	Y
CP3022	27	IDE AT	2,7 RLL	3.5 3H		50k		Y
CP3024	27	IDE AT	2,7 RLL	3.5 3H	8k	50k	3575	Y
CP3040	25	SCSI	2,7 RLL	3.5 3H	8k	50k	3557	Y
CP3041	25	IDE AT	2,7 RLL	3.5 HH		50k		Y
CP3044	25	IDE AT	2,7 RLL	3.5 3H	8k	50k	3557	Y
CP3181	25	IDE AT	2,7 RLL	3.5 HH		50k		
CP3100	25	SCSI	2,7 RLL	3.5 HH	32k	50k	3575	N
CP3102	25	IDE AT	2,7 RLL	3.5 HH	16k	50k		
CP3104	25	IDE AT	2,7 RLL	3.5 HH	16k	30k	3575	
CP3111		IDE AT	2,7 RLL	3.5 HH	16k	50k		
CP3114		IDE AT	2,7 RLL	3.5 HH				
CP3150	25	SCSI	2,7 RLL	3.5 HH		50k		
CP3180	25	SCSI	2,7 RLL	3.5 HH	32k	50k	3575	
CP3184	25	IDE AT	2,7 RLL	3.5 HH	32k	50k	3575	
CP3200	16	SCSI	2,7 RLL	3.5 HH	64k	50k	3485	
CP3200F	16	SCSI	2,7 RLL	3.5 HH	64k	50k	3485	N

Drive Model	Format Size MB	Head	Cyl	Sect/ Trac	Translate H/C/S	RWC/ WPC	Land Zone
CP3201I	215	8	1348	39	*UNIV T	NA/NA	AUTO
CP3204	209	8	1366	38	16/683/38	NA/NA	AUTO
CP3204F	212	8	1366	38	16/683/38	NA/NA	AUTO
CP3209F	212	8	1366	38	*UNIV T	NA/NA	AUTO
CP3304 (SUMMIT)	340	8	1806	46	16/659/63	NA/NA	AUTO
CP3360 (SUMMIT)	362	8	1806	49		NA/NA	AUTO
CP3364 (SUMMIT)	362	8	1808	49	16/702/63	NA/NA	AUTO
CP3500 (SUMMIT)	510	12	1806	49		NA/NA	AUTO
CP3504 (SUMMIT)	510	12	1806	46	16/987/63	NA/NA	AUTO
CP3505	510	12	1806	46		NA/NA	AUTO
CP3540 (SUMMIT)	543	12	1806	49		NA/NA	AUTO
CP3544 (SUMMIT)	544	12	1808	49	16/1024/63	NA/NA	AUTO
CP4024 (STUBBY)	21	2	627	34	4/615/17	NA/NA	AUTO
CP4044 (STUBBY)	43	2	1097	38	5/977/17	NA/NA	AUTO
CP4084 (GATOR)	85	2	1806	46		NA/NA	AUTO
CP30060 (HOPI)	60	2	1524	39		NA/NA	AUTO
CP30064 (HOPI)	60	2	1524	39	4/762/39	NA/NA	AUTO
CP30064H (HOPI)	60	2	1524	39	4/762/39	NA/NA	AUTO
CP30069 (HOPI)	60	2	1524	39		NA/NA	AUTO
CP30080 (HOPI)	84	4	1053	39		NA/NA	AUTO
CP30080E (JAGUAR)	85	4	1806	46		NA/NA	AUTO
CP30081	85	4	1058	39		NA/NA	AUTO
CP30084 (HOPI)	84	4	1053	39	8/526/39	NA/NA	AUTO
CP30084E (JAGUAR)	85	2	1806	46	4/903/46	NA/NA	AUTO
CP30100 (HOPI)	120	4	1524	39		NA/NA	AUTO
CP30101	122	4	1524	9		---/---	761
CP30101G	122	4	1524	9		---/---	761
CP30101 (HOPI)	121	8	761	39	*UNIV T	NA/NA	AUTO
CP30104 (HOPI)	121	4	1524	39	8/762/39	NA/NA	AUTO
CP30104H (HOPI)	121	4	1524	39	8/762/39	NA/NA	AUTO
CP30109 (HOPI)	120	4	1522	39		NA/NA	AUTO
CP30170E (JAGUAR)	170	4	1806	46		NA/NA	AUTO
CP30174E (JAGUAR)	170	4	1806	46	8/903/46	NA/NA	AUTO
CP30200 (COUGAR)	212	4	2124	49		NA/NA	AUTO
CP30204 (COUGAR)	212	16	683	38	16/683/38	NA/NA	683
CP30254	252	4	1985	62		NA/NA	AUTO
CP30544	543				16/989/63	---/---	

CORE INTERNATIONAL

Drive Model	Format Size MB	Head	Cyl	Sect/ Trac	Translate H/C/S	RWC/ WPC	Land Zone
3SHC230	230	5				NA/NA	AUTO
AT20	20	4	615	17		---/---	AUTO
AT26	26	3	988	17		---/---	
AT30	32	5	733	17		---/---	
AT30R	49	5	733	26		---/---	
AT32	32	5	733	17		---/---	
AT32R	49	5	733	26		---/---	
AT40F	40	4	564	35		---/---	AUTO
AT40	40	5	924	17		---/---	
AT40R	62	5	924	26		---/---	
ATPLUS43	43	5	988	17		---/---	
ATPLUS43R	66	5	988	26		---/---	
ATPLUS44	44	7	733	17		---/---	
ATPLUS44R	68	7	733	26		---/---	
ATPLUS56	56	7	924	17		---/---	
ATPLUS63	42	5	988	17		---/---	
ATPLUS63R	65	6	988	26		---/---	
ATPLUS72	73	9	924	17		---/---	
ATPLUS72R	107	5	924	26		---/---	
ATPLUS80	80	9	1024			---/---	
ATPLUS80R	132	9	1024			---/---	
ATPLUS82		5	968	35		---/---	AUTO
AT115		7	968	35		---/---	AUTO
AT145	58	7	968			---/---	

Drive Model	Seek Time	Interface	Encode	Form Factor	cache kb	mtbf	RPM	Obsolete?
CP3201I	19	IDE AT	2,7 RLL	3.5 HH	64k	150k		
CP3204		IDE AT	2,7 RLL	3.5 HH	64k	50k	3485	
CP3204F		IDE AT	2,7 RLL	3.5 HH	64k	50k	3485	
CP3209F	16	IDE AT	2,7 RLL	3.5 HH		150k		
CP3304 (SUMMIT)		IDE AT	1,7 RLL	3.5 HH		150k		N
CP3360 (SUMMIT)	12	SCSI-2	2,7 RLL	3.5 3H		150k		N
CP3364 (SUMMIT)	12	SCSI-2	2,7 RLL	3.5 3H	256k	150k	4498	N
CP3500 (SUMMIT)	12	SCSI	2,7 RLL	3.5 3H	256k	100k	3609	
CP3504 (SUMMIT)	12	SCSI	2,7 RLL	3.5 3H	256k	100k	3609	
CP3505	12	IDE AT	2,7 RLL	3.5 HH		150k		
CP3540 (SUMMIT)	12	SCSI-2	2,7 RLL	3.5 3H		150k		N
CP3544 (SUMMIT)	49	IDE AT	2,7 RLL	3.5 Factor	256k	150k	4498	N
CP4024 (STUBBY)		IDE AT	2,7 RLL	3.5 4H	8k	40k	2913	Y
CP4044 (STUBBY)		IDE AT	2,7 RLL	3.5 4H	8k	50k		Y
CP4084 (GATOR)	19	IDE AT	2,7 RLL	3.5 4H	32k			Y
CP30060 (HOPI)	19	SCSI	1,7 RLL	3.5 4H		150k		
CP30064 (HOPI)	19	IDE AT	1,7 RLL	3.5 4H	32k	150k	3400	
CP30064H (HOPI)	19	IDE AT	1,7 RLL	3.5 3H	32k	150k	3400	
CP30069 (HOPI)	19	MCA	1,7 RLL	3.5 4H		150k		
CP30080 (HOPI)	19	IDE AT	2,7 RLL	3.5 3H	8k			
CP30080E (JAGUAR)	17	SCSI	1,7 RLL	3.5 4H		150k		
CP30081	19	IDE AT	1,7 RLL	3.5 4H		150k		
CP30084 (HOPI)	19	IDE AT	1,7 RLL	3.5 4H	64k	150k	3400	
CP30084E (JAGUAR)	17	IDE AT	1,7 RLL	3.5 4H	64k	150k	3833	
CP30100 (HOPI)		SCSI	2,7 RLL	3.5 4H	64k	150k	3400	N
CP30101	19	IDE AT	2,7 RLL	3.5 3H				
CP30101G	19	IDE AT	2,7 RLL	3.5 3H				
CP30101 (HOPI)	10	IDE AT	2,7 RLL	3.5 3H				
CP30104 (HOPI)	19	IDE AT	1,7 RLL	3.5 4H	32k	100k	3400	
CP30104H (HOPI)		IDE AT	1,7 RLL	3.5 3H	32k	150k	3400	
CP30109 (HOPI)	19	MCA	2,7 RLL	3.5 4H	64k	150k	3400	
CP30170E (JAGUAR)	17	SCSI	1,7 RLL	3.5 4H		150k		
CP30174E (JAGUAR)	17	IDE AT	1,7 RLL	3.5 4H	32k	150k	3833	
CP30200 (COUGAR)	12	SCSI-2	1,7 RLL	3.5 4H	256k	150k	4500	
CP30204 (COUGAR)	12	IDE AT	2,7 RLL	3.5 4H	256k	150k	4498	
CP30254	14	IDE AT	1,7 RLL	3.5 3H		200k		
CP30544								

CORE INTERNATIONAL

Drive Model	Seek Time	Interface	Encode	Form Factor	cache kb	mtbf	RPM	Obsolete?
3SHC230	13	SCSI		3.5		150k		
AT20	20	ST412/506	MFM	5.25 FH		25k		
AT26	26	ST412/506	MFM	5.25 HH		25k		
AT30	21	ST412/506	MFM	5.25 FH		50k		
AT30R	21	ST412/506	2,7 RLL	5.25 FH		50		
AT32	21	ST412/506	MFM	5.25 FH		50k		
AT32R	21	ST412/506	2,7 RLL	5.25 FH		50k		
AT40F	10	ESDI		5.25 FH		33k	3597	
AT40	26	ST412/506	MFM	5.25 FH		50k		
AT40R	26	ST412/506	2,7 RLL	5.25 FH		50k		
ATPLUS43	26	ST412/506	MFM	5.25 HH		50k		
ATPLUS43R	26	ST412/506	2,7 RLL	5.25 HH		50k		
ATPLUS44	26	ST412/506	MFM	3.5 HH		50k		
ATPLUS44R	26	ST412/506	2,7 RLL	3.5 HH		50k		
ATPLUS56	26	ST412/506	MFM	5.25 FH		33k		
ATPLUS63	26	ST412/506	MFM	5.25 HH				
ATPLUS63R	26	ST412/506	2,7 RLL	5.25 HH				
ATPLUS72	26	ST412/506	MFM	5.25 FH		50k		
ATPLUS72R	26	ST412/506	2,7 RLL	5.25 FH		50k		
ATPLUS80	15	ST412/506	MFM	3.5 HH		50k		
ATPLUS80R	15	ST412/506	2,7 RLL	3.5 HH		50k		
ATPLUS82	16	ESDI		5.25 FH		33k	3597	
AT115	16	ESDI		5.25 FH		33k	3597	
AT145	17	ST412/506	MFM	5.25 FH				

Drive Model	Format Size MB	Head	Cyl	Sect/ Trac	Translate H/C/S	RWC/ WPC	Land Zone
AT150	156	9	968	35		--/--	AUTO
AT260		12	1212	35		--/--	AUTO
HC25	250					--/--	AUTO
HC40	40	4	564	35		NA/NA	AUTO
HC90	91	5	969	35		NA/NA	
HC100	101	15	379	35		--/--	
HC150	150	7	1250	35		--/--	AUTO
HC150S	155	9	969	35		--/--	AUTO
HC175	177	9	1072	35		--/--	
HC200	200	8				--/--	
HC230	230	5				NA/NA	AUTO
HC260	260	12	1212	35		NA/NA	
HC310	325	7	1747	52		NA/NA	AUTO
HC310S	330	8	1447	56		--/--	AUTO
HC315-20	340	8	1447	57		--/--	AUTO
HC380	376	15	1412	35		--/--	
HC650	658	15	1661	53		--/--	AUTO
HC650S	663	16	1447	56		--/--	AUTO
HC655-20	680	16	1447	57		--/--	AUTO
HC1000	1056	16	1787	77		NA/NA	AUTO
HC1000S	1005	16	1918	64		--/--	AUTO
HC1000-20	1056	15	1787	77		--/--	AUTO
MC60	60	4	928	32		NA/NA	AUTO
MC120	120	8	920	32		NA/NA	AUTO
OPTIMA 30	31	5	733	17		--/--	
OPTIMA 30R	48	5	733	26		--/--	
OPTIMA 40R	64	5	963	26		--/--	
OPTIMA 40	41	5	963	17		--/--	
OPTIMA 70R	109	9	918	17		--/--	
OPTIMA 70	71	9	918	17		--/--	
OPTIMA 80	80	9	1024	17		--/--	
OPTIMA 80R	132	9	1024	26		--/--	

DIGITAL EQUIPMENT CORP.

Drive Model	Format Size MB	Head	Cyl	Sect/ Trac	Translate H/C/S	RWC/ WPC	Land Zone
DSP2022A	220	5				--/--	
DSP2022S	220	5				--/--	
DSP3085	852	14				--/--	
DSP3105	1050	14				--/--	
DSP3160	1600	16				--/--	
DSP5200	2000	21				--/--	
DSP5350	3500	25				--/--	

DISC TEC

Drive Model	Format Size MB	Head	Cyl	Sect/ Trac	Translate H/C/S	RWC/ WPC	Land Zone
RHD-20 (REMOVABLE)	21	2	615	34		NA/NA	AUTO
RHD-60	62	2	1024	60		NA/NA	AUTO
RHD-80	81					NA/NA	AUTO
RHD-120	130					NA/NA	AUTO
RHD-180	183					NA/NA	AUTO
RHD-210	210					NA/NA	AUTO

DISCTRON (OTARI)

Drive Model	Format Size MB	Head	Cyl	Sect/ Trac	Translate H/C/S	RWC/ WPC	Land Zone
D214	11	4	306	17		128/128	
D503	3	2	153	17		--/--	
D504	4	2	215	17		--/--	
D506	5	4	153	17		--/--	
D507	5	2	306	17		128/128	
D509	8	4	215	17		128/128	
D512	11	8	153	17		--/--	
D513	11	6	215	17		128/128	
D514	11	4	306	17		128/128	
D518	15	8	215	17		128/128	
D519	16	6	306	17		128/128	

Drive Model	Seek Time	Interface	Encode	Form Factor	cache kb	Obsolete? mtbf	RPM
AT150	16	ESDI	2,7 RLL	5.25 FH		33k	3597
AT260	25	ESDI		5.25 FH		25k	3524
HC25		ESDI		5.25 FH			
HC40	9	ESDI	2,7 RLL	5.25 FH		50	
HC90	16	ESDI	2,7 RLL	5.25 HH		50k	
HC100	9	ESDI		5.25 FH		50k	
HC150	17	ESDI	2,7 RLL	5.25 HH		100k	3600
HC150S	16.5	SCSI	2,7 RLL	5.25 HH		150k	3597
HC175	14	ESDI	2,7 RLL	5.25 FH		50k	
HC200	16	IDE AT		5.25 FH		150k	
HC230	13	SCSI		3.5 FH		150k	
HC260	25	ESDI	2,7 RLL	5.25 FH			
HC310	18	ESDI	2,7 RLL	5.25 HH		100k	3600
HC310S	16.5	SCSI	2,7 RLL	5.25 HH		150k	4002
HC315-20	17	ESDI	2,7 RLL	5.25 FH		150k	4002
HC380	16	ESDI	2,7 RLL	5.25 FH		50k	
HC650	17	ESDI	2,7 RLL	5.25 FH		100k	3600
HC650S	16.5	SCSI		5.25 FH		150k	4002
HC655-20	17	SCSI		5.25 FH		150k	4002
HC1000	14	ESDI (24)	2,7 RLL	5.25 FH		150k	
HC1000S	15	SCSI	2,7 RLL	5.25 FH		150k	4002
HC1000-20	14	SCSI	2,7 RLL	5.25 FH		150k	3600
MC60	23	MCA		3.5 HH		45k	3600
MC120	23	MCA		3.5 HH		45k	3600
OPTIMA 30	21	ST412/506	MFM	5.25 HH			
OPTIMA 30R	21	ST412/506	2,7 RLL	5.25 HH			
OPTIMA 40R	26	ST412/506	2,7 RLL	5.25 HH		35k	
OPTIMA 40	26	ST412/506	MFM	5.25 HH		35k	
OPTIMA 70R	26	ST412/506	2,7 RLL	5.25 FH		35k	
OPTIMA 70	26	ST412/506	MFM	5.25 FH		35k	
OPTIMA 80	15	ST412/506	MFM	3.5 HH		35k	
OPTIMA 80R	15	ST412/506	2,7 RLL	3.5 HH		35k	

DIGITAL EQUIPMENT CORP.

Drive Model	Seek Time	Interface	Encode	Form Factor	cache kb	Obsolete? mtbf	RPM
DSP2022A		IDE AT	1,7 RLL	2.5 4H	512k	250k	5400
DSP2022S		SCSI-2 FAS	1,7 RLL	2.5 4H	512k	250k	5400
DSP3085	9	SCSI-2 FAS	1,7 RLL	3.5 HH	512k	250k	5400
DSP3105	9	SCSI-2 FAS	1,7 RLL	3.5 HH	512k	250k	5400
DSP3160		SCSI-2 FAS	1,7 RLL	3.5 HH	512k	300k	5400
DSP5200	12	SCSI-2 FAS	1,7 RLL	5.25 FH	512k	250k	5400
DSP5350	11	SCSI-2 FAS	1,7 RLL	5.25 FH	512k	300k	5400

DISC TEC

Drive Model	Seek Time	Interface	Encode	Form Factor	cache kb	Obsolete? mtbf	RPM
RHD-20 (REMOVABLE)	23	IDE AT	RLL	3.5 3H		20k	
RHD-60	22	IDE AT	RLL	3.5 3H		45k	
RHD-80	16	IDE AT	RLL	3.5 3H		150k	
RHD-120	17	IDE AT	RLL	3.5 3H		100k	
RHD-180	15	IDE AT	RLL	3.5 3H		100k	
RHD-210	19	IDE AT	RLL	3.5 3H		150k	

DISCTRON (OTARI)

Drive Model	Seek Time	Interface	Encode	Form Factor	cache kb	Obsolete? mtbf	RPM
D214		ST412/506	MFM	5.25 FH			
D503		ST412/506	MFM	5.25 FH			Y
D504		ST412/506	MFM	5.25 FH			Y
D506		ST412/506	MFM	5.25 FH			Y
D507		ST412/506	MFM	5.25 FH			Y
D509		ST412/506	MFM	5.25 FH			Y
D512		ST412/506	MFM	5.25 FH			Y
D513		ST412/506	MFM	5.25 FH			Y
D514		ST412/506	MFM	5.25 FH			Y
D518		ST412/506	MFM	5.25 FH			Y
D519		ST412/506	MFM	5.25 FH			Y

Drive Model	Format Size MB	Head	Cyl	Sect/ Trac	Translate H/C/S	RWC/ WPC	Land Zone
D526	21	8	306	17		128/128	

DMA

306	11	2	612	17		612/400	

ELOCH

DISCACHE10	10	4	320	17		321/321	
DISCACHE20	20	8	320	17		321/321	

EPSON

HD560	21	4	615	17		615/300	
HD830	10	2	612	17		---/---	
HD850	10	4	306	17		---/---	
HD860	21	4	612	17		---/---	
HMD710	10	2	615	17		---/---	
HMD720	21	4	615	17		---/---	
HMD726A	21	4	615	32		---/---	AUTO
HMD755	21	2	615	34		---/---	
HMD765	42	4	615	34		---/---	

FUJI

FK301-13	10	4	306	17		307/128	
FK302-13	10	2	612	17		613/307	
FK302-26	21	4	612	17		613/307	
FK302-39	32	6	612	17		613/307	
FK303-52	40	8	615	17		---/616	
FK305-26	21	4	615	17		---/616	
FK305-39	32	6	615	17		---/616	
FK305-39R	32	4	615	26		---/616	
FK305-58R	49	6	615	26		---/616	
FK308S-39R	45	6	615			---/---	
FK308S-58R	32	4	615	26		---/616	
FK309-26	21	4	615	17		---/616	
FK309-39R	32	4	615	26		---/616	
FK309S-50R	41	4	615			---/---	

FUJITSU AMERICA, INC.

M2225D	40	4	615	17		---/---	
M2225D2	20	4	615	17		---/---	
M2225DR	32	4	615	17		---/---	
M2226D	60	6	615	17		---/---	
M2226D2	30	6	615	17		---/---	
M2226DR	49	6	615	26		---/---	
M2227D	80	8	615	17		---/---	
M2227D2	42	8	615	17		---/---	
M2227DR	65	8	615	26		---/---	
M2230	5	2	320	17		320/180	
M2230AS	5	2	320	17		320/320	
M2230AT	5	2	320	17		320/320	
M2231	5	2	306	17		---/---	
M2233	10	4	320	17		320/128	
M2233AS	11	4	306	17		320/320	
M2233AT	11	4	306	17		320/320	
M2234	15	6	320	17		320/128	
M2234AS	16	6	306	17		320/320	
M2235	22	8	320	17		320/128	
M2235AS	22	8	306	17		320/320	
M2241AS	26	4	754	17		---/375	754
M2241AS2	24	4	754	32		---/375	AUTO
M2242AS	45	7	754	17		754/375	AUTO
M2242AS2	43	7	754	17		---/---	AUTO

Drive Model	Seek Time	Interface	Encode	Form Factor	cache kb	mtbf	Obsolete? RPM
D526		ST412/506	MFM	5.25 FH			Y
DMA							
306	170?	ST412/506	MFM	5.25 HH			
ELOCH							
DISCACHE10	65?	ST412/506	MFM	5.25 FH			
DISCACHE20	65?	ST412/506	MFM	5.25 FH			
EPSON							
HD560	78	ST412/506	MFM	5.25 HH			
HD830	93	ST412/506	MFM	5.25 HH			
HD850		ST412/506	MFM	5.25 HH			
HD860		ST412/506	MFM	5.25 HH			
HMD710	78	ST412/506	MFM	5.25 HH			
HMD720	78	ST412/506	MFM	5.25 HH			
HMD726A	80	SCSI	2,7 RLL	3.5 HH		20k	
HMD755	80	ST412/506	2,7 RLL	5.25 HH		20k	
HMD765	80	ST412/506	2,7 RLL	5.25 HH		20k	
FUJI							
FK301-13	65	ST412/506	MFM	3.5 HH		45k	Y
FK302-13	65	ST412/506	MFM	3.5 HH			Y
FK302-26	65	ST412/506	MFM	3.5 HH			Y
FK302-39	65	ST412/506	MFM	3.5 HH			Y
FK303-52	65?	ST412/506	MFM	3.5 HH		20k	Y
FK305-26	65	ST412/506	MFM	3.5 HH			Y
FK305-39	65	ST412/506	MFM	3.5 HH		20k	Y
FK305-39R	65	ST412/506	2,7 RLL	3.5 HH			Y
FK305-58R	65	ST412/506	2,7 RLL	3.5 HH		20k	Y
FK308S-39R	65	SCSI	2,7 RLL	3.5 HH		20k	Y
FK308S-58R	65	ST412/506	2,7 RLL	3.5 HH			Y
FK309-26	65	ST412/506	MFM	3.5 HH		20k	Y
FK309-39R	65	ST412/506	2,7 RLL	3.5 HH		20k	Y
FK309S-50R	45	SCSI	2,7 RLL	3.5 HH		20k	Y
FUJITSU AMERICA, INC.							
M2225D	40	ST412/506	MFM	3.5 HH		30k	Y
M2225D2	35	ST412/506	MFM	3.5 HH			N
M2225DR	35	ST412/506	2,7 RLL	3.5 HH			
M2226D	40	ST412/506	MFM	3.5 HH		30k	Y
M2226D2	35	ST412/506	MFM	3.5 HH			N
M2226DR	35	ST412/506	2,7 RLL	3.5 HH			
M2227D	40	ST412/506	MFM	3.5 HH		30k	Y
M2227D2	35	ST412/506	MFM	3.5 HH			N
M2227DR	35	ST412/506	2,7 RLL	3.5 HH			
M2230	85	ST412/506	MFM	5.25 FH			Y
M2230AS		ST412/506	MFM	5.25			
M2230AT		ST412/506	MFM	5.25			
M2231	85	ST412/506	MFM	5.25 FH			
M2233	80	ST412/506	MFM	5.25 FH			Y
M2233AS		ST412/506	MFM	5.25			
M2233AT		ST412/506	MFM	5.25			
M2234	85	ST412/506	MFM	5.25 FH			Y
M2234AS		ST412/506	MFM	5.25			
M2235	85	ST412/506	MFM	5.25 FH			Y
M2235AS		ST412/506	MFM	5.25			
M2241AS		ST412/506	MFM	5.25 FH			Y
M2241AS2	30	ST412/506	MFM	5.25 FH		20k	N
M2242AS	30	ST412/506	MFM	5.25 FH		30k	Y
M2242AS2	30	ST412/506	MFM	5.25 FH			N

Drive Model	Format Size MB	Head	Cyl	Sect/Trac	Translate H/C/S	RWC/WPC	Land Zone
M2243AS	72	11	754	17		754/375	AUTO
M2243AS2	67	11	754	17		---/---	AUTO
M2243R	110	7	1186	26		---/---	AUTO
M2243T	68	7	1186	17		---/---	AUTO
M2244E	73	5	823	35		NA/NA	AUTO
M2244SA	73	5	823	35		NA/NA	AUTO
M2245E	120	7	823	35		NA/NA	AUTO
M2245SA	120	7	823	35		NA/NA	AUTO
M2246E	138	10	823	35		NA/NA	AUTO
M2246SA	171	10	823	35		NA/NA	AUTO
M2247E	285	7	1243			NA/NA	AUTO
M2247S	289	7	1243	65		NA/NA	AUTO
M2247SA	160	7	1243	36		NA/NA	AUTO
M2247SB	169	7	1243			NA/NA	AUTO
M2248E	266	11	1243			NA/NA	AUTO
M2248S	227	11	1243			NA/NA	AUTO
M2248SA	252	11	1243	36		NA/NA	AUTO
M2248SB	266	11	1243			NA/NA	AUTO
M2249E	334	15	1243	35		NA/NA	AUTO
M2249S	334	15	1243	35		NA/NA	AUTO
M2249SA	334	15	1243	35		NA/NA	AUTO
M2249SB	362	15	1243			NA/NA	AUTO
M2261E	321	8	1658			NA/NA	AUTO
M2261HA	359	8	1658	53		NA/NA	AUTO
M2261S	321	8	1658			NA/NA	AUTO
M2262E	448	11	1658			NA/NA	AUTO
M2262HA	476	11	1658	51		NA/NA	AUTO
M2262SA	476	11	1658	51		NA/NA	AUTO
M2263E	650	15	1658			NA/NA	AUTO
M2263HA	674	15	1658	53		NA/NA	AUTO
M2263S	650	15	1658			NA/NA	AUTO
M2266A	1079	15	1658			---/---	
M2266E	674	15	1658	53		NA/NA	AUTO
M2266H	953	15	1658			NA/NA	AUTO
M2266HA	1079	15	1658			NA/NA	AUTO
M2266HB	1140	15	1658			NA/NA	AUTO
M2266S	953	15	1658			NA/NA	AUTO
M2266SA	1079	15	1658			NA/NA	AUTO
M2266SB	1140	15	1658			NA/NA	AUTO
M2344KS	690	27	624	NA		NA/NA	AUTO
M2511A	128					---/---	
M2611S (ES)	46	2	1334			NA/NA	AUTO
M2611SA	46	2	1334	34		NA/NA	AUTO
M2611SB (ESB)	46	2	1334	17		NA/NA	AUTO
M2611H	46	2	1334	34		NA/NA	AUTO
M2611S	46	2	1334	68		NA/NA	AUTO
M2611SA	46	2	1334	34		NA/NA	AUTO
M2611SB	46	2	1334	17		NA/NA	AUTO
M2611T	45	2	1334	33	4/667/33	NA/NA	AUTO
M2612ES	90	4	1334			NA/NA	AUTO
M2612ESA	90	4	1334	34		NA/NA	AUTO
M2612ESB	90	4	1334			NA/NA	AUTO
M2612SA	91	4	1334	33		NA/NA	AUTO
M2612ET	90	4	1334	33		NA/NA	AUTO
M2612S	92	4	1334	68		NA/NA	AUTO
M2612T	91	4	1334	33	8/667/33	NA/NA	AUTO
M2613ES	139	6	1334			NA/NA	AUTO
M2613ESA	139	6	1334	34		NA/NA	AUTO
M2613ESB	139	6	1334			NA/NA	AUTO
M2613ET	135	6	1334	33		NA/NA	AUTO
M2613S	139	6	1334	68		NA/NA	AUTO
M2613SA	137	6	1334			NA/NA	AUTO
M2613SB	139	6	1334	17		NA/NA	AUTO

Drive Model	Seek Time	Interface	Encode	Form Factor	cache kb	mtbf	RPM	Obsolete?
M2243AS	30	ST412/506	MFM	5.25 FH		30k		Y
M2243AS2	30	ST412/506	MFM	5.25 FH				N
M2243R	25	ST412/506	2,7 RLL	5.25 HH				
M2243T	25	ST412/506	MFM	5.25 HH				
M2244E	25	ESDI	2,7 RLL	5.25 FH		30k		N
M2244SA	25	SCSI	2,7 RLL	5.25 FH		35k		N
M2245E	25	ESDI	2,7 RLL	5.25 FH				N
M2245SA	25	SCSI	2,7 RLL	5.25 FH				N
M2246E	25	ESDI	2,7 RLL	5.25 FH		30k		N
M2246SA	25	SCSI	2,7 RLL	5.25 FH		30k		N
M2247E	18	ESDI	1,7 RLL	5.25 FH		30k		N
M2247S	18	SCSI	1,7 RLL	5.25 FH		30k		N
M2247SA	18	SCSI	1,7 RLL	5.25 FH		30k		N
M2247SB	18	SCSI	1,7 RLL	5.25 FH		30k		N
M2248E	18	ESDI	1,7 RLL	5.25 FH		130k		N
M2248S	18	SCSI	1,7 RLL	5.25 FH		130k		N
M2248SA	18	SCSI	1,7 RLL	5.25 FH		130k		N
M2248SB	18	SCSI	1,7 RLL	5.25 FH		130k		N
M2249E	18	ESDI	1,7 RLL	5.25 FH		30k		N
M2249S	18	SCSI	1,7 RLL	5.25 FH		30k		N
M2249SA	18	SCSI	1,7 RLL	5.25 FH		30k		N
M2249SB	18	SCSI	1,7 RLL	5.25 FH		30k		N
M2261E	16	ESDI	2,7 RLL	5.25 FH		200k		N
M2261HA	16	SCSI	1,7 RLL	5.25 FH		200k		N
M2261S	16	SCSI	2,7 RLL	5.25 FH		200k		N
M2262E	16	ESDI	1,7 RLL	5.25 FH		200k		
M2262HA	16	SCSI	1,7 RLL	5.25 FH		200k		
M2262SA	16	SCSI	1,7 RLL	5.25 FH		200k		
M2263E	16	ESDI	1,7 RLL	5.25 FH		30k		N
M2263HA	16	SCSI	1,7 RLL	5.25 FH		30k		
M2263S	16	SCSI	1,7 RLL	5.25 FH		30k		
M2266A	14	SCSI	1,7 RLL	5.25 FH	256k		3600	
M2266E	16	ESDI	1,7 RLL	5.25 FH		200k		
M2266H	14.5	SCSI	1,7 RLL	5.25 FH		200k	3600	N
M2266HA	14.5	SCSI	1,7 RLL	5.25 FH		200k	3600	N
M2266HB	14.5	SCSI	1,7 RLL	5.25 FH		200k	3600	N
M2266S	14.5	SCSI	1,7 RLL	5.25 FH		200k	3600	N
M2266SA	14.5	SCSI	1,7 RLL	5.25 FH	256k	200k	3600	N
M2266SB	14.5	SCSI	1,7 RLL	5.25 FH		200k	3600	N
M2344KS	16	SCSI/SMD	RLL	8				N
M2511A	30	SCSI-2		3.5 3H	256k	30k	3600	
M2611S (ES)	25	SCSI	1,7 RLL	3.5 HH		50k		Y
M2611SA	25	SCSI	1,7 RLL	3.5 HH	24k	50k	3490	Y
M2611SB (ESB)	25	SCSI	1,7 RLL	3.5 HH		50k		Y
M2611H	25	SCSI	1,7 RLL	3.5 HH		50k		
M2611S	25	SCSI	1,7 RLL	3.5 HH		50k		
M2611SA	25	SCSI	1,7 RLL	3.5 HH		50k		
M2611SB	25	SCSI	1,7 RLL	3.5 HH		50k		
M2611T	25	IDE AT	1,7 RLL	3.5 HH	64k	50k	3490	Y
M2612ES	20	SCSI	1,7 RLL	3.5 HH		50k		Y
M2612ESA	20	SCSI	1,7 RLL	3.5 HH		50k		Y
M2612ESB	20	SCSI	1,7 RLL	3.5 HH		50k		Y
M2612SA	20	SCSI	1,7 RLL	3.5 HH	24k	50k	3490	Y
M2612ET	20	IDE AT	1,7 RLL	3.5 HH		50k		Y
M2612ES	20	SCSI	1,7 RLL	3.5 HH		50k		
M2612T	20	IDE AT	1,7 RLL	3.5 HH	64k	50k	3490	Y
M2613ES	20	SCSI	1,7 RLL	3.5 HH		50k		Y
M2613ESA	20	SCSI	1,7 RLL	3.5 HH		50k		Y
M2613ESB	20	SCSI	1,7 RLL	3.5 HH		50k		Y
M2613ET	20	IDE AT	1,7 RLL	3.5 HH		50k		
M2613S	20	SCSI	1,7 RLL	3.5 HH		50k		
M2613SA	20	SCSI	1,7 RLL	3.5 HH	24k	50k	3490	Y
M2613SB	20	SCSI	1,7 RLL	3.5 HH		50k		

Drive Model	Format Size MB	Head	Cyl	Sect/ Trac	Translate H/C/S	RWC/ WPC	Land Zone
M2613T	135	6	1334	33	12/667/33	NA/NA	AUTO
M2614ES	185	8	1334			NA/NA	AUTO
M2614ESA	185	8	1334	34		NA/NA	AUTO
M2614ESB	185	8	1334			NA/NA	AUTO
M2614ET	180	8	1334	33		NA/NA	AUTO
M2614S	185	8	1334	68		NA/NA	AUTO
M2614SA	182	8	1334			NA/NA	AUTO
M2614SB	186	8	1334	17		NA/NA	AUTO
M2614T	180	8	1334	33	16/667/33	NA/NA	AUTO
M2614ET	104	4	1542	33		NA/NA	AUTO
M2616ESA	107	4	1542	34		NA/NA	AUTO
M2616ET	107	4	1542	34		NA/NA	AUTO
M2616SA	105	4	1542			NA/NA	AUTO
M2616T	105	4	1542			NA/NA	AUTO
M2621S	235	5	1435			NA/NA	AUTO
M2622FA	330	7	1435			---/---	
M2622S	330	7	1435			NA/NA	AUTO
M2622SA	329	7	1435			NA/NA	AUTO
M2622T	330	7	1435			NA/NA	AUTO
M2623F	425	9	1429	V		NA/NA	AUTO
M2623FA	425	9	1435			---/---	
M2623S	425	9	1435			NA/NA	AUTO
M2623SA	423	9	1435	64		NA/NA	AUTO
M2623T	425	9	1435			NA/NA	AUTO
M2624FA	521	11	1435			---/---	
M2624S	520	11	1435			NA/NA	AUTO
M2624SA	517	11	1435	64		NA/NA	AUTO
M2624T	520	11	1435			NA/NA	AUTO
M2635S	160	4	1569			---/---	
M2635T	160	4	1569			---/---	
M2637S	240	6	1569			---/---	
M2637T	240	6	1569			---/---	
M2651SA	1400	16	1944			---/---	
M2652H	1628	20	1893	84		NA/NA	AUTO
M2652HD	1628	20	1893	84		NA/NA	AUTO
M2652P	2000U	20	1893			---/---	
M2652S	1628	20	1893	84		NA/NA	AUTO
M2652SA	1750	20	1944			---/---	
M2654SA	2061	21	2179			---/---	
M2691EHA	645	9	1818	V		NA/NA	AUTO
M2691ESA	645	9	1818	V		NA/NA	AUTO
M2694EHA	1080	15	1818	V		NA/NA	AUTO
M2694ESA	1080	15	1818	V		NA/NA	AUTO

HEWLETT-PACKARD CO

Drive Model	Format Size MB	Head	Cyl	Sect/ Trac	Translate H/C/S	RWC/ WPC	Land Zone
D1296A	21	4	615	17		0/300	670
D1660A	340	8	1457	57		NA/NA	AUTO
D1661A	680	16	1457	57		NA/NA	AUTO
HP97530E	136	4				NA/NA	AUTO
HP97530S	204	6				NA/NA	AUTO
HP97532D	215	4	1643	64*V		NA/NA	AUTO
HP97532E	215	4	1643	64		NA/NA	AUTO
HP97532S	215	4	1643	64		NA/NA	AUTO
HP97532T	215	4	1643	64		NA/NA	AUTO
HP97533D	323	6	1643	64		NA/NA	AUTO
HP97533E	323	6	1643	64		NA/NA	AUTO
HP97533S	323	6	1643	64		NA/NA	AUTO
HP97533T	323	6	1643	64		NA/NA	AUTO
HP97536D	646	12	1643	64		NA/NA	AUTO
HP97536E	646	12	1643	64		NA/NA	AUTO
HP97536S	646	12	1643	64		NA/NA	AUTO
HP97536T	646	12	1643	64		NA/NA	AUTO
HP97544D	331	8	1447	56		NA/NA	AUTO

Drive Model	Seek Time	Interface	Encode	Form Factor	cache kb	Obsolete? mtbf	RPM	
M2613T	20	IDE AT	1,7 RLL	3.5 HH	64k	50k	3490	Y
M2614ES	20	SCSI	1,7 RLL	3.5 HH				Y
M2614ESA	20	SCSI	1,7 RLL	3.5 HH				Y
M2614ESB	20	SCSI	1,7 RLL	3.5 HH				Y
M2614ET	20	IDE AT	1,7 RLL	3.5 HH		50k		
M2614S	20	SCSI	1,7 RLL	3.5 HH		50k		
M2614SA	20	SCSI	1,7 RLL	3.5 HH	24k	50k	3490	Y
M2614SB	20	SCSI	1,7 RLL	3.5 HH		50k		
M2614T	20	IDE AT	1,7 RLL	3.5 HH	64k	50k	3490	Y
M2614ET	20	IDE AT	1,7 RLL	3.5 HH		50k		
M2616ESA	20	SCSI	1,7 RLL	3.5 HH				Y
M2616ET	20	IDE AT	1,7 RLL	3.5 HH				Y
M2616SA	20	SCSI	1,7 RLL	3.5 HH	24k	50k	3490	Y
M2616T	20	IDE AT	1,7 RLL	3.5 HH	64k	50k	3490	Y
M2621S	12	SCSI-2	1,7 RLL	3.5 HH				
M2622FA		SCSI-1/2	1,7 RLL	3.5 HH	240k			
M2622S	12	SCSI-2	1,7 RLL	3.5 HH				N
M2622SA	12	SCSI-2	1,7 RLL	3.5 HH	240k	200k	4400	
M2622T	12	IDE AT	1,7 RLL	3.5 HH	240k	200k	4400	
M2623F	12	SCSI 1/2	1,7 RLL	3.5 HH		200k		
M2623FA		SCSI-1/2	1,7 RLL	3.5 HH	240k			
M2623S	12	SCSI-2	1,7 RLL	3.5 HH	240k	200k	4400	N
M2623SA	12	SCSI-2	1,7 RLL	3.5 HH	240k	200k	4400	
M2623T	12	IDE AT	1,7 RLL	3.5 HH	240k	200k	4400	N
M2624FA		SCSI-1/2	1,7 RLL	3.5 HH	240k			
M2624S	12	SCSI-2	1,7 RLL	3.5 HH	240k		4400	N
M2624SA	12	SCSI-2	1,7 RLL	3.5 HH	240k	200k	4400	
M2624T	12	IDE AT	1,7 RLL	3.5 HH	240k	200k	4400	N
M2635S	14	SCSI-2		2.5	256k	150k	4500	
M2635T	14	IDE AT		2.5	256k	150k	4500	
M2637S	14	SCSI-2		2.5	256	150k	4500	
M2637T	14	IDE AT		2.5	256k	150k	4500	
M2651SA	11	SCSI-2	1,7 RLL	5.25 FH				
M2652H	11	SCSI-2	1,7 RLL	5.25 HH		200k		N
M2652HD	11	SCSI-2	1,7 RLL	5.25 HH		200k		N
M2652P		IPI-2		5.25 FH				
M2652S	11	SCSI-2	1,7 RLL	5.25 FH		200k		N
M2652SA		SCSI-2		5.25				
M2654SA	12	SCSI-2	1,7 RLL	5.25 FH	256k			
M2691EHA	9	SCSI-2	1,7 RLL	3.5 HH	256k	300k	5400	
M2691ESA	9	SCSI-2	1,7 RLL	3.5 HH	256k	300k	5400	
M2694EHA	10	SCSI-2 FAS	1,7 RLL	3.5 HH	256k	300k	5400	
M2694ESA	10	SCSI-2	1,7 RLL	3.5 HH	256k	300k	5400	

HEWLETT-PACKARD CO

Drive Model	Seek Time	Interface	Encode	Form Factor	cache kb	Obsolete? mtbf	RPM	
D1296A	65	ST412/506	MFM	5.25 HH		100k		
D1660A	16	ESDI (15)	2,7 RLL	5.25 HH		150k		
D1661A	16	ESDI (15)	2,7 RLL	5.25 HH		150k		
HP97530E	18	ESDI	2,7 RLL	5.25 FH				
HP97530S	18	SCSI	2,7 RLL	5.25 FH				
HP97532D	17	SCSI	2,7 RLL	5.25 HH	16k	99k	3348	
HP97532E	17	ESDI (10)	2,7 RLL	5.25 HH	16k	99k	3348	
HP97532S	17	SCSI	2,7 RLL	5.25 HH	16k	99k	3348	
HP97532T	17	SCSI	2,7 RLL	5.25 HH	16k	99k	3348	
HP97533D	17	SCSI	2,7 RLL	5.25 HH	16k	99k	3348	
HP97533E	17	ESDI	2,7 RLL	5.25 HH	16k	99k	3348	
HP97533S	17	SCSI	2,7 RLL	5.25 HH	16k	99k	3348	
HP97533T	17	SCSI	2,7 RLL	5.25 HH	16k	99k	3348	
HP97536D	17	SCSI	2,7 RLL	5.25 HH	16k	99k	3348	
HP97536E	17	ESDI	2,7 RLL	5.25 HH	16k	99k	3348	
HP97536S	17	SCSI	2,7 RLL	5.25 HH	16k	99k	3348	
HP97536T	17	SCSI	2,7 RLL	5.25 HH	16k	99k	3348	
HP97544D	16	SCSI	2,7 RLL	5.25 HH	64k	150k	4002	

Drive Model	Format Size MB	Head	Cyl	Sect/ Trac	Translate H/C/S	RWC/ WPC	Land Zone
HP97544E	337	8	1447	56		NA/NA	AUTO
HP97544P	331	8	1447	56		NA/NA	AUTO
HP97544S	331	8	1447	56		NA/NA	AUTO
HP97544T	331	8	1447	56		NA/NA	AUTO
HP97548D	663	16	1447	56		NA/NA	AUTO
HP97548E	675	16	1447	56		NA/NA	AUTO
HP97548P	663	16	1447	56		NA/NA	AUTO
HP97548S	663	16	1447	56		NA/NA	AUTO
HP97548T	663	16	1447	56		NA/NA	AUTO
HP97549T	1001	16	1911	64		NA/NA	AUTO
HP97549T	1001	16	1911	69		NA/NA	AUTO
HP97556E	688	11	1697	72		NA/NA	AUTO
HP97556P	677	11	1670	72		NA/NA	AUTO
HP97556T	677	11	1670	72		NA/NA	AUTO
HP97558E	1084	15	1962	72		NA/NA	AUTO
HP97558P	1069	15	1935	72		NA/NA	AUTO
HP97558T	1069	15	1935	72		NA/NA	AUTO
HP97560E	1374	19	1962	72		NA/NA	AUTO
HP97560P	1355	19	1935	72		NA/NA	AUTO
HP97560T	1355	19	1935	72		NA/NA	AUTO
HP2233	235	5	1546	V		NA/NA	AUTO
HPC2233S	234	5	1546	V		NA/NA	AUTO
HPC2233 ATA	238	5	1546	V		NA/NA	AUTO
HPC2234S	328	7	1546	V		NA/NA	AUTO
HPC2234 ATA	334	7	1546	V		NA/NA	AUTO
HPC2235S	422	9	1546	V		NA/NA	AUTO
HPC2247	1052	13	1981	V		NA/NA	AUTO
HPC3335 ATA	429	9	1546	V		NA/NA	AUTO

HITACHI AMERICA

Drive Model	Format Size MB	Head	Cyl	Sect/ Trac	Translate H/C/S	RWC/ WPC	Land Zone
DK301-1	10	4	306	17		---/---	
DK301-2	15	6	306	17		---/---	
DK312C-20	209	9	1076	38		---/---	
DK312C-25	251	11	1076	38		---/---	
DK314C-41	419	14		17		---/---	
DK315C-11	1100	15				NA/NA	AUTO
DK315C-14	1400	15				NA/NA	AUTO
DK505-2	21	4	615	17		---/---	
DK511-3	29	5	699	17		---/300	699
DK511-5	41	7	699	17		---/300	699
DK511-8	67	10	823	17		---/400	822
DK512-12	94	7	823			NA/NA	
DK512C-12	94	7	823			---/---	
DK512-17	94	10	823			NA/NA	
DK512C-17	134	10	819	35		---/---	
DK512-8	67	5	823			NA/NA	AUTO
DK512C-8	67	5	823			---/---	
DK514-38	330	14	903	51		NA/NA	
DK514C-38	322	14	898	50		---/---	
DK515-12	1229	15		69		NA/NA	AUTO
DK515-78	673	14	1361	69		---/---	
DK515C-78	670	14	1356	69		---/---	
DK515S-78	673	14				---/---	
DK515C-78D	673	14	1361	69		NA/NA	AUTO
DK516-12	1230					---/---	
DK516-15	1320	15				NA/NA	AUTO
DK516C-16	1340	15				---/---	
DK517C-26	2000	14				NA/NA	AUTO
DK517C-37	2900	21				NA/NA	AUTO
DK521-5	51	6	823	17		---/NA	822
DK522-10	91	6	823	36		---/---	
DK522C-10	87	6	819	35		---/---	

Drive Model	Seek Time	Interface	Encode	Form Factor	cache kb	mtbf	Obsolete? RPM ⇩
HP97544E	17	ESDI	2,7 RLL	5.25 FH	64k	150k	4002
HP97544P	17	SCSI-2	2,7 RLL	5.25 FH	64k	150k	4002
HP97544S	16	SCSI	2,7 RLL	5.25 FH	64k	150k	4002
HP97544T	17	SCSI-2	2,7 RLL	5.25 FH	64k	150k	4002
HP97548D	16	SCSI	2,7 RLL	5.25 FH	64k	150k	4002
HP97548E	17	ESDI	2,7 RLL	5.25 FH	64k	150k	4002
HP97548P	17	SCSI-2	2,7 RLL	5.25 FH	64k	150k	4002
HP97548S	16	SCSI	2,7 RLL	5.25 FH	64k	150k	4002
HP97548T	17	SCSI-2	2,7 RLL	5.25 FH	64k	150k	4002
HP97549P	17	SCSI-2	2,7 RLL	5.25 FH	128k	150k	4002
HP97549T	17	SCSI-2	2,7 RLL	5.25 FH	128k	150k	4002
HP97556E	14	ESDI	2,7 RLL	5.25 FH	128k	150k	4002
HP97556P	14	SCSI-2	2,7 RLL	5.25 FH	128k	150k	4002
HP97556T	14	SCSI-2	2,7 RLL	5.25 FH	128k	150k	4002
HP97558E	14	ESDI	2,7 RLL	5.25 FH	128k	150k	4002
HP97558P	14	SCSI-2	2,7 RLL	5.25 FH	128k	150k	4002
HP97558T	14	SCSI-2	2,7 RLL	5.25 FH	128k	150k	4002
HP97560E	14	ESDI	2,7 RLL	5.25 FH	128k	150k	4002
HP97560P	14	SCSI-2	2,7 RLL	5.25 FH	128k	150k	4002
HP97560T	14	SCSI-2	2,7 RLL	5.25 FH	128k	150k	4002
HP2233	12	SCSI-2	1,7 RLL	3.5 HH		150k	
HPC2233S	12	SCSI-2	2,7 RLL	3.5 HH	64k	150k	3600
HPC2233 ATA	12.6	IDE AT	2,7 RLL	3.5 HH	64k	150k	3600
HPC2234S	12	SCSI-2	2,7 RLL	3.5 HH	64k	150k	3600
HPC2234 ATA	12.6	IDE AT	2,7 RLL	3.5 HH	64k	150k	3600
HPC2235S	12	SCSI-2	2,7 RLL	3.5 HH	64k	150k	3600
HPC2247	10	SCSI-2	1,7 RLL	3.5 HH		150k	
HPC3335 ATA	12.6	IDE AT	2,7 RLL	3.5 HH	64k	150k	3600

HITACHI AMERICA

Drive Model	Seek Time	Interface	Encode	Form Factor	cache kb	mtbf	Obsolete? RPM ⇩
DK301-1	85	ST412/506	MFM	3.5 HH			
DK301-2	85	ST412/506	MFM	3.5 HH			
DK312C-20	17	SCSI	2,7 RLL	3.5 HH			40k
DK312C-25	17	SCSI	2,7 RLL	3.5 HH			40k
DK314C-41	17	SCSI	2,7 RLL	3.5 HH	64k	150k	
DK315C-11	11	SCSI-2		3.5 HH	256k	150k	
DK315C-14	11	SCSI-2		3.5 HH	256k	150k	
DK505-2	85	ST412/506	MFM	5.25 HH			
DK511-3	30	ST412/506	MFM	5.25 FH			
DK511-5	26	ST412/506	MFM	5.25 FH			
DK511-8	23	ST412/506	MFM	5.25 FH			
DK512-12	23	ESDI	2,7 RLL	5.25 FH			
DK512-12	23	SCSI	2,7 RLL	5.25 FH			
DK512C-12	23	SCSI	2,7 RLL	5.25 FH			
DK512-17	23	ESDI	2,7 RLL	5.25 FH			
DK512C-17	23	SCSI	2,7 RLL	5.25 FH			
DK512-8	23	ESDI	2,7 RLL	5.25 FH			
DK512C-8	23	SCSI	2,7 RLL	5.25 FH			
DK514-38	16	ESDI	2,7 RLL	5.25 FH			30k
DK514C-38	16	SCSI	2,7 RLL	5.25 FH			30k
DK515-12	14	ESDI	2,7 RLL	5.25 FH			150k
DK515C-78	16	ESDI	2,7 RLL	5.25 FH			150k
DK515C-78	16	SCSI	2,7 RLL	5.25 FH			150k
DK515S-78	16	E-SMD		5.25 FH			150k
DK515C-78D	16	SCSI	2,7 RLL	5.25 FH			150k
DK516-12	14	ESDI		5.25 FH			100k
DK516-15	14	ESDI		5.25 FH			150k
DK516C-16	14	SCSI-2	2,7 RLL	5.25 FH			150k
DK517C-26	12	SCSI-2		5.25 FH			150k
DK517C-37	12	SCSI-2		5.25 FH			150k
DK521-5	25	ST412/506	MFM	5.25 FH			
DK522-10	25	ESDI	2,7 RLL	5.25 HH			30kk
DK522C-10	25	SCSI	2,7 RLL	5.25 FH			30k

Drive Model	Format Size MB	Head	Cyl	Sect/ Trac	Translate H/C/S	RWC/ WPC	Land Zone
HYOSUNG							
HC8085	71	8	1024	17		NA/NA	AUTO
HC8128	109	8	1024	26		NA/NA	AUTO
HC8170E	150	8	1024	36		NA/NA	AUTO
IBM CORP. (STORAGE SYS DIV)							
0661-371	326	14	949	48		NA/NA	AUTO
0661-467	412	14	1199	48		NA/NA	AUTO
0663-E15	1206	16				--/--	
0663-E12	1044	14				--/--	
0663-H12	39	15	2051	66		NA/NA	AUTO
0663-L08	623	9	2051	66		NA/NA	AUTO
0663-L11	900	13	2051	66		NA/NA	AUTO
0663-L12	1039	15	2051	66		NA/NA	AUTO
0663-W2H	2412	15				--/--	
0664-CSH	4027	32				--/--	
0664-DSH	4027	32				--/--	
0664-ESH	4027	32				--/--	
0664-FSH	4027	32				--/--	
0664-M1H	2013	16		2870		--/--	
0664-N1H	2013	16				--/--	
0664-P1S	1741	15	2304			--/--	
0665-38	31	5	733	17		NA/NA	AUTO
0665-53	44	7	733	17		NA/NA	AUTO
0667-61	52	5	582	35		NA/NA	AUTO
0667-85	73	7	582	35		NA/NA	AUTO
0671-S11	234	11	1224	34		NA/NA	AUTO
0671-S15	319	15	1224	34		NA/NA	AUTO
0681-500	476	11	1458	58		NA/NA	AUTO
0681-1000	865	20	1458	58		NA/NA	AUTO
1430	21	4	615	17		320/128	307
1431	31	5	733	17		733/733	
1471	31	5	733	17		733/733	
WD-12	10	4	306	17		296/296	
WD-25	20	8	306	17		296/296	
WD-L40	41	2	1038	39		NA/NA	AUTO
WD-L40S	41	2	1038	39		NA/NA	AUTO
WD-240	42	2	1120	38		NA/NA	AUTO
WD-240	43	2	1122	38		NA/NA	AUTO
WD-240	42	2	1120	38		--/--	
WD-280	85	4	1120	38		--/--	
WD-325	21	4	615	17		--/--	
WD-380	81	4	1021	39		NA/NA	AUTO
WD-380	81	4	1021	39		NA/NA	AUTO
WD-387	60	4	928	32		NA/NA	AUTO
WD-2120	126	4	1248	50		--/--	
WD-3158	120	8	920	32		NA/NA	AUTO
WD-3160	163	8	1021	39		NA/NA	AUTO
WD-3160	163	8	1021	39		NA/NA	AUTO
WDA-L40	41	2	1040	39		--/--	
WDA-L42	42	2	1067	39		--/--	
WDA-L80	85	2	1923	44		--/--	
WDA-L160	171	4	1923	44		--/--	
WDA-240	43	2	1122	38		NA/NA	AUTO
WDA-240	43	2	1122	38		--/--	
WDA-260	63	2	1248	50		--/--	
WDA-280	87	4	1122	38		NA/NA	AUTO
WDA-380	81	4	1021	39		NA/NA	AUTO
WDA-2120	126	4	1248	50		--/--	
WDA-3160	81	4	1021	39		NA/NA	AUTO
WDS-L40	41	2	1038	39		NA/NA	AUTO

Drive Model	Seek Time	Interface	Encode	Form Factor	cache kb	Obsolete? mtbf	RPM
HYOSUNG							
HC8085	25	ST412/506		5.25 FH		28k	
HC8128	25	ST412/506		5.25 FH		28k	
HC8170E	25	ESDI		5.25 FH		28k	
IBM CORP. (STORAGE SYS DIV)							
0661-371	12.5	SCSI-2		3.5 HH	64k	300k	
0661-467	11.5	SCSI-2		3.5 HH	128k	300k	
0663-E15	11	SCSI-2 FAS		3.5 HH	256k	50k 4317	
0663-E12	11	SCSI-2 FAS		3.5 HH	256k	50k 4317	
0663-H12	9.8	SCSI-2		3.5 HH		400k	
0663-L08	9.8	SCSI-2		3.5 HH		400k	
0663-L11	11	SCSI-2		3.5 HH		400k	
0663-L12	11	SCSI-2		3.5 HH		880k	
0663-W2H	9	SCSI-2 FAS		5.25 FH	256k	300k 4317	
0664-CSH		SCSI-2 FAS		5.25 FH		375k 5400	
0664-DSH		SCSI-2 FAS		5.25 FH		375k 5400	
0664-ESH		SCSI-2 FAS		5.25 FH		375k 5400	
0664-FSH		SCSI-2 FAS		5.25 FH		375k 5400	
0664-M1H	10	SCSI-2 FAS		3.5 HH	512k	750k 5400	
0664-N1H	10	SCSI-2 FAS		3.5 HH	512k	750k 5400	
0664-P1S	9	IPI-2		3.5 HH		75k 5400	
0665-38	40	ST412/506	MFM	5.25 FH			
0665-53	40	ST412/506	MFM	5.25 FH			
0667-61	30	ESDI	RLL	5.25 FH			
0667-85	30	ESDI		5.25 FH			
0671-S11	21.5	SCSI		5.25 FH			
0671-S15	21.5	SCSI		5.25 FH			
0681-500	13	SCSI	RLL	5.25 FH		150k	
0681-1000	13	SCSI	RLL	5.25 FH		150k	
1430	80	ST412/506	MFM	5.25 FH			
1431	40	ST412/506	MFM	5.25 FH			
1471	40	ST412/506	MFM	5.25 FH			
WD-12		ST412/506	MFM	5.25 FH			
WD-25		ST412/506	MFM	5.25 FH			
WD-L40	17	MCA		3.5 HH		90k	
WD-L40S	17	MCA		3.5 HH		90k	
WD-240	19	MCA		2.5 4H		150k 3600	
WD-240	19			2.5 4H		150k	
WD-240	19	MCA		2.5 4H		150k 3600	
WD-280	17	MCA		2.5 4H		150k 3600	
WD-325	88	MCA		3.5 HH			
WD-380	16	MCA		3.5 HH		110k	
WD-380	16			3.5 HH		110k	
WD-387	23	MCA		3.5 HH		45k	
WD-2120	16	IDE AT		2.5 4H		150k 3600	
WD-3158	23	MCA		3.5 HH		45k	
WD-3160	16	MCA		3.5 HH		110k	
WD-3160	16			3.5 HH		110k	
WDA-L40	17	IDE AT	2,7 RLL	3.5 3H		90k	
WDA-L42	17	IDE AT	2,7 RLL	3.5 3H		90k	
WDA-L80	16	SCSI-2		3.5 4H		150k 3600	
WDA-L160	16	SCSI-2		3.5 4H		150k 3600	
WDA-240	19	IDE AT		2.5 4H		150k	
WDA-240	19	IDE AT		2.5 4H		150k 3600	
WDA-260	19	IDE AT		2.5 4H		150k 3600	
WDA-280	19	IDE AT		2.5 4H		150k 3600	
WDA-380	16	IDE AT		3.5 HH		110k	
WDA-2120	16	IDE AT		2.5 4H		150k 3600	
WDA-3160	16	IDE AT		3.5 HH		110k	
WDS-L40	17	SCSI-2		3.5 HH		90k	

Drive Model	Format Size MB	Head	Cyl	Sect/Trac	Translate H/C/S	RWC/WPC	Land Zone
WDS-L42	42	2	1066	39		NA/NA	AUTO
WDS-L80	85	2	1923	44		---/---	
WDS-L160	171	4	1923	44		---/---	
WDS-240	43	2	1120	38		NA/NA	AUTO
WDS-260	63	2	1248	50		---/---	
WDS-280	85	4	1120	38		---/---	
WDS-380	81	4	1021	39		NA/NA	AUTO
WDS-3100	104	2	1990	44		NA/NA	AUTO
WDS-3160	163	8	1021	39		NA/NA	AUTO
WDS-3200	209	4	1990	44		---/---	
IMI							
5006	5	2	306	17		307/214	
5012	10	4	306	17		307/214	
5018	15	6	306	17		307/214	
5021H	15					---/---	
INTERGRAL PERIPHERALS							
1862	64	3		V		NA/NA	AUTO
JCT (SEE MAXCARD)							
100	5			17		---/---	
105	5	2	306	17		---/---	
110	14			17		---/---	
120	20			17		---/---	
1000	5			17		---/---	
1005	7			17		---/---	
1010	14			17		---/---	
JVC COMPANIES OF AMERICA							
JD3842HA	21	2	436	48		---/---	
JD3848HA	43	4	436	48		---/---	
JD-E2042M	42	2	973	43		NA/NA	AUTO
JD-F2042M	42	2	973	43		NA/NA	AUTO
JD-E2085M	85	4	973	43		NA/NA	AUTO
JD-E2825P	21	2	581	36		---/---	AUTO
JD-E2825P	21	2	581	36		---/---	AUTO
JD-E2825P	21	2	581	36		---/---	AUTO
JD-E2850P	42	3	791	35		---/---	AUTO
JD-E2850P	42	3	791	35		---/---	AUTO
JD-E2850P	42	3	791	35		---/---	AUTO
JD-E3824TA	21	4	436	48		---/---	AUTO
JD-E3848HA	42	4	436	48		---/---	AUTO
JD-E3848P	42	2	862	48		---/---	AUTO
JD-E3848P	42	2	862	48		---/---	AUTO
JD-E3848P	42	2	862	48		---/---	AUTO
JD-E3896P	84	4	862	48		---/---	AUTO
JD-E3896P	84	4	862	48		---/---	AUTO
JD-E3896P	84	4	862	48		---/---	AUTO
JD-E3896V	84	4	862	48		NA/NA	AUTO
JD-E3896V	84	4	862	48		NA/NA	AUTO
JD-E3896V	84	4	862	48		NA/NA	AUTO
KALOK CORPORATION							
P5-125(A)	125	2	2048			NA/NA	AUTO
P5-125(S)	125	2	2048			NA/NA	AUTO
P5-250(A)	251	4	2048			NA/NA	AUTO
P5-250(S)	251	4	2048			NA/NA	AUTO
KL320	21	4	615	17		616/300	
KL330	33	4	615	26		617/617	
KL332	40	4	615			---/---	

Drive Model	Seek Time	Interface	Encode	Form Factor	cache kb	mtbf	RPM	Obsolete?
WDS-L42	17	SCSI-2		3.5 3H		80k		
WDS-L80	16	SCSI-2		3.5 4H		150k	3600	
WDS-L160	16	SCSI-2		3.5 4H		150k	3600	
WDS-240	19	SCSI		2.5		150k	3600	
WDS-260	16	SCSI-2		2.5 4H		150k	3600	
WDS-280	17	SCSI		2.5 4H		150k	3600	
WDS-380	16	SCSI-2		3.5 HH		110k		
WDS-3100	12	SCSI-2		3.5 4H	32k	150k	4320	
WDS-3160	16	SCSI-2		3.5 HH		110k		
WDS-3200	12	SCSI-2		3.5 4H	32k	150k	4320	

IMI

Drive Model	Seek Time	Interface	Encode	Form Factor	cache kb	mtbf	RPM	Obsolete?
5006		ST412/506	MFM					
5012		ST412/506	MFM					
5018		ST412/506	MFM					
5021H	85	ST412/506	MFM	5.25 FH				

INTERGRAL PERIPHERALS

Drive Model	Seek Time	Interface	Encode	Form Factor	cache kb	mtbf	RPM	Obsolete?
1862	18	IDE AT	1,7 RLL			100k		

JCT (SEE MAXCARD)

Drive Model	Seek Time	Interface	Encode	Form Factor	cache kb	mtbf	RPM	Obsolete?
100	110	ST412/506	MFM	5.25 HH				
105	110	ST412/506	MFM	5.25 HH				
110	130	ST412/506	MFM	5.25 HH				
120	100	ST412/506	MFM	5.25 HH				
1000	110	COMMODORE	MFM	5.25 HH				
1005	110	COMMODORE	MFM	5.25 HH				
1010	130	COMMODORE	MFM	5.25 HH				

JVC COMPANIES OF AMERICA

Drive Model	Seek Time	Interface	Encode	Form Factor	cache kb	mtbf	RPM	Obsolete?
JD3842HA	28		2,7 RLL	3.5 3H		20k		
JD3848HA	29		2,7 RLL	3.5 3H		20k		
JD-E2042M	16	IDE AT	1,7 RLL	2.5 4H	32k	130k	3118	
JD-F2042M	16	IDE AT	1,7 RLL	2.5 4H	32k	130k	3118	
JD-E2085M	16	IDE AT	1,7 RLL	2.5 4H	32k	130k	3118	
JD-E2825P	25	IDE AT	2,7 RLL	3.5 4H		30k	3109	N
JD-E2825P	25	IDE XT	2,7 RLL	3.5 4H		30k	3109	N
JD-E2825P	25	SCSI	2,7 RLL	3.5 4H		30k	3109	N
JD-E2850P	25	IDE AT	2,7 RLL	3.5 4H	32k	40k	3109	N
JD-E2850P	25	IDE XT	2,7 RLL	3.5 4H	32k	40k	3109	N
JD-E2850P	25	SCSI	2,7 RLL	3.5 4H	32k	40k	3109	N
JD-E3824TA	28			3.5 3H		20k		
JD-E3848HA	29			3.5 3H		20k		
JD-E3848P	25	SCSI	2,7 RLL	3.5 4H		30k	2332	N
JD-E3848P	25	IDE XT	2,7 RLL	3.5 4H		30k	2332	N
JD-E3848P	25	IDE AT	2,7 RLL	3.5 4H		30k	2332	N
JD-E3896P	25	IDE AT	2,7 RLL	3.5 4H		30k	3109	N
JD-E3896P	25	IDE XT	2,7 RLL	3.5 4H		30k	3109	N
JD-E3896P	25	SCSI	2,7 RLL	3.5 4H		30k	3109	N
JD-E3896V	25	IDE XT		3.5 3H		30k		
JD-E3896V	25	SCSI		3.5 3H		30k		
JD-E3896V	25	IDE AT		3.5 3H		30k		

KALOK CORPORATION

Drive Model	Seek Time	Interface	Encode	Form Factor	cache kb	mtbf	RPM	Obsolete?
P5-125(A)	17	IDE AT	1,7 RLL			100k		
P5-125(S)	17	SCSI-2	1,7 RLL			100k		
P5-250(A)	17	IDE AT	1,7 RLL			100k		
P5-250(S)	17	SCSI-2	1,7 RLL			100k		
KL320	40	ST412/506	MFM	3.5 HH		43.5	3600	N
KL330	40	ST412/506	2,7 RLL	3.5 HH		43.5	3600	N
KL332	48	MCA	2,7 RLL	3.5 HH				

Drive Model	Format Size MB	Head	Cyl	Sect/Trac	Translate H/C/S	RWC/WPC	Land Zone
KL340	43	6	820	17		---/---	
KL341	43	4	676	31		---/---	AUTO
KL342	42	4	676	31			
KL343	43	4	676	31		645/645	AUTO
KL360	66	6	820	26		---/---	
KL381	85	6	820			---/---	
KL383	84	4	815			NA/NA	
KL1000	105	6	978	35		---/---	AUTO
KL1100	105	6	820	48/35		NA/NA	AUTO
KL3120	121	6	820	55/40		NA/NA	AUTO
KL3250	252	4	2048	80		---/---	
KL3250	252	4	2048	80		---/---	

KYOCERA ELECTRONICS, INC.

Drive Model	Format Size MB	Head	Cyl	Sect/Trac	Translate H/C/S	RWC/WPC	Land Zone
KC20A	21	4	615	17		---/---	
KC20B	21	4	615	17		---/---	
KC30A	33	4	615	26		---/---	
KC30B	33	4	615	26		---/---	
KC40GA	40	2	1075			---/---	AUTO
KC80C	87	6	787	28		NA/NA	
KC80GA	78	4	1069	36		NA/NA	AUTO

LANSTOR

Drive Model	Format Size MB	Head	Cyl	Sect/Trac	Translate H/C/S	RWC/WPC	Land Zone
LAN-64		8	1024	17		---/NA	1023
LAN-115		15	918	17		---/NA	1023
LAN-140		8	1024	34		---/NA	1023
LAN-180		8	1024	26		---/NA	1023

LAPINE

Drive Model	Format Size MB	Head	Cyl	Sect/Trac	Translate H/C/S	RWC/WPC	Land Zone
LT10	10	2	615	17		616/---	
LT20	20	4	615	17		616/---	
LT100 (NOT VERIFIED)	10					---/---	
LT200	20	4	614	17		615/---	
LT300	32	4	614	17		615/---	
LT2000	20	4	614	17		615/---	
LT3065	10	4	306	17		306/128	
LT3512	10	4	306	17		306/128	
LT3522	10	4	306	17		307/---	
LT3532	32	4	614	26		---/615	
LT4000 (NOT VERIFIED)	40					---/---	
TITAN 20	21	4	615	17		---/---	615
TITAN 30	21	4	615			---/---	

MAXTOR CORPORATION

Drive Model	Format Size MB	Head	Cyl	Sect/Trac	Translate H/C/S	RWC/WPC	Land Zone
2585A	85	4	1092	NA	10/981/17	NA/NA	AUTO
2585S (NEVER MADE)						---/---	
25128A	128	4	1092	NA	14/1024/17	NA/NA	AUTO
3380	338	15	1224	NA		NA/NA	AUTO
7040A	42	2	1155	NA	5/981/17	NA/NA	AUTO
7040S	42	2	1155	36		NA/NA	AUTO
7060A	60	2	1498	NA	16/467/17	NA/NA	AUTO
7060S	60	2	1498	42		NA/NA	AUTO
7080A	81	4	1166	NA	10/981/17	NA/NA	AUTO
7080S	85	4	1166	36		NA/NA	AUTO
7120A	124	4	1498	NA	16/936/17	NA/NA	AUTO
7120S	124	4	1498	42	•	NA/NA	AUTO
7213A	212	4	1690	NA	16/683/38	NA/NA	AUTO
7213S	212	4	1690	NA		NA/NA	AUTO
8051A	41	4	745	26	5/981/17	NA/NA	AUTO
8051S	40	4	793	28		NA/NA	AUTO
EXT4175	234	11	1224	34		NA/NA	AUTO

Drive Model	Seek Time	Interface	Encode	Form Factor	cache kb	mtbf	RPM	Obsolete?
KL340	25	ST412/506	MFM	3.5 HH		50		
KL341	33	SCSI	2,7 RLL	3.5 HH	8k	40k	3375	N
KL342	30	MCA		3.5 HH		40k		
KL343	28	IDE AT	2,7 RLL	3.5 HH	8k	100k	3375	N
KL360	25	ST412/506	2,7 RLL	3.5 HH		50k		
KL381	25	SCSI	2,7 RLL	3.5 HH		50k		
KL383	25	SCSI	2,7 RLL	3.5 HH		50k		
KL1000	25	IDE AT	2,7 RLL	3.5 HH	32k	50k	3662	N
KL1100	19	IDE AT	2,7 RLL	3.5 HH		100k	3662	N
KL3120	19	IDE AT	2,7 RLL	3.5 HH		100k	3663	N
KL3250	16	IDE AT	1,7 RLL	3.5	128	250k	3600	
KL3250	16	SCSI-2	1,7 RLL	3.5	128	250k	3600	

KYOCERA ELECTRONICS, INC.

Drive Model	Seek Time	Interface	Encode	Form Factor	cache kb	mtbf	RPM	Obsolete?
KC20A	65	ST412/506	MFM	3.5 HH		40k		
KC20B	62	ST412/506	MFM	3.5 HH		40k		
KC30A	65	ST412/506	2,7 RLL	3.5 HH		40k		
KC30B	62	ST412/506	2,7 RLL	3.5 HH		40k		
KC40GA	28	IDE AT	2,7 RLL	3.5 HH		40k		
KC80C	28	SCSI	2,7 RLL	3.5 HH		28k		
KC80GA	23	IDE AT	2,7 RLL	3.5 HH		28k		

LANSTOR

LAN-64
LAN-115
LAN-140
LAN-180

LAPINE

Drive Model	Seek Time	Interface	Encode	Form Factor	cache kb	mtbf	RPM	Obsolete?
LT10		ST412/506	MFM	3.5 HH				
LT20		ST412/506	MFM	3.5 HH				
LT100 (NOT VERIFIED)	85	ST412/506		3.5 HH				
LT200	65	ST412/506		3.5 HH				
LT300		ST412/506	2,7 RLL	3.5 HH				
LT2000		ST412/506	MFM	3.5 HH				
LT3065	65	ST412/506	2,7 RLL	3.5 HH				
LT3512	65	ST412/506	2,7 RLL	3.5 HH				
LT3522		ST412/506	MFM	3.5 HH				
LT3532	65	ST412/506	2,7 RLL	3.5 HH				
LT4000 (NOT VERIFIED)		SCSI		3.5 HH				
TITAN 20		ST412/506	MFM	3.5 HH				
TITAN 30			RLL?	3.5 HH				

MAXTOR CORPORATION

Drive Model	Seek Time	Interface	Encode	Form Factor	cache kb	mtbf	RPM	Obsolete?
2585A	14	IDE AT	1,7 RLL	2.5 4H		250k	3600	N
2585S (Never made)								
25128A	14	IDE AT	1,7 RLL	2.5 4H		250k	3600	N
3380	27	SCSI	RLL	5.25 FH		20k	3600	Y
7040A	17	IDE AT	1,7 RLL	3.5 3H	32k	150k	3600	N
7040S	17	SCSI	1,7 RLL	3.5 3H	32k	150k	3600	N
7060A	15	IDE AT	1,7 RLL	3.5 3H		150k	3600	N
7060S	15	SCSI	1,7 RLL	3.5 3H		150k	3600	N
7080A	17	IDE AT	1,7 RLL	3.5 3H	32k	150k	3600	N
7080S	17	SCSI	1,7 RLL	3.5 3H	32k	150k	3600	N
7120A	15	IDE AT	1,7 RLL	3.5 3H	64k	150k	3600	N
7120S	15	SCSI	1,7 RLL	3.5 3H	64k	150k	3600	N
7213A	15	IDE AT	1,7 RLL	3.5 3H		150k	3600	N
7213S	15	SCSI	1,7 RLL	3.5 3H		150k	3600	N
8051A	28	IDE AT	2,7 RLL	3.5 HH	32k	150k	3484	N
8051S	28	SCSI	2,7 RLL	3.5 HH		30k	3600	Y
EXT4175	27	ESDI	RLL	5.25 FH		20k	3600	Y

Drive Model	Format Size MB	Head	Cyl	Sect/ Trac	Translate H/C/S	RWC/ WPC	Land Zone
EXT4280	157	7	1224	36		NA/NA	AUTO
EXT4380	319	15	1224	34		NA/NA	AUTO
LXT50S	48	4	733	32		NA/NA	AUTO
LXT100S	96	8	733	32		NA/NA	AUTO
LXT200A	207	7	1320	NA	15/816/32	NA/NA	AUTO
LXT200S	207	7	1320	33,53		NA/NA	AUTO
LXT213A	213	7	1320	NA	16/683/38	NA/NA	AUTO
LXT213S	213	7	1320	34-56		NA/NA	AUTO
LXT340A	340	7	1560	47-72	16/654/63	NA/NA	AUTO
LXT340S	340	7	1560	47-72		NA/NA	AUTO
LXT437A (Never made)						--/--	
LXT437S (Never made)						--/--	
LXT535A	535	16	1024	63	16/1036/63	NA/NA	AUTO
LXT535S	535	11	1560	47-72		NA/NA	AUTO
MXT1240S	1240	15	2512	NA		NA/NA	AUTO
MXT540SL	547	7		NA		NA/NA	AUTO
MXT540AL	547	7		NA		NA/NA	AUTO
P1-08E (Never made)	696	9	1778			NA/NA	AUTO
P1-12E (Never made)	1051	15	1778			NA/NA	AUTO
P1-13E (Never made)	1160	15	1778			NA/NA	AUTO
P1-16E (Never made)	1331	19	1778			NA/NA	AUTO
P1-17E (Never made)	1470	19	1778			NA/NA	AUTO
P1-17S PANTHER	1503	19	1778	70-101		NA/NA	AUTO
PO-12S PANTHER	1045	15	1632	61-103		NA/NA	AUTO
XT1050	38	5	902	17		NA/NA	AUTO
XT1065	52	7	918	17		NA/NA	AUTO
XT1085	71	8	1024	17		NA/NA	AUTO
XT1105	84	11	918	17		NA/NA	AUTO
XT1120R	105	8	1024	25		NA/NA	AUTO
XT1140	116	15	918	17		NA/NA	AUTO
XT1240R	196	15	1024	25		NA/NA	AUTO
XT2085	72	7	1224	17		NA/NA	AUTO
XT2140	113	11	1224	17		NA/NA	AUTO
XT2190	159	15	1224	17		NA/NA	AUTO
XT3170	129	9	1224	26		NA/NA	AUTO
XT3280	216	15	1224	26		NA/NA	AUTO
XT3380	277	15	1224	34		NA/NA	AUTO
XT4170E	153	7	1224	35/36		NA/NA	AUTO
XT4170S	157	7	1224	35-36		NA/NA	AUTO
XT4175	234	11	1224	34		NA/NA	AUTO
XT4230E	203	9	1224	35/36		NA/NA	AUTO
XT4280SF	338	15	1224	36		NA/NA	AUTO
XT4380E	322	15	1224	36		NA/NA	AUTO
XT4380S	338	15	1224	NA		NA/NA	AUTO
XT8380E	361	8	1632	53-54		NA/NA	AUTO
XT8380EH	360	8	1632	54		NA/NA	AUTO
XT8380S	361	8	1632	54		NA/NA	AUTO
XT8380SH	360	8	1632	NA		NA/NA	AUTO
XT8610E	541	12	1632	53-54		NA/NA	AUTO
XT8702S	616	15	1490	NA		NA/NA	AUTO
XT8760E	676	15	1632	53-54		NA/NA	AUTO
XT8760EH	676	15	1632	54		NA/NA	AUTO
XT8760S	670	15	1632	NA		NA/NA	AUTO
XT8760SH	670	15	1632	NA		NA/NA	AUTO
XT8800E	694	15	1274	71		NA/NA	AUTO
XT81000E	889	15	1632	71		NA/NA	AUTO

MEGA DRIVE SYSTEMS

Drive Model	Format Size MB	Head	Cyl	Sect/ Trac	Translate H/C/S	RWC/ WPC	Land Zone
M1-52	52	2	1219			--/--	
M1-105	105	4	1219			--/--	
M1-120	122	2	1818			--/--	
M1-240	245	4	1818			--/--	
MH-1G	1050	13	1974			--/--	

Drive Model	Seek Time	Interface	Encode	Form Factor	cache kb	mtbf	Obsolete? RPM
EXT4280	14	ESDI	RLL	5.25 FH		70k	3600 Y
EXT4380	27	ESDI	RLL	5.25 FH		20k	3600 Y
LXT50S	27	SCSI	2,7 RLL	3.5 HH		40k	3600 Y
LXT100S	27	SCSI	2,7 RLL	3.5 HH		150k	3600 Y
LXT200A	15	IDE AT	1,7 RLL	3.5 HH		150k	3600 N
LXT200S	15	SCSI	1,7 RLL	3.5 HH		150k	3600 N
LXT213A	15	IDE AT	1,7 RLL	3.5 HH	32k	150k	3600 N
LXT213S	15	SCSI	1,7 RLL	3.5 HH	32k	150k	3600 N
LXT340A	15	IDE AT	2,7 RLL	3.5 HH	128k	150k	3600 N
LXT340S	15	SCSI	2,7 RLL	3.5 HH	128k	150k	3600 N
LXT437A (Never made)							3600
LXT437S (Never made)							3600
LXT535A	15	IDE AT	2,7 RLL	3.5 HH	128k	150k	3600 N
LXT535S	13	SCSI	2,7 RLL	3.5 HH	128k	150k	3600 N
MXT1240S	9	SCSI-2	1,7 RLL	3.5 HH		300k	6300 N
MXT540SL	9	SCSI-2	1,7 RLL	3.5 3H		300k	6300 N
MXT540AL	9	IDE AT	1,7 RLL	3.5 3H		300k	6300 N
P1-08E (Never made)	12	ESDI	RLL	5.25 FH		100k	3600
P1-12E (Never made)	13	ESDI	RLL	5.25 FH		100k	3600
P1-13E (Never made)	13	ESDI	RLL	5.25 FH		100k	3600
P1-16E (Never made)	13	ESDI	RLL	5.25 FH		100k	3600
P1-17E (Never made)	13	ESDI	RLL	5.25 FH		100k	3600
P1-17S PANTHER	13	SCSI-2	RLL	5.25 FH	256k	150k	3600 N
PO-12S PANTHER	13	SCSI-2	RLL	5.25 FH	256k	150k	3600 N
XT1050	30	ST412/506	MFM	5.25 FH		20k	3600 Y
XT1065	30	ST412/506	MFM	5.25 FH		20k	3600 Y
XT1085	28	ST412/506	MFM	5.25 FH		70k	3600 Y
XT1105	27	ST412/506	MFM	5.25 FH		20k	3600 Y
XT1120R	27	ST412/506	2,7 RLL	5.25 FH		70k	3600 Y
XT1140	27	ST412/506	MFM	5.25 FH		70k	3600 Y
XT1240R	27	ST412/506	2,7 RLL	5.25 FH		70k	3600 Y
XT2085	30	ST412/506	MFM	5.25 FH		30k	3600 Y
XT2140	30	ST412/506	MFM	5.25 FH		30k	3600 Y
XT2190	29	ST412/506	MFM	5.25 FH		70k	3600 Y
XT3170	30	SCSI	RLL	3.5 FH		20k	3600 Y
XT3280	30	SCSI	RLL	5.25 FH		20k	3600 Y
XT3380	27	SCSI	RLL	5.25 FH		20k	3600 Y
XT4170E	14	ESDI	1,7 RLL	5.25 FH		30k	3600 Y
XT4170S	14	SCSI	1,7 RLL	5.25 FH		150k	3600 Y
XT4175	27	ESDI	RLL	5.25 FH		20k	3600 Y
XT4230E	16	ESDI	1,7 RLL	5.25 FH		150k	3600 N
XT4280SF	16	SCSI	1,7 RLL	5.25 FH		150k	
XT4380E	18	ESDI	1,7 RLL	5.25 FH		150k	3600 N
XT4380S	16	SCSI	1,7 RLL	5.25 FH		150k	3600 N
XT8380E	16	ESDI	1,7 RLL	5.25 FH		150k	3600 N
XT8380EH	13	ESDI	1,7 RLL	5.25 FH		150k	3600 N
XT8380S	14	SCSI	1,7 RLL	5.25 FH		150k	3600 N
XT8380SH	14	SCSI	1,7 RLL	5.25 FH	256k	150k	3600 N
XT8610E	16	ESDI	1,7 RLL	5.25 FH		150k	3600 N
XT8702S	17	SCSI	1,7 RLL	5.25 FH		150k	3600
XT8760E	16	ESDI	1,7 RLL	5.25 FH		150k	3600 N
XT8760EH	14	ESDI	1,7 RLL	5.25 FH		150k	3600 N
XT8760S	16	SCSI	1,7 RLL	5.25 FH		150k	3600 N
XT8760SH	14	SCSI	1,7 RLL	5.25 FH	256k	150k	3600 N
XT8800E	14	ESDI	1,7 RLL	5.25 FH		150k	3600 N
XT81000E	16	ESDI	1,7 RLL	5.25 FH		150k	3600

MEGA DRIVE SYSTEMS

M1-52	17	SCSI	2,7 RLL	3.5 HH	64k	60k	3662
M1-105	17	SCSI	2,7 RLL	3.5 HH	64k	60k	3662
M1-120	16	SCSI	1,7 RLL	3.5 HH	256k	250k	4306
M1-240	16	SCSI	1,7 RLL	3.5 HH	256k	250k	4306
MH-1G	10	SCSI	1,7 RLL	3.5 HH	256k	300k	5400

Drive Model	Format Size MB	Head	Cyl	Sect/ Trac	Translate H/C/S	RWC/ WPC	Land Zone
MH-340	338	9	1100			---/---	
MH-425	426	9	1520			---/---	
MH-535	525	9	1476			---/---	
P42	42	3	834	33		NA/NA	AUTO
P84	84	6	834	33		NA/NA	AUTO
P105	103	6	1019	33		NA/NA	AUTO
P120	120	5	1123			NA/NA	AUTO
P170	168	7	1123			NA/NA	AUTO
P210	210	7	1156			NA/NA	AUTO
P320	320	15	886			NA/NA	AUTO
P425	426	9	1512			NA/NA	AUTO

MEMOREX

Drive Model	Format Size MB	Head	Cyl	Sect/ Trac	Translate H/C/S	RWC/ WPC	Land Zone
321	5	2	320	17		321/128	
322	10	4	320	17		321/128	
323	15	6	320	17		321/128	
324	20	8	320	17		321/128	
450	10	2	612	17		321/350	
512	25	3	961	17		321/480	
513	41	5	961	17		321/480	
514	58	7	961	17		961?/480	

MICROPOLIS CORP

Drive Model	Format Size MB	Head	Cyl	Sect/ Trac	Translate H/C/S	RWC/ WPC	Land Zone
1302	20	3	830	17		831/831	AUTO
1303	35	5	830	17		831/831	AUTO
1304	40	6	830	17		831/831	AUTO
1323	35	4	1024	17		1025/1025	AUTO
1323A	44	5	1024	17		1025/1025	AUTO
1324	53	6	1024	17		1025/1025	AUTO
1324A	62	7	1024	17		1025/1025	AUTO
1325	71	8	1024	17		1025/1025	AUTO
1333A	44	5	1024	17		1025/1025	AUTO
1333	35	4	1024	17		1025/1025	AUTO
1334	53	6	1024	17		1025/1025	AUTO
1334A	62	7	1024	17		1025/1025	AUTO
1335	71	8	1024	17		1025/1025	AUTO
1352	32	2	1024	36		---/---	
1352A	41	3	1024	36		NA/NA	
1353	75	4	1024	36		NA/NA	
1353A	94	5	1024	36		NA/NA	
1354	113	6	1024	36		NA/NA	
1354A	131	7	1024	36		NA/NA	
1355	150	8	1024	36		NA/NA	
1373	72	4	1024	36		1017/1017	AUTO
1373A	91	5	1024	36		1017/1017	AUTO
1374	109	6	1024	36		1017/1017	AUTO
1374A	127	7	1024	36		1017/1017	AUTO
1374-6	135	6	1245	36		---/---	AUTO
1375	145	8	1024	36		1017/1017	AUTO
1516-10S	678	10	1840	72		NA/NA	
1517-13	922	13	1925	72		NA/NA	
1517-14	981	14	1925	71		---/---	
1517-15	1051	15	1925	71		---/---	
1518	1346					---/---	
1518-14	993	14	1925	72		NA/NA	
1518-15	1341	15	2104	83		NA/NA	AUTO
1528	1342	15	2100	84		---/---	
1528-15	1342	15	2100	84		NA/NA	AUTO
1538-15	910	15	1669	71		NA/NA	AUTO
1538	871	15	1669	68		NA/NA	AUTO
1548-15	1735	15	2099	V		NA/NA	AUTO
1554-07	157	7	1224	36		NA/NA	AUTO

Drive Model	Seek Time	Interface	Encode	Form Factor	cache kb	Obsolete? mtbf	RPM ⇓
MH-340	13	SCSI	1,7 RLL	3.5 HH	64k	150k	4412
MH-425	14	SCSI	1,7 RLL	3.5 HH	64k	150k	4412
MH-535	14	SCSI	1,7 RLL	3.5 HH	256k	150k	4412
P42	19	SCSI	2,7 RLL	3.5 HH		50k	
P84	19	SCSI	2,7 RLL	3.5 HH		50k	
P105	19	SCSI	2,7 RLL	3.5 HH		50k	
P120	14	SCSI	1,7 RLL	3.5 HH		50k	
P170	14	SCSI	1,7 RLL	3.5 HH		50k	
P210	14	SCSI	1,7 RLL	3.5 HH		50k	
P320	12.5	SCSI	1,7 RLL	3.5 HH		150k	
P425	12	SCSI	1,7 RLL	3.5 HH		75k	

MEMOREX

Drive Model	Seek Time	Interface	Encode	Form Factor	cache kb	Obsolete? mtbf	RPM
321		ST412/506	MFM				
322		ST412/506	MFM				
323		ST412/506	MFM				
324		ST412/506	MFM				
450		ST412/506	MFM				
512		ST412/506	MFM				
513		ST412/506	MFM				
514		ST412/506	MFM				

MICROPOLIS CORP

Drive Model	Seek Time	Interface	Encode	Form Factor	cache kb	Obsolete? mtbf	RPM
1302	30	ST412/506	MFM	5.25 FH		20k	3600
1303	30	ST412/506	MFM	5.25 FH		20k	3600
1304	30	ST412/506	MFM	5.25 FH		20k	3600
1323	28	SP412/506	MFM	5.25 FH		35k	3600
1323A	28	ST412/506	MFM	5.25 FH		35k	3600
1324	28	ST412/506	MFM	5.25 FH		35k	3600
1324A	28	ST412/506	MFM	5.25 FH		35k	3600
1325	28	ST412/506	MFM	5.25 FH		35k	3600
1333A	28	ST412/506	MFM	5.25 FH		25k	3600
1333	28	ST412/506	MFM	5.25 FD		25k	3600
1334	28	ST412/506	MFM	5.25 FH		25k	3600
1334A	28	ST412/506	MFM	5.25 FH		25k	3600
1335	28	ST412/506	MFM	5.25 FH		25k	3600
1352	23	ESDI	2,7 RLL	5.25 FH			
1352A	23	ESDI	2,7 RLL	5.25 FH			
1353	23	ESDI	2,7 RLL	5.25 FH		150k	3600
1353A	23	ESDI	2,7 RLL	5.25 FH		150k	3600
1354	23	ESDI	2,7 RLL	5.25 FH		150k	3600
1354A	23	ESDI	2,7 RLL	5.25 FH		150k	3600
1355	23	ESDI	2,7 RLL	5.25 FH		150k	3600
1373	23	SCSI	2,7 RLL	5.25 FH		30k	3600
1373A	23	SCSI	2,7 RLL	5.25 FH		30k	3600
1374	23	SCSI	2,7 RLL	5.25 FH		30k	3600
1374A	23	SCSI	2,7 RLL	5.25 FH		30k	3600
1374-6	16	SCSI		5.25 HH		40k	
1375	23	SCSI	2,7 RLL	5.25 FH		30k	3600
1516-10S	14	ESDI	2,7 RLL	5.25 FH		150k	
1517-13	14	ESDI	2,7 RLL	5.25 FH		150k	
1517-14	14	ESDI		5.25 FH		150k	
1517-15	14	ESDI		5.25 FH		150k	
1518	14.5	ESDI		5.25 FH		150k	N
1518-14	14	ESDI		5.25 FH		150k	
1518-15	14	ESDI	2,7 RLL	5.25 FH		150k	
1528	14.5	SCSI-2		5.25 FH	256k	150k	N
1528-15	14	SCSI-2		5.25 FH		150k	3600
1538-15	15	ESDI	2,7 RLL	5.25 FH		150k	3600 N
1538		ESDI	1,7 RLL	5.25 FH		150k	
1548-15	14	SCSI		5.25 FH	256k	150k	3600 N
1554-07	18	ESDI	2,7 RLL	5.25 FH		150k	3600

Drive Model	Format Size MB	Head	Cyl	Sect/ Trac	Translate H/C/S	RWC/ WPC	Land Zone
1555-08	180	8	1224	36		NA/NA	AUTO
1555-09	203	9	1224	36		NA/NA	AUTO
1556-10	225	10	1224	36		NA/NA	AUTO
1556-11	248	11	1224	36		NA/NA	AUTO
1557-12	270	12	1224	36		NA/NA	AUTO
1557-13	293	13	1224	36		NA/NA	AUTO
1557-14	315	14	1224	36		1225/1225	
1557-15	338	15	1224	36		1225/1225	
1558	338					--/--	
1558-14	315	14	1224	36		NA/NA	AUTO
1558-15	338	15	1224	36		NA/NA	AUTO
1560-8S	389	8	1632	54		--/--	
1564-07	315	7	1224	54		NA/NA	AUTO
1565-08	360	8	1224	54		NA/NA	AUTO
1565-09	406	9	1224	54		NA/NA	AUTO
1566-10	451	10	1224	54		NA/NA	AUTO
1566-11	496	11	1224	54		NA/NA	AUTO
1567-13	586	13	1224	54		NA/NA	AUTO
1567-12	541	12	1632	54		NA/NA	AUTO
1567-14	631	14	1632	54		--/--	
1568	676					--/--	
1568-14	631	14	1632	54		NA/NA	AUTO
1568-15	676	15	1632	54		NA/NA	AUTO
1574-07	155	7	1224	36		NA/NA	AUTO
1575-08	177	8	1224	36		NA/NA	AUTO
1575-09	199	9	1224	36		NA/NA	AUTO
1576-10	221	10	1224	36		1224/1224	AUTO
1576-11	243	11	1224	36		1224/1224	AUTO
1577-12	265	12	1224	36		1224/1224	AUTO
1577-13	287	13	1224	36		1224/1224	AUTO
1578	331					--/--	
1578-14	310	14	1224	36		1224/1224	AUTO
1578-15	332	15	1224	36		1224/1224	AUTO
1585-8S	344	8	1628	54		--/--	
1586-11	490	11	1628	54		1632/1632	AUTO
1587-13	585	13	1628	54		NA/NA	AUTO
1587-12	540	12	1628	54		1632/1632	AUTO
1587-13	579	13	1628	54		1632/1632	AUTO
1588	668					--/--	
1588-14	624	14	1628	54		1632/1632	AUTO
1588-15	667	15	1632	54		1632/1632	AUTO
1588T-15	676	15	1632	54		NA/NA	AUTO
1596-10S	668	10	1834	72		1835/1835	
1597-13	909	13	1919	72		1835/1835	
1598	1034					--/--	
1598-14	979	14	1919	72		1920/1920	
1598-15	1034	15	1928	71		1920/1920	AUTO
1624-7	667	7	2112	36		NA/NA	AUTO
1653-4	92	4	1249	36		NA/NA	AUTO
1653-5	115	5	1249	36		NA/NA	AUTO
1654	161					--/--	
1654-6	138	6	1249	36		NA/NA	AUTO
1654-7	161	7	1249	36		NA/NA	AUTO
1663-4	197	4	1780	54		NA/NA	AUTO
1663-5	246	5	1780	54		NA/NA	AUTO
1664	345					--/--	
1664-6	295	6	1780	54		NA/NA	AUTO
1664-7	344	7	1780	54		NA/NA	AUTO
1670-4	90	4	1245	36		--/--	
1673-4	90	4	1249	36		1250/1250	AUTO
1673-5	112	5	1249	36		1250/1250	AUTO
1674	158					--/--	
1674-6	135	6	1249	36		1250/1250	AUTO

Drive Model	Seek Time	Interface	Encode	Form Factor	cache kb	mtbf	RPM	Obsolete?
1555-08	18	ESDI	2,7 RLL	5.25 FH		150k	3600	
1555-09	18	ESDI	2,7 RLL	5.25 FH		150k	3600	
1556-10	18	ESDI	2,7 RLL	5.25 FH		150k	3600	
1556-11	18	ESDI	2,7 RLL	5.25 FH		150k	3600	
1557-12	18	ESDI	2,7 RLL	5.25 FH		150k	3600	
1557-13	18	ESDI	2,7 RLL	5.25 FH		150k	3600	
1557-14	18	ESDI		5.25 FH				
1557-15	18	ESDI		5.25 FH				
1558	19	ESDI		5.25 FH		150k		N
1558-14	18	ESDI	2,7 RLL	5.25 FH		150k	3600	
1558-15	18	ESDI	2,7 RLL	5.25 FH		150k	3600	
1560-8S	16	ESDI		5.25 FH		150k		
1564-07	18	ESDI	2,7 RLL	5.25 FH		150k	3600	
1565-08	18	ESDI	2,7 RLL	5.25 FH		150k	3600	
1565-09	18	ESDI	2,7 RLL	5.25 FH		150k	3600	
1566-10	18	ESDI	2,7 RLL	5.25 FH		150k	3600	
1566-11	18	ESDI	2,7 RLL	5.25 FH		150k	3600	
1567-13	18	ESDI	2,7 RLL	5.25 FH		150k	3600	
1567-12	18	ESDI	2,7 RLL	5.25 FH		150k	3600	
1567-14	16	ESDI		5.25 FH		150k		
1568	16	ESDI		5.25 FH		150k		N
1568-14	16	ESDI	2,7 RLL	5.25 FH		150k	3600	
1568-15	16	ESDI	2,7 RLL	5.25 FH		150k	3600	
1574-07	16	SCSI	2,7 RLL	5.25 FH		150k	3600	
1575-08	16	SCSI	2,7 RLL	5.25 FH		150k	3600	
1575-09	16	SCSI	2,7 RLL	5.25 FH		150k	3600	
1576-10	16	SCSI	2,7 RLL	5.25 FH		150k	3600	
1576-11	16	SCSI	2,7 RLL	5.25 FH		150k	3600	
1577-12	16	SCSI	2,7 RLL	5.25 FH		150k	3600	
1577-13	16	SCSI	2,7 RLL	5.25 FH		150k	3600	
1578	16	SCSI		5.25 FH	64k	150k		N
1578-14	16	SCSI	2,7 RLL	5.25 FH		150k	3600	
1578-15	16	SCSI	2,7 RLL	5.25 FH		150k	3600	
1585-8S	16	SCSI		5.25 FH		150k		
1586-11	16	SCSI	2,7 RLL	5.25 FH		150k		
1587-13	16	SCSI	2,7 RLL	5.25 FH		150k		
1587-12	16	SCSI	2,7 RLL	5.25 FH		150k		
1587-13	16	SCSI		5.25 FH		150k		
1588	16	SCSI		5.25 FH	256k	150k		N
1588-14	16	SCSI	2,7 RLL	5.25 FH		150k		
1588-15	16	SCSI	2,7 RLL	5.25 FH		150k	3600	
1588T-15	16	SCSI	2,7 RLL	5.25 FH		150k		
1596-10S	14	SCSI	2,7 RLL	5.25 FH				
1597-13	14	SCSI	2,7 RLL	5.25 FH		150k		
1598	14.5	SCSI-2		5.25 FH	256k	150k		N
1598-14	14	SCSI	2,7 RLL	5.25 FH		150k		
1598-15	14	SCSI-2	2,7 RLL	5.25 FH		150k	3600	
1624-7	15	SCSI-2 FAS		5.25 HH		150k	3600	
1653-4	16	ESDI	2,7 RLL	5.25 HH		150k	3600	
1653-5	16	ESDI	2,7 RLL	5.25 HH		150k	3600	
1654	16	ESDI		5.25 HH		150k		N
1654-6	16	ESDI	2,7 RLL	5.25 HH		150k	3600	
1654-7	16	ESDI	2,7 RLL	5.25 HH		150k	3600	
1663-4	14	ESDI	2,7 RLL	5.25 HH		150k		
1663-5	14	ESDI	2,7 RLL	5.25 HH		150k		
1664	15	ESDI		5.25 HH		150k		N
1664-6	14	ESDI	2,7 RLL	5.25 HH		150k		
1664-7	14	ESDI	2,7 RLL	5.25 HH		150k	3600	
1670-4	16	SCSI		5.25 HH		150k		
1673-4	16	SCSI	2,7 RLL	5.25 HH		150k	3600	
1673-5	16	SCSI	2,7 RLL	5.25 HH		150k	3600	
1674	16	SCSI		5.25 HH		150k		N
1674-6	16	SCSI	2,7 RLL	5.25 HH		150k	3600	

Drive Model	Format Size MB	Head	Cyl	Sect/ Trac	Translate H/C/S	RWC/ WPC	Land Zone
1674-7	157	7	1249	36		1250/1250	AUTO
1683-4	193	4	1776	54		1777/1777	AUTO
1683-5	242	5	1776	54		1777/1777	AUTO
1684	340					---/---	
1684-6	291	6	1776	54		1777/1777	AUTO
1684-7	339	7	1780	54		1777/1777	AUTO
1743-5	112	5	1140	28		NA/NA	
1744-6	135	6	1140	28		NA/NA	
1744-7	157	7	1140	28		NA/NA	
1745-8	180	8	1140	28		NA/NA	
1745-9	202	9	1140	28		NA/NA	
1773-5	112	5	1140	28		1141/1141	
1774-6	135	6	1140	28		1141/1141	
1774-7	157	7	1140	28		1141/1141	
1775-8	180	8	1140	28		1141/1141	
1775-9	202	9	1140	28		1141/1141	
1908-15	1381	15	2112	V		NA/NA	AUTO
1924-21	2100	21	2280	V		NA/NA	AUTO
2105-15	560	15	1747	V		NA/NA	AUTO
2105(A)	560	8	1745	V		NA/NA	AUTO
2105A-15	560	15	1747	V		NA/NA	AUTO
2105(S)	560	8	1745	V		NA/NA	AUTO
2108(A)	666	10	1745	V		NA/NA	AUTO
2108(S)	666	10	1745	V		NA/NA	AUTO
2112A-15	1050	15	1747	V		NA/NA	AUTO
2112(A)	1050	15	1745	V		NA/NA	AUTO
2112(S)	1050	15	1745	V		NA/NA	AUTO
2112-15	1050	15	1747	V		NA/NA	AUTO
2121(A)				V		NA/NA	AUTO
2121(S)				V		NA/NA	AUTO

MICROSCIENCE INTERNATIONAL COR

Drive Model	Format Size MB	Head	Cyl	Sect/ Trac	Translate H/C/S	RWC/ WPC	Land Zone
4050	44	5	1024	17		1025/1025	
4060	67	5	1024	26		---/---	
4070	62	7	1024	17		---/---	
4090	93	7	1024	26		---/---	
5100	110	7	855	36		NA/NA	
5100-20	120	7	960	35		NA/NA	AUTO
6100	110	7	855	36		---/---	
7040	47	3	855	36		NA/NA	
7100	100	7	855	36		NA/NA	
7100-20	120	7	960	35		NA/960	960
7200	200	7				---/---	
7400	304	8	1904			NA/NA	AUTO
8040	42	2	1024	40		NA/NA	AUTO
8080	85	2	1768	47		NA/NA	AUTO
8200	152	4	1904			NA/NA	AUTO
FH2414	366	8	1658	54		NA/NA	AUTO
FH2777	687	15	1658	54		NA/NA	AUTO
FH3414	366	8	1658	54		NA/NA	AUTO
FH3777	687	15	1658	54		NA/NA	AUTO
FH21200	1062	15	1921	72		NA/NA	AUTO
FH21600	1418	15	2147	86		NA/NA	AUTO
FH31200	1062	15	1921	72		NA/NA	AUTO
FH31600	1418	15	2147	86		NA/NA	AUTO
HH312	10	4	306	17		307/307	
HH315	10	4	306	17		307/307	
HH325	21	4	612	17		613/613	615
HH330	32	4	612	26		613/613	
HH612	10	4	306	17		307/307	
HH625	21	4	612	17		613/613	
HH712A	10	2	612	17		---/---	
HH712	10	2	612	17		613/613	

Drive Model	Seek Time	Interface	Encode	Form Factor	cache kb	mtbf	RPM	Obsolete?
1674-7	16	SCSI	2,7 RLL	5.25 FH		150k	3600	
1683-4	14	SCSI	2,7 RLL	5.25 FH		150k		
1683-5	14	SCSI	2,7 RLL	5.25 FH		150k		
1684	15	SCSI		5.25 FH		150k		N
1684-6	14	SCSI		5.25 FH		150k		
1684-7	14	SCSI	2,7 RLL	5.25 FH		150k	3600	
1743-5	15	IDE AT	2,7 RLL	3.5 HH				
1744-6	15	IDE AT	2,7 RLL	3.5 HH				
1744-7	15	IDE AT	2,7 RLL	3.5 HH				
1745-8	15	IDE AT	2,7 RLL	3.5 HH				
1745-9	15	IDE AT	2,7 RLL	3.5 HH				
1773-5	15	SCSI	2,7 RLL	3.5 HH				
1774-6	15	SCSI	2,7 RLL	3.5 HH				
1774-7	15	SCSI	2,7 RLL	3.5 HH				
1775-8	15	SCSI	2,7 RLL	3.5 HH				
1775-9	15	SCSI	2,7 RLL	3.5 HH				
1908-15	11	SCSI-2 FAS		5.25 FH		150k	5400	
1924-21	11	SCSI-2		5.25 FH		250k	5400	
2105-15	10	SCSI-2 FAS		3.5 FH		300k	5400	
2105(A)	10	IDE AT	RLL	3.5 FH		300k		
2105A-15	10	IDE AT		3.5 FH		300k	5400	
2105(S)	10	SCSI-2	RLL	3.5 HH		300k		
2108(A)	10	IDE AT	RLL	3.5 HH		300k		
2108(S)	10	SCSI-2	RLL	3.5 HH		300k		
2112A-15	10	IDE AT		3.5 FH		300k	5400	
2112(A)	10	IDE AT	RLL	3.5 FH		300k		
2112-15	10	SCSI-2 FAS		3.5 FH		300k	5400	
2112(S)	10	SCSI-2	RLL	5.25 FH		300k		
2121(A)	10	IDE AT	RLL	3.5 FH		300k		
2121(S)	10	SCSI-2	RLL	5.25 FH		300k		

MICROSCIENCE INTERNATIONAL COR

Drive Model	Seek Time	Interface	Encode	Form Factor	cache kb	mtbf	RPM	Obsolete?
4050	18	ST412/506	MFM	3.5 HH		36k		
4060	18	ST412/506	2,7 RLL	3.5 HH		36k		
4070	18	ST412/506	MFM	3.5 HH		36k		
4090	18	ST412/506	2,7 RLL	3.5 HH		36k		
5100	18	ESDI	2,7 RLL	3.5 HH		36k		
5100-20	18	ESDI	2,7 RLL	3.5 HH		60k		
6100	18	SCSI	2,7 RLL	3.5 HH		36k		
7040	18	IDE AT	2,7 RLL	3.5 HH				
7100	18	IDE AT	2,7 RLL	3.5 HH		36k		
7100-20	18	IDE AT	2,7 RLL	3.5 HH		60k	3600	
7200	18	IDE AT	2,7 RLL	3.5 HH				
7400	15	IDE AT		3.5 HH		100k		N
8040	25	IDE AT	2,7 RLL	3.5 3H		20k		N
8080	17	IDE AT		3.5 3H		100k		N
8200	16	IDE AT		3.5 3H		100k		N
FH2414	14	ESDI	2,7 RLL	5.25 FH		100k		
FH2777	14	ESDI	2,7 RLL	5.25 FH		50k	3600	N
FH3414	14	SCSI	2,7 RLL	5.25 FH		100k		
FH3777	14	SCSI	2,7 RLL	5.25 FH		100k	3600	N
FH21200	14	ESDI	2,7 RLL	5.25 FH		100k	3600	N
FH21600	14	ESDI	2,7 RLL	5.25 FH		100k	3600	N
FH31200	14	SCSI	2,7 RLL	5.25 FH		100k	3600	N
FH31600	14	SCSI	2,7 RLL	5.25 FH		100k	3600	N
HH312	65	ST412/506	MFM	5.25 HH				
HH315	65	ST412/506	MFM	5.25 HH				
HH325	80	ST412/506	MFM	5.25 HH				
HH330	105	ST412/506	2,7 RLL	5.25 HH				
HH612	85	ST412/506	MFM	5.25 HH				
HH625	65	ST412/506	MFM	5.25 HH				
HH712A	75	ST412/506	MFM	5.25 HH				
HH712	105	ST412/506	MFM	5.25 HH				

Drive Model	Format Size MB	Head	Cyl	Sect/Trac	Translate H/C/S	RWC/WPC	Land Zone
HH725	21	4	612	17		613/613	615
HH738	32	4	612	26		613/613	
HH825	21	4	615	17		616/616	
HH830	33	4	615	26		616/616	
HH1050	44	5	1024	17		1025/1025	1023
HH1060	65	5	1024	26		1025/1025	
HH1075	62	7	1024	17		1025/1025	
HH1080	65	5	1024	26		---/---	
HH1090	80	7	1314	17		1315/1315	
HH1095	95	7	1024	17		1025/1025	
HH1120	122	7	1314	26		1315/1315	
HH2012	10	4	306	17		---/---	
HH2120	128	7	1024	35		NA/NA	
HH2160	160	7	1276	35		NA/NA	
HH3120	121	5	1314	36		---/---	
HH3160	170	7	1314	36		---/---	

MINISCRIBE CORPORATION

Drive Model	Format Size MB	Head	Cyl	Sect/Trac	Translate H/C/S	RWC/WPC	Land Zone
80SC-MFM	21	4	615	17		---/---	
80SC-RLL	33	4	615	26		---/---	
1006	5	2	306	17		307/128	336
1012	10	2	306	17		307/128	336
2006	5	2	306	17		307/128	336
2012	10	4	306	17		307/128	336
3006	5	2	306	17		307/128	306
3012	10	2	612	17		613/128	656
3053	44	5	1024	17		1024/512	AUTO
3085	71	7	1170	17		1170/512	AUTO
3085E	72	3	1270	36		NA/NA	AUTO
3085S	72	3	1255	125		NA/NA	AUTO
3130S	115	5	1255	36		1256/512	AUTO
3130E	112	5	1250	36		NA/NA	AUTO
3180E	156	7	1250	35		1251/512	AUTO
3180S	153	7	1255	36		1256/512	AUTO
3180SM	161	7	1250	36		NA/NA	AUTO
3212	10	2	612	17		613/128	656
3212 PLUS	11	2	615	17		613/128	AUTO
3412	10	4	306	17		307/128	336
3425	21	4	615	17		616/128	656
3425 PLUS	21	4	615	17		616/128	656
3425S	21	4	612	17		615/128	656
3438	32	4	615	26		616/128	656
3438 PLUS	32	4	615	26		616/128	656
3650	42	6	809	17		819/128	852
3650F	42	6	809	17		810/128	852
3650R	64	6	809	26		809/128	852
3675	63	6	809	26		810/128	852
4010	8	2	480	17		481/128	520
4020	16	4	480	17		481/128	520
5330	25	6	480	17		481/128	
5338	32	6	612	17		613/306	
5440	32	8	480	17		481/128	
5451	43	8	612	17		613/306	
6032	26	3	1024	17		1024/512	AUTO
6053	45	5	1024	17		1024/512	AUTO
6074	62	7	1024	17		1025/512	
6079	68	5	1024	26		1024/512	AUTO
6085	71	8	1024	17		1024/512	AUTO
6128	110	8	1024	26		1024/512	AUTO
6170E	130	8	1024			NA/NA	AUTO
6212	10	2	612	17		613/128	
7040A	42	2	1159	36		NA/NA	AUTO
7040S	40	2	1156	36		NA/NA	AUTO

Drive Model	Seek Time	Interface	Encode	Form Factor	cache kb	mtbf	Obsolete? RPM ⇩
HH725	105	ST412/506	MFM	5.25 HH			
HH738	105	ST412/506	2,7 RLL	5.25 HH			
HH825	65	ST412/506	MFM	5.25 HH			
HH830	65	ST412/506	2,7 RLL	5.25 HH			
HH1050	28	ST412/506	MFM	5.25 HH		140k	
HH1060	28	ST412/506	2,7 RLL	5.25 HH		140k	
HH1075	28	ST412/506	MFM	5.25 HH			
HH1080	28	ST412/506	2,7 RLL	5.25 HH		50k	
HH1090	28	ST412/506	2,7 RLL	5.25 HH		40k	
HH1095	28	ST412/506	2,7 RLL	5.25 HH			
HH1120	28	ST412/506	2,7 RLL	5.25 HH		40k	
HH2012			MFM	5.25			
HH2120	28	ESDI (10)	2,7 RLL	5.25 HH		40k	
HH2160	28	ESDI (10)	2,7 RLL	5.25 HH		40k	
HH3120	28	SCSI	2,7 RLL	5.25 HH		40k	
HH3160	28	SCSI	2,7 RLL	5.25 HH		40k	

MINISCRIBE CORPORATION

Drive Model	Seek Time	Interface	Encode	Form Factor	cache kb	mtbf	Obsolete? RPM ⇩
80SC-MFM	68	ST412/506	MFM	3.5 HH		20k	3600 Y
80SC-RLL	68	ST412/506	2,7 RLL	3.5 HH		20k	3600 Y
1006	179	ST412/506	MFM	5.25 FH		8k	Y
1012	179	ST412/506	MFM	5.25 FH		8k	Y
2006	93	ST412/506	MFM	5.25 FH		10k	Y
2012	85	ST412/506	MFM	5.25 FH		10k	Y
3006		ST412/506	MFM	5.25 HH			Y
3012	155	ST412/506	MFM	5.25 HH		10k	Y
3053	25	ST412/506	MFM	5.25 HH		30k	3600 Y
3085	18	ST412/506	MFM	5.25 HH		40k	3600 Y
3085E	17	ESDI		5.25 HH			Y
3085S	17	SCSI		5.25 HH			Y
3130S	17	SCSI	2,7 RLL	5.25 HH		35k	3600 Y
3130E	17	ESDI	2,7 RLL	5.25 HH		35k	Y
3180E	17	ESDI	2,7 RLL	5.25 HH		35k	3600 Y
3180S	17	SCSI	2,7 RLL	5.25 HH		35k	3600 Y
3180SM	17	SCSI-MAC	RLL	5.25 HH		35k	Y
3212	85	ST412/506	MFM	5.25 HH		20k	3600 Y
3212 PLUS	53	ST412/506	MFM	5.25 HH		20k	3600 Y
3412	60	ST412/506	MFM	5.25 HH		11k	Y
3425	85	ST412/506	MFM	5.25 HH		20k	3600 Y
3425 PLUS	53	ST412/506	MFM	5.25 HH		20k	3600 Y
3425S	68	SCSI	MFM	5.25 HH		20k	Y
3438	85	ST412/506	2,7 RLL	5.25 HH		20k	3600 Y
3438 PLUS	53	ST412/506	2,7 RLL	5.25 HH		20k	3600 Y
3650	61	ST412/506	MFM	5.25 HH		25k	3600 Y
3650F	46	ST412/506	MFM	5.25 HH			Y
3650R	61	ST412/506	2,7 RLL	5.25 HH		25k	3600 Y
3675	61	ST412/506	2,7 RLL	5.25 HH		25k	Y
4010	133	ST412/506	MFM	5.25 FH		10k	Y
4020	133	ST412/506	MFM	5.25 FH		10k	Y
5330			MFM				
5338			MFM				
5440			MFM				
5451			MFM				
6032	28	ST412/506	MFM	5.25 FH		25k	3600 Y
6053	28	ST412/506	MFM	5.25 FH		25k	3600 Y
6074	28	ST412/506	MFM	5.25 FH			Y
6079	28	ST412/506	2,7 RLL	5.25 FH		25k	3600 Y
6085	28	ST412/506	MFM	5.25 FH		25k	3600 Y
6128	28	ST412/506	2,7 RLL	5.25 FH		25k	3600 Y
6170E	28	ESDI	RLL	5.25 FH			
6212		ST412/506	MFM	5.25 FH			
7040A	19	IDE AT	1,7 RLL	3.5 3H	32k	40k	3703 Y
7040S	19	SCSI	RLL	3.5 3H		40k	Y

Drive Model	Format Size MB	Head	Cyl	Sect/ Trac	Translate H/C/S	RWC/ WPC	Land Zone
7060A	65	2	1516	42		NA/NA	AUTO
7060S	65	2	1516	42		NA/NA	AUTO
7080A	81	4	1159	36		NA/NA	AUTO
7080S	81	4	1156	36		NA/NA	AUTO
7120A	131	2	1516	85		NA/NA	AUTO
7120S	131	2	1516	85		NA/NA	AUTO
7426	21	4	612	17		613/613	
8051A	42	4	745	28		746/128	AUTO
8051S	42	4	793	26		794/128	AUTO
8212	10	2	615	17		616/128	664
8225	20	2	771	26		772/128	810
8225XT	21	2	805	26		806/128	820
8225AT	21	2	747	26		748/128	820
8225S	21	2	804	26		805/128	820
8412	10	4	306	17		307/128	336
8425	21	4	615	17		616/128	664
8425F	21	4	615	17		616/128	664
8425S	21	4	615	17		616/128	664
8425XT	21	4	615	17		616/128	664
8434F	32	4	615	26		616/128	
8438	32	4	615	26		615/128	664
8438F	32	4	615	26		616/128	664
8438XT	31	4	615	26		NA/NA	664
8438 PLUS	31	4	615	26		615/128	664
8450	41	4	771	26		772/128	810
8450AT	42	4	745	28		746/128	820
8450XT	42	4	805	26		806/128	820
8450S	42	4	804	26		805/128	820
9000E	338	15	1224	36		NA/NA	AUTO
9000S	347	15	1220	36		NA/NA	AUTO
9230	203	9	1224	34		0/512	0
9230E	203	9	1224	36		NA/NA	AUTO
9230S	203	9	1224	36		NA/NA	AUTO
9380E	329	15	1224	36		NA/NA	AUTO
9380S	336	15	1224	36		NA/NA	AUTO
9380SM	319	15	1218			NA/NA	AUTO
9424E	360	8	1661			NA/NA	AUTO
9424S	355	8	1661			NA/NA	AUTO
9780E	645	15	1661	53		NA/NA	AUTO
9780S	668	15	1661	53		166/512	AUTO

MITSUBISHI ELECTRONICS

Drive Model	Format Size MB	Head	Cyl	Sect/ Trac	Translate H/C/S	RWC/ WPC	Land Zone
MR335	69	7	743	26		---/---	
MR521	10	2	612	17		---/---	
MR522	20	4	612	17		---/300	612
MR533	24	3	971	17		---/NONE	971
MR535	42	5	977	17		300/300	
MR535-U00	42	5	977	17		300/300	
MR535R	65	5	977	26		NA/NA	AUTO
MR535S	85	5	977	34		NA/NA	AUTO
MR537S	65	5	977	26		NA/NA	AUTO
MR5310E	65	5	977	26		NA/NA	AUTO

MITSUMI ELECTRONICS CORP.

Drive Model	Format Size MB	Head	Cyl	Sect/ Trac	Translate H/C/S	RWC/ WPC	Land Zone
HD2509AA	92	4		52		---/---	
HD2513AA	130	4		52		---/---	

MMI

Drive Model	Format Size MB	Head	Cyl	Sect/ Trac	Translate H/C/S	RWC/ WPC	Land Zone
M106	5	2	306	17		---/128	
M112	10	4	306	17		---/128	
M125	20	8	306	17		---/128	
M212	10	4	306	17		---/128	

Drive Model	Seek Time	Interface	Encode	Form Factor	cache kb	mtbf	RPM	Obsolete? ⇓
7060A	15	IDE AT	1,7 RLL	3.5 3H		150k		Y
7060S	15	SCSI	1,7 RLL	3.5 3H		150k		Y
7080A	19	IDE AT	1,7 RLL	3.5 3H	32k	40k	3703	Y
7080S	19	SCSI	1,7 RLL	3.5 3H		150k		Y
7120A	15	IDE AT	1,7 RLL	3.5 3H		150k		Y
7120S	15	SCSI	1,7 RLL	3.5 3H		150k		Y
7426		ST412/506	MFM					
8051A	28	IDE AT	2,7 RLL	3.5 HH	32k	150k	3484	Y
8051S	28	SCSI	2,7 RLL	3.5 HH	32k	150k	3484	Y
8212	68	ST412/506	MFM	3.5 HH		20k	3600	Y
8225	68	ST412/506	2,7 RLL	3.5 HH		30k	3600	Y
8225XT	68	IDE XT	2,7 RLL	3.5 HH		30k	3600	Y
8225AT	40	IDE AT	2,7 RLL	3.5 HH		30k	3600	Y
8225S	68	SCSI	2,7 RLL	3.5 HH		30k	3600	Y
8412	50	ST412/506	MFM	3.5 HH		20k		Y
8425	68	ST506/412	MFM	3.5 HH		20k	3600	Y
8425F	40	ST412/506	MFM	3.5 HH		20k	3600	Y
8425S	68	SCSI	MFM	3.5 HH		20k	3600	Y
8425XT	68	IDE XT	MFM	3.5 HH		20k	3600	Y
8434F	40	ST412/506	RLL	3.5 HH				Y
8438	68	ST412/506	RLL	3.5 HH		20k	3600	Y
8438F	40	ST412/506	2,7 RLL	3.5 HH		20k	3600	Y
8438XT	68	IDE XT	RLL	5.25 HH		20k	3600	Y
8438 PLUS	55	ST412/506	2,7 RLL	5.25 HH		20k		Y
8450	45	ST412/506	2,7 RLL	3.5 HH		30k	3600	Y
8450AT	40	IDE AT	2,7 RLL	3.5 HH		30k	3600	Y
8450XT	68	IDE XT	2,7 RLL	3.5 HH		20k	3600	Y
8450S	45	SCSI	2,7 RLL	3.5 HH		30k	3600	Y
9000E	16	ESDI		5.25 FH		30k		Y
9000S	16	SCSI		5.25 FH		30k		Y
9230	16	ESDI	RLL	5.25 FH				Y
9230E	16	ESDI		5.25 FH				Y
9230S	16	SCSI		5.25 FH				Y
9380E	16	ESDI	2,7 RLL	5.25 FH		50k	3600	Y
9380S	16	SCSI	2,7 RLL	5.25 FH		50k	3600	Y
9380SM	16	SCSI-MAC	RLL	5.25 FH		50k		Y
9424E	17	ESDI		5.25 FH				Y
9424S	17	SCSI		5.25 FH				Y
9780E	17	ESDI	1,7 RLL	5.25 FH		50k	3600	Y
9780S	17	SCSI	1,7 RLL	5.25 FH		50k	3600	Y

MITSUBISHI ELECTRONICS

Drive Model	Seek Time	Interface	Encode	Form Factor	cache kb	mtbf	RPM	Obsolete?
MR335	20	ST412/506	MFM	3.5 HH		30k		
MR521	85	ST412/506	MFM	5.25 HH				
MR522	85	ST412/506	MFM	5.25 HH				
MR533		ST412/506	MFM	5.25				
MR535	28	ST412/506	MFM	5.25 HH		30k	3600	N
MR535-U00	28	ST412/506	MFM	5.25 HH		30k		
MR535R	28	ST412/506	2,7 RLL	5.25 HH		30k	3600	N
MR535S	28	SCSI	2,7 RLL	5.25 HH		30k		
MR537S	28	SCSI		5.25 HH		30k		
MR5310E	28	ESDI		5.25 HH		30k		

MITSUMI ELECTRONICS CORP.

Drive Model	Seek Time	Interface	Encode	Form Factor	cache kb	mtbf	RPM	Obsolete?
HD2509AA	16	IDE AT	1,7 RLL	2.5 4H	32k	150k	3600	
HD2513AA	16	IDE AT	1,7 RLL	2.5 4H	32k	150k	3600	

MMI

Drive Model	Seek Time	Interface	Encode	Form Factor	cache kb	mtbf	RPM	Obsolete?
M106	75	ST412/506	MFM	3.5 HH				
M112	75	ST412/506	MFM	3.5 HH				
M125	75	ST412/506	MFM	3.5 HH				
M212	75	ST412/506	MFM	5.25 HH				

Drive Model	Format Size MB	Head	Cyl	Sect/ Trac	Translate H/C/S	RWC/ WPC	Land Zone
M225	20	8	306	17		---/128	
M306	5	2	306	17		---/128	
M312	10	4	306	17		---/128	
M325	20	8	306	17		---/128	

NCL AMERICA

SEE BRAND TECHNOLOGIES							---/---

NCR CORP

6091-5101	323	9				NA/NA	AUTO
6091-5301	675	15				NA/NA	AUTO
H6801-STD1-03-17	53	7	872	17		---/650	
H6801-STD1-07-17	45	3	868	34		NA/NA	AUTO
H6801-STD1-10-17	104	8	776	33		NA/NA	AUTO
H6801-STD1-12-17	42	2	1047	40		NA/NA	AUTO
H6801-STD1-46-46	21	4	615	17		616/128	664
H6801-STD1-47-46	71	8	1024	17		1025/128	AUTO
H6801-STD1-47-46	121	7	969	35		1025/128	AUTO

NEC TECHNOLOGIES INC

D3126	21	4	615	17		616/256	
D3142	42	8	642	17		---/---	
D3146H	40	8	615	17		---/---	
D3661	118	7	915	36		NA/NA	AUTO
D3735	45	2	1084	41		---/---	AUTO
D3755	105	4	1250	41		---/---	AUTO
D3761	114	7	915	35		---/---	AUTO
D3781	425	9	1464	63		---/---	AUTO
D3835	45	2	1084	41		---/---	AUTO
D3841	45	8	440			---/---	
D3855	105	4	1250	41		---/---	AUTO
D3861	114	7	915	35		---/---	
D3881	425	9	1464	63		---/---	AUTO
D5114	5	2	306	17		---/---	
D5124	10	4	309	17		310/310	664
D5126	20	4	612	17		613/NONE	664
D5126H	21	4	612	17		613/NONE	664
D5146H	42	8	615	17		616/NONE	664
D5146	40	8	615	17		616/NONE	664
D5392	1322	16	615	17		---/---	
D5652	143	10	823			NA/NA	
D5655	154	7	1224	35		NA/NA	
D5662	300	15	1224	35		NA/NA	
D5682	664	15	1633	53		NA/NA	AUTO
D5862	301	15	1224	53		NA/NA	
D5882	664	15	1633	53		---/---	AUTO
D5892	1404	19	1678	86		---/---	

NEI

RD3127	10	2	612	17		---/---	
RD3255	20	4	612	17		---/---	
RD4127	10	4	306	17		---/---	
RD4255	20	8	306	17		---/---	

NEWBURY DATA

NDR320	21	4	615	17		---/NONE	615
NDR340	42	8	615	17		---/NONE	615
PENNY 340	42	8	615	17		615/615	
NDR1065	55	7	918	17		---/---	
NDR1085	71	8	1024	17		---/NONE	1023
NDR1105	87	11	918	17		---/NONE	1023

Drive Model	Seek Time	Interface	Encode	Form Factor	cache kb	mtbf	RPM	Obsolete?
M225	75	ST412/506	MFM	5.25 HH				
M306	75	ST412/506	MFM	5.25 HH				
M312	75	ST412/506	MFM	5.25 HH				
M325	75	ST412/506	MFM	5.25 HH				

NCL AMERICA
SEE BRAND TECHNOLOGIES

NCR CORP
Drive Model	Seek Time	Interface	Encode	Form Factor	cache kb	mtbf	RPM	Obsolete?
6091-5101	27	SCSI	2,7 RLL	5.25				
6091-5301	25	SCSI	2,7 RLL	5.25				
H6801-STD1-03-17	28	ST412/506	MFM	3.5 HH		20k		
H6801-STD1-07-17	18	IDE AT	2,7 RLL	3.5 HH		20k		
H6801-STD1-10-17	25	IDE AT	2,7 RLL	3.5 HH		150k		
H6801-STD1-12-17	25	IDE AT	2,7 RLL	3.5 3H		150k		
H6801-STD1-46-46	68	ST412/506	MFM	3.5 HH		20k		
H6801-STD1-47-46	28	ST412/506	MFM	5.25 FH		40k		
H6801-STD1-47-46	16	ESDI (10)	2,7 RLL	5.25 FH		100k		

NEC TECHNOLOGIES INC
Drive Model	Seek Time	Interface	Encode	Form Factor	cache kb	mtbf	RPM	Obsolete?
D3126	85	ST412/506	MFM	3.5 HH				
D3142	28	ST412/506	MFM	3.5 HH		30k		
D3146H	35	ST412/506	MFM	3.5 HH				
D3661	20	ESDI (10)	2,7 RLL	3.5 HH		30k		
D3735	25	IDE AT	1,7 RLL	3.5 3H		50k	3456	N
D3755	25	IDE AT	1,7 RLL	3.5 3H		50k	3456	N
D3761	20	IDE AT	2,7 RLL	3.5 HH		30k		
D3781	15	IDE AT	1,7 RLL	3.5 HH	64k	50k	3600	N
D3835	25	SCSI	1,7 RLL	3.5 3H		50k	3456	N
D3841	28	SCSI	1,7 RLL	3.5 HH		30k		
D3855	25	SCSI	1,7 RLL	3.5 3H		50k	3456	N
D3861	20	SCSI		3.5 HH		30		
D3881	15	SCSI	1,7 RLL	3.5 HH	64k	50k	3600	N
D5114		ST412/506	MFM	5.25				
D5124	80	ST412/506	MFM	5.25 HH				
D5126	80	ST412/506	MFM	5.25 HH				
D5126H	40	ST412/506	MFM	5.25 HH				
D5146H	40	ST412/506	MFM	5.25 HH				
D5146	85	ST412/506	MFM	5.25 HH				
D5392	14	IPI-2		5.25 FH		100k		
D5652	23	ESDI	2,7 RLL	5.25 FH				
D5655	18	ESDI	2,7 RLL	5.25 FH		30k		
D5662	18	ESDI	2,7 RLL	5.25 FH		30k		
D5682	16	ESDI	RLL 1,7	5.25 FH		50k	3600	N
D5882	18	SCSI		5.25 FH		30k		
D5882	16	SCSI	RLL 1,7	5.25 FH		50k	3600	N
D5892	14	SCSI	1,7 RLL	5.25 FH		100k		

NEI
Drive Model	Seek Time	Interface	Encode	Form Factor	cache kb	mtbf	RPM	Obsolete?
RD3127		ST412/506	MFM	5.25				
RD3255		ST412/506	MFM	5.25				
RD4127		ST412/506	MFM	5.25				
RD4255		ST412/506	MFM	5.25				

NEWBURY DATA
Drive Model	Seek Time	Interface	Encode	Form Factor	cache kb	mtbf	RPM	Obsolete?
NDR320		ST412/506	MFM	5.25				
NDR340	40	ST412/506	MFM	3.5 HH				
PENNY 340		ST412/506	MFM	5.25 HH				
NDR1065	25	ST412/506	MFM	5.25 FH				
NDR1085	26	ST412/506	MFM	5.25 FH				
NDR1105	25	ST412/506	MFM	5.25 FH				

Drive Model	Format Size MB	Head	Cyl	Sect/ Trac	Translate H/C/S	RWC/ WPC	Land Zone
NDR1140	120	15	918	17		---/NONE	1023
NDR2085	74	7	1224	17		1224/1224	
NDR2140	117	11	1224	17		1224/1224	
NDR2190	160	15	1224	17		---/NONE	1223
NDR3170S	146	9	1224	26		NA/NA	AUTO
NDR3170S	146	9	1224	26		NA/NA	AUTO
NDR3280S	244	15	1224	26		---/---	
NDR3380S	319	15	1224	34		NA/NA	AUTO
NDR4175	179	7	1224	36		NA/NA	
NDR4380	338	15	1224	36		NA/NA	
NDR4380S	319	15	1224	34		---/---	

NPL

Drive Model	Format Size MB	Head	Cyl	Sect/ Trac	Translate H/C/S	RWC/ WPC	Land Zone
4064	5			17		---/---	
4127	10			17		---/---	
4191S	15			17		---/---	
4255	20			17		---/---	
4362	30			17		---/---	
NP02-13	11	4	320	17		NA/0	320
NP02-26A/26S	22	4	640	17		NA/0	640
NP02-52A	44	8	640	17		NA/640	640
NP03-20	16	6	306	17		NA/0	306
NP04-13T	10	6		17		---/---	
NP04-55	45	7	754	17		NA/0	754
NP04-85	72	11	754	17		NA/0	754

OKIDATA

Drive Model	Format Size MB	Head	Cyl	Sect/ Trac	Translate H/C/S	RWC/ WPC	Land Zone
OD526	31	4	640	26		651/651	
OD540	51	6	640	26		651/651	

OLIVETTI

Drive Model	Format Size MB	Head	Cyl	Sect/ Trac	Translate H/C/S	RWC/ WPC	Land Zone
XM5210	10			17		---/---	
XM5220/2	20			17		---/---	
HD662/12	20	4	612	17		---/---	
HD662/11	10	2	612	17		---/---	

OPTIMA TECHNOLOGY CORP

Drive Model	Format Size MB	Head	Cyl	Sect/ Trac	Translate H/C/S	RWC/ WPC	Land Zone
CONCORDE 635	640	14				NA/NA	AUTO
CONCORDE 1050	990	15				NA/NA	AUTO
CONCORDE 1350	1342					NA/NA	AUTO
DISKOVERY 40	45					NA/NA	AUTO
DISKOVERY 130	137					NA/NA	AUTO
DISKOVERY 200	200					NA/NA	AUTO
DISKOVERY 325	321					NA/NA	AUTO
DISKOVERY 420	416	8				NA/NA	AUTO
MINIPAK 40	45					---/---	AUTO
MINIPAK 100	104	4				NA/NA	AUTO
MINIPAK 200	209	8				NA/NA	AUTO
MINIPAK 300	320					NA/NA	AUTO

ORCA TECHNOLOGY CORP

Drive Model	Format Size MB	Head	Cyl	Sect/ Trac	Translate H/C/S	RWC/ WPC	Land Zone
320A	370	9				NA/NA	AUTO
320S	370	9				NA/NA	AUTO
400A	470	9				NA/NA	AUTO
400S	470	9				NA/NA	AUTO
760E	760	15				NA/NA	AUTO
760S	760	15				NA/NA	AUTO

Drive Model	Seek Time	Interface	Encode	Form Factor	cache kb	mtbf	Obsolete? RPM
NDR1140	25	ST412/506	MFM	5.25 FH			
NDR2085		ST412/506	MFM	5.25 FH			
NDR2140		ST412/506	MFM	5.25 FH			
NDR2190	28	ST412/506	MFM	5.25 FH			
NDR3170S	28	SCSI	2,7 RLL	5.25 FH			
NDR3170S	28	SCSI	2,7 RLL	5.25 FH			
NDR3280S	28	SCSI	2,7 RLL	5.25 FH			
NDR3380S	28	SCSI	2,7 RLL	5.25 FH		50k	
NDR4175	28	ESDI	2,7 RLL	5.25 FH			
NDR4380	28	ESDI	2,7 RLL	5.25 FH			
NDR4380S	28	SCSI	RLL	5.25 FH			

NPL

Drive Model	Seek Time	Interface	Encode	Form Factor	cache kb	mtbf	Obsolete? RPM
4064		ST412/506	MFM	5.25 FH			
4127		ST412/506	MFM	5.25 FH			
4191S		ST412/506	MFM	5.25 FH			
4255		ST412/506	MFM	5.25 FH			
4362		ST412/506	MFM	5.25 FH			
NP02-13	95	ST412/506	MFM	5.25 FH			
NP02-26A/26S	40	ST412/506	MFM	5.25 HH			
NP02-52A	40	ST412/506	MFM	5.25 HH			
NP03-20	85	ST412/506	MFM	3.5 FH			
NP04-13T	85	ST412/506	MFM	5.25 FH			
NP04-55	35	ST412/506	MFM	5.25 FH			
NP04-85	35	ST412/506	MFM	3.5 HH			

OKIDATA

Drive Model	Seek Time	Interface	Encode	Form Factor	cache kb	mtbf	Obsolete? RPM
OD526	85	ST412/506	2,7 RLL	5.25 HH			
OD540	85	ST412/506	2,7 RLL	5.25 HH			

OLIVETTI

Drive Model	Seek Time	Interface	Encode	Form Factor	cache kb	mtbf	Obsolete? RPM
XM5210	65	ST412/506	MFM	5.25 HH			
XM5220/2	85	ST412/506	MFM	5.25 FH			
HD662/12		ST412/506	MFM				
HD662/11		ST412/506	MFM				

OPTIMA TECHNOLOGY CORP

Drive Model	Seek Time	Interface	Encode	Form Factor	cache kb	mtbf	Obsolete? RPM
CONCORDE 635	16	SCSI	2,7 RLL	5.25		150k	N
CONCORDE 1050	15	SCSI	2,7 RLL	5.25		150k	N
CONCORDE 1350	14	SCSI	2,7 RLL	5.25		150k	N
DISKOVERY 40	25	SCSI	2,7 RLL	5.25		50k	N
DISKOVERY 130	20	SCSI	2,7 RLL	5.25		50k	N
DISKOVERY 200	15	SCSI	2,7 RLL	5.25		150k	N
DISKOVERY 325	14	SCSI	2,7 RLL	5.25		150k	N
DISKOVERY 420	16	SCSI	2,7 RLL	5.25		100k	N
MINIPAK 40	25	SCSI				30k	N
MINIPAK 100	25	SCSI	2,7 RLL	3.5 HH		30k	
MINIPAK 200	20	SCSI	2,7 RLL	3.5 HH		40k	
MINIPAK 300	13	SCSI	2,7 RLL	3.5 HH		150k	

ORCA TECHNOLOGY CORP

Drive Model	Seek Time	Interface	Encode	Form Factor	cache kb	mtbf	Obsolete? RPM
320A	12	IDE AT	2,7 RLL	3.5 HH		100k	
320S	12	SCSI	2,7 RLL	3.5 HH		100k	
400A	12	IDE AT	2,7 RLL	3.5 HH		100k	
400S	12	SCSI	2,7 RLL	3.5 HH		100k	
760E	14	ESDI	2,7 RLL	5.25		50k	
760S	14	SCSI	2,7 RLL	5.25		50k	

Drive Model	Format Size MB	Head	Cyl	Sect/ Trac	Translate H/C/S	RWC/ WPC	Land Zone
OTARI							
SEE DISCTRON						---/---	
PACIFIC MAGTRON							
MT3050	50	2	1062	46		---/---	
MT3100	100	4	1062	46		---/---	
MT4115E	115	4	1597			---/---	
MT4115S	115	4	1597			---/---	
MT4140E	140	5	1597			---/---	
MT4140S	140	5	1597			---/---	
MT4170E	170	6	1597			---/---	
MT4170S	170	6	1597			---/---	
MT5760E	676	15	1632	54		NA/NA	AUTO
MT5760S	673	15	1632	54		NA/NA	AUTO
MT6120S	1050	15	1927	71		NA/NA	AUTO
PANASONIC							
JU116	20	4	615	17		616/616	
JU128	42	7	733	17		734/734	
PLUS DEVELOPMENT							
HARDCARD 20	21	4	615	17		NA/NA	AUTO
HARDCARD 40	42	8	612	17		NA/NA	AUTO
HARDCARD II-40	40	5	925	17		NA/NA	AUTO
HARDCARD II-80	80	10	925	17		NA/NA	AUTO
HARDCARD II-XL50	52	10	601	17		---/---	
HARDCARD II-XL105	105	15	806	17		---/---	
IMPULSE 40AT	41	5	965	17		NA/NA	AUTO
IMPULSE 40S	42	3				---/---	AUTO
IMPULSE 52AT/LP	52	8	751	17		---/---	AUTO
IMPULSE 52S/LP	52	2				---/---	AUTO
IMPULSE 80AT	83	10	965	17		NA/NA	AUTO
IMPULSE 80AT/LP	85	16	616	17		---/---	AUTO
IMPULSE 80S	84	6				---/---	AUTO
IMPULSE 80S/LP	85	4				---/---	AUTO
IMPULSE 105AT/LP	105	16	755	17		---/---	AUTO
IMPULSE 105S	105	6				---/---	AUTO
IMPULSE 105S/LP	105	4	1056			---/---	AUTO
IMPULSE 120AT	120	5	1123	42		---/---	AUTO
IMPULSE 120S	120	5	1123	42		---/---	AUTO
IMPULSE 170AT	169	7	1123	42		---/---	AUTO
IMPULSE 170S	169	7	1123	42		---/---	AUTO
IMPULSE 210AT	174	7	1156	42		---/---	AUTO
IMPULSE 210S	174	7	1156	42		---/---	AUTO
IMPULSE 330AT	331					---/---	AUTO
IMPULSE 330S	331					---/---	AUTO
IMPULSE 425AT	425					---/---	AUTO
IMPULSE 425S	425					---/---	AUTO
PRAIRIETEK CORP							
PRAIRIE 120	21	2	615	34		---/---	
PRAIRIE 140	42	4	615	34		NA/NA	AUTO
PRAIRIE 220A	20	4	612	16		---/---	
PRAIRIE 220S	20	4	612	16		---/---	
PRAIRIE 240	42	4	615	34		---/---	
PRAIRIE 242A	42	4	615	34		NA/NA	AUTO
PRAIRIE 242S	42	4	615	34		NA/NA	AUTO
PRAIRIE 282A	82	4		34		NA/NA	AUTO
PRAIRIE 282S	82	4		34		NA/NA	AUTO

Drive Model	Seek Time	Interface	Encode	Form Factor	cache kb	mtbf	RPM

OTARI

SEE DISCTRON

PACIFIC MAGTRON

Drive Model	Seek Time	Interface	Encode	Form Factor	cache kb	mtbf	RPM
MT3050	20	IDE AT	2,7 RLL	5.25 HH		60k	
MT3100	20	IDE AT	2,7 RLL	5.25 HH		60k	
MT4115E	16	ESDI	2,7 RLL	5.25 HH		100k	
MT4115S	16	SCSI	2,7 RLL	5.25 HH		100k	
MT4140E	16	ESDI	2,7 RLL	5.25 HH		100k	
MT4140S	16	SCSI	2,7 RLL	5.25 HH		100k	
MT4170E	16	ESDI	2,7 RLL	5.25 HH		100k	
MT4170S	16	SCSI	2,7 RLL	5.25 HH		100k	
MT5760E	14	ESDI (15)	1,7 RLL	5.25 FH		150k	
MT5760S	14	SCSI	1,7 RLL	5.25 FH		150k	
MT6120S	14	SCSI	1,7 RLL	5.25 FH		150k	

PANASONIC

Drive Model	Seek Time	Interface	Encode	Form Factor	cache kb	mtbf	RPM
JU116	85	ST412/506	MFM	3.5 HH		5	
JU128	35	ST412/506	MFM	3.5 HH		5	

PLUS DEVELOPMENT

Drive Model	Seek Time	Interface	Encode	Form Factor	cache kb	mtbf	RPM
HARDCARD 20	40	IDE AT	2,7 RLL			60k	
HARDCARD 40	40	IDE AT	2,7 RLL			60k	
HARDCARD II-40	25	IDE AT	2,7 RLL				
HARDCARD II-80	25	IDE AT	2,7 RLL				
HARDCARD II-XL50	17	IDE AT	2,7 RLL	CARD 3H			
HARDCARD II-XL105	17	IDE AT	2,7 RLL	CARD 3H			
IMPULSE 40AT	19	IDE AT	2,7 RLL	3.5 HH		50k	
IMPULSE 40S	19	SCSI-2	2,7 RLL	3.5 HH		50k	
IMPULSE 52AT/LP	17	IDE AT	2,7 RLL	3.5 3H		60k	
IMPULSE 52S/LP	17	SCSI-2	2,7 RLL	3.5 3H		60k	
IMPULSE 80AT	19	IDE AT	2,7 RLL	3.5 3H		50k	
IMPULSE 80AT/LP	17	IDE AT	2,7 RLL	3.5 3H		60k	
IMPULSE 80S	19	SCSI-2	2,7 RLL	3.5 3H		50k	
IMPULSE 80S/LP	17	SCSI-2	2,7 RLL	3.5 3H		60k	
IMPULSE 105AT/LP	17	IDE AT	2,7 RLL	3.5 3H		60k	
IMPULSE 105S	17	SCSI-2	2,7 RLL	3.5 HH		50k	
IMPULSE 105S/LP	17	SCSI-2	2,7 RLL	3.5 3H		60k	
IMPULSE 120AT	15	IDE AT	1,7 RLL	3.5 HH		50k	
IMPULSE 120S	15	SCSI-2	1,7 RLL	3.5 HH		50k	
IMPULSE 170AT	15	IDE AT	1,7 RLL	3.5 HH		50k	
IMPULSE 170S	15	SCSI-2	1,7 RLL	3.5 HH		50k	
IMPULSE 210AT	15	IDE AT	1,7 RLL	3.5 HH		50k	
IMPULSE 210S	15	SCSI-2	1,7 RLL	3.5 HH		50k	
IMPULSE 330AT	14	IDE AT	1,7 RLL	3.5 HH		75k	
IMPULSE 330S	14	SCSI-2	1,7 RLL	3.5 HH		75k	
IMPULSE 425AT	14	IDE AT	1,7 RLL	3.5 HH		75k	
IMPULSE 425S	14	SCSI-2	1,7 RLL	3.5 HH		75k	

PRAIRIETEK CORP

Drive Model	Seek Time	Interface	Encode	Form Factor	cache kb	mtbf	RPM
PRAIRIE 120	23	IDE AT	2,7 RLL	2.5 4H		20k	
PRAIRIE 140	23		2,7 RLL	2.5 4H		20k	
PRAIRIE 220A	28	IDE AT	2,7 RLL	2.5 3H		20k	
PRAIRIE 220S	28	SCSI	2,7 RLL	2.5 3H		20k	
PRAIRIE 240	23	IDE AT	2,7 RLL	2.5 3H		20k	
PRAIRIE 242A	23	IDE XT-AT	2,7 RLL			20k	
PRAIRIE 242S	23	SCSI	2,7 RLL			20k	
PRAIRIE 282A	28		2,7 RLL			20k	
PRAIRIE 282S	23	SCSI	2,7 RLL			20k	

Drive Model	Format Size MB	Head	Cyl	Sect/ Trac	Translate H/C/S	RWC/ WPC	Land Zone
PRIAM CORPORATION							
502	46	7	755	17		756/756	
504	46	7	755	17		756/756	
514	117	11	1224	17		---/---	
519	160	15	1224	17		1225/1225	
519	244	11	1224	26		---/---	
617	153	7	1225			NA/NA	
628	241	11	1225			NA/NA	
638	329	15	1225			NA/NA	
717	153	7	1225			1226/1226	
728	241	11	1225			1226/1226	
738	329	15	1225			1226/1226	
3504	32	4	820	26		---/---	
ID20	25	3	987	17		---/---	
ID40AT	40	5	1018	17		---/---	
ID40	42	5	987	17		---/---	
ID45H	44	5	1024	17		---/---	
ID45	44	5	1018	17		---/---	
ID60AT	59	5	1018	17		---/---	
ID60	59	7	1018	17		---/---	
ID62	62	7	1166	17		---/---	
ID75	73	5	1166	25		---/---	
ID100	103	7	1166	25		---/---	
ID120	119	7	1024	33		NA/NA	
ID130	132	15	1224	17		---/---	
ID150	158	7	1276	35		NA/NA	
ID160H	156	7	1225	36		NA/NA	AUTO
ID160	158	7	1218	36		---/---	AUTO
ID230	233	15	1224	25		---/---	
ID250	246	11	1225	36		NA/NA	
ID330E	337	15	1218	36		---/---	
ID330	339	15	1218	36		---/---	
ID330D	337	15	1225	36		NA/NA	
ID330E-PS/2	330	15	1195	36		---/---	
ID330S	338	15	1225	36		NA/NA	AUTO
ID340H	340	7	1218	36		---/---	AUTO
ID660	660	15	1632	54		NA/NA	AUTO
ID1000	1034	15	1919	71		NA/NA	AUTO
ID/ED040	42	5	987	17		---/---	
ID/ED045	50	5	1166	17		---/---	
ID/ED060	62	7	1018	17		---/---	
ID/ED062	71	7	1166	17		---/---	
ID/ED075	74	5	1166	25		---/---	
ID/ED100	122	7	1314	26		---/---	
ID/ED120	121	7	1024	33		NA/NA	AUTO
ID/ED130	159	15	1224	17		---/---	
ID/ED150	160	7	1276	35		NA/NA	AUTO
ID/ED160	158	7	1225	36		NA/NA	AUTO
ID/ED230	235	15	1224	25		---/---	
ID/ED240	243	15	1220	26		---/---	
ID/ED250	248	11	1225	36		NA/NA	AUTO
ID/ED660	675	15	1628	54		---/---	AUTO
ID/ED1000	1046	15	1919	71		---/---	AUTO
V130	39	3	987	26		988/988	987
V150	42	5	987	17		988/988	987
V160	50	5	1166	17		1167/1167	
V170	60	7	987	17		988/988	987
V170R	91	7	987	26		988/988	987
V185	72	7	1166	17		1167/1167	1165
V519	159	15	1224	17		---/NONE	1223

Drive Model	Seek Time	Interface	Encode	Form Factor	cache kb	mtbf	Obsolete? RPM
PRIAM CORPORATION							
502	22	ST412/506	MFM	5.25 FH			
504	22	ST412/506	MFM	5.25 FH			
514	22	ST412/506	MFM	5.25 FH			
519	22	ST412/506	MFM	5.25 FH		40k	
519	22	ST412/506	2,7 RLL	5.25 FH		40	
617	20	ESDI	2,7 RLL	5.25 FH		40k	
628	20	ESDI	2,7 RLL	5.25 FH		40k	
638	20	SCSI	2,7 RLL	5.25 FH		40k	
717	20	SCSI	2,7 RLL	5.25 FH		40k	
728	20	SCSI	2,7 RLL	5.25 FH		40k	
738	20	SCSI	2,7 RLL	5.25 FH		40k	
3504	27	ST412/506	2,7 RLL	3.5 HH			
ID20	23	ST412/506	MFM	5.25 FH		40k	
ID40AT	23	ST412/506	MFM	5.25 FH		150k	
ID40	23	ST412/506	MFM	5.25 FH		40k	
ID45H	25	ST412/506	MFM	5.25 HH		40k	
ID45	23	ST412/506	MFM	5.25 FH		150k	
ID60AT	23	ST412/506	MFM	5.25 FH		150k	
ID60	30	ST412/506	MFM	5.25 FH		40k	
ID62	23	ST412/506	MFM	5.25 FH		40k	
ID75	23	ST412/506	2,7 RLL	5.25 FH		40k	
ID100	15	ST412/506	2,7 RLL	5.25 FH		40k	
ID120	28	ESDI	2,7 RLL	5.25 FH			
ID130	13	ST412/506	MFM	5.25 FH		40k	
ID150	28	ESDI	2,7 RLL	5.25 FH			
ID160H	28	ESDI	2,7 RLL	5.25 FH		150k	
ID160	28	SCSI		5.25 FH		150k	
ID230	11	ST412/506	2,7 RLL	5.25 FH		40k	
ID250	18	ESDI		5.25 FH			
ID330E	18	ESDI		5.25 FH			
ID330	18	SCSI		5.25 FH			
ID330D	18	ESDI	2,7 RLL	5.25 FH			
ID330E-PS/2	18	PS/2	2,7 RLL	5.25 FH			
ID330S	18	SCSI	2,7 RLL	5.25 FH			
ID340H	14	ESDI	2,7 RLL	5.25 FH		150k	
ID660	16	ESDI		5.25 FH		150k	
ID1000	14	ESDI		5.25 FH		150k	
ID/ED040	23	ST412/506	MFM	5.25 FH		40k	
ID/ED045	23	ST412/506	MFM	5.25 FH		40k	
ID/ED060	30	ST412/506	MFM	5.25 FH		40k	
ID/ED062	23	ST412/506	MFM	5.25 FH		40k	
ID/ED075	23	ST412/506		5.25 FH		40k	
ID/ED100	15	ST412/506	2,7 RLL	5.25 HH		40k	
ID/ED120	28	ESDI	2,7 RLL	5.25 HH			
ID/ED130	13	ST412/506	MFM	5.25 FH		40k	
ID/ED150	28	ESDI	2,7 RLL	5.25 FH			
ID/ED160	18	ESDI	2,7 RLL	5.25 FH			
ID/ED230	11	ST412/506		5.25 FH		40k	
ID/ED240	28	ST412/506	2,7 RLL	5.25 FH			
ID/ED250	18	ESDI		5.25 FH			
ID/ED660	16	SCSI		5.25 FH		150k	
ID/ED1000	14	SCSI		5.25 FH		150k	
V130		ST412/506	2,7 RLL	5.25 FH			
V150		ST412/506	MFM	5.25 FH			
V160		ST412/506	MFM	5.25 FH			
V170	28	ST412/506	MFM	5.25 FH			
V170R	28	ST412/506	MFM	5.25 FH			
V185	28	ST412/506	MFM	5.25 FH			
V519	20		MFM	5.25 FH			

Drive Model	Format Size MB	Head	Cyl	Sect/ Trac	Translate H/C/S	RWC/ WPC	Land Zone
PROCOM TECHNOLOGY							
BRAVOPAQ120	124	14	1024	17		---/---	AUTO
BRAVOPAQ40	42	5	977	17		---/---	AUTO
HIPER 20	21	4	615	17		---/---	
HIPER 30	33	4	615	26		---/---	
HIPER 48	48	6	615	26		---/---	
HIPER 145	150	8	1024	36		---/---	
HIPER 155	160	9	966	36		---/---	
HIPER 330	337	15	1224	36		---/---	
HIPER 380	388	16	755	63		---/---	
HIPER/II 155	157	64	150	32		---/---	
HIPER/II 65	65	9	925	17		---/---	
HIPER/II 380	383	64	365	32		---/---	
PROPAQ185-15	189	5				NA/NA	AUTO
SI1000S5	1037	8				NA/NA	AUTO
SI200/PS3	209	4				NA/NA	AUTO
SI585/PS5	601	8				NA/NA	AUTO
MD20	21	64	21	32		---/---	
MD30	30	64	30	32		---/---	
MD45	45	64	45	32		---/---	
MD80	83	64	80	32		---/---	
MD100	104	64	102	32		---/---	
MD200	209	32	200	32		---/---	
MD320	337	64	317	32		---/---	
MD420	433	64	415	32		---/---	
MTD320-10	337	64	317	32		---/---	
MTD585	601	64	573	32		---/---	
MTD650	676	64	650	32		---/---	
MTD1000	1037	64	989	32		---/---	
PAT40	42	4	805	26		---/---	AUTO
PAT100	110	14	535	29		---/---	AUTO
PH.D20	21	4	615	17		---/---	
PH.D30	33	4	615	26		---/---	
PH.D30-CE	33	4	615	26		---/---	
PH.D45	45	7	773	17		---/---	
PH.D48	49	6	615	26		---/---	
PH.D2520	21	4	615	17		---/---	
PH.D2545	45	7	733	17		---/---	
PH.D3020	21	4	615	17		---/---	
PH.D5045	45	7	773	17		---/---	
PIRA40	42	5	977	17		---/---	AUTO
PIRA 55-120	130					---/---	
PIRA 55-200	212					---/---	
PIRA 55-500	510					---/---	
PIRA 50-120	210	14	1024	36		---/---	AUTO
PIRA 50-200	210	12	954	36		---/---	AUTO
PIRA 100	101	8	776	33		---/---	AUTO
PIRA 120	124	14	1024	17		---/---	AUTO
PIRA 200	210	12	954	36		---/---	AUTO
PROPAQ40	40	4	805	26		---/---	AUTO
PROPAQ40N	40	6	560	26		---/---	AUTO
PROPAQ100	101	8	776	33		---/---	AUTO
PROPAQ120-19	124	14	1024	17		---/---	AUTO
PROPAQ185-15	189	12	1023	33		---/---	AUTO
PROPAQ/N40	40	4	805	26		---/---	AUTO
PROPAQ/N40N	40	6	560	26		---/---	AUTO
PROPAQ/N100	101	8	776	33		---/---	AUTO
PROPAQ/N120-19	124	14	1024	17		---/---	AUTO
PROPAQ/N185-15	189	12	1023	33		---/---	AUTO
PROPAQ/S40	40	4	805	26		---/---	AUTO
PROPAQ/S40N	40	6	560	26		---/---	AUTO
PROPAQ/S100	101	8	776	33		---/---	AUTO

Drive Model	Seek Time	Interface	Encode	Form Factor	cache kb	Obsolete? mtbf	RPM
PROCOM TECHNOLOGY							
BRAVOPAQ120	19	IDE AT	RLL	3.5 HH		150k	
BRAVOPAQ40	25	IDE AT	RLL	3.5 HH		150k	
HIPER 20	40	ST412/506	MFM			150k	
HIPER 30	28	ST412/506	RLL			150k	
HIPER 48	28	ST412/506	RLL			150k	
HIPER 145	23	ESDI		5.25 FH		30	
HIPER 155	16.5	SCSI	RLL	5.25 FH		100k	
HIPER 330	18	SCSI		5.25 FH		30k	
HIPER 380	16	SCSI	RLL	5.25 FH		100k	
HIPER/II 155	16.5	ESDI	RLL	5.25 FH		100k	
HIPER/II 65	28	ST412/506	MFM	5.25 FH		40k	
HIPER/II 380	16	ESDI	RLL	5.25 FH		100k	
PROPAQ185-15		IDE AT		3.5 HH		70k	
SI1000S5	15	SCSI		5.25		40k	
SI200/PS3	18	SCSI	2,7 RLL	3.5 HH		70k	
SI585/PS5	17	SCSI		5.25		100k	
MD20	28	SCSI	RLL			150k	
MD30	28	SCSI	RLL			150k	
MD45	28	SCSI	RLL			150k	
MD80	24	SCSI	RLL			150k	
MD100	28	SCSI	RLL			70k	
MD200	18	SCSI	RLL			70k	
MD320	12	SCSI	RLL			100k	
MD420	16	SCSI	RLL			100k	
MTD320-10	10.7	SCSI	RLL ZBR			100k	
MTD585	16.5	SCSI	RLL ZBR			100k	
MTD650	15.5	SCSI	RLL ZBR			100k	
MTD1000	15	SCSI	RLL ZBR			100k	
PAT40	25	IDE AT	RLL	5.25 HH		150k	
PAT100	15	IDE AT	RLL	3.5 HH		150	
PH.D20	40	ST412/506	MFM	3.5 HH		150	
PH.D30	28	ST412/506	RLL	3.5 HH		150	
PH.D30-CE	28	ST412/506	RLL	3.5 HH		150	
PH.D45	25	ST412/506	MFM	3.5 HH		150	
PH.D48	28	ST412/506	RLL	3.5 HH		150	
PH.D2520	40	ST412/506	MFM	3.5 HH		30k	
PH.D2545	25	ST412/506	RLL	3.5 HH		30k	
PH.D3020	40	ST412/506	MFM	3.5 HH		30k	
PH.D5045	25	ST412/506	MFM	3.5 HH		150k	
PIRA40	28	IDE AT	RLL	3.5 HH		150	
PIRA 55-120	16	IDE	2,7 RLL		32k	150k	3211
PIRA 55-200	15	IDE	1,7 RLL		64k	150k	3551
PIRA 55-500	12	IDE	2,7 RLL		256k	150k	4500
PIRA 50-120	19	IDE AT	RLL	3.5 HH		150	
PIRA 50-200	15	IDE AT	RLL	3.5 HH		150	
PIRA 100	25	IDE AT	RLL	3.5 HH		20k	
PIRA 120	18	IDE AT	RLL	3.5 HH		150	
PIRA 200	15	IDE AT	RLL	3.5 HH		150k	
PROPAQ40	25	IDE AT	RLL	3.5 HH		100k	
PROPAQ40N	25	IDE AT	RLL	3.5 HH		150k	
PROPAQ100	25	IDE AT	RLL	3.5 HH		150k	
PROPAQ120-19	19	IDE AT	RLL	3.5 HH		150k	
PROPAQ185-15	15	IDE AT	RLL	3.5 HH		150k	
PROPAQ/N40	25	IDE AT	RLL	3.5 HH		100k	
PROPAQ/N40N	25	IDE AT	RLL	3.5 HH		150k	
PROPAQ/N100	25	IDE AT	RLL	3.5 HH		100k	
PROPAQ/N120-19	19	IDE AT	RLL	3.5 HH		150k	
PROPAQ/N185-15	15	IDE AT	RLL	3.5 HH		150k	
PROPAQ/S40	25	IDE AT	RLL	3.5 HH		100k	
PROPAQ/S40N	25	IDE AT	RLL	3.5 HH		150k	
PROPAQ/S100	25	IDE AT	RLL	3.5 HH		20k	

Drive Model	Format Size MB	Head	Cyl	Sect/ Trac	Translate H/C/S	RWC/ WPC	Land Zone
PROPAQ/S120-19	124	14	1024	17		--/--	AUTO
PROPAQ/S185-15	189	12	1023	33		--/--	AUTO
SI45	48	64	45	32		--/--	
SI80	83	64	80	32		--/--	
SI100	104	64	102	32		--/--	
SI200	209	64	200	32		--/--	
SI200/PS3	209	4				NA/NA	AUTO
SI320-10	337	64	317	32		--/--	
SI320H	331	64	339	32		--/--	
SI420H	435	64	415	32		--/--	
SI585	601	64	415	32		--/--	
SI585/S5	601	8				NA/NA	AUTO
SI650	662	64	632	32		--/--	
SI1000/S5	1037	8				NA/NA	AUTO
SI1000	1037	64		32		--/--	

PTI (PERIPHERAL TECHNOLOGY)

Drive Model	Format Size MB	Head	Cyl	Sect/ Trac	Translate H/C/S	RWC/ WPC	Land Zone
PL32 TURBO	320	14				NA/NA	AUTO
PL100 TURBO	105	4				NA/NA	AUTO
PL200 TURBO	210	7				NA/NA	AUTO
PT225	21	4	615	17		--/--	
PT234	28	4	820	17		--/--	
PT238A	32	4	615	26		NA/NA	
PT238S	32	4	615	26		--/--	
PT251A	51	4	820	26		--/--	
PT251S	44	4	820	26		--/--	
PT251R	44	4	820	26		--/--	
PT238R	32	4	615	26		--/--	
PT338	32	6	615	17		--/--	
PT351	42	6	820	17		--/--	
PT357R	49	6	615	26		--/--	
PT357A	49	6	615	26		--/--	
PT357S	49	6	615	26		--/--	
PT376A	65	6	820	26		NA/NA	
PT376S	65	6	820	26		--/--	
PT376R	65	6	820	26		--/--	
PT468	57	8	820	17		--/--	
PT4102A	87	8	820	26		--/--	
PT4102S	87	8	820	26		--/--	
PT4102R	87	8	820	26		--/--	

QUANTUM CORPORATION

Drive Model	Format Size MB	Head	Cyl	Sect/ Trac	Translate H/C/S	RWC/ WPC	Land Zone
ELS42AT	42	1	1536	V	5/968/17	NA/NA	AUTO
ELS42S	42	1	1536	V		NA/NA	AUTO
ELS85AT	85	2	1536	V	10/977/17	NA/NA	AUTO
ELS85S	85	2	1536	V		NA/NA	AUTO
ELS127AT	128	2	1536	V	16/919/17	NA/NA	AUTO
ELS127S	128	2	1536	V		NA/NA	AUTO
ELS170AT	170	4	1536	V	15/1011/22	NA/NA	AUTO
ELS170S	170	4	1536	V		NA/NA	AUTO
GODRIVE 40AT	43	2	957		6/820/17	--/--	AUTO
GODRIVE 40S	43	2	957			NA/NA	AUTO
GODRIVE 60AT	63	2	1097	V		NA/NA	AUTO
GODRIVE 120AT	127	4	1097	V		NA/NA	AUTO
GODRIVE 120S	127	4	1097	V		NA/NA	AUTO
GODRIVE 80AT	84			NA	9/1024/17	NA/NA	AUTO
GODRIVE 80S	84					--/--	
HARDCARD EZ 42	42	5	977	17		NA/NA	AUTO
PRODRIVE 40AT	42	3	834		5/965/17	NA/NA	AUTO
PRODRIVE 40S	42	3	834			--/--	AUTO
PRODRIVE 80S	84	6	834			--/--	AUTO
PRODRIVE 80AT	84	6	834		10/965/17	NA/NA	AUTO

Drive Model	Seek Time	Interface	Encode	Form Factor	cache kb	mtbf	Obsolete? RPM
PROPAQ/S120-19	19	IDE AT	RLL	3.5 HH		150k	
PROPAQ/S185-15	15	IDE AT	RLL	3.5 HH		150k	
SI45	28	SCSI	RLL			150k	
SI80	24	SCSI	RLL			150k	
SI100	18	SCSI	RLL			70k	
SI200	18	SCSI	RLL			70k	
SI200/PS3	18	SCSI	2,7 RLL	3.5 HH		70k	
SI320-10	10.7	SCSI	RLL	5.25 HH		100k	
SI320H	14	SCSI	RLL	5.25 FH		100k	
SI420H	16	SCSI	RLL	5.25 FH		100k	
SI585	16.5	SCSI	RLL	5.25 FH		100k	
SI585/S5	17	SCSI		5.25		100k	
SI650	15.5	SCSI	RLL	5.25 FH		100k	
SI1000/S5	15	SCSI		5.25		40k	
SI1000	15	SCSI	RLL	5.25 FH		100k	

PTI (PERIPHERAL TECHNOLOGY)

Drive Model	Seek Time	Interface	Encode	Form Factor	cache kb	mtbf	Obsolete? RPM
PL32 TURBO	12	SCSI	2,7 RLL	3.5 HH		100k	
PL100 TURBO	19	SCSI	2,7 RLL	3.5 HH		60k	
PL200 TURBO	19	SCSI	2,7 RLL	3.5 HH		50k	
PT225	35	ST412/506	MFM	3.5 HH			
PT234	35	ST412/506	MFM	3.5 HH			
PT238A	35	IDE AT	2,7 RLL	3.5 HH			
PT238S	35	SCSI	2,7 RLL	3.5 HH			
PT251A	35	IDE AT		3.5 HH		25k	
PT251S	35	SCSI		3.5 HH		25k	
PT251R	35	ST412/506	2,7 RLL	3.5 HH		25k	
PT238R	35	ST412/506	2,7 RLL	3.5 HH			
PT338	35	ST412/506	MFM	3.5 HH			
PT351	35	ST412/506	MFM	3.5			
PT357R	35	ST412/506	2,7 RLL	3.5 HH		25k	
PT357A	35	IDE AT	2,7 RLL	3.5 HH		25k	
PT357S	35	SCSI	2,7 RLL	3.5 HH		25k	
PT376A	35	IDE AT	2,7 RLL	3.5 HH		25k	
PT376S	35	SCSI	2,7 RLL	3.5 HH		25k	
PT376R	35	ST412/506	2,7 RLL	3.5 HH		25k	
PT468	35	ST412/506	MFM	3.5 HH		25k	
PT4102A	35	IDE AT	2,7 RLL	3.5 HH		25k	
PT4102S	35	SCSI		3.5 HH		25k	
PT4102R	35	ST412/506	2,7 RLL	3.5 HH		25k	

QUANTUM CORPORATION

Drive Model	Seek Time	Interface	Encode	Form Factor	cache kb	mtbf	Obsolete? RPM
ELS42AT	19	IDE AT	2,7 RLL	3.5 3H		250k	
ELS42S	19	SCSI	2,7 RLL	3.5 3H		250k	
ELS85AT	17	IDE XT	2,7 RLL	3.5 3H		250k	
ELS85S	17	SCSI	2,7 RLL	3.5 3H		250k	
ELS127AT	17	IDE AT	1,7 RLL	3.5 3H		250k	
ELS127S	17	SCSI	1,7 RLL	3.5 3H		250k	
ELS170AT	17	IDE AT	1,7 RLL	3.5 3H		250k	
ELS170S	17	SCSI	1,7 RLL	3.5 3H		250k	
GODRIVE 40AT	19	IDE AT	1,7 RLL	2.5 4H	32k	80k	N
GODRIVE 40S	19	SCSI	1,7 RLL	2.5 4H	32k	80k	N
GODRIVE 60AT	19	IDE AT	1,7 RLL	2.5 3H		150k	
GODRIVE 120AT	19	IDE AT	1,7 RLL	2.5 3H		150k	
GODRIVE 120S	19	SCSI	1,7 RLL	2.5 3H		150k	
GODRIVE 80AT	19	IDE AT	1,7 RLL	2.5 4H		80k	
GODRIVE 80S	19	SCSI	1,7 RLL	2.5 4H		80k	
HARDCARD EZ 42		IDE AT					N
PRODRIVE 40AT	19	IDE AT	2,7 RLL	3.5 HH	64k	50k	N
PRODRIVE 40S	19	SCSI	2,7 RLL	3.5 HH	64k	50k	N
PRODRIVE 80S	19	SCSI	2,7 RLL	3.5 HH	64k	50k	Y
PRODRIVE 80AT	19	IDE AT	2,7 RLL	3.5 HH	64k	50k	Y

Drive Model	Format Size MB	Head	Cyl	Sect/ Trac	Translate H/C/S	RWC/ WPC	Land Zone
PRODRIVE 100E	103					NA/NA	
PRODRIVE 105AT	104	4	1219		16/755/17	NA/NA	AUTO
PRODRIVE 105S	105	6	1019			---/---	AUTO
PRODRIVE 120AT	120	5	1123		9/814/32	NA/NA	AUTO
PRODRIVE 120S	120	4	1123			---/---	AUTO
PRODRIVE 145E	145					NA/NA	
PRODRIVE 160AT	168	4	839			NA/NA	
PRODRIVE 160S	168	4	839			NA/NA	
PRODRIVE 170AT	168	7	1123		10/968/34	NA/NA	AUTO
PRODRIVE 170S	168	7	1123			---/---	AUTO
PRODRIVE 210AT	210	7	1156		13/873/36	NA/NA	AUTO
PRODRIVE 210S	210	7	1156			---/---	AUTO
PRODRIVE 330AT	331	7	1156			NA/NA	
PRODRIVE 330S	331	7	1156			---/---	AUTO
PRODRIVE 425AT	426	9	1156	NA	16/1021/51	NA/NA	AUTO
PRODRIVE 425S	426	9				---/---	AUTO
PRODRIVE 525S	525	6	2446	NA		NA/NA	AUTO
PRODRIVE 700S	700	8	2443	NA		NA/NA	AUTO
PRODRIVE 1050S	1050	12	2442	NA		NA/NA	AUTO
PRODRIVE 1225S	1225	14	2444	NA		NA/NA	AUTO
PRODRIVE LPS52AT	52	4	1219		8/751/17	NA/NA	AUTO
PRODRIVE LPS52S	52	2	1219			NA/NA	AUTO
PRODRIVE LPS80AT	80				16/611/17	NA/NA	AUTO
PRODRIVE LPS105 AT	105	4	1219		16/755/17	NA/NA	AUTO
PRODRIVE LPS105S	105	4	1219			---/---	AUTO
PRODRIVE LPS120AT	105	2			5/901/53	NA/NA	AUTO
PRODRIVE LPS240AT	240				13/723/51	NA/NA	AUTO
PRODRIVE LPS240S	245	4	1800	V	13/723/51	NA/NA	AUTO
Q160	200	12				---/---	
Q250	53	4	823			---/---	
Q280	80	6	823			---/---	
Q510	8	2	512	17		256/256	
Q520	18	4	512	17		256/256	512
Q530	27	6	512	17		256/256	512
Q540	36	8	512	17		256/256	512
Q2010	8	2	512	32		256/256	
Q2020	16	4	512	32		256/256	
Q2030	25	6	512	32		256/256	
Q2040	33	8	512	32		256/256	
Q2080	67	7	1172	32		256/256	

RICOH

Drive Model	Format Size MB	Head	Cyl	Sect/ Trac	Translate H/C/S	RWC/ WPC	Land Zone
RH5130	10	2	612	17		613/400	
RH5260	10	2	615	17		---/---	
RH5261	10	2	612	17		---/---	
RH5500	100	2	1285	76		NA/NA	AUTO
RS9150AR	100	2	1285	76		NA/NA	AUTO

RMS

Drive Model	Format Size MB	Head	Cyl	Sect/ Trac	Translate H/C/S	RWC/ WPC	Land Zone
RMS503	2.5	2	153	17		77/77	
RMS506	5	4	153	17		77/77	
RMS509	8	6	153	17		77/77	
RMS512	10	8	153	17		77/77	

RODIME SYSTEMS, INC

Drive Model	Format Size MB	Head	Cyl	Sect/ Trac	Translate H/C/S	RWC/ WPC	Land Zone
COBRA 40AT	40					---/---	AUTO
COBRA 80AT	80					---/---	AUTO
COBRA 110AT	110	4				---/---	AUTO
COBRA 210AT	210	5				---/---	AUTO
RO101	6	2	192	17		96/192	
RO102	12	4	192	17		96/192	
RO103	18	6	192	17		96/192	

Drive Model	Seek Time	Interface	Encode	Form Factor	cache kb	Obsolete? mtbf	RPM
PRODRIVE 100E	19	ESDI		3.5 HH			
PRODRIVE 105AT	17	IDE AT	2,7 RLL	3.5 HH		60k	
PRODRIVE 105S	19	SCSI	2,7 RLL	3.5 HH		50k	N
PRODRIVE 120AT	15	IDE AT	1,7 RLL	3.5 HH	64k	50k	N
PRODRIVE 120S	15	SCSI	1,7 RLL	3.5 HH	64k	50k	N
PRODRIVE 145E	19	ESDI		3.5 HH			
PRODRIVE 160AT	19	IDE AT	1,7 RLL	3.5 4H		80k	Y
PRODRIVE 160S	19	SCSI	1,7 RLL	3.5 4H		80k	
PRODRIVE 170AT	15	IDE AT	1,7 RLL	3.5 HH	64k	50k	N
PRODRIVE 170S	15	SCSI	1,7 RLL	3.5 HH	64k	50k	N
PRODRIVE 210AT	15	IDE AT	1,7 RLL	3.5 HH	64k	50k	N
PRODRIVE 210S	15	SCSI	1,7 RLL	3.5 HH	64k	50k	N
PRODRIVE 330AT	14	IDE AT	1,7 RLL	3.5 HH	64k	150k	N
PRODRIVE 330S	14	SCSI	1,7 RLL	3.5 HH	64k	150k	N
PRODRIVE 425AT	14	IDE AT	1,7 RLL	3.5 HH	64k	150k	Y
PRODRIVE 425S	14	SCSI		3.5 HH	64k	150k	N
PRODRIVE 525S		SCSI					N
PRODRIVE 700S		SCSI					N
PRODRIVE 1050S		SCSI					N
PRODRIVE 1225S		SCSI					N
PRODRIVE LPS52AT	17	IDE AT	2,7 RLL	3.5 3H	64k	60k	Y
PRODRIVE LPS52S	17	SCSI	2,7 RLL	3.5 3H	64k	60k	Y
PRODRIVE LPS80AT		IDE AT		3.5 3H			
PRODRIVE LPS105AT	17	IDE AT	2,7 RLL	3.5 3H	64k	60k	Y
PRODRIVE LPS105S	17	SCSI	2,7 RLL	3.5 3H	64k	60k	Y
PRODRIVE LPS120AT	16	IDE AT		3.5 3H	256k	250k	
PRODRIVE LPS240AT		IDE AT		3.5 3H	256k		
PRODRIVE LPS240S	17	SCSI	1,7 RLL	3.5 3H		na	
Q160	26	SCSI	2,7 RLL	5.25 HH			
Q250	26	SCSI	2,7 RLL	5.25 HH			
Q280	26	SCSI	2,7 RLL	5.25 HH			
Q510	30	ST412/506	MFM	5.25			
Q520		ST412/506	MFM	5.25			
Q530	40	ST412/506	MFM	5.25 FH			
Q540	45	ST412/506	MFM	5.25 FH			
Q2010	55		MFM	8		12k	Y
Q2020	60		MFM	8		12k	Y
Q2030	60		MFM	8		12k	Y
Q2040	65		MFM	8		12k	Y
Q2080	40		MFM	8		8k	Y

RICOH

RH5130	85	ST412/506	MFM				
RH5260	85	ST412/506	MFM				
RH5261	85	SCSI	MFM				
RH5500	25	SCSI	2,7 RLL	5.25 HH		20k	
RS9150AR	25	SCSI	2,7 RLL	5.25 HH		20k	

RMS

RMS503		ST412/506	MFM	5.25			
RMS506		ST412/506	MFM	5.25			
RMS509		ST412/506	MFM	5.25 FH			
RMS512		ST412/506	MFM	5.25			

RODIME SYSTEMS, INC

COBRA 40AT	19	IDE AT	2,7 RLL	3.5 HH		40k	
COBRA 80AT	20	IDE AT	2,7 RLL	3.5 HH		40k	
COBRA 110AT	19	IDE AT	2,7 RLL	3.5 HH		40k	
COBRA 210AT		IDE AT	2,7 RLL	3.5 HH		40k	
RO101		ST412/506	MFM	5.25 FH			
RO102		ST412/506	MFM	5.25 FH			
RO103	55	ST412/506	MFM	5.25 FH			

Drive Model	Format Size MB	Head	Cyl	Sect/Trac	Translate H/C/S	RWC/WPC	Land Zone
RO104	24	8	192	17		96/192	
RO200	11	4	320	17		---/132	
RO201	5	2	321	17		132/300	
RO201E	11	4	640	17		264/300	
RO202	10	4	321	17		132/300	
RO202E	21	4	640	17		264/300	640
RO203	15	6	321	17		132/300	321
RO203E	32	6	640	17		264/300	640
RO204	21	8	320	17		132/300	321
RO204E	43	8	640	17		264/300	640
RO251	5	2	306	17		307/307	
RO252	11	4	306	17		64/128	
RO351	5	2	306	17		307/307	
RO352	11	4	306	17		64/128	
RO365	21	4	612	17		613/613	
RO652A	20					---/---	
RO652B	20	4	306	33		---/---	
RO652	20	4	306	33		NA/NA	AUTO
RO752A	25					---/---	
RO752	20	4	306	33		NA/NA	AUTO
RO3045	37	5	872	17		873/---	
RO3055	45	6	872	17		873/---	
RO3055T	45	3	1053	26		NA/NA	AUTO
RO3057S	45	5	680			---/---	
RO3058A	45	3	868	17		---/---	
RO3058T	45	3	868	17		---/---	
RO3059A	46	2	1216	17		---/---	
RO3059T	46	2	1216	34		---/---	
RO3060R	50	2	1216	17		---/---	
RO3065	53	7	872	17		---/650	
RO3070S	71					---/---	
RO3075R	59	6	750			---/650	
RO3085R	69	7	750			---/650	
RO3085S	69	7	750			---/---	
RO3088A	75	5	868	34		---/---	
RO3088T	75	5	868	34		---/---	
RO3089A	70	3	1216	34		---/---	
RO3089T	70	3	1216	34		---/---	
RO3090T	75	5	1053	28		NA/NA	AUTO
RO3095A	80	3	1216	34		---/---	
RO3099A	80	4	1030			NA/NA	AUTO
RO3099AP	80	4	1030			NA/NA	AUTO
RO3128A	105	7	868			---/---	
RO3128T	105	7	868	17		---/---	
RO3129A	105	5	1090			---/---	
RO3129T	105	5	1090	17		---/---	
RO3130S	105	7	1047	30		---/---	
RO3130T	105	7	1053	28		NA/NA	AUTO
RO3135A	112	7	923	34		---/---	
RO3139A	112	5	1168	17		---/---	
RO3139AP	112	5	1168			NA/NA	AUTO
RO3139S	112	5	1148			NA/NA	AUTO
RO3139TP	112	5	1148			NA/NA	AUTO
RO3259A	210					---/---	
RO3259AP	212	9	1235			NA/NA	AUTO
RO3259T	210					---/---	
RO3259TS	210	9	1216			NA/NA	AUTO
RO5040S	38	3		17		---/---	
RO5065	63	5		17		---/---	
RO5075E	65	3	1224	35		---/---	
RO5075S	76					---/---	
RO5078S	62	3	1224	33		NA/NA	AUTO
RO5090	89	7	1224	17		---/---	

Drive Model	Seek Time	Interface	Encode	Form Factor	cache kb	mtbf	RPM
RO104		ST412/506	MFM	5.25 FH			
RO200		ST412/506	MFM	5.25 FH			
RO201	85	ST412/506	MFM	5.25 FH			
RO201E	55	ST412/506	MFM	5.25 FH			
RO202	85	ST412/506	MFM	5.25 HH			
RO202E	55	ST412/506	MFM	5.25 HH			
RO203	85	ST412/506	MFM	5.25 FH			
RO203E	55	ST412/506	MFM	5.25 FH			
RO204	85	ST412/506	MFM	5.25 FH			
RO204E	55	ST412/506	MFM	5.25 FH			
RO251	85	ST412/506	MFM	5.25 HH			
RO252	85	ST412/506	MFM	5.25 HH			
RO351	85	ST412/506	MFM	3.5 HH			
RO352	85	ST412/506	MFM	3.5 HH			
RO365		ST412/506	MFM	3.5 HH			
RO652A	85	SCSI		3.5 HH			
RO652B	85	SCSI	2,7 RLL	3.5 HH			
RO652	85	SCSI	2,7 RLL	3.5 HH			
RO752A	85	SCSI		5.25 HH			
RO752	85	SCSI		5.25 HH			
RO3045	28	ST412/506	MFM	3.5 HH			
RO3055	28	ST412/506	MFM	3.5 HH			
RO3055T		SCSI	RLL	3.5 HH			
RO3057S	28	SCSI	2,7 RLL	3.5 HH			
RO3058A	18	IDE AT	2,7 RLL	3.5 HH		20k	
RO3058T	18	SCSI	2,7 RLL	3.5 HH		20k	
RO3059A	18	IDE AT	2,7 RLL	3.5 HH		20k	
RO3059T	18	SCSI	2,7 RLL	3.5 HH		20k	
RO3060R	28	ST412/506	2,7 RLL	3.5 HH		20k	
RO3065	28	ST412/506	MFM	3.5 HH		20k	
RO3070S	28	SCSI		3.5 HH			
RO3075R	28	ST412/506	2,7 RLL	3.5 HH		20k	
RO3085R	28	ST412/506	2,7 RLL	3.5 HH		20k	
RO3085S	28	SCSI		3.5 HH			
RO3088A	18	IDE AT	2,7 RLL	3.5 HH		20k	
RO3088T	18	SCSI	2,7 RLL	3.5 HH		20k	
RO3089A	18	IDE AT	2,7 RLL	3.5 HH		20k	
RO3089T	18	SCSI	2,7 RLL	3.5 HH		20k	
RO3090T		SCSI		3.5 HH			
RO3095A	18	IDE AT	2,7 RLL	3.5 HH		20k	
RO3099A		IDE AT		3.5 HH			
RO3099AP		IDE AT		3.5 HH			
RO3128A	18	IDE AT	2,7 RLL	3.5 HH		20k	
RO3128T	18	SCSI	2,7 RLL	3.5 HH		20k	
RO3129A	18	IDE AT	2,7 RLL	3.5 HH		20k	
RO3129T	18	SCSI	2,7 RLL	3.5 HH		20k	
RO3130S	22	SCSI	2,7 RLL	5.25 HH		20k	
RO3130T	22	SCSI	2,7 RLL	5.25 HH		20k	
RO3135A	19	IDE AT	2,7 RLL	3.5 HH		20k	
RO3139A	18	IDE AT	2,7 RLL	3.5 HH		20k	
RO3139AP	18	IDE AT	2,7 RLL	3.5 HH		20k	
RO3139S		SCSI		3.5 HH			
RO3139TP		SCSI	RLL ZBR	3.5 HH			
RO3259A	18	IDE AT	2,7 RLL	3.5 HH			
RO3259AP		IDE AT		3.5 HH			
RO3259T	18	SCSI	2,7 RLL	3.5 HH			
RO3259TS	18	SCSI	2,7 RLL	3.5 HH			
RO5040S	28	SCSI	MFM				
RO5065	28	ST412/506	MFM	5.25 HH			
RO5075E	28	ESDI		5.25 HH			
RO5075S	28	SCSI		5.25 HH			
RO5078S		SCSI		5.25 HH			
RO5090	28	ST412/506	MFM	5.25 HH			

Drive Model	Format Size MB	Head	Cyl	Sect/Trac	Translate H/C/S	RWC/WPC	Land Zone
RO5095R	81	5	1224	26		NA/NA	AUTO
RO5125S	106	5	1219	34		NA/NA	AUTO
RO5125E	106	5	1224	34		---/---	
RO5125-1F2	106	5	1219	34		NA/NA	AUTO
RO5128S	103	5	1224	33		NA/NA	AUTO
RO5130R	114	7	1224	26		---/---	
RO5178S	144	7	1219			---/---	
RO5180E	149	7	1224	34		---/---	
RO5180S	144	7	1219	34		---/---	
RO5180-1F2	148	7	1219	34		NA/NA	AUTO

SAMSUNG

Drive Model	Format Size MB	Head	Cyl	Sect/Trac	Translate H/C/S	RWC/WPC	Land Zone
SHD2040N	44	4	820	26		---/544	819
SHD2041	47	4	820	28		NA/NA	AUTO
SHD3061A	60	2	1478	40		NA/NA	AUTO
SHD3062A	121	4	1479	40		NA/NA	AUTO
SHD3101	105	4	1282	40		NA/NA	AUTO
SHD3202	212	7	1376	43		NA/NA	AUTO
SHD3210S	212	7	1376	43		NA/NA	AUTO

SEAGATE TECHNOLOGIES

Drive Model	Format Size MB	Head	Cyl	Sect/Trac	Translate H/C/S	RWC/WPC	Land Zone
ELITE12G	1050	17				---/---	AUTO
SABRE368	368	10	1635			---/---	AUTO
SABRE500	500	10	1217			---/---	AUTO
SABRE736	741	15	1217			---/---	AUTO
SABRE850	851	15	1635			---/---	AUTO
SABRE1123	964	19				---/---	AUTO
SABRE1150	990	19				---/---	AUTO
SABRE1230	1050	15		1635		---/---	AUTO
SABRE2270	1948	19				---/---	AUTO
SABRE2500	2145	19				---/---	AUTO
ST124	21	4	615	17		NONE/-1	615
ST125-0	21	4	615	17		NONE/-1	AUTO
ST125-1	21	4	615	17		NONE/-1	AUTO
ST125A-0	21	4	404	26	4/615/17	NONE/-1	AUTO
ST125A-1	21	4	404	26	4/615/17	NONE/-1	AUTO
ST125N-0	21	4	407	26		NONE/-1	AUTO
ST125N-1	21	4	407	26		NONE/-1	AUTO
ST137R	33	4	615	26		---/---	AUTO
ST138-0	32	6	615	17		NONE/-1	AUTO
ST138-1	32	6	615	17		NONE/-1	AUTO
ST138A-0	32	4	604	26	6/615/17	NONE/-1	AUTO
ST138A-1	32	4	604	26	6/615/17	NONE/-1	AUTO
ST138N-0	32	4	615	26		NONE/-1	AUTO
ST138N-1	32	4	615	26		NONE/-1	AUTO
ST138R-0	32	4	615	26		NONE/-1	AUTO
ST138R-1	32	4	615	26		NONE/-1	AUTO
ST151	42	5	977	17		---/---	AUTO
ST157A-0	53	6	560	26	7/733/17	NONE/-1	AUTO
ST157A-1	53	6	560	26	7/733/17	NONE/-1	AUTO
ST157N-0	49	6	615	26		NONE/-1	AUTO
ST157N-1	49	6	615	26		NONE/-1	AUTO
ST157R-0	49	6	615	26		NONE/-1	AUTO
ST157R-1	49	6	615	26		NONE/-1	AUTO
ST177N	60	5	921	26		NA/NA	AUTO
ST206	5	2	306	17		307/128	
ST212	10	2	306	17		307/158	
ST213	10	2	615	17		613/300	615
ST224N	21	2				---/---	
ST225	21	4	615	17		300/660	615
ST225N	21	4	615	17		100K/---	
ST225R	21	2	667	31		NONE/-1	667

Drive Model	Seek Time	Interface	Encode	Form Factor	cache kb	mtbf	RPM	Obsolete?
RO5095R		ST412/506	2,7 RLL	5.25 HH				
RO5125S	28	SCSI	2,7 RLL	5.25 HH		20k		
RO5125E	18	ESDI	2,7 RLL	5.25 HH		25k		
RO5125-1F2	18	SCSI	2,7 RLL	5.25 HH		20k		
RO5128S		SCSI		5.25 HH				
RO5130R	28	ST412/506	2,7 RLL	5.25 FH		20k		
RO5178S	19	SCSI	2,7 RLL	5.25 HH				
RO5180E	18	ESDI	2,7 RLL	5.25 HH		25k		
RO5180S	28	SCSI	2,7 RLL	5.25 HH				
RO5180-1F2	19	SCSI	2,7 RLL	5.25 HH		20k		

SAMSUNG

Drive Model	Seek Time	Interface	Encode	Form Factor	cache kb	mtbf	RPM	Obsolete?
SHD2040N	39	ST412/506	2,7 RLL	3.5 HH		30k	3568	
SHD2041	29	IDE AT	2,7 RLL	3.5 HH		30k	3525	
SHD3061A	16	IDE AT	1,7 RLL	3.5 3H		200k		
SHD3062A	16	IDE AT	1,7 RLL	3.5 3H		200k		
SHD3101	16	IDE AT	1,7 RLL	3.5 3H		200k		
SHD3202	16	SCSI	1,7 RLL	3.5 HH		50k		
SHD3210S	16	SCSI	1,7 RLL	3.5 HH		50k		

SEAGATE TECHNOLOGIES

Drive Model	Seek Time	Interface	Encode	Form Factor	cache kb	mtbf	RPM	Obsolete?
ELITE12G	12	SMD	RLL	5.25 FH		100k		
SABRE368	182	SMD/SCSI	RLL	8.0 FH		100k		
SABRE500	18	SMD/SCSI	RLL	8.0 FH		100k		
SABRE736	15	SMD/SCSI	RLL	8.0 FH		50k		
SABRE850	15	SMD/SCSI	RLL	8.0 FH		50k		
SABRE1123	15	SMD	RLL	8.0 FH		100k		
SABRE1150	15	IPI-2	RLL	8.0 FH		100k		
SABRE1230	15	SMD/SCSI	RLL	8.0 FH		100k		
SABRE2270	12	SMD	RLL	8.0 FH		100k		
SABRE2500	12	SMD/SCSI	RLL	8.0 FH		100k		
ST124	40	ST412/506	MFM	3.5 HH		150k	3600	Y
ST125-0	40	ST412/506	MFM	3.5 HH		150k	3600	Y
ST125-1	28	ST412/506	MFM	3.5 HH		150k	3600	Y
ST125A-0	40	IDE AT	2,7 RLL	3.5 HH	2k	150k	3600	Y
ST125A-1	28	IDE AT	2,7 RLL	3.5 HH	2k	150k	3600	Y
ST125N-0	40	SCSI	2,7 RLL	3.5 HH	2k	150k	3600	Y
ST125N-1	28	SCSI	2,7 RLL	3.5 HH	2k	150k	3600	Y
ST137R	40	ST412/506	2,7 RLL	3.5 HH		70k		
ST138-0	40	ST412/506	MFM	3.5 HH		150k	3600	Y
ST138-1	28	ST412/506	MFM	3.5 HH		70k	3600	Y
ST138A-0	40	IDE AT	2,7 RLL	3.5 HH	2k	150k	3600	Y
ST138A-1	28	IDE AT	2,7 RLL	3.5 HH	2k	150k	3600	Y
ST138N-0	40	SCSI	2,7 RLL	3.5 HH	2k	150k	3600	Y
ST138N-1	28	SCSI	2,7 RLL	3.5 HH	2k	150k	3600	Y
ST138R-0	40	ST412/506	2,7 RLL	3.5 HH		150k	3600	Y
ST138R-1	28	ST412/506	2,7 RLL	3.5 HH		150k	3600	Y
ST151	24	ST412/506	MFM	3.5 HH		50k	3600	Y
ST157A-0	40	IDE AT	2,7 RLL	3.5 HH	2k	150k	3600	Y
ST157A-1	28	IDE AT	2,7 RLL	3.5 HH	2k	150k	3600	Y
ST157N-0	40	SCSI	2,7 RLL	3.5 HH		150k	3600	Y
ST157N-1	28	SCSI	2,7 RLL	3.5 HH		150k	3600	Y
ST157R-0	40	ST412/506	2,7 RLL	3.5 HH		150k	3600	Y
ST157R-1	28	ST412/506	2,7 RLL	3.5 HH		150k	3600	Y
ST177N	24	SCSI	2,7 RLL	3.5 HH	8k	150k	3600	Y
ST206		ST412/506	MFM	5.25 FH				
ST212		ST412/506	MFM	5.25 FH				
ST213	65	ST412/506	MFM	5.25 FH				
ST224N	70	SCSI	2,7 RLL	5.25 HH		100k		
ST225	65	ST412/506	MFM	5.25 HH		100k	3600	N
ST225N	65	SCSI	MFM	5.25 HH				
ST225R	70	ST412/506	2,7 RLL	5.25 HH		100k	3600	N

Drive Model	Format Size MB	Head	Cyl	Sect/Trac	Translate H/C/S	RWC/WPC	Land Zone
ST238R	32	4	615	26		NONE/-1	615
ST250R	42	4	667	31		NONE/-1	AUTO
ST250N	42	4				NA/NA	AUTO
ST251-0	43	6	820	17		NONE/-1	AUTO
ST251-1	42	6	820	17		NONE/-1	AUTO
ST251N-0	43	4	820	26		---/---	AUTO
ST251N-1	43	4	820	26		---/---	AUTO
ST251R	43	4	820	26		---/-1	AUTO
ST252	42	6	820	17		NONE/-1	AUTO
ST253	43	5	989	17		---/---	AUTO
ST274A	65	5	948	26	5/948/26	NA/NA	AUTO
ST277N-0	65	6	820	26		NONE/-1	AUTO
ST277N-1	65	6	820	26		NONE/-1	AUTO
ST277R-0	65	6	820	26		NONE/-1	AUTO
ST277R-1	65	6	820	26		NONE/-1	AUTO
ST278R	65	6	820	26		NONE/-1	AUTO
ST279R	65	5	989	26		---/---	AUTO
ST280A	71	5	1032	26	10/516/27	NA/NA	AUTO
ST296N	85	6	800	34		NA/NA	AUTO
ST325X	21	2	615	17		NA/NA	
ST325A,X	21	2	615	17	2/697/30	---/---	
ST325N	21	2	697	30		---/---	AUTO
ST351A,X	43	2	820	17	6/820/17	NA/NA	AUTO
ST406	5	2	306	17		307/128	
ST412	10	4	306	17		307/128	305
ST419	15	6	306	17		307/128	
ST425	20	8	306	17		307/128	
ST506	5	4	153	17		157/128	
ST706	5	2	306	17		307/128	
ST1057A	53	3	1024	17	6/1024/17	NA/NA	AUTO
ST1057N	49	3	940	34		---/---	AUTO
ST1090A	79	5	1072	29	16/335/29	NA/NA	
ST1090N	79	5	1068	29		---/---	
ST1096N	84	7	906	26		---/---	AUTO
ST1100	84	9	1072	17		---/---	AUTO
ST1102A	89	5	1024	17	10/1024/17	NA/NA	AUTO
ST1102N	84	5	965	34		---/---	AUTO
ST1106R	91	7	977	26		---/---	
ST1111A	98	5	1072	36	10/536/36	NA/NA	
ST1111E	98	5	1072	36		NA/NA	
ST1111N	98	5	1068	36		---/---	
ST1126A	111	7	1072	29	16/469/29	NA/NA	
ST1126N	107	7	1068	29		---/---	
ST1133A	113	7	1272	36	10/636/36	NA/NA	
ST1133NS	116	5	1268	36		---/---	
ST1144A	131	7	1024	32	15/1001/17	NA/NA	
ST1144N	126	7		32		---/---	
ST1150R	128	9	1072	26		---/---	
ST1156A	138	7	1072	36	14/536/36	NA/NA	
ST1156E	138	7	1072	36		NA/NA	
ST1156N	138	7	1068	36		---/---	
ST1156NS	138	7	1068	36		---/---	
ST1162A	143	9	1072	29	16/603/29	NA/NA	
ST1162N	138	9	1068	29		---/---	
ST1186A	164	7	1272	36	12/804/36	NA/NA	
ST1186NS	159	7	1268	36		---/---	
ST1201A	177	9	1072	36	9/804/48	NA/NA	
ST1201NS	177	9	1068	36		---/---	
ST1201E	177	9	1072	36		NA/NA	
ST1201N	172	9	1068	36		---/---	
ST1239A	211	9	1272	36	14/818/36	NA/NA	AUTO
ST1239NS	204	9	1268	36		NA/NA	AUTO
ST1274A	230	4	407	26		---/---	

Drive Model	Seek Time	Interface	Encode	Form Factor	cache kb	mtbf	RPM	Obsolete?
ST238R	65	ST412/506	2,7 RLL	5.25 HH		100k	3600	Y
ST250R	70	ST412/506	2,7 RLL	5.25 HH		100k	3600	N
ST250N	70	SCSI	2,7 RLL	5.25 HH		100k		
ST251-0	40	ST412/506	MFM	5.25 HH		100k	3600	N
ST251-1	28	ST412/506	MFM	5.25 HH		100k	3600	N
ST251N-0	40	SCSI	2,7 RLL	5.25 HH		100k		
ST251N-1	28	SCSI	2,7 RLL	5.25 HH		100k		
ST251R	28	ST412/506	2,7 RLL	5.25 HH		100k		
ST252	40	ST412/506	MFM	5.25 HH		100k	3600	N
ST253	28	ST412/506	MFM	5.25 HH		40k		
ST274A	28	IDE AT	2,7 RLL	5.25 HH		40k		
ST277N-0	40	SCSI	2,7 RLL	5.25 HH	2k	70k	3600	Y
ST277N-1	28	SCSI	2,7 RLL	5.25 HH	2k	70k	3600	Y
ST277R-0	40	ST412/506	2,7 RLL	5.25 HH		70k	3600	Y
ST277R-1	28	ST412/506	2,7 RLL	5.25 HH		70k	3600	Y
ST278R	28	ST412/506	2,7 RLL	5.25 HH		70k	3600	N
ST279R	28	ST412/506	2,7 RLL	5.25 HH		40k		
ST280A	28	IDE AT	2,7 RLL	5.25 HH		40k		
ST296N	28	SCSI	2,7 RLL	5.25 HH	8k	70k	3600	N
ST325X	45	IDE XT	2,7 RLL	3.5 HH	8/32k	150k	3600	Y
ST325A,X	28	IDE AT	2,7 RLL	3.5 HH	8/32k	150k	3048	Y
ST325N	28	SCSI	2,7 RLL	3.5 HH	8/32k	150k	3600	Y
ST351A,X	28	IDE AT	2,7 RLL	3.5 3H	32k	150k	3048	N
ST406	85	ST412/506	MFM	5.25 FH		110k		
ST412	85	ST412/506	MFM	5.25 FH		110k		
ST419	85	ST412/506	MFM	5.25 FH				
ST425		ST412/506	MFM	5.25 FH				
ST506	140							
ST706		ST412/506	MFM	5.25 FH				
ST1057A	19	IDE AT	RLL ZBR	3.5 HH	8/32k	50k	3528	Y
ST1057N	15	SCSI-2	2,7 RLL	3.5 HH	8/32k	50k	3528	N
ST1090A	15	IDE AT	2,7 RLL	3.5 HH		70k		
ST1090N	15	SCSI	2,7 RLL	3.5 HH		70k		
ST1096N	20	SCSI	2,7 RLL	3.5 HH	8k	150k	3600	Y
ST1100	15	ST412/506	MFM	3.5 HH		150k		Y
ST1102A	19	IDE AT	RLL ZBR	3.5 HH	8k	50k	3528	Y
ST1102N	19	SCSI-2	RLL ZBR	3.5 HH	8/32k	50k	3528	N
ST1106R	24	ST412/506	2,7 RLL	3.5 HH		50k		
ST1111A	15	IDE AT	2,7 RLL	3.5 HH		70k		
ST1111E	15	ESDI (10)	2,7 RLL	3.5 HH		150k		Y
ST1111N	15	SCSI	2,7 RLL	3.5 HH		70k		
ST1126A	15	IDE AT	2,7 RLL	3.5 HH	32k	150k		Y
ST1126N	15	SCSI	2,7 RLL	3.5 HH	64k	150k		Y
ST1133A	15	IDE AT	2,7 RLL	3.5 HH	64k	150k		Y
ST1133NS	15	SCSI-2	2,7 RLL	3.5 HH		150k		
ST1144A	19	IDE AT	RLL ZBR	3.5 HH	32k	150k	3528	Y
ST1144N	19	SCSI-2	RLL ZBR	3.5 HH	8/32k	50k	3528	N
ST1150R	15	ST412/506	2,7 RLL	3.5 HH		150k		Y
ST1156A	15	IDE AT	2,7 RLL	3.5 HH		70k		
ST1156E	15	IDE AT	2,7 RLL	3.5 HH		70k		
ST1156N	15	SCSI	2,7 RLL	3.5 HH		70k		
ST1156NS	15	SCSI-2	2,7 RLL	3.5 HH		70k		
ST1162A	15	IDE AT	2,7 RLL	3.5 HH	32k	150k		Y
ST1162N	15	SCSI	2,7 RLL	3.5 HH	64k	150k		Y
ST1186A	15	IDE AT	2,7 RLL	3.5 HH	32k	150k		Y
ST1186NS	15	SCSI-2	2,7 RLL	3.5 HH	64k	150k		Y
ST1201A	15	IDE AT	2,7 RLL	3.5 HH	32k	150k		Y
ST1201NS	15	SCSI-2	2,7 RLL	3.5 HH		70k		
ST1201E	15	ESDI (10)	2,7 RLL	3.5 HH		150k		Y
ST1201N	15	SCSI	2,7 RLL	3.5 HH	64k	150k		Y
ST1239A	15	IDE AT	2,7 RLL	3.5 HH	32k	150k		N
ST1239NS	15	SCSI-2	RLL ZBR	3.5 HH	64k	150k		Y
ST1274A	18	IDE AT	2,7 RLL	3.5 HH		70k		

Drive Model	Format Size MB	Head	Cyl	Sect/Trac	Translate H/C/S	RWC/WPC	Land Zone
ST1400A	331	7	1475	NA	12/1018/53	---/---	AUTO
ST1400N	331	7	1476	NA		---/---	AUTO
ST1401A	340	9	1100		15/726/61	---/---	
ST1401N	338	9	1100	NA		---/---	AUTO
ST1480A	426	9	1474	NA	15/895/62	---/---	AUTO
ST1480N	426	9	1476	NA		---/---	AUTO
ST1480NV	426	9	1478	V		NA/NA	AUTO
ST1481N	426	9	1476	NA		NA/NA	AUTO
ST1581N	525	9	1476	NA		NA/NA	AUTO
ST1980N	860	13	1730	NA		NA/NA	AUTO
ST1980ND	860	13	1730			---/---	
ST2106E	94	5	1024	34		NA/NA	AUTO
ST2106N	94	5	1022	35		NA/NA	AUTO
ST2106NM	94	5	1022	35		NA/NA	AUTO
ST2125N,NM,NV	107	3	1544	NA		NA/NA	AUTO
ST2182E	160	4	1455	54		NA/NA	AUTO
ST2209N	179	5	1544	NA		NA/NA	AUTO
ST2274A	241	5	1747	54	16/536/55	NA/NA	AUTO
ST2383A	338	7	1747	54	16/737/55	NA/NA	AUTO
ST2383E	338	7	1747	54		NA/NA	AUTO
ST2383N	338	7	1261	NA		NA/NA	AUTO
ST2383NM	332	7	1261	NA		NA/NA	AUTO
ST2383ND	332	7	1261	NA		NA/NA	AUTO
ST2502N	435	7	1765	NA		NA/NA	AUTO
ST2502NM	435	7	1765	NA		NA/NA	AUTO
ST2502ND	435	7	1765	NA		NA/NA	AUTO
ST2502NV	435	7	1765	NA		NA/NA	AUTO
ST3025A	21	1	615	17	2/808/26	NA/NA	AUTO
ST3025N	21	1	1616	26		NA/NA	AUTO
ST3051A	43	6	820	17		---/---	
ST3057A	53		*1024	17		NA/NA	AUTO
ST3057N	49	3	940	34		NA/NA	AUTO
ST3096A	90	10	1024	17	8/836/26	NA/NA	AUTO
ST3096N	84	3	1024	35		NA/NA	AUTO
ST3120A	107	12	1024	NA	12/1024/17	NA/NA	AUTO
ST3144A	130	15	1001	17	15/1001/17	NA/NA	AUTO
ST3243A	214	12	1024	34		---/---	
ST3283A	245				14/978/35	---/---	
ST3283N	248	5	1691	NA		---/---	
ST3385A	340	14	767	62	14/767/62	---/---	
ST3550A	452	14	1018	62		---/---	
ST3550N	456	NA	NA	NA		---/---	
ST3600ND	525	7	1872			---/---	
ST3600A	525					---/---	
ST3600N	525					---/---	
ST3610N	535	7	1872			---/---	
ST3610ND	535	7	1872			---/---	
ST4026	20	4	615	17		616/307	615
ST4038	31	5	733	17		---/732	733
ST4038N	30	5	733			---/-1	977
ST4051	40	5	977	17		---/-1	977
ST4053	44	5	1024	17		NONE/-1	AUTO
ST4077N	67	5	1024	26		1025/1025	
ST4077R	65	5	1024	26		1025/1025	
ST4085	71	8	1024	17		---/---	AUTO
ST4086	72	9	925	17		---/---	AUTO
ST4096	80	9	1024	17		NONE/-1	AUTO
ST4096N	83	4				---/---	AUTO
ST4097	80	9	1024	17		---/---	AUTO
ST4135R	115	9	960	26		NA/NA	AUTO
ST4144N	122	9	1024	26		NA/NA	1023
ST4144R	122	9	1024	26		NONE/-1	AUTO
ST4182E	160	9	969	36		NA/NA	AUTO

Drive Model	Seek Time	Interface	Encode	Form Factor	cache kb	mtbf	RPM	Obsolete?
ST1400A	14	IDE AT	2,7 RLL	3.5 HH	64k	150k	4412	N
ST1400N	14	SCSI-2	ZBR	3.5 HH	64k	150k	4412	N
ST1401A	12	IDE AT	2,7 RLL	3.5 HH		150k		
ST1401N	12	SCSI-2	ZBR	3.5 HH	64k	150k	4412	N
ST1480A	14	IDE AT	ZBR	3.5 HH	64k	150k	4412	N
ST1480N	14	SCSI-2	ZBR	3.5 HH	64k	150k	4412	N
ST1480NV	14	SCSI-2	1,7 RLL	3.5 HH		150k		
ST1481N	14	SCSI-2 FAS		3.5 HH	64k	150k	4412	N
ST1581N	14	SCSI-2 FAS		3.5 HH	64k	150k	4412	N
ST1980N	10	SCSI-2 FAS	1,7 RLL	3.5 HH	256k	200k	5400	N
ST1980ND	11	SCSI-2 FAS	1,7 RLL	3.5 HH	256k	200k	5400	N
ST2106E	18	ESDI (10)	2,7 RLL	5.25 HH		100k		
ST2106N	18	SCSI	2,7 RLL	5.25 HH	32k	100k		N
ST2106NM	18	SCSI	2,7 RLL	5.25 HH	32k	100k		Y
ST2125N,NM,NV	18	SCSI	RLL ZBR	5.25 HH	32k	100k		Y
ST2182E	16	ESDI (15)	2,7 RLL	5.25 HH		100k		N
ST2209N	16	SCSI	RLL ZBR	5.25 HH	32k	100k		Y
ST2274A	16	IDE AT	2,7 RLL	5.25 HH	32k	100k		N
ST2383A	16	IDE AT	2,7 RLL	5.25 HH	32k	100k		N
ST2383E	16	ESDI	2,7 RLL	5.25 HH		100k		N
ST2383N	14	SCSI	RLL ZBR	5.25 HH	64k	100k	3600	N
ST2383NM	14	SCSI	RLL ZBR	5.25 HH	64k	100k	3600	N
ST2383ND	14	SCSI	RLL ZBR	5.25 HH	64k	100k	3600	N
ST2502N	16	SCSI	RLL ZBR	5.25 HH	64k	100k		N
ST2502NM	16	SCSI	RLL ZBR	5.25 HH	64k	100k		N
ST2502ND	16	SCSI	RLL ZBR	5.25 HH	64k	100k		N
ST2502NV	16	SCSI	RLL ZBR	5.25 HH	64k	100k		N
ST3025A	19	IDE AT	2,7 RLL	3.5 3H	8/32k	50k	3600	N
ST3025N	19	SCSI-2	2,7 RLL	3.5 3H	8/32k	50k	3600	N
ST3051A	16	IDE AT	2,7 RLL	3.5 3H	32k	150k	3211	
ST3057A	18	IDE AT	2,7 RLL	3.5 3H	8/32k	50k	3600	N
ST3057N	19	SCSI-2	2,7 RLL	3.5 3H	8/32k	50k	3600	N
ST3096A	17	IDE AT	2,7 RLL	3.5 3H	32k	150k	3528	N
ST3096N	20	SCSI-2	2,7 RLL	3.5 3H	8/32k	50k	3528	N
ST3120A	15	IDE AT	RLL ZBR	3.5 3H	32k	150k	3528	N
ST3144A	16	IDE AT	2,7 RLL	3.5 3H	32k	150k		N
ST3243A	16	IDE AT	1,7 RLL	3.5 3H	128k	150k	3811	
ST3283A	12	IDE AT	1,7 RLL	3.5 3H	128k	200k		N
ST3283N	12	SCSI-2 FAS	RLL ZBR	3.5 3H	128k	250k		
ST3385A	12	IDE AT	1,7 RLL	3.5 3H	256k	250k	4500	
ST3550A	12	IDE AT	1,7 RLL	3.5 3H	256k	250k	4500	
ST3550N	12	SCSI-2 FAS	1,7 RLL	3.5 3H	256k	250k	4500	
ST3600ND	12	SCSI-2 FAS	1,7 RLL	3.5 3H	256k	200k	4500	
ST3600A	11	IDE AT		3.5 3H	256k	200k	4500	N
ST3600N	11	SCSI-2		3.5 3H	256k	200k	4500	
ST3610N	10	SCSI-2 FAS	1,7 RLL	3.5 3H	256k	200k	5411	
ST3610ND	12	SCSI-2 FAS	1,7 RLL	3.5 3H	256k	200k	5411	
ST4026	40	ST412/506	MFM	5.25 FH				
ST4038	40	ST412/506	MFM	5.25 FH		20k		Y
ST4038N		SCSI		5.25 FH				
ST4051	40	ST412/506	MFM	5.25 FH		40k		
ST4053	28	ST412/506	MFM	5.25 FH		40k	3600	N
ST4077N	28	SCSI	2,7 RLL	5.25 FH				
ST4077R	28	ST412/506	2,7 RLL	5.25 FH				
ST4085	28	ST412/506	MFM	5.25 FH		40k		Y
ST4086	28	ST412/506	MFM	5.25 FH		40k		Y
ST4096	28	ST412/506	MFM	5.25 FH		40k	3600	Y
ST4096N	17	SCSI		5.25 FH				
ST4097	28	ST412/506	MFM	5.25 FH		40k		Y
ST4135R	28	ST412/506	2,7 RLL	5.25 FH		40k		N
ST4144N	28	SCSI		5.25 FH				
ST4144R	28	ST412/506	2,7 RLL	5.25 FH		40k	3600	N
ST4182E	16	ESDI	2,7 RLL	5.25 FH		100k		Y

Drive Model	Format Size MB	Head	Cyl	Sect/ Trac	Translate H/C/S	RWC/ WPC	Land Zone
ST4182N,NM	155	9	967	36		NA/NA	AUTO
ST4192E	169	8	1147	36		NA/NA	
ST4192N	168	8	1147	36		1148/1148	
ST4350N	307	9	1412	NA		NA/NA	AUTO
ST4350NM	307	9	1412	NA		NA/NA	AUTO
ST4376N	330	9	1549	NA		NA/NA	AUTO
ST4376NM	330	9	1549	NA		NA/NA	AUTO
ST4376NV	330	9	1549	NA		NA/NA	AUTO
ST4383E	338	13	1412	34		NA/NA	AUTO
ST4384E	338	15	1224	34		NA/NA	AUTO
ST4385N	330	15	791	NA		NA/NA	AUTO
ST4385NM	330	15	791	NA		NA/NA	AUTO
ST4385NV	330	15	791	NA		NA/NA	AUTO
ST4442E	380	15	1412	34		NA/NA	AUTO
ST4702N	601	15	1546	NA		NA/NA	AUTO
ST4702NM	601	15	1546	NA		NA/NA	AUTO
ST4766E	676	15	1632	54		NA/NA	AUTO
ST4766N	663		1632	54		NA/NA	AUTO
ST4766NM	663		1632	54		NA/NA	AUTO
ST4766NV	663		1632	54		NA/NA	AUTO
ST4767E	676	15	1399	63		NA/NA	AUTO
ST4767N	665	15	1356	64		NA/NA	AUTO
ST4767NM	665	15	1356	64		NA/NA	AUTO
ST4767ND	665	15	1356	64		NA/NA	AUTO
ST4767NV	665	15	1356	64		NA/NA	AUTO
ST4769E	691	15	1552	58		NA/NA	AUTO
ST6344J	344	24	711			---/---	AUTO
ST6515J	516	24	711			---/---	AUTO
ST8368N	316			NA		NA/NA	AUTO
ST8500N	427			NA		NA/NA	AUTO
ST8741N	637			NA		NA/NA	AUTO
ST8851J	727	15	1381			---/---	AUTO
ST8851K	727	15	1381			---/---	
ST8851N	727	15	1381			NA/NA	AUTO
ST8885N	727			NA		NA/NA	AUTO
ST9025A	21	4	1024			NA/NA	AUTO
ST9051A	43	6	1024			NA/NA	AUTO
ST9052A	42	16	1024	63	5/980/17	---/---	
ST9077A	64	17	802	39	11/699/17	NA/NA	AUTO
ST9080A	64	4	823	38	4/823/38	---/---	
ST9096A	85	3	940	34	10/980/17	NA/NA	AUTO
ST9100AG	85	16	1024	63	16/651/16	---/---	
ST9144A	128	3			15/980/17	NA/NA	AUTO
ST9235AG	209	13	985	32	13/985/32	---/---	
ST9235N	209	NA	NA	NA		---/---	
ST9295AG	261	16	1024	63		---/---	
ST9295N	250	NA	NA	NA		---/---	
ST11200N	1050	15	1877			NA/NA	AUTO
ST11200ND	1050	15	1877			---/---	
ST11201N	1050	15	1877			---/---	
ST11201ND	1050	15	1877			---/---	
ST11700N	1430	13	2626			---/---	
ST11700ND	1430	13	2626			---/---	
ST11701N	1430	13	2626			---/---	
ST11701ND	1430	13	2626			---/---	
ST11750N	1437		2756			---/---	
ST11750ND	1437		2756			---/---	
ST11751N	1437		2756			---/---	
ST11751ND	1437		2756			---/---	
ST12400N	2100	19	626			---/---	AUTO
ST12400ND	2100	19	2626			---/---	
ST12401N	2100	19	2626			---/---	
ST12401ND	2100	19	2626			---/---	

Drive Model	Seek Time	Interface	Encode	Form Factor	cache kb	mtbf	RPM	Obsolete?
ST4182N,NM	16	SCSI	RLL ZBR	5.25 FH	32k	100k		Y
ST4192E	17	ESDI	2,7 RLL	5.25 FH		20k		
ST4192N	17	SCSI	2,7 RLL	5.25 FH		20k		
ST4350N	16	SCSI	RLL ZBR	5.25 FH	32k	100k		Y
ST4350NM	16	SCSI	RLL ZBR	5.25 FH	32k	100k		Y
ST4376N	17	SCSI	RLL ZBR	5.25 FH	32k	100k		Y
ST4376NM	17	SCSI	RLL ZBR	5.25 FH	32k	100k		Y
ST4376NV	17	SCSI	RLL ZBR	5.25 FH	32k	100k		Y
ST4383E	18	ESDI	2,7 RLL	5.25 FH		100k		N
ST4384E	14	ESDI	2,7 RLL	5.25 FH		100k		N
ST4385N	10	SCSI	RLL ZBR	5.25 FH	32k	100k		N
ST4385NM	10	SCSI	RLL ZBR	5.25 FH	32k	100k		N
ST4385NV	10	SCSI	RLL ZBR	5.25 FH	32k	100k		N
ST4442E	16	ESDI	2,7 RLL	5.25 FH		100k		N
ST4702N	16	SCSI	RLL ZBR	5.25 FH	32k	100k		N
ST4702NM	16	SCSI	RLL ZBR	5.25 FH	32k	100k		N
ST4766E	15	ESDI (15)	2,7 RLL	5.25 FH		150k		N
ST4766N	15	SCSI	2,7 RLL	5.25 FH	32k	150k		N
ST4766NM	15	SCSI	2,7 RLL	5.25 FH	32k	150k		N
ST4766NV	15	SCSI	2,7 RLL	5.25 FH	32k	150k		N
ST4767E	11	ESDI (24)	2,7 RLL	5.25 FH		150k	4800	N
ST4767N	11	SCSI-2	RLL ZBR	5.25 FH	256k	150k	4800	N
ST4767NM	11	SCSI-2	RLL ZBR	5.25 FH	256k	150k	4800	N
ST4767ND	11	SCSI-2	RLL ZBR	5.25 FH	256k	150k	4800	N
ST4767NV	11	SCSI-2	RLL ZBR	5.25 FH	256k	150k	4800	N
ST4769E	13	ESDI	2,7 RLL	5.25 FH		150k	4800	N
ST6344J	18	SMD		9		30k		
ST6515J	18	SMD		9		30k		
ST8368N	18	SCSI		8		30k		
ST8500N	18	SCSI		8		30k		N
ST8741N	15	SCSI		8		50k		N
ST8851J	12	SMD-O/E		8		100k		
ST8851K	15	IPI-2	2,7 RLL	8		100k	3600	
ST8851N	12	SCSI		8		100k		
ST8885N	15	SCSI		8		150k		N
ST9025A		IDE AT	2,7 RLL	2.5		150k	3631	N
ST9051A		IDE AT	2,7 RLL	2.5	32k	150k	3631	Y
ST9052A	16	IDE AT	2,7 RLL	2.5 4H	32k	150k	3450	
ST9077A	19	IDE AT	2,7 RLL	2.5	32k	150k		N
ST9080A	16	IDE AT	2,7 RLL	2.5 4H	32k	150k	3450	
ST9096A	16	IDE AT	2,7 RLL	2.5	64k	150k		
ST9100AG	16	IDE XT	1,7 RLL	2.5 4H	120k	300k	3545	
ST9144A	16	IDE AT	2,7 RLL	2.5	64k	150k		N
ST9235A	16	IDE AT	2,7 RLL	2.5 4H	64k	150k	3450	
ST9235N	16	SCSI	2,7 RLL	2.5 4H	64k	150k	3450	
ST9295AG	16	IDE AT	2,7 RLL	2.5 4H	120k	300k	3450	
ST9295N	16	SCSI	2,7 RLL	2.5 4H	64k	150k	3450	
ST11200N	11	SCSI-2 FAS	1,7 RLL	3.5 HH	256k	200k	5400	N
ST11200ND	12	SCSI-2 FST	1,7 RLL	3.5 HH	256k	200k	5400	
ST11201N	10	SCSI-2 FAS	1,7 RLL	3.5 HH	256k	200k	5400	
ST11201ND	12	SCSI-2 FST	1,7 RLL	3.5 HH	256k	200k	5400	
ST11700N	9	SCSI-2 FAS	1,7 RLL	3.5 HH	256k	500k	5400	
ST11700ND	10	SCSI-2 FST	1,7 RLL	3.5 HH	256k	500k	5400	
ST11701N	9	SCSI-2 FAS	1,7 RLL	3.5 HH	256k	500k	5400	
ST11701ND	10	SCSI-2 FST	1,7 RLL	3.5 HH	256k	500k	5400	
ST11750N	8	SCSI-2 FAS	1,7 RLL	3.5 HH	1024k	500k	7200	
ST11750ND	9	SCSI-2 FST	1,7 RLL	3.5 HH	1024k	500k	7200	
ST11751N	8	SCSI-2 FAS	1,7 RLL	3.5 HH	1024k	500k	7200	
ST11751ND	9	SCSI-2 FST	1,7 RLL	3.5 HH	1024k	500k	7200	
ST12400N	9	SCSI-2 FAS	1,7 RLL	3.5 HH	256k	500k	5400	
ST12400ND	10	SCSI-2 FST	1,7 RLL	3.5 HH	256k	500k	5400	
ST12401N	9	SCSI-2 FAS	1,7 RLL	3.5 HH	256k	500k	5400	
ST12401ND	10	SCSI-2 FST	1,7 RLL	3.5 HH	256k	500k	5400	

Drive Model	Format Size MB	Head	Cyl	Sect/Trac	Translate H/C/S	RWC/WPC	Land Zone
ST12550N	2100		2756			---/---	
ST12550ND	2100		2756			---/---	
ST12551N	2100		2756			---/---	
ST12551ND	2100		2756			---/---	
ST31200N	1050	9	2626			---/---	
ST31200ND	1050	9	2626			---/---	
ST41097J	1097	17	2101			NA/NA	AUTO
ST41200N	1037	15	1931	NA		NA/NA	AUTO
ST41200NM	1037	15	1931	NA		NA/NA	AUTO
ST41200ND	1037	15	1931	NA		NA/NA	AUTO
ST41200NV	1037	15	1931	NA		NA/NA	AUTO
ST41201J	1200U	17	2101	NA		NA/NA	AUTO
ST41201K	1200U	17	2101	NA		NA/NA	AUTO
ST41520N	1370	17	2101	NA		NONE/-1	AUTO
ST41520ND	1370	17	2101	NA		NONE/-1	AUTO
ST41600N	1370	17	2101	NA		NONE/-1	AUTO
ST41600ND	1370	17	2101	NA		NONE/-1	AUTO
ST41601N	1370	17	2101	V		NA/NA	AUTO
ST41601ND	1370	17	2101	V		NA/NA	AUTO
ST41650N	1415	15	2107	NA		NA/NA	AUTO
ST41650ND	1415	15	2107	NA		NA/NA	AUTO
ST41651N	1415	15	2107	NA		NA/NA	AUTO
ST41651ND	1415	15	2107	NA		NA/NA	AUTO
ST41800K	1986U	18	2262	NA		NA/NA	AUTO
ST42000N,ND	1792	16	2627	NA		NA/NA	AUTO
ST42100N	1900			NA		NA/NA	AUTO
ST42400N,ND	2129	19	2627	NA		NA/NA	AUTO
ST43200N	3338			NA		---/---	
ST43200K	3385U	20	2738			NA/NA	AUTO
ST43400N,ND	2912	21	2738	NA		NA/NA	AUTO
ST43401N/ND	2904			NA		NA/NA	AUTO
ST43402N/ND	2904			NA		NA/NA	AUTO
ST81123J	1123U	15	1635			---/---	AUTO
ST81154K	1154U	14	1635			---/---	AUTO
ST81236J	1056	15	1635			NA/NA	AUTO
ST81236N	1056	15	1635	NA		NA/NA	AUTO
ST81236K	1056	15	1635			---/---	
ST82030U	2030U	19	2120			---/---	
ST82030K	2030U	19	2120			---/---	
ST82038U	2038U	19	2611			---/---	AUTO
ST82105K	2105U	16	2611			---/---	AUTO
ST82272J	2272U	19	2611			---/---	
ST82368K	2368U	18	2611			---/---	AUTO
ST82500J	2140	19	2611			NA/NA	AUTO
ST82500N	2140	19	2611	NA		NA/NA	AUTO
ST82500ND	2140	19	2611	NA		NA/NA	AUTO
ST83050K	3050U	19	2655	NA		NA/NA	AUTO
ST83050N	3050U	18	2655	NA		NA/NA	AUTO
ST83220K	3220U	19	2655	NA		NA/NA	AUTO
SHUGART							
604	5	4	160	17		128/128	
606	7	6	160	17		128/128	
612	10	4	306	17		307/128	
706	6	2	320	17		321/128	
712	10	4	320	17		321/128	
1002	5			17		---/---	
1004	10			17		---/---	
1004	30			17		---/---	
4004	14			17		---/---	
4008	29			17		---/---	
4100	56			17		---/---	

Drive Model	Seek Time	Interface	Encode	Form Factor	cache kb	mtbf	RPM	Obsolete?
ST12550N	8	SCSI-2 FAS	1,7 RLL	3.5 HH	1024k	500k	7200	
ST12550ND	8	SCSI-2 FAS	1,7 RLL	3.5 HH	1024k	500k	7200	
ST12551N	8	SCSI-2 FAS	1,7 RLL	3.5 HH	1024k	500k	7200	
ST12551ND	9	SCSI-2 FAS	1,7 RLL	3.5 HH	1024k	500k	7200	
ST31200N	9	SCSI-2 FAS	1,7 RLL	3.5 3H	256k	500k	6300	
ST31200ND	10	SCSI-2 FAS	1,7 RLL	3.5 3H	256k	500k	6300	
ST41097J	11	SMD		5.25 FH		150k	5400	
ST41200N	15	SCSI-2	RLL ZBR	5.25 FH	256k	150k		N
ST41200NM	15	SCSI-2	RLL ZBR	5.25 FH	256k	150k		N
ST41200ND	15	SCSI-2	RLL ZBR	5.25 FH	256k	150k		N
ST41200NV	15	SCSI-2	RLL ZBR	5.25 FH	256k	150k		N
ST41201J	11	SMD		5.25 FH		150k	5400	
ST41201K	11	IPI-2		5.25 FH		150k	5400	N
ST41520N	11	SCSI-2	ZBR	5.25 FH	48k	150k	5400	
ST41520ND	11	SCSI-2	ZBR	5.25 FH	48k	150k	5400	
ST41600N	11	SCSI-2	ZBR	5.25 FH	48k	150k	5400	
ST41600ND	11	SCSI-2	ZBR	5.25 FH	48k	150k	5400	
ST41601N	11	SCSI-2 FAS	2,7 RLL	5.25 FH	256k	150k	5400	
ST41601ND	11	SCSI-2 FAS	2,7 RLL	5.25 FH	256k	150k	5400	
ST41650N	15	SCSI-2	RLL ZBR	5.25 FH	256k	150k		N
ST41650ND	15	SCSI-2 DIF	RLL ZBR	5.25 FH	256k	150k		N
ST41651N	15	SCSI-2		5.25 FH	256k	150k		N
ST41651ND	15	SCSI-2 DIF	1,7 RLL	5.25 FH	256k	150k		N
ST41800K	11	IPI-2		5.25 FH		150k	5400	
ST42000N,ND	11	SCSI-2 FAS	2,7 RLL	5.25 FH		200k	5400	N
ST42100N	13	SCSI-2 FAS		5.25 FH		200k		
ST42400N,ND	11	SCSI-2 FAS	2,7 RLL	5.25 FH	512k	200k	5400	N
ST43200N	11	IPI-2	RLL ZBR	5.25 FH		300k		N
ST43200K	11	IPI-2	1,7 RLL	5.25 FH	512k	200k	5400	N
ST43400N,ND	11	SCSI-2 FAS	1,7 RLL	5.25 FH	512k	200k	5400	N
ST43401N/ND	11	SCSI-2 1PO		5.25 FH	394k	300k	5400	N
ST43402N/ND	11	SCSI-2 2PO		5.25 FH	394k	300k	5400	N
ST81123J	12	SMD-O/E		8		150k		
ST81154K	15	IPI-2	2,7 RLL	8		150k	3600	
ST81236J	12	SMD		8		150k		
ST81236N	12	SCSI		8		150k		
ST81236N	15	SCSI		8		250k		N
ST81236K	15	IPI-2	2,7 RLL	8		150k	3600	
ST82030J	11	SMD-O/E	2,7 RLL	8		150k	3600	
ST82030K	11	IPI-2	2,7 RLL	8		150k	3600	
ST82038J	12	SMD-E		8		150k		
ST82105K	12	IPI-2	2,7 RLL	8		80k	3600	
ST82272J	12	SMD-E		8		150k		
ST82368K	12	IPI-2	2,7 RLL	8		80k	3600	
ST82500J	12	SMD-O/E		8		150k		
ST82500N	12	SCSI		8		150k		
ST82500N	12	SCSI		8		250k		N
ST83050K	12	IPI-2	1,7 RLL	8		150k	4365	N
ST83050N	12	IPI-2	1,7 RLL	8		150k	4365	N
ST83220K	12	IPI-2		8		150k		N

SHUGART

604		ST412/506	MFM	5.25 FH				Y
606		ST412/506	MFM	5.25 FH				Y
612		ST412/506	MFM	5.25 FH				Y
706		ST412/506	MFM	5.25 FH				Y
712		ST412/506	MFM	5.25 FH				Y
1002		ST412/506	MFM	8.0 FH				
1004		ST412/506	MFM	8.0 FH				
1004		ST412/506	MFM	8.0 FH				
4004		ST412/506	MFM					
4008		ST412/506	MFM					
4100		ST412/506	MFM					

Drive Model	Format Size MB	Head	Cyl	Sect/Trac	Translate H/C/S	RWC/WPC	Land Zone
SIEMENS							
1200	174	8	1216	35		NA/NA	AUTO
1300	261	12	1216	35		NA/NA	AUTO
2200	174	8	1216			NA/NA	AUTO
2300	261	12	1216	35		NA/NA	AUTO
4410	322	11	1100	52		NA/NA	AUTO
4420	334	11	1100	54		NA/NA	AUTO
5710	655	15				NA/NA	AUTO
5720	655	15				NA/NA	AUTO
5810	777	16				NA/NA	AUTO
5820	777	16				NA/NA	AUTO
6200	1200					NA/NA	AUTO
7520	655	15				NA/NA	AUTO
STORAGE DIMENSIONS							
AT40	44	5	1024	17		---/NONE	1023
AT70	70			17		---/---	
AT100S	105	3				---/---	
AT100	109	8	1024	26		---/NONE	1023
AT120	119	15	918	17		---/---	
AT133	133	15	1024	17		---/NONE	1023
AT140	142	8	1024	34		---/NONE	1023
AT155E	158	9	1224	36		---/---	
AT155S	156	9	1224	36		---/---	
AT160	160	15	1224	17		---/NONE	1023
AT200S	204	7				---/---	
AT200	204	15	1024	26		---/NONE	1023
AT320S	320	15	1224	36		---/---	
AT335E	338	15	1224	36		---/---	
AT650E	651	15	1632	54		---/---	
AT650S	651	15	1632	54		---/---	
AT1000S	1000	15				---/---	
MAC-195	195	7				NA/NA	AUTO
PS155E	156	9	1224	36		---/---	
PS155S	156	9	1224	36		---/---	
PS320S	320	15	1224	36		---/---	
PS335E	338	15	1224	36		---/---	
PS650S	651	15	1632	16		---/---	
XT40	44	5	1024	17		---/NONE	1023
XT70	71	8	1024	17		---/NONE	1023
XT100	109	8	1024	26		---/NONE	1023
XT120	119	15	918	17		---/NONE	
XT200	204	15	1024	26		---/NONE	1023
SYQUEST TECHNOLOGY							
SQ225F	20			17		---/---	
SQ306R	5	2	306	17		---/---	
SQ306RD	3	2	306	17		307/307	
SQ306F	5			17		---/---	
SQ312	10	2	615	17		616/616	
SQ312RD	10	2	615	17		616/616	
SQ319	10	2	612	17		---/---	
SQ325	21	4	612	17		612/612	
SQ325F	20	4	615	17		616/616	
SQ338F	30	6	615	17		616/616	
SQ340AF	38	6	640	17		616/616	
TANDON COMPUTER CORPORATION							
TM244	41	4	782	26		783/783	
TM246	62	6	782	26		783/783	

Drive Model	Seek Time	Interface	Encode	Form Factor	cache kb	mtbf	Obsolete? RPM

SIEMENS

Drive Model	Seek Time	Interface	Encode	Form Factor	cache kb	mtbf	RPM
1200	25	ESDI	2,7 RLL	5.25 FH			
1300	25	ESDI	2,7 RLL	5.25 FH			
2200	25	ESDI	2,7 RLL	5.25 FH			
2300	25	ESDI	2,7 RLL	5.25 FH			
4410	18	ESDI	2,7 RLL	5.25 FH		30k	
4420	16	SCSI	2,7 RLL	5.25 FH		40k	
5710	16	ESDI	2,7 RLL	5.25 FH			
5720	16	SCSI	2,7 RLL	5.25 FH			
5810	18	ESDI	2,7 RLL	5.25 FH			
5820	18	SCSI	2,7 RLL	5.25 FH			
6200	14	SCSI	2,7 RLL	5.25 FH			
7520	16	SCSI	2,7 RLL	5.25 FH			

STORAGE DIMENSIONS

Drive Model	Seek Time	Interface	Encode	Form Factor	cache kb	mtbf	RPM
AT40		ST412/506	MFM				
AT70	27	ST412/506	MFM	5.25 FH		40k	
AT100S	19	SCSI	2,7 RLL	3.5 HH		150k	
AT100		ST412/506	2,7 RLL				
AT120	26	ST412/506	MFM	5.25 FH		40k	
AT133		ST412/506	MFM				
AT140							
AT155E	14	ESDI	2,7 RLL	5.25 FH		40k	
AT155S	17	SCSI	2,7 RLL	5.25 FH		40k	
AT160	28	ST412/506	MFM	5.25 FH		40k	
AT200S	16	SCSI	2,7 RLL	3.5 HH		150k	
AT200		ST412/506	2,7 RLL				
AT320S	17	SCSI	2,7 RLL	5.25 FH		40k	
AT335E	16	ESDI	2,7 RLL	5.25 FH		40k	
AT650E	16	ESDI	2,7 RLL	5.25 FH		40k	
AT650S	16	SCSI	2,7 RLL	5.25 FH		40k	
AT1000S		SCSI				100k	
MAC-195	15	SCSI	2,7 RLL	3.5 HH		150k	
PS155E	14	ESDI	2,7 RLL	5.25 FH		70k	
PS155S	14	SCSI	2,7 RLL	5.25 FH		70k	
PS320S	16	SCSI	2,7 RLL	5.25 FH		150k	
PS335E	15	ESDI	2,7 RLL	5.25 FH		70k	
PS650S	15	SCSI	2,7 RLL	5.25 FH		100k	
XT40		ST412/506	MFM				
XT70		ST412/506	MFM				
XT100		ST412/506	2,7 RLL				
XT120		ST412/506	MFM				
XT200		ST412/506	2,7 RLL				

SYQUEST TECHNOLOGY

Drive Model	Seek Time	Interface	Encode	Form Factor	cache kb	mtbf	RPM
SQ225F	99	ST412/506	MFM	5.25 HH			
SQ306R	99	ST412/506	MFM	5.25 HH			
SQ306RD	99	ST412/506	MFM	5.25 HH			
SQ306F	99	ST412/506	MFM	5.25 HH			
SQ312	80	ST412/506	MFM	5.25 HH			
SQ312RD	80	ST412/506	MFM	5.25 HH			
SQ319	80	ST412/506	RLL	5.25 HH			
SQ325	80	ST412/506	MFM	5.25 HH			
SQ325F	99	ST412/506	MFM	5.25 HH			
SQ338F	80	ST412/506	MFM	5.25 HH			
SQ340AF	80	ST412/506	MFM	5.25 HH			

TANDON COMPUTER CORPORATION

Drive Model	Seek Time	Interface	Encode	Form Factor	cache kb	mtbf	RPM
TM244		ST412/506	2,7 RLL				
TM246		ST412/506	2,7 RLL				

Drive Model	Format Size MB	Head	Cyl	Sect/ Trac	Translate H/C/S	RWC/ WPC	Land Zone
TM251	5	2	306	17		---/---	
TM252	10	4	306	17		307/307	
TM261	10	4	615	17		616/616	
TM262	21	4	615	17		616/616	AUTO
TM262R	20	2	782	26		783/783	
TM264	41	4	782	26		783/783	
TM344	41	4	782	26		783/783	
TM346	62	6	782	26		783/783	
TM361	10	2	615	17		616/616	
TM362	20	4	615	17		616/616	615
TM362R	20	2	782	26		783/783	
TM364	41	4	782	26		783/783	
TM501	5	2	306	17		128/153	
TM502	10	4	306	17		128/153	
TM503	15	6	306	17		128/153	
TM602S	5	4	153	17		128/128	
TM602SE	12			17		---/---	
TM603S	10	6	153	17		128/128	
TM603SE	12	6	230	17		128/128	
TM702	20	4	615	26		616/616	
TM702AT	21	4	615	17		616/616	615
TM703	30	5	733	17		734/734	695
TM703AT	31	5	733	17		733/733	733
TM703C	25	17				---/---	
TM705	41	5	962	17		---/NONE	962
TM755	42	5	981	17		982/982	981
TM2085	74	9	1004	17		1005/1005	
TM2128	115	9	1004	26		1005/1005	
TM2170	154	9	1344	26		1345/1345	
TM3085	71	8	1024	17		1024/1024	
TM3085R	105	8	1024	26		1024/1024	

TANDY CORP

25-1045	28					---/---	AUTO
25-1046	43	4	782	27		NA/NA	AUTO
25-4130	100	4	1219			NA/NA	AUTO

TEAC AMERICA, INC.

SD240	43	2	1000	42		NA/NA	AUTO
SD260	63	2	1226	50		NA/NA	AUTO
SD340A	43	2	1050	40		NA/NA	AUTO
SD340S	43	2	1050	40		---/---	AUTO
SD340HS	43	2	1050	40		---/---	AUTO
SD340HA	43	2	1050	40		NA/NA	AUTO
SD380	86	4	1050	40		NA/NA	AUTO
SD380(S)		4	1050	40		---/---	AUTO
SD380H(A)		4	1050	40		NA/NA	AUTO
SD380H(S)		4	1050	40		---/---	AUTO
SD510	10	4	306	17		128/128	
SD520	20	4	615	17		128/128	
SD3105A	105	4	1282	40		NA/NA	AUTO
SD3105S	105	4	1282	40		NA/NA	AUTO
SD3210(A)	215	4	1695	62		NA/NA	AUTO
SD3210(S)	215	4	1695	62		NA/NA	AUTO
SD3240	245	4	1930			---/---	

TEXAS INSTRUMENTS

TI5	5	4	153	17		64/64	

TOKICO

DK503-2	10	4	306	17		---/---	

Drive Model	Seek Time	Interface	Encode	Form Factor	cache kb	mtbf	RPM	Obsolete?
TM251		ST412/506	MFM	5.25				
TM252	85	ST412/506	MFM	5.25 HH				
TM261		ST412/506	MFM	5.25				
TM262	65	ST412/506	MFM	3.5 HH				
TM262R	85	ST412/506	2,7 RLL	3.5 HH				
TM264	85	ST412/506	2,7 RLL	3.5 HH				
TM344	35	ST412/506	2,7 RLL	3.5 HH				
TM346	35	ST412/506	2,7 RLL	3.5 HH				
TM361		ST412/506	MFM	5.25				
TM362		ST412/506	MFM	5.25				
TM362R	85	ST412/506	2,7 RLL	3.5 HH				
TM364	85	ST412/506	2,7 RLL	3.5 HH				
TM501		ST412/506	MFM	5.25 FH				
TM502	85	ST412/506	MFM	5.25 FH				
TM503	85	ST412/506	MFM	5.25 FH				
TM602S	85	ST412/506	MFM	5.25 FH				
TM602SE		ST412/506	MFM	5.25 FH				
TM603S		ST412/506	MFM	5.25 FH				
TM603SE		ST412/506	MFM	5.25 FH				
TM702		ST412/506	MFM	5.25				
TM702AT		ST412/506	MFM	5.25 FH				
TM703		ST412/506	MFM	5.25 FH				
TM703AT	35	ST412/506	MFM	5.25 FH				
TM703C		ST412/506	MFM	5.25 FH				
TM705		ST412/506	MFM	5.25 FH				
TM755		ST412/506	MFM	5.25 FH				
TM2085	25	SCSI	MFM	5.25				
TM2128	25	SCSI	2,7 RLL	5.25				
TM2170	25	SCSI	2,7 RLL	5.25				
TM3085	35	ST412/506	MFM	5.25				
TM3085R	35	ST412/506	2,7 RLL	5.25				

TANDY CORP

Drive Model	Seek Time	Interface	Encode	Form Factor	cache kb	mtbf	RPM	Obsolete?
25-1045		IDE XT		3.5 HH				
25-1046	28	IDE XT	2,7 RLL	3.5 HH		40k		
25-4130	17		2,7 RLL	3.5 HH				

TEAC AMERICA, INC.

Drive Model	Seek Time	Interface	Encode	Form Factor	cache kb	mtbf	RPM	Obsolete?
SD240	19	IDE AT	1,7 RLL	2.5	32k	100k	3600	N
SD260	19	IDE AT	1,7 RLL	2.5	32k	100k	3600	N
SD340A	23	IDE AT	2,7 RLL	3.5 3H		30k	2358	N
SD340S	23	SCSI	2,7 RLL	3.5 3H		30k	2358	N
SD340HS	19	SCSI	2,7 RLL	3.5 3H		30k	2358	N
SD340HA	19	IDE AT	2,7 RLL	3.5 3H		30k	2358	N
SD380	22	IDE AT	2,7 RLL	3.5 3H		30k	2358	N
SD380(S)	22	SCSI	2,7 RLL	3.5 3H		30k	2358	N
SD380H(A)	19	IDE AT	2,7 RLL	3.5 3H		30k	2358	N
SD380H(S)	19	SCSI	2,7 RLL	3.5 3H		30k	2358	N
SD510		ST412/506	MFM	5.25 FH				
SD520		ST412/506	MFM	5.25 FH				
SD3105A	19	IDE AT	2,7 RLL	3.5 3H	64k	30k	3600	N
SD3105S	19	SCSI	2,7 RLL	3.5 3H	64k	30k	3600	N
SD3210(A)	17	IDE AT	1,7 RLL	3.5 3H		100k	3600	
SD3210(S)	17	SCSI	1,7 RLL	3.5 3H		100k	3600	
SD3240	17	IDE AT	1,7 RLL	3.5 3H		100k	3600	

TEXAS INSTRUMENTS

Drive Model	Seek Time	Interface	Encode	Form Factor	cache kb	mtbf	RPM	Obsolete?
TI5		ST412/506	MFM	5.25 FH				

TOKICO

Drive Model	Seek Time	Interface	Encode	Form Factor	cache kb	mtbf	RPM	Obsolete?
DK503-2		ST412/506	MFM	5.25				

Drive Model	Format Size MB	Head	Cyl	Sect/ Trac	Translate H/C/S	RWC/ WPC	Land Zone
TOSHIBA AMERICA, INC.							
MK53FA(R)	43	5	830	26		831/831	
MK53FA(M)	36	5	830	17		830/512	830
MK53FA	36	5	830	17		---/512	830
MK53FB-I	36	5	830	17		830/512	
MK53FB(M)	36	5	830	17		830/512	
MK53FB(R)	64	5	830	26		831/831	
MK53FB	36	5	830	17		830/512	
MK54FA(R)	90	7	830	26		831/831	
MK54FA(M)	60	7	830	17		831/512	830
MK54FB-I	50	7	830	17		830/512	830
MK54FB(M)	60	7	830	17		830/512	
MK54FB(R)	90	7	830	26		831/831	
MK56FA(M)	86	10	830	17		831/831	
MK56FA(R)	129	10	830	26		---/512	830
MK56FB-I	72	10	830	17		830/512	830
MK56FB(M)	86	10	830	17		830/512	
MK56FB(R)	129	10	830	26		831/831	
MK72	72			17		---/---	
MK72PCR	109			26		---/---	
MK130	53	7	733			---/---	
MK134FA	44	7	733	17		---/---	
MK134FA(R)	65	7	733	26		---/---	
MK153FA	74	5	830	35		NA/NA	
MK153FA-I	74	5	830	35		NA/NA	AUTO
MK153FB	74	5	830	35		---/---	
MK154FA	104	7	830	35		NA/NA	
MK154FA-I	104	7	830	35		NA/NA	AUTO
MK154FB	104	7	830	35		---/---	
MK156FA	148	10	830	35		NA/NA	
MK156FB	148	10	830	35		---/---	
MK232FB	45	3	845	35		---/---	AUTO
MK232FBS	45	3	845	35		---/---	
MK232FC	45	3	845	35		NA/NA	
MK233FB	75	5	845	35		---/---	AUTO
MK234FB	106	7	845	35		---/---	AUTO
MK234FBS	106	7	845	35		---/---	
MK234FC	106	7	845	35		---/---	AUTO
MK234FCH	106	7	845	35		---/---	
MK250FA	382	10	1224	35		NA/NA	
MK250FB	382	10	1224	35		NA/NA	
MK286FC	374	11	823			---/---	
MK288FC	510	15	823			---/---	
MK355FA	405	9	1661	53		---/---	
MK355FB	405	9	1661	53		---/---	
MK358FA	675	15	1661	53		---/---	
MK358FB	675	15	1661	53		---/---	
MK388FA	720	15	1162			---/---	
MK438FB	877	15	1691			NA/NA	AUTO
MK537FB	1064	13	1980	NA		NA/NA	AUTO
MK538FB	1230	15	1980	NA		NA/NA	AUTO
MK556FA	152	10	830			NA/NA	
MK1034FC	107	4	1345			---/---	
MD1122FC	43	2	977			---/---	
MK2024FC	86	4	977	43		NA/NA	AUTO
MK2124FC	130	4	1155	55		NA/NA	AUTO
MKM0351E	36	5	830	17		830/512	830
MKM0351J	36	5	830	17		830/512	830
MKM0352E	50	7	830	17		---/512	830
MKM0352J	50	7	830	17		---/512	830
MKM0353E	72	10	830	17		830/512	830
MKM0353J	72	10	830	17		830/512	830

Drive Model	Seek Time	Interface	Encode	Form Factor	cache kb	mtbf	Obsolete? RPM

TOSHIBA AMERICA, INC.

Drive Model	Seek Time	Interface	Encode	Form Factor	cache kb	mtbf	RPM
MK53FA(R)	30	ST412/506	2,7 RLL	5.25 FH		20k	
MK53FA(M)	25	ST412/506	MFM	5.25 FH		20k	
MK53FA	30	ST412/506	MFM	5.25 FH		20k	
MK53FB-I	25	ST412/506	MFM	5.25 FH		20k	
MK53FB(M)	25	ST412/506	MFM	5.25 FH		20k	
MK53FB(R)	25	ST412/506	2,7 RLL	5.25 FH		20k	
MK53FB	25	ST412/506	MFM	5.25 FH		20k	
MK54FA(R)	25	ST412/506	2,7 RLL	5.25 FH		20k	
MK54FA(M)	30	ST412/506	MFM	5.25 FH		20k	
MK54FB-I	25	ST412/506	MFM	5.25 FH		20k	
MK54FB(M)	25	ST412/506	MFM	5.25 FH		20k	
MK54FB(R)	25	ST412/506	2,7 RLL	5.25 FH		20k	
MK56FA(M)	30	ST412/506	MFM	5.25 FH		20k	
MK56FA(R)	30	ST412/506	2,7 RLL	5.25 FH		20k	
MK56FB-I	25	ST412/506	MFM	5.25 FH		20k	
MK56FB(M)	25	ST412/506	MFM	5.25 FH		20k	
MK56FB(R)	25	ST412/506	2,7 RLL	5.25 FH		20k	
MK72	25	ST412/506	MFM	3.5 HH			
MK72PCR	25	ST412/506	2,7 RLL	3.5 HH			
MK130	25	ST412/506	MFM	3.5 HH		30k	
MK134FA	25	ST412/506	MFM	3.5 HH		30k	
MK134FA(R)	23	ST412/506	2,7 RLL	3.5 HH			
MK153FA	23	ESDI	2,7 RLL	5.25 FH		30k	
MK153FA-I	23	ESDI	2,7 RLL	5.25 FH		30k	
MK153FB	23	SCSI	2,7 RLL	5.25 FH		30k	
MK154FA-I	23	ESDI	2,7 RLL	5.25 FH		30k	
MK154FB	23	SCSI	2,7 RLL	5.25 FH		30k	
MK156FA	23	ESDI	2,7 RLL	5.25 FH		30k	
MK156FB	23	SCSI	2,7 RLL	5.25 FH		30k	
MK232FB	25	SCSI		3.5 HH		30k	
MK232FBS	19	SCSI	2,7 RLL	3.5 HH		30k	3600 N
MK232FC	25	IDE AT	2,7 RLL	3.5 HH		30k	
MK233FB	25	SCSI	2,7 RLL	3.5 HH			30 3600 N
MK234FB	25	SCSI	2,7 RLL	3.5 HH		30k	3600 N
MK234FBS	19	SCSI	2,7 RLL	3.5 HH		30k	
MK234FC	25	IDE AT	2,7 RLL	3.5 HH		30k	3600 N
MK234FCH	25	IDE AT	2,7 RLL	3.5 HH		30k	
MK250FA	18	ESDI	2,7 RLL	5.25 FH		30k	
MK250FB	18	SCSI	2,7 RLL	5.25 FH		30k	
MK286FC	18	HSMD	2,7 RLL	8.00 FH		35k	
MK288FC	18	HSMD	2,7 RLL	8.00 FH		35k	
MK355FA	16	ESDI	2,7 RLL	5.25 FH		30k	
MK355FB	16	SCSI	2,7 RLL	5.25 FH		30k	
MK358FA	16	ESDI	2,7 RLL	5.25 FH		30k	
MK358FB	16	SCSI-2	2,7 RLL	5.25 FH		30k	
MK388FA	18	HSMD	2,7 RLL	8.00 FH		35k	
MK438FB	12	SCSI-2	1,7 RLL	3.5 HH		200	N
MK537FB	12	SCSI-2	1,7 RLL	3.5 HH	512k	200k	N
MK538FB	12	SCSI-2	1,7 RLL	3.5 HH	512k	200k	N
MK556FA	23	ESDI		5.25 FH		30k	
MK1034FC	16	IDE AT	2,7 RLL	3.5 3H		40k	
MD1122FC	23	IDE AT	2,7 RLL	2.5 4H		40k	N
MK2024FC	19	IDE AT	2,7 RLL	2.5 4H		80k	N
MK2124FC	17	IDE AT	2,7 RLL	2.5 4H		80k	N
MKM0351E	25	ST412/506	MFM	5.25 FH		20k	
MKM0351J	25	ST412/506	MFM	5.25 FH		20k	
MKM0352E	30	ST412/506	MFM	5.25 FH		20k	
MKM0352J	30	ST412/506	MFM	5.25 FH		20k	
MKM0353E	25	ST412/506	MFM	5.25 FH		20k	
MKM0353J	25	ST412/506	MFM	5.25 FH		20k	

Drive Model	Format Size MB	Head	Cyl	Sect/Trac	Translate H/C/S	RWC/WPC	Land Zone
MKM0363A	74	5	830	35		NA/NA	AUTO
MKM0363J	74	5	830	35		NA/NA	AUTO
MKM0364A	104	7	830	35		NA/NA	AUTO
MKM0364J	104	7	830	35		NA/NA	AUTO
MKM0381E	36	5	830	17		830/512	
MKM0381J	36	5	830	17		830/512	830
MKM0382E	50	7	830	17		---/512	830
MKM0382J	50	7	830	17		---/512	830
MKM0383E	72	10	830	17		830/512	830
MKM0383J	72	10	830	17		830/512	830

TULIN

Drive Model	Format Size MB	Head	Cyl	Sect/Trac	Translate H/C/S	RWC/WPC	Land Zone
TL213	10	2	640	17		656/656	640
TL226	22	4	640	17		656/656	656
TL238	22	4	640	17		---/NONE	640
TL240	33	6	640	17		656/656	656
TL258	32	6	640	17		---/NONE	640
TL326	22	4	640	17		641/641	640
TL340	33	6	640	17		641/641	640

VERTEX (SEE PRIAM)

WESTERN DIGITAL

Drive Model	Format Size MB	Head	Cyl	Sect/Trac	Translate H/C/S	RWC/WPC	Land Zone
PIRANHA 105A	1104	4				NA/NA	AUTO
PIRANHA 105S	1104	4				NA/NA	AUTO
WD262	20	4	615	17		616/616	616
WD344R	40	4	782	26		783/783	783
WD362	20	4	615	17		616/616	616
WD382R	20	2	782	26		783/783	782
WD383R	30	4	615	17		616/616	616
WD384R	40	4	782	26		783/783	783
WD544R	40	4	782	26		783/783	783
WD562-5	21	4	615	17		---/---	
WD582R	20	2	782	26		783/783	783
WD583R	30	4	615	17		616/616	616
WD584R	40	4	782	26		783/783	783
WDAB130 (TIDBIT)	31	5	733	17		734/734	AUTO
WDAB260 (TIDBIT)	62	4	1020	17		NA/NA	AUTO
WDAC140 (CAVIAR)	42	2	1082	39		NA/NA	AUTO
WDAC160 (CAVIAR)	62	7	1024	17		1023/1023	AUTO
WDAC280 (CAVIAR)	85	10	980	17	10/980/17	NA/NA	981
WDAC1170 (CAVIAR)	170	2	2233	56-96	6/1010/55	NA/NA	AUTO
WDAC2120 (CAVIAR)	125	8	872	35	8/872/35	872/872	AUTO
WDAC2170 (CAVIAR)	171	4	1584	48-56	6/1010/55	NA/NA	AUTO
WDAC2200 (CAVIAR)	213	4	1971	48-56	12/989/35	NA/NA	AUTO
WDAC2250 (CAVIAR)	256	3	2233	56-96	9/1010/55	NA/NA	AUTO
WDAC2340 (CAVIAR)	341	4	2233	56-96	12/1010/55	NA/NA	AUTO
WDAH260 (TIDBIT)	62	4	1024	17		NA/NA	AUTO
WDAH280	86	4	1390	V		NA/NA	AUTO
WDAP2120 (PIRANHA)	125	8	872	35		NA/NA	AUTO
WDAP4200 (PIRANHA)	212	8	1280	41		NA/NA	AUTO
WDMI130-44 (44 PIN)	31	2	920	33		NA/NA	AUTO
WDMI130-72 (72 PIN)	30	2	928	32		NA/NA	AUTO
WDMI4120-72 (72 PIN)	125	8	925	33		NA/NA	AUTO
WDSC8320 (CONDOR)	320	14	949	48		NA/NA	AUTO
WDSC8400 (CONDOR)	400	15	1199	48		NA/NA	AUTO
WDSP2100 (PIRANHA)	104	4	1265	41		NA/NA	AUTO
WDSP4200 (PIRANHA)	209	8	1265	41		NA/NA	AUTO
WDTM262R (TANDON)	20	2	782	26		783/783	784
WDTM364 (TANDON)	41	4	782	26		783/783	784
WD93020-XE1	20	4	615	17		NA/NA	616

Drive Model	Seek Time	Interface	Encode	Form Factor	cache kb	mtbf	RPM	Obsolete?
MKM0363A	23	ESDI	2,7 RLL	5.25 FH		30k		
MKM0363J	23	SCSI	2,7 RLL	5.25 FH		30k		
MKM0364A	23	ESDI	2,7 RLL	5.25 FH		30k		
MKM0364J	23	ESDI	2,7 RLL	5.25 FH		30k		
MKM0381E	25	ST412/506	MFM	5.25 FH		20k		
MKM0381J	25	ST412/506	MFM	5.25 FH		20k		
MKM0382E	30	ST412/506	MFM	5.25 FH		20k		
MKM0382J	30	ST412/506	MFM	5.25 FH		20k		
MKM0383E	25	ST412/506	MFM	5.25 FH		20k		
MKM0383J	25	ST412/506	MFM	5.25 FH		20k		

TULIN

Drive Model	Seek Time	Interface	Encode	Form Factor	cache kb	mtbf	RPM	Obsolete?
TL213		ST412/506	MFM	5.25				Y
TL226	85	ST412/506	MFM	5.25				Y
TL238		ST412/506	MFM	5.25				Y
TL240	85	ST412/506	MFM	5.25				Y
TL258		ST412/506	MFM	5.25				Y
TL326	40	ST412/506	MFM	5.25				Y
TL340	40	ST412/506	MFM	5.25				Y

VERTEX (SEE PRIAM)

WESTERN DIGITAL

Drive Model	Seek Time	Interface	Encode	Form Factor	cache kb	mtbf	RPM	Obsolete?
PIRANHA 105A	15	IDE AT	2,7 RLL	3.5 HH		50k		
PIRANHA 105S	15	SCSI	2,7 RLL	3.5 HH		50k		
WD262	80	ST412/506	MFM	3.5 HH				Y
WD344R	40	ST412/506	2,7 RLL	3.5 HH				Y
WD362	80	ST412/506	MFM	3.5 HH				Y
WD382R	85	ST412/506	2,7 RLL	3.5 HH				Y
WD383R	85	ST412/506	2,7 RLL	3.5 HH				Y
WD384R	85	ST412/506	2,7 RLL	3.5 HH				Y
WD544R	40	ST412/506	2,7 RLL	3.5 HH				Y
WD562-5	80	ST412/506	MFM	3.5 HH		40k		
WD582R	85	ST412/506	2,7 RLL	3.5 HH				Y
WD583R	85	ST412/506	2,7 RLL	3.5 HH				Y
WD584R	85	ST412/506	2,7 RLL	3.5 HH				Y
WDAB130 (TIDBIT)	19	IDE AT-XT	2,7 RLL	2.50 4H	32k			N
WDAB260 (TIDBIT)	19	IDE XT-AT	2,7 RLL	2.5 4H		50k		N
WDAC140 (CAVIAR)	18	IDE AT	2,7 RLL	3.5 3H	32k	50k		N
WDAC160 (CAVIAR)	17	IDE AT	2,7 RLL	3.5 3H			3605	N
WDAC280 (CAVIAR)	18	IDE AT	2,7 RLL	3.5 3H	32k	100k	3595	N
WDAC1170 (CAVIAR)	13	IDE AT	1,7 RLL	3.5 3H	32k	200k	3322	N
WDAC2120 (CAVIAR)	15	IDE AT	2,7 RLL	3.5 3H	32k	100k	3600	N
WDAC2170 (CAVIAR)	14	IDE AT	2,7 RLL	3.5 3H	32k	100k	3652	N
WDAC2200 (CAVIAR)	14	IDE AT	2,7 RLL	3.5 3H	64k	100k	3652	N
WDAC2250 (CAVIAR)	13	IDE AT	1,7 RLL	3.5 3H	64k	250k	3322	N
WDAC2340 (CAVIAR)	13	IDE AT	1,7 RLL	3.5 3H	64k	200k	3322	N
WDAH260 (TIDBIT)	19	IDE XT-AT	2,7 RLL	2.5 4H		50k	3383	N
WDAH280	19	IDE XT-AT	2,7 RLL	2.5 4H		50k		N
WDAP2120 (PIRANHA)	15	IDE AT	2,7 RLL	3.5 3H		100k	3605	N
WDAP4200 (PIRANHA)	14	IDE AT	2,7 RLL	3.5 HH	64k	50k		N
WDMI130-44 (44 PIN)	19	MCA	RLL	3.5 3H		45k		Y
WDMI130-72 (72 PIN)	19	MCA	RLL	3.5 3H		45k		Y
WDMI4120-72 (72 PIN)	23	MCA	2,7 RLL	3.5 3H		45k		Y
WDSC8320 (CONDOR)	12	SCSI-2	1,7 RLL	3.5 HH	64k	150k	4316	N
WDSC8400 (CONDOR)	16	SCSI-2	1,7 RLL	3.5 HH	128k	150k	4316	N
WDSP2100 (PIRANHA)	14	SCSI-2	2,7 RLL	3.5 HH	64k	50k		N
WDSP4200 (PIRANHA)	14	SCSI-2	2,7 RLL	3.5 HH	64k	50k		N
WDTM262R (TANDON)	85	ST412/506	2,7 RLL	3.5 HH				Y
WDTM364 (TANDON)	85	ST412/506	2,7 RLL	3.5 HH				Y
WD93020-XE1	85	IDE XT	2,7 RLL	3.5 HH				Y

Drive Model	Format Size MB	Head	Cyl	Sect/ Trac	Translate H/C/S	RWC/ WPC	Land Zone
WD93024-A	21	2	782	27		NA/NA	783
WD93024-X	21	2	782	27		NA/NA	783
WD93028-A	21	2	782	27		NA/NA	783
WD93028-AD	21	2	782	27		NA/NA	783
WD93028-X	21	2	782	27		NA/NA	783
WD93034-X	32	3	782	27		NA/NA	783
WD93038-X	32	3	782	27		NA/NA	783
WD93044-A	43	4	782	27		NA/NA	783
WD93044-X	43	4	782	27		NA/NA	862
WD93048-A	40	4	782	27		NA/NA	783
WD93048-AD	43	4	782	27		NA/NA	783
WD93048-X	43	4	782	27		NA/NA	783
WD95024-A	21	2	782	27		783/783	783
WD95024-X	21	2	782	27		NA/NA	783
WD95028-A	20	2	782	27		783/783	783
WD95028-AD	21	2	782	27		783/783	783
WD95028-X	20	2	782	27		NA/NA	783
WD95034-X	32	3	782	27		783/783	783
WD95038-X	30	3	782	27		NA/NA	783
WD95044-A	43	4	782	27	4/782/27	783/783	783
WD95044-X	43	4	782	27	4/782/27	783/783	783
WD95048-A	40	4	782	27	4/782/27	NA/NA	783
WD95048-AD	43	4	782	27	4/782/27	NA/NA	783
WD95048-X	40	4	782	27	4/782/27	NA/NA	783

XEBEC

Drive Model	Format Size MB	Head	Cyl	Sect/ Trac	Translate H/C/S	RWC/ WPC	Land Zone
OWL I	25	4				---/---	
OWL II	38	4				---/---	
OWL III	52	4				---/---	

Y-E DATA AMERICA, INC

Drive Model	Format Size MB	Head	Cyl	Sect/ Trac	Translate H/C/S	RWC/ WPC	Land Zone
YD3042	43	4	788	28		789/789	AUTO
YD3081B	45	2	1057	42		NA/NA	AUTO
YD3082	87	8	788	28		789/789	AUTO
YD3082B	90	4	1057	42		NA/NA	AUTO
YD3083B	136	6	1057	42		NA/NA	AUTO
YD3084B	181	8	1057	42		NA/NA	AUTO
YD3161B	45	2	1057	42		NA/NA	AUTO
YD3162B	90	4	1057	42		NA/NA	AUTO
YD3181B	45	2	1057	42		NA/NA	AUTO
YD3182B	90	4	1057	42		NA/NA	AUTO
YD3530	32	5	731	17		732/732	AUTO
YD3540	42	7	733	32		732/732	AUTO
YD3541	45	8	731	15		732/732	AUTO

Drive Model	Seek Time	Interface	Encode	Form Factor	cache kb	mtbf	RPM	Obsolete?
WD93024-A	28	IDE AT	2,7 RLL	3.5 HH		40k		Y
WD93024-X	39	IDE XT	2,7 RLL	3.5 HH		40k		Y
WD93028-A	70	IDE AT	2,7 RLL	3.5 HH	1k	50k		Y
WD93028-AD	69	IDE AT	2,7 RLL	3.5 HH		40k		Y
WD93028-X	70	IDE XT	2,7 RLL	3.5 HH		40k		Y
WD93034-X	39	IDE XT	2,7 RLL	3.5 HH		40k		Y
WD93038-X	70	IDE XT	2,7 RLL	3.5 HH	1k	50k		Y
WD93044-A	28	IDE AT	2,7 RLL	3.5 HH		40k		Y
WD93044-X	39	IDE XT	2,7 RLL	3.5 HH	1k	50k		Y
WD93048-A	69	IDE AT	2,7 RLL	3.5 HH		40k		Y
WD93048-AD	69	IDE AT	2,7 RLL	3.5 HH		40k		Y
WD93048-X	70	IDE XT	2,7 RLL	3.5 HH		40k		Y
WD95024-A	28	IDE AT	2,7 RLL	5.25 HH		40k		Y
WD95024-X	39	IDE XT	2,7 RLL	3.5 HH	1k	50k		Y
WD95028-A	70	IDE AT	2,7 RLL	5.25 HH		40k		Y
WD95028-AD	69	IDE AT	2,7 RLL	5.25 HH		40k		Y
WD95028-X	70	IDE XT	2,7 RLL	5.25 HH		40k		Y
WD95034-X	39	IDE XT	2,7 RLL	3.5 HH	1k	50k		Y
WD95038-X	70	IDE XT	2,7 RLL	5.25 HH		40k		Y
WD95044-A	28	IDE AT	2,7 RLL	5.25 HH		40k		Y
WD95044-X	39	IDE XT	2,7 RLL	3.5 HH	1k	50k		Y
WD95048-A	70	IDE AT	2,7 RLL	5.25 HH		40k		Y
WD95048-AD	69	IDE AT	2,7 RLL	5.25 HH		40k		Y
WD95048-X	70	IDE XT	2,7 RLL	5.25 HH		40k		Y

XEBEC

Drive Model	Seek Time	Interface	Encode	Form Factor	cache kb	mtbf	RPM	Obsolete?
OWL I	55	SCSI	MFM	5.25 HH				
OWL II	40	SCSI	MFM	5.25 HH				
OWL III	38	SCSI	MFM	5.25 HH				

Y-E DATA AMERICA, INC

Drive Model	Seek Time	Interface	Encode	Form Factor	cache kb	mtbf	RPM	Obsolete?
YD3042	28	SCSI	2,7 RLL	3.5 HH		40k		Y
YD3081B	28	SCSI	2,7 RLL	3.5 HH		30k		
YD3082	28	SCSI	2,7 RLL	3.5 HH		40k		Y
YD3082B	28	SCSI	2,7 RLL	3.5 HH		30k		
YD3083B	28	SCSI	2,7 RLL	3.5 HH		30k		
YD3084B	28	SCSI	2,7 RLL	3.5 HH		30k		
YD3161B	19	IDE AT	2,7 RLL	3.5 3H		40k		
YD3162B	19	IDE AT	2,7 RLL	3.5 3H		40k		
YD3181B	19	SCSI	2,7 RLL	3.5 3H		40k		
YD3182B	19	SCSI	2,7 RLL	3.5 3H		40k		
YD3530	26	ST412/506	MFM	3.5 HH				
YD3540	29	ST412/506	MFM	3.5 HH		20k	3600	
YD3541	29	SCSI	2,7 RLL	3.5 HH		20k	3600	

Hard Drive Specifications Notes

Information contained in the hard drive section was derived from numerous sources, including the manufacturers of the drives. When compiling tables this large, the chance for typing and resource error is great. The authors and publisher would greatly appreciate being notified of any inaccurate or missing information. Some of the older drives (especially those from companies who have gone out of business) are very difficult to obtain accurate and verifiable specifications for. If you have access to old specification sheets, etc please send us a copy so that we may add the information to future editions.

The following are important resources:

ONTRACK Computer Systems Disk Manager Series
   Eden Prairie, Minnesota, 1985 to 1990
The Hard Disk Technical Guide by Douglas T. Anderson
   PCS Publications, Clearwater, FL, 1990, 1991
The Micro House Encyclopedia of Hard Drives edited
   by Douglas T. Anderson, Boulder, CO, 1990,1991,1992
Numerous public domain and BBS hard drive listings.
SpeedStor Hard Disk Preparation/Diagnostics
   Storage Dimensions, 1985, 1988
Numerous manufacturer specification sheets
Reseller's Resource - Hard Drives, Volume 2, No 1
   Technology Publishing, Inc, Livonia, MI   January 1990
Buyer's Guide-Hard Drives 40MB to 400MB
   Computer Shopper, March 1990
THEREF by F. Robert Falbo, Rome, New York, 1991
Western Digital BBS Listing, 6-6-91

POCKET PCRef

Floppy Drive Specifications

Sequoia needs your help! If you have specifications on new or obsolete floppy drives, please send them to us for future editions of PCRef.

GENERAL FLOPPY DRIVE SPECS

Formatted Capacity	Sides	Tracks	Sectors	ID Byte	Media Type*	Doping Agent
5-1/4 inch diameter						
160 k	1	40	8	FE	SSDD	Ferite
180 k	1	40	9	FC	SSDD	Ferite
320 k	2	40	8	FF	DSDD	Ferite
360 k	2	40	9	FD	DSDD	Ferite
1.2 meg	2	80	15	F9	DSHD	Cobalt
3-1/2 inch diameter						
720 k	2	80	9	F9	DSDD	Cobalt
1.44 meg	2	80	18	F0	DSHD	Cobalt
2.8 meg	2	80	36		DSEHD	Barium

* SS=Single Sided, DS=Double Sided
  DD=Double Density
  HD=High Density
  EHD=Extra High Density

Maximum Entries in the Root Directory:
  5-1/4 DD and 3.5 DD = 112 Entries
  5-1/4 HD and 3.5 HD = 224 Entries
  3.5 EHD = 240 Entries

All floppy drives currently produced rotate at 300 RPM, except for the 1.2meg, 5-1/4 HD drives, which rotate at 360 RPM.

All floppy drives are formatted at 512 Bypes Per Sector.

Floppys have 2 FATs, 12 Bit Type

Sequoia needs your help! If you have specifications on new or obsolete floppy drives, please send them to us for future editions of PCRef.

FLOPPY DRIVE SPECS BY MODEL

Manufacturer	Model Number	Width (Inch)	Height (Inch)	Format Capacity	Comments

Sequoia needs your help! If you have specifications on new or obsolete floppy drives, please send them to us for future editions of PCRef.

Manufacturer	Model Number	Width (Inch)	Height (Inch)	Format Capacity	Comments
Alps Electric	DFL713A	3.50	Half	1.4Mb	
	FDD2124	5.25	Half	180Kb	
Aurora Tech	FD350 (SCSI)	3.50	Half		
	FD525 (SCSI)	5.25	Half		
Cannon	531	5.25	Half	360Kb	
	5501	5.25	Half		
CDC	9409	5.25	Full	360Kb	
	BR8B1A	5.25	Full	360Kb	
Chinon.....	C354	3.50	Half	720Kb	
	FX354	3.50	1.0"	720Kb	
	FZ357	3.50	1.0"	1.4Mb	
	C359	3.50	Half	1.4Mb	
	F, FZ, C502	5.25	Half	360Kb	
	C506	5.25	Half	1.2Mb	
Epson	SMD-1040	3.50	0.7"	1.4Mb	
	SMD-1060	3.50	0.7"	2.8Mb	
	SMD-340	3.50	1.0"	1.4Mb	
	SMD-349	3.50	Half	1.4Mb	
	SMD-380	3.50	1.0"	720Kb	
	SMD-389	3.50	Half	720Kb	
	SD-520	5.25	Half	360Kb	
	SD-521	5.25	Half	360Kb	
	SD-581	5.25	Half		
	SD-621L	5.25	Half	360Kb	
	SD-680L	5.25	Half	1.2Mb	Dual speed
Fuji/Toshiba	FDD4206A0K	3.50	Half	720Kb	
	FDD4216G0K	3.50	1.0"	720Kb	
	FDD5452B0K	5.25	Half	360Kb	
	FDD6471L0K	5.25	Half	360Kb	
Fujitsu	M2551A	5.25	Half	360Kb	
	M2553A,K	3.50	Half	1.4Mb	

FLOPPY DRIVE SPECS BY MODEL

Manufacturer	Model Number	Width (Inch)	Height (Inch)	Format Capacity	Comments
Mitsubishi ..	MF353B,C	3.50	Half	720Kb	
	MF355A,B,C	3.50	1.0"	1.4Mb	
	M4851	5.25	Half	360Kb	
	M4852	5.25	Full	360Kb	
	M4854	5.25	Half	1.2Mb	
	MF501A,B	5.25	Half	360Kb	
	MF504A,B	5.25	Half	1.2Mb	Dual speed
Mitsumi		3.50		720Kb	
		3.50		1.4Mb	
	D503V	5.25	Half	360Kb	
	D509V	5.25	Half	1.2Mb	
MPI	51-S	5.25	Full	180Kb	
	52-S	5.25	Full	360Kb	
NEC........	FD-1157C	5.25	Half	1.2Mb	Dual speed
Olivetti	XM4311	5.25	Half	360Kb	
Pacific Rim..	U1.44	3.50		1.4Mb	
	U4	3.50	1.0"	2.8Mb	
	U720	3.50		720Kb	
	U1.2	5.25	Half	1.2Mb	
	U360	5.25	Half	360Kb	
Panasonic ..	JU257	3.5	1.0	1.4Mb	
	JU455	5.25	Half	360Kb	
	JU475	5.25	Half	1.2Mb	
Qume	142	5.25	Half	360Kb	
	542	5.25	Full	360Kb	
Sanyo	FDA-5200	5.25	Half	360Kb	
Shugart	SA400L	5.25	Full	180Kb	
	SA455	5.25	Half	360Kb	
	SA460	5.25	Full	360Kb	
Siemens	FDD100-5	5.25	Full	180Kb	
Tandon	65-8	5.25	Half	1.2Mb	
	TM100-1A	5.25	Full	180Kb	
	TM100-2A	5.25	Full	360Kb	
	TM965-2	5.25	Full	360Kb	

FLOPPY DRIVE SPECS BY MODEL

Manufacturer	Model Number	Width (Inch)	Height (Inch)	Format Capacity	Comments
Teac	FD-235F	3.50	1.0"	720Kb	
	FD-235HF	3.50	1.0"	1.4Mb	
	FD-235HS	3.50	1.0"	1.4Mb	* SCSI *
	FD-235J	3.50	1.0"	2.9Mb	Vert.rec. reads reg.
	FD-235JS	3.50	1.0"	2.9Mb	* SCSI *
	FD-335F	3.50	0.75"	720Kb	
	FD-335HF	3.50	0.75"	1.4Mb	
	FD-335HS	3.50	0.75"	1.4Mb	* SCSI *
	FD-335J	3.50	0.75"	2.9Mb	Vert.rec. reads reg.
	FD-335JS	3.50	0.75"	2.9Mb	Vert/reg. * SCSI *
	FD-50A	5.25	Full	180Kb	
	FD-54B	5.25	Half	360Kb	
	FD-55A	5.25	Half	180Kb	1-Side
	FD-55B	5.25	Half	360Kb	
	FD-55BR	5.25	Half	360kb	
	FD-55E	5.25	Half	360Kb	1-Side
	FD-55GFR	5.25	Half	1.2Mb	Dual speed
	FD-55GR	5.25	Half	1.2Mb	
	FD-55GS	5.25	Half	1.2Mb	Dual speed * SCSI *
	FD-505	5.25/3.5 Half		1.2Mb/1.4Mb	Combo
	FB501	5.25	Half	180Kb	
Toshiba	ND-352T,S	3.50	1.0"	720Kb	
	ND-354A	3.50	1.0"	720Kb	
	ND-356T,Y,S	3.50	1.0"	1.4Mb	
	PD-211	3.50	1.0"	2.9Mb	Vert.rec. r/w reg.s
	ND-04DEG	5.25	Half	360Kb	
	ND-04DT	5.25	Half	360Kb	
	ND-0801DEG	5.25	Half	1.2Mb	Dual speed

FLOPPY DRIVE SPECS BY MODEL

Manufacturer	Model Number	Width (Inch)	Height (Inch)	Format Capacity	Comments
NON DOS Floppy Drives					
DEC Operating system (not IBM or MSDOS compatible)					
AT&T.......	KS-23144	5.25	Half	720k	
Fujitsu	M2552A	5.25	Half	720k	
Mitsubishi ..	4853	5.25	Half	720k	
Seiko.......	8640	5.25	Half	720k	
8" Floppy Drives					
Mitsubishi ..	2896-63	8.00	Half		
NEC........	FD-1165FQ	8.00	Half		
Qume	842	8.00	Full		1-Side
Shugart.....	SA800-1	8.00	Full		1-Side
	SA800-2	8.00	Full		1-Side
	SA860	8.00	Half		
	SA900-1	8.00	Full		1-Side
Tandon	848-02	8.00	Half		

POCKET PCRef

PC Industry
Phone Book

Want to Register in the
PC Industry Phone Book?
Call 1-800-873-7126
Sequoia Publishing, Inc
For
Pricing and Availability.

Company and :State	Main Phone	Tech Phone
1776 Inc :CA	(310) 215-1776	(310) 216-4398
1st Intl Computer Of America :CA	(510) 475-7885	
3Com Corp :CA	(800) 876-3266	(800) 876-3266
	BBS (408) 980-8204	
3D Visions Coroporation :CA	(800) 729-4723	
3E Corporation :MA	(800) 682-5175	
3G Graphics :	(800) 456-0234	(800) 456-0234
3M Corp :MN	(800) 263-3456	(800) 362-3455
3M Electrical Products Division :TX	(800) 225-5373	
3PM Inc :IA	(319) 393-7932	
7-Sigma :MN	(612) 721-4280	
A Bit Better Software Publishing :WA	(206) 627-6111	
A C Technology :CA	(714) 228-1633	
A Cad-Group :GA	(404) 315-8901	
A J Computer Supplies :CA	(714) 895-5802	
A-Comm Electronics :	(201) 334-3017	
A-Matic International Inc :CA	(818) 855-8888	
A.C. Pwerline :NY	(716) 288-6870	
AA Computech :CA	(800) 360-6801	(805) 257-6804
AAA International Co :CA	(714) 951-0747	
Aadtech Micro Systems Inc :CA	(415) 659-0756	
Aamazing Technologies :CA	(714) 255-1688	
ABA Systems/USA, Inc :UT	(801) 561-8681	
Abacus Accounting Systems Inc :AB	(403) 489-5994	
Abacus Concepts :CA	(510) 540-1949	(510) 540-1949
	BBS (616) 698-8106	
Abacus Concepts + :MI	(800) 666-7828	
Abaton :	(800) 821-0806	(510) 498-4433
	BBS (510) 438-4650	
Abbeon Cal :CA	(800) 922-0977	
Abbott Systems :	(800) 552-9157	(914) 747-4171
ABC Computer Corp :CA	(310) 325-4005	
ABC Products :CA	(714) 373-9898	
ABC Systems & Development Inc :MA	(508) 463-8602	
Aberdeen :CA	(800) 552-6868	(213) 725-3360
ABL Electronics Corp :MD	(410) 584-2700	
Above Dariana Software Inc :CA	(800) 892-9950	
Above Software, Inc. :CA	(800) 344-0116	(714) 851-2283
Abra Cadabra Software :FL	(813) 525-4400	
Abra MacDabra Software :CA	(408) 737-9454	
Abracadata :OR	(800) 451-4871	(503) 342-3030
Abrams Creative Services :CA	(818) 343-6365	
ABS Computer Technologies :CA	(800) 876-8088	(800) 876-8088
AC & DC :CA	(818) 336-1388	
ACC - Alamo City Computer :TX	(512) 545-1010	
ACC Microelectronics Corp :CA	(408) 980-0622	
Access Computer Components :TX	(800) 332-3778	(214) 380-8010
Access Software :UT	(800) 800-4880	(800) 793-8324
Access Technology, Inc :MA	(508) 655-9191	
Acco USA Inc :IL	(708) 541-9500	

Company and :State	Main Phone	Tech Phone
Accolade :....................	(800) 245-7744	(408) 296-8400
.... BBS	(408) 296-8800	
Accountants Microsystems, Inc :...	(206) 643-2050	
Accton Technology Corp :CA	(800) 926-9288	(510) 226-9800
.... BBS	(510) 226-9832	
Accufast Products :NY	(800) 447-9990	
Acculogic Inc :CA..............	(714) 454-2441	
AccuTel, Inc :CA	(707) 778-7182	
Ace Software Corp :CA	(408) 451-0100	(408) 451-0112
Acecad Inc :CA	(408) 655-1900	
Acer America Corp :CA	(800) 733-2237	
.... BBS	(800) 833-8241	
Acer Peripheral/ASIC Bus. Group :NJ	(609) 924-1153	
Achieva Computer :CA	(800) 388-2918	(408) 894-0200
Acius, Inc :CA................	(408) 252-4444	(408) 252-4444
ACL Inc :IL	(800) 782-8420	
ACM Inc :MD	(800) 342-6626	
Acme Electric Corp :NY	(716) 968-2400	
Across The Ocean Import Export :ON	(415) 660-7804	
Action Communication Inc :MN	(612) 636-3559	
Action Electronics Co Ltd :CA	(818) 813-1500	
Action Multimedia :CA	(800) 322-3132	
Action Plus Software Inc :UT	(801) 255-0600	(801) 255-0600
ACTIVISILIN :CA	(310) 207-4500	
Activision :CA	(310) 207-4500	(310) 207-4500
Actix Systems Inc :CA	(800) 927-5557	
Acucobol Inc :CA	(800) 262-6585	
Acumos Inc :CA	(415) 570-0535	
Acxiom Corp :AZ	(501) 329-6836	
AD Costas Projects :CA.........	(415) 462-3111	(415) 426-5040
Ad Lib Inc :MA	(800) 463-2686	(418) 529-6252
Ad Lib Multimedia Inc :PQ	(418) 529-9676	
AD Research :CA	(800) 926-7365	(800) 873-7365
Adaptec :CA..................	(408) 945-8600	(800) 959-7274
.... BBS	(408) 945-7727	
ADDA Technologies Inc :CA	(510) 770-9899	
Addison-Wesley Publishing :CA ...	(800) 447-2226	
ADDS :NY	(800) 645-5406	
AddStor Inc :CA	(800) 732-3133	(415) 688-0471
.... BBS	(415) 324-4077	
AddTech Group :CA.............	(510) 623-7583	
ADI Systems, Inc :CA	(800) 228-0530	
ADI/Execufold :CA	(209) 683-2126	
ADIC :WA	(206) 881-8004	
Adisoft Inc :CA	(510) 483-5605	
Adobe Systems, Inc :CA	(800) 833-6687	(800) 292-3623
AdRem Technologies :ON	(416) 886-7899	
Adtran/PTT :AL	(205) 971-8000	
Adv. Institutional Mgmt. Soft. :NY .	(516) 496-7700	

Company and :State	Main Phone	Tech Phone
Advanced Computer Cable :FL	(800) 626-3608	
Advanced Computer Innovations :NY	(716) 383-1939	
Advanced Computer Techniques :NY	(212) 679-4040	
Advanced Digital Systems :CA	(800) 888-5244	
Advanced Electr. Support Product :FL	(800) 446-2377	
Advanced Gravis :WA	(800) 663-8558	(604) 431-1807
Advanced Gravis Computer :BC	(604) 431-5020	
Advanced Hardware Architecture :ID	(208) 883-8000	(208) 883-8001
Advanced Input Devices :ID	(208) 765-8000	
Advanced Integration Research :CA	(408) 428-0800	
Advanced Logic Research, Inc :CA	(800) 444-4257	(714) 458-1952
	BBS (714) 458-6834	
Advanced Matrix Technology :CA	(800) 637-7878	
Advanced Micro Computer Syst :DE	(800) 866-0829	(302) 368-9300
Advanced Micro Devices :CA	(408) 732-2400	
Advanced Micro Technology :CA	(714) 598-6120	
Advanced Microcomputer Syst :FL	(305) 784-0900	
Advanced Network :CA	(408) 779-2209	
Advanced Software :	(800) 346-5392	(800) 346-5392
Advanced Technologies :CA	(408) 942-1780	
Advanced Technologies & Services :CA	(310) 676-0487	(310) 676-0487
Advanced Vision Research :CA	(800) 544-6243	
Adweeks Marketing Computers :NY	(800) 722-6658	
AEC Management :	(800) 346-9413	(703) 450-2318
AER Energy Resources Inc :GA	(404) 433-2127	
AESP Inc :FL	(305) 944-7710	
Aetech :CA	(619) 755-1277	
Affinity :CO	(800) 367-6771	(303) 442-4840
After Hours Software :	(818) 780-2220	(818) 780-2220
AgData :CA	(209) 784-5500	
AGE Logic Inc :CA	(619) 455-8600	
Agfa Division :NY	(914) 365-0190	
Agfa Division :MA	(800) 424-8973	(800) 937-7787
Ags Computers :NJ	(908) 654-4321	
AGSADIVISION :MA	(508) 658-5600	
Ahead Systems Inc :CA	(510) 623-0900	
AI Today :WV	(304) 965-5548	
Aicom Corp :CA	(408) 453-8251	
Aim Motherboard Corp :NY	(800) 786-2566	
Aim Tech :	(603) 883-0220	(603) 883-0220
AIQ Systems :NV	(800) 332-2999	(702) 831-2999
Aitech International :CA	(800) 882-8184	
AJM, Inc :CA	(408) 980-8631	
AJS Publishing :CA	(310) 215-9145	
AI Expert Magazine :CA	(415) 905-2200	
Alacrity Systems Inc :NJ	(908) 813-2400	
Aladdin Software Security :NY	(516) 424-5100	
Aladdin Systems :CA	(408) 761-6200	
Alamo Components :TX	(800) 890-8800	
Aldridge Company, The :TX	(800) 548-5019	

Company and :State	Main Phone	Tech Phone
Aldus Corp :WA	(800) 685-3540	(206) 628-2320
Alexander Batteries :IA	(515) 423-8955	
Alf Products Inc :CO	(800) 321-4668	
ALfa Power Inc :CA	(818) 937-6529	
Alisa Systems :CA	(800) 992-5472	
Alki Software Corp :WA	(206) 286-2600	
All Computers :OT	(800) 387-2744	
	BBS (416) 960-8679	
All Electronics :CA	(818) 904-0524	
Allegro Microsystems Inc :MA	(508) 853-5000	
Allen Communication, Inc :UT	(801) 537-7800	
AllMicro :FL	(800) 653-4933	
Alloy Computer Products :	(508) 481-8200	(508) 486-0900
	BBS (508) 460-8140	
Allsop Inc :WA	(206) 734-9090	
Allstate Office Supply Corp :CA	(714) 692-9100	
Alltech Electronics :CA	(714) 543-5011	
Alltel Corp :OH	(216) 650-7000	
Alpha Research Corp :TX	(512) 836-0709	
Alpha Software Corp :MA	(800) 451-1018	(617) 272-3680
	BBS (617) 229-2915	
Alpha Systems Lab, Inc :CA	(714) 252-0117	
Alpha Technologies :WA	(206) 647-2360	
Alpha Wire Corp :NJ	(908) 925-8000	
Alps America :CA	(800) 950-2577	(800) 825-2577
Alsoft :	(800) 257-6381	(713) 353-1510
Alsys :MA	(617) 270-0030	
Altec Lansing Consumer Prod :PA	(717) 296-1272	
Altech Inc :MO	(314) 576-5100	
Alternative Computer Products :TX	(805) 522-4984	
Altex Electronics (Austin) :TX	(512) 832-9131	
Altex Electronics (Corp) :TX	(512) 655-8882	
Altex Electronics (Dallas) :TX	(214) 386-8882	
Altex Electronics (Mail Order) :TX	(800) 531-5369	
Altex Electronics (San Antonio) :TX	(512) 655-8882	
Altima Systems, Inc :CA	(800) 356-9990	
	BBS (510) 356-2456	
Altos Computer Systems :CA	(800) 258-6787	
Altron, Inc :MN	(800) 678-8802	
Altsys :	(214) 680-2060	(214) 680-2093
	BBS (214) 680-8592	
Altus Systems :CA	(800) 522-5887	(909) 598-7769
Aluminum Filter Company :CA	(805) 684-7651	
Alumni Computer Group :NY	(800) 387-9785	
Always Technology Corp :CA	(818) 597-1400	
Alywa Computer Corp :TX	(713) 440-1393	
AM Electronics, Inc (AME) :MA	(408) 955-9666	
Ama Inc :ON.	(416) 897-2153	
Amatix Inc :CA	(800) 869-0744	
Amax Applied Technology Inc :CA	(818) 300-8828	

Company and :State	Main Phone	Tech Phone
Amax Engineering Corp :CA	(800) 888-2629	
AMAZEI, Inc :WA	(800) 367-4802	(206) 820-4102
AMBI Circuit Board Electronics :MA	(800) 879-2624	
Ambra Computer Corp :NC	(800) 252-6272	
Amcom Corporation :MN	(800) 328-7723	
Amdahl Corp :CA	(800) 538-8460	
Amdek :CA	(800) 722-6335	(800) 800-9973
Amdek Corporation :CA	BBS (408) 922-4400	
AME, Inc :CA	(800) 955-9666	
AMEC Computer Ergonom DL :CA	(800) 759-5060	
Americal Group Computer Products :CA	(800) 288-8025	(818) 765-3887
American Business System :MA	(508) 250-9600	
American Computer Engineers :CA	(619) 587-9002	
American Computer Express :FL	(800) 533-4604	
American Computer Hardware Corp :CA	(800) 447-1237	
American Computer Repair Inc :PA	(211) 539-1010	
American Computer Resources :CT	(203) 380-4600	
American Covers, Inc :UT	(800) 228-8987	
American Cybernetics :AZ	(800) 221-9280	
	BBS (602) 968-1082	
American Databankers :CA	(800) 323-7767	
American Digicom Corp :CA	(408) 245-1580	
American Digital :MA	(617) 449-9292	
American Educational Services :VA	(703) 256-5315	
American Enhance Inc :CA	(510) 438-9180	
American Fundware, Inc :CO	(800) 551-4458	
American Healthware Systems :NY	(718) 435-6300	
American Ink Jet Corp :MA	(508) 667-0600	
American Laubscher Corp :NY	(516) 694-5900	
American Magnetics Corp :CA	(213) 775-8651	
American Management Systems :VA	(800) 826-4395	
American Megatrends, Inc :GA	(800) 828-9264	(404) 263-8181
	BBS (404) 246-8780	
American Microsystems :TX	(800) 648-4452	
American Power Conversion :RI	(800) 800-4272	(401) 789-5735
American ProImage, Inc :CA	(310) 949-9797	
American Reliance Inc :CA	(800) 654-9838	
American Research Corp :CA	(800) 423-3877	
American Ribbon :FL	(800) 327-1013	
American Services Resources :CA	(800) 333-1157	
American Small Business Computer :OK	(918) 825-4844	(918) 825-4844
American Software, Inc :GA	(404) 261-4381	(404) 261-4381
American Suntek Intl Corp :CA	(800) 888-7813	
American Systec Corp :CA	(714) 993-0882	
American Trader's Post :MD	(301) 695-8438	
Ameritech :IL	(312) 750-5000	
Ames Supply Company :IL	(800) 323-3856	
Ameteck, Inc :NY	(212) 935-8640	
Amherst International Corp :NH	(800) 547-5600	
Amita Corp :TX	(512) 218-8857	

Company and :State	Main Phone	Tech Phone
Amkly Systems Inc :CA	(714) 727-0788	
AMP :PA	(800) 522-6752	
Ampex :CA	(310) 640-0150	(310) 640-0150
Amphenol Canada Corp :ON	(416) 291-4401	
Amplicom :CA	(619) 693-9127	
Ampro Computers, Inc :CA	(800) 966-5200	(408) 522-2100
Amprobe Instrument :NY	(516) 593-5600	
Amptron International Inc :CA	(818) 912-5789	
AmRam :CA	(408) 559-0603	
Amrel Technology Inc :CA	(818) 575-5110	
AMRIS Training Systems :TX	(800) 842-3693	
AMS :CA	(800) 886-2671	(800) 886-3536
Amstrad Inc :TX	(800) 999-0174	
AMT International :CA	(408) 432-1790	
Amtec Computer Services :IA	(515) 270-2480	
AmTech Organization Inc :MA	(617) 344-1550	
Amtron Inc :CA	(213) 721-1717	
Anacapa Micro Products Inc :CA	(805) 339-0305	
Anacom General Corp :CA	(714) 774-8080	
Anacomp, Inc :IN	(317) 844-9666	
Analog & Digital Peripherals Inc :OH	(513) 339-2241	
Analog Devices, Inc :MA	(800) 426-2564	
Analog Technology Center Inc :NH	(603) 673-0404	
Analog Technology Corp :CA	(818) 357-0098	
Analogic Corp. :MA	(800) 343-8333	
Analysts Intl Corp :MN	(800) 328-9929	
Analytical Software :WA	(206) 362-2855	
AnaTek Corporation :NH	(800) 999-0304	
Ancot Corp :CA	(415) 322-5322	
Anderson Bell :CO	(303) 940-0595	
Andgate Systems Corp :CA	(714) 468-3084	
Ando Corporation :MD	(301) 294-3365	
Andor Systems Inc :CA	(408) 996-9010	
Andrew Corp :CA	(310) 320-7126	
Andromeda Systems Inc :CA	(818) 709-7600	
Angelica Uniform Group :MO	(800) 222-3112	
Angia Communications :UT	(801) 288-0488	
Anix Tech Corp :CA	(408) 737-9935	
Anixter Brothers Inc :IL	(708) 677-2600	
Anjene International :NJ	(908) 704-0304	
Ann Arbor Software :MI	(800) 345-6777	
Answer Computer :CA	(800) 677-2679	
AnswerSet Corporation :CA	(408) 996-8683	
Antec, Inc :CA	(510) 770-9591	(510) 770-9590
Antex Electronics Corp :CA	(310) 532-3092	
Anthes Universal Inc :AZ	(800) 828-0308	
Anthro Co :OR	(800) 325-3841	
Anvil Cases :CA	(800) 359-2684	
AOC International (USA) Ltd :TN	(800) 443-7516	
Aox Inc :MA	(800) 232-1269	(800) 726-0269

Company and :State	Main Phone	Tech Phone
Apex Computer :WA	(800) 654-8222	
Apex Software :PA	(800) 858-2739	(412) 681-4343
Apian Software :CA	(800) 237-4565	
Aplus Computer :CA	(800) 886-2671	(800) 886-3536
APM Technologies :GA	(404) 476-3596	
Apogee Software :MA	(508) 365-2359	(508) 368-7036
	BBS (508) 365-2359	
Appian :WA	(800) 422-7369	
	BBS (206) 454-0511	
Appian Technology Inc :CA	(408) 730-5400	
Apple Computer Inc :CA	(800) 776-2333	
	FAX Back (180) 046-2436	
Application Techniques Inc :MA	(800) 433-5201	(508) 433-5201
Applied Business Technology :NY	(212) 219-8945	
Applied Computer Sciences, Inc :WA	(800) 525-5512	(800) 525-2400
Applied Computer Technology :TX	(214) 271-6550	
Applied Concepts Inc :FL	(800) 393-2277	
Applied Data Communications Inc :CA	(714) 731-9000	(800) 422-3635
Applied Design Company :MN	(612) 378-0094	
Applied Engineering :	(214) 241-6060	(214) 241-6084
	BBS (214) 241-6677	
Applied Instruments :CA	(510) 490-7117	
Applied Magnetics Corp :CA	(800) 328-5640	
Applied Microsystems Corp :WA	(800) 426-3925	
Applix, Inc :MA	(508) 870-0300	
Appoint :CA	(800) 448-1184	
APPRO International :CA	(408) 985-5359	(408) 732-6093
Approach Software :CA	(800) 277-7622	(415) 306-0646
Apricorn :CA	(619) 271-4880	
APS Packaging Systems :NJ	(201) 575-1040	
Aptech Systems :WA	(800) 443-3732	
Aquidneck Systems International :RI	(401) 295-2691	
Arbor Image Corp :MI	(313) 741-8700	
Arche Technologies, Inc :CA	(800) 422-4674	(800) 322-2724
Archive Corporation :CA	(714) 890-8602	
Archive Software :FL	(800) 821-8782	(800) 227-6296
Archive Technology :CA	(714) 641-1230	
Archtek America Corp :CA	(818) 912-9800	
Arcom Electronics Inc :CA	(408) 452-0678	
Area TV & Computers :PA	(814) 453-3918	
Areal Technology, Inc :CA	(408) 436-6800	(408) 436-6843
ARES Microdevelopment :MI	(800) 322-3200	
Ares Software :	(415) 578-9090	(415) 578-9090
Arion Technologies Inc :CT	(203) 775-6939	
Aris Entertainment :CA	(310) 821-0234	
Aristo Computers Inc :OR	(800) 327-4786	
Aristosoft Inc :CA	(800) 338-2629	
Arity :MA	(800) 722-7489	
Arix Corp :CA	(408) 432-1200	
ARK Multimedia Publishing :VA	(804) 220-4722	

Company and :State	Main Phone	Tech Phone
Arkay Technologies, Inc :NH	(800) 786-2419	
Arkenstone Inc :CA	(408) 752-2200	
Arkwright Inc :RI	(800) 638-8032	
Arlington Computer Products :IL	(800) 548-5105	(708) 228-1470
Arlington Electronic Wholesale :VA	(703) 524-2412	
Arnet Corp :TN	(800) 377-6686	(800) 366-8844
Aropa Corp :CA	(408) 734-2001	
Array Analysis :NY	(800) 451-8514	
Arrow Electronics, Inc :NY	(800) 932-7769	
Ars Nova Software :	(800) 445-4866	(206) 889-0927
Artek Computer Systems :CA	(510) 490-8402	
Artful Applications :OT	(416) 920-7395	
	BBS (416) 538-3107	
Arthur Andersen & Co :IL	(800) 458-8851	
Arthur Dent Associates Inc :MA	(508) 858-3742	
Articulate Systems :	(800) 443-7077	(617) 935-2220
Artisoft, Inc :AZ	(800) 846-9726	(602) 670-7000
	BBS (602) 293-0065	
Artist Graphics :MA	(612) 631-7832	
	BBS (612) 631-7669	
Artnet International Inc :CT	(203) 348-1141	
Asahi Chemical Industry Co Inc :NY	(212) 536-0540	
Asante Technologies :	(800) 662-9686	(800) 622-7464
ASCII Group Inc., The :MD	(301) 718-2600	
Ascom Timeplex Inc :NJ	(800) 669-2298	
ASD Software, Inc :CA	(714) 624-2594	
Asean Computer Technologies :CA	(909) 598-2828	(909) 598-5498
Ashby Industries, Inc :OK	(405) 722-1705	
Ashton-Tate :CA	(800) 437-4329	(408) 438-8400
Asia Communications :PQ	(514) 434-9373	
Asia Source Inc :CA	(510) 226-8000	(510) 226-8878
Asian Micro Sources, Inc :CA	(510) 376-9111	
Asian Sources Computer Products :IL	(708) 475-1900	
Asiatek Inc :CA	(818) 333-3802	
ASJ Support Services Inc :FL	(800) 262-0089	
Ask Computer Systems, Inc :CA	(415) 969-4442	
Ask-Me Information Center :MN	(612) 531-0603	
AskSam Systems :FL	(800) 800-1997	
	BBS (904) 584-8287	
Aslan Computer Corp :CA	(818) 575-5271	
ASP Computer Products, Inc :CA	(800) 445-6190	(408) 746-2965
Aspect Telecommunications :CA	(800) 541-7799	
Aspen Imaging International :CO	(800) 955-5555	
AspenSoft Inc :CA	(415) 508-1840	
Associated Data Services Inc :MD	(800) 772-9812	
Associated Distribution Logistis :NY	(800) 443-3443	
Associated Research Inc :IL	(800) 858-8378	
Associates Computer Supply :NY	(718) 543-3364	(718) 543-3386
Association Of Shareware Prof. :IN	(317) 322-2000	
AST Computer :CA	(800) 876-4278	(714) 727-4141

Company and :State	Main Phone	Tech Phone
....	BBS (714) 727-4723	
AST Research :.............	(800) 876-4278	(800) 727-1278
....	BBS (717) 727-4723	
Astea International Inc :MA......	(617) 275-5440	
Astec Co :NJ.............	(201) 595-7001	
Astra Computer Products :CA	(619) 278-2682	
Astro Memory Products :TX	(800) 652-7876	
Astrocom Corp :MN	(612) 227-8651	
Astrotech Intl Corp :PA	(412) 391-1896	
Asymetrix :WA	(800) 624-8999	(206) 637-1600
....	BBS (206) 451-1173	
AT&T :NJ.............	(201) 331-4134	
AT&T Capital Corp :TX.............	(800) 874-7123	
AT&T Language Line Services :CA	(800) 752-6096	
AT&T Microelectronics :NJ	(908) 771-2825	
AT&T SRC :IL	(708) 955-4208	
Atari Corp :CA	(800) 443-8020	
Atasi Technology	-Out Of Business :	
Atech Software :CA.............	(818) 765-5311	(818) 765-5561
Aten Research Inc :CA.............	(800) 755-0561	(714) 255-9726
Athana Inc :CA	(800) 421-1591	
ATI Technologies :OT.............	(416) 882-2600	(416) 882-2600
....	BBS (416) 764-9404	
ATI Technologies Inc :CA.......	(800) 955-5284	(213) 823-1129
Atkins/Jones Computer Service Ic :CA	(714) 953-4351	
Atlantic Computer Products :CA...	(800) 245-2284	
Atlantic Inc :CA	(310) 273-3163	
Atlantic Scientific Corporation :FL	(800) 544-4737	
Atlantis Laser Center :GA	(800) 733-9155	
Atlas Business Solutions :IL	(708) 208-1373	
Atlas Micro Distributing Inc :CA ...	(310) 530-6300	
Atrix International Inc :MN	(800) 222-6154	
Attachmate Corp :WA.............	(800) 426-6283	
Attain :MA	(617) 776-1110	(617) 776-2711
Attitash Software :.............	(800) 736-4198	(800) 736-2803
Attitude Inc :CA.............	(714) 680-8112	
ATTO Technology Inc :NY	(716) 688-4259	
Audio Digital Imaging, Inc. :IL	(708) 439-1335	
Aura Associates :CA.............	(408) 252-2872	
Aurora Computer & Accessories :CA	(800) 852-3344	
Aurum Software Inc :CA	(408) 562-6370	
Austek Microsystems :CA.............	(408) 988-8556	
Austin Computer Systems :TX	(800) 752-1577	(800) 752-4171
Austin.Marsh Communications :ON	(416) 840-7840	
Auto Trol Technology :CO	(303) 452-4919	
AutoDesk Inc :CA	(800) 445-5415	
Autodesk Retail Products :WA	(206) 487-2233	
Automap :.............	(602) 893-2400	(602) 893-2400
Automated Cartridge Libraries :CO	(800) 536-2251	
Automated Design Systems :GA ...	(800) 366-2552	

Company and :State	Main Phone	Tech Phone
.... BBS	(404) 394-7448	
Automated Technology Systems :NY	(516) 231-7777	
Automatic Data Processing, Inc :NJ	(201) 994-5000	
Automatic Tool & Connector :NJ	(800) 524-2857	
Automation Technologies :UT	(800) 777-6368	(801) 566-5544
Automatrix Inc :MA.............	(508) 667-7900	
Automecha Ltd :NY	(800) 447-9990	
AutoSoft Inc :GA	(404) 594-8855	
Autrec, Inc :NC	(919) 759-9493	
Autumn Hill Software :CO	(303) 494-8865	
.... BBS	(303) 494-8868	
Auva Computer, Inc :CA	(714) 562-6999	
Ava Instrumentation Inc :CA	(408) 336-2281	
Avalan Technology :MA.........	(800) 441-2281	
Avalon Hill Game Company :MD...	(410) 254-9200	
Avance Logic Inc :CA............	(510) 226-9555	
Avanpro :CA...................	(213) 454-3866	
Avant Industries Inc :CA	(818) 330-0166	
Avant-Garde Computing, Inc :NJ...	(609) 778-7000	
Avantek Security :CA............	(408) 727-0700	
Avantos Performance Systems :CA	(510) 654-4600	(510) 657-4729
Avatar :	(800) 282-8276	
Avery Dennison :CA............	(818) 858-8214	
Avery International :	(800) 252-8379	(818) 792-2102
Avex Electronics Corporation :PA ...	(800) 877-7623	
AVI Systems Inc :CA	(510) 535-1020	
Avnet, Inc. :NY	(516) 466-7000	
Avocet :ME....................	(800) 448-8500	(207) 236-6010
AVR Technology Inc :CA	(408) 434-1115	
Award Software Inc :CA..........	(408) 370-7979	(408) 370-7979
.... BBS	(408) 371-3139	
AXA Corp :CA	(714) 757-1500	
Axelen Inc :WA................	(206) 643-2781	
Axik Computer Inc :CA..........	(408) 735-1234	(408) 735-1437
Axis Communications Inc :MA.....	(508) 777-7957	
Axonix Corp :UT	(800) 866-9797	
Axxion Group Corp :TX	(800) 828-6475	
Aydin Corp :PA...............	(215) 657-7510	
Az-Tech Software :MO..........	(816) 776-2700	
Azerty Inc :NY	(800) 888-8080	(716) 662-7616
Azure Technologies Inc :MA	(800) 233-3800	
B&B Eletronics Mfg Co :IL	(815) 434-0846	
B&K Precision :IL..............	(312) 889-1448	
Babbages Inc :TX..............	(800) 288-9020	
Back Thru Future Microcomputers :NJ	(201) 644-9587	
Baggerly & Associates Inc :HI	(808) 875-2510	
Baler Software :IL..............	(800) 327-6108	(708) 506-1770
Ball Aerospace :NM	(505) 298-5445	
Balt, Inc :TX	(817) 697-4953	
Banctec Inc :TX	(800) 527-5918	

Company and :State	Main Phone	Tech Phone
Banctec Service Corp :TX	(800) 435-7832	
Bandy Inc :TX	(214) 272-5455	
Banner Band :IL	(800) 333-0549	
Banner Blue Software :CA	(510) 794-6850	(510) 794-6850
Bantam Electronic Publishing :NY	(212) 765-6500	
Banyan Systems Inc :MA	(508) 898-1000	
Bar-Tec Inc :TX	(800) 433-1409	(800) 356-1695
Barbados Industrial Development :NY	(212) 867-6420	
Barbey Electronics :PA	(215) 376-7451	
Barcode Industries, Inc :MD	(301) 498-5400	(301) 498-6498
Barouh Easton Ltd :ON	(800) 268-9955	
Barrister Information Systems :NY	(716) 845-5010	
Barrons Educational Services :NY	(800) 645-3476	
Baseline Publishing :	(901) 682-9676	(901) 682-9676
Basf :MA	(800) 343-4600	(800) 225-3326
Basic + Micro Products :CA	(510) 887-8186	
Basic Computer :OH	(216) 873-1000	
Basic Needs :CA	(800) 633-3703	(800) 633-3703
Basic Systems, Inc :FL	(305) 584-5422	
Basmark :OH	(216) 621-7650	
Battelle Memorial Institute :OH	(614) 424-6424	
Battery Biz :CA	(800) 848-6782	
Battery Power Inc :IL	(800) 949-1000	
Battery Specialties :CA	(800) 854-5759	
Battery Technology Inc :CA	(213) 728-7874	
Bay Technical Associates :MS	(800) 523-2702	
Baysoft :CA	(415) 527-3300	
Bayware Inc :CA	(415) 312-0980	
BCC :CA	(408) 944-9000	
BCM Advanced Research :CA	(714) 752-0526	
BCTOP Inc :CA	(213) 383-0791	
Beacon Software, Inc :OH	(800) 753-2322	
Beacon Technology :	(719) 594-4884	(719) 594-4884
Beagle Brothers :	(800) 451-5151	(801) 228-9901
Beame & Whiteside Software Ltd :ON		(416) 765-0822
Bear Rock Technologies :CA	(916) 622-4640	
Beaver Computer Corp :CA	(800) 827-4222	
BEC :CA	(714) 731-6116	
BEC Computer :CA	(408) 954-8828	
BEC Inc/Cert. Calibration Labs :PA	(800) 523-3808	
BEC Lynkers :CA	(714) 731-6117	
Bedford Computer Systems Inc :MA	(508) 671-0870	
Bel Merit Corp :CA	(714) 586-3700	
Belgian Foreign Trae Office :CA	(213) 857-1244	
Belkin Components :CA	(800) 223-5546	
Bell & Howell Products Co :IL	(708) 933-3125	
Bell Atlantic Bus. Systems Serv. :PA	(800) 634-9827	(215) 296-6180
Bell Atlantic Corp :PA	(215) 963-6000	
Bell Atlantic CTS :MA	(800) 688-1492	
Bell Atlantic CTS :CA	(800) 345-7950	

Company and :State	Main Phone	Tech Phone
Bell Atlantic CTS :CA	(500) 350-3475	
Bell Atlantic CTS :PA	(800) 888-2622	
Bell Atlantic CTS-ESS :WI	(800) 888-2622	
Bell Industries, Inc :CA	(310) 826-2355	
Bell Of Pennsylvania :PA	(215) 466-7978	
Belmont Distributing :CO	(303) 936-5758	
Bendata Management Systems :CO	(719) 531-5007	
Benedict Computers :CA	(800) 346-5186	
Benefit Concepts Systems :RI	(401) 438-7100	
Bentley Company :MA	(617) 221-8590	
Berkeley Systems Design Inc :CA	(800) 877-5535	(510) 540-5535
Best Computer Supplies :NV	(800) 544-3470	(702) 826-4393
Best Data Products, Inc :CA	(818) 773-9600	
Best PC Supply, Inc :CA	(415) 875-6888	
Best Power Technology Inc :WI	(800) 356-5794	(800) 356-5737
Best Programs Inc :VA	(703) 820-9300	
Beta Automation Inc :CA	(800) 421-8462	
Bethesda Softworks :MD	(301) 926-8300	(301) 963-2002
Better Business Systems :CA	(800) 829-9991	(818) 373-7525
Better Software Technology Inc :MA	(508) 879-0744	
BGS Systems :MA	(617) 891-0000	
BGW Systems Inc :CA	(310) 973-8090	
Bi-Link Computer, Inc :CA	(800) 888-5369	(310) 695-5166
Biblesoft :WA	(206) 824-0547	
Big Blue Products Inc :NY	(516) 261-1000	
Binary Research :PA	(215) 233-3200	
Biomation :CA	(800) 934-2466	
Birmingham Data Systems :MI	(313) 362-0860	
Bis Technology Inc :CA	(818) 856-5888	
Bit 3 Computer Corp :MN	(612) 881-6955	
BIT Computer Inc :CA	(800) 935-0209	
Bit Software Inc :CA	(510) 490-2928	(510) 490-2928
Bits Technical Corp :TX	(713) 981-1166	
Bitstream Inc :MA	(800) 223-3176	(617) 497-7514
Bitwise Designs, Inc :NY	(800) 367-5906	
Biz Base, Inc. :	(800) 833-8892	(619) 673-7355
BJS Electonics Inc :CA	(408) 456-8989	
Black & White International :NY	(800) 932-9202	
Black Box Accessories :PA	(800) 321-0746	(412) 746-5565
Black Box Corp :PA	(412) 746-5565	
BlackCurrant Technology :CA	(714) 432-6514	
Blackship Computer Systems :CA	(800) 877-6249	
Blaise Computing :CA	(800) 333-8087	
Bleuel Associates Inc :CA	(818) 907-7162	
BLOC Publishing Corp :FL	(800) 888-6111	(305) 445-6304
Blue Fin Technologies Inc :NH	(603) 433-2223	
Blue Line Communications :CA	(800) 258-7810	
Blue Rose Computer :PA	(800) 685-3035	
Blue Sky Software Corp :CA	(800) 677-4946	
Bluebird Systems :CA	(619) 438-2220	

Company and :State	Main Phone	Tech Phone
Bluelynx :MD	(800) 832-4526	(800) 642-5888
Bluesky Software :CA	(800) 677-4946	
Blyth Software :CA	(800) 346-6647	
BMI Inc :CA	(415) 570-5355	
Board Xchange Inc :FL	(407) 678-2269	
Boardwatch Magazine :CO	(303) 973-6038	
	BBS (303) 973-4222	
Boca Research :FL	(407) 997-6227	(407) 241-8088
	BBS (407) 241-1610	
BodyCello :CA	(619) 578-6969	
Bogen Communications Inc :NJ	(201) 934-8500	
Bolt Beranek & Newman, Inc :MA	(617) 873-2000	
Bolt Systems :MD	(301) 656-7133	
Bondhus Corporation :MN	(800) 328-8310	
Bondwell Industrial Co, Inc :CA	(800) 627-6888	(800) 288-4388
Book Tech Distributing, Inc :CO	(303) 329-0300	
Boole And Babbage, Inc :CA	(800) 222-6653	
Boonton Electronics Corp :NJ	(201) 584-1077	
Borland International :CA	(800) 331-0877	(408) 461-9155
	BBS (408) 439-9096	
Bostek :MA	(800) 926-7835	
Boston Business Computing :MA	(508) 470-0444	
Boston Computer Exchange :MA	(800) 262-6399	
Botton Line Industries Inc :CA	(818) 700-1922	
Bourbaki :ID	(208) 342-5849	
	BBS (209) 342-5823	
Bowers Development :MA	(508) 369-8175	
Brand Technologies :CA	(818) 407-4040	(818) 407-4040
Braun Media Services, Inc :MN	(612) 943-4033	
Bravo Communications Inc :CA	(800) 366-0297	
Bravo Technology :	(510) 841-8552	(510) 841-8552
BRC Electronics :TX	(800) 255-3027	
Bretford Manufacturing Inc :IL	(708) 678-2545	
Brian Instruments, Inc :CA	(714) 992-5540	
Brian R. White Co Inc :CA	(707) 462-9795	
Brier Technology :CA	(408) 435-8463	(404) 564-5550
Bright Star Technology :WA	(206) 451-3697	
Brightwork Development :NJ	(800) 552-9876	(908) 530-9650
	BBS (914) 667-4759	
Brightwork Development Inc :NJ	(908) 530-0440	
Brim Electronics Inc :NJ	(201) 796-2886	
Britton Lee, Inc :CA	(800) 372-7111	
Broadtech International :CA	(714) 773-1820	
Broadview Associates :NJ	(201) 461-7929	
Brock Control Systems Inc :GA	(800) 221-0775	
Broderbund Software :CA	(415) 382-4400	(415) 382-4700
Brooks Electronics :PA	(800) 052-3010	
Brooks Power Systems Inc :PA	(800) 523-1551	
Brother International :NJ	(908) 356-8880	
Brown Bag Software, Inc :CA	(408) 559-4545	

Company and :State	Main Phone	Tech Phone
. . . .	BBS (408) 371-7654	
Brown-Wagh :CA	(408) 378-3838	
Brown-Wagh Publishing :CA	(408) 378-3838	
Brunelle Instruments Inc :QC.	(800) 567-3506	
BSE Company :CA	(714) 258-8722	
BSI (Broadax Systems Inc.) :CA . . .	(800) 872-4547	(818) 442-7038
BSM Computers :TX	(800) 888-3475	
BTC Corp :CA	BBS (510) 657-1859	
BTECH Inc :NJ.	(201) 428-1779	
Budget Computer :MA	(800) 370-1212	(800) 370-1313
Buffalo Products Inc :OR	(800) 345-2356	(800) 345-2027
Bull HN Information Systems :MA . .	(800) 999-2181	(800) 226-4357
Bull Information Systems :MA	(800) 233-2855	
Bulldog Computer Products :GA . . .	(800) 438-6039	
Bullseye Software :	(702) 831-2523	
Bureau Development :NJ.	(201) 808-2700	(201) 808-2700
Bureau Of Electronic Publishing :NJ	(201) 808-2700	
Burndy Corp :CT	(203) 838-4444	
Burr-Brown Corp :AZ	(800) 227-3947	
Burroughs Corp :MI	(800) 247-5617	
Bus Computer Systems, Inc :NY . . .	(212) 627-4485	
Buse Communications :MO	(800) 521-1117	
Business Computer Systems :VA . . .	(800) 333-2955	(804) 420-6658
Business Credit Leasing :MN	(800) 328-5371	
Business Development Int'l :NJ. . . .	(201) 891-1040	
Business Logistics Services :TN . . .	(901) 395-7112	
Business Sense Inc :WY	(801) 963-1384	
Business Systems Direct :NY	(800) 777-4068	
BusinessVision Management Syst :ON	(414) 629-3233	
BusinessWare Inc :CA	(714) 492-8958	
BusinessWise Inc :CA	(408) 866-5960	
BusLogic Inc :CA	(408) 492-9090	
Button Ware Inc :WA	(800) 528-8866	(900) 454-8000
. . . .	BBS (206) 454-7875	
Bux Tek Corp :CA	(408) 492-9090	
Buzzwords, Int'l :MO	(314) 334-6317	
Byte Brothers :WA	(206) 271-9567	
BYTE Magazine :NH	(603) 924-2627	
Bytel Corp :CA	(415) 527-1157	
Bytronix Corp :CA	(714) 879-0810	
C C Steven & Associates, Inc :CA. .	(805) 658-0207	
C H Products :CA	(619) 598-2518	
C Hoelzle Associates Inc :CA	(714) 251-9000	
C J Carrigan Enterprises Inc :CA . .	(714) 598-1276	
C Source :MO	(816) 478-1888	
. . . .	BBS (816) 478-0944	
C&D Charter Power Systems :PA . .	(215) 828-9000	
C&F Associates :NH	(800) 688-9112	
C&S Sales Inc :IL	(800) 292-7711	
C-88 International Corp :CA	(408) 956-8345	

Company and :State	Main Phone	Tech Phone
C-Tech Associates Inc :NJ	(201) 726-9000	
C-Tech Electronics, Inc :CA	(800) 347-4017	
C2 Micro Systems Inc :CA	(510) 683-8888	
CA Retail Solutions :ON	(800) 668-3767	
CA Technology, Ltd :NY	(212) 260-7661	
Cabinets Galore Inc :CA	(619) 586-0555	
Cable Connection :CA	(408) 395-6700	
Cable Systems Inc :MA	(617) 389-7080	
Cables To Go :OH	(800) 225-8646	
Cabletron Systems :NH	(603) 332-9400	
CableWorks :CA	(619) 450-1929	
CablExpress :NY	(315) 476-3000	
Cache Computers Inc :CA	(510) 226-9922	
Caching Technology Corp :CA....	(714) 777-2818	
CACI Int'l Inc :VA	(703) 841-7800	
CAD & Graphics Computers :CA ..	(800) 288-1611	(415) 647-9671
CAD Warehouse :OH	(800) 487-0485	(216) 487-0631
Cadec Systems, Inc :NH........	(800) 223-3220	
Cadence Design Systems, Inc :CA	(408) 943-1234	
CADRE Technology Inc :RI	(800) 548-7645	
Caere Corp :CA	(800) 535-7226	(800) 462-2373
CAF Technology Inc :CA	(800) 289-8299	
Cahners Publishing Co :MA	(617) 964-3030	
Caig Laboratories :CA	(619) 451-1799	
Calan, Inc :PA	(800) 544-3392	
CalComp :CA	(800) 541-7877	(800) 225-2667
....	BBS (714) 821-2359	
Calculus :CA....................	(305) 481-2334	
Calculus :FL	(305) 481-2334	
Calera Recognition Systems :CA..	(800) 544-7051	(408) 720-0999
....	BBS (408) 773-9068	
Caliber Computer Corp :CA	(408) 942-1220	
California Peripherals Corp :CA ..	(213) 538-1030	
California Software Products :CA..	(714) 973-0440	
California Switch & Signal, Inc :CA	(310) 538-9830	
CalSOFT Technology, Inc :CA	(805) 497-8054	
Caltex Software :TX	(214) 522-9840	
Caltronix :NY....................	(716) 359-3780	
Calyx Corp :WI	(800) 558-2208	(800) 866-1008
Calzone Case Co :CT........	(203) 367-5766	
Cambria Corp :NJ	(609) 665-3600	
Cambridge Electronics Labs :MA..	(617) 629-2805	
Cameo Communications, Inc :NH .	(603) 465-2940	
Caminton Corp :CA........	(800) 843-8336	
Campbell Services Inc :MI	(800) 345-6747	
....	BBS (313) 559-6434	
Canada, External Affairs :ON	(613) 993-6576	
Canon USA Inc :NY	(516) 488-6700	
CanTech :UT....................	(800) 255-3999	
Capital Data :MI	(517) 371-7100	

Company and :State	Main Phone	Tech Phone
Capricorn Systems :VA	(804) 355-9371	
Capstone :FL	(305) 591-5900	
Cardiff Software Inc :CA	(800) 659-8755	
Cardinal Technologies :	(800) 233-0187	(717) 293-3124
	BBS (717) 293-3074	
Cardinal Technologies Inc :PA	(800) 722-0094	(717) 293-3124
	BBS (717) 293-3074	
Caritech Computer Corp :TX	(915) 584-9817	
Carlisle Memory Products :TX	(800) 433-7632	
CarNel Enterprises Inc :CA	(800) 962-1450	
Carroll Touch :TX	(512) 244-3500	
Cartridge Technologies Inc :MD	(800) 869-8570	
Casady Co :CA	(408) 484-9228	
Case Logic Inc :CO	(303) 530-3800	
Casecom Inc :CA	(408) 942-5416	
Casecom Technology Inc :CA	(510) 490-7122	
Caseworks, Inc :GA	(800) 635-1577	
Casio :NJ	(201) 361-5400	
Castelle :CA	(408) 496-0474	
Catalytix :MA	(617) 738-1516	
Catspaw :CO	(719) 539-3884	
	BBS (719) 539-4830	
Cayman Systems :	(617) 494-1999	(617) 494-1999
CBM America Corp :CA	(800) 421-6516	(310) 767-7838
CC:Mail Inc :CA	(800) 448-2500	(415) 961-9871
	BBS (415) 691-0401	
CCI :BC	(604) 465-1540	
CD Systems :CA	(909) 595-5736	
CD-ROM Direct :MA	(800) 332-2404	
CDC :MN	(800) 345-6628	
CDCE Inc :CA	(714) 630-4633	
CE Software :IA	(515) 224-1995	(515) 224-1953
Cellular Data Inc :CA	(415) 856-9800	
Cellular Digital Packet Data :WA	(206) 828-8691	
Cellular Products Distributors :CA	(310) 312-0909	
CenTech :UT	(800) 255-3999	
Centel Corp :IL	(800) 323-2174	
Centon Electronics Inc :CA	(714) 855-9111	
Central Computer Products :CA	(800) 456-4123	(805) 524-4189
Central Data :IL	(800) 482-0315	
Central Point/MAXA :OR	(503) 690-8088	(503) 690-8080
	BBS (503) 690-6650	
Centrepoint S-W Technologies:ON	(613) 235-7054	
Centron Software :	(800) 848-2424	
Century Computer Marketing :CA	(310) 827-0999	
Century Data Systems Inc :NC	(919) 821-5696	
Century Micro Electronics :CA	(408) 748-7788	
Century Software :	(801) 268-3088	
CERA Inc :TX	(800) 966-3070	
Ceres Software :	(800) 877-4292	(503) 245-9011

Company and :State	Main Phone	Tech Phone
Cermetek Microelectronics, Inc :CA	(408) 752-5000	
Cerner Corp :MO	(816) 221-1024	
Certified Management Software :UT	(801) 534-1231	
Certus International Corp :	(800) 722-8737	(800) 729-6684
CH Ellis Company Inc :IN	(317) 636-3351	
CH Products :CA	(619) 598-2518	
Chain Store Guide Information :FL.	(800) 927-9292	
Champion Business Systems :CO.	(303) 792-3606	
Champion Duplicators :CA	(800) 752-2145	
CHAMPS Inc :FL.	(904) 795-2362	
Chancery Software Ltd :BC	(604) 294-1233	
Chang Laboratories :CA	(408) 727-8096	(408) 727-8096
Chaplet Systems U S A :CA :CA	(408) 732-7950	
Chapman Corporation :ME	(207) 773-4726	
Charles Charles & Associates :KS.	(800) 348-1354	
Chatsworth Products Inc :CA	(818) 882-8595	
CheckFree :	(614) 899-7500	(614) 898-6000
CheckMark Software :	(303) 484-3541	
CheckSum :WA.	(206) 653-4861	
CHEM Corp :CA	(510) 226-6280	
Chemtronics, Inc :GA	(800) 645-5244	(800) 424-9300
Chen & Associates :LA	(504) 928-5765	
CHEQsys :ON.	(416) 475-4121	
Cherry Corp :IL	(708) 662-9200	
Cheyenne Software :NY	(516) 484-5110	
	BBS (516) 484-3445	
CHI/COR Information Management :IL	(312) 322-0150	
Chic Technology Corp :WA	(206) 833-4836	
Chicago Case Co :IL.	(312) 927-1600	
Chicony America Inc :CA	(714) 380-0928	
Chinon America, Inc :CA	(800) 441-0222	
Chips And Technologies, Inc :CA.	(408) 434-0600	
Chips For Less :TX	(214) 250-0009	(214) 250-9335
ChipSoft Inc :CA	(800) 622-6829	(619) 453-4842
	BBS (619) 453-5232	
Chishom :CA.	(800) 888-4210	
Chloride Power Electronics :NY	(800) 333-0529	
Choice Courier Systems Inc :NY	(212) 370-1999	
Choice Technical Services :CA	(714) 522-8123	
CHRONOS Software :CA	(415) 626-4244	
Chrysler First Commercial Corp :PA	(215) 437-8680	
Chuck Atkinson Programs :TX	(800) 826-5009	
Chwatal Development Co :	BBS (318) 487-0800	
Ci Design Co, Inc :CA.	(714) 261-5524	
CIBD :CA.	(510) 676-6466	
CIE America, Inc :CA	(714) 833-8445	
Cimmetry Systems Inc :PQ	(514) 735-3219	
Cincinnati Bell Inc :OH	(513) 397-9900	
Cincinnati Milacron Inc :OH	(513) 841-8100	
Cincom Systems Inc :OH	(513) 662-2300	

Company and :State	Main Phone	Tech Phone
CIO Publishing :MA	(508) 872-8200	
Cipher Data Products :CA	(800) 424-7437	
Cipher Data Products, Inc :CA. . . .	(800) 424-7437	
Ciprico Inc :MN	(612) 551-4000	
Circle Computer Inc :MA	(617) 821-4114	
Circo Computer System :CA	(800) 678-1688	
Circuit Repair Corp :MA.	(508) 948-7973	
Circuit Test :CA	(510) 463-2432	
Cirris Systems Corp :UT	(800) 441-9910	
Cirrus Logic, Inc :CA	(510) 623-8500	
Cirvis Inc :CA	(714) 891-2000	
Citel America Inc :FL	(800) 248-3548	
Citizen America :CA.	(310) 453-0614	
. . . .	BBS (310) 453-7564	
Citrix Systems :FL	(305) 755-0559	(305) 345-3666
. . . .	BBS (305) 346-9004	
CJF Enterprises Inc :FL.	(305) 491-1850	
Clarify Inc :CA	(408) 428-2000	
Clarion Software :FL	(800) 354-5444	(305) 785-4556
. . . .	BBS (305) 785-9172	
Claris Corp :CA	(408) 987-7000	
Clark Development Company :UT. .	(801) 261-1686	
. . . .	BBS (801) 261-8976	
Clary Corp :CA.	(818) 359-4486	
. . . .	BBS (801) 261-8976	
Clear Software :MA	(800) 338-1759	
. . . .	BBS (617) 965-5406	
Cleo Communications :	(800) 233-2536	
Cliff Notes :NE	(800) 228-4078	(402) 421-8324
Clipper Products :OH.	(513) 528-7011	
Clone Technologies :MO	(314) 365-2050	
Club American Technologies:CA . .	(510) 683-6088	
CMD Technology Inc :CA	(714) 454-0800	
CMG Computer Products :TX	(512) 329-8220	
CMI	Out Of Business :	
CMI Communications Inc :MI.	(800) 825-5150	
CMO :PA	(800) 233-8950	(800) 221-4283
CMP Publications :NY	(516) 562-5000	
CMS Enhancements, Inc :CA	(714) 222-6000	(800) 222-6617
. . . .	BBS (714) 222-0805	
CMX-Computer Module Exchange :ON	(800) 668-6413	(800) 285-2699
CNet Technology, Inc :CA	(408) 954-8000	
. . . .	BBS (408) 954-1787	
CNS :MN	(800) 843-2978	
CNS Inc :NJ	(201) 625-4056	
Coast Computer Power :CA	(800) 822-2587	
Coastal Electronics :GA.	(912) 352-1444	
Cobalt Blue :GA	(404) 518-1116	
Coda Music Software :MN	(612) 854-1288	(612) 854-9649
Coefficient Systems :NY	(800) 833-4220	

Company and :State	Main Phone	Tech Phone
Cogito	Out Of Business :	
Cognitive Systems, Inc :CT	(203) 773-0726	
Cognitronics Corp :CT	(800) 243-2594	
Colad Group Inc :NY.	(716) 849-1776	
Color Age Incorporation :MA	(800) 873-4367	
Colorado Memory Systems :CO . . .	(303) 635-1500	
. . . .	BBS (303) 679-0650	
Colorado Tech Designs Inc :CO . . .	(303) 449-0963	
Colorocs Corp :GA	(404) 564-5520	
Columbia Data Products :FL	(407) 869-6700	
. . . .	BBS (407) 862-4724	
Comarco, Inc :CA	(714) 921-0672	
Comclok Inc :CA	(714) 991-1580	
Comdale Technologies :OT	(416) 252-2424	
Comdisco Parts :IL	(800) 635-2211	
Comedge Inc :CA	(818) 336-7522	
Comlite Systems Inc :GA	(800) 354-3821	
Command Communications Inc :CO	(303) 751-7000	
Command Computer Corp :NJ	(201) 288-7000	
Command Software Systems :FL. .	(407) 575-3200	
Command Technology :CA	(800) 336-3320	
Commax Technologies, Inc :CA . . .	(800) 526-6629	(408) 435-8272
Commodore Business Machines:PA	(800) 448-9987	(800) 874-4811
Common Cents Software :CA	(719) 481-4682	
Commonwealth Of Puerto Rico :NY	(212) 245-1200	
Communication Automation,Control :PA	(215) 776-6669	
Communication Horizons :NY	(212) 724-0150	
Communications Research Group :LA	(504) 923-0888	
. . . .	BBS (504) 926-5625	
Communications Technology Group :IL	(800) 626-2715	
Communications Test Design :PA .	(800) 223-3910	
COMP USA :TX	(800) 541-7638	
COMPAC Microelectronics :CA . . .	(510) 656-3333	
Compact Disk Products :NJ	(908) 290-8687	(212) 737-8400
Compaq Computer Corp :TX	(800) 888-5858	(800) 345-1518
CompEd Inc :VA	(800) 456-5338	
Compeq USA Ltd :CA	(800) 852-0105	(714) 404-1619
Compex Technology Inc :CA	(818) 855-7988	
Compex, Inc :CA	(714) 630-7302	
Complementary Solutions :GA . . .	(404) 454-8033	
Complete Computer :	(415) 549-3153	
Complete PC, The :CA	(800) 229-1753	(408) 434-9600
. . . .	BBS (408) 434-9703	
Compo Group Inc :CT.	(203) 222-1335	
Component Sales Corp :CA	(408) 894-1870	
Comprehensive Software :CA . . .	(213) 318-2561	(213) 214-1461
Compro Computer Services :FL. . .	(412) 255-3616	
Compsee, Inc :NC.	(407) 724-4321	
Compteck Research, Inc :NY	(716) 842-2700	
Compton's NewMedia :CA	(800) 532-3766	(619) 929-2626

Company and :State	Main Phone	Tech Phone
Comptronics :NC	(919) 779-7268	
Compu-D International Inc :CA	(818) 787-3282	
Compu-Gard Inc :MA	(508) 761-4520	
Compu-Tek International :TX	(800) 531-0190	(214) 994-0193
CompuAdd Corp :TX	(800) 925-3000	(800) 925-0995
CompuCase By Incom America:TX.	(800) 255-9617	
CompuClassics :CA	(800) 733-3888	
CompuClean :TX	(800) 444-9038	
Compucom Systems :NJ	(609) 848-2300	
CompuCover :FL	(800) 874-6391	(904) 863-2200
CompuD International :CA	(800) 929-9333	(818) 787-3282
Compudyne :TX	(800) 862-3083	(800) 447-3895
CompuLan Technology Inc :CA	(800) 486-8810	(408) 954-8864
Compulaw :CA	(800) 559-4991	(800) 533-7839
CompuLink Management :CA	(310) 212-5465	
Compulits Inc :IN	(317) 581-7600	
CompuMedia Technology Inc :CA..	(510) 656-9811	
Compumetrics Incorporated :NY	(212) 323-8150	
CompuRegister Corp :MO	(314) 365-2050	
CompuServe :OH.	(800) 848-8990	(800) 848-8990
Compusol Inc :CA	(714) 253-9533	
ComputAbility Consumer Electr. :WI	(800) 588-0003	
Compute Publications, Inc :NY	(212) 496-6100	
Computeach :	(800) 448-3224	(800) 448-3224
Computer & Control Solutions :GA .	(800) 782-3525	
Computer & Monitor Maintenance :GA	(800) 466-4411	
Computer Aided Management:CA..	(707) 795-4100	
Computer Aided Technology Inc :TX	(214) 350-0888	
Computer Aided Technology, Inc :TX	(214) 350-0888	
Computer Analysis :HI	(808) 848-4878	
Computer Assistance Inc :OR	(503) 895-3347	
Computer Associates :IL	(708) 505-6000	
Computer Associates Int'l Inc :NY..	(800) 342-5224	
Computer Automation :CA	(714) 833-8830	
Computer Auxiliary Products :CA ..	(714) 465-0911	
Computer Bay :WI	(414) 357-7705	
Computer Book Club, The :PA	(717) 794-2191	
Computer Business Services :IN	(800) 343-8014	(317) 758-9612
Computer Buyers Guide :NY	(212) 807-8220	
Computer Buying World :MA	(617) 246-3800	
Computer Cable & Connector Co :NJ	(201) 993-9285	
Computer Care :VA	(703) 528-8700	
Computer Care Inc :WV	(800) 552-4283	
Computer Channel Inc :NY	(516) 921-5170	
Computer Clipboard :VA	(800) 777-4932	
Computer Commodities Int'l :MN..	(800) 365-3475	
Computer Communications :CA	(800) 421-1178	
Computer Communications Specials :GA	(404) 441-3114	
Computer Component Source Inc :NY	(516) 496-8727	
Computer Components :NY	(800) 356-1227	

Company and :State	Main Phone	Tech Phone
Computer Connection :WI	(800) 552-2331	
Computer Connection Corp :MN ..	(612) 884-0758	
Computer Control Systems :FL	(904) 752-0912	
Computer Covers Unlimited :CA ..	(800) 722-6837	
Computer Coverup, Inc :IL	(312) 327-9200	
....	BBS (312) 327-9078	
Computer Craftsmen Ltd :WI	(414) 567-1700	
Computer Currents :CA	(415) 547-6800	
Computer Data Systems :MD	(301) 921-7000	
Computer DataVault :CA	(714) 362-3839	
Computer Design Magazine :MA ..	(800) 225-0556	
....	BBS (508) 392-2265	
Computer Discount Warehouse :IL	(800) 726-4239	(708) 291-7575
Computer Doctor :TX	(512) 467-9355	
Computer Doctors :MD	(301) 474-3095	
Computer Dynamics :SC	(803) 877-8700	
Computer Exchange :GA	(404) 446-7980	
Computer Expressions :PA	(800) 443-8278	
Computer Factory Outlet :AZ	(800) 486-9975	(602) 829-7751
Computer Field Services Inc :MA..	(617) 246-4090	
Computer Fixer :PA	(215) 568-1100	
Computer Friends, Inc :OR	(800) 547-3303	
Computer Fun :CA	(619) 279-1919	
Computer Gate International :CA..	(408) 730-0673	
Computer Hand Holding :CA	(415) 882-0517	
Computer Horizons Corp :NY	(800) 847-4097	
Computer Hot Line :TX.........	(214) 233-5131	
Computer Identics Corp :MA	(800) 343-0846	
Computer Innovations :NJ	(908) 542-5920	(201) 542-5920
Computer Intelligence :CA	(619) 450-1667	(619) 450-0255
Computer Labs Inc :NY	(315) 635-7236	
Computer Language Magazine :CA	(800) 525-0643	
Computer Law & Tax Report :NY..	(212) 879-3325	
Computer Law Strategist :NY	(212) 741-8300	
Computer Law Systems Inc :MN ..	(612) 941-3801	
Computer Law Systems, Inc :MN..	(800) 328-1913	
Computer Library :NY	(212) 503-4400	
Computer Locators International :FL	(407) 627-7797	
Computer Logic Ltd :OH	(800) 359-0599	
Computer Logics Ltd :OH	(216) 349-8600	
Computer Maintenance Plus :CO..	(303) 427-5181	
Computer Maintenance Service :PA	(800) 333-4267	
Computer Maintenance Training:MA	(800) 952-5977	
Computer Management Services :CA	(510) 732-0644	
Computer Media & Services Corp :CO	(800) 798-9078	
Computer Modules Inc :CA......	(408) 496-1881	
Computer Monthly/Reseller World :AL	(205) 988-9708	
Computer Music Supply :CA	(714) 594-5051	(714) 594-6821
Computer Network Technology :MN	(800) 638-8324	
Computer Parts Outlet, Inc :FL....	(800) 475-1655	

Company and :State	Main Phone	Tech Phone
Computer Parts Unlimited :CA.	(818) 879-1100	
Computer Peripheral Repair :FL . . .	(407) 586-0011	
Computer Peripherals Inc :CA.	(800) 854-7600	(805) 499-6021
. . . .	BBS (805) 499-9646	
Computer Place, The :AZ	(602) 962-1030	
Computer Power, Inc :NJ.	(800) 526-5088	(908) 638-8600
Computer Products :FL	(305) 974-5500	
Computer Products Corp :CO	(800) 338-4273	
Computer Products Plus :CA.	(714) 847-1799	
Computer Products Plus, Inc :CA . .	(800) 274-4277	(714) 847-1799
Computer Publishers :IL	(708) 390-7000	
Computer Publishing & Adver. :NY	(914) 833-0600	
Computer Publishing Enterprises :CA	(619) 576-0353	
Computer Publishing Enterprises :CA	(619) 576-0353	
Computer Recyclers :TX	(800) 466-6449	
Computer Reference Products :WA	(206) 869-7840	
Computer Renaissance Inc :MN . . .	(612) 942-5062	
Computer Representatives Assn :FL	(407) 788-3666	
Computer Research :PA	(800) 245-2710	
Computer Reset :TX	(214) 276-8072	
Computer Resources :CO	(800) 662-0034	
Computer Sales Professional :NJ .	(800) 950-6660	
Computer Sciences Corp :CA	(213) 615-0311	
Computer Service & Maintenance :CA	(619) 944-1228	
Computer Service Center Inc :NJ .	(201) 843-6290	
Computer Service Express Corp :KY.	(502) 366-3188	
Computer Service Labs Inc :PA. . .	(800) 220-6860	
Computer Service Supply :NH. . . .	(800) 255-7815	
Computer Service Technology:TX .	(214) 241-2662	
Computer Services Group Inc :NY .	(212) 819-0122	
Computer Site Technologies Inc :FL	(305) 425-0638	
Computer Solutions Inc :NJ.	(201) 672-6000	
Computer Support :TX.	(214) 661-8960	
. . . .	BBS (214) 404-8652	
Computer Support Products :MA. .	(508) 281-6554	
Computer Systems Advisors :NJ. .	(800) 537-4262	
Computer Systems Associates :NC	(704) 871-8367	
Computer Systems News :NY	(516) 365-4600	
Computer Systems Repair :CA . . .	(310) 217-8901	
Computer Task Group :NY	(716) 882-8000	
Computer Technology Review :CA .	(310) 208-1335	
Computer Technology Services:CA	(714) 855-8667	
Computer Terminal Services :CA .	(916) 368-4300	
Computer Time Of America :PA . . .	(800) 456-1159	(614) 759-0100
Computer Trade Exchange :NJ. . . .	(201) 226-1528	
Computer Trading International :CA	(818) 764-0615	
Computer Trend Inc :AL.	(205) 442-6376	
ComputerEasy International Inc :AZ	(602) 829-9614	
ComputerGear :KS	(800) 234-3434	
Computerland Corp :CA.	(510) 734-4000	(800) 922-5263

Company and :State	Main Phone	Tech Phone
ComputerLand Corp :NJ	(201) 575-7110	
Computerland Depot Repair Servis :NJ	(800) 445-6879	
Computers For Less :CA	(800) 634-1415	(714) 975-0542
Computers Inc :NJ	(800) 637-4832	
Computers Plus :RI.	(401) 434-9180	
Computerwise Inc :KS	(913) 829-0600	
Computerworld :MA	(508) 879-0700	
Computime Inc :MO	(800) 423-8826	
Computone :PA.	(800) 541-9915	
Computone Corp :GA	(404) 475-2725	(404) 475-2725
Computrac, Inc :TX.	(214) 234-4241	
CompuTrend Systems Inc :CA	(818) 333-5121	
Comshare :MI	(313) 994-4800	
Comtech Publishing :NV.	(702) 825-9000	
Comtrade :CA.	(800) 969-2123	(800) 899-4508
Comtrol Corp :MN.	(800) 926-6876	
. . . .	BBS (612) 631-9310	
Concentric Data :MA.	(508) 366-1122	
Concept Omega Corp :NJ	(800) 524-0430	
Conceptual Software :TX	(713) 667-4222	
Concurrent Computer :NJ.	(908) 758-7000	
Concurrent Computer Corporation :NJ	(908) 870-4128	
Concurrent Controls, Inc :CA	(800) 487-2249	
. . . .	BBS (415) 873-6256	
Conde Systems :AL	(800) 826-6332	(205) 633-3876
Conductive Containers Inc :IL	(800) 327-2329	
Conlux USA Corp :MO	(800) 792-0101	
Connect :.	(415) 435-7446	
Connect Software :WA	(800) 234-9497	
Connect Tech Inc :ON	(519) 836-1291	
Connect-Air International, Inc :WA . .	(800) 247-1978	
Connectix Corp :CA	(800) 950-5880	
Conner Peripherals, Inc. :CA	(800) 851-4200	(408) 456-3388
FAX back (408) 456-4903 . .	BBS (408) 456-4415	
Conner/Maynard Electronics :FL . .	(800) 227-6296	
. . . .	BBS (407) 263-3502	
Connexperts :TX	(800) 433-5373	(214) 352-2281
Consmi Development :	(310) 835-9687	(800) 654-8829
Consolidated Electronics :OH. . . .	(513) 252-5662	
Consultex :CA.	(800) 243-3338	
Consulting Spectrum :TX	(214) 484-9330	
Consultronics :ON.	(800) 267-7255	
Consumer Technology Northwest :OR	(800) 356-3983	
Consumers Software Inc :BC	(604) 688-4548	
Contact East :MA	(800) 225-5334	
Contact Software International :TX.	(800) 365-0606	(214) 484-4349
Contek International Corp :CT	(203) 853-4313	
Contemporary Computer Services :NY	(516) 563-8800	
Continental Information Systems :NY	(315) 437-1900	
Continental Resources Inc :MA . . .	(800) 937-4688	

Company and :State	Main Phone	Tech Phone
Contingency Planning Research :NY.	(516) 997-1100	
Control Cable :MD	(410) 298-4411	
Control Concepts Corp :NY	(800) 288-6169	
Control Data Corp :MN	(612) 853-8100	
Control Technology Inc :OK.	(405) 840-3163	
Controlled Power Company :MI.	(313) 528-3700	
Convergent World :	(800) 888-5093	
Conversion Systems :CA.	(714) 870-1626	
Conway Engineering Inc :CA.	(510) 568-4028	
Cook's Computer Maintenance :CA	(805) 323-6036	
Cooper Industries :IN.	(317) 983-5200	
Coordinated Service :MA.	(508) 486-0388	
Copam USA, Inc :CA	(800) 828-4200	
Copia International :IL	(708) 682-8898	
Copy Technologies :CA	(714) 975-1477	
Cordata :CA	(213) 603-2901	
Core International :FL	(800) 688-9910	(407) 997-6033
	BBS (407) 241-2929	
Core Software Inc :TX	(713) 292-2177	
Corel Systems Corp :ON	(800) 836-3729	(613) 728-1990
	BBS (613) 728-4752	
Corim International Corporation :NY	(212) 883-0030	
Cornell Computer Systems :CA.	(800) 886-7200	
Cornerstone Data Systems :CA	(714) 772-5527	
Cornerstone Technology :CA	(800) 562-2552	
	BBS (408) 435-8943	
Corollary Inc :CA	(714) 250-4040	
Coromandel Industries Inc :NY	(800) 535-3267	(718) 793-7966
Corporate Management & Marketing :NJ	(201) 989-0229	
Corporate Microsystems Inc :NH.	(603) 448-5193	
Corporate Software :MA	(617) 821-4500	
Cortex Corp :MN	(612) 894-3354	
Corvus Systems, Inc :CA.	(800) 426-7887	
	BBS (408) 972-9154	
Cosmic Enterprises :MA	(800) 292-6967	
Costa Distributing, West :CA	(800) 926-7829	
CoStar :	(800) 426-7827	(203) 661-9700
Costas Systems :CA	(510) 443-2332	
Costem :CA	(408) 734-9235	
Cougar Mountain Software :ID	(800) 388-3038	(800) 727-9912
Courseware Technology :CA	(800) 736-1936	
Courseware Technology :	(619) 452-2726	
Courtland Group Inc :MD.	(410) 730-7668	
Covox Inc :OR	(503) 342-1271	
	BBS (503) 342-4135	
CP+ :	(800) 274-4277	
CPE Inc :TX	(214) 313-1133	
Cpt Corp :MN	(612) 937-8000	
CPU Products :KS	(316) 788-3749	

Company and :State	Main Phone	Tech Phone
Cranel Inc :MA	(800) 727-2635	
Cray Research :MN	(612) 452-6650	
CRC Systems Ltd :CO	(800) 231-0743	
Creative Computer Applications :CA	(818) 880-6700	
Creative Controllers Inc :MS.	(800) 950-6224	
Creative Data Products Inc :CA	(800) 366-1020	
Creative Labs, Inc. :CA.	(800) 998-5227	(408) 428-6622
	BBS (408) 428-6660	
Creative Multimedia Corp :OR	(503) 241-4351	
Creative Programming :TX	(214) 416-6447	
	BBS (214) 418-0059	
Creotec Corp :TX	(214) 717-1272	
Crescent Project Management :CA	(415) 493-4787	
Crescent Software :CT	(203) 438-5300	
Cresta Batteries :CA	(800) 638-7120	
Crisis Computer Corp :CA	(800) 726-0726	(800) 729-0729
CRM Computer Parts Inc :ON	(800) 284-2865	
CRM Computer Parts Inc :FL	(800) 759-5539	
Crosby Creations :WA	(800) 842-8445	
Crosfield Dicomed :MN.	(612) 895-3000	
Crossley Group Inc, The :GA	(404) 751-3703	
Crosstalk Communications :GA	(404) 442-4000	
	BBS (404) 740-8428	
Crown Mats & Matting :OH	(800) 628-5463	
Crump Electronics :CO	(303) 936-4407	
Crutchfield-Hardware :VA	(800) 537-4050	
Crutchfield-Software :VA	(800) 538-4050	
Crystal Computer Systems :CA	(310) 946-1447	
Crystal Semiconductor Corp :TX	(512) 445-7222	
Crystal Services :BC	(604) 681-3435	
CrystalGraphics Inc :CA	(408) 496-6175	
CSC CompuSource Inc :NC	(919) 460-1234	
CSP Inc :MA	(617) 272-6020	
CSR :NJ	(201) 617-7711	
CSS Laboratories, Inc :CA	(714) 852-8161	
	BBS (714) 852-9231	
CST Inc :TX.	(214) 241-2662	
CTC Corp :CA.	(510) 770-8787	
CTI :VA	(703) 264-8900	
CTS Services :MA.	(508) 528-7720	
CTSI International Inc :NY	(516) 467-1281	
CTX International Inc :CA	(714) 595-6146	
Cubix Corp :NV	(800) 829-0550	
	BBS (702) 882-8737	
CUE Paging Corp :CA	(800) 858-8828	
Cuesta Systems Corp :CA	(800) 332-3440	
CUI :CA	(800) 458-6686	(408) 988-2703
Cullinet Software :MA	(617) 329-7700	
Cumulus :OH	(216) 464-2211	
	BBS (216) 464-3019	

Company and :State	Main Phone	Tech Phone
Curtis Manufacturing :NH	(603) 532-4123	
Curtis Manufacturing Co :NH	(800) 955-5544	
Custom Application :	(508) 667-8585	(508) 663-8213
Custom Computer Cable Inc :MN	(612) 941-5651	
Custom Real-Time Software :NJ	(201) 228-7623	
Customer Satisfaction Research :KS	(913) 894-6166	
Customer Service Institute :MD	(301) 585-0730	
Cut Craft Inc :TX	(817) 332-6151	
CW Electronics :CO	(303) 832-1111	
CWay Software :PA	(215) 368-9494	(215) 368-7233
CXR Digilog :CA	(408) 435-8520	
CyberTechnics Corporation :CA	(408) 986-9686	
Cybex Corp :AL	(205) 534-0011	
Cyborg Corporation :MA	(617) 964-9020	
Cycare Systems :AZ	(800) 545-2483	
Cyclades Corp :CA	(510) 770-9727	
Cyco International :GA	(800) 323-2926	
	BBS (404) 634-1441	
Cylix Corporation :CA	(805) 379-3155	
Cyma Systems Inc :AZ	(800) 292-2962	
Cypress Research :	(408) 752-2700	
Cyrix Corp :TX	(800) 462-9749	
D-C-Drives :TX	(800) 473-0960	(713) 333-2099
D-Link Systems, Inc :CA	(714) 455-1688	
	BBS (714) 445-1779	
Da Vinci Systems :NC	(919) 781-5924	
DAC Software :	BBS (214) 931-6617	
DacEasy, Inc :TX	(800) 322-3279	(214) 248-0205
	BBS (214) 931-6617	
Daewoo International Corp :NJ	(201) 935-8700	
Dairyland Computer & Consulting :MN	(800) 323-6987	
Daisy Disc Corporation :MA	(800) 537-3475	
Daisycom :TX	(214) 881-4700	
DakTech Inc :PA	(800) 325-3238	
Dalco Electronics :OH	(800) 445-5342	(800) 543-2526
Dallas Digital Corporation :TX	(800) 842-6333	
Dallas Fax Inc :TX	(214) 699-8999	
Dana Commercial Credit Corp :MI	(313) 689-7000	
Danish Consulate General :CA	(213) 387-4277	
Danpex Corp :CA	(408) 437-7557	
Dantona Industries Inc :NY	(516) 596-1515	
Dantz Development :	(510) 849-0293	(510) 849-0372
Danwill Industrial Ltd :CA	(818) 810-8880	
Dariana Software :CA	(714) 236-1380	
	BBS (714) 994-7410	
Darius Technology Inc :WA	(206) 483-8889	
Dash Computer Inc :CA	(408) 773-1488	
Dat Entry Inc :FL	(407) 339-5062	
Data 3 Systems :CA	(707) 528-6560	
Data Access Corp :FL	(305) 238-0012	(305) 232-3142

Company and :State	Main Phone	Tech Phone
. . . .	BBS (305) 238-0640	
Data Accessories Corp :ON	(416) 292-9963	
Data Base Solutions :CA	(800) 336-6060	
. . . .	BBS (619) 270-2042	
Data Code :NY	(516) 331-7848	
Data Communications :NY	(212) 512-6950	
Data Communications 2000 Inc :CA	(714) 255-7090	
Data Connections :NC	(800) 225-1855	
Data Depot Inc :FL	(800) 767-3424	
Data Devices International :CA . . .	(818) 727-2335	
Data Engineering :NH	(603) 893-3374	
Data Entry Systems, Inc :AL	(205) 539-2483	
Data Envelope & Packaging :CA . .	(800) 544-4417	
Data Exchange Corp :CA	(805) 388-1711	
Data General Corp :MA	(508) 366-8911	
Data I/O Corp :WA	(206) 881-6444	
Data Mate North America Inc :CA .	(310) 316-5161	
Data Pad Corp :UT	(800) 755-8218	
Data Plus, Inc :TX	(713) 641-6158	
Data Pro :NJ	(908) 756-7300	
Data Pro Accounting Software :FL .	(800) 836-6377	(813) 888-5847
Data Processing Security Inc :TX. .	(817) 457-9400	
Data Quest Hawaii :HI	(808) 545-5482	
Data Recording Products Ltd :CA .	(310) 633-7198	
Data Retrieval Services Inc :FL . . .	(800) 952-7530	
Data Retrieval Services Inc :CA . . .	(800) 942-4472	
Data Services Corporation :GA . . .	(404) 246-3700	
Data Set Cable Company :CT	(800) 344-9684	
Data Solutions :CA	(714) 637-5060	
Data Spec :CA	(818) 772-9977	(818) 772-9977
Data Storage Marketing :CO	(800) 543-6090	(800) 543-6098
Data Storage Marketing :NJ	(800) 424-2203	
Data Storage Marketing :TX	(800) 654-6311	
Data Switch Corp :CT	(203) 926-1801	
Data Systems/Micro Connect :MI. .	(800) 445-3282	
Data Technology :CA	(408) 262-7700	(408) 262-7700
. . . .	BBS (408) 942-4197	
Data Transforms :CO	(303) 832-1501	
Data Translation :MA	(508) 481-3700	(508) 481-3700
Data Viz :CT	(800) 733-0030	
Data Watch :NC	(919) 490-1277	
Data-Cal Corp :AZ	(800) 223-0123	
Data-Doc Electonics, Inc :TX	(512) 928-8926	(512) 928-8926
Data/Ware Development Inc :CA . .	(619) 453-7660	
Database Applications :NJ	(609) 924-2900	
Database Programming & Dsign :CA	(415) 905-2200	
Database Technologies :MA	(617) 739-3390	
Datability Software Systems Inc :NJ	(212) 807-7800	
Datacap Inc :NY	(914) 332-7515	
Datacap Systems, Inc :PA	(215) 699-7051	

Company and :State	Main Phone	Tech Phone
Datacom Technologies Inc :WA ...	(800) 468-5557	
Datadesk International :CA	(818) 998-4200	
DataEase International :CT	(800) 243-5123	(203) 374-2825
.... BBS (203) 374-6302		
DataExpert Corp :CA	(408) 737-0880	
Datafix Inc :AR	(501) 562-3554	
Datagate Inc :CA	(408) 946-6222	
Dataguard Recovery Services:KY	(800) 325-3977	
DataJets International Inc :CA ...	(714) 630-6662	
Datalynx Marketing Inc :BC	(604) 765-1162	
Datamar Systems :CA	(800) 223-9963	
Datamate :OK	(918) 664-7276	
Datamation :MA	(617) 964-3030	
Datapath Technologies Inc :CA ...	(510) 651-5580	
Datapoint Corp :TX	(512) 593-7000	
Datapro Information Services :NJ ..	(609) 764-0100	
Datapro Research Group :NJ	(800) 328-2776	
Dataproducts :CA..............	(818) 887-8440	
Dataproducts :NH	(603) 673-9100	
Dataq Instruments Inc :OH	(216) 668-1444	
Dataquest/Ledgeway :MA	(508) 370-5555	
Datasouth Computer Corp :NC ...	(800) 476-2450	
DataSpec :	(800) 431-8124	
Datastorm Technologies, Inc :MO..	(314) 443-3282	
.... BBS (314) 875-0503		
Datasure Technologies Inc :CA ...	(510) 935-9899	
DataSym Inc :ON	(519) 758-5800	
Datatech Depot Inc :CA	(714) 970-1600	
Datatek Peripheral Services:CA ...	(800) 829-2099	
Datatran Corporation :CO	(303) 778-0870	
DataTrek Corp :IN	(219) 522-8000	
Datatronics Inc :TX	(713) 367-0567	
Dataviz :	(800) 733-0030	(203) 268-0030
Dataware :TX	(800) 426-4844	
DATEC :WA	(800) 525-9905	
DATEC :OR	(503) 641-6644	
Datel :MA	(508) 339-3000	
Dauphin Technology, Inc :IL	(708) 627-4004	
David Smith Software :MA	(508) 249-9056	
David Systems, Inc :CA.........	(408) 720-6867	(408) 720-6884
.... BBS (408) 720-0406		
Davidson & Associates :CA	(800) 545-7677	
Davox Corp :MA..............	(508) 667-4455	
DayFlo Software :CA	(714) 474-1364	
Dayna Communications :UT	(801) 269-7200	
.... BBS (801) 535-4205		
DayStar Digital :	(800) 962-2077	
DBMS :CA	(415) 358-9500	
DC Battery Products :MN	(612) 616-7478	

Company and :State	Main Phone	Tech Phone
DCA :GA	(404) 442-4000	(404) 740-0300
. . . .	BBS (404) 740-8428	
DCA/Crosstalk Communications :	(404) 442-3210	
DCI Companies :NY	(800) 234-2202	
DCM Data Products :TX	(817) 870-2202	
DCSI :VA.	(703) 823-9886	
DD & TT Enterprise USA Co :CA . .	(213) 780-0099	
DDC Publishing :NY	(212) 683-9028	(800) 528-3897
DEC Professional :PA.	(215) 957-1500	
Decision Inc :TX	(903) 586-0557	
Decision Industries :PA.	(215) 674-3300	
Dee One Systems :CA	(800) 831-8808	
Dee Van Enterprise USA Inc :CA. .	(800) 878-0691	
Deerfield Systems Inc :NY	(800) 356-8170	
Dees Communications Engineering :BC	(604) 946-8433	
Deico Electronics, Inc :CA	(510) 651-7800	
Delkin Devices Inc :CA.	(619) 571-1234	
Dell Computer Corp :TX	(800) 426-5150	(800) 624-9896
. . . .	BBS (512) 338-8528	
DeLorme Mapping :ME.	(207) 865-1234	
Delphi :MA.	(800) 695-4005	
Delrina Technology :OT	(800) 268-6082	(416) 441-1026
Delta Computer Inc :NJ	(201) 440-8585	
Delta Phase International :CA . .	(714) 768-6842	
Delta Products Corp :IL	(708) 487-1037	
Delta Technology International :WI	(715) 832-7575	
Delta Warranty :WA	(206) 391-2000	
DeltaPoint Inc :CA.	(408) 648-4000	(408) 375-4700
Deltec Corp :CA	(800) 854-2658	
Deltron Inc :PA	(800) 523-2332	
DemoSource :CA	(800) 283-4759	
Dempa Publications :NY	(212) 752-3003	
Deneba Software :FL	(800) 622-6827	
Departmental Technologies, Inc :NJ	(201) 786-5838	
Depot America :NJ	(800) 648-6833	
Desco Industries :CA	(714) 598-2753	
DeScribe, Inc :CA	(916) 646-1111	
Design Creations :CA	(209) 532-8413	
Design Science :CA	(800) 827-0685	(213) 433-6969
DesignCAD :OK	(918) 825-4844	
Desk Top Graphics :	(817) 346-0556	
Deskin Research Group Inc :CA . .	(408) 496-5300	
Desktop AI :CT	(203) 255-3400	
Desktop Sales Inc :IL	(708) 272-9695	
Dest Corp :CA	(408) 436-2700	
Destiny Technology Corp :CA . . .	(408) 262-9400	
DEW International Corp :CA.	(800) 326-7114	
DF Blumberg & Associates :PA . .	(215) 643-9060	
DFM Systems, Inc :IA.	(800) 922-4336	
DH Serv :CA	(800) 548-7862	

Company and :State	Main Phone	Tech Phone
DH Technology :CA	(619) 451-3485	
DI/AN Controls :MA	(800) 878-3134	
Diagnostic Technologies :ON	(416) 542-8674	
DiagSoft Inc :CA	(800) 342-4763	
Diamond Computer Systems :CA . .	(408) 736-2000	
. . . .	BBS (408) 730-1100	
Diamond Data Management, Inc :WI	(800) 955-3330	
Diamond Flower Electric Inst. :CA .	(916) 568-1234	
Dianachart Inc :NJ	(201) 625-2299	
DIC Digital :NJ	(201) 224-9344	
Dick Berg & Associates :CA	(619) 452-2745	
Diebold :OH	(216) 489-4110	
Digi-Data Corp :MD	(800) 782-6395	
DIGI-KEY :MN	(800) 344-4539	
Digiboard, Inc :MN	(800) 344-4273	
. . . .	BBS (612) 943-0812	
Digicom Systems Inc :CA	(408) 262-1277	
. . . .	BBS (508) 262-1412	
Digital Communications Assoc. :GA	(800) 348-3221	
. . . .	BBS (404) 740-8428	
Digital Computer Services :PA . . .	(215) 358-6045	
Digital Data Recovery :WI	(414) 353-1219	
Digital Data Systems Inc :FL	(800) 762-7811	
Digital Equipment Corp :MA	(800) 332-7378	
Digital Equipment Corp :MA	(800) 332-4636	
Digital Equipment Corp :MA	(508) 841-6286	
Digital Equipment Corp :NH.	(603) 884-2004	
Digital Equipment Corp :MA	(508) 841-3627	
Digital Mind :FL	(407) 354-0045	
Digital News & Revies :MA	(617) 964-3030	
Digital Processing Systems Inc :KY	(606) 371-5533	
Digital Products Inc :MA.	(800) 243-2337	
Digital Products, Inc :MA	(800) 243-3333	
Digital Research :CA	(408) 649-3896	(408) 646-6464
. . . .	BBS (408) 649-3443	
Digital Review :MA.	(617) 964-3030	
Digital Solutions Inc :CA	(916) 773-1551	
Digital Storage Inc :OH	(800) 232-3475	
Digital Typeface Corp :MN	(612) 944-9264	(612) 941-8652
Digital Vision :MA	(617) 329-5400	
. . . .	BBS (617) 329-8387	
Digitalk :CA	(800) 531-2344	(310) 337-3135
Digitech Industries Inc :CT	(203) 797-2676	
Digitronix Inc :NE	(402) 339-5340	
Digitz :NC	(919) 828-5227	
DigiVox Corp :CA.	(415) 494-6200	
Digix America Corp :FL	(305) 593-8070	
Direct Drives :IL	(708) 481-1111	
DISC :CA	(800) 669-2333	
Disc & Tape Services :NH	(603) 889-5722	

Company and :State	Main Phone	Tech Phone
Disc Distributing Corp :CA	(800) 688-4545	
Disc Manufacturing Inc :DE	(302) 479-2500	
Discimagery :	(212) 675-8500	
Discis Knowledge Research :ON	(416) 250-6537	
Discount Micro :UT	(800) 574-3325	(714) 827-7090
Discoversoft Inc :CA	(510) 814-1690	
Disctec :FL	(407) 671-5500	
Disctron, Inc	Out Of Business :	
Discus Knowledge Research :ON	(416) 250-6537	
Disk Drive Repair Inc :WA	(206) 575-3181	
Disk Software :TX	(800) 635-7760	
Disk Technician Corp :CA	(619) 274-5000	(619) 274-5000
	BBS (619) 272-9240	
Disk's & Labels To Go, Inc :NJ	(800) 426-3303	
Diskette Connection :OK	(800) 654-4058	
Diskettes Unlimited :TX	(800) 364-3475	
Disks And Labels To Go, Inc :NJ	(609) 265-1500	
Disney Computer Software :	(818) 841-3326	
Display Technologies :IL	(708) 931-2136	
Distinct Corp :CA	(408) 741-0781	
Distributed Logic Corp :CA	(714) 476-0303	
Distributed Processing Tech :	(407) 830-5522	
	BBS (407) 831-6432	
Distributed Technologies :WA	(206) 395-7800	
Ditek International :ON	(416) 479-1990	
DiVA :MA	(617) 491-4147	(617) 491-6913
Diverse Business Group :BC	(604) 596-6088	
Diversified Case Company :NY	(315) 736-3028	
Dlesko Associates :NJ	(201) 435-8401	
DMA :NY	(516) 462-0440	
DMS :CA	(800) 821-3354	
DNA Networks, Inc :PA	(800) 999-3622	
	BBS (215) 296-9558	
Document Management :AZ	(602) 224-9777	
Document Storage Systems Inc :CO	(303) 757-1455	
DocuPoint Inc :CA	(510) 770-1189	
Dolch Computer Systems :CA	(800) 538-7506	
Dominion Blueline Inc :ON	(416) 444-6621	
DotShop Inc :OR	(800) 487-6025	
Dove Computer :NC	(919) 343-5648	(919) 343-5610
	BBS (919) 343-5616	
Dover Electronics Manufacturing :CO	(303) 772-5933	
Dovetail Communications :CA	(800) 432-1414	
Dow Jones & Company :	(609) 520-4000	
Dow Jones Service :NJ	(800) 922-0358	
DP Nemeth Associates :NJ	(609) 737-1166	
DP Tech :TX	(713) 492-1894	
DP-Tek, Inc :KS	(800) 727-3130	
DPT - Distrbt. Processing Techn. :FL	(407) 830-5522	
	BBS (407) 831-6432	

Company and :State	Main Phone	Tech Phone
Dr. Dobb's Journal :CA	(415) 358-9500	
Dragon Systems Inc :MA	(617) 965-5200	
Dranetz Technologies Inc :NJ	(800) 372-6832	
Dresselhaus Computer Products :CA	(800) 368-7737	
Drexler Technology :CA	(415) 969-7277	
Drive Repair Service Co :CA	(510) 430-0595	
DSA Systems :MA	(508) 477-2540	
DSC Communications :TX	(214) 519-3000	
DSE Inc :HI	(808) 578-0237	
DSG Communications Inc :SK	(306) 665-6107	
DSK Inc :UT	(801) 224-4828	
DST Systems :MO	(816) 221-5545	
DTK Computer Inc :CA	(818) 810-8880	
	BBS (818) 333-6548	
Du Pont Connector Systems :DE	(302) 992-5009	
Dual Group, Inc :CA	(310) 542-0788	
Dubl-Click Software :	(800) 266-9525	
Dudley Software :TN	(615) 966-3667	
	BBS (615) 966-3574	
Duffy Consulting Group Inc :ON	(416) 966-4015	
Dumont Oscilloscope :NJ	(201) 575-8666	
Duplication Technology, Inc :CO	(303) 444-6157	
Duracell Inc :CT	(203) 796-4000	
Dustin Discount Software :CA	(800) 274-6611	
DW Smith & Associates :CA	(415) 349-7725	
Dyatron Corp :AL	(800) 334-3471	
Dyna Micro, Inc :CA	(408) 943-0100	
Dynamic Electronics Inc :CA	(714) 855-0411	
Dynamic Pathways :	(714) 720-8462	
Dynamic Power Systems :NY	(800) 422-0708	
Dynatech Corp :MA	(617) 272-6100	
DynaTek Automation Systems:OT	(416) 636-3000	
Dynaware USA :	(415) 349-5700	
Dytel Inc :IL	(708) 519-9850	
E-Cam Technology Inc :AZ	(602) 443-1949	
E-Comms :WA	(800) 247-1431	
E-Machines :OR	(800) 344-7274	(503) 626-5163
E-Systems :TX	(214) 661-1000	
E-Tech Research Inc :CA	(408) 730-1388	
E-Toor Corp :CA	(818) 333-5521	
Eagle Electronics :CA	(800) 992-3191	
Eagle Performance Software :TX	(214) 539-7855	
Eagle Technology :WI	(800) 388-3268	
Easel Corp :MA	(617) 221-2100	
Eastern Time Designs Inc :NH	(603) 645-6578	
Easterntech Corp :NY	(800) 289-8128	(800) 685-5006
Eastman Kodak :NY	(716) 724-4000	
Easy Automation Systems, Inc :GA	(800) 627-3274	(404) 840-0475
EAZY :PA	(412) 746-5500	
EBS Consulting :NY	(215) 493-7315	

Company and :State	Main Phone	Tech Phone
Eclipse Marketing Inc :OR	(800) 284-0779	
Eclipse Marketing Inc :OR	(800) 284-0779	(503) 598-9640
Eclipse Systems :IL	(312) 541-0260	
Ecol 2 :CA	(408) 456-0272	
Edgell Enterprises :NJ	(201) 895-3300	
Edimax Computer Company :CA . . .	(408) 496-1105	
Edison Technologies :CA	(800) 334-7668	
EDP Research & Development :CT . .	(203) 399-5018	
EDS Corp :TX	(214) 661-6000	
Edsun Laboratories, Inc :MA	(617) 647-9300	
Educom USA Inc :CA	(618) 693-4344	
Eductional Systems, Inc :IL	(800) 553-2212	
EECO Inc :CA	(714) 835-6000	
EF Industries :CA	(310) 523-2290	
EFA Corp Of America :MD	(301) 670-6166	
EFAR Microsystems Inc :CA	(408) 452-1888	
Efficient Field Service Corp :MA . . .	(800) 257-4745	
Effron Sales: CA	(714) 962-1016	
EFI Electronics :UT	(800) 877-1174	
Egghead Discount Software :WA . . .	(206) 391-0800	
Eicon Technology :PQ	(514) 631-2592	
EID Center :	(408) 733-5501	
Eight Hundred Software :CA	(800) 888-4880	
EJ Bilingual Inc :CA	(310) 320-8139	
EKD Computer Sales & Supplies :NY	(516) 736-0500	
El Camino Resources Ltd :CA	(818) 226-6600	
Elan Computer Group :CA	(415) 964-2200	
Elan Software Corp :CA	(800) 654-3526	(818) 999-1184
Elan Software Corp :CA	(818) 999-9872	
Elcee Computek, Inc :FL	(407) 750-8061	
Elco Computers :CA	(818) 284-3281	(818) 284-7018
Elecom Computer Products Inc :CA	(310) 802-0077	
Electrified Discounters :CT	(800) 678-8585	
Electro Media Publishing Inc :CA . .	(408) 374-9804	
Electro Products Inc :WA	(800) 423-0646	
Electro Standards Laboratory Inc :RI	(401) 943-1164	
Electro Static Technology Inc :ME .	(207) 795-6416	
Electro Tech Industries Inc :CA . . .	(619) 745-3575	
Electro Test Industries Inc :MA . . .	(617) 341-0781	
Electro-Tech Systems Inc :PA	(215) 887-2196	
Electrodata Inc :OH.	(800) 441-6336	
Electrografics Intrntl. Corp :PA	(215) 443-5190	(215) 443-9564
Electrohome Projection Systems :ON	(519) 744-7111	
Electromatic :IL	(708) 882-5757	
Electronic Arts Distribution :	(800) 448-8822	(415) 572-2787
Electronic Assistance Corp :TX . . .	(817) 778-7978	
Electronic Associates :NJ	(908) 229-1100	
Electronic City :AZ	(602) 622-1173	
Electronic Data Associates :MO . . .	(816) 966-0669	
Electronic Marketing Group :PA . . .	(800) 955-2688	

Company and :State	Main Phone	Tech Phone
Electronic News :	(800) 883-6397	
Electronic Products Service Inc :GA	(404) 448-0748	
Electronic Services Technologies :MI	(313) 341-1821	
Electronic Specialists Inc :MA	(508) 655-1532	
Electronic Speech Systems :CA	(510) 783-3100	
Electronics Of Salina :KN	(913) 827-7377	
Electronics Unlimited Inc :OH	(216) 835-0520	
Electroservice Laboratories :CA	(800) 336-4375	
Electrospec Inc :NJ	(800) 631-9616	
Elegant Graphics Corp :CO	(303) 879-4334	
ELEK-TEK :IL	(800) 395-1000	
Elektro Assemblies Inc :MN	(800) 533-1558	
Elenco Electronics :IL	(708) 541-3800	
Elesys :	(800) 637-0500	
Eletch Electonics, Inc :CA	(714) 385-1707	
Eletech Electronics Inc :CA	(714) 385-1707	
Elgar Corp :CA	(619) 450-0085	
Elisa Technology Inc :CA	(510) 651-5817	
Elite :CA	(310) 370-2762	
Elite High Technology :	(800) 874-6698	
Elite Microelectronics, Inc :CA	(408) 943-0500	
Elitegroup Computer Systems :CA	(510) 226-7333	
Elographics, Inc :TN	(615) 482-4100	
ELSA America Inc :CA	(415) 615-7799	
ELT Systems Of California :CA	(510) 226-9057	
Eltrex Industries Inc :NY	(716) 454-6100	
Elvo :NY	(914) 241-1008	
Elxsi Corp :.	(408) 994-9301	
EMAC/EVEREX :	(510) 498-4499	(510) 498-4440
	BBS (510) 226-9694	
Emax International Inc :CA	(310) 637-6380	
EMC Corp :MA	(800) 222-3622	
Emerald Intelligence :MI	(313) 663-8757	
Emerald Systems :	(800) 366-4349	
	BBS (619) 673-4617	
Emerging Technology Cons. :CO	(303) 447-9495	
Emerson Computer Corp :CA	(800) 222-5877	
Emerson Computer Power :CA	(714) 457-3600	
Emerson Electric :MO	(314) 553-2000	
Emery World Wide :CA	(800) 443-6379	
EML Associates :MA	(617) 341-0781	
Empac International Corp :CA	(510) 683-8800	
Empire Security Int'l :NY	(516) 466-3786	
Empress Software Inc :MD	(301) 220-1919	
Emulex :CA	(800) 854-7112	
Enable Software :NY	(800) 766-7079	(518) 877-8236
	BBS (518) 877-6316	
ENCAD Inc :CA	(619) 578-4070	
Enclosure Technologies, Inc :MI	(313) 481-2200	(313) 481-0597
Encore Computer Corp :MA	(508) 460-0500	

Company and :State	Main Phone	Tech Phone
Enertronics Research Inc :MO	(314) 427-7578	
Engage Communications :CA	(408) 688-1021	
Engineered Data Products, Inc :CO	(800) 432-1337	
Engineering Computers & Appl :NY	(800) 950-1217	
Engineering Services :NJ	(800) 525-5608	
English Knowledge Systems :GA..	(408) 438-6922	
Enhance Memory Products Inc :CA	(818) 343-3066	
Enlight Corp. USA :CA	(310) 693-8885	
Enterprise Systems Journal :TX...	(214) 343-3717	
Entrepreneur :CA	(714) 261-2325	
Entropy Engineering :MD	(301) 770-6886	
Envelope Manager :CA..........	(415) 321-2640	
Envisio :.	(612) 628-6288	
Envisions Solutions Technology :CA	(800) 365-7226	(415) 692-9067
EOS Distributing :KN	(913) 827-7377	
EOS Technology Inc :CA	(408) 727-0111	
EPE Technologies, Inc :CA	(714) 557-1636	
EPrinceton Computer Support :NJ.	(609) 921-8889	
Epsilon Data Management :MA ...	(800) 225-3333	
Epson America, Inc. :CA........	(800) 289-3776	(800) 922-8911
	BBS (408) 947-8777	
Epson Direct :CA	(800) 374-7300	(800) 922-8911
Equinox :FL..................	(305) 255-3500	
	BBS (305) 378-1696	
Equinox Systems Inc :FL	(305) 797-3873	
ERA :IL	(312) 649-1333	
Ergo Computing, Inc :MA	(508) 535-7510	
	BBS (508) 535-7228	
Ergo Management Co :MO......	(800) 348-8633	
Ergodyne :MN................	(612) 642-9889	
Ergotron :.	(800) 888-8458	
ErgoView Technologies Corp :NY .	(212) 995-2673	
ERM/Crazy Bob's :MA	(800) 776-5865	(617) 662-2046
Ero Surge Inc :NJ	(908) 766-4220	
ERS Electronic Repair Service :TX	(210) 623-4420	
Esca Corp :WA	(206) 822-6800	
ESCOD Industries :MA.........	(800) 533-4736	
Esico-Triton :CT	(203) 526-5361	
Esker :CA	(415) 341-9065	
ESoft Product Support :CO	(303) 699-6565	
	BBS (303) 699-8222	
ESP Inc :RI	(800) 338-4353	
Etak Inc :CA	(415) 328-3825	
ETC Computer Inc :CA.........	(510) 226-6250	
ETCON Corp :IL	(708) 325-6100	
Eteq Microsystems, Inc :CA	(408) 432-8147	
ETN Corporation :PA	(800) 326-9273	
ETS Incorporated :UT..........	(801) 265-2490	
	BBS (801) 265-0919	
European Computer Marketplace :CA	(619) 929-0955	

Company and :State	Main Phone	Tech Phone
European Computer Sources :IL	(708) 475-1900	
Evans & Sutherland Company :UT	(801) 582-5847	
Everest Computer Corp :CA	(408) 997-1674	
Everex Systems Inc :CA	(800) 821-0806	(510) 498-1115
	BBS (510) 438-4650	
Everfit Computer Supply Inc :CA	(408) 894-9003	
Evergreen Technologies :OR	(800) 733-0934	
	BBS (503) 757-8869	
Eversource International Corp :CA	(408) 745-0462	
Evolution Computing :AZ	(602) 967-8633	(800) 874-4028
Evtek Corp :OH	(216) 267-8499	
Ex Machina Inc :NY	(718) 965-0309	
Ex-Cel Solutions :NE	(402) 333-6541	
Exabyte Corp :CO	(800) 767-8273	
Excelan (Novell) :CA	(408) 434-2300	(800) 638-9273
Excelta Corp :CA	(805) 686-4686	
Executive Systems Inc :CA	(805) 541-0604	
EXFO Electro-Optical Engineering :QC	(800) 663-3936	
Exide Electronics Group Inc :NC	(919) 870-3285	
Exima International :CA	(408) 970-9225	
ExMachina :	(718) 965-0309	
EXP Computer, Inc :NY	(516) 496-3703	
Experience In Software :CA	(800) 678-7008	
Experience Software :CO	(303) 798-0790	
ExperVision Inc :CA	(408) 428-9988	(408) 428-0660
Expo Tech :IL	(800) 284-3976	
Exponent Corp :NJ	(201) 808-9423	
Express Computer Supply :CA	(800) 342-4542	
Exsel Inc :NY	(800) 624-2001	(800) 624-2001
Exsel Inc :NY	(716) 272-8770	
Exsel, Inc :NY.	(716) 272-8770	
Exsys :NM	(505) 256-8356	
Extech Instruments :MA	(617) 890-7440	
Extended Systems Inc :ID	(800) 235-7576	
Exxus Direct :CA	(800) 557-1000	(800) 557-4000
EyeTel Communications Inc :BC	(604) 984-2522	
EZX Publishing :TX	(713) 280-9900	
	BBS (713) 280-8180	
F Systems Industries :NJ	(800) 432-8051	
Facit,Inc :NH	(603) 647-2700	
Fairchild Defense :MD	(301) 428-6677	
Faircom :MO	(314) 445-6833	(800) 234-8180
Falltech Electronics :CA	(714) 543-5011	
Family & Home Office Computing :NY	(212) 505-3580	
Family Scrapbook :FL	(904) 247-0062	
	BBS (904) 249-9515	
Farallon Computing :	(510) 814-5000	
Fargo Electronics Inc :MN	(612) 941-9470	
FarPoint Communications :CA	(805) 726-4420	
FAST Electronic US Inc :MA	(508) 655-3278	

Company and :State	Main Phone	Tech Phone
Faultless Starch/Bon Ami :MO	(816) 842-1230	
FAX-Stor, Corp :CA	(408) 287-2700	
Faxback Inc :OR	(503) 645-1114	
FCC Public Access BBS :MD	BBS (301) 725-1072	
FDP Corp :FL	(305) 858-8200	
FEC :CA	(714) 692-1170	
Fedco Electronics, Inc :WI	(800) 542-9761	
Federal Computer International :VA	(703) 689-7711	
Federal Computer Week :VA	(703) 876-5100	
Federal Express :TN.............	(800) 238-5355	
Fellowes :IL	(708) 893-1600	
Fessenden Technologies :MO	(417) 485-2501	
FFE Software :CA...............	(510) 232-6800	
Fiber Instrument Sales :NY.......	(800) 445-2901	
FiberOptic Network Solutions :MA .	(508) 842-4744	
Fidelity International :NJ	(908) 828-7948	
Fidelity Professional Develop. :MN	(612) 897-3875	
Fieldpiece Instruments :CA.......	(714) 992-1239	
Fieldtex Products Inc :NY	(716) 473-5237	
Fifth Generation Systems Inc :LA.	(800) 873-4384	(504) 295-3344
....	BBS (504) 295-3344	
Filenet Corp :CA	(714) 966-3400	
Finalsoft Corp :FL	(800) 232-8228	
First Byte :CA	(800) 545-7677	(800) 556-6141
First Financial Management :GA ...	(404) 321-0120	
First International Computer :CA ...	(510) 475-7885	
First Source International :CA.....	(800) 535-5892	
First United Leasing Corp :IL	(708) 615-0992	
Fischer International :FL	(813) 643-1500	
Fiserv, Inc :WI	(800) 558-8413	
Flagship Accounting :TX.........	(214) 248-0305	
Flagship Group Inc, The :TX......	(214) 342-2801	
Flagstaff Engineering :AZ	(602) 779-3341	
Flambeaux Software,Inc :CA	(800) 833-7355	
Fleetmasters-Comtech :CA	(310) 539-7900	
Fleming Software :VA............	(703) 591-6451	
Flexistand Inc :NJ	(908) 754-6868	
FlexStar Technology :CA	(510) 440-0170	
Flight Form Cases Inc :WA	(206) 435-6688	
Flip Track OneOnOne Comp. Train. :IL	(800) 424-8668	
Floating Point Systems Computing :OR	(503) 641-3151	(503) 641-3151
Flytech Technology Co Ltd :CA ...	(408) 727-7373	
....	BBS (408) 727-0730	
Focus Electronics Corp :CA	(714) 468-5533	
Focus Information Systems Inc :CA	(510) 657-2845	
Folex Film Systems :NJ	(800) 631-1150	
Folio Corp :UT.................	(801) 375-3700	
....	BBS (801) 375-9907	
Footprint Software Inc :ON	(416) 860-0477	
Fora Inc :CA	(408) 944-0393	

Company and :State	Main Phone	Tech Phone
Foresight Resources Corp :MO	(800) 231-8574	(816) 891-8418
. . . .	BBS (816) 891-8465	
FormalSoft :UT	(800) 962-7118	
FormGen Corp :OT	(416) 857-4141	
Fornax Computer Corp :NJ	(908) 874-7122	
Fort's Software :KS	(913) 537-2897	
Forte Computer Services Inc :IL . .	(708) 985-7222	
Fortron/Source Corp :CA	(510) 373-1008	
Forval America Inc :CA	(408) 452-8887	
Forval America, Inc :UT	(801) 561-8080	
Fotec Inc :MA	(800) 537-8254	
Foundationware (Certus Intn'l) :OH.	(216) 752-8181	
Fountain Technologies, Inc :NJ	(908) 563-4800	
Four Seasons Publishing :NY	(212) 599-2141	
Fourgen Software, Inc :WA	(800) 333-4436	(800) 444-3398
Fourth Party Maintenance Co :ON . .	(416) 479-1910	
Fox Software :OH.	(419) 874-0162	
Fractal Design Corp :CA	(408) 688-8800	
Frame Technology :CA	(408) 433-3311	
Franklin Datacom, Inc :CA	(805) 373-8688	
Franklin Electronic Publishers :NJ. .	(609) 261-4800	
Franklin Quest Co :UT.	(801) 975-9992	
Frederick Engineering :MD	(410) 290-9000	
Free Computer Technology :CA . . .	(408) 945-1118	
Fremont Communications Co :CA . .	(510) 438-5000	
French Expositions In The US:NY. .	(212) 265-5676	
Fresh Technology Group :AZ	(800) 545-8324	
. . . .	BBS (602) 497-4235	
Fridays Electronics :CA	(800) 488-6575	(408) 294-5295
Friendly Software Store :CA	(800) 848-0486	(415) 593-8275
Frontline Network Systems :MA . . .	(508) 393-1911	
Frontline Systems :CA.	(800) 451-0303	
. . . .	BBS (415) 327-7319	
Frontline Test Equipment :IL	(708) 653-8570	
Frost & Sullivan, Inc :NY	(800) 435-1080	
FRS Inc :CA	(916) 928-1107	
Frye Computer :MA	(617) 451-5400	
FTG Data Systems :CA	(800) 962-3900	
FTP Software Inc :MA	(508) 685-4000	
Fuji Electric Corp. :CA	(510) 651-0811	(415) 651-0811
Fuji Photo Film USA, Inc :NY.	(914) 789-8100	
Fujikama U S A Inc :IL	(708) 832-1166	
Fujikama USA :IL	(708) 832-1166	
Fujikura America, Inc :GA	(404) 956-7200	
Fujitsu America, Inc. :CA	(800) 626-4686	
. . . .	BBS (408) 944-9899	
Fujitsu Computer Products :CA	(408) 432-6333	
Fujitsu Microelectronics Inc :CA . . .	(800) 637-0683	(800) 642-7616
Fujitsu Personal Systems Inc :CA . .	(408) 982-5900	
Funk Software, Inc :MA	(617) 497-6339	

Company and :State	Main Phone	Tech Phone
Futaba Corp. Of America :CA	(714) 455-9888	
Future Domain :CA	(714) 253-0400	
	BBS (714) 253-0432	
Future Graphics Inc :CA	(818) 341-6314	
Future Soft Engineering Inc :TX	(713) 496-9400	
	BBS (713) 588-6870	
Future Solutions :CA	(800) 886-1278	(510) 440-1210
FutureComm, Inc :CT	(203) 932-4881	
FutureSoft Inc :TX	(713) 496-9400	
Futurmaster USA :FL	(305) 371-4555	
Futurus Corp :GA	(404) 392-7979	
FWB, Inc :CA	(415) 474-8055	(415) 474-8055
G & H Ribbons,Inc :PA	(215) 953-1970	
G C I :NM	(505) 522-4600	(800) 874-2383
Galacticomm Inc :FL	(305) 583-5990	
	BBS (305) 583-7808	
Galaxy Applied Engineering :CA	(415) 347-9953	
Galaxy Computer Services Inc :MN	(612) 688-7454	
Galaxy Computers :VA	(800) 771-4049	
Galizia Inc :CA	(310) 763-2184	
Gallant Intelligent Computers :CA	(800) 848-8088	(818) 575-3781
Gama Computers Inc :AZ	(602) 741-9550	
Gametek :FL	(305) 935-3995	(800) 927-4263
GammaLink :CA	(408) 744-1430	(408) 745-2250
Gandalf :IL	(708) 517-3615	
Gandalf Technologies :OT	(613) 723-6500	
Gap Development :CA	BBS (714) 493-3819	
Gartech :MN	(612) 379-7930	
Gates Distributing :CA	(800) 332-2222	
Gates FA Distributing :SC	(800) 332-2222	
Gateway 2000 :SD	(800) 846-2000	
Gateway Book Binding :MB	(204) 663-9214	
Gateway Communications :CA	(800) 367-6555	
	BBS (714) 863-7097	
Gateway Electronics :MO	(314) 427-6116	
Gateway Electronics :CO	(303) 458-5444	
Gateway Electronics :CA	(619) 279-6802	
Gateway Systems :NC	(919) 929-8983	
Gazelle Systems :UT	(800) 786-3278	
	BBS (801) 375-2548	
GBC Technologies :NJ	(800) 229-2296	
GBM Design/COS :CA	(310) 677-8801	
GC/Thorsen :IL	(800) 435-2931	
GCC Technologies :MA	(800) 422-7777	(617) 890-0822
GDT Softworks :	(604) 291-9121	(604) 299-3379
GE Rental/Lease :GA	(800) 437-3687	
GE Rental/Lease :GA	(800) 437-3688	
GEC Plessey Semiconductors :CA	(408) 438-2900	
Geist Inc :NE	(800) 432-3219	
Geller Software Laboratories :NJ	(201) 746-7402	

Company and :State	Main Phone	Tech Phone
Gemini INc :MN	(800) 533-3631	
Gemplus Card International :MD . .	(301) 990-8800	
Gen 2 Ventures :CA	(408) 446-2277	
Genamation Industries Inc :ON . .	(416) 475-9434	
Genemax Monitoring Systmes :ON.	(416) 823-9000	
General Computer Corp :OH	(800) 521-4548	
General Datacomm Industries :CT .	(203) 574-1118	
General Diagnostics Inc :CA	(310) 715-1222	
General Disk Corp :CA	(408) 432-0505	
General Electric :GA	(800) 543-0440	
General Motors Corp :MI	(313) 556-5000	
General Parametrics :CA.	(510) 524-3950	
General Peripherals, Inc :CA.	(714) 770-1223	
General Power Corp :CA	(800) 854-3469	
General Ribbon :CA.	(800) 423-5400	
General Sales Equipment :CA. . . .	(310) 828-2577	
General Semiconductor Industries :AZ	(602) 968-3101	
General Signal Corp :CT	(203) 357-8800	
Generation Systems :	(800) 325-5811	(800) 323-9285
Generic Software, Inc :WA	(800) 228-3601	
Genesis Development Corp :UT . . .	(801) 568-1212	
Genesis Integrated Systems Inc :MN	(612) 544-4445	
Genesis Technology :CA	(510) 782-4800	
Genesoft :CA	(714) 394-0010	
Genicom :VA	(800) 535-4364	
Genigraphics Corp :CT	(800) 638-7348	(203) 925-1919
Genisco Technology Corp :CA	(619) 661-5100	
Genoa Systems Corp :CA	(408) 432-9090	
	BBS (408) 943-1231	
Genovation, Inc :CA.	(714) 833-3355	
Gentek International, Inc :CT.	(202) 683-1160	
Genus Microprogramming :TX	(800) 227-0918	(713) 977-0680
Geocomp :MA	(800) 822-2669	
Georgens Industries Inc :CA	(800) 255-5350	
GeoSystems :PA	(717) 293-7500	
GeoWorks :CA	(510) 644-0883	
Gerber Scientific :CT	(203) 644-1551	
Gestetner Corp :CT	(203) 863-5561	
GETC :BC	(604) 684-3230	
Gibson Research :CA	(800) 736-0637	
Giga-Byte Technology Co Ltd :CA .	(818) 814-0949	
Gigatek Memory Systems :CA	(619) 438-9010	
GigaTrend Inc :CA.	(619) 931-9122	
. . . .	BBS (619) 566-0361	
Gimpel Software :PA	(215) 584-4261	
Gizmo Technologies :	(510) 623-7899	
Glenco Engineering Inc :IL.	(800) 562-2543	(708) 808-0315
Glendale Technologies Corp :IL . .	(708) 305-9100	
Glenn A Barber & Associates:CA . .	(818) 951-4744	
Global Specialties :CT	(800) 345-6251	

Company and :State	Main Phone	Tech Phone
Global Village Communication : . . .	(415) 390-8300	
. . . .	BBS (415) 390-8397	
Globalink, Inc :VA	(800) 255-5660	
GlobeTech International :AZ	(800) 654-7314	
GMC Technology Corp :CA	(818) 401-3743	
GMP :PA	(215) 357-5500	
GN Navtel :ON	(800) 262-8835	
GN Navtel Limited :GA	(800) 262-8835	
Go Corp :CA	(415) 345-7400	
GO Technology :	(702) 831-3100	(702) 832-7762
God Disk Inc :CA	(213) 320-5080	
Gold Disk :CA	(310) 320-5080	
Gold Disk Inc :OT	(800) 465-3375	
Gold Hill Computers :MA	(617) 621-3300	
Golden Bow Systems :CA	(619) 298-9349	
Golden Coast Electronics Inc :CA .	(619) 268-8447	
Golden Image Technology Corp :CA	(800) 327-4482	
Golden Power Systems :CA	(805) 582-4400	
Golden Ribbon :CO.	(303) 443-6966	
Golden Star Inc :MO	(800) 821-2792	
Golden Triangle :	(800) 326-1858	
Golden-Lee Book Distributors :NY .	(718) 857-6333	
Goldstar Precision Co Ltd :CA . . .	(619) 268-8447	
GoldStar Technology Corp :CA . . .	(408) 432-1331	
. . . .	BBS (408) 432-0236	
Goldstein & Blair :	(800) 283-9444	
Good Software :TX	(800) 925-5700	
Gorrell's Computer Services :KY . .	(606) 299-8468	
Gotoless Conversion :TX	(214) 625-2323	
. . . .	BBS (214) 625-6905	
Gould Inc :OH	(216) 328-7000	
Government Computer News :MD .	(301) 650-2000	
Gradco Inc :CA	(714) 770-1223	
GrafPoint :CA	(800) 426-2230	
Graham Magnetics Inc :TX	(817) 868-5000	
Granite Corp :CA	(818) 887-5533	
Grapevine LAN Products, Inc :WA .	(206) 869-2707	
Graphic Enterprises Of Ohio, Inc :OH	(800) 321-9874	(216) 456-5107
Graphic Software Systems :OR . . .	(503) 641-2200	
GRAPHIC TECH :MA	(413) 536-7800	
Graphic Utilities Inc :ME	(800) 669-4723	
Graphic Utilities, Inc :ME	(207) 473-7587	
Graphics Develpmnt International :CA	(800) 989-4434	
Graphics Simulations :TX	(214) 699-7400	
Graybar Electric Company :MO . . .	(800) 825-5517	
Great American Software Inc :NH .	(603) 889-5400	
. . . .	BBS (603) 889-7292	
Great Eastern Technology :MA . . .	(800) 875-0025	
Great Plain Software :ND	(701) 281-0550	(800) 456-0025
Great Software Ideas :CA	(800) 486-7800	(714) 261-9744

Company and :State	Main Phone	Tech Phone
Great Tek Inc :CA	(408) 943-1005	
Great Wave Software :CA	(408) 438-1990	
Greatlink Electronics USA Inc :CA	(510) 683-0655	
Greco Systems :CA	(800) 234-7326	
Greengage Development Corp :CA.	(408) 243-8980	
Greenleaf International Inc :CA	(800) 523-9830	
	BBS (214) 250-3778	
Greenleaf International Inc :CA	(408) 734-8888	
Greenleaf Software :TX	(800) 523-9830	
GRiD Systems :CA	(800) 326-4743	
Group 1 Software :MD	(301) 982-2000	(800) 367-6950
Group 4 Electronics :CA	(800) 229-7189	
Group One Electronics Co Inc :CA	(818) 993-4575	
Group Technologies :	(800) 476-8781	(703) 841-4357
Group Three Electronics Inc :CA..	(310) 781-9191	
Gruber Industries Inc :AZ	(602) 863-2655	
Gryphon Software :CA	(619) 536-8815	
GST, Inc :CA	(714) 739-0106	
GTCO Corp :MD	(301) 381-6688	
GTE Corp :CT	(203) 965-2000	
GTE Electronic Repair Services :CA	(714) 945-2313	
GTE Supply Electronic Repair :TX .	(214) 615-7599	
GUIS America, Inc :CA	(714) 590-0801	
Gupta Technologies :CA	(800) 876-3267	(415) 321-4484
	BBS (415) 321-0549	
GVC Technologies, Inc :NJ	(800) 289-4821	(201) 579-3630
	BBS (201) 579-2380	
GW Computer Systems Inc :BC	(604) 244-7118	
H & H Enterprises :NV	(702) 876-6292	
H&J Electronics International :FL	(800) 275-2447	
H. Allen & Co :IL	(708) 769-4040	
H. Co. Memory Products :CA	(714) 833-3222	
H.Co. Memory Upgrades :CA	(800) 726-2477	(714) 833-3364
Ha-Lo Advertising Specialties :IL..	(708) 676-5305	
Haba/Arrays :CA	(818) 994-1899	
Hadron, Inc :VA	(703) 359-6201	
Hahn & Company :OR	(503) 248-0262	
Halcyon Software :CA	(408) 378-9898	
Hale Systems :	(415) 369-8890	
Haliburton NUS Environmental :MD	(301) 258-6000	
Haltek Electronics :CA	(415) 969-0510	
Hamilton Digital Controls Inc :NY .	(315) 797-2370	
Hampton Business Machines/System :IL	(800) 974-2402	
Hand Held Products :NC	(704) 541-1380	
Hand Tool Industries :OH	(216) 678-8787	
Handok Co, Ltd :CA	(408) 736-3191	
Hands On Learning :MA	(617) 272-0088	
Handtop Computers :CA	(818) 884-4076	
Hanson Data Systems Inc :MA	(800) 879-1371	
Hard Drive Associates Inc :OR	(503) 233-2821	

Company and :State	Main Phone	Tech Phone
Hard Drive Super Source :CA	(800) 252-9777	(408) 739-4110
Hard Drive Wholesalers :CA.	(408) 559-1773	
Hard Drives International :AZ	(800) 927-7848	
Hardigg Cases :MA.	(413) 665-2163	
HARDISK Technology :CA.	(408) 374-5157	
Hardware House :AR	(501) 225-4477	
Hardware House :IN	(317) 842-8244	
Hardware House :KY	(502) 425-1402	
Hardware House :NE	(402) 498-5677	
Hardware House :OH	(513) 489-0868	
Hardware House (Memphis) :TN . .	(901) 756-6677	
Hardware House (Nashville) :TN . .	(615) 356-2888	
Harley Systems Inc :NJ	(800) 237-2885	
Harmony Computers :NY	(718) 692-2828	(800) 441-1144
Harris Adacom Network Services :TX	(214) 386-2000	
Harris Corp :FL	(407) 727-9100	
Harvard Business Systems :CA . . .	(800) 288-7750	(310) 207-7750
Harvard Softworks :OH.	(513) 748-0390	
Hauppauge Computer Works :NY . .	(516) 434-1600	
HavenTree Software Ltd :NY	(800) 267-0668	
Hawaii Software Service Center :HI	(808) 733-2042	
Hawk Computers :CA	(408) 436-8999	
Hawk Data Systems :CA	(805) 371-1764	
Hayes Microcomputer Products :GA	(404) 840-9200	(404) 441-1617
. . . .	BBS (404) 446-6336	
HB Computer Technology Co :CA .	(310) 644-2602	
HBO & Company :	(404) 393-6092	
HCI :CA.	(800) 486-0001	
HCR Corp :OT	(416) 922-1937	(800) 567-4357
HD Computer :CA	(800) 347-0493	(800) 676-0164
HDC Computer Corp :WA.	(206) 885-5550	
. . . .	BBS (206) 869-2418	
Headland Technology :CA	(510) 683-6290	(800) 248-1850
. . . .	BBS (415) 656-0503	
Health Care Keyboard Co Inc :WI .	(414) 253-4131	
Health Software, Inc :OH	(216) 759-2103	
Hedge Systems :CA	(818) 243-2235	
HEI FastPoint Light Pens :MN . . .	(612) 443-2500	
Helix Software Co, Inc :MA.	(718) 392-3100	(718) 392-3735
Help Desk Institute :CO	(800) 248-5667	
Hercules Computer Technology :CA	(510) 623-6030	
. . . .	BBS (510) 540-0621	
Heritage Computer Parts :MN	(800) 828-8266	
Hermeneutika :WA	(206) 824-9673	
Hersey Micro Consulting :MI	(313) 994-3259	
Hetra Computer & Communication :FL	(800) 327-0661	
Hewlett-Packard :CA	(800) 544-9976	
Hewlett-Packard :MA	(617) 221-5285	
Hewlett-Packard Co :ID	(208) 396-6000	(208) 323-2551
Hewlett-Packard Co :CA.	(619) 592-4522	

Company and :State	Main Phone	Tech Phone
Hewlett-Packard Worldwide :CA . . .	(415) 968-5600	
Hexacon Electric Co :NJ	(908) 245-6200	
Hi Tech Expressions :NY	(212) 941-1224	(305) 581-4240
Hi-Tech Asset Recovery :CA	(805) 966-5454	
Hi-Tech Computer Products, Inc :FL	(800) 950-6991	
Hi-TECH Connections Inc :PA.	(215) 372-1401	
Hi-Tech USA :CA	(800) 831-2888	(408) 956-8285
Hi-Techniques Inc :WI	(800) 248-1633	
HI-TEK Services Inc :CA	(800) 285-3508	
High Technology Development:HI. . .	(808) 625-5293	
Highland Products Inc :NJ	(201) 366-0156	
Hilgraeve :MI	(313) 243-0576	(313) 243-0576
Hillside Electronics Corp :MA	(413) 238-5566	
Hitachi :NY	(516) 921-7200	
Hitachi America :CA.	(800) 448-2244	
Hitachi America :NY	(914) 332-5800	(800) 323-9712
HMC-HUB Material Company :MA . .	(800) 482-4440	
Hogan Systems :	(214) 386-0200	
Hokkins Systemation Inc :CA	(408) 436-8303	
Holmes Microsystems, Inc :UT	(801) 975-9929	
Home Office Computing :NY	(212) 505-3688	
Honeywell :MN	(612) 870-5431	(612) 782-7646
Honeywell Keyboard Division :TX . . .	(915) 544-5511	
Honeywell-IAC :AZ.	(602) 789-5393	
Hooleon Corp :AZ	(800) 937-1337	
Hooper International,Inc :.	(407) 851-3100	(407) 851-3100
Hoppecke Battery Systems Inc :NJ.	(201) 492-0045	
Horizon Technology :TX	(800) 888-9600	
Horizon USA Data Supplies Inc :CA	(800) 325-1199	(702) 826-4393
Horizons Technology Inc :CA	(619) 292-7100	
Hornet Technology USA Corp :CA :CA .	(818) 333-9667	(818) 572-3784
Hotronic Inc :CA.	(408) 378-3688	
House Of Batteries :CA	(800) 432-3385	
Houston Computer Services Inc :TX	(713) 493-9900	
Houston Data Center Inc :TX.	(713) 880-0042	
Houston Instrument :TX.	(800) 444-3425	
Howard W. Sams :IN	(800) 428-7267	
Howe Industries Inc :FL	(800) 322-1830	
HSC Software :CA	(310) 392-8441	
Hubbell Inc :CT	(203) 337-3100	
Hughes Lan Systems (Sytek) :CA. .	(415) 966-7300	
Humana Computer Publications :AB	(403) 245-2194	
Huron Computer Of PA Inc :PA. . . .	(412) 776-6110	
Husky Computers Inc :FL	(800) 486-7774	
Hutchinson Technology :MN	(612) 587-3797	
Hy-Tronix Instruments Inc :KS.	(800) 835-1005	
Hydra Systems :CA	(408) 253-5800	
Hyper Glot Software :	(615) 558-8270	
Hyperception Inc :TX	(214) 343-8525	
Hyperdoc, Inc :CA	(408) 764-9938	

Company and :State	Main Phone	Tech Phone
Hyperkinetic :CA	(714) 935-0823	
Hyperpress Publishing :	(800) 633-4252	(415) 345-4620
Hypro Systems :CA	(310) 473-2937	
Hyundai Electronics America :CA	(408) 473-9200	
I-Data Inc :NY	(516) 351-1333	
I/O Design :	(800) 241-2122	
IBC :CA	(800) 654-3790	
IBC/Integrated Business Computer :CA	(818) 882-9007	
IBEX Inc :CT	(203) 393-1610	
IBEX Technologies Inc :CA	(916) 621-4342	
Ibis Software :	(415) 546-1917	(415) 546-0405
IBM :NY	(914) 766-3722	
IBM Choice Software :ON	(416) 946-9000	
IBM Corp :NY	(914) 288-3000	
	FAX Back (800) 456-4329	
IBM Corp :GA	(800) 426-9402	
	BBS (404) 835-6600	
IBM Corp. :AZ	(800) 426-2968	(800) 426-7763
IBM Corp. (Storage Sys Div) :MN.	(507) 253-1897	(507) 253-5005
IBM Corp.-Customer Satisfaction :	(800) 772-2227	
IBM Corp.-Dealer Locator :	(800) 426-3377	
IBM Corp.-Hardware Service :	(800) 426-7378	
IBM Corp.-Independent Remarketer :TX	(800) 426-3333	
IBM Corp.-OS2 Info Line :	(800) 342-6672	
IBM Corp.-Software Center :	(800) 237-5511	
IBM Corp.-Telemarketing Ops :	(800) 426-2468	
IBM Personal System Card Repair :TX	(800) 759-6995	
IC Designs :WA.	(206) 821-9202	(206) 821-8218
Icarus Corp :MD	(301) 881-9350	
ICM International Components :CA	(800) 748-6232	
Icom Simulations :IL	(800) 877-4266	
Icon Computer Corp :CA	(800) 966-4266	
ICON CS Canada Inc :ON	(613) 722-0115	
Icons International :OR	(800) 959-4266	
Icot Corp :CA.	(800) 227-8068	
ICS Electro-Pac Division :IL	(708) 543-6200	
ICS Inc :CA	(805) 257-6900	
ID Systems :NH	(603) 924-9631	
IDE :MN.	(612) 946-4100	
Idea Courier :AZ	(800) 528-1400	
IDEA Servcom Inc :AZ	(602) 894-7000	
Ideal Industries Inc :IL.	(800) 435-0705	
Ideassociates :MA.	(508) 663-6878	
Idek-Iiyama North America :PA	(800) 394-4335	
Identica :CA.	(408) 727-2600	(408) 727-2600
Identity Systems Technology :TX	(214) 235-3330	
IDER :CA.	(800) 622-4337	(818) 288-4008
IDG Communications :MA	(508) 879-0700	
IEEE Computer Graphics :CA	(714) 821-8380	
IET Labs :NY.	(800) 899-8438	

Company and :State	Main Phone	Tech Phone
IEV Corp :UT	(800) 438-6161	
Ilcon Corporation :CA	(408) 779-7466	
Iliad Group :CA	(415) 563-2053	
Image Club Graphics :AB	(403) 262-8008	
Image Research Corp :AZ	(602) 998-1113	
Image Systems :CA	(714) 833-0155	
Image-In :MN	(800) 345-3540	
	BBS (612) 888-2324	
ImageSoft Inc :NY	(800) 245-8840	
	BBS (516) 767-7094	
ImageWare Software Inc :CA	(619) 457-8600	
Imagine Club Graphics :	(403) 262-8008	
Imagine That :	(408) 365-0305	
Imaging Magazine :NY	(212) 691-8215	
IMC Networks Corp :CA	(800) 624-1070	
	BBS (714) 724-0930	
Impact :TX	(800) 777-4323	(512) 966-3621
Implements :MA	(508) 358-5858	
Imprimis Drives	- See Seagate :	
Impulse Software :MN	(800) 328-0184	(612) 566-0221
Impulse Systems :CA	(415) 641-9197	
IMSI :CA	(415) 454-7101	
	BBS (415) 454-2893	
In Focus Systems Inc :OR	(800) 327-7231	
In Shape Co Ltd :CA	(408) 432-9025	
In Win Development Inc :CA	(818) 333-1986	
InaCom :NE	(402) 392-3900	
Inacomp Computer Centers :MI	(313) 649-5580	
Inbit :CA	(415) 967-1788	
Incas Corp :CA	(818) 332-3443	
Incas Corp USA :NJ	(609) 424-7811	
Incider :NH	(603) 924-9471	
Incomm Data Systems, Inc :IL	(708) 459-8881	
	BBS (708) 459-9331	
Incomnet :CA	(818) 887-3400	
Independent Computer Support :PA	(215) 687-0900	
Index Applications :TX	(512) 822-4818	
Indiana Cash Drawer Co :IN	(317) 398-6643	
Indigo Software Corp :CA	(415) 312-0770	
Individual Software Inc :CA	(800) 822-3522	(800) 331-3313
Inductel, Inc :CA	(800) 367-4497	
Indus International, Inc :WI	(608) 786-0300	
Indus-Tool :IL	(800) 662-5021	
Industrial Commercial Electronic :NY	(800) 442-3462	
Industrial CPU Systems Intern. :CA	(714) 957-2815	
Industrious Software Solutions :CA	(310) 330-7602	
Inference Corporation :CA	(310) 322-0200	
Infinite Solutions :TX	(713) 492-1894	
Infiniti Manufacturing Inc :CA	(818) 960-4509	
InfoChip Systems :CA	(408) 436-8300	

Company and :State	Main Phone	Tech Phone
....	BBS (408) 727-2496	
Infodata :VA	(703) 578-3430	
Infoextend :CA	(619) 587-9140	
Infomatic Power Systems Corp :CA	(310) 948-2217	
Infonetics :MA	(508) 393-8088	
Inforite Corp :CA	(415) 571-8766	
Information Builders :NY	(800) 444-4303	
Information Center :MA	(617) 542-0146	
Information Concepts :	(202) 682-0330	
Information Consultants, Inc :CA	(714) 859-7123	
Information Machines :CA	(818) 884-5779	
Information Packaging Corp :NY	(800) 776-7633	
Information Procesing, Inc :FL ...	(407) 331-5200	
Information Research :VA	(804) 979-8191	
Information Science :NJ	(201) 592-0009	
Information Strategies :NY	(212) 971-5000	
Information Systems Consulting :TX	(214) 490-1881	
Informationweek :NY..............	(516) 365-4600	
Informix Software Inc :CA	(800) 438-7627	(415) 926-6593
Informix Software/IBM :KS	(800) 274-8184	
....	BBS (913) 492-2089	
Informtech International Inc :CA..	(310) 836-8993	
InfoShare :VA	BBS (703) 803-8000	
Infoworld :CA.........................	(415) 572-7341	
Ingram Micro :CA	(714) 566-1000	
Ingram/Micro D :CA	(714) 566-1000	
Inland Data Pak :MI	(313) 583-6220	
Inline Design :	(203) 435-4995	
Innotech Inc :ON....................	(416) 492-3838	
Innovative Concepts :CA	(408) 436-1777	
Innovative Data Design :..........	(510) 680-6818	
Innovative Manufacturing Corp :FL	(305) 836-1035	
Innovative Resources :MN	(612) 377-5701	
Innovative Technologies Inc :TX	(713) 583-1141	
Innovative Technology Inc :FL	(800) 647-8877	
Innovative Technology Ltd :OK ..	(800) 253-4001	(405) 243-0030
Inovatic :VA...........................	(703) 522-3053	
Inputer, The :........................	(818) 842-8581	
Inset Systems :CT..................	(800) 828-0068	(203) 740-8846
....	BBS (203) 740-0063	
Insight Development :CA	(800) 825-4115	(510) 626-9558
Insight International :AZ	(800) 927-7848	
Insight Resource Inc :NY	(914) 332-1589	
Insignia Solutions :CA	(800) 848-7677	(415) 694-7694
Insite Peripherals, Inc :CA	(408) 946-8080	
Instant Replay :UT	(801) 272-0671	
Instaplan :CA.........................	(415) 389-1414	
Institute For VAR Development :NV	(702) 656-7611	
Institute, The :NY	(212) 705-7555	
Instructware Inc :ON	(800) 267-0101	

Company and :State	Main Phone	Tech Phone
Instrument Repair Labs, Inc :CO . . .	(800) 345-6140	
Instrument Specialties Co Inc :PA . .	(717) 424-8510	
InstrumentMart :NY	(516) 487-7430	
Instruments & Equipment :NJ	(201) 579-0009	
Int'l. Journal Of Parallel Prg. :	(801) 581-5586	
Intcomex :FL	(305) 477-6230	
Intec Computer Service :NJ.	(800) 225-1187	
Integral Systems :CA	(510) 939-3900	
Integrated Circuit Systems Inc :PA .	(215) 666-1900	
Integrated Computer Services :CA . .	(818) 960-1921	
Integrated Computer Solutions :NJ .	(201) 808-9646	
Integrated Data Technologies :PA. .	(215) 726-6124	
Integrated Development Corp :NH . .	(603) 329-5522	
Integrated Device Technology:CA. .	(408) 727-6116	
Integrated Infor. Technology Inc :CA	(408) 727-1885	
Integrated Workstations, Inc :CA . . .	(800) 832-6526	
Intek :WA	(206) 455-9935	
Intel Corp :CA.	(800) 538-3373	
FAX Back (800) 525-3019		
Intel PCEO :OR	(503) 629-7000	
. . . .	BBS (503) 645-6275	
Intelecsis, Inc :TX.	(512) 682-0649	
Intelect :CA.	(310) 828-7310	
Intellicom :CA.	(818) 407-3900	
Intellicorp :CA	(415) 965-5500	
Intelligence Technology Corp :TX . . .	(214) 250-4277	
Intelligenceware :CA	(310) 417-8896	
Intelligent Controls Inc :WA	(206) 771-8107	
Intelligent Electronics :PA	(215) 458-5500	
Intelligent Instrumentation :AZ.	(602) 624-2434	
Intelligent Systems Master, LP :GA. .	(404) 381-2900	
IntelliPower Inc :CA	(714) 587-0155	
Intellisystems, Inc :CA	(818) 341-7000	
Intelogic Trace Inc :TX.	(800) 531-7186	
InterAct :WV	(304) 258-1611	
Interacter Inc :CT	(203) 630-0199	
Interactive Imaging Inc :FL.	(813) 996-4316	
InterActive Inc :SD	(605) 363-5117	
Interactive Multimedia Assoc. :MD . .	(410) 626-1380	
Interactive Software Engineering :CA	(805) 685-1006	
Interactive Systems Corp :CA	(213) 453-8649	
Interactive Training Tech. :OR.	(503) 681-0343	
Interchange Standards Corp :CA. . . .	(800) 423-7823	
InterComp Inc :CA	(408) 928-1588	
Intercon Associates, Inc :NY	(716) 244-1250	
Interex Computer Products :KS	(316) 524-4747	
Interface Electronics :OR	(503) 393-2838	
Interface Group, The :MA	(617) 449-6600	
Interface Systems :MI	(800) 544-4072	
Interface Technologies :MO.	(314) 434-0046	

Company and :State	Main Phone	Tech Phone
Intergraph :CA.	(213) 479-3400	
Interleaf, Inc :MA	(617) 290-0710	
Intermatic Inc :IL	(815) 675-2321	
Intermec :WA	(206) 348-2600	
Intermetrics :MA	(617) 661-1840	
Internat'l Power Machines Corp :TX	(214) 272-8000	
International Business Software :. .	(408) 522-8001	
International Buyers Market :NV . . .	(702) 647-3632	
International Compliance Corp :TX	(817) 491-3696	
International Computer Center :CA	(818) 894-2222	
International Computer Power :CA.	(818) 443-7557	
International Data Corp :MA	(508) 879-0700	
International Data Engineering :MN	(602) 946-4100	
International Data Sciences :RI . . .	(800) 437-3282	
International Keytech Corp :CA . . .	(714) 598-6219	
International Meta Systems, Inc :CA	(213) 375-4700	
International Open Systems :MA . .	(508) 535-2080	
International Power Machines :TX .	(800) 527-1208	
International Software :.	(305) 823-8088	
International Tech. Systems:WA . . .	(206) 486-9031	
International Transware :	(415) 903-2300	
Intemtl Computers & Communictns :CA	(310) 836-7561	
Interphase Corp :TX	(214) 919-9000	
InterPlay Productions :	(714) 549-2411	
Interpos Systems Inc :ON.	(416) 513-9209	
Interpreter :CO	(303) 431-8991	
Intersecting Concepts :CA	(805) 373-3900	
Intersolv (Sage Software) :MD . . .	(301) 230-3200	(800) 443-1601
Intersolve (Polytron) :OR	(503) 645-1150	(800) 548-4000
Intex Solutions Inc :MA	(617) 449-6222	
Intra Electronics USA, Inc :CA . . .	(408) 744-1706	
Intuit :CA.	(800) 624-8742	(415) 858-6010
InView System Inc :MA.	(508) 428-5688	
Invisible Software :CA.	(415) 570-5967	
Invisible Software Inc :FL	(800) 982-2962	
IOcomm International Technology :CA	(213) 644-6100	
Ioline :WA	(206) 821-2140	
IOMEGA :UT.	(800) 456-5522	
. . . .	BBS (801) 778-4400	
Ion Systems :CA	(800) 367-2452	
IPC Corp Ltd :GA	(404) 594-8281	
IPL Systems, Inc :MA	(800) 338-8475	(617) 487-2057
IPUA Journal :.	(408) 353-2231	
IPX Infomatic Power Systems:CA .	(310) 948-2217	
IQ Engineering :CA.	(800) 765-3668	
IQ Software :GA	(404) 446-8880	
IQ Technologies Inc :WA	(206) 823-2273	
IQI Accessories :CA	(415) 567-3500	
IQV Corp :IL	(708) 253-5196	
Iris Software Products, Inc :MA . . .	(617) 341-1990	

Company and :State	Main Phone	Tech Phone
Iron Mountain :MA	(800) 883-8000	
Irons Group Inc, The :NY	(212) 645-4737	
ISC Systems :WA	(509) 927-5600	
ISCO/MSC Ribbons :NY	(718) 706-8833	
ISI Systems :MA	(800) 255-1580	(508) 682-5500
ISICAD, Inc :CA	(800) 634-1223	
Island Graphics :CA	(415) 491-1000	
Islandview/MGI :VA	(804) 673-5601	
ITC :	(719) 593-7377	(719) 593-7377
Iterated Systems Inc :GA	(404) 840-0633	
Ithaca Software :CA	(510) 523-5900	
Itron,Inc :WA	(509) 924-9900	
Itronix Inc :WA	(800) 441-1309	
ITS :CA	(818) 882-7747	
ITT Commercial Finance Corp :MO.	(800) 727-9090	
ITT Consumer Financial :MN	(612) 540-8799	
ITT Corp :NY	(212) 258-1000	
ITT Pomona Electronics :CA	(909) 623-3463	
ITT PowerSystems Corp :AZ	(602) 889-7600	
ITW Linx :IL	(708) 952-8844	
Iverson Technology :VA	(703) 749-1200	(800) 677-7881
J & S Custom Computer Services :CA	(800) 995-5840	
J B Technologies Inc :CA	(805) 529-0908	
J Bond Computer Systems:CA	(408) 946-9622	
J Bond Computer Systems :CA	(510) 490-8290	
J P N Corp :CA	(510) 770-3962	
J-Mark Computer Corp. :CA	(818) 814-9472	
Jabert USA Inc :TX	(214) 644-2084	
Jactech Corp :CA	(714) 228-1633	
Jade Computer :CA	(800) 421-5500	
Jain Tools For Sales :	(415) 941-9191	
JAM Enterprises :CA	(619) 673-8180	
Jameco Electronics Computer Prod :CA	(800) 831-0084	(415) 592-8097
James Burn/American Inc :NY	(914) 454-8200	
Jameslee Corp :IL	(312) 271-6000	
Jasick Designs :	(510) 322-1386	
Javelin Software Corp :	(617) 890-1100	
JAZ Designs :TX	(512) 659-8946	
JB Saunders :CO	(303) 442-1212	
JB Technologies, Inc :CA	(800) 688-0908	
JC Enterprises :CA	(818) 773-0296	
JDR Microdevices :CA	(800) 538-5000	(800) 538-5002
	BBS (408) 559-0253	
JDV Engineering Company :NJ	(201) 796-1720	
Jem Computers :MA	(617) 254-5500	
Jenistar Inc :MA	(508) 230-2414	
Jensen Tools, Inc :AZ	(602) 968-6231	
Jensen-Jones Inc :NJ	(800) 688-7080	(908) 530-7788
JET FAX :CA	(415) 324-0600	
	BBS (415) 324-1259	

Company and :State	Main Phone	Tech Phone
JetFill Inc :TX	(713) 933-1900	
JetForm Corp :MA.	(800) 267-9976	
Jetpad Systems :MA.	(617) 536-7526	
JH America Inc :CA.	(310) 328-0051	
Ji-Haw :CA	(310) 328-0051	
Jian :CA.	(415) 941-9191	
Jimi Software :PA	(215) 628-0840	
Jinco Computers, Inc :CA	(800) 253-2531	(818) 309-1103
JMR Electronics, Inc :CA	(818) 993-4801	
Jo-Dan International Inc :MI	(313) 340-0300	
John Anderson Associates :AZ	(602) 474-9555	
John Fluke Manufacturing :WA	(800) 443-5853	
John Wiley & Sons, Inc :NY	(212) 850-6000	
Johnson Controls :WI	(414) 274-4000	
Johnson Controls :WI	(414) 961-6500	
Joindata Systems Inc :CA.	(818) 330-6553	
Joindata Systems Inc. :CA	(818) 330-6553	
Jones Business Systems Inc :TX.	(800) 225-1923	
Jordan Industries Corporation :NY	(914) 793-0700	
Joseph Electronics :IL.	(708) 297-4200	
Journal Of Information Systems :NY	(212) 971-5000	
Journal Of Scientific Com :	(609) 258-6227	
Jovian Logic Corp :CA	(510) 651-4823	
Julie Associates Inc :MA.	(508) 667-1958	
Jump Microsystems Inc :CA	(510) 440-8006	
Juno Technical Services Inc :CA.	(510) 487-7601	
JVC Companies Of America :CA.	(714) 965-2610	(714) 965-2610
JVC Information Products Co :CA .	(408) 988-7506	
JWP :CA	(408) 437-0400	
JWP Information Systems :MA.	(617) 821-4100	
JYACC :NY	(800) 458-3313	
K & A Mfg, Inc :AZ	(800) 678-3805	
K D I Precision Products Corp :OH	(513) 943-2000	
K&R International Inc :CA	(714) 598-8738	
K-N Electronics :OH	(216) 724-9953	
Kaetron Software :	(713) 890-6171	
Kalglo Electronics Co, Inc :PA	(800) 524-0400	
Kalok Corp :CA	(408) 747-1315	(408) 747-1315
Kanix Inc :CA	(714) 693-1888	
Kantek Inc :NY	(516) 593-3212	
Kao Infosystems :MA	(800) 274-5520	
Kart-A-Bag :IL	(815) 723-1940	
Kay Elemetrics Corp :NJ.	(201) 227-2000	
Kazcom Inc :IL	(800) 444-0543	
KCI Canada :ON.	(416) 633-0351	
KCI Computing, Inc :CA	(310) 478-6100	
KDM Associates Inc :IL.	(800) 553-5171	
KEA Systems Ltd :BC.	(604) 431-0727	
Keane, Inc :MA	(617) 241-9200	
Kedwell Software :CA	(415) 899-8525	

Company and :State	Main Phone	Tech Phone
Kelly Computer Systems :CA	(415) 960-1010	
Kelly Microsystems :CA	(714) 859-3900	
Kenfil Distribution :CA	(800) 487-9889	
Kennsco :MN	(800) 229-1758	
Kenosha Computer Corp :WI	(800) 255-2989	(414) 697-9595
Kensington Microware :CA	(800) 535-4242	(800) 535-4242
Kent Marsh :	(713) 522-8906	
	BBS (713) 522-8921	
Kenwood USA :CA	(310) 639-4200	
Kepler Co :MN	(612) 522-0756	
Kepner-Tregoe Inc :NJ.	(800) 257-0404	
Key Computers, Inc :GA	(404) 565-0089	
Key Lime Systems :FL	(800) 789-5463	(407) 627-5322
Key Power, Inc :CA	(310) 948-2084	
Key Services Inc :NC	(919) 768-4400	
Key Tronic :WA	(800) 262-6006	
Keydata International :NJ	(800) 486-7010	(800) 486-9100
Keyfile :NH	(603) 883-3800	
Keylogic USA/Europe :CA	(619) 242-7722	
Keypoint Technology :CA	(310) 944-3041	
KFC USA Inc :CA	(714) 546-0336	
KGK Automated Systems :	(914) 681-1336	
Kidasa Software Inc :TX	(800) 765-0167	
Kidde-Fenwal Inc :MA	(508) 881-2000	
Kikusui International Corp :CA.	(800) 545-8784	
Killer Tracks :CA	(714) 435-2600	
Kimpsion International :CA	(408) 988-8808	
Kings Electronics :NY	(914) 793-5000	
Kingston Technology :CA	(714) 435-2600	
Kinzuid, Inc :NY	(716) 665-3087	
Kiss Software Corp :NJ	(800) 472-5477	
Kiwi Software :	(805) 685-4031	
Klein Tools Inc :IL	(708) 677-9500	
Klever Computers, Inc :CA	(408) 735-7723	
KLM Services :CA	(805) 376-2825	
Knowledge Access :CA	(415) 969-0606	
Knowledge Adventure :CA.	(818) 542-4200	
Knowledge Dynamics :TX	(800) 331-2783	
	BBS (512) 964-3929	
Knowledge Garden :NY	(516) 246-5400	
KnowledgePoint :CA	(800) 727-1133	
Knozall Systems Inc :AZ	(800) 333-8698	
Koala Acquisitions :	(408) 776-8181	
Kobetron Inc :OH	(513) 298-8244	
Kodak :	(800) 255-3434	(800) 344-0006
Kodiak Technology :CA	(800) 888-8084	(800) 777-7704
	BBS (408) 452-0677	
Kofax Image Products Inc :CA.	(714) 727-1733	
Konami :	(708) 215-5111	
Konic Electronics :CA	(714) 770-3267	

Company and :State	Main Phone	Tech Phone
Konica Business Machines USA:CT	(203) 683-2222	
Kontrax Software Inc :ON	(416) 451-1610	
Korea Trade Center :CA	(213) 954-9500	
Koss Stereo Phones :WI	(414) 964-5000	
Koutech Systems, Inc :CA	(310) 699-5340	
KPT :CA	(714) 468-5555	
Kraft Systems :CA	(619) 724-7146	
Kres Engineering :CA	(818) 957-6322	
Kris Technologies :CA	(415) 875-6728	
Krystaltech International Inc :NY	(212) 385-1900	
KS Brotherbox (USA) Co :CA	(818) 814-0516	
KTV Inc :NJ	(201) 440-9090	
Kurta :AZ	(602) 276-5533	
	BBS (602) 243-9440	
Kurzweil :MA	(617) 890-2929	
KW Control Systems Inc :NY	(914) 355-5000	
KYE International Corp :CA	(714) 590-3940	
Kye International Corp :CA	(714) 923-3510	
Kyocera Electronics Inc :NJ	(908) 560-3400	
Kyocera Electronics, Inc. :CA	(619) 576-2669	
L & M Computer Products :FL	(800) 544-2910	
L-Com Inc :MA	(800) 343-1455	
L-Cube Innovative Solution :CT	(203) 378-1343	
L-Tech :	(201) 288-1608	
La Cie :OR	(800) 999-0143	(800) 288-9919
LA Computer :CA	(310) 533-7177	
La Jolla Software Company :CA	(619) 454-7015	
LA Trade :CA	(800) 433-3726	(310) 539-0019
Labtec Enterprises Inc :WA	(206) 896-2000	
LacTek USA Co :CA	(714) 545-4916	
LaFrance Corp :PA	(215) 365-8000	
Lahey Computer Systems :NV	(702) 831-2500	
	BBS (702) 831-8023	
Lake Erie Systems And Services :PA	(814) 898-074	
Lamp Technology :NY	(516) 567-1800	
LAN Magazine :CA	(415) 905-2200	
Lan Systems :NY	(212) 995-7700	
LAN Technology :CA	(415) 358-9500	
Lan Times :UT	(801) 565-1060	
LANCAST :NH	(603) 880-1833	
Landmark :FL	(800) 683-6696	(800) 683-0854
Lane Service Company :TX	(800) 231-0861	
Lang Chao Group :CA	(916) 638-8900	
Language Systems :VA	(703) 478-0181	
LANpoint Systems :AZ	(800) 328-2526	
LanSource Technologies Inc :ON	(416) 866-8575	
Lantana Tech :CA	(619) 565-6400	
LANtek Computer :CA	(800) 462-0436	
Lantell Systems :CA	(800) 526-8355	
LANWorks :ON	(416) 238-5528	

Company and :State	Main Phone	Tech Phone
. . . .	BBS (416) 238-0253	
Lapis Technologies :	(510) 748-1600	
Larson-Davis Information Systems :UT	(801) 375-8855	
Laser Computer, Inc :IL	(708) 540-8086	
Laser Digital Inc :CA	(408) 737-2666	
Laser Magnetic Storage Int'l :CO. . . .	(719) 593-7900	
Laser Master Corp :MN	(800) 950-6868	
Laser Precision :NY	(800) 443-6154	
Laser Printers Accessories :CA . . .	(619) 485-8411	
Laser Source :NY.	(315) 463-6090	
Laser Supply :PA	(800) 422-0080	
Laser Tek Industries :IL	(800) 322-8137	
Laser's Edge, Inc :IA	(515) 472-7850	
LaserCard Systems Corp :CA	(415) 969-4428	
Laserex Inc :AZ	(800) 225-5503	
LaserGo, Inc :CA	(619) 450-4600	
. . . .	BBS (617) 450-9370	
Lasermaster Corp :MN.	(612) 944-9457	
Lasertechnics Inc :NM	(505) 822-1123	
Lasertek :NV	(800) 252-7374	
LaserTools :CA	(510) 420-8777	(800) 767-8005
Lattice, Incorporated :IL	(708) 769-4060	
. . . .	BBS (708) 916-1200	
Laudholm Automation Services :ME	(207) 761-5657	
Laura Technologies :AZ.	(602) 940-9800	
Lava Computer Mfg Inc :ON	(416) 674-5942	
Law Cypress Distributing :CA	(800) 344-3044	
LAWN O'Neill Communications:NJ	(908) 329-4100	
Lawson Associates :MN	(612) 379-2633	
LCS Industries :NJ	(201) 778-5588	
LCT Technology Inc :CA	(818) 575-5000	
LDI Retail Services :OH	(800) 874-3209	
Lead Electronics :NY	(315) 699-6099	
Lead Technologies :NC	(704) 549-5532	
Leader Instruments Corp :NY	(800) 645-5104	
Leading Edge :MA	(508) 836-4800	(900) 370-4800
. . . .	BBS (508) 836-3967	
Leading Technology, Inc :OR	(503) 646-3424	
League For Programming Freedom :MA	(617) 243-4091	
LearnKey Inc :UT.	(801) 224-8210	
Leasametric :CA	(800) 553-2255	
LeCroy Corp :NY	(800) 553-2769	
Lectronix Computer Service :WV	(304) 736-8035	
Lectronix Distribution & Service :MO	(800) 325-3348	
Lee Data/IIS :MN	(800) 533-3282	
Legacy Storage Systems Inc :MA	(508) 435-4700	
Legacy Technology :CA.	(800) 832-8883	
Legend Micro :OH	(800) 366-6333	
Legent Corp :VA	(703) 734-9494	
LEGEON CORP :CA	(714) 546-4900	

Company and :State	Main Phone	Tech Phone
Leisure Products :...............	(408) 448-7020	
Lek Technologies Inc :TX......	(806) 355-7900	
Lenel Systems International :....	(716) 248-9720	
Lermer Packaging Corp :NJ	(908) 789-0900	
LES International :CA	(714) 595-7299	
Letraset :NJ.................	(800) 343-8973	(800) 634-3463
Level Computers :CA	(714) 974-6427	
Leviton Mfg Inc :WA	(206) 486-2222	
Lexidyne Of Penn :PA..........	(412) 661-4526	
Lexmark International Inc :KY...	(606) 232-2000	
....	BBS (800) 453-9223	
Liberty Research Group Inc :MT ..	(406) 771-7736	
Liberty Systems Inc :CA	(408) 983-1127	
Libra Corp :UT	(800) 453-3827	
Library Software Review :CT	(203) 226-6967	
Librex Computer Systems Inc :CA .	(408) 894-6800	
Librex Computer Systems, Inc :CA	(408) 441-8500	
Lifeboat Associates :NJ	(908) 389-8950	
Light Brigade :WA	(206) 251-1240	
Light Source :CA.............	(415) 461-8000	(415) 461-3030
Lighthorse Technologies, Inc :CA..	(800) 443-3446	
Lighting Word Corp :CA	(408) 241-1990	
Lightning Communications Inc :CA	(714) 457-8001	
Likom Group :CA	(408) 954-8070	
Linco Computer :CA	(213) 903-1299	
Lind Electronic Design :MN	(612) 927-6303	
Link Computer, Inc :CA.........	(714) 993-0800	
Link Technologies :CA	(800) 448-5465	
Link-Up :NJ	(609) 654-6266	
Linkon Corp :NY	(212) 753-2544	
Linksys :CA.................	(800) 326-7114	
LIPS Inc :NY	(516) 673-2255	
Lite-On, Inc :CA..............	(408) 946-4873	
Literature Display Systems, Inc :IN	(800) 669-4399	
Litton Industries :CA	(310) 859-5000	
Liuski International, Inc :NY	(516) 454-8220	
LJ Enterprises :NY	(800) 296-5536	
Llon USA Inc :CA	(818) 991-4330	
Lloyd Bush, Inc :NY	(212) 962-4004	
LMT Marketing Inc :CA	(805) 644-1797	
Localnetter :................	(612) 435-2035	
Lockheed :CA................	(818) 876-2000	
Locus Computing :CA..........	(800) 423-2586	
Logica North America :MA	(617) 890-7730	
Logical Connection, Inc. :OR	(800) 238-9415	(503) 390-9375
....	BBS (504) 295-3344	
Logical Operations Inc :NY	(716) 482-7700	
Logical Systems Corporation :FL...	(813) 885-7179	
Logicode Technology Inc :CA....	(805) 491-9000	
Logicon, Inc :CA	(213) 373-0220	

Company and :State	Main Phone	Tech Phone
Logitech :CA	(800) 231-7717	
	BBS (510) 795-0408	
Longshine Microsystems Inc :CA	(310) 903-0899	
Longshine Technology, Inc :CA	(408) 942-1746	
LookUp Software :NV	(702) 786-4242	
Loop Computer Products :CA	(714) 549-5818	
Loral Commercial Systems :MI	(313) 390-2601	
Lortec Power Systems :OH	(800) 927-5051	
Lotus Development Corp :MA	(800) 343-5414	(800) 223-1662
	BBS (617) 693-7000	
Lotus Publishing :MA	(617) 494-1192	
Lousig-Nont & Associates,Inc :NV	(800) 477-3211	
Lowry Computer Products :MI	(800) 733-0010	
LPA Software Inc :NY	(800) 248-9602	
LSI Logic Corp :CA	(408) 433-8000	
LSW Inc :MD	(301) 772-8700	
Lucas Deeco Corp :CA	(510) 471-4700	
Lucasey Mfg Corp :CA	(510) 534-1435	
Lucid :CA	(800) 843-4204	(800) 223-9322
Lucky Star International :TX	(214) 690-1825	
Luctor Corp :AZ	(602) 582-5503	
Lugaru Software :PA	(412) 421-5911	
Luxor Corp :IL	(708) 244-1800	
Lxycon :CA	(818) 281-3957	
Lyco Computer Marketing :PA	(800) 233-8760	(717) 494-1670
Lynx Technology Inc :ON	(416) 886-7315	
Lysis Corp :GA	(404) 373-3359	
Lyte Optronics Inc :CA	(310) 450-8551	
Lytec Systems Inc :UT	(801) 562-0111	
M & P Services :CA	(714) 359-6011	
M Global :TX	(713) 960-0205	
M Technology Inc :CA	(408) 748-8701	
M USA Business Systems :TX	(214) 386-6100	(214) 490-0100
M&T Publishing :CA	(415) 358-9500	
M-S Cash Drawer Corp :CA	(818) 792-2111	
M-Test Equipment :CA	(800) 334-4293	
M-USA Business Systems :TX	(800) 933-6872	
M/A-Com LCS :NH	(800) 669-1769	
M1 Electronic Industries :PQ	(514) 956-7834	
MA Labs Inc :CA	(408) 954-8188	
Mac America :CA	(408) 434-0433	(800) 832-4003
Macazine :	(512) 467-4550	
Mace, Paul Software :OR	(503) 488-2322	
	BBS (503) 482-7435	
Machine Design :OH	(216) 696-7000	
Machine Independent :	(703) 435-0413	
	BBS (703) 437-8557	
MACRACON SYSTMES :CA	(510) 651-9115	
Macromedia :CA	(800) 288-8108	
Macromind :CA	(415) 442-0200	

| --- | --- | --- |
Macronix Inc :CA	(408) 453-8088	
Macrotron Systems Inc :CA	(510) 651-9115	
MacShack Inc :NY	(716) 344-9230	
Macuser :CA	(415) 378-5600	
MAG InnoVision Inc :CA	(800) 827-3998	
Magee Enterprises, Inc :GA	(800) 662-4330	(404) 662-5387
	BBS (404) 446-6650	
Magic RAM :CA	(213) 413-9999	
Magic Software Enterprises :CA	(714) 250-1718	
Magic Solutions, Inc :NJ	(201) 529-5533	
Magma Software Systems :NJ	(201) 912-0192	
	BBS (201) 912-0668	
Magna :	(408) 282-0900	
Magnavox/Philips Consumer Elec :TN	(615) 521-4316	
Magnetic Data, Inc :MN	(800) 328-3441	
Magnetic Recovery Technology :CA	(805) 257-2262	
Magni Systems, Inc :OR	(503) 626-8400	
Magretech Inc :CA	(805) 685-4551	
Magus Data Technology Inc :ON	(416) 513-0823	
MAI Systems :CA	(714) 731-5100	
Main Boards :NY	(800) 359-0201	
Main Source Electronics :CA	(818) 882-7500	
Main Street Computer :FL	(800) 456-6246	(813) 351-8420
MainLan Inc :TX	(214) 248-0305	
Mainlan, Inc :FL	(407) 331-4400	
	BBS (407) 331-7433	
Mainline Computer Repair Inc :PA	(215) 644-0534	
Mainstay Software :CA	(818) 991-6540	
Mainstream Software :TX	(214) 934-8906	
Maintech :NY	(800) 426-8324	
Maintenance Etc :TX	(713) 520-6567	
Maintenance Troubleshooting :DE	(302) 738-0532	
Man & Machine Inc :MD	(301) 277-3760	
Mandax Computer, Inc :WA	(206) 867-1973	
Manhattan Electric Cable Corp :NY	(800) 228-6322	
Mannesmann Tally :WA	(206) 251-5609	
Mansfield Software Group, Inc :CT	(203) 429-8402	
Mantis Computer Parts Inc :NH	(800) 252-9989	
Manugistics :MD	(800) 592-0050	(301) 984-5489
Manusoft Corp. :CA	(818) 304-2762	
Manzanita Software Systems :CA	(916) 781-3880	(800) 447-5700
Maple Systems :CA	(408) 456-0355	
MapInfo Corp :NY	(518) 274-6000	
Marclyn :CA	(408) 739-2443	
Marconi Circuit Technology:NY	(516) 293-8686	
Mark IV Industries, Inc :NY	(716) 689-4972	
Mark Of The Unicorn :MA	(617) 576-2760	
Market Intelligence Research :CA	(415) 961-9000	
Marlin P. Jones & Assoc :FL	(407) 848-8236	
Marshall Industries :CA	(800) 522-0084	

Company and :State	Main Phone	Tech Phone
Marstek Inc :CA	(714) 833-7740	
Martin Information Systems Ltd :HI	(808) 733-2003	
Martin Marietta Corp :MD	(301) 897-6000	
Masque Publishing :CO	(800) 765-4223	
Mass Memory Systems, Inc :FL	(800) 347-5722	
Mass Micro Systems :CA	(800) 522-7979	(800) 442-7979
Masstor Systems Corp :CA	(408) 955-0160	
Master Bond Inc :NJ	(201) 343-8983	
Masterclip Graphics :FL	(305) 983-7440	
Mastersoft :AZ	(602) 277-0900	
Mastertronics :CA	(714) 833-8710	(714) 833-8710
Matesys :	(415) 925-2900	
Math Soft Inc :MA	(800) 628-4223	
Mathematica :FL	(813) 682-1128	(813) 682-1130
MathSoft, Inc :MA	(617) 577-1017	(800) 628-4223
Matrix Digital Products, Inc :CA	(818) 566-8567	
Matrox Electronic Systems Ltd :PQ.	(514) 685-2630	
Matter Of FAX :NY	(800) 433-3329	(212) 431-5426
Maui Research & Technology Cntr :HI	(808) 875-2320	
Max Software Consulting :MD	(301) 828-5935	
Max Systems :FL	(407) 877-3807	
Maxcard :OR	(503) 593-6027	
Maxell :CA	(800) 325-7717	(800) 533-2836
Maxell Corp Of America :NJ	(201) 794-5900	
Maxi Switch, Inc :AZ	(602) 294-5450	
Maxim Technology :KS	(800) 755-1008	
Maximus :CA	(800) 394-6299	(800) 894-0142
Maxis :CA	(510) 254-9700	
Maxoptix Corp :CA	(408) 954-9700	
Maxspeed :CA	(415) 345-5447	
Maxtor Colorado (Miniscribe) :CO	(303) 651-6000	(800) 356-5333
	FAX Back (303) 678-2618	BBS (303)
Maxtor Corp :CA	(408) 432-1700	(800) 356-5333
	BBS (303) 678-2222	
Maxtron :CA	(818) 350-5706	
MAXX Memory Products :CA	(800) 748-6629	
Maya Electronic Products Co :TX	(915) 590-8880	
Mayesys Corp NA :MD	(301) 961-4899	
Maynard Electronics Inc :FL	(800) 222-5871	
Maysteel Corp :WI	(414) 629-5535	
MBS :MD	(800) 944-3808	(301) 762-7405
MBS Technologies :PA	(800) 860-8700	(800) 860-8703
McArthur Associates :CT	(914) 279-8049	
McCarty Associates :CT	(203) 388-6994	
MCCI :CA	(408) 954-8070	
McClure Consultants Ltd :IL	(708) 382-6233	
McDonnell Douglas Corp :MO	(314) 232-0232	
McGraw Hill :PA	(800) 262-4729	
McGraw- Hill TechNet Group :NY	(212) 512-4604	
McGraw-Hill Computer Publication :CA	(415) 513-6800	

Company and :State	Main Phone	Tech Phone
McGraw-Hill, Inc/Data Communictn :NJ	(609) 426-5000	
MCI Communications Corp :	(202) 872-1600	
MCM Electronics :OH	(800) 543-4330	
McNeil & Associates :MN	(612) 428-4068	
MCR Computer Services Inc :NC	(800) 849-9595	
MCR Marketing Inc :OH	(513) 861-3046	
MCSI Technologies, Inc :MD	(301) 495-4444	
McWains Chelsea :NJ	(201) 993-5700	
Mead Training Systems :CT	(800) 621-8711	
Mead-Hatcher, Inc :NY	(716) 877-1185	
Measurement & Control Products :NY	(212) 662-6012	
Measurex Corp :CA	(408) 255-1500	
MECA Software :	(800) 288-6322	(203) 255-7562
MECC :MN	(612) 569-1529	(612) 569-1529
Meckler Corp :CT	(203) 226-6967	
Mectel International Inc :CA	(800) 248-0255	
Media 4 Less :CA	(800) 621-6827	
Media Cybernetics :MD	(800) 992-4256	
Media Factory :CA	(800) 879-9536	(408) 456-9182
Media Products :CA	(408) 432-1711	
Media Resources :CA.	(714) 256-5048	
Media Source :GA	(800) 356-2553	
Media Value :CA	(800) 845-3472	
Media Vision Resource :CA	(800) 684-6699	(800) 638-2807
	BBS (510) 770-0968	
MediaLogic, Inc :MA	(508) 695-2006	
MediaShare Corp :CA.	(619) 931-7171	
Medical Systems & Management :CA	(310) 914-1600	
Mega Drive Systems :CA	(800) 322-4744	(310) 556-1663
Mega Drive Systems Inc :CA	(310) 847-0006	
Mega PC Technology Inc :CA	(714) 850-1044	
Megadata Corp :NY	(516) 589-6800	
MegaHaus :TX	(800) 426-0560	(713) 333-1944
Megahertz :UT	(800) 527-8677	
Megasource :VA	(800) 473-9728	
Megatel Computer Corp :ON	(416) 245-2953	
MEI/Micro Center :OH	(800) 634-3478	
Meirick Inc :MO	(800) 735-5069	
Melard Technologies Inc :NY	(914) 273-4488	
Meltek Inc :CA.	(408) 438-4986	
Memorex Technologies Inc :CA	(408) 957-1421	
Memorex Telex Corp :OK	(918) 627-2333	
Memory Express :CA	(800) 877-8188	
Memory Media Products :CA	(714) 669-1800	
Memory Media Products :CA	(714) 669-1800	
Memory Products And More :CA	(714) 753-1200	
Memory Technology Inc :CO	(303) 786-8080	
Memsoft, Inc :FL	(407) 997-6655	
Mendon Optronics Inc :NY	(716) 248-8480	
Mentor Graphics Corp :OR	(503) 685-7000	

Company and :State	Main Phone	Tech Phone
Mentor Market Research :CA	(408) 268-6333	
Merchant Systems :AZ.	(602) 951-9390	
Mercury Computer Systems Inc :MA	(508) 458-3100	
Mercury Technologies :QU	(514) 747-0254	
Meridian Data :	(800) 755-8324	
Meridian Technologies :	(404) 551-1999	
Merisel :CA.	(800) 637-4735	
Merit Software:TX	(214) 385-2353	
Merlin Software :WA	(206) 361-0093	
Merrill & Bryan Enterprises :CA	(619) 689-8611	
Merritt Computer Products, Inc :TX.	(214) 339-0753	
MESA Distribution Inc :MN	(800) 388-3339	
Mesa Systems Inc :CA.	(510) 462-9491	
Meta Software :MA.	(617) 576-6920	
Metagraphics :CA	(408) 438-1550	
	BBS (408) 438-5368	
Metaware :	(719) 429-6382	
Metc Software :WA	(800) 767-6292	
Metcan Information Technologies :ON	(416) 881-9955	
Metheus Corp :OR	(800) 638-4387	
Methode Electronics Inc :IL	(800) 323-6858	
Metra Information Systems :CA.	(408) 730-9188	
Metrix Customer Support Systems :WI	(414) 798-8560	
Metrix Network Systems Inc :NH.	(603) 888-7000	
Metro Data-Vac :NY.	(914) 357-1600	
Metromedia Paging Services Inc :NJ	(201) 462-4966	
Metropolis Software :	(415) 322-2001	
Metropolitan Vacuum Cleaner :NY	(914) 357-1600	
MetroTel Corp :NY	(516) 937-3420	
MetroVision Microsystems :NY	(800) 875-2099	
Metrum Instrumentation Services :CA	(415) 969-5500	
Metz Software :WA	(206) 441-4525	
Mextel :IL	(708) 595-4146	
MFS Inc :VA	(800) 456-2159	
MGI Group International Inc :CA	(310) 352-3100	
MGV Manufacturing Inc :AL	(205) 772-1100	
MIC Media Corp :CA	(510) 226-0606	
Micom Systems, Inc :CA	(805) 583-8600	
Micro 2000 Inc :CA	(818) 547-0125	
Micro Accessories Inc :CA	(800) 777-6687	
Micro Accessories, Inc. :CA.	(408) 441-1242	
Micro Care Corp :CT	(800) 638-0125	
Micro Central :NJ	(800) 836-4276	
Micro Channel Developers Assoc. :CA	(916) 222-2262	
Micro Connectors Inc :CA	(510) 839-8112	
Micro Data Base Systems, Inc :IN.	(317) 463-2581	
Micro Design Inc :PA	(215) 884-1112	
Micro Design International, Inc. :FL.	(407) 677-8333	
Micro Digital :OH	(714) 891-2363	
Micro Direct :FL	(407) 677-8333	

Company and :State	Main Phone	Tech Phone
Micro Display :MN.	(612) 437-2233	
. . . .	BBS (612) 438-3513	
Micro Edge, Inc :	(919) 831-0662	
Micro Electronic Technologies :MA	(508) 435-9057	
Micro Electronics WinBook :OH . . .	(800) 468-0252	
Micro Exchange Corp :NJ.	(201) 284-1200	
Micro Fine International Inc :NY . . .	(718) 358-3870	
Micro Focus :CA	(415) 856-4161	
Micro House :CO	(303) 443-3388	(303) 443-3389
. . . .	BBS (303) 443-9957	
Micro Industries Corp :OH	(614) 548-7878	
Micro Informatica Corp :FL.	(305) 377-1930	
Micro League Sports :DE	(302) 368-9990	
Micro Mart Inc :MA	(508) 888-2225	
Micro Media International :CA	(714) 588-9882	
Micro Medic Inc :CA	(714) 581-3651	
Micro Medics :MI.	(313) 759-0231	
Micro Palm Computers, Inc :FL . . .	(813) 530-0128	
Micro Power Electronics :OR	(800) 642-7612	
Micro Professionals :IL	(800) 800-8300	
Micro Security Systems, Inc :UT . .	(801) 575-6600	
Micro Service Express :TX	(214) 239-7033	
Micro Solutions :IL	(815) 756-3411	
Micro Star :CA.	(619) 931-4949	
Micro Systems :PA	(800) 548-5182	
Micro Technology :NJ.	(201) 340-0442	
Micro X-Press :IN	(800) 875-9737	(317) 328-5784
Micro-Integration Corp :MD	(301) 777-3307	
Micro-Integration, Inc :MD	(301) 746-5888	
Micro-Term, Inc :MO.	(314) 822-4111	
MicroAge Computer Centers Inc :AZ	(602) 929-2416	
Microbase Information Systems :CA	(310) 479-1239	
Microbilt Corp :GA.	(404) 955-0313	
MicroBiz Corp :NY	(800) 637-8268	(914) 425-3789
MicroClean Inc :CA	(408) 745-0611	
Microcom :MA	(800) 822-8224	
Microcomputer Accessories :CA . . .	(310) 645-9400	
Microcomputer Concepts :CA.	(800) 772-3914	
Microcomputer Industry :CA.	(415) 941-6679	
Microcomputer Technical Services :MA	(508) 798-9912	
Microdynamics Inc :TX	(214) 343-1170	
Microdyne Corp :FL	(800) 456-8667	
. . . .	BBS (703) 739-0432	
Microfield Graphics, Inc :OR.	(503) 626-9393	
MicroGate Corp :TX	(512) 345-7791	
Micrografx, Inc :TX	(800) 733-3729	(214) 234-2694
Microlog Corp :MD	(800) 333-6564	
Micrologic :NJ	(201) 342-6518	
MicroLogic Software :CA	(510) 652-5464	
MicroLogic Systems :TX.	(903) 561-0007	

Company and :State	Main Phone	Tech Phone
Microlytics :NY	(716) 248-9150	
MicroMaid Inc :TX	(800) 369-7079	
MicroMaps Software :	(800) 334-4291	(609) 397-1611
Micromation Technology Inc :CA	(408) 739-2999	
Micromax Distribution :OH	(800) 795-6299	
Micron Computer :ID	(800) 438-3343	
Micron Technology Inc :ID	(208) 386-3800	
	BBS (208) 368-4530	
Micronet Computer Systems:CA	(714) 739-2244	
MicroNet Technology, Inc :CA	(714) 837-6033	(714) 837-6033
Micronics Computers, Inc :CA	(510) 651-2300	
	BBS (510) 651-6837	
MicroPen Computer Corp :CA	(408) 734-4181	
Microplex Systems Ltd :BC	(604) 875-1461	
Micropolis Corp :CA	(800) 395-3300	(818) 709-3325
	BBS (818) 709-3310	
Micropost Corp :BC	(604) 682-6258	
MicroProcessors Unlimited :OK	(918) 267-4961	(918) 267-3879
Microprose Software :MD	(410) 771-1151	
Microref/Educational Systems Inc :IL	(708) 498-3780	
Microrim :WA	(800) 248-2001	(206) 649-9551
	BBS (206) 649-9836	
Micros Systems, Inc :MD	(301) 210-6000	
Microscience International Cor :CA	(408) 441-1456	(408) 433-9898
Microseconds International Inc :CA	(619) 756-0765	
Microseeds Publishing :	(813) 882-8635	
MicroServ Inc :WA	(800) 736-3599	
MicroSlate Inc :PQ	(514) 444-3680	
Microsoft Corp :WA	(800) 426-9400	
	BBS (206) 637-9009	
Microsoft Press :	(800) 426-9400	(206) 454-2030
Microsoft Systems Journal :CA	(411) 535-8950	
Microsoft University :	(800) 426-9400	(206) 646-5104
Microsoft-Text Phone For Deaf :	(206) 635-4948	
Microspeed :CA	(800) 232-7888	
Microspot :	(800) 622-7568	(408) 257-4000
MicroStep Inc :CA	(818) 336-8991	
Microsystems Development :CA	(408) 296-4000	
MicroTac Software :CA	(619) 272-5700	
Microtech International :CT	(800) 626-4276	(800) 626-4276
	BBS (203) 469-6430	
Microtech International :	(800) 666-9689	
Microtek Lab :CA	(213) 321-2121	(310) 352-3300
Microtek Lab :	(213) 321-2121	
Microtest :AZ	(800) 526-9675	
Microtimes :CA	(510) 934-3700	
MicroTouch Systems, Inc :MA	(508) 694-9900	
Microtrace Inc :IN	(317) 842-0772	
Microvitec Inc :GA	(404) 991-2246	
Microvoice Corp :CA	(714) 588-2739	

Company and :State	Main Phone	Tech Phone
Microware Distributors :OR	(800) 777-9511	(800) 888-4797
Microware Technology Distrib. :NY	(800) 382-2405	
Microway :MA	(508) 746-7341	
MicroWest Spacesaver Software :CA	(800) 969-9699	
MICS Computers Inc :CA	(310) 325-4520	
Midern Computer Inc :CA	(818) 964-8682	
MIDI Land Inc :CA	(714) 595-0708	
Midisoft Corporation :WA	(800) 776-6434	
Midland ComputerMart :IL	(800) 407-0700	(708) 967-0746
Midwest Computer Support :OH	(419) 259-2600	
Midwest Computer Works :IL	(800) 669-5208	
Midwest Micro :OH	(800) 312-8822	(800) 243-0313
Midwestern Diskette :IA	(800) 221-6332	(515) 782-5190
Migraph, Inc :WA	(206) 838-4677	
Mikael Blaisdell & Associates :CA	(510) 865-4515	
Miles Computing :	(818) 341-1411	
Miller Freeman Publications,Inc :CA	(415) 397-1881	
Miltope Corp :NY	(516) 420-0200	
Mind Path Technologies :TX	(214) 233-9296	
Mind's Eye :MA	(617) 935-2679	
Mindflight Technology Inc :BC	(604) 434-6463	
Mini-Micro Supply Co, Inc :CA	(408) 456-9500	
Mini-Vac :CA	(818) 244-6777	
Minolta Corp :NJ	(201) 825-4000	
Minta Technologies Co :NJ	(201) 329-2020	
Minuteman UPS :TX	(800) 238-7272	
MIPS Technologies, Inc :CA	(415) 960-1980	
MIPSI Systems, Inc :OK	(800) 727-6774	
Mirage Computer :CA	(800) 666-8098	(909) 598-2602
Miramar Systems :	(805) 966-2432	
Mirror Technologies :MN	(800) 654-5294	(612) 633-2105
Mirus :CA	(408) 944-9770	
MIS Computer Systems :CA	(408) 730-9188	
Misco :NJ	(908) 876-4726	
MissionSix Development Corp :CA	(408) 722-9211	
Mita Copystar America, Inc :NJ	(201) 808-8444	
Mitac :CA	(510) 623-5300	
Mitel Corp :OT	(613) 592-2122	
Mitsuba Corp :CA	(714) 392-2000	
Mitsubishi Electronics :CA	(800) 843-2515	(800) 344-6352
	BBS (714) 636-6216	
Mitsubishi Electronics America :CA	(714) 220-2500	
Mitsubishi International Corp :NY	(914) 997-4960	
Mitsubishi Rayon Co Ltd :CA	(213) 627-7120	
Mitsui Petrochemicals :CA	(415) 572-2333	
Mitsumi Electronics Corp :NY	(516) 752-7730	(408) 970-9699
Mitsumi Electronics Corp :TX	(214) 550-7300	
Mix Software :TX	(800) 333-0330	(214) 783-6001
MM Newman Corporation :MA	(617) 631-7100	
MMC Ad Systems :CA	(408) 263-0781	

Company and :State	Main Phone	Tech Phone
MMF Industries :IL	(708) 537-7890	
Mobile Computer Recovery:NJ	(800) 688-6262	
Mod-Tap :MA	(508) 772-5630	
Modern Office Technology :OH	(216) 696-7000	
Modgraph,Inc :MA	(617) 229-4800	
Modumend :CA	(800) 350-5558	
Monitech Inc :NJ	(800) 332-9349	
Moniterm Corp :MN	(800) 343-4969	
Monitor Maintenance Corp :MA	(617) 961-2600	
Monogram Media :WI	(414) 887-7744	
Monolithic Systems	Out Of Business. :	
Monotype Typography :IL	(800) 666-6897	
Monster Design :	(415) 871-6000	
Montech :MA	(508) 663-5015	
Monterey Computer Consulting :CA	(408) 646-1147	
Monterey Electronics Inc :CA	(408) 437-5496	
Monterey Electronics Inc :CA	(408) 437-5496	
Moon Valley Software :AZ	(800) 473-5509	
Moore Bus. Forms & Systems Div. :IL	(708) 480-3000	
Moore Bus. Forms & Systme Div. :IL	(708) 615-6000	
Morelli Associates :MA	(508) 543-4105	
Morris Video :CA	(310) 533-4800	(310) 320-3171
Morrow Computer Corp :OH	(800) 859-6849	(212) 360-0580
Morse Technology, Inc :CA	(818) 854-8688	
Mortice Kern Systems :OT	(519) 884-2251	(519) 884-2270
Morton Management Inc :MD	(800) 548-5744	
Moses Computers :CA	(408) 358-1550	
MOST Inc :CA	(714) 898-9400	
Motherboard Warehouse :AZ	(800) 486-9975	(602) 829-7751
Motion Works Inc :BC	(602) 685-9975	
Motorola Codex :MA	(508) 261-4307	
Motorola Inc :IL	(708) 576-5304	(800) 311-6456
Motorola Inc :TX	(512) 891-2000	
Motorola Mobile Data Division :BC	(800) 247-2346	
Mountain Network Solutions :CA	(800) 458-0300	(408) 438-7897
	BBS (408) 438-2665	
Mouse Systems Corp :CA	(510) 656-1117	
	BBS (510) 683-0617	
Mouser Electronics :TX	(800) 346-6873	
Movonics :CA	(415) 960-1250	
MP Systems :TX	(214) 385-2221	
MPS Multimedia :CA	(800) 533-4677	(602) 829-7751
Mr. Software, Inc :NY	(212) 947-6272	
MSC Technologies, Inc :CA	(408) 988-0211	
MSI Data Corp :CA	(714) 549-6000	
MST Distribution :OH	(216) 248-2533	
Mueller :OH	(216) 771-5225	
Multi Connection Technology :CA	(510) 670-0633	
Multi-Dimension Research Inc :CA	(818) 337-6860	
Multi-Industry Tech, Inc :CA	(310) 921-6669	

Company and :State	Main Phone	Tech Phone
Multi-Link Inc :KY	(800) 535-4651	
Multi-Tech Systems, Inc :MN	(800) 328-9717	
	BBS (612) 785-9875	
MultiLing International Inc :UT	(801) 377-7077	
Multimedia Direct :PA	(800) 386-3342	
Multimedia Warehouse :MA	(800) 683-2868	
Multiscope :CA	(800) 888-5945	
MultiTech Systems :MN	(800) 328-9717	
MultiWriter Software :NJ	(201) 833-1333	
Murata Business Systems Inc :TX	(214) 403-3300	
Mustang Software, Inc :CA	(805) 395-0223	
	BBS (805) 395-0650	
Mustek Inc :CA	(800) 468-7835	
Mux Lab :QC	(800) 361-1965	
Mylex Corp :CA	(510) 796-6100	
Myoda Inc :IL	(708) 369-5199	
Myriad Inc :CA	(510) 659-8782	
MySoftware Company :CA	(415) 325-4222	
Nada Concepts Inc :MN	(612) 623-0711	
Nanao USA Corp :CA	(213) 325-5202	
Nantucket Corp :CA	(310) 390-7923	
Nashua Corporation :NH	(800) 258-1370	
Nat'l Assoc Of Service Managers :IL	(708) 310-9930	
Nat'l Micronetics, Inc :NY	(914) 338-0333	
National Advancement Corp :CA	(800) 832-4787	
National Business Association :TX	(214) 991-5381	
National Communications :NJ	(201) 733-9200	
National Computer Distributors :FL	(305) 967-2397	
National Computer Systems:MN	(612) 829-3000	
National Cristina Foundation :NY	(914) 738-7494	
National Customer Engineering :CA	(619) 452-7974	
National Data Corp :GA	(404) 728-2000	
National Datacomputer Inc :MA	(508) 663-7677	
National Design Inc :TX	(512) 329-5055	
National Instruments :TX	(800) 433-3488	
National Instruments :TX	(800) 433-3488	
National Inventory Exchange :AZ	(800) 633-2869	
National Peripheral Services :CA	(800) 628-9025	
National Semiconductor :CA	(408) 721-5000	
	BBS (408) 245-0671	
National Service Network Inc :WA	(206) 845-1288	
National Software Testing Labs :PA	(215) 941-9600	
National TeleVAR :MN	(800) 468-1732	
Nationwide Computer Distributors :NJ	(800) 777-1054	(201) 659-2977
Natl Software Testing Lab. Inc. :PA	(215) 941-9600	
Natter Manufacturing Inc :UT	(801) 561-9261	
Natural Micro Systems :	(617) 655-0700	
Navacor InCorp :CA	(408) 441-6500	
NavPress Software :CO	(719) 598-1212	
NBI, Inc :CO	(303) 444-5710	(800) 225-5624

Company and :State	Main Phone	Tech Phone
NCI :CO	(303) 650-5522	
NCL America :CA	(408) 956-1040	
NCL America :CA	(408) 734-1006	
NCR Corp :KS	(316) 636-8000	
NCR Corporation-Education Svcs. :OH	(800) 845-2273	
NCR Direct Connect :OH.	(800) 627-8076	(800) 531-2222
NCR Worldwide Service Parts Ctr. :GA	(800) 367-1842	
NDC Communications :CA	(408) 428-9108	
Nearnco :MA	(617) 269-7600	
NEC Technologies Inc :MA	(800) 388-8888	(508) 264-4300
FAX Back (800) 366-0476	BBS (508) 635-6328	
Needham's Electronics :CA	(916) 924-8037	
Nesco Battery Systems :CA	(800) 423-2664	
Net Computers International :TX	(214) 386-9310	(214) 386-9337
Net Soft :CA	(818) 572-0607	
NET-Source Inc :CA	(408) 246-6679	
Netalliance :WA	(206) 637-3305	
Netline :VA	(703) 760-0660	
NETS Electronics Inc :NH	(800) 633-7999	
Network :MA.	(508) 568-0933	
Network Communications Corp :MN	(800) 451-1984	
Network Equipment Technologies :CA	(415) 366-4400	
Network Express :FL	(800) 333-9899	(813) 359-2876
Network General :IL	(708) 574-3399	
Network Interface Corp :KS	(913) 894-2277	
Network Security Systems Inc :CA	(619) 587-7950	
Network Systems Corp :MN	(612) 424-4888	
Network Technologies :OH	(800) 742-8324	
Neuralytic Systems :CA	(415) 321-3777	
Nevada Computer :NV.	(800) 654-7762	
New England Software :CT	(203) 625-0062	
New Horizons Computer Lrning Ctr :CA	(714) 556-1220	
New Media Corp :CA	(714) 453-0100	
New Media Graphics Corp :MA	(508) 663-0666	
	BBS (508) 663-7612	
New MMI :PA	(800) 221-4283	
New Quest Technologies :	(801) 975-9992	
New Vision Technology Inc :ON	(613) 727-8184	
New World Technologies :MA	(800) 443-8885	
Newbury Data :CA	(213) 372-3775	
Newer Technology :KS	(316) 685-4904	
NewGen Systems Corp :CA	(714) 641-8600	(714) 436-5150
NewMedia Magazine :CA	(415) 573-5170	
Neworg Inc :VA	(804) 358-5626	
NewQuest Technology Inc :UT	(613) 727-8184	
Nexgen Microsystems Inc :CA	(408) 435-0202	
Next Computer Corp :CA	(415) 366-0900	
Next Generation Software, Inc :GA	(404) 365-8258	
Nial Systems :OT	(613) 234-4188	
Nichimen America Inc :IL	(312) 938-8887	

Company and :State	Main Phone	Tech Phone
Nikon Electronic Imaging :NY	(516) 547-4350	
Nimax Inc :CA	(619) 566-4800	
Ninga Software Corp :AB	(403) 265-6611	
Nisca Inc :TX	(800) 245-7226	
	BBS (214) 446-0646	
Nissei Sangyo America, Ltd. :MA	(617) 893-5700	
Nissho Electronics (USA) Corp :CA	(714) 261-8811	
Nisus :CA	(619) 481-1477	
Nitek Inc :AZ	(602) 285-5662	
NKR Research Inc :CA	(408) 149-2612	
NMB Technologies :CA	(818) 341-3355	
No-Brainer Software :UT	(800) 748-4499	
Noetic Technologies :FL	(800) 780-6343	
Nolo Press :CA	(800) 992-6656	
NOMDA/NIA :MO	(816) 941-3100	
NoRad Corp :CA	(800) 262-3260	
Norcom :AK	(907) 780-6464	
Nordisk Systems :CA	(805) 485-4778	
Norick Data Systems :OK	(405) 947-7560	
Nortek Computers :ON	(705) 474-2058	
Nortek Computers :FL	(305) 421-4500	
North American Business :	(800) 325-1485	
North American InfoNet, Inc :CA	(707) 765-1999	
North American Phillips :CA	(212) 697-3600	
North Hills Electronics :NY	(516) 671-5700	
North-East Microcomputer :ON	(416) 513-6800	
Northeast Technical Services :NH	(800) 647-9725	
Northeastern Sonics :CT	(800) 243-2452	
Northern Technologies :WA	(800) 727-9119	
Northern Telecom Ltd :OT	(416) 897-9000	
Northgate Computer Systems :MN	(800) 548-1993	(800) 446-5037
Northgate Computer Systems:MN	(612) 943-6009	
	BBS (612) 943-8341	
Northstar Matrix-Serv :MN	(800) 969-0009	
Northstar Matrixserv :MN	(612) 785-1075	
Norton-Lambert :CA	(805) 964-6767	
	BBS (805) 683-2249	
Noteable Computers Inc :CA	(800) 274-4124	
NoteStar Computers :NJ	(908) 651-8686	
Notework Corp :MA	(617) 734-4317	
Nova Technology Services :MD	(800) 523-2773	
Novacor Inc :CA	(800) 486-6682	
Novation :CA	(818) 998-5060	(818) 998-5060
Novell Inc :UT	(801) 429-7000	
FAX Back (801) 429-5363		
Now Software :OR	(800) 237-3611	
Noyes Fiber Systems :NH	(603) 528-7780	
NPA Systems :NY	(800) 873-6724	
NPA West :CA	(800) 999-4672	
NRD Inc :NY	(716) 773-7634	

Company and :State	Main Phone	Tech Phone
NRG Data Corp :CA	(408) 727-9700	
NRI :DC	(202) 244-1600	
NSM Information Systems :NY	(516) 261-7700	
NSSI :CA	(800) 755-7078	
NSTS :GA	(404) 923-1383	
NTE Electronics Inc :NJ	(800) 631-1250	
Ntergaid, Inc :CT	(203) 368-0632	
NTR Computer :CA	(408) 727-4500	
Nu Data :NJ	(908) 842-5757	
Number Nine Computer Corp :MA	(617) 674-0009	
	BBS (617) 497-6463	
Numonics Corp :PA	(215) 362-2766	
NUS :ID	(800) 247-8818	
NUS Training Corp :MD	(800) 848-1717	
Nuvotech :	(800) 232-9922	
NView Corp :VA	(800) 736-8439	
Nynex Corp :NY	(914) 741-4700	
Nyquan Research :	(416) 427-4042	
O'Neill Communications :NJ	(800) 624-5296	(215) 957-5408
O.K. Industries :NY	(914) 969-6800	
Oakland Group :MA	(617) 491-7311	
OAZ Communications, Inc :CA	(408) 745-1750	
OBI Distributors Inc :CA	(714) 259-1925	
Objective Software :CA	(415) 324-3333	
Objective Systems :CA	(415) 929-0964	
Ocean Interface Co, Inc :CA	(714) 595-1212	
Ocean Isle Software :NC	(407) 770-4777	
OCEAN Microsystems, Inc :CA	(408) 374-8300	
OCLI (Optical Coating Lab. Inc) :CA	(707) 545-6440	
OCR Systems, Inc :	BBS (215) 938-7245	
Ocron, Inc. :CA	(408) 980-8900	
Octocom Systems Inc :MA	(508) 441-2181	
Octophase Technology Corp :CA	(408) 954-1240	
OCTuS Inc :CA	(619) 452-9400	
Odesta Group :IL	(708) 498-5615	(708) 498-8852
Odetics Inc :CA	(714) 774-6900	
Odyssey Development Inc :CO	(303) 394-0091	
OEM Parts Repair Depot :ON	(800) 422-2115	
Office Automation Systems, Inc :CA	(619) 452-9400	
Office Publications, Inc :CT	(203) 327-9670	
OFTI :MA	(508) 692-6606	
Ogg Software :CA	(213) 274-4402	(213) 274-4402
Okidata Corp :NJ	(800) 654-3282	
	BBS (800) 283-5474	
Okna :	(201) 909-8600	
Olduvai :FL	(800) 822-0772	(305) 665-4665
Olivetti Office USA :NJ	(201) 526-8200	
Olivetti/ISC :WA	(509) 927-5622	
Olson Metal Products :TX	(512) 379-2799	
Omega Technology Of Taiwan:FL.	(305) 597-5564	

Company and :State	Main Phone	Tech Phone
Omni CEO :MA	(508) 937-5004	
Omni Labs :CA	(800) 706-3342	(415) 788-1345
Omni-Data Communications :KS	(800) 922-2329	
Omnicomp Graphics Corp :TX	(713) 464-2990	
Omniprint Inc :CA	(800) 878-6880	
Omnitech Gencorp :FL	(305) 599-9898	
OmniTel Inc :CA	(510) 490-2202	
Omnium Corp :WI	(715) 268-8500	
Omron Electronics, Inc :IL	(708) 843-7900	
Omron Office Automation Products :CA	(408) 727-1444	
On Board Computer Services :CT	(203) 881-0555	
ON Technology :	(800) 548-8871	(615) 876-5122
On Time Mac Service :CA	(415) 367-6263	
On-Line Data :	(519) 579-3930	
On-Line Power Co :CA	(213) 721-5017	
On-Line Software International :NJ	(201) 592-0009	
On-Line/AAA Power :CA	(213) 721-5017	
OnDisk Information Systems Inc :TX	(800) 654-3146	
Oneac Corp :IL	(708) 816-6000	
Online Press Inc :WA	(206) 641-3434	
Online, USA :CO	(303) 932-1900	
	BBS (303) 932-1400	
Ontrack Computer Systems :MN	(800) 872-2599	
Open Systems :MN	(800) 328-2276	(800) 582-5000
Open Text Corporation :CN	(519) 571-7711	
Opt-Tech Data Processing :NV	(702) 588-3737	
OPTi, Inc :CA	(408) 980-8178	
	BBS (408) 980-9774	
Optibase, Inc. :CA	(818) 719-6566	
Optical Cable Corporation :VA	(703) 265-0690	
Optical Data Systems, Inc :TX	(214) 234-6400	
Optical Devices, Inc :CA	(805) 987-8801	
Optical Storage Corp :CA	(310) 791-2028	
Optical Storage Trade Assn. :CA	(805) 569-2541	
Optima Technology Corp :CA	(714) 476-0515	
	BBS (714) 476-0626	
Optiquest, Inc. :CA	(310) 948-1185	
Opus Computer Products :OH	(216) 248-9264	
OR Computer Keyboards, Ltd. :CN	(604) 879-9815	
ORA Electronics :CA	(818) 772-2700	
Oracle Corp :CA	(415) 506-2200	
Orange Micro, Inc :CA	(714) 779-2772	
Orbit Industries, Inc. :CN	(604) 852-6301	
Orchid Technology :CA	(510) 683-0300	
	BBS (510) 683-0327	
Oregon Software :OR	(503) 624-6883	
Orevox USA Corp. :CA	(818) 333-6803	
Orientec Corp Of America :CA	(818) 442-1818	
Origin Systems, Inc :TX	(512) 328-0282	
	BBS (512) 328-8402	

Company and :State	Main Phone	Tech Phone
OS Computer City :CA	(800) 938-6722	
OS/2 2.0 Applications :TX	(800) 426-3333	
Osborne/McGraw Hill :CA	(800) 227-0900	
Osborne/McGraw-Hill :CA	(800) 227-0900	
Oscan Electro-Optics, Inc. :CN	(613) 745-4600	
Oscar International :CA	(909) 595-0339	
OSI Netter, The :MN	(612) 935-2035	
Osicom Technologies :NJ	(201) 586-2550	
Our Business Machines, Inc :CA	(818) 337-9614	
Outbound Systems, Inc. :CO	(303) 786-9200	
Output Tech Corp :WA	(800) 468-8788	
Overdrive Systems :	(216) 292-3425	(216) 292-3410
Overland Data, Inc :CA	(619) 571-5555	
Overseas Trade Group :MI	(313) 340-0300	
Owl International :	(206) 747-3203	
OWP :NH	(603) 880-5100	
P.A. Computer Accessories :CA	(818) 448-9221	
P.M. Ware :	(619) 738-6633	
P.N.Y. Electronics, Inc. :NJ	(201) 438-6300	
PACE Custom Cases :UT	(801) 753-1067	
Pace Inc :MD	(301) 490-9860	
Pacer Industries :WI	(800) 283-1141	
Pacer Software :	(508) 454-0565	(508) 898-3300
Pacific Computer Products, Inc :CA	(714) 549-7535	
Pacific Data Products :CA	(619) 552-0880	
	BBS (619) 452-6329	
Pacific Dataware Inc :OR	(800) 234-4734	
Pacific Decision Sciences Corp :CA	(714) 832-2200	
Pacific Electro Data Inc :CA	(800) 676-2468	
Pacific Gold Coast Corp. :NY	(800) 732-3002	
Pacific Image Communications Inc :CA	(818) 441-0104	
Pacific International Center :HI	(808) 539-1533	
Pacific Magnetics Corp :CA	(619) 474-8216	
Pacific Magtron, Inc. :CA	(408) 744-1188	
Pacific Micro Data, Inc. :CA	(714) 838-8900	
Pacific Micro Marketing(Magnavox :CA	(510) 438-0100	
Pacific Microelectronics, Inc. :CA	(415) 948-6200	
Pacific Northwest Partnership :WA	(206) 682-6900	
Pacific Power Source Corp :CA	(714) 898-2691	
Pacific Rim Systems, Inc. :CA	(800) 722-7461	
Pacific Telecom, Inc :WA	(206) 696-0983	
Pacific Telesis Group :CA	(415) 394-3000	
Packintell Electronics :CA	(916) 635-2784	
Padware :MA	(617) 848-7310	
Page Computer :CA	(800) 886-0055	
PageAhead Software Corp :WA	(206) 441-0340	
PagePlus :NH	(800) 697-3743	
Paladin Corp :CA	(800) 272-8665	
Palindrome Corp :IL	(708) 505-3300	
	BBS (708) 505-3336	

Company and :State	Main Phone	Tech Phone
Palo Alto Design Group, Inc. :CA ..	(415) 327-9444	
Palomar Software :	(619) 721-7000	
Pam-Pacific Associates, Inc :CA ..	(818) 333-3009	
Panacea Inc :NH	(800) 729-7420	
Panamax :CA	(800) 472-5555	
Panasonic Comm. & Systems Co. :NJ	(201) 348-7000	
....	BBS (201) 863-7847	
Panasonic Industrial Co :NJ	(800) 848-3979	
Panduit Corp :IL	(800) 777-3300	
Pantex Computer, Inc :TX	(713) 988-1688	
Par Technology Corp :NY.........	(315) 738-0600	
Para Systems :TX................	(214) 446-7363	
Paradigm Systems :NY...........	(607) 748-5966	
Paradyne Corp :FL	(813) 530-2000	
Paragon Concepts :CA...........	(619) 481-1477	
Paragon Memory Corp :CA	(714) 454-6444	
Parallel Peripherals Tech., Inc. :CA	(714) 394-7244	
Parana Supplies Corp :CA	(800) 472-7262	
Parcplace Systems :CA	(415) 691-6700	(800) 822-8259
Parity Systems :CA	(408) 378-1000	
Parker Systems, Inc :NV..........	(800) 458-1049	
Parts Express :AZ...............	(800) 377-6543	
Parts Now Inc :WI	(800) 866-6688	
Parts Port Ltd :VA	(800) 253-0515	
Passport Designs, Inc. :CA.......	(415) 726-0280	
Pastel Development :	(212) 431-3421	(212) 941-7500
Patco Electronics Inc :FL	(407) 268-0205	
Pathfinder Associates :CA	(408) 984-2256	
....	BBS (408) 246-0164	
Patton & Patton Software Corp :CA	(408) 778-6557	
....	BBS (408) 778-9697	
Patton Consultants :NY	(716) 334-2554	
Paul Mace Software Inc :OR	(800) 523-0258	
....	BBS (714) 240-4759	
Paxr Test Systems :CA...........	(800) 825-7297	
Paychex :NY	(716) 385-6666	
PBS Inc :NH	(603) 889-6512	
PC & C Research Corporation :CA	(805) 484-1865	
PC America/The General Store :NY	(800) 722-6374	(804) 523-6600
PC Catalog :NE.................	(402) 477-8900	
PC CompoNet, Inc. :CA	(310) 943-9878	
PC Computer Source Book :CA ...	(408) 446-0551	
PC Computing :NY	(212) 503-5449	
PC Concepts Inc :CA	(818) 768-6033	
PC Concepts, Inc. :CA...........	(818) 768-6033	
PC Discount Center :IL...........	(800) 245-7453	(708) 390-7451
PC DOCS, Inc. :FL..............	(904) 942-3627	
PC Dynamics, Inc :CA	(818) 889-1741	
PC Express, Inc. :CA	(818) 307-0288	
PC Globe, Inc :AZ...............	(602) 730-9000	

Company and :State	Main Phone	Tech Phone
PC Guardian :CA	(800) 288-8126	
PC House :CA	(213) 324-8621	
PC Importers :OH.	(800) 886-5155	(216) 464-5641
PC Laptop Magazine :CA	(310) 858-7155	
PC Letter :CA	(415) 592-8880	
PC Link Corp :NY	(212) 730-8036	
PC Logic, Inc. :PA	(717) 399-2399	
PC Magazine :NY	(212) 503-5446	
PC Manager, Inc :VA	(703) 356-4600	
PC Novice :NE	(402) 477-8900	
PC Parts Express :TX	(214) 406-8583	
PC Power & Cooling Inc :CA	(800) 722-6555	
PC Publishing Inc :MA	(617) 661-8050	
PC QUICK CORP :OR.	(503) 644-5644	
PC Serviceland Inc :GA	(404) 934-0440	
PC Technology :	(313) 996-9690	
PC Today :NE	(402) 477-8900	
PC Weeks Labs :MA	(617) 393-3700	
PC Wholesale :IL	(708) 307-1700	
PC World :CA.	(415) 243-0500	
PC-Kwik Corp. :OR	(800) 274-5945	
PC-Sig :CA.	(408) 730-9291	
PC/Nametag :WI	(608) 273-4300	
PCMCIA :CA	(408) 720-0107	
PCPI :CA	(800) 225-4098	
PCs Compleat :MA	(800) 669-4727	
PCS/Professional Computer Sys. :CA	(408) 263-0222	
PCUBID Computer Technology :CA	(619) 793-1328	
PDA Engineering :CA	(714) 540-8900	
PDI :OR	(503) 646-5024	
Peachtree Software :GA	(404) 564-5700	(800) 346-5317
Peachtree Software, Inc. :GA	(404) 564-5700	
Peak Technologies Group :MD	(800) 627-6372	
Peaktron Computer, Inc. :CA	(310) 634-3911	
Pearson Technologies :GA	(404) 591-2484	
PedCom Inc :CA	(800) 733-4488	
Pedro Cos :MN.	(800) 328-9284	
Peed Corp. :NE	(402) 477-8900	
Peer Logic :CA	(415) 626-4545	
Pelikan, Inc. :TN.	(800) 874-5898	
Pen Systems, Inc. :CA	(714) 489-0047	
Pengo Computer Accessories :CA	(818) 350-4990	
Penta Systems Int'l, Inc :	(301) 685-7258	
Pentax Technologies Corp :CO	(303) 460-1600	
	BBS (303) 460-1637	
Pentel Of America Ltd :CA	(310) 320-3831	
Penton Publishing :OH.	(216) 696-7000	
PenWare, Inc. :CA	(415) 858-4920	
Peoplesmith Software :MA	(617) 545-7300	
Peradata Technology Corp :NY	(516) 588-2216	

Company and :State	Main Phone	Tech Phone
Perception Technologies :MA....	(617) 821-0320	
Perceptive Solutions, Inc :TX	(214) 954-1774	
Perco, Inc :OR.....	(503) 344-1189	
Percom Technology, Inc. :CA...	(510) 656-2866	
Percon, Inc :OR.....	(800) 873-7266	
PereLine Data Systems, Inc :CA ..	(408) 364-2770	
Perfect Data Corp. :CA.........	(805) 581-4000	
PerfectData Corp :CA.........	(805) 581-4000	
Pericomp Corp :MA.............	(508) 655-7660	
Peripheral Computer Support :CA .	(408) 263-4043	
Peripheral Land Inc :CA	(800) 288-8754	(800) 288-8754
Peripheral Maintenance Inc :NJ ...	(201) 227-8411	
Peripheral Parts Support :MA.....	(617) 890-9101	
Peripheral Repair Corp :CA	(800) 627-3475	
Peripheral Service Products :CA ..	(800) 247-4733	
Peripheral Solutions INc :CA	(408) 425-8280	
Peripheral Vision :CA	(800) 441-0933	
Peripherals Plus :NJ............	(800) 444-7369	(908) 363-6270
Periscope :GA................	(800) 722-7006	
Perkin-Elmer Corp :CT	(203) 762-1000	
Perma Power Electronics, Inc :IL ..	(800) 323-4255	
Persoft :WI..................	(608) 273-6000	
Personal Computer Products, Inc. :CA	(619) 485-8411	
Personal Computer Sol. :TX......	(214) 661-8144	
Personal Computing Tools :CA ...	(800) 767-6728	
Personal Library Software :MD....	(301) 926-1402	
Personal Publishing :IL	(708) 665-1000	
Personal Tex :CA	(415) 388-8853	
Personal Training Systems :CA ...	(800) 832-2499	
Personal Travel Technologies :NH.	(516) 538-1234	
Personics Corp :MA	(617) 897-1575	
Peter Norton Computing, Inc :CA ..	(310) 453-4600	
Phar Lap Software :MA.........	(617) 661-1510	
Pheecom Technology Corp :CA...	(714) 668-9550	
PHIHONG USA :CA	(408) 263-2200	
Philips Consumer Electronics :TN .	(615) 521-4316	
Philips ECG :PA	(800) 526-9354	
Philips Key Modules :CA	(714) 453-7373	
Philips Labs :NY	(800) 628-0363	
Philtek Power Corp :WA.........	(800) 727-4877	
Phoenix Contact :PA...........	(717) 944-1300	
Phoenix Contact Inc :PA.'......	(717) 944-1300	
Phoenix Technologies :MA.......	(617) 551-4000	
Physician Micro Systems, Inc :WA..	(206) 441-8490	
Physiotronics Corp USA :NY	(212) 887-9555	
PI Manufacturing Corp :CA	(714) 598-3718	
Pick Systems :CA.............	(714) 261-7425	
Pico Electronics :NY...........	(800) 431-1064	
PictureWare, Inc :PA...........	(215) 667-0880	
Pilot Corp Of America :CT	(203) 377-8800	

Company and :State	Main Phone	Tech Phone
Pilot Software Inc :MA	(800) 944-0094	
Pine Computer Systems, Inc :CA	(619) 569-7463	
Pinnacle Data Systems INc :OH	(614) 487-1150	
Pinnacle Micro :CA	(714) 727-3300	
Pinnacle Publishing :WA	(206) 251-1900	
	BBS (206) 251-6217	
Pinpoint Publishing :CA	(707) 935-3217	
	BBS (707) 523-0468	
Pioneer Communications Of Amer. :NJ	(201) 327-6400	
Pioneer Computer, Inc :CA	(510) 623-0808	
Pioneer Magnetics :CA	(800) 233-1745	
Pioneer Software :NC	(800) 876-3101	
Pioneer Standard Electronics :OH.	(216) 587-3600	
Pitney Bowes Inc :CT.	(203) 351-7226	
Pivar Computing Services,Inc :IL	(708) 459-6010	
Pixar :	(800) 937-3179	(510) 236-4000
PKware, Inc :WI	(414) 354-8699	
	BBS (414) 354-8670	
Plainview Batteries Inc :NY	(800) 642-2354	
Plamer Systems :OR	(503) 690-1100	
Plasmaco, Inc. :NY	(914) 883-6800	
Plasmon Data Systems :CA	(408) 432-0570	
Plastic Systems Inc :MA	(508) 485-7390	
Platinum Desktop Software Inc :CA	(714) 727-3775	(714) 727-2110
Platinum Software Corp :CA	(714) 727-1250	
Plato Products Inc :CA.	(818) 965-8044	
Platt Luggage :IL	(800) 222-1515	
Plesman Publications, Ltd. :ON.	(416) 497-9562	
PLI :CA.	(800) 288-8754	
	BBS (510) 651-5948	
Plotworks :CA.	(619) 457-5090	
Plus 5 Engineering Ltd :MD	(301) 977-4048	
Plus Development :CA.	(408) 434-6900	(900) 740-4433
	BBS (408) 434-1664	
Plus Development Corp :CA	(408) 434-6900	
Plustek USA, Inc. :CA	(800) 685-8088	
PMR Corporation :CT	(800) 456-6480	
Pocket Soft, Inc :	(800) 456-7032	
Point 4 Data Corp :CA	(714) 259-0777	
Polar Instruments :WA.	(800) 328-0817	
Polaris Service Inc :MA	(800) 541-5831	
Polaris Software :CA	(800) 722-5728	(619) 674-6500
Polaris Software :CA	(800) 722-5728	
Polaroid :MA.	(617) 577-2000	(800) 225-1618
Polaroid Corp. :MA.	(800) 225-1618	
Policy Management Systems :SC	(803) 735-4000	
Polygon, Inc :MO	(314) 576-7709	
Polytel Computer Products Corp :CA	(408) 745-1540	
Polytele Computer Products :CA.	(408) 745-1540	
Polytronics :LA	(318) 797-2952	

Company and :State	Main Phone	Tech Phone
Polywell Computers :CA	(415) 583-7222	
Popking Software & Systems Inc :NY	(212) 571-3434	
Popular Programs, Inc :TX	(800) 447-678	
Poqet Computer Corp :CA	(800) 624-8999	
Porelon, Inc :TN	(615) 432-4042	
Portable Warehouse, The :CA	(714) 993-1095	(714) 993-1096
Portacom Technologies, Inc. :CA	(415) 390-8507	
Portfolio Systems :	(408) 252-0420	(802) 865-9558
Positive Software Solutions :CA	(310) 301-8446	
Postcraft International :	(805) 257-1797	(416) 641-0768
Power Clinic Inc :TX	(214) 245-4016	
Power General :MA.	(617) 828-6216	
Power Integrity Corp :NC	(800) 237-6260	
Power Line :CA	(800) 234-2444	
Power Plus :TX	(800) 875-5530	
Power Pros :NC	(800) 788-0070	
Power Up! Software Corp :CA	(800) 851-2917	(415) 345-0551
Powercard Supply :FL	(305) 251-5855	
Powercom America, Inc. :CA	(714) 252-8241	
Powercore Inc :IL	(815) 468-3737	
PowerPro Software :CA	(415) 345-9278	
PowerTek Industries, Inc. :CO	(303) 680-9400	
Powervar Inc :IL	(800) 369-7179	
PQ Systems :OH.	(513) 885-2255	
Practical Peripherals :CA	(800) 442-4774	(818) 991-8200
Practical Peripherals :CA	(805) 497-4774	
....	BBS (805) 496-4445	
PrairieTek Corp :CO	(800) 825-2511	
PRC :VA	(703) 556-1000	
Pre-Owned Electronics Inc :MA	(800) 274-5343	
Pre-Owned Electronics, Inc. :MA	(617) 275-4600	
Precise Power Corp :FL	(813) 746-3515	
Precision Data Products :MI	(800) 968-0888	
Precision Line Inc :MN	(612) 475-3550	
Precision Line Inc. :MN.	(612) 475-3550	
Precision Methods, Inc :VA	(703) 752-2800	
Precision Methods, Inc. :VA	(703) 752-2800	
Precision Micro Research Corp :CA	(408) 727-9697	
Precision Motion :CA	(805) 546-8294	
Precision Plus Software :OT.	(519) 657-0633	
Preferred Computer Services :IL	(708) 268-9150	
Preh Electronic Industries, Inc :IL	(708) 438-4000	
Preh Electronics Industries :IL	(708) 438-4000	
Prema Precision Electronics Inc :CA	(800) 441-0305	
Prentice Hall Computer Publish. :IN	(317) 573-2500	
Prentice Hall, Inc :NJ	(201) 767-5937	
Prescience :	(415) 543-2252	
Present Technologies Company :OR	(503) 641-1370	
Prestance Corp :WA	(206) 448-5052	
Priam Corp :CA.	(408) 946-4600	

Company and :State	Main Phone	Tech Phone
Priam Systems :CA	(408) 954-8680	
....	BBS (408) 434-1646	
Prima International :CA	(408) 727-2600	
Prima International, Inc :CA	(408) 727-2600	
Primages Inc :NY	(516) 585-8200	
Primavera Systems, Inc :PA	(800) 423-0245	(215) 668-3030
Primax Electronics :CA	(800) 338-3693	
Prime Computer, Inc :	(508) 879-2960	
Prime Portable Manufacturer :CA	(800) 966-7237	
Prime Solutions :CA	(619) 274-5000	(619) 272-4000
....	BBS (619) 272-9240	
PrimeService :MA	(508) 620-2800	
Princeton Graphics :GA	(800) 241-1490	(404) 664-1010
....	BBS (404) 664-1210	
Princeton Technology, Inc. :CA	(714) 847-2477	
Principia Products :PA	(215) 429-1359	
Print Products International :MD	(800) 638-2020	
Printech Enterprises Inc :MI	(800) 346-2618	
Printech Ribbons Inc :QB	(514) 684-8450	
Printer Connection :VA	(800) 622-7060	
Printer Products :MA	(617) 254-1200	
Printer Source :PA	(215) 538-3188	
Printer Systems Corp :MD	(301) 258-5060	
Printer Works :CA	(800) 225-6116	
Printers Plus :MO	(800) 562-2727	
Printers Plus National Sales :VA	(800) 877-4683	(800) 258-2661
Printing Technology Center :OH	(800) 285-6496	(216) 524-1291
Printronix, Inc :CA	(714) 863-1900	(714) 863-1900
Prism Imaging Systems :CA	(510) 490-9360	
Pro Active Software :CA	(415) 691-1500	
Pro Tools Inc :OR	(800) 743-4335	
Pro-C Ltd :ON	(519) 725-5173	
Pro-Mation, Inc :UT	(801) 566-4655	
Pro-Serv Development Inc :DE	(302) 234-2733	
Pro-Tech Cases :UT	(800) 638-3789	
Pro-TecT Computer Products :UT	(801) 295-7739	
Processing Telecom Technologies :AL	(205) 971-8001	
Processor, The :NE	(800) 247-4880	
Procom Technology :CA	(714) 549-9449	(714) 549-9449
Procom Technology :CA	(714) 852-1000	
Procomp USA, Inc :OH	(216) 234-6387	
....	BBS (216) 234-6581	
Prod-Art Marketing (U.S.A.) Inc :NY	(516) 223-9800	
Prodatel Communications Inc :QC	(800) 561-4019	
Prodem Technology America :CA	(408) 984-2850	
Prodigy Services Co :NY	(914) 993-8000	
Product Safety Engineering Inc :FL	(813) 989-2360	
Productivity Enhancement Product :CA	(714) 348-1011	
Productivity Software :NY	(212) 818-1144	
Professional Computer Service :GA	(404) 998-7776	

| --- | --- | --- |
Professional Management Inst :OK	(800) 383-1296	
Professional MicroCare :OH	(513) 223-2348	
Profit Press :AZ	(800) 843-7990	
Profitability Of Hawaii :HI	(808) 536-6167	
Progen Technology Inc :CA	(714) 549-5818	
Prognostics :CA	(415) 424-8711	
Programmer's Paradise :NJ	(908) 389-8950	
Programmer's Warehouse :AZ	(800) 323-1809	
Progress Software Corp :MA	(617) 275-4500	
Progressive Computer Services :LA	(504) 831-9717	
Progressive Micro Systems :GA	(800) 220-9888	(800) 220-9898
Progressive Ribbon, Inc :OH	(800) 800-7426	
ProHance Technologies, Inc :CA	(408) 746-0950	
Prolink Computer Inc :CA	(213) 780-7978	
ProMaccomuters Inc :OR	(503) 691-0304	
Promark Ltd :NM	(505) 345-7701	
Prometheus Products :OR	(503) 692-9600	(503) 624-0953
	BBS (503) 691-5199	
Promise Technology Inc :CA	(408) 452-0948	
Promise Technology, Inc :CA	(408) 452-0948	
ProSoft :CA	(818) 765-4444	
Prosonus :CA	(818) 766-5221	
ProSource Power :IL	(800) 949-4797	
Protec Microsystems Inc :PQ	(514) 630-5832	
Protech Inc :TX	(210) 614-1690	
Protective Closures Co Inc :NY	(716) 876-9855	
Protek Inc :NJ	(201) 767-7242	
Proteon, Inc :MA	(508) 898-2800	
	BBS (508) 366-7827	
Protolab :UT	(801) 785-5000	
Proton Corp :CA	(714) 952-6900	
ProtoView Development Co :NJ	(908) 329-8588	
ProVUE Development :	(714) 892-8199	(714) 892-8599
Proworks :OR	(503) 567-1459	(503) 567-8836
Proxim Inc :CA	(415) 960-3876	
Proxima Corp :CA	(800) 582-0852	
PS Solutions, Inc :TX	(214) 980-2632	
PSI :CA	(800) 622-1722	
Psion Inc :MA	(508) 371-0310	
PSN :NY	(212) 696-9476	
PSSI Plug-In Storage Systems Inc :CT	(800) 231-5952	
Psygnosis Limited :MA	(617) 497-7794	
PTN Publishing :NY	(516) 845-2700	
Publishers Group West :CA	(510) 658-3453	
Publishing Perfection :WI	(800) 782-5974	
Publishing Technologies, Inc :TX	(512) 246-2835	
Pulizzi Engineering Inc :CA	(714) 540-4229	
Pulse Metric Inc :CA	(619) 546-9461	
Pup-Pak :CA	(310) 568-1790	
Purart :NH	(603) 772-9907	

Company and :State	Main Phone	Tech Phone
Puretek Industrial Co, Ltd :CA	(510) 656-8083	
Pycon Inc :CA	(800) 949-0349	
Pyramid Data :CA	(800) 972-7972	(415) 312-7080
Pyramid Software Technology, Inc :CA	(714) 832-7577	
Pyramid Technology Corp :CA	(415) 965-7200	
Q/Media Software Corp :BC	(604) 879-6886	
Qantel Business Systems, Inc :CA	(510) 887-7777	
QDI Computer Inc :CA	(310) 908-1029	
QMS Inc :AL	(205) 633-4300	(205) 633-4500
	BBS (205) 633-3632	
QSound Ltd :AB	(403) 291-2492	
Qtronix Corp :CA	(408) 954-8040	
Qtronix Inc :CA	(213) 383-8088	
Quadbase Systems :CA	(408) 738-6989	
Quadram Corp :GA	(404) 564-5537	
	BBS (404) 564-5678	
Quadrant Components Inc :CA	(510) 656-9988	
Quadtel Corp :CA	(714) 754-4422	
Qualitas :MD	(800) 676-8386	(301) 907-7470
	BBS (301) 907-8030	
Quality Computer Accessories Inc :CA	(818) 964-3398	
Quality Power Products :GA	(800) 525-7502	
Quality Repair Services :CA	(510) 651-8486	
Quality Software Products :	(310) 410-0303	
Quality Systems, Inc :CA	(714) 731-7171	
Qualstar Corp :CA	(818) 882-5822	
Qualtec Data Products, Inc :CA. . .	(800) 628-4413	
Quanta :CA	(800) 682-1738	
Quantum Corp :CA	(800) 345-3377	(408) 894-4000
	BBS (408) 894-3214	
Quantum Data :IL	(708) 888-0450	
Quantum Software Systems, Inc :OA	(613) 591-0931	
Quark Inc :CO	(303) 894-8888	(303) 894-8899
Quarterdeck Office Systems :CA. . .	(310) 392-9851	
	BBS (213) 396-3904	
Quarterdeck Office Systems :CA. . .	(310) 393-9851	
	BBS (310) 341-3227	
Quatech, Inc :OH	(216) 434-3154	
Quaterdeck Office Systems :CA . . .	(310) 392-9851	
Que Corp :IN	(317) 573-2500	
Que Software/Prentice Hall Comp. :IN	(800) 992-0244	(317) 581-3833
Questronics INc :UT	(801) 262-9923	
Quick Comm :CA	(408) 956-8236	
	BBS (408) 956-1358	
Quickpath Systems Inc :CA	(510) 440-7288	
Quicksoft :WA	(800) 888-8088	
Quintar Corp :CA	(310) 320-5700	
Quintus Corporation :CA	(800) 542-1283	
Quixale America Inc :IL	(815) 399-3608	
Qumax Corp :CA	(408) 954-8040	

Company and :State	Main Phone	Tech Phone
Qume Corp :CA	(408) 942-4242	
Quotron Systems, Inc :CA	(310) 827-4600	
QVS, Inc :MI	(313) 946-1120	
R & D Business Systems Ltd :WA	(604) 872-1118	
R & K Supply Co :OH	(800) 362-6780	
R & R Electronics :GA	(800) 736-3644	(404) 368-1159
R Co :CA	(310) 441-0447	
R&K Supply :OH	(800) 362-6780	
R's Data Services :CA	(818) 700-8766	
R.J. Swantek & Associates :	(203) 953-0236	
R.R. Software :WI	(608) 251-3133	
Rabbit Software :PA	(800) 445-4357	
Racal-Datacom Inc :FL	(800) 572-2255	
RaceCom :FL	(800) 638-8088	
Racore Computer Products, Inc :CA	(800) 635-1274	(801) 596-0265
	BBS (801) 363-8720	
Radiant Communications Corp. :NJ	(201) 757-7444	
Radiometrics Midwest Corp :IL	(708) 932-7262	(708) 932-7262
Radius Inc :CA	(800) 227-2795	(408) 434-1012
Radix Group International, Inc :CA	(310) 338-2525	
RAG Electronics Inc :CA	(818) 998-6500	
Raima :WA	(206) 747-5570	(206) 562-2622
Rainbow Technologies :CA	(800) 852-8569	
Ralin Wholesaler :NY	(800) 752-9512	
RAM Mobile Data :NY	(212) 303-7800	
Ram Solutions Inc :AZ	(602) 759-5520	
Ramp Industries :NY	(607) 729-5256	
Ramtek Corp :CA	(408) 954-2700	(408) 954-2750
Ranch Technology Inc :CA	(714) 987-3966	
Rand Information Systems, Inc :CA	(415) 391-2213	
Random House Inc :MD	(301) 848-1900	(301) 857-9460
Randomex Inc :CA	(310) 595-8301	
Raosoft Inc :WA	(206) 525-4025	
Rapid Systems INc :WA	(206) 547-8311	
Rapid Technology Corp :NY	(716) 833-8533	
RARE Systems Inc :TX	(214) 991-7273	
Raster OPS :CA	(800) 729-2656	
Rational Data Systems Inc :CA	(415) 499-3354	
Rational Systems :MA	(508) 653-6194	
Ratliff Software :	(818) 546-3850	
Ray Dream :	(415) 960-0765	(415) 960-0767
Raynet Electronics :TX	(713) 578-3802	
Rayovac Corp :WI	(608) 275-4932	
Raytheon :MA	(617) 862-6600	
Raytheon :RI	(401) 847-8000	
Rayton Comm. (U.S.A) Inc :CA	(800) 472-9866	
Rayven Inc :MN	(800) 627-3776	
RC Electronics :CA	(800) 882-3475	
RCI :NJ	(908) 874-4072	
RDN & Associates :NY	(800) 647-6747	

Company and :State	Main Phone	Tech Phone
React Computer Services INc :IL	(800) 662-9199	
Reactor :IL	(312) 573-0800	
Read/Right Products Division :NJ	(201) 327-9100	
Real Applications Ltd :CA	(818) 226-6600	
Realia :IL	(312) 346-0642	
Reality Technologies :	(800) 521-2471	(215) 277-7600
RealWorld Corp :NH	(800) 678-6336	(603) 288-3432
Recognita Corp Of America :CA	(408) 749-9935	
Recognition Equipment, Inc :TX	(214) 579-6000	
Recordex Corp :CA	(619) 467-9068	
Recoton :NY	(800) 223-6009	
Recovery Management :MA	(508) 486-8866	
Recovery Plus Planning Products :IL	(800) 356-7586	
Recovery Resources Inc :FL	(407) 851-7657	
Red Wing Business Systems:MN	(800) 732-9464	
	BBS (612) 388-9605	
Redysoft Software GmbH :CA	(714) 626-4070	
Reference Software :CA	(800) 872-9933	
Reflection Systems :CA	(408) 432-0943	
Reflection Technology :MA	(617) 890-5905	
Regent Peripherals :WA	(509) 662-8848	
Relational Courseware :MA	(617) 262-4933	
Relay Communications, Inc :	(203) 798-3800	
Relialogic Corp :CA	(510) 770-3990	
Relisys :CA	(408) 945-9000	
REM :CA	(408) 655-1111	
Remote Control International :CA	(800) 992-9952	
	BBS (619) 431-4030	
Rena Informationstehnik :PA	(215) 265-8420	
RenaSonce Group Inc :CA	(619) 287-3348	
Renewable Resources Inc :CA	(800) 832-1400	
Rent-A-Computer :CA	(408) 727-7800	
Repeat-O-Type Manufacturing Corp :NJ	(800) 288-3300	
Reply Corp :CA	(800) 955-5295	
Reseller Management :NJ	(201) 292-5100	
Reset Inc :CA	(805) 584-4900	
Resource Analysis International :CA	(213) 390-7661	
Resource Spectrum :TX	(214) 484-9330	
Retix :CA	(310) 828-3400	
Revelation Technologies, Inc :NY	(206) 746-1629	
	BBS (206) 641-8110	
Revolution Software, Inc :NJ	(908) 879-7038	
Rexon Corp :CA	(805) 583-5255	
Reynolds & Reynolds Company :OH	(513) 443-2000	
RFF Electronics :CO	(303) 663-5767	
RFG Onyx :MI	(800) 946-8324	(800) 766-2711
RG Software Systems :AZ	(602) 423-8000	
RGB Spectrum :CA	(510) 848-0180	(510) 848-0180
Ribbon Tek USA :CO	(719) 578-0506	
Ribbon Tree USA Inc :WA	(800) 862-9499	

Company and :State	Main Phone	Tech Phone
Richmond Technology Inc :CA	(714) 794-2111	
Ricks RamStar, Inc :GA	(800) 327-2303	
Ricoh Corp :CA	(714) 259-1310	(714) 566-3584
Ricoh Corp :CA	(408) 432-8800	
Rimage Corp :MN	(800) 445-8288	(612) 934-5432
Rimawi Intl. Import & Export Inc :QB	(514) 337-2503	
Ring King Visibles, Inc :IA	(319) 263-8144	
Ripe C&C Technologies Inc :CA	(408) 492-9585	
Riser-Bond Instruments :NE	(800) 688-8377	
RISO, Inc :MA	(508) 777-7377	
Rite-Off Inc :NY	(800) 645-5853	
Rittenhouse :IL	(800) 323-4265	
River Data :CA	(818) 222-7191	
Rix Softworks, Inc :CA	(800) 345-9059	
	BBS (714) 476-0728	
RJ Stearns Associates :MA	(508) 263-3426	
RO Associates :ID	(208) 772-2781	
Road Scholar :	(713) 266-7623	
Robec Distributors :PA	(800) 223-7087	
Robec Distributors - Eastern :	(800) 223-7081	(800) 223-7087
Robec Distributors - Western :	(800) 433-5061	
Robert J Victor & Assoc :NJ	(201) 875-3600	
Roberts Express :OH	(800) 762-3787	
Robitron Software :GA	(404) 684-5855	
Rochelle Communications, Inc :TX	(800) 542-8808	(512) 794-0088
Rockwell International :IL	(708) 960-8000	
Rockwell International :CA	(714) 833-4700	
Roctec Electronics Ltd :CA	(408) 379-1713	(408) 379-1713
Rodax Inc :WA	(206) 885-9999	
Rodime Systems, Inc :FL	(800) 227-4144	
Rohde & Sshwartz Inc :MD	(301) 459-8800	
Roland Corp US :CA	(213) 685-5141	
Roland Digital Group :CA	(714) 975-0560	
Rose Electronics :TX	(713) 933-7673	
ROSH Intelligent Systems :MA	(800) 677-7674	
Rotating Memory Services :CA	(916) 939-7500	(916) 939-7500
Roundhill :IL	(708) 690-3737	
Royal Computer :CA	(818) 333-7628	(818) 330-2717
Royal Seating Corp :TX	(817) 697-6421	
Roykore Inc :CA	(415) 563-9175	
RPA :NJ	(800) 879-5860	
RQDQ Corp :NY	(315) 437-2631	
RT&C Systems Inc :CA	(510) 655-1993	
Rundel Products :OR	(800) 547-7061	
Rupp Technology Corporation :AZ	(602) 224-9922	(602) 224-0898
Rupp Technology Corporation :CA	(213) 850-5394	
Ryan Mc Farland :TX	(512) 343-1010	
Rybs Electronics :CO	(303) 444-6073	
	BBS (303) 443-7437	
S & W Computers & Electronics :NY	(800) 874-1235	(212) 463-8330

Company and :State	Main Phone	Tech Phone
S-MOS Systems Inc :CA	(408) 922-0200	
S1 Computers :CA	(800) 886-3210	(818) 912-0166
S3 Inc. :CA	(408) 980-5400	
Saber Software :TX	(800) 338-8754	(800) 526-8086
	BBS (214) 361-1883	
Sabina International :CA	(800) 272-2462	
SAG Electronics :MA	(800) 989-3475	(800) 899-5752
Sager Computer :CA	(800) 669-1624	
SAIC Imaging Solutions :CA	(800) 442-7242	
Salient :CA	(800) 766-7283	
Samna Corp :GA	(800) 831-9679	(404) 256-2272
Sampo Corp Of America :GA	(404) 449-6220	
Sampson MIDI Source :TX	(214) 328-2730	
Sams/New Rider-MCP :	(800) 428-5331	
Samsonite Corp :CO	(303) 373-2000	(303) 373-6666
Samsung :NJ	(201) 592-7900	
Samsung Electronics America :NJ	(800) 446-0262	(201) 691-6214
Samsung Info. Systems America :CA	(800) 446-0262	(800) 446-0262
	BBS (408) 434-5684	
Samtron :CA	(310) 802-8425	(714) 522-1282
Sankyo Seiki (America) Inc :CA	(714) 724-1505	
Santa Cruz Operations :CA	(408) 425-7222	(800) 347-4381
Santos Technology Inc :CA	(310) 320-8888	
Sanyo Business Systems Corp :NJ.	(800) 524-0048	(201) 440-9300
Sanyo Energy (USA) Corp :CA	(619) 661-6620	
Sanyo Energy Corp :CA.	(619) 661-6620	
Sapro-Impact Software :CA	(800) 369-8649	(714) 541-2202
SaRonix :CA	(415) 856-6900	
SAS Electronics Inc :CA	(108) 245-5000	
SAS Industries :OR	(800) 245-4657	
SAS Institute, Inc :NC	(919) 677-8000	(919) 677-8008
Save Rite Technologies Inc :ON	(800) 668-7972	
Savin Corp :CT.	(203) 967-5000	
Sayett Technology, Inc :NY	(800) 836-7730	(800) 533-6803
SBE, Inc :CA	(510) 680-7722	(800) 827-2245
SBT :CA	(415) 331-9900	(415) 332-9308
Scan-Optics, Inc :CT	(800) 854-8412	
Scanbase Graphics :	(908) 536-9653	
Scandinavian PC Systems, Inc :MD	(301) 294-7450	(301) 294-7453
Scandura Intelligent Systems :PA	(215) 664-1207	
Scantech Computer Systems Inc :CA	(818) 960-2999	
Sceptre Technologies Inc :CA	(714) 993-9193	
Scherrer Resources Inc :PA	(215) 836-1830	
Schlumberger Ltd :NY	(212) 350-9400	
Schlumberger Technologies :MA	(800) 225-5765	
Schnellmann America Inc :CA	(408) 441-6026	
Scholastic, Inc :MO	(314) 636-5271	
SCI Systems, Inc :AL	(205) 882-4755	
SCI/CAD Scan Inc :NM	(505) 881-4872	
Scicom Data Service :MN	(612) 933-4200	

Company and :State	Main Phone	Tech Phone
Science Appl. International Corp :CA	(800) 442-7242	(619) 766-7242
Science Lab SW :MA	(617) 769-5153	
Scientific Endeavors :TN	(615) 376-4146	
Scientific Logics :CA	(408) 446-3575	
Scientific Micro Systems :CA	(408) 954-1633	
Scientific Software Inc :CO	(303) 292-1111	
Scitor Corp :CA	(415) 570-7700	
Scopus Technology Inc :CA	(510) 428-0500	
Script Systems, Inc :NJ	(201) 343-8500	(800) 724-8400
Scriptel Corp :OH	(614) 276-8402	
SCS/Compute, Inc :MO	(314) 966-1040	
SD Enterprises :	(805) 566-1317	
SDA Corporation :IL	(800) 833-5020	
SDB Systems :FL	(813) 481-0224	
Seagate Technologies :CA	(408) 438-6550	(408) 438-8222
FAX Back (408) 438-2620	BBS (408) 438-8771	
Seagull Scientific Systems :WA	(800) 758-2001	
Sears Business Systems :	(800) 777-0375	
Sears Industrial Sales :OH	(800) 776-8666	
Seco Industries :CA	(213) 726-9721	
Sector Computer Services Inc :OH	(216) 524-5858	
Secura Technologies :CA	(714) 248-1544	
Secure Telecom Inc :CA	(408) 992-0572	
Secured Communication Int'l Inc :ON	(416) 888-1580	
Security Microsystems Inc :NY	(800) 345-7390	
SEEQ Technology, Inc :CA	(408) 432-7400	
SEI (National FSI Inc) :TX	(214) 689-3200	
Seiko Instruments USA :CA	(408) 922-5900	(408) 922-1917
Seikosha America Inc :NJ	(201) 327-7227	(201) 327-7227
Sejin America :CA	(408) 752-8447	
Selecterm, Inc :MA	(800) 877-7586	(800) 767-7586
Selective Software :CA	(408) 423-3556	(800) 423-3556
Selectronics & Microlytics :NY	(716) 248-9150	
Selfware :	(703) 352-2977	
Semiconductor Industry Update :	(408) 429-5850	
SemiTech International :MA	(617) 628-8880	
Semware :GA	(404) 641-9002	
	BBS (404) 641-8968	
Sencore Inc :SD	(800) 736-2673	
Seneca Data Distributorrs :NY	(800) 227-3432	
Sensible Software :MI	(313) 528-1950	
Sensible Solutions Inc :MA	(508) 830-0130	
Senstron Electronic Co :NJ	(908) 561-8585	(908) 561-8585
Sentinel Computer Services :IL	(708) 990-8060	
Sequel Inc :CA	(408) 987-1401	
Sequent Computer Systems :OR	(503) 626-5700	
Sequitter :	(403) 439-8171	
Sequoia Data Corp :CA	(415) 696-8750	
Sequoia Publishing, Inc :CO	(303) 972-4167	
Sercomp Corp :CA	(800) 428-2635	(800) 428-2635

Company and :State	Main Phone	Tech Phone
Serif Inc :NH	(800) 697-3743	
Serigraph Inc :WI	(414) 335-7200	
Serius :	(800) 876-6847	
Servatek :MD	(410) 760-7337	
Server Technology :CA	(408) 988-0142	
Service 2000 :MN	(800) 466-2000	
Service InfoSystems Inc :NY	(716) 334-9126	
Service Management Corp :NH	(603) 882-7783	
Service Management Group :MD	(410) 992-9975	
Service Partner Inc :NJ	(201) 770-4949	
Service System International :KS	(913) 661-0190	
Serviceland Of Upstate NY, Inc :NY	(716) 427-0880	
ServiceScope Corp :CT	(203) 265-2624	
ServiceWare :NY	(716) 842-1611	
Servicing Systems-Profile Tech :NH	(800) 659-9649	
Servitech Inc :IL	(708) 620-8750	
Servonics Corporation :MA	(508) 295-6372	
Set Laboratories :OR	(503) 289-4574	
Setpoint, Inc :TX	(713) 584-1000	
Shafer's Full Service Systems :CA	(619) 440-5421	(619) 440-5421
Shaffstall Corp :IN	(800) 248-3475	(317) 842-2077
Shana Corp :AB	(403) 463-3330	
Shape Electronics Inc :IL	(800) 367-5811	
Shape Electronics Inc :IL	(800) 367-5811	
Shapeware :WA	(800) 446-3335	(206) 467-6740
Shared Medical Systems :PA	(215) 296-6300	
Shareware Testing Laboratories :IN	(317) 322-2000	
Sharp Electronics Corp :NJ	(800) 447-4700	
Sharpe Systems Corp :CA	(909) 596-0070	
Shattuck Industries :CA	(408) 336-5145	
Sheilds Business Machines Inc :NJ	(800) 759-6161	
Shereff Systems, Inc :OR	(503) 626-2022	(503) 626-2022
Sherlock Software	(608) 257-0802	
Sherwood Kimtron :CA	(800) 777-8755	
Shining Technology :CA	(310) 802-3081	
Shiva :	(617) 252-6300	(617) 252-6400
	BBS (617) 621-0190	
Shreve Systems :LA	(800) 227-3971	
Shuttle Computer International :CA	(510) 623-8876	(510) 623-8876
SI Dynamics Inc :CA	(619) 322-2761	
Sicon International Inc :CA	(408) 432-8585	(408) 432-8585
Sidco Software International :NY	(212) 627-4475	
Sidon Data Systems :CA	(714) 553-1131	
Sidus :ON	(416) 882-1600	
Siecor Corporation :NC	(800) 633-7432	
Siemens Communications Test Equp :NC	(704) 327-5051	
Siemens Information Systems:FL	(818) 706-8872	
Siemens Nixdorf Infor. Systems :MA	(617) 273-0480	(617) 273-0480
Siemon Company :CT	(203) 274-2523	
Sierra Computers :NV	(702) 322-6455	

Company and :State	Main Phone	Tech Phone
Sierra On-Line :CA	(800) 326-6654	
....	BBS (209) 683-4463	
Sigen :CA	(408) 737-3904	
Sigma Designs :CA	(510) 770-0100	
....	BBS (510) 770-0111	
Sigma International Inc :VA	(800) 658-8893	
Sigmatronics, Inc :MN	(800) 852-6322	
Sigsmall/PC :	(212) 869-7440	
SIIG, Inc :CA	(510) 657-8688	(510) 657-8688
Silcom Manufacturing Technology :ON	(416) 238-8822	
Silicom :NJ	(201) 529-1100	
Silicon Beach Software :CA	(619) 695-6956	
SILICON GRAPHICS :CA	(415) 960-1980	
Silicon Graphics, Inc :CA	(800) 676-6272	(800) 676-6272
Silicon Integrated Systems :CA	(408) 735-1362	
Silicon Star International Inc :CA	(510) 623-0500	
Silicon Systems, Inc :CA	(714) 573-6000	(714) 731-7110
Silvar-Lisco :CA	(408) 991-6000	
Silver Reed (U.S.A) Inc :CA	(800) 733-7333	(800) 733-7333
Silverware :TX	(214) 247-0131	
....	BBS (214) 247-2177	
Sim-Trade Co :CA	(800) 435-7482	(800) 435-7482
Simon & Schuster Software :NY	(800) 624-0023	(212) 373-8500
Simon & Schuster Software :NY	(800) 922-0579	
Simple Software :NY	(914) 297-5858	(914) 297-5868
Simplex Tim Recorder Co :MA	(508) 632-2500	
Singapore Trade Develpmnt Board :CA	(213) 617-7358	(213) 617-7358
Sir-Tech Software :	(315) 393-6633	
SitBack Technologies, Inc :KS	(913) 894-0808	
Sixgraph Computing Ltd :PQ	(514) 332-1331	
Skill Dynamics :GA	(404) 835-1969	
SkiSoft Publishing :	(617) 863-1876	
SkyTel :DC	(800) 759-3375	(800) 759-3375
SL Waber Inc :NJ	(800) 634-1485	(800) 257-8384
Slinger Sierra :CA	(209) 295-5595	
SLR Systems :PA	(412) 282-0864	
....	BBS (412) 282-2799	
Small Computer Company, The :NY	(914) 769-3160	
Small Computers In Library :	(203) 226-6967	
Smart Modular Technologies :CA	(510) 623-1231	
Smart Technologies Inc :AB	(403) 233-9333	
SmartMicro Technologies :CA	(800) 766-2467	(805) 495-1385
SMC :NY	(800) 762-4968	
SMH Electronics :MA	(508) 291-7447	
Smith Design :PA	(215) 661-9107	
Smith Micro Software Inc :CA	(714) 362-5800	
SMK Electronics Corp USA :CA	(714) 996-0960	
SNA Communications Report :VA	(703) 760-0660	
Snow Software :FL	(813) 784-8899	
Social Software Inc :NY	(212) 956-2707	

Company and :State	Main Phone	Tech Phone
SofNet :	(404) 984-8088	
	BBS (404) 984-9926	
Sofpak Inc :OT	(613) 591-1555	
Sofsolutions :TX	(512) 735-0746	
Soft Cable :CA	(310) 828-2577	
Soft Warehouse, Inc :HI	(808) 734-5801	
Soft-Age Publishing :CA	(805) 945-0051	(805) 945-0051
Soft-Com Inc :NY	(212) 242-9595	
Soft-Hard Systems :CA	(818) 999-9531	
Soft-Letter :MA	(617) 924-3944	
Softa Group Inc, The :IL	(708) 291-4000	(800) 874-0045
Softbridge, Inc :MA.	(617) 576-2257	(617) 576-2257
SoftCraft, Inc :WI	(800) 351-0500	(608) 257-3300
SofTest Designs Corporation :TX	(210) 697-8828	
Softfocus :OT	(416) 825-0903	
Softhead :	(414) 498-5909	
SoftKat :CA.	(800) 641-1057	(818) 700-8061
Softkey Software Productions:FL	(407) 367-0005	
Softklone :FL	(904) 878-8564	
	BBS (904) 878-9884	
SoftLogic Solutions, Inc :NH	(603) 627-9900	(603) 644-5555
	BBS (603) 644-5556	
Softsoulutions :UT	(801) 226-6000	
Softsystems :	(714) 860-2070	
Software Academy, Inc :CA	(619) 464-2500	
Software Add-Ons :PA	(800) 822-8088	
Software AG Systems, Inc :VA	(703) 860-5050	
Software Alliance :CA	(800) 443-5152	
Software Artistry :IN.	(317) 876-3042	
Software City, Inc :NJ	(800) 222-0918	
Software Creations, Inc :FL	(800) 767-3279	(800) 767-3279
Software Developer's Company :MA	(800) 421-8006	
Software Development Factory :MD	(301) 666-8129	
Software Digest :PA.	(215) 878-9300	
Software Directions, Inc :NJ	(201) 584-8466	(201) 584-3882
Software Etc. :	(612) 893-7821	
Software Factory :TX	(214) 490-0835	
Software Grove :WA	(206) 823-0833	
Software Interphase :RI	(401) 397-2340	
Software Link :GA	(404) 448-5465	(404) 263-8676
Software Machine, The :UT	(801) 561-9393	
Software Magazine :MA.	(508) 366-2031	
Software Matters Inc :IN	(800) 253-5274	(317) 253-8088
Software Of The Future, Inc :TX	(800) 766-7355	(214) 264-2626
Software Partners :CA	(415) 857-1110	
Software Plumbers Inc :MD	(301) 963-8423	(301) 963-8423
Software Plus :MD	(301) 261-0264	
Software Products Internationa :CA	(800) 937-4774	
	BBS (619) 450-2179	
Software Products International :	(800) 937-4774	

Company and :State	Main Phone	Tech Phone
Software Publishers Assoc. :DC...	(800) 388-7478	
Software Publishing Corp:CA	(408) 986-8000	(408) 988-4005
Software Resource :CA	(415) 883-0600	
Software Security Inc :CT	(203) 329-8870	
....	BBS (203) 329-7263	
Software Shop Systems :NJ	(908) 938-3200	(800) 654-8923
Software Solutions, Inc :GA	(404) 418-2000	(404) 418-2000
Software Support :FL	(800) 873-4357	
Software Support Professionals :CA	(619) 674-4864	
Software Toolworks, The :CA.....	(415) 883-3000	
Software Ventures :CA	(510) 644-3232	(510) 644-1325
....	BBS (510) 849-1912	
Sola Electric :IL..............	(800) 289-7652	
Solartech :NJ................	(800) 367-1132	
Solder Absorbing Technology :MA.	(413) 788-6191	
Solea Systems Inc :CA.........	(714) 768-7736	
Solectek Corp :CA	(619) 450-1220	
Solectron Corp :CA	(408) 942-1943	
Solidex :CA	(714) 599-2666	
Solidstate Controls, Inc :OH	(800) 635-7300	(800) 222-9079
Solomat Instrumentation :CT	(203) 849-3111	
Soltec :CA	(800) 423-2344	
Solution Development Assn :PA..	(215) 362-2611	
Solutions Incorporated :	(802) 865-9220	(802) 658-5506
Solutions Systems :MA.........	(800) 821-2492	(800) 999-9663
....	BBS (617) 237-8530	
Solutronix Corp :MN	(800) 875-2580	
Sonera Technologies :NJ	(800) 932-6323	
SonicAir Couriers :AZ	(800) 528-6052	
Sony Corp Of America :NJ	(800) 222-7669	
Soricon Corp :CO	(303) 440-2800	
SOS Computer :NH	(800) 767-2554	
Sound Electro Flight :CA	(800) 777-3475	(805) 527-0046
Sound Ideas :ON	(416) 886-5000	
Sound Minds Technology Inc :CA .	(408) 374-7070	
Sound Source Unlimited :CA	(805) 494-9996	
Soundware Corp :CA	(800) 333-4554	
Source & Solution :FL.........	(813) 962-8911	
Source Graphics :CA	(800) 553-5285	
Source Services Corp :TX	(214) 717-5005	
SourceMate Information Systems :CA	(800) 877-8896	(415) 381-1793
South East Computer Brokers :FL .	(305) 792-3780	
South Hills Datacom VAR Program :PA	(800) 624-1770	
Southdale :OT...............	(416) 455-9533	
Southern New England Telephone :CT	(203) 771-5204	
Southern Technical :KY	(502) 585-5635	
Southwest Data Products, Inc : ...	(713) 461-0100	
Soyo USA Inc :CA............	(818) 330-1712	(818) 330-1712
SPA News :.................	(202) 452-1600	
Spacepage Inc :CT............	(800) 332-7243	

Company and :State	Main Phone	Tech Phone
Spain, Industrial Development :CA	(310) 203-5411	
Spartan Electronics :NY	(516) 499-9500	
Spea/Video Seven :CA	(510) 683-6201	
Spear Technology Inc :IL	(800) 852-4202	
Specialix :CA	(800) 423-5364	(800) 423-5364
Specialix Inc :CA	(408) 378-7919	
Specialized Business Solutions :CA	(800) 359-3458	
Specialized Products Co :TX	(800) 527-5018	
Specom Technologies Corp :CA	(408) 736-7832	
Spectra Logic :CO	(303) 449-7759	
SpectraFAX :FL	(800) 833-1329	
Spectragraphics :CA	(619) 450-0611	
Spectrum Computer Corp :CA	(800) 959-1030	
Spectrum Holobyte :	(510) 522-1164	
Spectrum Information Tech. :NY	(516) 627-8992	
Speedbird Data Systems Inc :CO	(303) 440-9983	
Spencer Industries :IN	(812) 937-4561	
Spencer Industries Inc :IN	(812) 937-4561	
Spindrift Laboratories :	(708) 255-6909	
Spinnaker Software :MA	(800) 323-8088	
Sprague Magnetics :CA	(818) 994-6602	
Spring Circle Computer, Inc :CA	(310) 944-2287	(213) 698-5961
Sprite, Inc :CA	(408) 773-8888	
SPSS, Inc :IL	(800) 543-2185	
Square D/Topaz :CA	(619) 279-0111	
SRW Computer Components :CA	(714) 963-5500	
Stac Electronics :CA	(619) 431-7474	(800) 522-5335
	BBS (619) 431-5956	
Staco Energy Products :OH	(513) 253-1191	
Stallion Technologies, Inc :CA	(408) 395-5775	
Standard Computer Corp :CA	(800) 662-6111	
Standard Microsystems :NY	(516) 273-3100	(800) 992-4762
Standard Rate & Data Service :IL	(708) 256-6067	
Stanley-Vidmar :PA	(215) 797-6600	
Star Gate Technologies Inc. :OH	(216) 349-1860	
Star Micronics America :NY	(212) 986-6770	(714) 768-3192
Star Path System :MI	(517) 332-1137	(517) 332-1256
Star Software Systems :CA	(310) 533-1190	(800) 443-5737
Star-Tek Inc :MA	(508) 393-9393	
StarGate Computers :OH	(800) 945-0202	
Startech Computer Accessories :ON	(519) 438-8529	
Starware Publishing Corp :FL	(800) 354-5353	
Stat-Tech International Corp :CO	(719) 543-5005	
State Of Texas :TX	(512) 320-9625	
State Street Discount :NH	(800) 212-1519	(800) 242-1519
Static Control Components Inc :NC	(800) 356-2728	
Statpower Technologies Corp. :BC	(604) 420-1585	
StatSoft :OK	(918) 583-4149	
Statx Brands Co. :IL	(708) 520-0007	
STB Systems Inc. :TX	(214) 234-8750	

Company and :State	Main Phone	Tech Phone
....	BBS (214) 437-9615	
Stellar Computer, Inc :MA	(508) 369-7666	
Sterling Castle Software :........	(800) 323-6406	
Stevenson Software (RoseSoft) :WA	(206) 562-0225	
STI-Certified Products :CA	(800) 274-3475	
Stingray Computer International :TN	(615) 355-0242	
Stockholder Systems, Inc :GA	(404) 441-3387	
Stone & Associates :CA	(619) 459-9173	
Stonehouse & Company :TX	(214) 960-1566	
Storage Concepts, Inc :CA	(800) 525-9217	
Storage Devices Inc. :CA	(714) 562-5500	
Storage Dimensions :CA	(408) 354-0710	(408) 954-0710
....	BBS (408) 944-1220	
Storage Technology Corp :CO	(303) 673-5151	
Storage Tek :CO	(303) 673-6761	
Storage USA :PA	(800) 538-3475	
Storm Technology :............	(800) 275-5734	
StrandWare, Inc. :WI.	(715) 833-2331	
Strata :......................	(800) 869-6855	(801) 628-9751
Strategic Mapping Inc :CA	(408) 985-7400	
Strategic Simulations :CA	(408) 737-6800	(408) 737-6850
Strategic Solutions :CT	(203) 221-1334	
Stratus Computer, Inc :MA	(508) 460-2000	
Strawberry Tree :CA	(408) 736-8800	
Stride Software, Inc :CA	(213) 433-6977	
Strohl Systems :PA	(800) 634-2016	
Structural Dynamics Research :OH	(513) 576-2400	
Structured Software Solutions :TX .	(214) 985-9901	
STSC :MD	(301) 984-5000	(301) 984-5489
Studebaker-Worthington Leasing :NY	(800) 645-7242	
Sub Systems :................	(617) 438-8901	
SubLOGIC :IL	(217) 359-8482	(800) 637-4983
Success Trainers Inc :GA.......	(800) 229-4708	
Summagraphics :CT............	(822) 729-7866	(203) 881-5318
Summit Memory Systems :CA	(408) 438-2660	(800) 523-4767
Summit Micro Design :CA.	(408) 739-6348	(408) 739-6348
Summus Corp :TX	(713) 492-6611	
Sun Country Software :NM......	(505) 873-2220	
....	BBS (505) 877-8354	
Sun Microsystems Inc :CA	(415) 960-1300	(800) 872-4876
Sun Moon Star :CA.............	(408) 452-7811	(408) 452-7811
Sun Remarketing :UT	(800) 821-3221	(800) 992-7631
Sun River Corp :TX.............	(512) 835-8001	
Suncom Technologies :IL........	(708) 647-4040	(708) 647-4040
SunData Inc :GA	(404) 449-6116	
Sundog Software :NY	(718) 855-9141	
Sunflex L.P. :CA..............	(408) 522-8850	
Sungard Data Systems, Inc :PA ...	(215) 341-8700	
Sunhill Distributing :WA	(800) 544-1361	
Sunny Hill Software :WA.	(800) 367-0651	(206) 857-2666

Company and :State	Main Phone	Tech Phone
Sunnyvale Memories, Inc :CA	(800) 262-3475	(800) 262-3475
SunRace Technology Corp. :CA	(714) 468-2955	(800) 872-4786
Sunrise Computer Supplies :FL	(813) 877-7866	
Sunrise Imaging :CA	(510) 657-6250	
Sunshine Video & Computers :FL	(800) 828-2992	(407) 368-2992
Sunwell International Corp :CA	(408) 436-9797	(408) 436-1107
Super Computer Inc :CA	(213) 532-2133	
Super PC Market :FL	(800) 426-6669	
Supercom :CA	(408) 456-8888	
Supercomputer Systems, Inc :WI	(715) 839-8484	
Superior Electric :CT	(203) 582-9561	
Superior IS :TX	(713) 662-8500	(713) 662-8500
SuperMac Technology :CA	(408) 245-2202	(408) 245-0646
Superpower Supply Inc. :CA	(310) 903-4528	
Supersell Software :GA	(404) 889-7807	
Supersoft :CA	(408) 745-0234	(408) 745-0234
SuperTime Inc. :ON	(416) 499-3288	
Support Systems :CA	(800) 777-6269	(209) 734-9090
Support Systems International :CA	(800) 777-6269	
Supra Corp :OR	(800) 727-8772	(503) 967-2440
	BBS (503) 967-2444	
Survivor Software :CA	(213) 410-9527	
Sutrasoft :TX	(713) 491-2088	
Sutton Designs :NY	(800) 326-8119	
SW Training Services :NJ	(609) 751-5481	
Swedish Trade Council :IL	(312) 781-6222	
Swifte International :DE	(800) 237-9383	(302) 234-1750
Switchcraft Inc :IL	(312) 792-2700	
Sybex, Inc. :CA	(800) 227-2346	
SyDOS :	(407) 998-5400	(800) 536-7936
Symantec Corp (Tech Support):CA.	(503) 345-3322	
FAX Back (800) 554-4403	BBS (503) 484-6699 (2400baud)	
Symantec Corp (Corporate):CA	(408) 253-9600	
Symbol Technologies, Inc :NY	(516) 563-2400	
Symbolics Inc :MA	(617) 221-1000	
SymbologicCorp :WA	(800) 448-9292	(800) 448-9292
Symmetry Software :AZ	(800) 624-2485	(800) 624-2485
Symphony Laboratories :CA	(408) 986-1701	
SymSoft :NV	(702) 832-4300	
Symtech :CA	(619) 569-6800	
Synchronics :TN	(901) 761-1166	
Syncom Technologies Inc. :SD	(605) 996-8200	
Syncomp International Corp :CA	(213) 690-1011	(213) 694-0555
Synergetics International, Inc :CO	(303) 678-5200	
Synergy Computer Services Inc :ON	(416) 273-9565	
Synergy Software :	(215) 779-0522	
Synergy Software :PA	(215) 779-0522	
Synergystex International Inc. :OH	(216) 225-3112	
SynOptics Communications :CA	(800) 776-8023	(800) 473-4911
Syntrex, Inc :NJ	(908) 542-1500	

Company and :State	Main Phone	Tech Phone
Syquest Technology :CA	(510) 226-4000	(510) 226-4000
	BBS (510) 656-0470	
Sys Technology, Inc :CA	(213) 493-6888	
Sys-Com :CA	(800) 343-0100	
Sysgen, Inc :CA	(800) 821-2151	(408) 263-1171
	BBS (408) 946-5032	
Sysgration USA Inc :CA	(415) 306-7860	(415) 348-5663
SysKonnect :CA	(408) 725-4667	
Sysnet Computer Systems Inc :ON	(800) 627-8964	
Systat, Inc :IL	(708) 864-5670	
	BBS (708) 492-3570	
Systech Corp :CA	(619) 453-8970	
System Connection :UT	(800) 877-1985	
System Dynamic Group :CA	(800) 373-6467	
System General Corp :CA	(408) 263-6667	(408) 236-6667
System Industries :CA	(800) 333-2220	
System Integrators, Inc :CA	(916) 929-9481	
System Security Technology :NV	(702) 454-7009	
Systematics, Inc :AR	(501) 220-5100	(501) 220-5653
Systems & Computer Technology :PA	(215) 647-5930	
Systems And Software :CA	(714) 833-1700	(714) 833-1700
Systems Compatability Corp :IL	(800) 333-1395	
	BBS (312) 670-4239	
Systems Enhancement Corp :MO	(314) 532-2855	
Systems Integration :MA	(617) 964-3030	
Systems Integration Associates :IL	(312) 440-1275	(312) 440-1275
Systems Plus,Inc. :CA	(415) 969-7047	
Systems Software Assoc. Inc :IL	(312) 641-2900	
Systems Strategies Inc. :NY	(212) 279-8400	
Sytron Corp :MA	(508) 898-0100	
T & T Computer Inc :CA	(714) 594-1420	
T & W Computer Service :MO	(314) 272-200	
T/Maker Company :CA	(415) 962-0195	
Tab Books/McGraw-Hill :PA	(800) 233-1128	
Tactic Software :	(305) 665-4665	
Tadiran Electronic Industries :NY	(516) 621-4980	
Tae II Media :CA	(510) 657-1244	
Tagram Systems :CA	(800) 824-7267	
Tall Tree Systems :CA	(415) 493-1980	
Tally Systems :NH	(800) 262-3877	
Tally Systems Corp. :NH	(800) 262-3877	
Talon Instruments :CA	(909) 599-0690	
Tamrac, Inc. :CA	(818) 407-9500	
Tandberg Data Inc. :CA	(805) 495-8384	
Tandem Computers, Inc :TX	(800) 255-5010	
Tandon Computer Corp :CA	(805) 523-0340	(800) 487-8324
Tandy Corp :TX	(817) 390-3011	
Tangent Computer, Inc :CA	(415) 342-9388	(415) 342-9388
Tapette Corp. :CA	(714) 638-7960	
Tardis Technology Inc. :CA	(310) 490-3150	

Company and :State	Main Phone	Tech Phone
Target Micro Inc. :IL	(800) 883-8830	
Target Systems Corp :MA	(800) 233-3493	
Targus :CA	(714) 523-5429	
Tasco Inc :CO	(800) 999-9952	
Tatung Company Of America:CA	(800) 829-2850	(800) 827-2850
Tatung Science & Technology :CA	(408) 435-0140	
Tau-Tron :MA	(800) 828-8766	
Tauber Electronics Inc :CA	(619) 274-7242	
Taxan America, Inc. :CA	(408) 748-0900	
Taxan USA Corp :CA	(408) 946-3400	
Taylored Graphics :	(408) 761-2481	
TC Computer :LA	(800) 723-8282	(800) 723-6380
TCE Co :IL	(800) 383-8001	
TCS Distributors :CA	(800) 488-0589	
TDK Electronics Corp :NY	(516) 625-0100	
TDX Peripherals, Inc :NY	(800) 842-0708	(800) 842-0708
Teac America, Inc. :CA	(213) 726-0303	
Teachware, Inc :PA	(814) 696-2530	
Team Systems Inc :CA	(800) 338-1981	
TEC Computer Systems :	(617) 964-3890	
Tech 101 Office Automation:CA	(714) 261-5141	
Tech Assist Inc :FL	(800) 274-3785	
Tech Data Corp :FL	(800) 237-8931	
Tech Data Corp. :FL	(813) 539-7429	
Tech Spray Inc :TX	(806) 372-8523	
Tech Tronic Fabrications Inc. :MO	(417) 745-2195	
Tech-Cessories Inc :FL	(800) 637-0909	
Tech-Sa-Port :PA	(800) 543-2233	
Techanalysis Corp :MN	(612) 925-5900	
Techmart Inc :GA	(404) 772-9811	
Techni-Tool :PA	(215) 941-2400	
Techni-Tool Inc :PA	(215) 825-4990	
Technical & Logistical Consult. :MA	(508) 478-8211	
Technical Computer Support :CA	(619) 792-8216	
Technical Parts Inc :CA	(619) 552-2288	
Technicom Computer Service :CA	(800) 621-8229	
Techniserv :TX	(512) 289-9060	
Techno Inc :IL	(312) 567-9200	
Technologic Systems :OH	(513) 644-2230	
Technology Concepts, Inc. :	(800) 477-3473	(503) 692-9601
Technology Congress, Ltd, The :MN	(612) 420-9800	(612) 420-9800
Technology Enhancement Group :AZ	(602) 464-4494	
Technology Integrated Products :CA	(408) 980-5191	
Technology Marketing, Inc :CA	(714) 863-1100	
Technology Works :	(800) 688-7466	
Technoserv Inc :MN	(800) 553-1984	
TechPlus Electronics Corp :CA	(800) 776-8160	
TechSoft Systems :	(800) 825-8386	
Tecmar :OH	(800) 624-8560	
	BBS (216) 349-0853	

Company and :State	Main Phone	Tech Phone
Tecnet Canada Inc :BC	(604) 388-6677	
Tecnocorp, Inc :FL	(305) 477-5862	
TECsupport :FL	(813) 540-2775	
Ted Dasher & Associates :AL	(800) 638-4833	
Tekcom-Prentice Corp :CA	(408) 435-9515	
Tekelec :CA	(818) 880-5656	
Teklogix :NY	(800) 633-3040	
Teklogix Inc :IN	(317) 849-1390	
Teknosys :FL	(800) 873-3494	
Teknowledge, Inc :CA	(415) 424-0500	
Tekra Corp :WI	(800) 448-3572	
Tekserv :MA	(508) 459-9480	
Teksyn, Inc :IN	(317) 875-9750	(317) 875-9750
Tektronix :OR	(800) 835-6100	
Tektronix, Inc. :OR	(503) 682-3411	
Tekworks Inc :NJ	(201) 540-1096	
TEL Electronics Inc :UT	(800) 824-7451	(800) 824-7451
TEL Electronics Inc :UT	(801) 756-9606	
Tel-Tex Computer Products :TX	(713) 868-6000	
Telcor, Inc. :NJ	(908) 852-7000	
Tele-Art Instruments :NY	(516) 594-0952	
Telebit :CA	(800) 835-3248	
	BBS (408) 745-3803	
Telebyte Technology :NY	(516) 423-3232	
Telecommunications Techniques :MD	(301) 353-1550	
Telecomputer, Inc :CA	(800) 637-9695	
Teleconnect :	(319) 366-6600	
TeleDynamics Corp :TX	(800) 847-5629	
Teledyne, Inc :CA	(213) 277-3311	
Teleglobe Communications Inc :MA	(508) 681-0600	
Telegnostics Corporation :CA	(805) 544-8588	
Telemart :AZ	(800) 537-4735	
Telematics International, Inc :FL	(305) 772-3070	
Telenex Corp :NJ	(609) 234-7900	
Telenex Corp :VA	(800) 368-3261	
Telesystems SLW Inc :ON	(416) 441-9966	
Teletutor :NH	(800) 542-2242	
Televideo Systems, Inc :CA	(408) 954-8333	
Teleware Inc :NJ	(800) 322-6962	(201) 586-2269
Telex Communications Inc :MN	(612) 774-4051	
Telindus Inc :NY	(212) 682-2595	
Telix :NC	(919) 460-4556	
	BBS (919) 481-9399	
Telos Corp :CA	(213) 450-2424	
Teltron Inc :PA	(215) 582-2711	
Telxon Corp :OH	(216) 867-3700	
Tempest Technologies, Inc :VA	(703) 471-0157	
Temptronic Corp :MA	(617) 969-2501	
Ten Times Sales :AZ	(602) 438-0889	(602) 438-0889
Tenera, L.P. :CA	(510) 845-5200	

Company and :State	Main Phone	Tech Phone
Teradata Corp :	(213) 827-7777	
Teradyne, Inc :MA	(617) 482-2700	
TeraTech :MD	(800) 447-9120	
Terminal Data Corp :CA	(805) 529-1500	
Test Engineering Services :CA	(800) 842-0333	
Test Probes Inc :CA	(800) 368-5719	
Texas Instruments :TX	(800) 232-3200	
	BBS (512) 250-6112	
Texas Instruments :TX	(800) 477-8924	
Texas Instruments Inc :TX	(800) 527-3500	
Texas Micro :TX	(713) 933-8050	
Texas Microwystems, Inc :TX	(713) 933-8050	
Texel :CA	(408) 980-1838	
Textronix, Inc :OR	(503) 627-7111	
TextWare Corp :UT	(801) 645-9600	(801) 645-9600
Texwipe Company :NJ	(800) 284-5577	
Thaumaturge Resource Corp :IN	(317) 870-5666	
The AG Group :CA	(510) 937-7900	
The Austrian Trade Commission :CA	(310) 477-9988	
The Boeing Company :WA	(206) 655-3897	
The Boston Computer Society :MA	(617) 232-0600	
The Brimble Group Of Companies :TX	(512) 478-6678	
The Chair Works :TX	(409) 693-7000	
The Complete PC :	(408) 434-9600	
The Computer Factory Inc :NY	(914) 347-5000	
The Continuum Company :TX	(512) 345-5700	
The Foxboro Company :MA	(508) 543-8750	
The Interface Group :MA	(617) 449-6600	
The JLR Group Inc :MA	(617) 254-9109	
The Learning Company :CA	(800) 852-2255	
The Maxximum Co :ID	(800) 766-6299	
The Old Publication :	(614) 771-0006	
The One-Off CD Shop Inc :AB.	(800) 387-1633	
The Programmer's Shop :MA	(800) 421-8006	
The Protector Corp :CO	(303) 939-8100	
The Stolas Group :CA	(800) 521-7666	
The Stone Group :CA	(408) 982-9999	
The Technology Congress, Ltd :MN	(612) 420-9800	
The Ultimate Corp :	(201) 877-9222	
The Vidicode US, Inc. :NC	(919) 452-5600	
The Voyager Company :CA.	(310) 451-1383	
THEOS Software Corp :CA	(510) 935-1118	(510) 935-1118
Thermodyne International Ltd :CA.	(310) 603-1976	
Thinx Software Inc :MD	(301) 604-2588	
Third Party Industries :CA	(510) 713-0392	
Thirdware Computer Products :FL	(800) 446-5987	(800) 446-5987
Thomas & Betts Electronics :SC	(803) 676-2900	
Thomas-Conrad Corp :TX	(800) 332-8683	(800) 334-4112
	BBS (512) 836-8012	
Thompson & Thompson :CA	(714) 855-3838	

Company and :State	Main Phone	Tech Phone
Thomson Consumer Electronics :NJ	(609) 853-2525	
Thought I Could :NY	(212) 673-9724	
Three Com Corp :CA	(800) 876-3266	
Thunderware, Inc :CA	(510) 254-6581	
TI Computing :	(817) 883-9201	
TIE/Communications, Inc :CT	(203) 888-8000	
TIEX :TX	(214) 392-0647	
Tiger Software :FL	(800) 888-4437	
Tigon Corporation :TX	(800) 962-2330	
Timberline Software :OR	(503) 626-6775	
Time Arts Inc :CA	(707) 576-7722	
Time Design Software :CO	(303) 693-3425	
Time Motion Tools :CA	(619) 679-0303	
Timekeeping Systems :OH	(216) 361-9995	
Timeplex, Inc :NJ	(201) 391-1111	
Timeslips Corp :MA	(800) 285-0999	(508) 768-7490
TimeValue Software :CA	(714) 727-1800	
Timeworks Inc :IL	(708) 559-1300	(708) 559-1331
Titan Corp :CA	(619) 453-9592	
TKC :FL	(813) 544-2594	
TLCSE Inc :CA	(408) 986-8300	
TMC Research Corp :CA	(408) 262-0888	
TMS Computer Maintenance :TX	(210) 492-8827	
TMS Inc :CA	(415) 903-2252	
Todd SCI :CA	(818) 331-7377	
Togai InfraLogic, Inc :CA	(714) 975-8522	
Token Perspectives, The :MN	(612) 935-2035	
Tokyo Electric Co Ltd :CA	(510) 651-5333	
Tokyo Electric Co., Ltd. :MA	(617) 235-4422	
Tool Kit Specialists Inc :CA	(800) 722-1123	
Tool Makers :	(408) 458-0690	
Tool Technology Publishing :CA	(415) 459-3700	
Tools & Techniques :TX	(800) 444-1945	
Top Data :CA	(800) 888-3318	(408) 734-9343
Top Microsystems :CA	(408) 980-9813	
Top-Link Computers Inc :CA	(408) 263-2200	
Topline Technology Inc :CA	(714) 524-6900	
TOPS Computer Company :MA	(508) 887-5915	
Toshiba America Consumer Prod. :IL	(708) 541-9400	(800) 999-4273
Toshiba America Electronic Comp. :CA	(800) 999-4273	(800) 456-8649
	BBS (714) 837-2116	
Toshiba America, Inc. :CA	(800) 457-7777	(714) 455-0407
Tosoh USA, Inc :CA	(415) 588-5200	
Total Assets Protect, Inc :	(817) 640-8800	
Total Computer Concepts, Inc :WA	(206) 867-9050	
Total Concept Sales :CA	(800) 488-0589	
Total Maintenance Concepts :IL	(708) 834-7351	
Total Multimedia :CA.	(805) 371-0500	
Total Peripheral Repair :CA	(619) 552-2288	
Total Peripherals Inc :MA	(508) 480-8327	

Company and :State	Main Phone	Tech Phone
Total Power International :MA	(508) 453-1503	
Total Software Inc :MB.	(204) 947-5699	
Total Systems House, Inc :CA	(805) 582-3240	
Total Systems Serv's. Inc :GA	(404) 649-2387	
Total Technologies, Ltd :CA	(714) 241-0406	
Touch Technology :TX.	(512) 328-9284	
TouchStone Software Corp :CA	(800) 531-0450	
Toyogo :	(800) 869-6469	
TPS Electronics :CA	(415) 856-6833	
Trace Products :CA	(800) 872-2318	
Trade Winds :CA	(818) 700-6920	
Trade Winners Net Marketing :WA	(206) 694-1765	
Trans Datacorp :CA	(415) 327-2692	
Trans Leasing International :IL	(800) 323-1180	
Trans PC Systems, Inc :CA	(213) 868-6930	
Trans-Micro Inc :FL	(407) 464-5335	
Transamerica Commercial :CA	(510) 847-2008	
Transcend Information Inc :CA	(714) 598-5500	
TransComputer, Inc :CA	(408) 747-1355	
Transform Logic Corp :AZ	(602) 948-2600	
Transition Engineering Inc :MN	(612) 941-7600	
Transitional Technology Inc :CA	(714) 693-1133	
Transtector Systems :ID	(800) 829-2901	
Trantor Systems, Ltd :CA.	(510) 770-1400	
	BBS (510) 656-5159	
Traveling Software :WA	(800) 343-8080	
	BBS (206) 485-1736	
Travis-Helwig Inc :AZ.	(602) 745-5452	
Treasure Chest Peripherals :LA	(800) 677-9781	(504) 468-2010
Tredex California Inc :CA	(800) 338-0939	(310) 551-3139
Trellis Communications Corp :NH	(603) 668-1213	
Trenton Terminals, Inc :GA	(404) 381-6031	
Tri State Computer :NY	(800) 433-5199	(212) 608-2308
Tri-Star Computer Corp :AZ	(800) 800-7400	
Triad System Corp :CA	(415) 449-0606	
Triad Systems Corp :CA	(510) 449-0606	
Tribe Computer Works :	(510) 547-7145	
Tribeca Peripherals :NJ	(800) 445-6222	
Trident Microsystems, Inc :CA.	(415) 691-9211	
	BBS (415) 691-1016	
TriGem :CA	(800) 359-0491	
Trilogy Magnetics :CA	(800) 873-4323	
Trimarchi Inc :PA	(800) 356-6638	
TriMark Engineering (Doorway) :TN	(615) 966-3667	
	BBS (615) 675-3282	
Trimm Industries :CA	(800) 272-3557	
Trinzic/Channel Computing, Inc :NH	(800) 289-0053	
Trio Information Systems Inc :NC	(919) 783-6682	
Trio Systems :	(818) 798-5567	
Tripp Lite :IL	(312) 329-1777	

Company and :State	Main Phone	Tech Phone
Tripp-Lite :IL	(312) 329-1601	
TriSoft Inc :TX	(800) 366-6873	(512) 219-8103
	BBS (512) 331-9611	
Tritech Information Systems :CA	(408) 252-5441	
Triton Technologies, Inc :NJ	(908) 855-9440	
Triwef Corp :NJ	(201) 770-2800	
Trompeter Electronics, Inc :CA	(818) 707-2020	
TRON Association :AZ	(602) 249-3388	
Tron Computer :ME	(800) 397-8909	
Tronix Peripherals, Inc :CA	(408) 727-4191	
True Basic Inc :NH	(800) 872-2742	
TrueData Products :MA	(800) 635-0300	(508) 278-6555
TrueTech :MN	(612) 944-8712	
Truevision :IN	(317) 841-0332	
	BBS (317) 577-8783	
TRW Customer Service Division :NJ	(800) 722-2736	
TS Micro Tech, Inc :CA	(310) 787-1640	
TSA Inc :TX	(800) 422-4872	
Tseng Laboratories Inc :PA	(215) 968-0502	
TSR Systems :NY	(516) 331-6336	
	BBS (516) 331-6682	
Tucker Electronics :TX	(800) 527-4642	
Turbo Technologies Inc :CA	(310) 641-4622	
Turbopower Software :CO	(719) 260-6641	
Turtle Beach Systems :PA	(717) 843-6916	
	BBS (717) 845-4835	
Tutankhamon Electronics :CA	(800) 998-4888	
TVM Professional Monitor Corp :CA	(800) 822-8168	
Twelve Tone Systems :MA	(617) 926-2480	
TWICE :NY	(212) 133-6900	
Twilight Express :NY	(800) 376-4797	
Twincom :NJ	(201) 935-8880	
Twinhead Corp :CA	(408) 945-0808	
TWIX :TX	(800) 344-8949	
Twix International Corp :CO	(303) 789-5333	
Tyan Computer Corp :CA	(408) 720-1200	(408) 720-1200
Tyan Computer Corp :CA	(408) 956-8000	
Tycor International :AB	(403) 259-3200	
Tyler Corp :TX	(214) 754-7800	
Typerite Ribbon Mfg., Inc :NY	(800) 328-8028	
Tystar Electronics Co, Ltd :MO	(816) 842-7900	
U S Robotics :IL	(800) 342-5877	(800) 982-5151
	BBS (708) 982-5092	
U S West, Inc :CO	(303) 793-6500	
U-Lead Systems, Inc. :CA	(310) 523-9393	
U-Tron Technologies Inc :CA	(800) 933-7775	
U.S. Computer :FL	(305) 477-2288	
U.S. Robotics, Inc. :IL	(800) 342-5877	
UDP Data Products, Inc :CA	(213) 782-9800	
UDP Fonts :CA	(310) 782-9800	

Company and :State	Main Phone	Tech Phone
UDS Motorola :AL	(205) 430-8000	
ULSI Systems :CA	(408) 943-0562	
Ulta Computers :WV	(800) 755-7518	(304) 748-1891
Ultima Electronics Corp. :CA	(510) 659-1580	
Ultimate Corp :NJ	(201) 887-9222	
Ultimedia Tool Series, IBM :CA	(415) 694-3090	
Ultra-X Inc :CA	(800) 772-3789	
UltraStor Corp :CA	(714) 581-4100	
Ungermann-Bass, Inc :CA	(408) 496-0111	
Uni-CGS, Inc :CA	(714) 468-1577	
Uni-Rep :CA	(619) 662-1271	
Unibind USA Inc :WA	(800) 874-7579	
Unicomp Inc :CA	(714) 571-1900	
Unicore Software :MA	(800) 800-2467	(508) 686-2204
Unicorn Software :NV	(702) 597-0818	
Unidata :CA	(916) 362-1239	
Uniform Industrial Corp (U.S.A.) :CA	(510) 549-0817	
Uniplex :	(214) 717-0068	(800) 338-9940
Unipress Software :NJ	(908) 985-8000	
Uniq Technology, Inc :CA	(415) 226-9988	(415) 226-9996
UniQube Corporation :CO	(800) 334-4990	
Unison Technologies, Inc :CA	(714) 855-8700	
Unisphere :TX	(214) 343-3717	
UniStor :	(800) 422-2115	
Unisys :	(800) 547-8362	
Unit Tech America Inc :CA	(310) 602-2392	
United Barcode Industries, Inc. :MD	(301) 210-3000	
United Business Machines :CA	(800) 722-7703	(909) 279-1298
United Computer Express :NY	(800) 448-3738	
United Computer Supply, Inc :CA	(714) 468-2680	
United Innovations :MA	(413) 733-3333	
United Microelectronics Corp :CA	(408) 727-2100	
United Networks Inc :CA	(408) 433-0900	
United Parcel Service :GA	(404) 913-7047	
United Software Security :VA	(703) 556-0007	
United Systems And Software:FL	(407) 875-2120	
United Technology Corp :CT	(203) 728-7000	
United Telecomm, Inc :KS	(913) 624-3000	
Unitek Technology :CA	(800) 944-5650	
Unitron Computer USA Inc :CA	(818) 333-0280	
Universal Computer Corp :FL	(800) 457-4433	(305) 446-9905
Universal Enterprises :OR	(800) 547-5740	
Universal Fiber Optics :VA	(703) 389-9844	
Universal Technical Systems :IL	(815) 963-2220	
Universal Vectors Corp :VA	(703) 435-2500	
Unix International :NJ	(201) 263-8400	
Unix Review Magazine :CA	(415) 905-2200	
Unix Today :NY	(516) 562-5000	
Unlimited Systems Corp Inc. :CA	(619) 277-3300	
Up Time Disaster Recovery :CA	(800) 366-1282	

Company and :State	Main Phone	Tech Phone
Upsonic :CA	(800) 877-6642	
Uptime Computer Support Services :CA	(805) 254-3384	
URS Information Systems :MA	(508) 657-6100	
US Computer :FL	(305) 477-2288	
US Computer Maintenance :NY	(800) 473-8650	
US Logic :CA	(619) 467-1100	
US Paging Corporation :NJ	(201) 305-6000	
US Technologies :NJ	(201) 288-8200	
USA Electronics :TX	(214) 631-1574	(214) 631-1693
USA Flex :IL	(800) 872-3539	(708) 351-7172
USA Microsystems :MD	(800) 365-4774	(301) 881-8974
Use 'R Computers, Inc :MN	(800) 624-2480	
Useful Software Inc :CA	(818) 880-9128	
User Friendly Computers :CO	(303) 444-0770	
USIT :CA	(800) 543-2294	
UVC Corp :CA	(714) 261-5336	
V Communications :CA	(408) 296-4224	
Valcom, Inc :NE	(402) 392-3900	
Valid Logic Systems, Inc :CA	(408) 432-9400	
Valiteck, Inc :MA	(800) 825-4835	
Valitek :MA	(413) 549-2700	
Vallesverd Co., Inc :MN	(612) 933-0023	
Valor Software :CA	(408) 559-1100	
Valtron Technologies :CA	(805) 257-0333	
Valtronix :CA	(714) 261-6671	
Value Added Inc :GA	(404) 662-5800	
ValueStor :CA	(800) 873-8258	(408) 945-4188
Van Nostrand Reinhold :NY	(212) 254-3232	
Vantage Technologies :NH	(800) 487-5678	
Varbusiness :NY	(516) 365-4600	
Varta Batteries :NY	(800) 468-2782	
Varta Batteries Inc. :NY	(914) 592-2500	
Vector Automation, Inc :MD	(301) 433-4200	
Vector Information Systems Inc :CT	(203) 797-0558	
Vektron International :TX	(800) 725-0020	(214) 606-2843
Ven-Tel Inc :CA	(800) 538-5121	
	BBS (408) 922-0988	
Ventek Corp :CA	(818) 991-3868	
Ventura Software :CA	(800) 822-8221	(619) 673-6000
	BBS (619) 673-7691	
Verbatim :CA	(800) 538-8589	
Verbatim Corp. :NC	(704) 547-6500	
Verbum :CA	(619) 644-9977	
Verdix Corp :VA	(703) 378-7600	
Verilink Corp :CA	(408) 945-1199	
Veritas :CA	(408) 727-1222	
Verite :CA	(310) 326-5040	
VeriTest, Inc. :CA	(310) 450-0062	
Vermont Creative Software :VT	(802) 848-7731	(802) 848-7571
	BBS (802) 848-7581	

Company and :State	Main Phone	Tech Phone
Vermont Database :VT	(802) 253-4437	
Versacad Corp :MA	(800) 488-7228	
Vestronix :OT	(519) 745-2700	
VI & C Technology, Inc :MA	(617) 861-8877	
VI&C Technology, Inc. :MA	(617) 275-1284	
VIA Technologies, Inc. :CA	(510) 770-0370	
ViaGrafix :OK	(918) 825-6700	
Vic's Computer Service Inc :TX	(800) 999-1827	
Victor Technologies, Inc :PA	(215) 251-5000	(800) 628-2420
Victory Enterprises Technology :TX	(512) 450-0801	
Video Display Corp :GA	(800) 241-5005	
Video Express Productions:WI	(414) 644-7042	
Video Seven :CA	BBS (510) 656-0503	
Video Works :CA	(800) 838-1031	
VideoLogic, Inc :MA	(617) 494-0530	
	BBS (617) 494-4960	
Videomail, Inc. :CA	(408) 747-0223	
Videomedia, Inc :CA	(408) 227-9977	
Videx, Inc :OR	(503) 758-0521	
Videx, Inc. :CA	(503) 758-0521	
VidTech Microsystems, Inc. :MN	(800) 752-8033	
Vienna Software Publishing Inc. :FL	(800) 392-7724	
View Sonic :CA	(714) 869-7976	
Viewpoint Software :CA	(800) 635-5621	
Viewsonic :CA	(800) 888-8583	
Viking Acoustical Corp :MN	(800) 328-8385	
Viking Components, Inc. :CA	(714) 643-7255	
Viking Technologies Inc :	(401) 847-2455	
VIP Computer, Inc. :CA	(714) 562-6999	
VIP Data Systems :MI	(800) 352-1150	
Viratec Thin Films, Inc. :MN	(507) 334-0051	
Virgin Games :	(714) 833-8710	
Visage, Inc. :MA	(508) 620-7100	
Visalia Computer Technology :CA	(209) 625-1480	
Visi-Tron, Inc :NJ	(609) 424-0400	
Visible Systems Corp :MA	(617) 969-4100	
Vision Computer Remarketers :MA	(800) 242-5224	
Vision Imaging :CA	(714) 965-7122	
Visionary Software :	(503) 246-6200	
Visionetics International Corp. :CA	(310) 316-7940	
Visionex :CA	(408) 954-0640	
Visitech Software :NC	(919) 676-8474	
Vista Microsystems :MA	(508) 695-8459	
Vistron, Inc :CA	(408) 522-8900	
Visual Business Systems :	(404) 956-0325	
	BBS (404) 953-1613	
Visual Computer :	(201) 348-4033	
Visual Technology Inc :	(617) 459-4903	
Vita Enterprise Int'l. Corp. :CA	(818) 458-0282	
Vital Communications :NY	(516) 437-4400	

Company and :State	Main Phone	Tech Phone
Vital Records Inc :NJ	(908) 369-6900	
Viziflex Seels, Inc :NJ	(201) 487-8080	
Viziflex Seels, Inc. :NJ	(201) 487-8080	
VLSI Technology, Inc :AZ	(602) 752-8574	
VM Software, Inc :	(703) 264-8010	
VocalTec Inc. :NJ	(201) 784-0993	
Voice-It Software Inc. :BC	(604) 589-1086	
VoiceFax Information Systems :BC	(604) 732-9771	
Voicetek Corp :MA	(508) 250-9393	
Volkswriter, Inc :CA	(408) 648-3000	
	BBS (408) 648-3015	
Volt-Guard Inc :FL	(800) 237-0769	
Voltura Enterprises :NJ	(908) 879-5803	
Vortex Computer Laboratories :AZ	(800) 486-4586	(800) 883-8008
Voyetra Technologies :NY	(914) 738-4500	
Vu-Data Corp :CA	(619) 452-7670	
VXIbus Associates :NJ	(201) 299-8321	
Vycor Corp :MD	(800) 888-9267	
VZ Corp :UT	(801) 595-1352	
W & T Products Corp :FL	(800) 628-2086	
W Systems :CA	(800) 344-8335	
Wacom Technology Corp :WA	(206) 750-8882	
Wadsworth :KY	(606) 525-2230	
Walker Richer & Quinn Inc :WA	(206) 324-0407	
Wall Data Inc :WA	(800) 927-8622	
Wall Street Computer Rev. :NY	(212) 869-1300	
Wallaby Software Corp :NJ	(201) 934-9333	
Wallace Comp. Serv's. Inc. :IL	(312) 626-2000	
Wallsoft Systems :NY	(212) 406-7026	
	BBS (212) 962-1923	
Walnut Creek CDROM :CA	(800) 786-9907	(510) 674-0783
Wandel & Goltermann Inc :NC	(800) 277-7404	
Wang In The News :	(817) 883-2453	
Wang Laboratories Taiwan Ltd. :NY	(212) 308-5862	
Wang Laboratories, Inc :MA	(508) 459-5000	
WangDAT, Inc :CA	(714) 753-8900	
Wangtek, Inc :CA	(805) 583-5255	(800) 992-9916
	BBS (805) 582-3370	
Warner Computer Systems, Inc :NJ	(201) 794-4800	
Warner Electronics Inc :OH	(216) 661-0304	
Warner New Media :	(818) 955-9999	
Warrantech :CT	(203) 975-1100	
Watcom Products :OT	(800) 265-4555	
Waterloo Furniture Components :ON	(519) 748-5060	
Watson Information Systems Corp :TX	(512) 476-4665	
Wavetek Corp :CA	(619) 279-2955	
Wavetek Corp :CA	(800) 223-9885	
Wayzata Technology :MN	(218) 326-0597	(800) 377-7321
Wearnes Technology Corp :CA	(408) 456-8838	
Webcorp :CA	(415) 331-1449	

Company and :State	Main Phone	Tech Phone
Weetech Inc :MA	(800) 232-5152	
Weitek Corp :CA	(408) 738-8400	
	BBS (408) 522-7517	
Welch Allyn :NY	(315) 685-8945	
Welling Electronics :NE	(402) 342-6564	
Wells American Corp :	(801) 796-7800	
Wen Technology Corp :NY	(914) 347-4100	
Wescorp :CA	(800) 537-7828	
Wescorp Statis Control Product :CA	(800) 537-7828	
Wespercorp :CA	(714) 261-0606	
Western Digital :CA	(800) 228-6488	(714) 932-0952
	BBS (714) 753-1068	
Western Engineering Consultants :CA	(805) 375-4025	
Western Micro :OR	(800) 634-2248	
Western Telematic Inc :CA	(714) 586-9950	
Western Telematic Inc :CA	(714) 586-9950	
Western Union Corp :NJ	(201) 818-5000	
Western Wares :	(303) 327-4898	
Westinghouse Electric Corp :PA	(412) 244-2000	
Westlake Data Corp :TX	(512) 328-1041	
Wetex International (USA) Corp :CA	(800) 759-3839	(213) 728-3156
Weyerhauser Recovery Services :WA	(800) 654-9347	
White Pine Software :	(603) 886-9050	
White Sciences Inc :	(602) 967-8257	
Whitewater Group :	(708) 328-3800	
	BBS (708) 328-9442	
Wicat Systems, Inc :UT	(801) 224-6400	
Wilcom Inc :NH	(800) 222-1898	
Williams & Macius :	(509) 235-2012	
Willies Computer Software :TX	(800) 966-4832	
Willow Creek Technologies Inc :ON	(519) 836-1532	
Willow Peripherals :	(800) 444-1585	
Wilson Laboratories :CA	(714) 998-1980	
Wilson WindowWare :WA	(206) 937-9335	
WIN Group :CA	(213) 903-1440	
Wincom International Network Inc :CA	(909) 594-2218	
Windowdos Publications :	(817) 467-4103	
Windows User Magazine :NY	(212) 302-2626	
WindSoft Inc :NJ	(201) 586-4400	
Windsor Technologies :CA	(415) 456-2200	
Wink Data Products Corp :WA	(206) 742-4145	
Winner Products (USA) :CA	(714) 595-2490	
Winners Only Inc :CA	(619) 549-2249	
WinSoft :WA	(800) 275-7638	
Winsryg Corp, The :AZ	(602) 431-9118	
Wintec Industries Inc :CA	(510) 770-9239	
Wintime Corp :CA	(310) 375-5930	
WinWare :TX	(214) 458-0540	
WIP Technology :CA	(800) 743-2318	
Wise Components :CT	(800) 543-4333	

Company and :State	Main Phone	Tech Phone
Wise-Ware :CA	(714) 556-6523	
Wiseport Data :	(714) 725-9263	
WIT :CA.	(408) 433-0188	
Wizard Works Group, Inc. :	(612) 544-8581	
Wizardworks :MN	(612) 544-8581	
Wolff Forbes & Associates :CA	(914) 478-5048	
Wolfram Research, Inc :IL	(800) 441-6284	
Wollongong Group, Inc :CA	(415) 962-7100	
Wonder Corporation :MA	(617) 965-8400	
Wonderware :CA.	(714) 727-9779	
Woolf Software :	(818) 703-8112	
Word Star International :CA	(800) 227-5609	(812) 323-8814
Wordata Inc :OH	(800) 543-1922	
WordPerfect Corp :UT	(800) 451-5151	(800) 541-5096
	BBS (801) 225-4444	

Word Perfect Corporation

Amiga Word Perfect	(801) 226-4147	(800) 321-3204
Apple Word Perfect for IIe/IIc/IIGS	(801) 226-8300	(800) 752-7744
Atari Word Perfect	(801) 321-3271	(800) 226-8660
Corporate Accounts	(801) 222-2035	
Data General Products	(801) 222-4100	
Data Perfect	(801) 225-5700	(800) 321-3749
DEC Products	(801) 222-5500	(801) 226-4180
Developer's Toolkit	(801) 228-7710	
Draw Perfect	(801) 226-8766	(800) 541-5098
Education	(801) 222-2300	
General Information	(801) 225-5000	(800) 451-5151
Government	(801) 222-2100	
Interim Release/Upgrade Info	(801) 226-4444	(800) 321-5906
International	(801) 222-4200	
Letter Perfect	(801) 228-9902	(800) 321-2185
NeXT Word Perfect	(801) 228-9910	
Office Gateways/Cross Platform	(801) 226-6944	
Office Software	(801) 226-4440	(800) 321-3523
OS/2 Word Perfect	(801) 225-4900	(800) 321-1230
Plan Perfect	(801) 226-2690	(800) 321-3248
Printer-Dot Matrix & Other	(800) 541-5160	
Printer-Laser of Postscript	(800) 541-5170	
Reseller Information	(800) 321-0034	
Rhymer	(801) 228-9901	(800) 321-2196
System 370	(801) 222-5100	
UNIX Products	(801) 222-5300	(801) 226-5333
VMS Products	(801) 222-5500	(801) 226-4180
Word Perfect Executive	(801) 228-9903	(800) 321-2186
Word Perfect Features	(801) 226-7900	(800) 541-5096
Word Perfect for Macintosh	(801) 226-5522	(800) 336-3614
Word Perfect Graphics	(801) 226-7900	(800) 321-3383
Word Perfect Installation	(801) 226-5444	(800) 533-9605
Word Perfect Macro/Merge	(800) 541-5129	
Word Perfect on Networks	(801) 226-4777	(800) 321-3253

Company and :State	Main Phone	Tech Phone
WordStar International :CA	(800) 227-5609	
WordStar International :CA	(415) 382-8000	
WordTech Systems, Inc :CA	(510) 254-0900	
	BBS (510) 254-1141	
WorksWare :	(818) 989-2298	
Worlco Data Systems :PA	(215) 630-9500	
World Richman Corp :IL	(708) 298-1188	
Worldata :FL	(407) 393-8200	
Worldcomm :NC	(800) 472-0438	
Worldnet Marketing :CA	(714) 545-7118	
Worldwide Computer Service :NJ	(201) 694-8876	
Worldwide Technologies :PA	(800) 457-6937	(215) 922-4640
Worthington Data Solutions :CA	(800) 345-4220	
Wrist Pro :MO	(800) 348-8633	
WV Computronics :WV	(304) 882-3086	
Wyle Laboratories :CA	(213) 322-1763	
Wynit :NY	(800) 999-9648	
Wyse Technologies :CA	(800) 800-9973	
	BBS (408) 922-4400	
X-10 (USA) Inc :NJ	(201) 784-9700	
Xcel Computer Systems :MA	(508) 799-9494	
XDB Systems :MD	(301) 317-6800	
XDB Systems Inc :MD	(301) 317-6800	
Xebex	Out Of Business :	
Xeltek :CA	(800) 541-1975	
XenoSoft :CA	(510) 564-4936	
Xentek Inc :CA	(619) 727-0940	
Xerox Corp :CA	(800) 832-6979	
Xerox Corporation :CT	(203) 968-3000	
Xerox Imaging Systems :	(800) 248-6550	
Xerox International Partners :CA	(415) 813-7700	
Xinetron :CA	(408) 727-5509	
Xionics, Inc :CA	(714) 971-4717	(714) 971-4717
Xircom :	(800) 874-4428	
	BBS (818) 878-7618	
Xircom Inc :CA	(818) 878-7600	
XL/Datacomp Inc :IL	(800) 323-3289	
XOR Corp :	(612) 831-8640	
Xpect Trading Corp :CA	(800) 332-5555	
XScribe Corp :CA	(619) 457-5091	
XtraCom Inc :ON	(416) 427-6612	
XTree Company :CA	(800) 964-2490	(900) 903-9873
	BBS (805) 546-9150	
Xtron Computer Equipment Corp :NJ	(201) 798-5000	
Xuron Corporation :ME	(207) 283-1401	
XXCAL, Inc :CA	(800) 879-9225	
Xxera Technologies :CA	(818) 286-5569	
Xylogics, Inc :MA	(800) 225-3317	(617) 272-8140
XYQuest :MA	(508) 671-0888	
	BBS (508) 667-5669	

Company and :State	Main Phone	Tech Phone
XYXIS Corp :MN	(612) 949-2388	
Y-E Data America Inc :GA	(404) 446-8655	
Y.E.S. Systems Corp :CA	(510) 657-8886	
Yamaha LSI :CA	(800) 543-7457	
Yamaha Systems Technology :CA.	(800) 543-7457	
Yamaichi Electronics Inc :CA	(408) 452-0797	
Yangs International Corp :CA	(510) 651-4305	
Yokogawa Corporation Of America :GA	(800) 258-2552	
Young Micro Systems :CA	(310) 946-3450	
Yuasa-Exide Inc :PA	(215) 378-0333	
Z Soft :	(404) 428-0008	
Z-International, Inc :MO	(816) 474-8400	
Z-Mar Technology :NC	(704) 841-8845	
Z-Ram :CA	(714) 454-1500	
Z-World :CA	(916) 753-3722	
Zaptec International Corp :CA	(714) 792-2229	
Zedcor :AZ	(800) 482-4561	(602) 881-2310
Zemaitis, Inc :CA.	(408) 436-1530	
Zenith Data Systems :IL	(800) 227-3360	
Zenographics, Inc :CA	(800) 366-7494	
	BBS (714) 851-3860	
Zenon Computer Systems :CA.	(800) 899-6119	(800) 229-7898
Zentao Corp :IL	(708) 350-9040	
Zentek Storage Of America Inc :CA	(408) 946-4464	
Zeny Computer Systems, Inc :CA	(510) 659-0386	
Zeos International :MN	(800) 423-5891	
Zericon, Inc :	(800) 727-8380	
Zi-Tech Instrument Corp :CA	(415) 326-2151	
Ziff Davis Technical Info. Sys :MA	(617) 393-3200	
Ziff-Davis Publishing CO :NY	(212) 503-5446	
Zippertubing :CA	(310) 527-0488	
Zirco :	(303) 421-2013	
Zirco Inc :CO	(303) 421-2013	
Zitel Corp :CA	(408) 946-9600	
Zoltrix Inc :CA	(510) 657-1188	
Zoom Telephonics :MA	(800) 631-3116	(617) 423-1076
	BBS (617) 451-5284	
Zorn Industries :NH	(603) 894-4950	
Zortech :MA	(617) 937-0696	
ZSoft Corp :GA	(800) 444-4780	
	BBS (404) 427-1045	
Ztest Electronics :NY	(416) 238-3543	
Zucker America :	(408) 720-1942	
Zykronix :CO	(303) 799-4944	
ZyLAB Corp :IL	(800) 544-6339	
ZyMOS Corp :CA	(408) 730-5400	(800) 422-7369
Zytec Corporation :MN	(612) 941-1100	
ZyXEL USA :CA	(800) 255-4101	
	BBS (714) 693-0762	

POCKET PCRef

Boardwatch Magazine Top 100 Bulletin Boards for 1993
Readers' Choice Awards

Boardwatch Magazine is a top notch guide to BBSs (Electronic Bulletin Boards) and Online Information Services. It provides a critical information link between millions of computer BBS users and a world of rapidly changing computer and communications technology. The magazine is published monthly, at an annual subscription rate of $36 ($99 Overseas), by Boardwatch Magazine, 8500 W. Bowles Ave, Suite 210, Dept. 111, Littleton, Colorado 80123. Phone: (303) 973-6038 BBS: (303) 973-4222

Boardwatch Magazine Top 100 BBSs

Rank	Board Name	BBS Phone	Location
1	Software Creations	508-368-7139	Clinton, MA
2	EXEC-PC	414-789-4210	Elm Grove, WI
3	delta Comm BBS	919-481-9399	Cary, NC
4	PC-OHIO	216-381-3320	Cleveland, OH
5	GLIB	703-578-4542	Arlington, VA.
6	Westside	213-933-4050	Los Angeles, CA
7	Albuquerque ROS	505-299-5974	Albuquerque, NM
8	Odyssey	818-358-6968	Monrovia, CA
9	Wizard's Gate BBS	614-224-1635	Columbus, OH
10	Pleasure Dome	804-490-5878	Norfolk, VA
11	Blue Ridge Express	804-790-1675	Richmond, VA
12	Deep Cove BBS	604-536-5885	White Rock, BC
13	Totem Pole BBS	313-238-1178	Flint, MI
14	Planet BMUG	510-849-2684	Berkeley, CA
15	Prostar BBS	206-941-0317	Auburn, WA
16	Chrysalis	214-690-9295	Plano, TX
17	OS/2 Shareware	703-385-4325	Fairfax, VA
18	Microfone Infoservice	908-494-8666	Metuchen, NJ
19	Nashville Exchange	615-383-0727	Nashville, TN
20	Eagle's Nest BBS	303-933-0701	Littleton, CO
21	Plains Bulletin service	701-281-3390	Fargo, ND
22	City Lights	612-633-1366	Arden Hills, MN
23	Lifestyle	516-689-5390	Lake Grove, NY
24	Monterey Gaming System	408-655-5555	Monterey, CA
25	Windy City Freedom Fort	708-564-1069	Northbrook, IL
26	Micro Message Service	919-779-6674	Raleigh, NC
27	Liberty BBS	714-996-7777	Anaheim Hills, CA
28	File Bank	303-534-4646	Denver, CO
29	Cracker Barrel	703-899-0020	Falmouth, VA
30	Source BBS	310-371-3737	Torrance, CA
31	America's Suggestion Box	516-471-8625	Ronkonkoma, NY
32	Garbage Dump BBS	505-294-5675	Albuquerque, NM
33	Windows On Line	510-736-8343	Danville, CA
34	Springfield Public Access	413-536-4365	Springfield, MA

Boardwatch Magazine Top 100 BBSs

Rank	Board Name	BBS Phone	Location
35	O.U. BBS	405-325-6128	Norman, OK
36	AlphaOne	708-827-3619	Park Ridge, Il
37	Advanced System BBS	702-334-3308	Reno, NV
38	Godfather	813-289-3314	Tampa, FL
39	Fantasy Party Line	713-596-7101	Houston, TX
40	Hello Central	206-641-7218	Bellevue, WA
41	Datamax/Satelite	215-443-9434	Ivyland, PA
42	Tampa Connection	813-961-8665	Tampa, FL
43	H H Infonet	203-738-0342	New Hartford, CT
44	Radio Wave BBS	609-764-0812	Delran, NJ
45	Executive Network	914-667-4567	Mount Vernon, NY
46	Invention Factory	212-274-8110	New York City, NY
47	Father and Son BBS	215-439-1509	Whitehall, PA
48	Legend of Roseville BBS	313-776-1975	Roseville, MI
49	Radio Daze BBS	219-256-2255	Mishawaka, IN
50	CoSNUG BBS	719-578-6088	Colorado Springs, CO
51	Rusty and Edies BBS	216-726-2620	Youngstown, OH
52	Space BBS	415-323-4193	Menlo Park, CA
53	Techtalk	407-635-8833	Cocoa, FL
54	Hotlanta BBS	404-992-5345	Roswell, GA
55	24th Street Exchange	916-448-2483	Sacramento, CA
56	Mog-UR's EMS	818-366-1238	Granada Hills, CA
57	After Hours	512-320-1650	Austin, TX
58	Starship II BBS	201-935-1485	Lyndhurst, NY
59	Prime Time BBS	818-982-7271	Burbank, CA
60	3rd Eye BBS	615-227-6155	Nashville, TN
61	Arizona Online	602-294-9447	Tuscon, AZ
62	Digicom BBS	812-479-1310	Evansville, IN
63	Cajun Clickers BBS	504-756-9658	Banton Rouge, LA
64	Channel 1	617-354-8873	Cambridge, MA
65	KBBS Los Angeles	818-886-0872	Canoga Park, CA
66	Eagles Nest Communications	401-732-5290	Providence, RI
67	Argus	617-674-2345	Lexington, MA

Boardwatch Magazine Top 100 BBSs

Rank	Board Name	BBS Phone	Location
68	TCSNet	206-692-2388	Silverdale, WA
69	S-Tek	514-597-2409	Montreal, QC
70	Infoquest	618-453-8511	Carbondale, IL
71	One Stop PCBoard BBS	509-943-0211	Richland, WA
72	Kandy Shack	714-636-2667	Garden Grove, CA
73	Texas Talk	214-497-9100	Richardson, TX
74	BCS BBS	213-962-2902	Hollywood, CA
75	Higher Powered BBS	408-737-7040	Sunnyvale, CA
76	Zoo BBS	312-907-1831	Chicago, IL
77	Toolkit	219-696-3415	Lowell, IN
78	Electronic Tribune	505-823-7700	Albuquerque, NM
79	YA WEBECAD	812-428-3870	Evansville, IN
80	Wayne's World	918-665-0061	Tulsa, Ok
81	TGC Services	812-284-1321	Clarksville, IN
82	Computers & Dreams	212-888-6565	New York City, NY
83	WinPlus	206-630-8203	Kent, WA
84	U S A BBS	501-753-8575	N. Little Rock, AR
85	Capital City Online	206-956-1206	Lacey, WA
86	Nightbreed	512-345-5099	Austin, TX
87	Cloud 9	619-737-3097	Escondido, CA
88	Mercury Opus	813-321-0734	St. Petersburg, FL
89	Wolverine	517-695-9952	Midland, MI
90	Heat In The Night	515-386-6227	Kent, WA
91	BMUG Boston	617-721-5840	Boston, MA
92	Seaside	805-964-4766	Santa Barbara, CA
93	Psycho Ward BBS	203-371-8769	Bridgeport, CT
94	File Shop BBS	816-587-3311	Kansas City, MO
95	Aces Place	209-357-8424	Afwater, CA
96	Frog Pond	716-461-1924	Rochester, NY
97	CRS	416-213-6002	Mississauga, ON
98	Studs	415-495-2929	San Francisco, CA
99	Collector's Edition	214-351-9859	Dallas, TX
100	Batboard	314-446-0475	Columbia, MO

POCKET PCRef

Index

E

F

G

H

I

J

K

L

M

Q

R

S

Index